MW00618782

The **2015/2016**
Comprehensive Vintage Motorcycle Price Guide

Antique, classic, and
special interest motorcycles

Model years 1901 through 1996

Data compiled by the
Motorcycle and Model Railroad Museum of Wisconsin

Whitehorse Press
Center Conway, New Hampshire

Whitehorse Press books are also available at discounts in bulk quantity for sales and promotional use. For details about special sales or for a catalog of Whitehorse Press motorcycling books, write to the publisher:

Whitehorse Press
107 East Conway Road
Center Conway, New Hampshire 03813
Phone: 603-356-6556 or 800-531-1133
E-mail: CustomerService@WhitehorsePress.com
Internet: www.WhitehorsePress.com

ISBN: 978-1-884313-95-0

5 4 3 2 1

Printed in the United States

CONTENTS

THE PRICE MART SHOWROOM

What Do the "Experts" See with Prices for 2015–2016?

For the ninth year in a row, here it is! We present to you the 2015/2016 edition of the *Comprehensive Vintage Motorcycle Price Guide* (CVMPG). Through hundreds of hours of research, data entry, and the opinions of many dealers, auctioneers, collectors, and experts in the vintage field, we feel this is the most accurate price guide written for vintage motorcycles. It also contains more data than any other, as all major marques (and many lesser known marques) are included with data through 1996. It is also our intent to add additional marques each year, and data for any motorcycles 15 years old and older when possible. This year, we have added listings for Douglas motorcycles, with more marques to come in future editions. We will also continue to work on adding manufacturing numbers to each marque to help determine rarity and value. These numbers are found in parenthesis right after the model and year, when available. Additionally, it is our goal to add the very early years of some of the marques for which little if any data may exist. The CVMPG will continue to grow and evolve, and we appreciate your comments and input!

   In addition to what is in this guide, we have collected data about at least 50 other marques, but the years and information for these is scattered. Consequently, we will continue to do research and add these marques to the CVMPG as this data becomes more complete.

   As we have gone through the task of evaluating thousands

of prices, remember that this is a *guide;* these prices are not etched in stone. Rarity, demand, and condition are all factors that drive prices. These prices have been determined through research using other pricing sources, dealer sales, auctions, private sales, eBay sales, and experts from each marque. With this in mind, we have come to the following conclusions and have spotted the following trends that have emerged over the past 12 months:

1. It seems like every time BSA motorcycles come up for sale, they are snapped up quickly, and often at new record prices. These motorcycles still continue to be a great investment. There is a lot of demand and every major vintage dealer we speak to is in agreement.

2. The scooter craze which we thought in our last issue might be coming to a plateau seems to be having a resurgence. Cushmans, Vespas, and Mustangs are still drawing good money. With the popularity of the new models all over the streets, it seems as if there is acceptance, and even an increased interest in these little bikes. While people are still restoring them, there is still the question of whether a person can restore one for less than the actual retail value. The popularity of TV shows like "American Pickers" and others where many of these little machines are uncovered, may be helping to drive the market and increase interest.

3. Ducatis continue to have a high demand right now, and perhaps that is because so few good models come up for sale. Those that are available get snapped up quickly.

4. Early Harley-Davidson models seem to be holding solid prices. Perhaps now may be the time to invest. There

seems to be a demand for Knuckleheads and the 1936–1940 pre-war models.

5. In the Japanese market as a whole, the early-year bikes, especially in the 1960–1980 range, seem to be continuing to climb, and some dramatically. If a 1960s Yamaha, Suzuki, Honda, or Kawasaki comes up for sale in condition 1 or 2, there is a very high probability that it is going to set some sort of record price. We have seen people sitting at auctions, shaking their heads in amazement, especially when some of these small displacement bikes go through the roof. There continues to be a high demand for some of the "big bikes" of the 70s: the Honda CB750s, Kawasaki Z1 and KZ1000, and Yamaha 650s.

6. We consider Norton motorcycles a continued good investment. Top examples draw top money.

7. Early Triumphs are holding their value, while mid-1960s and 1970s models still do not draw the prices they did 10 years ago. That said, top quality models in these years are steady. We see a demand for early models, and are hoping continued research back to the early years of Triumph will help unearth some of these models and help drive prices upward for the marque.

8. Looking at a specific Japanese marque, we think Kawasaki may still be the way to go. We have seen 1973 Z1s trade at over $25,000 for excellent specimens, and 1973 H2s go at $20,000. The 1975 H2 actually has the lowest manufactured number of the series and is hard to find in top condition. When they do become available, we have seen them sell for close to $18,000.

9. BMW prices are an interesting study. A few choice

models have come up for sale; otherwise all we have seen are common models or examples in poor condition. This is hard to explain, as the supply of older, excellent models has dried up in public sales for several years—especially original motorcycles that have not been restored. Could this be an indication that there might be a price spike for these models in the upcoming year? We are unsure, but are cautiously optimistic.

10. We continue to like the investment potential for old, obscure marques, in original, unrestored condition. When we mention names like Pope, Cleveland, Crocker, Minneapolis, New Imperial, Pierce, Reading, Sparkbrook, or Thor, many people do not realize that in the United States, back in the early part of the 20th century, there were more than 200 motorcycle manufacturers, not to mention many more overseas. Most have since gone by the wayside. Find a rare gem in a barn, and you might have the next $100K motorcycle! Watch for pre-1920s bikes in original condition—we have seen them set a record price in one sale, only to be sold again a few months later for another record price!

11. As a whole, the market has continued to jump for top quality motorcycles, whether original or restored, and rarities. Compared to four years ago, when buyers were being very cautious in a down economy, there seems to be a lot more optimism now, and cash is flowing more freely for good quality and rare vintage motorcycles. While some buyers are always in evidence, this feeling seems to be spreading across the market. That said, people are still sitting on choice pieces, or rare early pieces in any condition, waiting to see if the market jumps more. When they do, we

predict that the prices set for these motorcycles will help to bring along the rest of the market.

You can help us to update and improve the *Comprehensive Vintage Motorcycle Price Guide* by becoming a member of our pricing network!

The Motorcycle and Model Railroad Museum of Wisconsin includes a body of staffers who are responsible for the production and gathering of data for the *Comprehensive Vintage Motorcycle Price Guide.* We are always looking to add dealers, auction services, and experts in each marque to our network of businesses and individuals who contribute their data from sales of motorcycles to us as we update and improve this publication each year. Qualifications to be a part of this network are: your interest in learning how to fairly grade motorcycles in an unbiased way, as well as sending us a list of motorcycles that you have sold or have seen sold in the last calendar year.

We also are looking for experts who deal in some of the lesser marques, who can help us gather model information, displacements, and manufacturing numbers so that we can improve the CVMPG with more factual data each year and make it more useful. If you are an expert in Adler, Cyclone, Crocker, Flying Merkel, Flanders, Zundapp, or anything in between, we'd love to have you join us.

If you would like to join us in this effort, please contact us at 920-865-1217.

Thank you!

HOW TO GRADE AND EVALUATE A MOTORCYCLE

The *Comprehensive Vintage Motorcycle Price Guide* uses a six-level grading scale to determine the value of a vintage motorcycle. By using this scale, you should be able to make a reasonably accurate assessment of the condition and value of any motorcycle in your collection or for sale. We recommend that you consult with experts in the field if questions arise, and recommend certification by such firms as the Vintage Motorcycle Certification Service (VMCS) for major purchases in order to be assured that the bike you are purchasing meets these criteria. The VMCS can be found at major vintage events, such as Vintage Days at Mid-Ohio, the Barber Vintage Festival, and most major auctions. The VMCS can be reached at 920-865-1217.

Condition 1 – PERFECT/NEW

New, unused motorcycles or perfect restorations. It should be noted that there are almost no Condition 1 motorcycles on the road. These are bikes that would have just left the showroom floor, or have been restored to showroom condition with proper factory specifications. Everything runs and operates perfectly. These bikes are rarely ridden, and often will be show winners. Many people save these bikes in climate-controlled rooms or museums as investment pieces or works of art. Note that in relationship to this price guide, there are often differences in prices between a Condition 1 original bike, and a Condition 1 restored bike, related to the demand and rarity. This is a factor that must be taken into consideration when purchasing a Condition 1 motorcycle.

Condition 2 – EXCELLENT

Without close examination, many Condition 2 motorcycles may appear as Condition 1. It may be a bike that is ridden, but usually for limited miles. It may be a well-restored bike, or a well-preserved original. There is almost no wear, or very minimal wear, on these motorcycles.

Condition 3 – VERY GOOD

Most bikes that are seen on the road are in Condition 3 or Condition 4. They are operable original bikes, or perhaps older restorations that have some wear. It may look good as you gaze at it in a parking lot, but as you get closer, you may see paint nicks or light fading; wear on the plastic, rubber, or leather parts; or light dulling of the chrome. All components of the bike are in working order.

Condition 4 – GOOD

This is a basic, usable motorcycle. This can be an original, well-used model, or a restoration that has been ridden and has begun to deteriorate. This bike may need some minor work, but most of the systems should function. Even from a distance, it is obvious that there are chips and fading in the paint, small dents, rust, poor chrome, or other areas of the motorcycle that need attention. Again, it is important to note that most motorcycles on the road would grade out as Condition 3 or Condition 4.

Condition 5 – FAIR

This is a motorcycle that needs close to a full restoration. It may or may not be running, but is in better shape than a Condition 6 motorcycle. These bikes usually have all of the original parts, or the parts may be available from the owners if they have modified the bike and have not discarded the original equipment. It has rust, faded or scratched paint, pitted or dull chrome, but not throughout the entire bike. This is a bike that would be considered as a good base for a restoration and would not present the restorer with a huge chore to find parts and supplies.

Condition 6 – POOR

These bikes are not running. They may be missing parts, may have been wrecked, and are in poor shape throughout, with faded and scratched paint, lots of rust, badly pitted or rusted chrome, tears in seats, cracked plastic and leather, worn or torn rubber pieces, and other problems. These bikes are usually good for parts to be used on other restorations, but can also be in the form of a complete bike in bad shape.

What to Look for When Inspecting a Bike for Condition

Helpful hints

- Cracked or worn footpeg rubbers/grips
- Torn seat covers, bad seat foam
- Holes in the mufflers/rusted mufflers. Run your hand underneath them, behind them and see what's there
- Paint fade, paint chips, paint bubbling, poor repainting
- Chrome pitting or peeling, rust in all areas
- Leaks of oil, forks, brake fluid, master cylinder, caliper, head gaskets, exhaust leaks
- Excessive play in levers, brakes, clutch, throttle
- Electrical: Is there a lot of electrical tape? Are there a lot of spliced wires? Exposed wires? Hanging wires? Do the electrics work?
- Decal and badge chipping and wear, bent badges
- Tire condition (cracks, wear, hole plugs)
- Bent wheels, bent forks, rusted or poorly maintained chains
- Look under the seat and side covers! Is the battery full of corrosion? Is there rust? Is there a lot of dirt and grime?
- How does the wiring look? Examine areas hidden to the eye!
- Pull the spark plugs. Plug condition can tell a lot.

PRICE GUIDE

Notes:

- Prices that have gone up since the last edition (2013/2014) are in **bold,** while prices that have gone down have a minus sign (–) in front of them.

- Where available, we have included production quantity in parentheses after some model names; see for example, early Harley-Davidson.

- To save space in the listings, we have substituted the letter "K" for thousands, in prices 100,000 and higher. Thus 240,000 is abbreviated 240K; 1,000,000 is abbreviated 1,000K.

- All prices are in U.S. dollars.

- As this book goes to press, the exchange rates for certain currencies are as follows:

TO CONVERT A PRICE

From	To	Multiply by
US dollars	British pounds	.65
US dollars	Euros	.88
US dollars	Canadian dollars	1.24
US dollars	Australian dollars	1.29
US dollars	Mexican pesos	14.9
British pounds	US dollars	1.54
Euros	US dollars	1.14
Canadian dollars	US dollars	.80
Australian dollars	US dollars	.78
Mexican pesos	US dollars	.07

	6	5	4	3	2	1
ACE						
1920						
Ace Four (78-cid, inline 4-cyl.).	13,000	20,000	30,000	40,000	55,000	70,000
1921						
Ace Four (78-cid, inline 4-cyl.).	13,000	20,000	30,000	40,000	55,000	70,000
1922						
Ace Four (78-cid, inline 4-cyl.).	13,000	20,000	30,000	40,000	55,000	70,000
1923						
Ace Four (78-cid, inline 4-cyl.).	13,000	20,000	30,000	40,000	55,000	70,000
Sporting Solo (78-cid, inline 4-cyl, alloy						
pistons)	13,000	20,000	30,000	45,000	60,000	75,000
1924						
Ace Four (78-cid, inline 4-cyl.).	13,000	20,000	30,000	40,000	55,000	70,000
Sporting Solo (78-cid, inline 4-cyl, alloy						
pistons)	13,000	20,000	30,000	45,000	60,000	75,000
1926						
Ace Four (78-cid, inline 4-cyl.).	13,000	20,000	30,000	40,000	55,000	70,000
Sporting Solo (78-cid, inline 4-cyl, alloy						
pistons)	13,000	20,000	30,000	45,000	60,000	75,000
1927						
Ace Four (78-cid, inline 4-cyl.).	14,000	20,000	31,000	41,000	55,000	70,000
Sporting Solo (78-cid, inline 4-cyl, alloy						
pistons)	14,000	21,000	31,000	45,000	60,000	75,000
AJS						
1915						
Model A (550cc).	5,000	10,000	20,000	30,000	40,000	50,000
Model D (750cc).	5,000	10,000	20,000	30,000	40,000	50,000
1923						
B1 Single (350cc)	1,500	3,000	6,000	9,000	12,000	15,000
1924						
Model B5	1,000	2,000	4,000	6,000	8,000	10,000
1925						
Model G6 (350cc)	2,500	5,000	10,000	15,000	20,000	25,000
Model E1 (800cc)	5,000	10,000	20,000	30,000	40,000	50,000
1927						
V-Twin.	6,000	10,000	13,000	16,000	19,000	22,000
Belt Drive Single H4.	1,500	3,000	6,000	9,000	12,000	15,000
Big Port H6	6,000	10,000	13,000	16,000	19,000	22,000
1929						
Model M (996cc)	3,000	6,000	9,000	12,000	16,000	20,000
1930						
R7.	1,800	3,600	5,400	8,000	12,000	16,000
R12	1,800	3,600	5,400	8,000	12,000	16,000
1931						
V-Twin.	2,000	4,000	8,000	12,000	16,000	20,000
1933						
Model 10 (495cc)	5,000	10,000	15,000	20,000	25,000	30,000
1935						
Model 22 (245cc)	1,800	3,600	5,400	8,000	12,000	16,000
1936						
Model 22 (245cc)	1,800	3,600	5,400	8,000	12,000	16,000
1939						
Dual Port (350cc single).	3,500	70,000	10,000	14,500	17,500	20,500
1942						
16M Military (350cc single)	2,000	2,500	3,500	4,600	6,800	8,000
18 (500cc single)	2,000	2,600	3,600	4,700	7,000	8,500
1943						
16M Military (350cc single)	2,000	2,500	3,500	4,600	6,800	8,000
18 (500cc single)	2,000	2,600	3,600	4,700	7,000	8,500

	6	5	4	3	2	1
1944						
16M Military (350cc single)	2,000	2,500	3,500	4,600	6,800	8,000
18 (500cc single)	2,000	2,600	3,600	4,700	7,000	8,500
1945						
18 (500cc single)	1,500	2,300	3,400	4,500	6,000	7,500
1946						
16M (350cc single)	1,400	2,100	3,200	4,200	5,600	7,000
16MC (350cc single)	1,400	2,100	3,200	4,200	5,600	7,000
18 (500cc single)	1,500	2,300	3,400	4,500	6,000	7,500
1947						
16M (350cc single)	1,400	2,100	3,200	4,200	5,600	7,000
16MC (350cc single)	1,400	2,100	3,200	4,200	5,600	7,000
18 (500cc single)	1,500	2,300	3,400	4,500	6,000	7,500
18C (500cc single)	1,500	2,300	**4,000**	**5,500**	**7,000**	**8,500**
1948						
7R Racer (350cc single).	5,000	7,500	14,000	21,000	28,000	35,000
16M (350cc single)	1,400	2,100	3,200	4,200	5,600	7,000
16MC (350cc single)	1,500	2,200	3,300	4,400	5,900	7,400
18 (500cc single)	1,300	2,000	2,900	3,900	5,200	6,500
18C (500cc single)	1,400	2,200	**4,000**	**5,500**	**7,000**	**8,500**
1949						
7R Racer (350cc single).	5,000	7,500	14,000	21,000	28,000	35,000
16M (350cc single)	1,400	2,100	3,200	4,200	5,600	7,000
16MC (350cc single)	1,500	2,200	3,300	4,400	5,900	7,400
16MS (350cc single)	1,400	2,100	3,200	4,200	5,600	7,000
18 (500cc single)	1,300	2,000	2,900	4,500	6,000	7,200
18C (500cc single)	1,400	2,200	**4,000**	**5,500**	**7,000**	**8,500**
20 (500cc twin)	1,200	1,900	**3,000**	**4,500**	**6,000**	**7,500**
20CSR (500cc twin).	**1,500**	**2,500**	**4,000**	**5,500**	**7,000**	**8,500**
1950						
7R Racer (350cc single).	5,000	7,500	11,300	15,000	20,000	25,000
16M (350cc single)	1,400	2,100	3,200	4,200	5,600	7,000
16MC (350cc single)	1,500	2,200	3,300	4,400	5,900	7,400
16MCS (350cc single).	1,400	2,100	3,100	4,100	5,500	6,900
16MS (350cc single)	1,400	2,100	3,200	4,200	5,600	7,000
18 (500cc single)	1,300	2,000	2,900	3,900	5,200	6,500
18C (500cc single)	1,400	2,200	**4,000**	**5,500**	**7,000**	**8,500**
18CS (500cc single).	1,400	2,200	4,000	6,000	7,500	9,000
18S (500cc single)	1,200	1,900	**3,000**	**4,400**	**5,800**	**7,200**
20 (500cc twin)	1,200	1,900	**3,000**	**4,500**	**6,000**	**7,500**
20CSR (500cc twin).	**1,500**	**2,500**	**4,000**	**5,500**	**7,000**	**8,500**
1951						
7R Racer (350cc single).	5,000	7,500	11,300	15,000	20,000	25,000
16M (350cc single)	1,400	2,100	3,200	4,200	5,600	7,000
16MC (350cc single)	1,500	2,200	3,300	4,400	5,900	7,400
16MCS (350cc single).	1,400	2,100	3,100	4,100	5,500	6,900
16MS (350cc single)	1,400	2,100	3,200	4,200	5,600	7,000
18 (500cc single)	1,300	2,000	2,900	3,900	5,200	6,500
18C (500cc single)	1,400	2,200	**4,000**	**5,500**	**7,000**	**8,500**
18CS (500cc single).	1,400	2,200	4,000	6,000	7,500	9,000
18S (500cc single)	1,200	1,900	**3,000**	**4,400**	**5,800**	**7,200**
20 (500cc twin)	1,200	1,900	**3,000**	**4,500**	**6,000**	**7,500**
20CSR (500cc twin).	**1,500**	**2,500**	**4,000**	**5,500**	**7,000**	**8,500**
1952						
7R Racer (350cc single).	5,000	7,500	11,300	15,000	20,000	25,000
16M (350cc single)	1,400	2,100	3,200	4,200	5,600	7,000
16MC (350cc single)	1,500	2,200	3,300	4,400	5,900	7,400
16MCS (350cc single).	1,400	2,100	3,100	4,100	5,500	6,900
16MS (350cc single)	1,400	2,100	3,200	4,200	5,600	7,000
18 (500cc single)	1,300	2,000	2,900	3,900	5,200	6,500

	6	5	4	3	2	1
18C (500cc single)	1,400	2,200	**4,000**	**5,500**	**7,000**	**8,500**
18CS (500cc single)	1,400	2,200	4,000	6,000	7,500	9,000
18S (500cc single)	–1,200	–1,900	**3,000**	**4,400**	**5,800**	**7,200**
20 (500cc twin)	1,200	1,900	**3,000**	**4,500**	**6,000**	**7,500**
20CSR (500cc twin)	**1,500**	**2,500**	**4,000**	**5,500**	**7,000**	**8,500**
1953						
7R Racer (350cc single)	5,600	8,400	12,600	16,800	22,400	28,000
16M (350cc single)	1,400	2,100	3,200	4,200	5,600	7,000
16MC (350cc single)	1,500	2,200	3,300	4,400	5,900	7,400
16MCS (350cc single)	1,400	2,100	3,100	4,100	5,500	6,900
16MS (350cc single)	1,400	2,100	3,200	4,200	5,600	7,000
18 (500cc single)	1,300	2,000	2,900	3,900	5,200	6,500
18C (500cc single)	1,400	2,200	**4,000**	**5,500**	**7,000**	**8,500**
18CS (500cc single)	1,400	2,200	4,000	6,000	7,500	9,000
18S (500cc single)	–1,200	–1,900	**3,000**	**4,400**	**5,800**	**7,200**
20 (500cc twin)	1,200	1,900	**3,000**	**4,500**	**6,000**	**7,500**
20CSR (500cc twin)	**1,500**	**2,500**	**4,000**	**5,500**	**7,000**	**8,500**
1954						
7R Racer (350cc single)	6,000	9,000	13,500	18,000	24,000	30,000
16M (350cc single)	1,400	2,100	3,200	4,200	5,600	7,000
16MC (350cc single)	1,500	2,200	3,300	4,400	5,900	7,400
16MCS (350cc single)	1,400	2,100	3,100	4,100	5,500	6,900
16MS (350cc single)	1,400	2,100	3,200	4,200	5,600	7,000
18 (500cc single)	1,300	2,000	2,900	3,900	5,200	6,500
18C (500cc single)	1,400	2,200	**4,000**	**5,500**	**7,000**	**8,500**
18CS (500cc single)	1,400	2,200	4,000	6,000	7,500	9,000
18S (500cc single)	–1,200	–1,900	**3,000**	**4,400**	**5,800**	**7,200**
20 (500cc twin)	1,200	1,900	**3,000**	**4,500**	**6,000**	**7,500**
20CSR (500cc twin)	**1,500**	**2,500**	**4,000**	**5,500**	**7,000**	**8,500**
20B (545cc twin)	**1,500**	**2,500**	**4,000**	**5,500**	**7,000**	**8,500**
1955						
7R Racer (350cc single)	6,000	9,000	13,500	18,000	24,000	30,000
16M (350cc single)	1,400	2,100	3,200	4,200	5,600	7,000
16MC (350cc single)	1,500	2,200	3,300	4,400	5,900	7,400
16MCS (350cc single)	1,400	2,100	3,200	4,200	5,600	7,000
16MS (350cc single)	1,400	2,100	3,200	4,300	5,700	7,100
18 (500cc single)	1,300	2,000	3,000	4,000	5,400	6,700
18C (500cc single)	1,400	2,200	**4,000**	**5,500**	**7,000**	**8,500**
18CS (500cc single)	1,400	2,200	4,000	6,000	7,500	9,000
18S (500cc single)	1,300	2,500	4,000	6,000	7,000	8,000
20 (500cc twin)	1,200	1,900	**3,000**	**4,500**	**6,000**	**7,500**
20CSR (500cc twin)	**1,500**	**2,500**	**4,000**	**5,500**	**7,000**	**8,500**
20B (545cc twin)	**1,500**	**2,500**	**4,000**	**5,500**	**7,000**	**8,500**
1956						
7R Racer (350cc single)	6,000	9,000	13,500	18,000	24,000	30,000
16MCS (350cc single)	1,400	2,100	3,200	4,200	5,600	7,000
16MS (350cc single)	1,400	2,200	3,200	4,300	5,800	7,200
18CS (500cc single)	1,400	2,200	4,000	6,000	7,500	9,000
18S (500cc single)	1,300	2,000	3,000	4,000	5,300	6,600
20 (500cc twin)	1,200	1,900	2,800	3,700	5,000	6,200
20CSR (500cc twin)	–1,200	–1,900	–3,000	**4,500**	**6,000**	**7,500**
30 (600cc twin)	1,300	**2,000**	**3,500**	**5,000**	**6,500**	**8,000**
30CSR (600cc twin)	**1,500**	**2,500**	**4,000**	**5,500**	**7,000**	**8,500**
1957						
7R Racer (350cc single)	6,000	9,000	13,500	18,000	24,000	30,000
16MCS (350cc single)	1,400	2,200	3,200	4,300	5,800	7,200
18CS (500cc single)	1,400	2,200	4,000	6,000	7,500	9,000
18S (500cc single)	1,300	2,000	3,000	4,000	5,300	6,600
20 (500cc twin)	1,200	1,900	2,800	3,700	5,000	6,200

	6	5	4	3	2	1
20CSR (500cc twin)	−1,200	−1,900	−3,000	**4,500**	**6,000**	**7,500**
30 (600cc twin)	1,300	**2,000**	3,500	5,000	6,500	8,000
30CSR (600cc twin)	**1,500**	**2,500**	4,000	5,500	7,000	8,500
1958						
14 (250cc single)	800	1,200	1,800	2,400	3,200	4,000
7R Racer (350cc single).	6,000	9,000	13,500	18,000	24,000	30,000
16MCS (350cc single)	1,400	2,200	3,200	4,300	5,800	7,200
18CS (500cc single)	1,400	2,200	4,000	6,000	7,500	9,000
18S (500cc single)	1,300	2,000	3,000	4,000	5,300	6,600
20 Deluxe (500cc twin)	1,200	1,900	**3,000**	**4,500**	**6,000**	**7,500**
20 (500cc twin)	**1,400**	**2,100**	**3,200**	**4,200**	**5,600**	**7,000**
20CSR (500cc twin)	**1,500**	**2,500**	4,000	5,500	7,000	8,500
30 (600cc twin)	**1,400**	**2,100**	**3,200**	**4,200**	**5,600**	**7,000**
30CSR (600cc twin)	**1,500**	**2,500**	4,000	5,500	7,000	8,500
1959						
14 (250cc single)	700	1,100	1,600	2,100	2,800	3,500
14CS (250cc single).	800	1,200	1,800	2,300	3,100	3,900
7R Racer (350cc single).	6,000	9,000	13,500	18,000	24,000	30,000
16 (350cc single)	1,100	1,600	2,400	3,200	4,300	5,400
16C (350cc single)	1,300	2,000	3,000	4,000	5,400	6,700
16CS (350cc single).	1,300	2,000	3,000	4,000	5,400	6,700
18CS (500cc single)	1,400	2,200	4,000	6,000	7,500	9,000
18S (500cc single)	−1,200	−1,900	3,000	**4,500**	**6,000**	**7,500**
20 Deluxe (500cc twin)	1,200	1,900	**3,000**	**4,500**	**6,000**	**7,500**
20 (500cc twin)	**1,400**	**2,100**	**3,200**	**4,200**	**5,600**	**7,000**
20CSR (500cc twin).	−1,200	−1,900	−3,000	**4,500**	**6,000**	**7,500**
31 Deluxe (650cc twin)	**1,300**	**2,000**	3,500	5,000	6,500	8,000
31 (650cc twin)	1,200	**1,900**	**3,000**	**4,500**	**6,000**	**7,500**
31CSR (650cc twin).	**1,500**	**2,500**	4,000	5,500	7,000	8,500
1960						
14 (250cc single)	700	1,000	1,500	2,000	2,600	3,300
14CS (250cc single).	700	1,100	1,700	2,200	3,000	3,700
7R Racer (350cc single).	6,000	9,000	13,500	18,000	24,000	30,000
8 (350cc single)	900	1,300	2,000	2,600	3,500	4,400
16 (350cc single)	1,100	1,600	2,400	3,200	4,300	5,400
16C (350cc single)	1,300	2,000	3,000	4,000	5,400	6,700
18CS (500cc single)	**1,500**	**3,000**	**4,500**	**6,000**	**7,500**	**9,000**
18S (500cc single)	−1,200	−1,900	−3,000	**4,500**	**6,000**	**7,500**
20 (500cc twin)	1,200	1,900	**3,000**	**4,500**	**6,000**	**7,500**
20CSR (500cc twin).	−1,300	−2,000	3,500	5,000	6,500	8,000
31 Deluxe (650cc twin)	**1,300**	**2,000**	3,500	5,000	6,500	8,000
31 (650cc twin)	1,200	**1,900**	**3,000**	**4,500**	**6,000**	**7,500**
31CSR (650cc twin).	**1,500**	**2,500**	4,000	5,500	7,000	8,500
1961						
14 (250cc single)	700	1,000	1,500	2,000	2,600	3,300
14CS (250cc single).	700	1,100	1,700	2,200	3,000	3,700
14S (250cc single)	800	1,200	1,800	2,300	3,100	3,900
7R Racer (350cc single).	6,000	9,000	13,500	18,000	24,000	30,000
8 (350cc single)	900	1,300	2,000	2,600	3,500	4,400
16 (350cc single)	1,100	1,600	2,400	3,200	4,300	5,400
16C (350cc single)	1,400	2,100	3,100	4,100	5,500	6,900
18CS (500cc single).	**1,500**	**3,000**	**4,500**	**6,000**	**7,500**	**9,000**
18S (500cc single)	−1,200	1,900	**3,000**	**4,500**	**6,000**	**7,500**
20 (500cc twin)	**1,400**	**2,100**	**3,200**	**4,200**	**5,600**	**7,000**
20CSR (500cc twin).	−1,200	−1,900	−3,000	**4,500**	**6,000**	**7,500**
31 Deluxe (650cc twin)	**1,300**	**2,000**	3,500	5,000	6,500	8,000
31 (650cc twin)	1,200	**1,900**	**3,000**	**4,500**	**6,000**	**7,500**
31CSR (650cc twin).	2,000	−3,500	−5,000	−6,500	−8,000	−9,500

	6	5	4	3	2	1
1962						
14 (250cc single)	700	1,000	1,500	2,000	2,600	3,300
14CS (250cc single).	700	1,100	1,700	2,200	3,000	3,700
14CSR (250cc single).	800	1,300	1,900	2,500	3,400	4,200
14S (250cc single)	800	1,200	1,800	2,300	3,100	3,900
7R Racer (350cc single).	6,000	9,000	13,500	18,000	24,000	30,000
8 (350cc single)	900	1,300	2,000	2,600	3,500	4,400
16 (350cc single)	1,000	1,600	2,300	3,100	4,200	5,200
16C (350cc single)	1,400	2,100	3,100	4,100	5,500	6,900
16S (350cc single)	1,000	1,600	2,300	3,100	4,200	5,200
18CS (500cc single).	1,500	**3,000**	**4,500**	**6,000**	**7,500**	**9,000**
18S (500cc single)	1,200	1,900	**3,000**	**4,500**	**6,000**	**7,500**
31 (650cc twin)	**1,500**	**2,500**	**4,000**	**5,500**	**7,000**	**8,500**
31CSR (650cc twin)	**2,000**	**3,500**	**5,000**	**6,500**	**8,000**	**9,500**
1963						
14 (250cc single)	700	1,000	1,500	2,000	2,600	3,300
14CSR (250cc single).	800	1,300	1,900	2,500	3,400	4,200
7R Racer (350cc single).	6,000	9,000	13,500	18,000	24,000	30,000
16 (350cc single)	1,000	1,600	2,300	3,100	4,200	5,200
16C (350cc single)	1,300	2,000	3,000	4,000	5,400	6,700
18CS (500cc single).	1,500	**3,000**	**4,500**	**6,000**	**7,500**	**9,000**
18S (500cc single)	1,200	**1,900**	**3,000**	**4,500**	**6,000**	**7,500**
31 (650cc twin)	**1,500**	**2,500**	**4,000**	**5,500**	**7,000**	**8,500**
31CSR (650cc twin)	**2,000**	**3,500**	**5,000**	**6,500**	**8,000**	**9,500**
1964						
14CSR (250cc single).	800	1,300	1,900	2,500	3,400	4,200
16 (350cc single)	1,000	1,600	2,300	3,100	4,200	5,200
16C (350cc single)	1,300	2,000	3,000	4,000	5,400	6,700
18CS (500cc single).	**1,500**	**3,000**	**4,500**	**6,000**	**7,500**	**9,000**
18S (500cc single)	1,200	**1,900**	**3,000**	**4,500**	**6,000**	**7,500**
31 (650cc twin)	**1,500**	**2,500**	**4,000**	**5,500**	**7,000**	**8,500**
31CSR (650cc twin)	**2,000**	**3,500**	**5,000**	**6,500**	**8,000**	**9,500**
33 (750cc twin)	**1,500**	**3,000**	**4,500**	**6,000**	**7,500**	**9,000**
33CSR (750cc twin)	**2,000**	**3,500**	**5,000**	**6,500**	**8,000**	**9,500**
1965						
14CSR (250cc single).	800	1,300	1,900	2,500	3,400	4,200
16 (350cc single)	1,000	−1,500	**2,500**	**3,900**	**5,300**	**6,700**
18CS (500cc single).	**1,500**	**3,000**	**4,500**	**6,000**	**7,500**	**9,000**
18S (500cc single)	1,200	**1,900**	**3,000**	**4,500**	**6,000**	**7,500**
31 (650cc twin)	**1,500**	**2,500**	**4,000**	**5,500**	**7,000**	**8,500**
31CSR (650cc twin)	**2,000**	**3,500**	**5,000**	**6,500**	**8,000**	**9,500**
33 (750cc twin)	**1,500**	**3,000**	**4,500**	**6,000**	**7,500**	**9,000**
33CSR (750cc twin)	**2,000**	**3,500**	**5,000**	**6,500**	**8,000**	**9,500**
1966						
14CSR (250cc single).	800	1,300	1,900	2,500	3,400	4,200
16 (350cc single)	1,000	1,600	2,300	3,100	4,200	5,200
18S (500cc single)	**1,200**	**1,900**	**3,000**	**4,500**	**6,000**	**7,500**
31 (650cc twin)	**1,500**	**2,500**	**4,000**	**5,500**	**7,000**	**8,500**
31CSR (650cc twin)	**2,000**	**3,500**	**5,000**	**6,500**	**8,000**	**9,500**
33 (750cc twin)	**1,500**	**3,000**	**4,500**	**6,000**	**7,500**	**9,000**
33CSR (750cc twin)	**2,000**	**3,500**	**5,000**	**6,500**	**8,000**	**9,500**
1967						
33 (750cc twin)	**1,500**	**3,000**	**4,500**	**6,000**	**7,500**	**9,000**
33CSR (750cc twin)	**2,000**	**3,500**	**5,000**	**6,500**	**8,000**	**9,500**
1968						
37A Trials (250cc single)	1,000	1,500	2,300	3,000	4,000	5,000
33 (750cc twin)	**1,500**	**3,000**	**4,500**	**6,000**	**7,500**	**9,000**
33CSR (750cc twin)	**2,000**	**3,500**	**5,000**	**6,500**	**8,000**	**9,500**

	6	5	4	3	2	1
1969						
37A Trials (250cc single)	1,000	1,500	2,300	3,000	4,000	5,000
33 (750cc twin)	**1,500**	**3,000**	**4,500**	**6,000**	**7,500**	**9,000**
33CSR (750cc twin)	**2,000**	**3,500**	**5,000**	**6,500**	**8,000**	**9,500**
1970						
Y40 Stormer (250cc single)	600	900	1,400	1,800	2,400	3,000
Y50 Stormer (370cc single)	700	1,000	1,500	2,000	2,700	3,300
1971						
Y41 Stormer	500	700	1,200	2,000	2,700	3,300
Y51 Stormer	600	800	1,300	2,200	3,000	3,600

APRILIA

	6	5	4	3	2	1
1988						
TRX 312	100	300	600	900	1,200	1,500
1989						
Climber 300	100	300	700	1,000	1,300	1,600
1990						
Climber 300	100	300	700	1,100	1,300	1,600
1991						
Climber 300	100	200	400	900	1,300	1,600
1992						
Climber 280R	100	200	500	1,000	1,400	1,800
1993						
Climber 280R	100	200	500	1,000	1,400	1,800
1994						
Climber 280R	100	200	500	1,000	1,500	1,900

ARIEL

	6	5	4	3	2	1
1920						
Solo (498cc single)	1,200	1,800	3,000	4,500	6,000	7,500
Solo (586cc single)	1,400	2,000	3,000	4,500	6,000	7,500
Solo/SC (670cc V-twin)	3,000	4,500	6,800	9,000	12,000	15,000
Solo/SC (795cc V-twin)	3,000	4,500	6,800	9,000	12,000	15,000
1921						
Solo (498cc single)	1,200	1,800	2,700	4,500	6,000	7,500
Solo (586cc single)	1,500	2,300	3,400	4,500	6,000	7,500
Solo/SC (670cc V-twin)	3,000	4,500	6,800	9,000	12,000	15,000
Solo/SC (795cc V-twin)	3,000	4,500	6,800	9,000	12,000	15,000
1922						
Solo (498cc single)	1,200	1,800	2,700	4,500	6,000	7,500
Solo (665cc single)	1,500	2,300	3,400	4,500	6,000	7,500
Solo/SC (795cc V-twin)	2,800	4,200	6,300	9,000	12,000	15,000
Solo/SC (993cc V-twin)	3,600	5,400	8,100	10,800	14,400	18,000
1923						
Solo (249cc single)	1,100	1,700	2,500	4,500	6,000	7,500
Solo (498cc single)	1,200	1,800	2,700	4,500	6,000	7,500
Solo (665cc single)	1,500	2,300	3,400	4,500	6,000	7,500
Solo/SC (795cc V-twin)	2,800	4,200	6,300	9,000	12,000	15,000
Solo/SC (993cc V-twin)	3,600	5,400	8,100	10,800	14,400	18,000
1924						
Solo (249cc single)	1,100	1,700	3,000	4,500	6,000	7,500
Solo 1 (498cc single)	1,200	1,800	3,000	4,500	6,000	7,500
Solo 2 (498cc single)	1,200	1,800	3,000	4,500	6,000	7,500
Solo 3 (498cc single)	1,200	1,800	3,000	4,500	6,000	7,500
Solo/SC (993cc V-twin)	3,600	5,400	8,100	10,800	14,400	18,000
1925						
Solo (249cc single)	1,100	1,700	3,000	4,500	6,000	7,500
Sports (498cc single)	1,500	2,300	3,400	4,500	6,000	7,500
1926						
Sports C (500cc single)	1,200	1,800	3,000	4,500	6,000	7,500
Touring D (500cc single)	1,200	1,800	3,000	4,500	6,000	7,500
Sports A (557cc single)	1,600	2,400	3,600	4,800	6,400	8,000

	6	5	4	3	2	1
Touring B (557cc single)	1,600	2,400	3,600	4,800	6,400	8,000
1927						
Sports C (500cc single)	1,200	1,800	4,000	6,000	7,500	9,000
Sports E (500cc single)	1,200	1,800	4,000	6,000	7,500	9,000
Touring D (500cc single)	1,200	1,800	4,000	6,000	7,500	9,000
Sports A (557cc single)	1,600	2,400	4,000	6,000	7,500	9,000
Touring B (557cc single)	1,600	2,400	4,000	6,000	7,500	9,000
1928						
Sports C (500cc single)	1,200	1,800	4,000	6,000	7,500	9,000
Sports E (500cc single)	1,200	1,800	4,000	6,000	7,500	9,000
Touring D (500cc single)	1,200	1,800	4,000	6,000	7,500	9,000
Sports A (557cc single)	1,600	2,400	4,000	6,000	7,500	9,000
Touring B (557cc single)	1,600	2,400	4,000	6,000	7,500	9,000
1929						
LB Colt (250cc single).	1,300	2,000	3,500	4,500	6,000	7,500
LF Colt (250cc single).	1,300	2,000	3,500	4,500	6,000	7,500
Deluxe F (500cc single)	1,500	2,500	4,000	5,500	7,000	8,500
Model E (500cc single)	1,600	2,400	3,600	4,800	6,400	8,000
Deluxe B (500cc single)	1,600	2,400	3,600	4,800	6,400	8,000
Model A (557cc single)	1,600	2,400	3,600	4,800	6,400	8,000
1930						
LB Colt (250cc single).	1,300	2,000	3,500	4,500	6,000	7,500
LF Colt (250cc single).	1,300	2,000	3,500	4,500	6,000	7,500
LG Colt (250cc single).	1,300	2,000	2,900	3,900	5,200	6,500
Deluxe F (500cc single)	1,500	2,500	4,000	5,500	7,000	8,500
Model E (500cc single)	1,600	2,400	3,600	4,800	6,400	8,000
Model G (500cc single)	1,500	2,300	3,400	4,500	6,000	7,500
Deluxe B (557cc single)	1,600	2,400	3,600	4,800	6,400	8,000
Model A (557cc single)	1,600	2,400	3,600	4,800	6,400	8,000
1931						
LB31 (250cc single)	1,200	2,000	3,500	5,000	6,500	7,500
L1F31 (250cc single)	1,200	2,000	3,500	5,000	6,500	7,500
L2F31 (250cc single)	1,200	2,000	3,500	5,000	6,500	7,500
MF (250cc single)	1,200	2,000	3,500	5,000	6,500	7,500
VF (500cc single)	1,200	2,000	3,500	5,000	6,500	8,000
SF31 (500cc single).	1,200	2,000	3,500	5,000	6,500	8,000
SG31 (500cc single).	1,200	2,000	3,500	5,000	6,500	8,000
4F Square Flour (500cc four)	3,000	5,000	10,000	15,000	25,000	35,000
VG31 (500cc single).	1,100	1,700	3,500	5,000	6,500	8,000
SB31 (557cc single)	1,400	2,100	3,500	5,000	6,500	8,000
VB (557cc single)	1,400	2,100	3,500	5,000	6,500	8,000
1932						
LB32 (249cc single)	1,200	2,000	3,500	5,000	6,500	7,500
LF32 (249cc single)	1,200	2,000	3,500	5,000	6,500	7,500
MB32 (348cc single)	1,200	2,000	3,500	5,000	6,500	7,500
MF32 (348cc single)	1,200	2,000	3,500	5,000	6,500	7,500
MH32 (348cc single)	1,200	2,000	3,500	5,000	6,500	7,500
VG32 (499cc single).	1,200	2,000	3,500	5,000	6,500	8,000
SG32 (499cc single).	1,200	2,000	3,500	5,000	6,500	8,000
VH32 RH (499cc single).	1,700	2,600	3,900	5,100	6,800	8,500
VB32 (557cc single).	1,200	2,000	3,500	5,000	6,500	8,000
SB32 (557cc single).	1,200	2,000	3,500	5,000	6,500	8,000
4F/6 Square Four (601cc four)	3,000	5,000	10,000	15,000	25,000	35,000
1933						
LH (248cc single)	1,200	2,000	3,500	5,000	6,500	7,500
NF (346cc single)	1,200	2,000	3,500	5,000	6,500	7,500
NH (346cc single)	1,200	**2,000**	**3,500**	**5,000**	**6,500**	**7,500**
VF (499cc single)	1,200	2,000	3,500	5,000	6,500	8,000
VH (499cc single)	1,700	2,600	3,800	5,100	6,800	8,500
VA (557cc single)	1,200	2,000	3,500	5,000	6,500	8,000

	6	5	4	3	2	1
VB Deluxe (557cc single)	1,300	2,000	3,500	5,000	7,000	9,000
4F/6 Square Four (601cc four)	3,000	5,000	10,000	15,000	25,000	35,000
1934						
LF (248cc single)	1,200	2,000	3,500	5,000	6,500	7,500
LH/RH Sport (248cc single)	1,200	2,000	3,500	5,000	6,500	7,500
NF (346cc single)	1,200	2,000	3,500	5,000	6,500	7,500
NH/RH Sport (346cc single).	1,200	2,000	3,500	5,000	6,500	7,500
VF (499cc single)	1,200	2,000	3,500	5,000	6,500	8,000
VH/RH Sport (499cc single).	1,700	2,600	3,800	5,100	6,800	8,500
VA (557cc single)	1,200	2,000	3,500	5,000	6,500	8,000
VB Deluxe (557cc single)	1,300	2,000	3,500	5,000	7,000	9,000
4F/6 Square Four (601cc four)	3,000	5,000	10,000	15,000	25,000	35,000
1935						
LF (248cc single)	1,200	2,000	3,500	5,000	6,500	7,500
LH/RH Sport (248cc single)	1,200	2,000	3,500	5,000	6,500	7,500
NF (346cc single)	1,200	2,000	3,500	5,000	6,500	7,500
NH/RH Sport (346cc single).	1,200	2,000	3,500	5,000	6,500	7,500
VF (499cc single)	1,200	2,000	3,500	5,000	6,500	8,000
VG Deluxe (499cc single)	1,200	2,000	3,500	5,000	6,500	8,000
VH/RH Sport (499cc single).	1,700	2,600	3,800	5,100	6,800	8,500
VA (557cc single)	1,200	2,000	3,500	5,000	6,500	8,000
VB Deluxe (557cc single)	1,300	2,000	3,500	5,000	7,000	9,000
4F/6 Square Four (601cc four)	3,000	5,000	10,000	15,000	25,000	35,000
1936						
LG Deluxe (248cc single)	1,200	2,000	3,500	5,000	6,500	7,500
LH/RH Sport (248cc single)	1,200	2,000	3,500	5,000	6,500	7,500
NG Deluxe (346cc single).	1,200	2,500	5,000	7,000	8,500	10,000
NH/RH Sport (346cc single).	1,200	2,000	3,500	5,000	6,500	7,500
VG Deluxe (499cc single)	1,200	2,000	3,500	5,000	6,500	8,000
VH/RH Sport (499cc single).	1,700	2,600	3,800	5,100	6,800	8,500
VB Deluxe (557cc single)	1,300	2,000	3,500	5,000	7,000	9,000
4F/6 Square Four (601cc four)	3,000	5,000	10,000	15,000	25,000	35,000
4G Square Four (1,000cc four)	3,000	5,000	10,000	15,000	25,000	35,000
1937						
LG Deluxe (248cc single)	1,200	2,000	3,500	5,000	6,500	7,500
LH/RH Sport (248cc single)	1,200	2,000	3,500	5,000	6,500	7,500
NG Deluxe (346cc single).	1,200	2,500	5,000	7,000	8,500	10,000
NH/RH Sport (346cc single).	1,200	2,000	3,500	5,000	6,500	7,500
VG Deluxe (499cc single)	1,200	2,000	3,500	5,000	6,500	8,000
VH/RH (499cc single).	1,700	2,600	3,800	5,100	6,800	8,500
VB Deluxe (598cc single)	1,300	2,000	3,500	5,000	7,000	9,000
4F/6 Square Four (601cc four)	3,000	5,000	10,000	15,000	25,000	35,000
4G Square Four (1,000cc four)	**5,000**	**12,000**	**18,000**	**23,000**	**28,000**	**33,000**
1938						
LG Deluxe (248cc single)	1,200	2,000	3,500	5,000	6,500	7,500
LH/RH (248cc single)	1,200	2,000	3,500	5,000	6,500	7,500
NG Deluxe (346cc single).	1,200	2,500	5,000	7,000	8,500	10,000
NH/RH (346cc single)	1,200	2,000	3,500	5,000	6,500	7,500
VG Deluxe (499cc single)	1,200	2,000	3,500	5,000	6,500	8,000
VH/RH (499cc single).	1,700	2,600	3,800	5,100	6,800	8,500
VB Deluxe (598cc single)	1,400	2,100	3,500	5,000	7,000	9,000
4F Square Four (600cc four)	3,000	5,000	10,000	15,000	25,000	35,000
4G Square Four (995cc four)	**5,000**	**12,000**	**18,000**	**23,000**	**28,000**	**33,000**
4H Square Four (995cc four)	**5,000**	**12,000**	**18,000**	**23,000**	**28,000**	**33,000**
1939						
OG Deluxe (248cc single).	1,200	2,000	3,500	5,000	6,500	7,500
OH/RH (248cc single).	1,200	2,000	3,500	5,000	6,500	7,500
NG Deluxe (346cc single).	1,200	2,500	5,000	7,000	8,500	10,000
NH/RH (346cc single)	1,200	2,000	3,500	5,000	6,500	7,500
VG Deluxe (499cc single)	1,200	2,000	3,500	5,000	6,500	8,000

	6	5	4	3	2	1
VH/RH (499cc single)	1,700	2,600	3,800	5,100	6,800	8,500
VB Deluxe (598cc single)	1,400	2,100	3,500	5,000	7,000	9,000
4F Square Four (600cc four)	3,000	5,000	10,000	15,000	25,000	35,000
4G Square Four (995cc four)	**5,000**	**12,000**	**18,000**	**23,000**	**28,000**	**33,000**
4H Square Four (995cc four)	**5,000**	**12,000**	**18,000**	**23,000**	**28,000**	**33,000**
1940						
OG Deluxe (248cc single)	1,200	2,000	3,500	5,000	6,500	7,500
OH/RH (248cc single)	1,200	2,000	3,500	5,000	6,500	7,500
NG Deluxe (346cc single)	1,200	2,500	5,000	7,000	8,500	10,000
NH/RH (346cc single)	1,200	2,000	3,500	5,000	6,500	7,500
VG Deluxe (500cc single)	1,200	2,000	3,500	5,000	6,500	8,000
VH/RH (500cc single)	1,700	2,600	3,800	5,100	6,800	8,500
VA Deluxe (598cc single)	1,200	2,000	3,500	5,000	6,500	8,000
VB Deluxe (598cc single)	1,400	2,200	3,500	5,000	7,000	9,000
4F Square Four (600cc four)	3,000	5,000	10,000	15,000	25,000	35,000
4G Square Four (995cc four)	**5,000**	**12,000**	**18,000**	**23,000**	**28,000**	**33,000**
4H Square Four (995cc four)	**5,000**	**12,000**	**18,000**	**23,000**	**28,000**	**33,000**
1941-1945 (military production)						
Model W/NG (346cc single)	1,700	2,600	3,800	5,100	6,800	8,500
1946						
NG Deluxe (346cc single)	1,300	2,500	5,000	−6,500	−8,000	−9,500
NH (346cc single)	1,200	2,000	3,500	5,000	6,500	**8,000**
VG Deluxe (500cc single)	1,200	2,000	3,500	5,000	6,500	8,000
VH (500cc single)	1,600	2,400	3,600	4,800	6,400	8,000
VB Deluxe (598cc single)	1,300	2,000	3,500	5,000	7,000	9,000
4G Square Four (995cc four)	**5,000**	**12,000**	**18,000**	**23,000**	**28,000**	**33,000**
1947						
NG (347cc single)	**1,300**	2,500	5,000	−6,500	−8,000	−9,500
NH (347cc single)	1,200	2,000	3,500	5,000	6,500	**8,000**
VG (497cc single)	1,200	2,000	3,500	5,000	6,500	7,500
VH (497cc single)	1,600	**2,500**	**4,000**	**5,500**	**7,000**	**8,500**
VB (598cc single)	1,600	**2,500**	**4,000**	**5,500**	**7,000**	**8,500**
4G Square Four (997cc four)	**5,000**	**12,000**	**18,000**	**23,000**	**28,000**	**33,000**
1948						
NG (347cc single)	**1,300**	2,500	5,000	−6,500	−8,000	−9,500
NH (347cc single)	1,200	2,000	3,500	5,000	6,500	**8,000**
VH (497cc single)	1,600	**2,500**	**4,000**	**5,500**	**7,000**	**8,500**
KG Deluxe (498cc twin)	−1,600	−2,500	**4,000**	**5,500**	**7,000**	**8,500**
KH (498cc twin)	1,800	2,800	4,100	5,500	7,400	9,200
VB (598cc single)	1,300	2,000	3,500	5,000	7,000	9,000
4G Mk. 1 Square Four (997cc four)	**5,000**	**12,000**	**18,000**	**23,000**	**28,000**	**33,000**
1949						
NG (347cc single)	**1,300**	2,500	5,000	−6,500	−8,000	−9,500
NH (347cc single)	1,200	2,000	3,500	5,000	6,500	**8,000**
VG (497cc single)	**1,600**	**2,500**	**4,000**	**5,500**	**7,000**	**8,500**
VH (497cc single)	1,600	**2,500**	**4,000**	**5,500**	**7,000**	**8,500**
KH (498cc twin)	1,800	2,800	4,100	5,500	7,400	9,200
VB (598cc single)	1,600	**2,500**	**4,000**	**5,500**	**7,000**	**8,500**
4G Mk. 1 Square Four (997cc four)	**5,000**	**12,000**	**18,000**	**23,000**	**28,000**	**33,000**
1950						
NH (347cc single)	1,200	2,000	3,500	5,000	6,500	**8,000**
VCH (497cc single)	**1,300**	2,000	3,500	5,000	**7,000**	**9,000**
VG (497cc single)	**1,300**	2,000	3,500	5,000	**7,000**	**9,000**
VH (497cc single)	1,600	**2,500**	**4,000**	**5,500**	**7,000**	**8,500**
KG Deluxe (498cc twin)	−1,300	−2,000	−3,500	−5,000	**7,000**	**9,000**
KH (498cc twin)	1,900	2,900	4,300	5,700	7,600	9,500
VB (598cc single)	1,600	**2,500**	**4,000**	**5,500**	**7,000**	**8,500**
4G Mk. 1 Square Four (997cc four)	**5,000**	**12,000**	**18,000**	**23,000**	**28,000**	**33,000**

	6	5	4	3	2	1
1951						
NH (347cc single)	1,200	2,000	3,500	5,000	6,500	8,000
VCH (497cc single)	−1,300	−2,000	−3,500	5,000	7,000	9,000
VH (497cc single)	−1,300	−2,000	−3,500	5,000	7,000	9,000
KG Deluxe (498cc twin)	1,900	2,900	4,300	5,700	7,600	9,500
KH (498cc twin)	1,800	2,700	4,100	5,400	7,200	9,000
VB (598cc single)	1,600	2,500	4,000	5,500	7,000	8,500
4G Mk. 1 Square Four (997cc four)	5,000	12,000	18,000	23,000	28,000	33,000
1952						
NH (347cc single)	1,200	2,000	3,500	5,000	6,500	8,000
VCH (497cc single)	−1,300	−2,000	−3,500	5,000	7,000	9,000
VH (497cc single)	−1,300	−2,000	−3,500	5,000	7,000	9,000
VHA (497cc single)	1,800	2,700	4,100	5,400	7,200	9,000
KH (498cc twin)	1,900	2,900	4,300	5,700	7,600	9,500
VB (598cc single)	1,800	2,700	4,100	5,400	7,200	9,000
4G Mk. 1 Square Four (997cc four)	5,000	12,000	18,000	23,000	28,000	33,000
4G Mk. 2 Square Four (997cc four)	5,000	12,000	18,000	23,000	28,000	33,000
1953						
LH (197cc single)	1,200	2,000	3,500	5,000	6,500	7,500
NH (347cc single)	1,200	2,000	3,500	5,000	6,500	8,000
HT5 Trials (497cc single)	2,000	3,000	4,500	6,000	8,000	10,000
VH (497cc single)	1,800	2,700	4,100	5,400	7,200	9,000
KH (498cc twin)	1,900	2,900	4,300	5,700	7,600	9,500
VHA (500cc single)	2,000	3,000	4,500	6,000	8,000	10,000
KHA (500cc single)	2,000	3,000	4,500	6,000	8,000	10,000
VB (598cc single)	1,300	2,000	3,500	5,000	7,000	9,000
4G Mk. 1 Square Four (997cc four)	5,000	12,000	18,000	23,000	28,000	33,000
4G Mk. 2 Square Four (997cc four)	5,000	12,000	18,000	23,000	28,000	33,000
1954						
LH (197cc single)	1,000	1,500	2,500	4,000	5,500	7,000
NH (347cc single)	1,200	2,000	3,500	5,000	6,500	8,000
HS Scrambler (497cc single)	2,000	3,000	4,500	6,000	8,000	10,000
HT5 Trials (497cc single)	2,000	3,000	4,500	6,000	8,000	10,000
VH (497cc single)	1,800	2,700	4,100	5,400	7,200	9,000
KH (498cc twin)	1,800	2,700	4,100	5,400	7,200	9,000
VB (598cc single)	1,700	2,600	3,800	5,100	6,800	8,500
FH (650cc twin)	1,900	2,900	4,300	5,700	7,600	9,500
4G Mk. 2 Square Four (997cc four)	5,000	12,000	18,000	23,000	28,000	33,000
1955						
LH (197cc single)	1,000	1,500	2,500	4,000	5,500	7,000
LM (197cc single)	1,000	1,500	2,500	4,000	5,500	7,000
NH (347cc single)	1,200	2,000	3,500	5,000	6,500	8,000
HS Scrambler (497cc single)	1,700	2,600	3,800	5,100	6,800	8,500
HT5 Trials (497cc single)	2,000	3,000	4,500	6,000	8,000	10,000
VH (497cc single)	2,000	3,000	4,500	6,000	8,000	10,000
KH (498cc twin)	1,800	2,700	4,100	5,400	7,200	9,000
VB (598cc single)	1,700	2,600	3,800	5,100	6,800	8,500
FH (650cc twin)	1,900	2,900	4,300	5,700	7,600	9,500
4G Mk. 2 Square Four (997cc four)	5,000	12,000	18,000	23,000	28,000	33,000
1956						
LH (197cc single)	1,000	1,500	2,500	4,000	5,500	7,000
LM (197cc single)	1,000	1,500	2,500	4,000	5,500	7,000
HT3 Trials (347cc single)	1,600	2,400	3,600	4,800	6,400	8,000
NH (347cc single)	1,200	2,000	3,500	5,000	6,500	8,000
HS Mk.3 (497cc single)	2,000	4,000	6,000	8,000	10,000	12,000
HT5 Trials (497cc single)	2,000	3,000	4,500	6,000	8,000	10,000
VH (497cc single)	1,900	2,900	4,300	5,700	7,600	9,500
KH (498cc twin)	1,800	2,700	4,100	5,400	7,200	9,000
VB (598cc single)	1,800	2,700	4,100	5,400	7,200	9,000

	6	5	4	3	2	1
FH (650cc twin)	1,800	2,700	4,100	5,400	7,200	9,000
Cyclone (650cc twin)	1,400	2,100	4,000	6,000	9,000	12,000
4G Mk. 2 Square Four (997cc four)	5,000	12,000	18,000	23,000	28,000	33,000
1957						
LH (197cc single)	1,000	1,500	2,500	4,000	5,500	7,000
HT3 Trials (347cc single)	1,600	2,400	3,600	4,800	6,400	8,000
NH (347cc single)	1,600	2,400	3,600	–4,800	–6,400	8,000
HS Mk.3 (497cc single)	2,000	4,000	6,000	8,000	10,000	12,000
HT5 Trials (497cc single)	2,000	3,000	4,500	6,000	8,000	10,000
VH (497cc single)	1,900	2,900	4,300	5,700	7,600	9,500
KH (498cc single)	1,800	2,700	4,100	5,400	7,200	9,000
VB (598cc single)	1,800	2,700	4,100	5,400	7,200	9,000
FH (650cc twin)	1,800	2,700	4,100	5,400	7,200	9,000
Cyclone (650cc twin)	1,400	2,100	4,000	6,000	9,000	12,000
4G Mk. 2 Square Four (997cc four)	5,000	12,000	18,000	23,000	28,000	33,000
1958						
LH (197cc single)	1,000	1,500	2,500	4,000	5,500	7,000
Leader (247cc twin)	1,000	1,500	2,500	4,000	5,500	7,000
HT3 Trials (347cc single)	1,600	2,400	3,600	4,800	6,400	8,000
NH (347cc single)	1,600	2,400	3,600	–4,800	–6,400	8,000
HS Mk.3 (497cc single)	2,000	4,000	6,000	8,000	10,000	12,000
HT5 Trials (497cc single)	2,000	3,000	4,500	6,000	8,000	10,000
VH (497cc single)	1,900	2,900	4,300	5,700	7,600	9,500
VB (598cc single)	1,800	2,700	4,100	5,400	7,200	9,000
FH (650cc twin)	1,800	2,700	4,100	5,400	7,200	9,000
Cyclone (650cc twin)	1,400	2,100	4,000	6,000	9,000	12,000
4G Mk. 2 Square Four (997cc four)	5,000	12,000	18,000	23,000	28,000	33,000
1959						
Arrow (247cc twin)	1,600	2,400	3,600	4,800	6,400	8,000
Leader (247cc twin)	1,700	2,600	3,800	5,100	6,800	8,500
1960						
Arrow (247cc twin)	1,600	2,400	3,600	4,800	6,400	8,000
Arrow Sport (247cc twin)	1,700	2,600	3,800	5,100	6,800	8,500
Leader (247cc twin)	1,600	2,400	3,600	4,800	6,400	8,000
1961						
Fieldmaster	2,000	4,000	6,000	8,000	10,000	12,000
1962						
Golden Arrow	1,500	2,000	4,000	6,000	8,000	10,000
1963						
Pixie (49cc single)	500	1,000	1,800	2,700	3,600	4,500
Arrow (197cc twin)	1,600	2,400	3,600	4,800	6,400	8,000
Arrow (247cc twin)	1,700	2,600	3,800	5,100	6,800	8,500
Arrow Sport (247cc twin)	1,700	2,600	3,800	5,100	6,800	8,500
Leader (247cc twin)	1,300	2,000	3,500	5,000	7,000	9,000
ATK						
1985						
560	100	200	300	400	500	700
1986						
560	100	200	300	400	500	700
1987						
560	100	200	300	400	500	700
1988						
200	100	200	300	400	500	700
250	100	200	300	400	500	700
406	100	200	300	400	500	700
604	100	200	300	500	700	900
1989						
250	100	200	300	400	500	700
406	100	200	300	400	500	700
604	100	200	300	500	700	900

	6	5	4	3	2	1
604 ES	100	200	300	600	900	1,200
1990						
250	100	200	300	500	800	1,100
406	100	200	300	400	600	900
604 Electric Start	100	200	300	600	900	1,200
604 Kick Start	100	200	300	600	800	1,000
1991						
250 CC	100	200	300	700	1,000	1,300
250 MX	100	200	300	500	700	900
350 Electric Start	100	200	400	800	1,200	1,600
350 ES CC	100	200	500	1,000	1,500	2,000
350 ES MX	100	200	300	600	900	1,200
350 MX	100	200	300	500	800	1,100
350 STD.	100	200	400	700	1,000	1,300
406 CC	100	200	400	700	1,000	1,300
406 MX	100	200	300	500	700	900
604 ES	100	200	400	800	1,300	1,700
604 ES CC	100	200	500	1,000	1,500	2,000
604 ES MX	100	200	300	700	1,000	1,300
604 MX	100	200	300	600	900	1,200
604 STD.	100	200	400	800	1,100	1,400
1992						
250 CC	100	200	400	700	1,000	1,300
250 MX	100	200	300	500	700	900
350 ES	100	200	500	900	1,300	1,700
350 ES CC	100	200	600	1,100	1,600	2,100
350 ES CC EFI	100	200	600	1,100	1,700	2,300
350 ES EFI	100	200	500	1,000	1,500	2,000
350 ES MX	100	200	400	700	1,000	1,300
350 ES MX EFI	100	200	400	800	1,100	1,400
350 MX	100	200	300	600	900	1,200
350 MX EFI	100	200	300	700	1,000	1,300
350 STD.	100	200	400	800	1,100	1,400
350 STD EFI	100	200	500	900	1,300	1,700
406 CC	100	200	400	700	1,000	1,300
406 MX	100	200	300	500	700	900
604 ES	100	200	500	900	1,400	1,900
604 ES CC	100	200	600	1,100	1,700	2,300
604 ES CC EFI	100	200	600	1,100	1,600	2,100
604 ES EFI	100	200	500	1,000	1,500	2,000
604 ES MX	100	200	400	800	1,100	1,400
604 ES MX EFI	100	200	400	800	1,200	1,600
604 MX	100	200	300	600	900	1,200
604 MX EFI	100	200	400	700	1,000	1,300
604 STD.	100	200	400	800	1,200	1,600
604 STD EFI	100	200	500	900	1,400	1,900
1993						
250 CC	100	200	400	800	1,100	1,400
250 MX	100	200	300	500	800	1,100
350 ES	100	200	500	1,000	1,500	2,000
350 ES CC	100	200	600	1,100	1,700	2,300
350 ES CC EFI	100	200	600	1,200	1,800	2,400
350 ES EFI	100	200	600	1,100	1,700	2,300
350 ES MX	100	200	400	800	1,100	1,400
350 ES MX EFI	100	200	400	800	1,100	1,400
350 MX	100	200	300	700	900	1,100
350 MX EFI	100	200	400	800	1,100	1,400
350 STD.	100	200	400	900	1,300	1,700
350 STD EFI	100	200	500	1,000	1,500	2,000
406 CC	100	200	400	800	1,100	1,400

	6	5	4	3	2	1
406 MX	100	200	300	500	800	1,100
605 ES	100	200	600	1,100	1,600	2,100
605 ES CC	100	200	600	1,200	1,800	2,400
605 ES CC EFI	100	200	700	1,300	2,000	2,700
605 ES EFI	100	200	600	1,200	1,800	2,400
605 ES MX	100	200	400	800	1,200	1,600
605 ES MX EFI	100	200	500	900	1,300	1,700
605 MX	100	200	400	700	1,000	1,300
605 MX EFI	100	200	400	800	1,200	1,600
605 STD.	100	200	500	900	1,300	1,700
605 STD EFI	100	200	600	1,100	1,600	2,100
1994						
250 CC	100	200	400	800	1,200	1,600
350 CC	100	200	500	1,000	1,500	2,000
350 DS	100	200	600	1,100	1,700	2,300
350 ES CC	100	200	600	1,100	1,700	2,300
350 ES DS	100	200	700	1,300	1,900	2,500
406 CC	100	200	400	900	1,200	1,500
605 CC	100	200	600	1,100	1,600	2,100
605 DS	100	200	600	1,300	1,800	2,300
605 ES CC	100	200	600	1,300	1,900	2,500
605 ES DS	100	300	700	1,400	2,100	2,800

BENELLI

	6	5	4	3	2	1
1938						
Single (250cc).	1,000	2,000	4,000	6,000	8,000	10,000
Grand Prix (500cc)	2,000	4,000	8,000	12,000	16,000	20,000
1954						
90cc.	1,000	2,000	3,000	4,000	5,000	6,000
Leoncino (125cc)	1,000	2,000	3,000	4,000	5,000	6,000
1960						
Trail Sport (48cc)	300	500	700	1,600	3,400	5,500
Touring OHV (125cc)	300	500	800	1,700	3,800	5,600
Sprite OHV (200cc)	300	500	900	1,900	4,000	6,000
1961						
Trail Sport (48cc)	300	500	700	1,600	3,400	5,500
Touring OHV (125cc)	300	500	800	1,700	3,800	5,600
Sprite OHV (200cc)	300	500	900	1,900	4,000	6,000
1962						
Trail Sport (48cc)	300	500	700	1,600	3,400	5,500
Touring OHV (125cc)	300	500	800	1,700	3,800	5,600
Sprite OHV (200cc)	300	500	900	1,900	4,000	6,000
Sprite OHV (250cc)	300	500	900	2,100	4,500	6,500
1963						
Trail Sport (48cc)	300	500	700	1,600	3,200	4,800
Touring OHV (125cc)	300	500	800	1,700	3,600	5,400
Sprite OHV (200cc)	300	500	900	1,900	3,800	5,500
Sprite OHV (250cc)	400	600	900	2,100	4,300	6,500
1964						
Trail Sport (48cc)	300	500	700	1,600	3,200	4,800
Touring OHV (125cc)	300	500	800	1,700	3,600	5,400
Sprite OHV (200cc)	300	500	900	1,900	3,800	5,500
Sprite OHV (250cc)	400	600	900	2,100	4,300	6,500
1965						
Trail Sport (48cc)	300	500	700	1,500	3,000	4,500
Touring OHV (125cc)	300	500	800	1,600	3,200	4,800
Sprite OHV (200cc)	300	500	900	1,800	3,400	5,000
Sprite OHV (250cc)	400	600	900	2,000	3,700	5,400
1966						
Trail (50cc)	200	400	600	1,100	2,300	3,500
Fireball (50cc).	200	400	600	1,100	2,400	3,700

	6	5	4	3	2	1
Cobra (125cc)	300	500	800	1,500	2,700	3,900
Cobra Scrambler (125cc)	300	500	900	1,600	3,100	4,600
Sprite (125cc)	200	400	600	1,200	2,500	3,800
Sprite (200cc)	200	400	700	1,300	2,700	4,000
Barracuda (250cc)	500	1,000	1,500	3,000	4,500	6,000
1967						
Automatic (50cc)	200	300	500	900	1,900	2,900
Fireball (50cc)	200	400	600	1,100	2,400	3,700
Mini Bike (50cc)	100	200	400	800	1,300	1,800
Trail (50cc)	200	400	600	1,100	2,300	3,500
Mini Sprite (100cc)	200	300	600	900	1,600	2,300
Cobra (125cc)	300	500	800	1,500	2,700	3,900
Cobra California (125cc)	300	500	900	1,600	2,800	4,000
Cobra Scrambler (125cc)	300	500	900	1,700	3,000	4,300
Sprite (125cc)	200	400	600	1,200	2,500	3,800
Sprite (200cc)	200	400	700	1,300	2,700	4,100
Barracuda (250cc)	500	1,000	1,500	3,000	4,500	6,000
Barracuda California (250cc)	500	1,000	1,500	3,000	4,500	6,000
1968						
Buzzer (50cc)	200	400	600	1,000	1,900	2,800
Dynamo Compact (50cc)	200	400	500	900	1,800	2,700
Fireball Trail (50cc)	200	400	500	900	1,800	2,700
Mini Sprite (100cc)	200	300	600	900	1,500	2,100
Cobra Scrambler (125cc)	300	500	900	1,600	2,800	4,000
Sprite 4 Speed (125cc)	200	400	500	900	2,200	3,500
Sprite 5 Speed (125cc)	200	400	600	1,100	2,300	3,500
Sprite (200cc)	300	500	700	1,200	2,400	3,600
Barracuda (250cc)	500	1,000	1,500	3,000	4,500	6,000
Barracuda 5 Speed (250cc)	500	1,000	1,500	3,000	4,500	6,000
Scorcher (360cc)	300	500	800	1,400	2,600	3,800
Tornado (650cc twin)	500	700	1,200	2,800	4,500	6,200
1969						
Buzzer (50cc)	200	400	600	1,000	1,900	2,800
Dynamo (50cc)	200	400	500	900	1,800	2,700
Dynamo Scrambler (50cc)	300	500	800	1,100	2,000	3,000
Fireball (50cc)	200	400	500	900	1,800	2,700
Hornet (50cc)	200	400	500	900	1,800	2,700
Maverick (50cc)	200	400	500	900	1,800	2,700
Cobra California (125cc)	400	600	700	1,100	2,100	3,100
Cobra Scrambler (125cc)	300	500	900	1,600	2,800	4,000
El Diablo 4 Speed (125cc)	200	400	600	1,100	2,300	3,500
El Diablo California (125cc)	200	400	600	1,100	2,300	3,500
Sprite 4 Speed (125cc)	200	400	500	900	2,200	3,500
Sprite 5 Speed (125cc)	200	400	600	1,100	2,300	3,500
Sprite California (125cc)	200	400	500	900	2,200	3,500
El Diablo 4 Speed (200cc)	300	500	700	1,100	2,400	3,700
Sprite (200cc)	300	500	700	1,200	2,400	3,600
Sprite California (200cc)	200	400	500	900	2,200	3,500
Barracuda 4 Speed (250cc)	500	1,000	1,500	3,000	4,500	6,000
Barracuda 5 Speed (250cc)	500	1,000	1,500	3,000	4,500	6,000
Barracuda California 4 Speed (250cc)	500	1,000	1,500	3,000	4,500	6,000
Barracuda California 5 Speed (250cc)	500	700	1,000	1,800	3,500	5,200
El Diablo 4 Speed (250cc)	300	500	700	1,200	2,500	3,800
El Diablo 5 Speed (250cc)	400	600	700	1,200	2,600	4,000
Tornado (650cc twin)	500	700	1,200	2,800	4,500	6,200
1970						
Buzzer-Hornet (60cc)	200	400	600	1,000	1,900	2,800
Cougar (60cc)	200	400	600	1,000	1,900	2,800
Dynamo Compact (65cc)	300	500	700	1,000	2,000	3,000
Dynamo Scrambler (65cc)	300	500	700	1,000	2,000	3,000

	6	5	4	3	2	1
Dynamo Woodsbike (65cc)	300	500	700	1,000	2,000	3,000
Cobra Scrambler (125cc)	300	500	700	1,000	2,100	3,200
Sprite 5 Speed (125cc)	200	400	600	1,100	2,300	3,500
Volcano (180cc)	300	500	700	1,100	2,100	3,100
Sprite El Diablo (200cc)	300	500	700	1,200	2,400	3,600
Barracuda Supersport (250cc)	500	1,000	1,500	3,000	4,500	6,000
Tornado (650cc twin)	500	700	1,200	2,800	4,500	6,200
1971						
Buzzer-Hornet (60cc)	200	400	600	1,000	1,900	2,800
Cougar (60cc)	200	400	600	1,000	1,900	2,800
Dynamo Compact (65cc)	300	500	700	1,000	2,000	3,000
Dynamo Scrambler (65cc)	300	500	700	1,000	2,000	3,000
Dynamo Woodsbike (65cc)	300	500	700	1,000	2,000	3,000
Hurricane (65cc)	300	500	700	1,000	2,000	3,000
Sprite 5 Speed (125cc)	300	500	600	1,100	2,300	3,500
Motocross (175cc)	300	500	700	1,000	2,000	3,000
Motocross (180cc)	300	500	700	1,100	2,100	3,100
Volcano (180cc)	300	500	700	1,100	2,100	3,100
Barracuda Supersport (250cc)	500	1,000	1,500	3,000	4,500	6,000
Tornado (650cc twin)	500	700	1,200	2,800	4,500	6,200
1972						
Buzzer (65cc)	200	400	600	900	1,900	2,900
Buzzer Jr (65cc)	300	500	700	1,000	2,000	3,000
Cougar (65cc)	200	400	600	900	1,900	2,900
Dynamo Compact (65cc)	200	400	600	900	1,900	2,900
Dynamo Trail (65cc)	200	400	600	900	1,900	2,900
Dynamo Woodsbike (65cc)	200	400	600	900	1,900	2,900
Hornet (65cc)	200	400	600	900	1,900	2,900
Hurricane (65cc)	200	400	600	900	1,900	2,900
Banshee (90cc)	300	500	700	1,000	2,100	3,200
Mini Enduro (90cc)	300	500	700	1,000	2,100	3,200
Panther (125cc)	300	500	700	1,100	2,100	3,100
Road Trail (125cc)	300	500	700	1,000	2,100	3,200
Enduro (175cc)	300	500	700	1,000	2,100	3,200
Volcano (180cc)	300	500	700	1,100	2,100	3,100
Twin Super Sport (250cc)	400	600	800	1,100	2,300	3,500
Tornado (650cc twin)	500	700	1,200	2,800	4,500	6,200
1973						
Buzzer (65cc)	200	400	600	900	1,900	2,900
Compact Chopper (65cc)	300	500	700	1,100	2,100	3,100
Dynamo Compact (65cc)	200	400	600	900	1,900	2,900
Dynamo Sidehack (65cc)	200	400	600	900	1,900	2,900
Dynamo Trail (65cc)	200	400	600	900	1,900	2,900
Dynamo Woodsbike (65cc)	200	400	600	900	1,900	2,900
Hornet (65cc)	200	400	600	900	1,900	2,900
Hurricane (65cc)	200	400	600	900	1,900	2,900
Mini Enduro (65cc)	200	400	600	900	1,900	2,900
Banshee (90cc)	300	500	700	1,000	2,100	3,200
Panther (125cc)	300	500	700	1,100	2,100	3,100
Enduro (175cc)	300	500	700	1,100	2,100	3,100
Volcano (180cc)	300	500	700	1,100	2,100	3,100
Phantom (250cc twin)	300	500	700	1,100	2,100	3,100
Supersport (250cc)	400	600	800	1,200	2,300	3,500
Tornado (650cc twin)	600	800	1,200	2,800	4,500	6,200
1974						
Dynamo Compact (65cc)	200	300	500	900	1,900	2,900
Dynamo Trail (65cc)	200	300	500	900	1,900	2,900
Dynamo Woodsbike (65cc)	200	300	500	900	1,900	2,900
Mini Enduro (65cc)	200	300	500	900	1,900	2,900
Banshee (90cc)	200	400	600	900	1,900	2,900

	6	5	4	3	2	1
Panther (125cc)	200	400	600	1,000	2,100	3,200
Enduro (175cc)	200	400	600	900	1,900	2,900
Volcano (180cc)	200	400	600	900	1,900	2,900
Phantom (250cc twin)	200	400	600	1,000	2,100	3,200
Supersport (250cc)	400	600	800	1,200	2,300	3,500
Quattro 4 Cylinder (500cc)	1,000	1,600	2,500	3,000	5,000	7,000
Tornado (650cc twin)	500	700	1,100	2,100	4,000	5,900
SEI 6 Cylinder (750cc)	**1,500**	**3,000**	**6,000**	**9,000**	**12,000**	**15,000**
1975						
Dynamo Compact (65cc)	200	300	500	900	1,900	2,900
Dynamo Trail (65cc)	200	300	500	900	1,900	2,900
Dynamo Woodsbike (65cc)	200	300	500	900	1,900	2,900
Mini Enduro (65cc)	200	300	500	900	1,900	2,900
Banshee (90cc)	200	400	600	900	1,900	2,900
Enduro (175cc)	200	400	600	900	1,900	2,900
Volcano (180cc)	200	400	600	900	1,900	2,900
Phantom (250cc twin)	200	400	600	1,000	2,100	3,200
Quattro 4 Cylinder (500cc)	800	1,200	2,000	3,000	5,000	7,000
Tornado (650cc twin)	300	500	900	1,800	3,500	5,200
SEI 6 Cylinder (750cc)	**1,500**	**3,000**	**6,000**	**9,000**	**12,000**	**15,000**
1976						
Dynamo Trail (65cc)	200	300	500	900	1,900	2,900
Dynamo Woodsbike (65cc)	200	300	500	900	1,900	2,900
Mini Enduro (65cc)	200	300	500	900	1,900	2,900
Banshee (90cc)	200	400	600	900	1,900	2,900
Panther (125cc)	200	400	600	1,000	2,100	3,200
Enduro (175cc)	200	400	600	900	1,900	2,900
Phantom (250cc twin)	200	400	600	1,000	2,100	3,200
Quattro 4 Cylinder (500cc)	800	1,200	2,000	3,000	5,000	7,000
Tornado (650cc twin)	300	500	900	1,800	3,500	5,200
SEI 6 Cylinder (750cc)	**1,500**	**3,000**	**6,000**	**9,000**	**12,000**	**15,000**
1977						
Dynamo Trail (65cc)	200	300	500	900	1,900	2,900
Dynamo Woodsbike (65cc)	200	300	500	900	1,900	2,900
Mini Enduro (65cc)	200	300	500	900	1,900	2,900
Enduro (175cc)	200	400	600	900	1,900	2,900
Phantom (250cc twin)	200	400	600	1,000	2,100	3,200
Quattro 4 Cylinder (500cc)	700	1,000	2,000	3,000	5,000	7,000
Tornado (650cc twin)	300	500	900	1,800	3,500	5,200
SEI 6 Cylinder (750cc)	**1,500**	**3,000**	**6,000**	**9,000**	**12,000**	**15,000**
1978						
Dynamo Woodsbike (65cc)	200	300	500	900	1,900	2,900
Phantom (250cc twin)	200	400	600	1,000	2,100	3,200
Quattro 4 Cylinder (500cc)	700	1,000	2,000	3,000	5,000	7,000
Tornado (650cc twin)	300	500	900	1,800	3,500	5,200
SEI 6 Cylinder (750cc)	**1,500**	**3,000**	**6,000**	**9,000**	**12,000**	**15,000**
1979						
Dynamo Woodsbike (65cc)	200	300	500	900	1,900	2,900
Phantom (250cc twin)	200	400	600	1,000	2,100	3,200
Quattro 4 Cylinder (500cc)	900	1,500	3,000	5,000	7,000	9,000
Tornado (650cc twin)	300	500	900	1,800	3,500	5,200
SEI 6 Cylinder (750cc)	**1,500**	**3,000**	**6,000**	**9,000**	**12,000**	**15,000**
1980						
Quattro 4 Cylinder (250cc)	300	500	900	1,600	3,200	4,800
Quattro 4 Cylinder (500cc)	700	1,000	2,000	3,000	5,000	7,000
SEI 6 Cylinder (750cc)	**1,500**	**3,000**	**6,000**	**9,000**	**12,000**	**15,000**
1981						
C2 Long St (50cc single)	200	300	500	900	1,900	2,900
250/4 (250cc four)	500	900	1,800	3,500	5,200	2,700
Quattro 4 Cylinder (500cc)	700	1,000	2,000	3,000	5,000	7,000

	6	5	4	3	2	1
SEI 6 Cylinder (750cc)	1,500	3,000	6,000	9,000	12,000	15,000
1982						
SEI 6 Cylinder (750cc)	1,500	3,000	6,000	9,000	12,000	15,000
1983						
SEI 6 Cylinder (750cc)	1,500	3,000	6,000	9,000	12,000	15,000
1984						
SEI 6 Cylinder (750cc)	1,500	3,000	6,000	9,000	12,000	15,000
1985						
G2 (50cc single).	200	300	500	900	1,900	2,900
BETA						
TR32 Trials	100	200	400	600	1,000	1,500
1986						
TR32 Trials	100	200	400	600	1,000	1,500
TR33 Trials	100	200	400	600	1,000	1,500
Trekking 230	100	200	500	700	1,200	1,800
1987						
TR33 Trials	100	200	400	600	1,000	1,500
TR34 Trials	100	200	400	600	1,000	1,500
TR50 Trials	100	200	400	600	1,000	1,500
Trekking 230	100	200	400	600	1,000	1,500
1988						
TR34 Trials	100	200	400	600	1,000	1,500
Trekking	100	200	400	600	1,100	1,600
1989						
Mini Trail 50 .	100	200	300	600	1,000	1,400
Alp 240	100	300	600	900	1,500	2,100
TR 34 Campionato	100	200	300	600	1,000	1,400
TR 34 Replica	100	200	500	700	1,200	1,700
1990						
Alp	100	300	500	800	1,200	1,600
TR34C 125	100	300	600	900	1,500	2,100
TR34C 240	100	300	600	900	1,500	2,100
TR34C 260	200	500	800	1,200	1,800	2,400
1991						
TR35 50	100	200	300	600	1,000	1,400
TR35 125	100	300	600	900	1,500	2,100
TR35 240	100	300	600	900	1,500	2,100
TR35 260	300	500	1,000	1,400	2,000	2,600
Trial Mini	100	200	300	600	1,000	1,400
Trial-Alp 260.	300	500	1,000	1,400	2,000	2,600
Zero 240	100	300	600	900	1,500	2,100
Zero 260	300	500	1,000	1,400	2,000	2,600
1992						
Trial Mini	100	200	300	600	1,000	1,400
Alp 240	100	300	600	900	1,500	2,100
Supertrial 240	100	300	700	1,200	1,800	2,400
Synt 260.	300	500	1,000	1,400	2,000	2,600
Zero 260	300	500	1,000	1,400	2,000	2,600
1993						
Alp 240	100	300	600	900	1,500	2,100
Supertrial 240	100	300	700	1,200	1,800	2,400
Gara 260	300	500	1,000	1,400	2,000	2,600
Synt 260.	100	300	600	900	1,500	2,100
1994						
Alp 50	100	200	300	600	1,000	1,400
MX 50R	100	200	300	600	1,000	1,400
RK 6 50	100	200	300	600	1,000	1,400
Super Trial 50	100	200	300	600	1,000	1,400
Trial Mini 50	100	200	300	600	1,000	1,400
Trial Mini Auto 50	100	200	300	600	1,000	1,400

	6	5	4	3	2	1
Zero 50	100	200	300	600	1,000	1,400
Synt 125	100	200	500	700	1,200	1,700
Alp 240	100	300	600	900	1,500	2,100
Super Trial 240	100	200	700	1,200	1,800	2,400
Techno 250	300	500	1,000	1,400	2,000	2,600
Synt 260	100	300	600	900	1,500	2,100

BIMOTA

1979

	6	5	4	3	2	1
SB2	2,500	5,000	10,000	15,000	20,000	25,000

1983

HB2	150	250	400	700	1,100	1,500
KB2	100	200	300	650	1,000	1,300
KB2/TT	150	250	400	700	1,100	1,500
KB3	100	200	400	700	1,100	1,500
SB3	100	200	300	600	900	1,200

1984

HB2	100	200	400	900	1,300	1,700
KB2	100	200	400	800	1,300	1,900
KB3	100	200	400	900	1,300	1,700
SB3	100	200	400	700	1,100	1,500
SB4	100	200	400	900	1,300	1,700

1985

HB3	100	200	600	1,200	1,700	2,200
KB2	100	200	500	1,100	1,600	2,100
KB3	100	200	600	1,200	1,700	2,200
SB4	100	200	600	1,200	1,700	2,200
SB5	100	200	600	1,300	2,000	2,700

1986

DB1	100	200	600	1,300	1,900	2,500

1987

DB1	100	300	700	1,500	2,200	2,900

1988

DB1	200	300	900	1,900	2,800	3,600
YB4	200	400	1,200	2,500	3,700	4,900
YB6	200	400	1,100	2,300	3,400	4,500

1989

DB1-F1B	200	400	1,000	2,200	3,200	4,200
DB1-SR750	400	600	1,700	3,500	5,300	7,100
YB4-EL750	300	600	1,600	3,200	4,800	6,400
YB5	200	400	1,000	2,100	3,200	4,300
YB6	300	500	1,300	2,700	4,000	5,300

1990

DB1	200	400	1,200	2,500	3,800	5,100
DB1-SR	400	800	2,200	4,400	6,600	8,800
YB4	400	700	1,800	3,700	5,500	7,300
YB4-ELR	700	1,200	3,300	6,800	10,000	13,000
YB5	200	400	1,200	2,500	3,700	4,900
YB6	300	600	1,500	3,100	4,600	6,100

1991

Bellaria	500	800	2,100	4,400	6,600	8,800
Dieci	800	1,200	2,500	6,000	8,000	10,000
Tesi 1D 851	800	1,200	3,300	6,800	10,000	13,000
Tesi 1D 906	900	1,300	3,700	7,700	11,500	15,500
Tuatara EL	700	1,000	2,900	5,900	8,900	12,000
YB4-EL	600	900	2,600	5,300	7,800	10,000
YB4-EXUP	500	800	2,200	4,500	6,700	8,900
YB5	300	600	1,700	3,500	5,200	6,900

1992

Dieci	800	1,200	2,500	6,000	8,000	10,000
Tesi 1D 906 IE	900	1,300	3,700	7,700	11,500	15,500

	6	5	4	3	2	1
YB8	500	800	2,000	4,200	6,300	8,400
1993						
DB2	400	700	1,700	3,600	5,400	7,200
Dieci	800	1,200	2,500	6,000	8,000	10,000
Tesi 1D 906 IE	1,000	1,400	4,000	8,200	12,000	16,000
YB8	500	800	2,200	4,500	6,800	9,000

BMW						
1923						
R32 (494cc twin)	5,000	10,000	20,000	30,000	40,000	50,000
1924						
R32 (494cc twin)	5,000	10,000	20,000	30,000	40,000	50,000
1925						
R32 (494cc twin)	5,000	10,000	20,000	30,000	40,000	50,000
R37 (494cc twin)	10,000	25,000	50,000	100K	150K	200K
R39 (247cc single)	1,400	2,100	3,100	4,100	5,500	6,900
1926						
R32 (494cc twin) (3,090-4 yrs)	5,000	10,000	16,000	24,000	32,000	40,000
R37 (494cc twin) (152-2 yrs)	10,000	25,000	50,000	100K	150K	200K
R39 (247cc single)	1,400	2,100	3,100	4,100	5,500	6,900
R42 (494cc twin)	5,000	10,000	15,000	20,000	26,000	32,000
1927						
R39 (247cc single) (855-3 yrs)	1,400	2,100	3,100	4,100	5,500	6,900
R42 (494cc twin)	5,000	10,000	15,000	20,000	26,000	32,000
R47 (494cc twin)	5,000	10,000	15,000	20,000	26,000	32,000
1928						
R42 (494cc twin) (6,502-3 yrs)	5,000	10,000	15,000	20,000	26,000	32,000
R47 (494cc twin) (1,720-2 yrs)	5,000	10,000	15,000	20,000	26,000	32,000
R52 (486cc twin)	5,000	10,000	20,000	30,000	40,000	50,000
R57 (494cc twin)	5,000	10,000	18,000	25,000	30,000	36,000
R62 (745cc twin)	4,000	7,000	11,000	14,000	18,000	25,000
R63 (735cc twin)	4,000	6,000	9,000	11,000	14,000	18,000
1929						
R11 (745cc twin)	4,000	6,000	9,000	11,000	14,000	18,000
R16 (736cc twin)	4,000	6,000	9,000	11,000	14,000	18,000
R52 (486cc twin) (4,377-2 yrs)	2,600	3,900	5,900	7,800	11,000	13,000
R57 (494cc twin)	5,000	10,000	15,000	20,000	26,000	32,000
R62 (745cc twin) (4,355-2yrs)	4,000	7,000	11,000	14,000	18,000	25,000
R63 (735cc twin) (794-2 yrs)	4,000	6,000	9,000	11,000	14,000	18,000
1930						
R11 (745cc twin)	4,000	6,000	9,000	11,000	14,000	18,000
R16 (736cc twin)	4,000	6,000	9,000	11,000	14,000	18,000
R57 (494cc twin) (1,005-3 yrs)	5,000	10,000	15,000	20,000	26,000	32,000
1931						
R2 (198cc single) (4,161)	1,400	2,500	4,000	6,000	7,500	9,000
R11 (745cc twin)	4,000	6,000	9,000	11,000	14,000	18,000
1932						
R2 (198cc single) (1,850)	1,400	2,500	4,000	6,000	7,500	9,000
R4 (398cc single) (1,101)	2,600	3,900	5,900	7,800	10,000	13,000
R11 (745cc twin)	4,000	6,000	9,000	11,000	14,000	18,000
R16 (736cc twin)	4,000	6,000	9,000	11,000	14,000	18,000
1933						
R2 (198cc single) (2,000)	1,400	2,500	4,000	6,000	7,500	9,000
R4 (398cc single) (1,737)	2,600	3,900	5,900	7,800	10,000	13,000
R11 (745cc twin)	4,000	6,000	9,000	11,000	14,000	18,000
R16 (736cc twin)	4,000	6,000	9,000	11,000	14,000	18,000
1934						
R2 (198cc single) (2,077)	1,400	2,500	4,000	6,000	7,500	9,000
R4 (398cc single) (3,671)	2,600	3,900	5,900	7,800	11,000	13,000
R11 (745cc twin) (7,500-6 yrs)	4,000	6,000	9,000	11,000	14,000	18,000
R16 (736cc twin) (1,006-5 yrs)	4,000	6,000	9,000	11,000	14,000	18,000

	6	5	4	3	2	1
1935						
R2 (198cc single) (2,700)	1,400	2,500	4,000	6,000	7,500	9,000
R4 (398cc single) (3,651)	2,600	3,900	5,900	7,800	11,000	13,000
R12 (745cc twin)	4,000	6,000	9,000	11,000	14,000	18,000
R17 (735cc twin)	4,000	6,000	10,000	12,000	15,000	20,000
1936						
R2 (198cc single) (2,500)	1,400	2,500	4,000	6,000	7,500	9,000
R3 (305cc single) (740)	2,600	3,900	5,900	7,800	11,000	13,000
R4 (398cc single) (5,033)	2,600	3,900	5,900	7,800	11,000	13,000
R12 (745cc twin)	4,000	6,000	9,000	11,000	14,000	18,000
R17 (735cc twin)	4,000	6,000	10,000	12,000	15,000	20,000
1937						
R20 (192cc single)	1,400	2,100	3,200	4,200	5,600	7,000
R35 (342cc twin)	1,800	2,700	4,100	5,400	7,200	9,000
R4 (398cc single)	3,800	5,700	8,600	11,000	15,000	19,000
R5 (494cc twin)	2,500	5,000	10,000	15,000	20,000	25,000
R6 (598cc twin)	2,000	3,000	4,500	6,000	8,000	10,000
R17 (735cc twin) (434-3 yrs)	3,400	5,100	10,000	12,000	15,000	20,000
R12 (745cc twin)	2,600	3,900	5,900	7,800	11,000	13,000
1938						
R20 (192cc single) (5,000-2 yrs)	1,400	2,100	3,200	4,200	5,600	7,000
R23 (247cc single)	1,400	2,100	3,100	4,100	5,500	6,900
R35 (342cc twin)	1,800	2,700	5,500	7,000	9,000	11,000
R51 (494cc twin)	**5,000**	**10,000**	**15,000**	**20,000**	**25,000**	**30,000**
R66 (597cc twin)	3,400	5,100	7,700	10,000	14,000	17,000
R61 (599cc twin)	1,600	2,400	3,600	4,800	6,400	8,000
R12 (745cc twin)	2,400	3,600	5,400	7,200	9,600	12,000
R71 (745cc twin)	3,000	4,500	6,800	9,000	12,000	15,000
1939						
R23 (247cc single)	1,400	2,100	3,100	4,100	5,500	6,900
R35 (342cc single)	1,800	2,700	4,100	5,400	7,200	9,000
R51 (494cc twin)	**5,000**	**10,000**	**15,000**	**20,000**	**25,000**	**30,000**
R61 (597cc twin)	2,400	3,600	5,400	7,200	9,600	12,000
R66 597cc twin)	3,200	4,800	7,200	9,600	13,000	16,000
R12 745cc twin)	2,400	3,600	5,400	7,200	9,600	12,000
R71 (745cc twin)	3,000	4,500	6,800	9,000	12,000	15,000
1940						
R23 (247cc single) (8,021-3 yrs)	1,400	2,100	3,100	4,100	5,500	6,900
R35 (342cc single) (15,386-4 yrs)	1,800	2,700	4,100	5,400	7,200	9,000
R51 (494cc twin) (3,775-3 yrs)	**5,000**	**10,000**	**15,000**	**20,000**	**25,000**	**30,000**
R61 (597cc twin)	2,200	3,300	5,000	6,600	8,800	11,000
R66 (597cc twin)	3,200	4,800	7,200	9,600	13,000	16,000
R12 (745cc twin)	2,400	3,600	5,400	7,200	9,600	12,000
R71 (745cc twin)	3,400	5,100	7,700	10,000	14,000	17,000
1941						
R61 (597cc twin) (3,747-4yrs)	2,200	3,300	5,000	6,600	8,800	11,000
R66 (597cc twin) (1,669-4 yrs)	3,200	4,800	7,200	9,600	13,000	16,000
R12 (745cc twin)	2,400	3,600	5,400	7,200	9,600	12,000
R71 (745cc twin) (3,458-4 yrs)	3,400	4,500	5,500	8,000	12,000	14,000
R75 (745cc twin) (3,747-4 yrs)	**3,000**	**6,000**	**9,000**	**12,000**	**15,000**	**18,000**
1942						
R12 (745cc twin) (36,000-8 yrs)	2,400	3,600	5,400	7,200	9,600	12,000
R75 (745cc twin)	**3,000**	**6,000**	**9,000**	**12,000**	**15,000**	**18,000**
1943						
R75 (745cc twin)	**3,000**	**6,000**	**9,000**	**12,000**	**15,000**	**18,000**
1944						
R75 (745cc twin) (18,000-4 yrs)	**3,000**	**6,000**	**9,000**	**12,000**	**15,000**	**18,000**
1945						

NOTE: 1945-1947 (no civilian production). .

	6	5	4	3	2	1
1948						
R24 (247cc single)	1,300	2,000	2,900	3,900	5,200	6,500
1949						
R24 (247cc single)	1,300	2,000	2,900	3,900	5,200	6,500
1950						
R24 (247cc single) (12,020-3 yrs)	1,300	2,000	2,900	3,900	5,200	6,500
R25 (247cc single)	1,200	1,800	2,700	3,600	4,800	6,000
R51/2 (494cc twin)	2,000	3,000	4,500	6,000	8,000	10,000
1951						
R25 (247cc single) (23,040-2 yrs)	1,200	1,800	2,700	3,600	4,800	6,000
R25/2 (247cc single)	1,200	1,800	2,700	3,600	4,800	6,000
R51/2 (494cc twin) (5,000-2 yrs)	2,000	3,000	4,500	6,000	8,000	10,000
R51/3 (494cc twin)	2,500	4,000	7,500	10,000	13,000	16,000
R67 (594cc twin) (1,470)	1,600	2,400	3,600	4,800	6,400	8,000
1952						
R25/2 (247cc single)	1,200	1,800	2,700	3,600	4,800	6,000
R51/3 (494cc twin)	2,500	4,000	7,500	10,000	13,000	16,000
R67/2 (594cc twin)	1,400	2,100	3,200	4,200	5,600	7,000
R68 (594cc twin)	3,000	4,500	6,800	9,000	12,000	15,000
1953						
R25/2 (247cc single) (38,651-3 yrs)	1,200	1,800	2,700	3,600	4,800	6,000
R25/3 (247cc single)	1,200	1,800	2,700	4,000	5,000	6,500
R51/3 (494cc twin)	2,500	4,000	7,500	10,000	13,000	16,000
R67/2 (594cc twin)	1,400	2,100	3,200	4,200	5,600	7,000
R68 (594cc twin)	3,000	6,000	9,000	12,000	15,000	18,000
1954						
R25/3 (247cc single)	1,200	1,800	2,700	3,600	4,800	6,000
R51/3 (494cc twin) (18,420-4 yrs)	2,400	3,600	5,400	7,200	9,600	12,000
R67/2 (594cc twin) (4,234-3 yrs)	1,400	2,100	3,200	4,200	5,600	7,000
R68 (594cc twin) (1,452-3 yrs)	3,200	4,800	7,200	9,600	13,000	16,000
1955						
R25/3 (247cc single)	1,200	1,800	2,700	3,600	4,800	6,000
R50 (494cc twin)	1,200	1,800	2,700	3,600	4,800	6,000
R67/3 (594cc twin) (700-2 yrs)	1,600	2,400	3,600	4,800	6,400	8,000
R69 (594cc twin)	1,400	2,100	3,200	4,200	5,600	7,000
1956						
R25/3 (247cc single) (47,700-4 yrs)	1,200	1,800	2,700	3,600	4,800	6,000
R26 (247cc single)	1,000	1,500	2,300	3,000	4,000	5,000
R50 (494cc twin)	1,300	2,000	3,000	4,000	6,000	8,000
R60 (594cc twin)	1,500	2,200	3,300	4,400	5,900	7,400
R67/3 (594cc twin)	1,600	2,400	3,600	4,800	6,400	8,000
R69 (594cc twin)	1,400	2,100	4,000	6,000	9,000	12,000
1957						
R50 (494cc twin)	1,300	2,000	3,000	4,000	6,000	8,000
R60 (594cc twin)	1,500	2,200	3,300	4,400	5,900	7,400
R69 (594cc twin)	1,400	2,100	4,000	6,000	9,000	12,000
1958						
R26 (247cc single)	1,000	1,500	2,300	3,000	4,000	5,000
R50 (494cc twin)	1,500	2,300	3,400	4,500	6,000	7,500
R60 (594cc twin)	1,500	2,200	3,300	4,400	5,900	7,400
R69 (594cc twin)	1,400	2,100	4,000	6,000	9,000	12,000
1959						
R26 (247cc single)	1,000	1,500	2,300	3,000	4,000	5,000
R50 (494cc twin)	1,500	2,300	3,400	4,500	6,000	7,500
R60 (594cc twin)	1,500	2,200	3,300	4,400	5,900	7,400
R69 (594cc twin)	1,400	2,100	4,000	6,000	9,000	12,000
1960						
R26 (247cc single) (30,236-5 yrs)	1,000	1,500	2,300	3,000	4,000	5,000
R27 (247cc single)	1,500	2,500	3,500	5,000	6,500	8,000
R50 (494cc twin) (13,510-6 yrs)	1,500	2,300	3,400	4,500	6,000	7,500
R50/2 (494cc twin)	2,400	3,600	5,400	7,200	9,600	12,000

	6	5	4	3	2	1
R50S (494cc twin).	2,400	3,600	5,400	7,200	9,600	12,000
R60 (594cc twin) (3,530-5 yrs)	2,000	4,000	6,000	8,000	10,000	12,000
R60/2 (594cc twin)	1,900	2,900	6,000	9,000	12,000	15,000
R69 (594cc twin) (2,956-6 yrs)	2,500	4,000	7,000	10,000	13,000	16,000
R69S (594cc twin).	**2,500**	**4,500**	**7,500**	**10,500**	**13,500**	**16,500**
1961						
R27 (247cc single)	1,500	2,500	3,500	5,000	6,500	8,000
R50/2 (494cc twin).	2,400	3,600	5,400	7,200	9,600	12,000
R50S (494cc twin).	2,400	3,600	5,400	7,200	9,600	12,000
R60/2 (594cc twin)	1,900	2,900	4,300	6,000	9,000	12,000
R69S (594cc twin).	**2,500**	**4,500**	**7,500**	**10,500**	**13,500**	**16,500**
1962						
R27 (247cc single)	1,500	2,500	3,500	5,000	6,500	8,000
R50/2 (494cc twin).	2,400	3,600	5,400	7,200	9,600	12,000
R50S (494cc twin) (1,634-3 yrs).	2,400	3,600	5,400	7,200	9,600	12,000
R60/2 (594cc twin)	1,900	2,900	6,000	9,000	12,000	15,000
R69S (594cc twin).	**2,500**	**4,500**	**7,500**	**10,500**	**13,500**	**16,500**
1963						
R27 (247cc single)	1,500	2,500	3,500	5,000	6,500	8,000
R50/2 (494cc twin).	2,400	3,600	6,000	9,000	12,000	15,000
R60/2 (594cc twin)	1,900	3,000	6,000	9,000	12,000	15,000
R69S (594cc twin).	**2,500**	**4,500**	**7,500**	**10,500**	**13,500**	**16,500**
1964						
R27 (247cc single)	1,500	2,500	3,500	5,000	6,500	8,000
R50/2 (494cc twin).	2,400	3,600	5,400	7,200	9,600	12,000
R60/2 (594cc twin)	1,900	2,900	6,000	9,000	12,000	15,000
R69S (594cc twin).	**2,500**	**4,500**	**7,500**	**10,500**	**13,500**	**16,500**
1965						
R27 (247cc single)	1,500	2,500	3,500	5,000	6,500	8,000
R50/2 (494cc twin).	2,400	3,600	5,400	7,200	9,600	12,000
R60/2 (594cc twin)	1,900	2,900	6,000	9,000	12,000	15,000
R69S (594cc twin).	**2,500**	**4,500**	**7,500**	**10,500**	**13,500**	**16,500**
1966						
R27 (247cc single) (15,364-7 yrs)	1,500	2,500	3,500	5,000	6,500	8,000
R50/2 (494cc twin).	2,400	4,000	6,000	9,000	12,000	15,000
R60/2 (594cc twin)	1,900	3,000	6,000	9,000	12,000	15,000
R69S (594cc twin) (11,317-10 yrs)	**2,500**	**4,500**	**7,500**	**10,500**	**13,500**	**16,500**
1967						
R50US (294cc twin)	1,000	2,000	3,000	5,000	7,000	9,000
R50/2 (494cc twin)	2,400	3,600	6,000	9,000	12,000	15,000
R60/2 (594cc twin)	1,900	2,900	6,000	9,000	12,000	15,000
R60US (594cc twin).	1,000	1,500	2,300	3,000	4,000	5,000
R69US (594cc twin).	1,600	**3,000**	**6,000**	**9,000**	**12,000**	**15,000**
1968						
R50US (294cc twin).	1,400	2,100	2,000	4,000	6,000	8,000
R50/2 (494cc twin).	2,400	3,600	5,400	7,200	9,600	12,000
R60/2 (594cc twin)	2,400	3,600	6,000	9,000	12,000	15,000
R60US (594cc twin).	1,400	2,100	3,200	4,200	5,600	7,000
R69US (594cc twin) (Incl in R69/S)	1,600	**3,000**	**6,000**	**9,000**	**12,000**	**15,000**
1969						
R50US (294cc twin) (Incl in R50/2)	1,400	2,100	3,200	4,200	5,600	7,000
R50/2 (494cc twin) (19,036-10 yrs)	2,400	3,600	5,400	7,200	9,600	12,000
R50/5 (496cc twin)	1,100	1,700	2,500	3,300	4,400	5,500
R60/5 (594cc twin)	900	1,400	2,100	2,800	3,800	4,700
R60/2 (594cc twin) (17,306-10 yrs)	2,400	3,600	6,000	9,000	12,000	15,000
R60US (594cc twin) (Incl in R60/2)	1,400	2,100	3,200	4,200	5,600	7,000
R69US (594cc twin).	1,600	**3,000**	**6,000**	**9,000**	**12,000**	**15,000**
R75/5 (745cc twin)	1,000	1,500	2,300	3,000	4,000	5,000
1970						
R50/5 (496cc twin)	1,100	1,700	2,500	3,300	4,400	5,500

	6	5	4	3	2	1
R60/5 (594cc twin)	900	1,400	2,100	2,800	3,800	4,700
R75/5 (745cc twin)	1,200	1,800	2,700	3,600	4,800	6,000
1971						
R50/5 (496cc twin)	1,100	1,700	2,500	3,300	4,400	5,500
R60/5 (594cc twin)	1,000	1,400	2,200	2,900	3,800	4,800
R75/5 (745cc twin)	1,200	1,800	2,700	3,600	4,800	6,000
1972						
R50/5 (496cc twin)	1,100	1,700	2,500	3,300	4,400	5,500
R60/5 (594cc twin)	1,000	1,400	2,200	2,900	3,800	4,800
R75/5 (745cc twin)	1,200	1,800	2,700	3,600	4,800	6,000
1973						
R50/5 (496cc twin) (7,865-5 yrs)	1,100	1,700	2,500	3,300	4,400	5,500
R60/5 (594cc twin) (22,721-5 yrs).	900	1,400	2,000	2,700	3,600	4,500
R75/5 (745cc twin) (38,370-5 yrs).	1,200	1,800	2,700	3,600	4,800	6,000
1974						
R60/6 (599cc twin)	800	1,200	1,800	2,400	3,200	4,000
R75/6 (745cc twin)	800	1,200	1,900	2,500	3,300	4,100
R90/6 (898cc twin)	1,300	2,000	**4,000**	**6,000**	8,000	10,000
R90S (898cc twin).	1,900	**3,000**	6,000	9,000	12,000	15,000
1975						
R60/6 (599cc twin)	800	1,200	2,000	3,000	3,500	4,200
R75/6 (745cc twin)	800	1,200	1,900	2,500	3,300	4,100
R90/6 (898cc twin)	900	1,400	2,500	3,000	3,600	4,500
R90S (898cc twin).	1,900	2,900	4,300	5,700	7,600	9,500
1976						
R60/6 (599cc twin) (13,511-4 yrs)	800	1,200	1,800	2,400	3,200	4,000
R60/7 (599cc twin)	800	1,200	1,800	2,400	3,200	4,000
R75/6 (745cc twin) (17,587-4 yrs)	800	1,200	1,900	2,500	3,300	4,100
R75/7 (745cc twin)	900	1,300	1,900	2,600	3,400	4,300
R75/7 (745cc twin)	900	1,300	1,900	2,600	3,400	4,300
R90/6 (898cc twin) (21,097-4 yrs).	900	1,300	2,000	2,600	3,500	4,400
R90S (898cc twin) (17,465-4 yrs)	1,900	2,900	4,300	5,700	7,600	9,500
R100/7 (980cc twin).	800	1,100	1,700	2,300	3,000	3,800
R100RS (980cc twin)	800	1,200	1,800	2,400	3,200	4,000
R100S (980cc twin)	800	1,100	1,700	2,300	3,000	3,800
1977						
R60/7 (599cc twin)	800	1,200	1,800	2,400	3,200	4,000
R75/7 (745cc twin) (6,264-4 yrs)	800	1,300	1,900	2,500	3,400	4,200
R80/7 (797cc twin)	800	1,200	1,800	2,400	3,200	4,000
R100/7 (980cc twin).	800	1,100	2,000	2,500	3,000	3,800
R100RS (980cc twin)	800	1,200	1,800	2,400	3,200	4,000
R100S (980cc twin)	900	1,500	2,500	3,000	3,800	4,500
1978						
R60/7 (599cc twin)	800	1,200	1,800	2,400	3,200	4,000
R65 (649cc twin)	800	1,100	1,700	2,300	3,000	3,800
R80/7 (797cc twin)	800	1,200	1,800	2,400	3,200	4,000
R100RS (980cc twin)	900	1,400	2,100	2,800	3,800	4,700
R100RT (980cc twin)	900	1,400	2,100	2,800	3,800	4,700
R100S (980cc twin) (11,762-5yrs).	700	1,100	1,600	2,100	2,800	3,500
R100T (980cc twin) (5,463-3 yrs)	700	1,100	1,600	2,100	2,800	3,500
R100/7 (980cc twin) (12,056-5 yrs)	600	1,000	1,400	1,900	2,600	3,200
1979						
R60/7 (599cc twin)	800	1,200	1,800	2,400	3,200	4,000
R65 (649cc twin)	800	1,100	1,700	2,300	3,000	3,800
R80/7 (797cc twin)	800	1,200	1,800	2,400	3,200	4,000
R100RS (980cc twin)	900	1,400	2,100	2,800	3,800	4,700
R100RT (980cc twin)	900	1,400	2,100	2,800	3,800	4,700
R100T (980cc twin)	800	1,200	1,800	2,400	3,200	4,000
1980						
R60/7 (599cc twin)	800	1,200	1,800	2,400	3,200	4,000

	6	5	4	3	2	1
R65 (649cc twin)	800	1,100	1,700	2,300	3,000	3,800
R80G/S (797cc twin)	800	1,200	1,800	2,400	3,200	4,000
R80/7 (797cc twin) (18,522-8 yrs)	800	1,200	1,800	2,400	3,200	4,000
R100RS (980cc twin)	900	1,400	2,100	2,800	3,800	4,700
R100RT (980cc twin)	900	1,400	2,100	2,800	3,800	4,700
R100T (980cc twin)	800	1,200	1,800	2,400	3,200	4,000
1981						
R60/7 (599cc twin)	800	1,200	1,800	2,400	3,200	4,000
R65 (650cc twin)	800	1,200	1,800	2,400	3,200	4,000
R80G/S (800cc twin)	900	1,400	2,100	2,800	3,300	3,900
R100 (1000cc twin)	900	1,400	2,100	2,900	4,000	5,300
R100CS (1000cc twin)	900	1,400	2,100	2,800	3,800	4,700
R100RS (1000cc twin)	900	1,400	2,100	3,500	4,500	5,500
R100RT (1000cc twin)	900	1,400	2,100	2,800	3,800	4,700
1982						
R60/7 (599cc twin) (11,163-7yrs)	800	1,200	1,800	2,400	3,200	4,000
R65 (650cc twin)	700	1,000	1,500	2,000	2,700	3,400
R65LS (650cc twin)	800	1,100	1,700	2,300	3,000	3,800
R100 (1000cc twin)	800	1,400	2,100	2,800	3,900	5,000
R100TR (1000cc twin)	900	1,400	2,100	2,800	3,800	4,700
R100RS (1000cc twin)	900	1,400	2,100	2,800	3,800	4,700
R100RT (1000cc twin)	900	1,400	2,100	2,800	3,800	4,700
1983						
R65 (650cc twin)	700	1,000	1,600	2,200	2,900	3,600
R65LS (650cc twin)	700	1,000	1,600	2,200	2,900	3,600
R80G/S (800cc twin)	800	1,400	2,100	2,800	3,500	4,200
R80ST (800cc twin)	800	1,400	2,100	2,800	3,500	4,200
R80RT (800cc twin)	800	1,400	2,100	2,800	3,600	4,400
R100 (1000cc twin)	900	1,500	2,200	2,900	3,800	4,800
R100S (1000cc twin)	900	1,500	2,200	2,900	3,800	4,800
R100RS (1000cc twin)	900	1,500	2,200	2,900	3,800	4,800
R100RT (1000cc twin)	900	1,500	2,200	2,900	3,800	4,800
1984						
R65 (650cc twin) (29,454-9yrs)	700	1,000	1,600	2,200	2,900	3,700
R65LS (650cc twin)	700	1,000	1,600	2,200	2,900	3,700
R80G/S (800cc twin)	800	1,400	2,100	2,900	3,600	4,300
R80ST (800cc twin) (5,963-3 yrs)	800	1,400	2,100	2,900	3,600	4,300
R80RT (800cc twin)	800	1,400	2,100	2,800	3,600	4,400
R100 (1000cc twin) (10,111-5 yrs)	900	1,500	2,200	2,900	3,800	4,800
R100CS (1000cc twin) (4,038-5 yrs)	900	1,500	2,200	2,900	3,800	4,800
R100RS (1000cc twin) (33,648-9 yrs)	1,000	2,000	3,000	3,900	4,800	5,500
R100RT (1000cc twin) (18,015-7 yrs)	900	1,500	2,200	2,900	3,800	4,800
1985						
R80G/S (800cc twin)	800	1,400	2,100	2,900	3,600	4,300
R80 (800cc twin)	800	1,400	2,100	2,900	3,600	4,300
R80RT (800cc twin) (7,315-3 yrs)	800	1,400	2,100	2,900	3,600	4,300
K100 (987cc four).	900	1,600	2,300	3,000	3,900	4,900
K100RS (987cc four)	900	1,600	2,300	3,000	3,900	4,900
K100RT (987cc four)	900	1,600	2,300	3,000	3,900	4,900
1986						
R65 (650cc twin)	700	1,100	1,700	2,300	3,000	3,800
K75T (750cc triple)	900	1,500	2,200	2,900	3,700	4,500
K75C (750cc triple)	900	1,500	2,200	2,900	3,700	4,500
K75S (750cc triple)	900	1,500	2,200	2,900	3,700	4,500
R80 (800cc twin)	800	1,400	2,100	2,800	3,600	4,400
R80G/S (800cc twin) (21,864-8 yrs)	800	1,400	2,100	2,900	3,600	4,300
R80RT (800cc twin)	800	1,400	2,100	2,800	3,600	4,400
K100 (1000cc four) (12,871-9 yrs)	900	1,600	2,300	3,000	4,000	5,000
K100RS (1000cc four).	900	1,600	2,300	3,000	4,000	5,000
K100RT (1000cc four).	900	1,600	2,300	3,000	4,000	5,000

	6	5	4	3	2	1
1987						
R65 (650cc twin)	800	1,200	1,800	2,400	3,200	4,100
K75C (750cc triple)	900	1,500	2,200	2,900	3,700	4,500
K75S (750cc triple)	900	1,500	2,200	2,900	3,700	4,500
K75T (750cc triple) (Incl in K75C)	900	1,500	2,200	2,900	3,700	4,500
R80 (800cc twin) (13,815-12 yrs)	900	1,500	2,200	2,900	3,800	4,800
R80RT (800cc twin)	1,000	1,700	2,400	2,900	3,800	4,700
K100RS (1000cc four) (34,804-7 yrs)	900	1,600	2,300	3,000	4,000	5,000
K100RT (1000cc four)	900	1,600	2,300	3,000	4,000	5,000
K100LT (1000cc four)	900	1,600	2,300	3,000	4,000	5,000
1988						
K75C (750cc triple)	900	1,500	2,200	2,800	3,700	4,600
K75 (750cc triple)	900	1,500	2,200	2,800	3,700	4,600
K75S (750cc triple)	1,000	1,700	2,400	2,900	3,800	4,700
R100 GS (1000cc twin)	900	1,600	2,300	3,000	4,000	5,000
R100RS (1000cc twin)	900	1,600	2,300	3,000	4,000	5,000
R100RT (1000cc twin)	900	1,600	2,300	3,000	4,000	5,000
K100RS (1000cc four)	900	1,600	2,300	3,000	4,000	5,000
K100RS ABS Spcl Ed (1000cc four)	1,400	2,000	2,600	3,500	4,700	6,000
K100RT (1000cc four) (22,335-7 yrs)	900	1,600	2,300	3,000	4,000	5,000
K100LT (1000cc four) (14,899-6 yrs)	1,400	2,000	2,600	3,500	4,700	6,000
1989						
K75 (750cc triple)	900	1,500	2,200	2,800	3,700	4,600
R100 GS (1000cc twin)	900	1,600	2,300	3,100	4,100	5,100
R100RS (1000cc twin)	900	1,600	2,300	3,100	4,100	5,100
R100RT (1000cc twin)	900	1,600	2,300	3,100	4,100	5,100
K100RS ABS (1000cc four)	1,400	2,000	3,000	4,000	5,000	6,100
K100LT ABS (1000cc four)	1,400	2,000	3,000	4,100	5,100	6,200
1990						
K75 (750cc triple)	1,000	1,700	2,400	2,900	3,800	4,700
K75S (750cc triple)	1,000	1,700	2,400	2,900	3,800	4,700
K75RT (750cc triple)	1,000	1,700	2,400	2,900	3,800	4,700
R100GS (1000cc twin)	900	1,600	2,300	3,100	4,100	5,100
R100GS Paris-Dakar (1000cc twin)	1,000	1,700	2,400	3,200	4,200	5,200
R100RT (1000cc twin)	900	1,600	2,300	3,100	4,100	5,100
K1 (1000cc four) (6,921-6 yrs)	2,000	3,000	4,200	6,000	7,000	9,000
K100LT ABS (1000cc four)	1,400	2,000	3,000	4,100	5,100	6,200
1991						
K75 (750cc triple)	900	1,500	2,200	2,900	3,800	4,800
K75S (750cc triple)	900	1,500	2,200	2,900	3,800	4,800
K75S ABS (750cc triple)	1,000	1,600	2,300	2,900	3,900	4,900
K75RT (750cc triple)	900	1,500	2,200	2,900	3,800	4,800
K75RT ABS (750cc triple)	1,000	1,600	2,300	2,900	3,900	4,900
R100GS (1000cc twin)	1,000	1,700	2,400	3,200	4,200	5,200
R100GS Paris-Dakar (1000cc twin)	1,200	1,800	2,300	3,300	4,300	5,300
R100 (1000cc twin)	1,200	1,800	2,300	3,300	4,300	5,300
R100RT (1000cc twin)	1,200	1,800	2,300	3,300	4,300	5,300
K100RS (1000cc four)	1,200	1,800	2,300	3,300	4,300	5,300
K100RS ABS (1000cc four)	1,400	2,000	2,600	3,500	4,700	6,000
K1 ABS (1000cc four)	2,100	3,200	4,200	5,200	6,200	7,200
K100LT ABS (1000cc four)	1,400	2,000	3,000	4,100	5,100	6,200
1992						
K75C (750cc triple) (9,566-6 yrs)	900	1,500	2,200	2,900	3,800	4,800
K75 (750cc triple)	900	1,500	2,200	2,900	3,800	4,800
K75RT ABS (750cc triple)	900	1,600	2,300	3,000	4,000	5,000
K75S (750cc triple)	900	1,500	2,200	2,900	3,800	4,800
K75S ABS (750cc triple)	1,000	1,700	2,400	3,200	4,200	5,200
R100GS (1000cc twin)	1,200	1,800	2,300	3,300	4,300	5,300
R100GS Paris-Dakar (1000cc twin)	1,000	1,700	2,400	3,400	4,400	5,400
R100R (1000cc twin)	1,000	1,700	2,400	3,400	4,400	5,400

	6	5	4	3	2	1
R100RS Sport (1000cc twin)	1,300	1,900	2,800	3,800	4,800	5,800
K100RS ABS (1000cc four) (12,666-4 yrs) .	1,100	1,800	2,500	3,500	4,500	5,600
K1 ABS (1000cc four)	2,200	3,400	4,400	5,400	6,400	7,400
R100RT (1000cc twin)	1,400	2,000	3,000	4,100	5,100	6,200
K100LT ABS (1000cc four)	1,900	2,700	3,700	4,700	5,700	6,700
1993						
K75 (750cc triple)	900	1,500	2,200	2,900	3,800	4,800
K75RT ABS (750cc triple)	900	1,600	2,300	3,000	4,000	5,000
K75S (750cc triple)	900	1,500	2,200	2,900	3,800	4,800
K75S ABS (750cc triple)	1,000	1,700	2,400	3,200	4,200	5,200
R100GS (1000cc twin)	1,200	1,800	2,300	3,300	4,300	5,300
R100GS Paris-Dakar (1000cc twin)	1,000	1,700	2,400	3,400	4,400	5,400
R100R (1000cc twin)	1,000	1,700	2,400	3,400	4,400	5,400
R100RS w/fairing (1000cc twin)	1,300	1,900	2,800	3,800	4,800	5,800
K1 ABS (1000cc four)	2,200	3,400	4,400	5,400	6,400	7,400
R100RT (1000cc twin)	1,400	2,000	3,000	4,100	5,100	6,200
K1100RS ABS w/fairing (1100cc four) . . .	2,000	3,000	4,000	5,300	6,300	7,300
K1100LT ABS (1100cc four)	1,600	2,600	3,600	4,800	5,800	7,000
1994						
K75 (750cc triple) (18,485-13 yrs)	900	1,500	2,200	2,900	3,800	4,800
K75RT ABS (750cc triple) (21,264-8 yrs) . .	900	1,600	2,300	3,000	4,000	5,000
K75A (750cc triple)	300	600	900	2,000	2,900	4,000
K75S (750cc triple) (18,649-12 yrs)	900	1,500	2,200	2,900	3,800	4,800
R100R (1000cc twin) (20,589-6 yrs)	1,000	1,700	2,400	3,400	4,400	5,400
R100GS (1000cc twin) (34,007-12 yrs) . . .	1,000	1,700	2,400	3,400	4,400	5,400
R100GS Paris-Dakar (1000cc twin)	1,000	1,700	2,400	3,400	4,400	5,400
R100RT	1,400	2,000	3,000	4,100	5,100	6,200
K1100LT ABS (1100cc four)	1,600	2,600	3,600	4,800	5,800	7,000
K1100RS ABS w/fairing (1100cc four) . . .	2,000	3,000	4,000	5,300	6,300	7,300
R1100RS	1,300	1,900	2,800	3,800	4,800	5,800
R1100RSL	400	600	1,700	3,500	5,200	7,000
1995						
K75 (750cc triple)	600	1,000	1,900	2,800	3,700	4,600
K75/3 (750cc triple)	600	1,000	1,900	3,000	4,100	5,200
K75/3 ABS (750cc triple)	700	1,200	2,200	3,200	4,200	5,200
K75S (750cc triple)	700	1,200	2,400	3,600	4,800	6,000
K75RT ABS (750cc triple)	700	1,200	2,400	3,600	4,800	6,000
R100GS (1000cc twin)	800	1,500	2,600	3,700	4,800	6,000
R100GS Paris-Dakar (1000cc twin)	700	1,200	2,700	4,000	5,300	6,600
R100GS Paris-Dakar Clas (1000cc twin) . .	800	1,500	2,800	4,100	5,400	6,700
R100RT (1000cc twin)	700	1,200	2,400	3,600	4,800	6,000
R100M Mystic (1000cc twin)	600	1,300	2,500	3,700	4,900	6,100
R100R Classic (1000cc twin)	600	1,300	2,500	3,700	4,900	6,100
R1100GS (1100cc twin)	700	1,200	2,500	3,800	5,100	6,400
R1100GS ABS (1100cc twin)	800	1,500	3,000	4,300	5,600	6,900
R1100R (1100cc twin)	600	1,100	2,300	3,500	4,700	5,900
R1100RA/S ABS (1100cc twin)	700	1,200	2,400	3,600	4,800	6,000
R1100R ABS (1100cc twin)	700	1,400	2,500	3,600	4,700	5,800
R1100RS ABS Special Edition (1100cc twin)	600	1,300	2,500	3,700	4,900	6,100
R1100RS ABS (1100cc twin)	600	1,300	2,500	3,700	4,900	6,100
R1100RSL ABS Special Edition (1100cc twin)	600	1,300	2,800	4,300	5,800	7,300
R1100RSL ABS (1100cc twin)	600	1,300	2,800	4,300	5,800	7,300
K1100LT ABS (1100cc four)	700	1,400	2,800	4,200	5,600	7,000
K1100RS ABS w/fairing (1100cc four) . . .	600	1,300	2,800	4,300	5,800	7,300
R1100RT (1100cc twin)	600	1,300	2,800	4,300	5,800	7,300
R1100RT Classic Edition (1100cc twin) . . .	700	1,400	2,900	4,400	5,900	7,400
1996						
R850R (850cc twin)	600	1,500	3,000	5,000	7,000	9,000
R850R ABS (850cc twin)	800	2,000	4,000	6,000	8,000	10,700

	6	5	4	3	2	1
R1100GS ABS (1100cc twin)	800	2,000	4,000	6,000	8,000	13,000
R1100R (1100cc twin).	800	2,000	4,000	6,000	8,000	10,300
R1100R ABS (1100cc twin)	800	2,000	4,000	6,000	9,000	12,290
R1100R ABS Spoke Wheel (1100cc twin). .	800	2,000	4,000	6,000	9,000	12,700
R1100RS ABS (1100cc twin)	1,200	2,500	5,000	8,000	11,000	14,800
R1100RSL ABS (1100cc twin)	1,500	3,000	6,000	9,000	12,000	15,100
K1100RS ABS (1100cc four)	1,500	3,000	6,000	9,000	12,000	15,400
K1100RS ABS Special Edition (1100cc four)	1,500	3,000	6,000	9,000	12,000	15,600
R1100RT ABS (1100cc twin)	1,500	3,000	6,000	9,000	12,000	15,400
R1100RTL ABS (1100cc twin)	1,500	3,000	6,000	9,000	12,000	16,000
K1100LT ABS (1100cc four)	1,500	3,000	6,000	9,000	12,000	16,600

BRIDGESTONE

	6	5	4	3	2	1
1963						
Bridgestone 7 (48cc single)	300	500	700	1,000	1,300	1,600
1964						
50 Homer (48cc single)	300	500	800	1,000	1,400	1,700
Bridgestone 7 (48cc single)	300	500	700	1,000	1,300	1,600
Bridgestone 90 (88cc single)	400	600	1,000	1,300	1,700	2,100
1965						
50 Sport (48cc single).	300	500	800	1,000	1,400	1,700
50 Homer (48cc single)	300	500	800	1,000	1,400	1,700
60 Sport (60cc single).	400	600	900	1,100	1,500	1,900
90 Deluxe (88cc single)	400	600	900	1,200	1,600	2,000
90 Mountain (88cc single).	400	600	900	1,200	1,600	2,000
90 Racer (88cc single)	400	600	900	1,200	1,600	2,000
90 Sport (88cc single).	400	600	1,000	1,300	1,700	2,100
1966						
50 Sport (48cc single).	300	500	800	1,000	1,400	1,700
50 Homer (48cc single)	300	500	800	1,000	1,400	1,700
60 Sport (60cc single).	400	600	900	1,100	1,500	1,900
90 Deluxe (88cc single)	400	600	900	1,200	1,600	2,000
90 Mountain (88cc single).	400	600	900	1,200	1,600	2,000
90 Racer (88cc single)	400	600	900	1,200	1,600	2,000
90 Sport (88cc single).	400	600	1,000	1,300	1,700	2,100
DT 175 (177cc dual twin)	600	900	1,300	1,700	2,300	2,900
1967						
50 Sport (48cc single).	300	500	800	1,000	1,400	1,700
50 Homer (48cc single)	300	500	800	1,000	1,400	1,700
60 Sport (60cc single).	400	600	900	1,100	1,500	1,900
90 Deluxe (88cc single)	400	600	900	1,200	1,600	2,000
90 Mountain (88cc single).	400	600	900	1,200	1,600	2,000
90 Racer (88cc single)	400	700	1,000	1,300	1,800	2,200
90 Sport (88cc single).	400	600	900	1,200	1,600	2,000
90 Trail (88cc single)	400	600	1,000	1,300	1,700	2,100
DT 175 (177cc dual twin)	600	900	1,300	1,700	2,300	2,900
Hurricane Scrambler (177 cc dual twin) . . .	600	900	1,300	1,700	2,300	2,900
1968						
50 Sport (48cc single).	300	500	800	1,000	1,400	1,700
50 Step-thru (48cc single).	300	500	800	1,000	1,400	1,700
60 Sport (60cc single).	400	500	800	1,100	1,400	1,800
90 Deluxe (88cc single)	400	600	900	1,200	1,600	2,000
90 Mountain (88cc single).	400	600	900	1,200	1,600	2,000
90 Racer (88cc single)	400	700	1,000	1,300	1,800	2,200
90 Sport (88cc single).	400	600	1,000	1,300	1,700	2,100
90 Trail (88cc single)	400	600	1,000	1,300	1,700	2,100
DT 175 (177cc dual twin)	600	900	1,300	1,700	2,300	2,900
Hurricane Scrambler (177 cc dual twin) . . .	600	900	1,300	1,700	2,300	2,900
350 GTR (345cc twin).	800	1,200	1,800	2,300	3,100	3,900
1969						
60 Sport (60cc single).	400	600	900	1,100	1,500	1,900

	6	5	4	3	2	1
SR 90 (90cc single)	400	700	1,000	1,300	1,800	2,200
SR 100 (100cc single)	900	1,400	2,000	2,700	3,600	4,500
100 GP (100cc single)	500	800	1,100	1,500	2,000	2,500
100 TMX (100cc single)	500	800	1,200	1,600	2,200	2,700
SR 175 (175cc twin)	1,400	2,100	3,200	4,200	5,600	7,000
350 GTR (345cc twin)	800	1,200	1,800	2,300	3,100	3,900
350 GTO (345cc twin)	1,000	1,500	2,300	3,000	4,000	5,000
1970						
60 Sport (60cc single)	400	600	900	1,100	1,500	1,900
SR 90 (90cc single)	400	700	1,000	1,300	1,800	2,200
SR 100 (100cc single)	900	1,400	2,000	2,700	3,600	4,500
100 Sport (100cc single)	600	800	1,200	1,600	2,200	2,700
350 GTR (345cc twin)	800	1,200	1,800	2,300	3,100	3,900
350 GTO (345cc twin)	1,000	1,500	2,300	3,000	4,000	5,000
1971						
SR 90 (90cc single)	400	700	1,000	1,300	1,800	2,200
SR 100 (100cc single)	900	1,400	2,000	2,700	3,600	4,500
350 GTR (345cc twin)	800	1,200	1,800	2,300	3,100	3,900
350 GTO (345cc twin)	1,000	1,500	2,300	3,000	4,000	5,000

BROUGH SUPERIOR

	6	5	4	3	2	1
1921						
Mk. I (side-valve J.A.P. twin, 976cc)	8,000	12,000	18,000	24,000	32,000	40,000
1922						
Mk. I (side-valve J.A.P. twin, 976cc)	8,000	12,000	18,000	24,000	32,000	40,000
SS80 (side valve J.A.P. twin, 976cc)	8,000	12,000	18,000	24,000	32,000	40,000
1923						
Mk. I (side-valve J.A.P. twin, 976cc)	8,000	12,000	18,000	24,000	32,000	40,000
SS80 (side valve J.A.P. twin, 976cc)	9,000	13,000	19,000	25,000	34,000	43,000
1924						
Mk. I (side-valve J.A.P. twin, 976cc)	8,000	12,000	18,000	24,000	32,000	40,000
SS80 (side valve J.A.P. twin, 976cc)	9,000	13,000	19,000	25,000	34,000	43,000
SS100 (OHV J.A.P. twin, 984cc)	31,000	50,000	75,000	100K	150K	200K
1925						
SS80 (side valve J.A.P. twin, 976cc)	9,000	14,000	20,000	27,000	36,000	45,000
SS100 (OHV J.A.P. twin, 984cc)	31,000	50,000	75,000	100K	150K	200K
1926						
SS80 (side valve J.A.P. twin, 976cc)	9,000	14,000	20,000	27,000	36,000	45,000
SS100 (OHV J.A.P. twin, 984cc)	31,000	50,000	75,000	100K	150K	200K
Model 680 (OHV J.A.P. twin, 676cc)	9,000	15,000	25,000	35,000	45,000	55,000
1927						
SS80 (side valve J.A.P. twin, 976cc)	9,000	14,000	20,000	27,000	36,000	45,000
SS100 (OHV J.A.P. twin, 984cc)	31,000	50,000	75,000	100K	150K	200K
Model 680 (OHV J.A.P. twin, 676cc)	9,000	15,000	25,000	35,000	45,000	55,000
1928						
SS80 (side valve J.A.P. twin, 976cc)	9,000	14,000	20,000	27,000	36,000	45,000
SS100 (OHV J.A.P. twin, 984cc)	31,000	50,000	75,000	100K	150K	200K
Model 680 (OHV J.A.P. twin, 676cc)	9,000	15,000	25,000	35,000	45,000	55,000
1929						
SS80 (side valve J.A.P. twin, 976cc)	9,000	14,000	20,000	27,000	36,000	45,000
SS100 (OHV J.A.P. twin, 984cc)	31,000	50,000	75,000	100K	150K	200K
Model 680 (OHV J.A.P. twin, 676cc)	9,000	15,000	25,000	35,000	45,000	55,000
1930						
SS80 (side valve J.A.P. twin, 976cc)	9,000	14,000	20,000	27,000	36,000	45,000
SS100 (OHV J.A.P. twin, 984cc)	29,000	50,000	75,000	100K	150K	200K
Model 680 (OHV J.A.P. twin, 676cc)	9,000	15,000	25,000	35,000	45,000	55,000
1931						
SS80 (side valve J.A.P. twin, 976cc)	9,000	14,000	20,000	27,000	36,000	45,000
SS100 (OHV J.A.P. twin, 984cc)	29,000	44,000	65,000	87,000	120K	150K
Model 680 (OHV J.A.P. twin, 676cc)	9,000	15,000	25,000	35,000	45,000	55,000

	6	5	4	3	2	1
1932						
SS80 (side valve J.A.P. twin, 976cc)	9,000	14,000	20,000	27,000	36,000	45,000
SS100(OHV J.A.P. twin, 984cc)........	29,000	50,000	75,000	100K	150K	200K
Model 680 (OHV J.A.P. twin, 676cc)	9,000	15,000	25,000	35,000	45,000	55,000
1933						
SS80 (side valve J.A.P. twin, 976cc)	9,000	14,000	20,000	27,000	36,000	45,000
SS100(OHV J.A.P. twin, 984cc)........	29,000	50,000	75,000	100K	150K	200K
Model 680 (OHV J.A.P. twin, 676cc)	9,000	15,000	25,000	35,000	45,000	55,000
Model 1150 (side-valve J.A.P. twin, 1150cc)	7,000	10,000	15,000	23,000	32,000	40,000
1934						
SS80 (side valve J.A.P. twin, 976cc) (630 from 1921-34)	9,000	14,000	20,000	27,000	36,000	45,000
SS100(OHV J.A.P. twin, 984cc)........	29,000	50,000	75,000	100K	150K	200K
Model 680 (OHV J.A.P. twin, 676cc)	9,000	15,000	25,000	35,000	45,000	55,000
Model 1150 (side-valve J.A.P. twin, 1150cc)	7,000	10,000	15,000	20,000	27,000	35,000
1935						
SS80 (side valve Matchless twin, 998cc) ..	**15,000**	**20,000**	**35,000**	**55,000**	**75,000**	**95,000**
SS100(OHV J.A.P. twin, 984cc)........	29,000	50,000	75,000	100K	150K	200K
Model 680 (OHV J.A.P. twin, 676cc)	9,000	15,000	25,000	35,000	45,000	55,000
Model 1150 (side-valve J.A.P. twin, 1150cc)	7,000	10,000	15,000	20,000	27,000	35,000
1936						
SS80 (side valve Matchless twin, 998cc) ..	**15,000**	**20,000**	**35,000**	**55,000**	**75,000**	**95,000**
SS100 (OHV Matchless twin, 998cc)	25,000	50,000	75,000	125K	175K	225K
Model 1150 (side-valve J.A.P. twin, 1150cc)	7,000	10,000	15,000	20,000	27,000	35,000
1937						
SS80 (side valve Matchless twin, 998cc) ..	**15,000**	**20,000**	**35,000**	**55,000**	**75,000**	**95,000**
SS100 (OHV Matchless twin, 998cc)	25,000	50,000	75,000	125K	175K	225K
Model 1150 (side-valve J.A.P. twin, 1150cc)	7,000	10,000	15,000	20,000	27,000	35,000
1938						
SS80 (side valve Matchless twin, 998cc) ..	**15,000**	**20,000**	**35,000**	**55,000**	**75,000**	**95,000**
SS100 (OHV Matchless twin, 998cc)	25,000	50,000	75,000	125K	175K	225K
Model 1150 (side-valve J.A.P. twin, 1150cc)	6,000	9,000	14,000	18,000	24,000	30,000
1939						
SS80 (side valve Matchless twin, 998cc) (460 from 1935-39)	**15,000**	**20,000**	**35,000**	**55,000**	**75,000**	**95,000**
SS100 (OHV Matchless twin, 998cc)	25,000	50,000	75,000	125K	175K	225K
Model 1150 (side-valve J.A.P. twin, 1150cc)	8,000	11,000	17,000	23,000	31,000	40,000
BSA						
1914						
Model 557H	3,000	5,000	7,000	11,000	15,000	19,000
1915						
Model K	2,500	5,000	10,000	15,000	20,000	25,000
1916						
Model K	2,500	5,000	10,000	15,000	20,000	25,000
1921						
Model H 557.	1,500	2,500	5,000	8,000	11,000	14,000
1924						
Flat Tank	2,000	4,000	5,500	7,000	8,500	10,000
Single Valve	3,000	6,000	9,000	12,000	15,000	18,000
Model B	2,000	4,000	5,500	7,000	8,500	10,000
Model L (349cc).	2,000	4,000	5,500	7,000	8,500	10,000
1927						
Model B Deluxe	2,000	4,000	5,500	7,000	8,500	10,000
Model S27 (500cc)	2,000	4,000	5,500	7,000	8,500	10,000
1928						
Model A28 (175cc)	1,000	2,000	3,000	4,000	5,000	6,000
Model L28 (350cc)	2,000	4,000	6,000	8,000	10,000	12,000
Model M28 (500cc)	2,000	4,000	5,500	7,000	8,500	10,000
Model S28 (500cc)	2,000	4,000	5,500	7,000	8,500	10,000

	6	5	4	3	2	1
1929						
S-29 Deluxe (493cc)	2,000	4,000	8,000	12,000	16,000	20,000
Sloper Side Valve (500cc)	2,000	4,000	5,500	7,000	8,500	10,000
Colonial (770cc)	1,000	2,000	3,000	4,000	5,000	6,000
1930						
A-2 (150cc single)	1,100	1,700	2,500	3,400	4,500	5,600
B-3 (250cc single)	1,200	1,700	2,600	3,500	4,600	5,800
B-4 (250cc single)	1,200	1,700	2,600	3,500	4,600	5,800
L-11 (350cc single)	1,200	1,800	2,700	3,600	4,800	6,000
L-5 (350cc single)	1,200	1,800	2,700	3,600	4,800	6,000
L-6 (350cc single)	1,200	1,800	2,700	3,600	4,800	6,000
S-12 (500cc single)	1,200	2,200	3,200	4,200	5,200	7,200
S-13 Deluxe (500cc single)	1,200	1,900	3,000	4,500	6,000	7,500
S-18 Light (500cc single)	1,200	1,900	3,000	4,500	6,000	7,500
S-19 Light (500cc single)	1,200	1,900	3,000	4,500	6,000	7,500
S-7 (500cc single)	1,200	1,900	3,000	4,500	6,000	7,500
S-9 Deluxe (500cc single)	1,200	1,900	3,000	4,500	6,000	7,500
H-10 (550cc single)	1,400	2,000	3,500	5,000	6,400	7,800
H-8 (550cc single)	1,400	2,000	3,100	4,100	5,400	6,800
E-14 (750cc twin)	1,400	2,500	3,500	5,000	6,500	8,000
G-15 (1000cc twin)	2,000	4,500	6,500	8,500	10,500	12,500
G-16 World Tour (1000cc twin)	2,000	4,500	6,500	8,500	10,500	12,500
1931						
B-1 (250cc single)	1,200	1,700	2,600	3,500	4,600	5,800
B-2 (250cc single)	1,200	1,700	2,600	3,500	4,600	5,800
B-3 (250cc single)	1,200	1,800	2,700	3,600	4,800	6,000
L-4 (350cc single)	1,200	1,800	2,800	3,700	4,900	6,100
L-5 Deluxe (350cc single)	1,200	1,800	2,800	3,700	4,900	6,100
L-6 Deluxe (350cc single)	1,200	1,900	2,800	3,700	5,000	6,200
S-10 Deluxe (500cc single)	1,200	1,900	2,500	4,000	5,500	7,000
S-7 (500cc single)	1,200	1,900	2,500	4,000	5,500	7,000
S-9 (500cc single)	1,200	1,900	2,500	4,000	5,500	7,000
H-8 (550cc single)	1,200	1,900	3,000	4,500	6,000	7,500
E-11 (750cc twin, 3-gal.tank)	1,400	2,000	3,500	5,000	6,400	7,800
1932						
B-1 (250cc single)	1,200	1,700	2,600	3,500	4,600	5,800
L-2 (350cc single)	1,300	2,000	2,900	3,900	5,200	6,500
L-3 (350cc single)	1,300	2,000	2,900	3,900	5,200	6,500
L-4 Deluxe (350cc single)	1,300	2,000	2,900	3,900	5,200	6,500
L-5 Blue Star (350cc single)	1,500	2,200	3,300	4,400	5,900	7,400
L-5 Deluxe (350cc single)	1,300	2,000	2,900	3,900	5,200	6,500
S-8 Deluxe (500cc single)	1,200	1,900	2,500	4,000	5,500	7,000
W-6 (500cc single)	1,200	1,900	2,500	4,000	5,500	7,000
W-7 Blue Star (500cc single)	1,900	2,900	4,300	6,000	9,000	12,000
H-9 Deluxe (550cc single)	1,200	1,900	3,000	4,500	6,000	7,500
G-10 (1000cc twin)	2,000	3,000	6,000	9,500	13,500	16,500
1933						
B-1 (250cc single)	1,200	1,800	2,700	3,600	4,800	6,000
B-2 S.P. (250cc single)	1,200	1,800	2,700	3,600	4,800	6,000
B-3 Blue Star Jr. (250cc single)	1,200	1,800	2,700	3,600	4,800	6,000
R-4 (350cc single)	1,300	2,000	3,000	4,000	5,300	6,600
R-5 Blue Star (350cc single)	1,500	2,200	3,300	4,400	5,900	7,400
W-6 (500cc single)	1,200	1,900	2,500	4,000	5,500	7,000
W-6 Post Office (500cc single)	1,200	1,900	2,500	4,000	5,500	7,000
W-7 (500cc single)	1,200	1,900	2,500	4,000	5,500	7,000
W-8 Blue Star (500cc single)	1,900	2,900	4,300	6,000	9,000	12,000
W-9 Special (500cc single)	1,200	1,900	3,000	4,500	6,000	7,500
M-10 (600cc single)	1,200	1,900	2,500	4,000	5,500	7,000
M-11 (600cc single)	1,200	1,900	2,500	4,000	5,500	7,000
G-13 Light (1000cc twin)	2,000	3,000	4,500	6,500	8,500	11,500

	6	5	4	3	2	1
G-13 World Tour (1000cc twin)	1,900	2,900	4,300	6,000	9,000	12,000
G-14 War Office (1000cc twin)	1,900	2,900	4,300	6,000	9,000	12,000
1934						
X-0 (150cc single).	1,500	2,500	4,000	5,000	6,000	7,000
B-1 (250cc single).	1,200	1,800	2,700	3,600	4,800	6,000
B-17 Sports (250cc single)	1,200	1,800	2,700	3,600	4,800	6,000
B-2 (250cc single).	1,200	1,800	2,700	3,600	4,800	6,000
B-3 Blue Star Jr. (250cc single)	1,200	1,800	2,700	3,600	4,800	6,000
R-4 (350cc single).	1,300	2,000	3,000	4,000	5,300	6,600
R-5 Blue Star (350cc single)	1,500	2,300	3,400	4,500	6,000	7,500
R-6 Special (350cc single)	1,300	2,000	3,000	4,000	5,300	6,600
W-7 (500cc single)	1,200	1,800	2,700	3,500	5,000	6,500
W-8 (500cc single)	1,200	1,900	2,500	4,000	5,500	7,000
W-9 Blue Star (500cc single)	1,900	2,900	4,500	6,500	8,500	10,500
W-10 Special (500cc single).	1,500	2,300	3,400	4,500	6,000	7,500
J-11 (500cc single)	1,900	2,900	4,300	6,000	8,000	10,000
M-12 (600cc single)	1,200	1,900	2,500	4,000	5,500	7,000
M-13 (600cc single)	1,200	1,900	2,500	4,000	5,500	7,000
G-14 World Tour (1000cc twin)	2,200	3,300	5,000	6,500	9,500	12,500
1935						
X-0 (150cc single).	1,500	2,500	4,000	5,000	6,000	7,000
B-1 (250cc single).	1,200	1,800	2,700	3,600	4,800	6,000
B-2 (250cc single).	1,200	1,800	2,700	3,600	4,800	6,000
B-3 Deluxe (250cc single).	1,200	1,800	2,700	3,600	4,800	6,000
R-4 Deluxe (350cc single).	1,300	2,000	2,900	3,900	5,200	6,500
R-5 Blue Star (350cc single)	1,400	2,100	3,200	4,200	5,600	7,000
R-17 Twin Port (350cc single)	1,300	2,000	2,900	3,900	5,200	6,500
W-6 (500cc single)	1,500	2,300	3,400	4,500	6,000	7,500
J-12 (500cc single)	1,900	2,900	4,500	6,500	8,500	10,500
W-7 (500cc single)	1,300	2,000	2,900	3,900	5,200	6,500
W-8 Blue Star (500cc single)	1,900	2,900	4,300	5,700	7,600	9,500
W-9 Special (500cc single)	1,200	1,900	2,500	4,000	5,500	7,000
M-10 (600cc single)	1,200	1,900	2,500	4,000	5,500	7,000
J-15 War Office (750cc twin)	**2,000**	**3,000**	**5,000**	**8,000**	**11,000**	**14,000**
G-14 (1000cc twin)	–2,000	–3,000	5,000	**8,000**	**11,000**	**14,000**
1936						
X-0 (150cc single).	1,500	2,500	4,000	5,000	6,000	7,000
B-1 (250cc single).	1,200	1,800	2,700	3,600	4,800	6,000
B-18 Light Deluxe (250cc single)	1,200	1,800	2,700	3,600	4,800	6,000
B-2 (250cc single).	1,200	1,800	2,700	3,600	4,800	6,000
B-3 Deluxe (250cc single).	1,200	1,800	2,700	3,600	4,800	6,000
R-4 Deluxe (350cc single).	1,300	2,000	2,900	3,900	5,200	6,500
R-17 (350cc single)	1,300	2,000	2,900	3,900	5,200	6,500
R-19 Comp. (350cc single)	1,600	2,400	3,600	4,800	6,400	8,000
R-20 New Blue Star (350cc single)	1,400	2,100	3,200	4,200	5,600	7,000
R-5 Empire Star (350cc single)	1,500	2,300	3,400	4,500	6,000	7,500
Q21 New Blue Star (500cc single)	2,200	3,300	5,000	7,000	9,000	12,000
Q7 (500cc single)	1,600	3,000	4,500	6,000	7,500	9,000
Q8 Empire Star (500cc single)	2,200	3,300	5,000	6,600	8,800	11,000
J-12 (500cc single)	2,200	3,300	5,000	7,000	9,000	11,500
W-6 (500cc single)	1,500	2,300	3,400	4,500	6,000	7,500
M-10 (600cc single)	1,400	2,100	3,200	4,200	5,600	7,000
Y-13 (750cc twin)	–2,000	–3,000	5,000	**8,000**	**11,000**	**14,000**
G-14 (1000cc twin)	–2,000	–3,000	5,000	**8,000**	**11,000**	**14,000**
1937						
B20 Tourer (250cc single).	1,200	1,800	2,700	3,600	4,800	6,000
B21 Sports (250cc single).	1,200	1,800	2,700	3,600	4,800	6,000
B22 Empire star (250cc single)	1,300	2,000	2,900	3,900	5,200	6,500
B23 Tourer (350cc single).	1,200	1,800	2,700	3,600	4,800	6,000
B24 Empire Star (350cc single)	1,500	2,300	3,400	4,500	6,000	7,500

	6	5	4	3	2	1
B25 Comp. (350cc single)	1,600	2,400	3,600	4,800	6,400	8,000
B26 Sports (350cc single)	1,400	2,200	3,200	4,300	5,800	7,200
M19 Deluxe (350cc single)	1,200	1,800	2,700	3,600	4,800	6,000
M20 Tourer (500cc single)	1,600	2,400	3,600	4,800	6,400	8,000
M22 Sports (500cc single)	1,400	2,100	3,200	4,200	5,600	7,000
M23 Empire Star (500cc single)	1,800	2,700	4,050	5,400	7,200	9,000
M21 Tourer (600cc Single)	1,200	1,800	3,000	4,000	6,000	8,000
Y13 (750cc twin)	–2,000	–3,000	5,000	**8,000**	**11,000**	**14,000**
G14 (1000cc twin)	–2,000	–3,000	5,000	**8,000**	**11,000**	**14,000**
1938						
B20 Tourer (250cc single)	1,200	1,800	2,700	3,600	4,800	6,000
B21 Sports (250cc single)	1,200	1,800	2,700	3,600	4,800	6,000
B22 Empire star (250cc single)	1,300	2,000	2,900	3,900	5,200	6,500
C10 (250cc single)	900	1,400	2,000	2,700	3,600	4,500
C11 (250cc single)	900	1,400	2,000	2,700	3,600	4,500
B23 Tourer (350cc single)	1,300	2,000	2,900	3,900	5,200	6,500
B24 Empire Star (350cc single)	1,600	2,400	3,600	4,700	6,300	7,900
B25 Comp. (350cc single)	1,700	2,600	3,800	5,100	6,800	8,500
B26 Sports (350cc single)	1,400	2,200	3,200	4,300	5,800	7,200
M19 Deluxe (350cc single)	1,100	1,700	2,500	3,300	4,400	5,500
M22 Sports (500cc single)	1,400	2,100	3,200	4,200	5,600	7,000
M23 Empire Star (500cc single)	1,800	2,700	5,000	7,000	9,000	12,000
M24 Gold Star (500cc single)	2,200	3,300	5,000	6,500	9,500	12,500
M21 Tourer (600cc Single)	1,600	2,400	3,600	4,800	6,400	8,000
Y13 (750cc twin)	–2,000	–3,000	5,000	**8,000**	**11,000**	**14,000**
G14 (1000cc twin)	–2,000	–3,000	5,000	**8,000**	**11,000**	**14,000**
1939						
B21 Deluxe (250cc single)	**1,200**	**1,800**	**2,700**	**3,600**	**4,800**	**6,000**
B21 (250cc single)	**1,200**	**1,800**	**2,700**	**3,600**	**4,800**	**6,000**
C10 Deluxe (250cc single)	**1,200**	**1,800**	**2,700**	**3,600**	**4,800**	**6,000**
C10 (250cc single)	**1,200**	**1,800**	**2,700**	**3,600**	**4,800**	**6,000**
C11 (250cc single)	**1,200**	**1,800**	**2,700**	**3,600**	**4,800**	**6,000**
B23 (350cc single)	1,200	1,800	2,700	3,600	4,800	6,000
B25 Comp. (350cc single)	2,000	3,000	4,500	6,000	8,000	10,000
B26 (350cc single)	1,500	2,300	3,500	4,600	6,200	7,700
B23 Deluxe (350cc single)	1,200	1,800	2,700	3,600	4,800	6,000
B24 Silver Star (350cc single)	1,700	2,600	3,800	5,100	6,800	8,500
M20 Deluxe (500cc single)	1,600	2,400	3,600	4,800	6,400	8,000
M20 (500cc single)	1,600	2,400	3,600	4,800	6,400	8,000
M22 (500cc single)	1,400	2,100	3,200	4,200	5,600	7,000
M23 Silver Star (500cc single)	2,200	3,300	5,000	6,500	9,500	12,500
M24 Gold Star (500cc single)	2,200	3,300	5,000	6,500	9,500	12,500
M21 (600cc Single)	1,600	2,400	3,600	4,800	6,400	8,000
G14 (1000cc twin)	–2,000	–3,000	5,000	**8,000**	**11,000**	**14,000**
1940						
WD/M20 (500cc single)	1,600	**3,000**	**4,500**	**6,000**	**7,500**	**9,000**
1941						
WD/M20 (500cc single)	1,600	**3,000**	**4,500**	**6,000**	**7,500**	**9,000**
1942						
WD/M20 (500cc single)	1,600	**3,000**	**4,500**	**6,000**	**7,500**	**9,000**
1943						
WD/M20 (500cc single)	1,600	**3,000**	**4,500**	**6,000**	**7,500**	**9,000**
1944						
WD/M20 (500cc single)	1,600	**3,000**	**4,500**	**6,000**	**7,500**	**9,000**
1945						
C10 (250cc single)	**1,300**	**2,000**	**2,900**	**3,900**	**5,200**	**6,500**
C11 (250cc single)	**1,300**	**2,000**	**2,900**	**3,900**	**5,200**	**6,500**
B31 (350cc single)	**1,300**	**2,000**	**2,900**	**3,900**	**5,200**	**6,500**
M20 (500cc single)	1,600	**3,000**	**4,500**	**6,000**	**7,500**	**9,000**

	6	5	4	3	2	1
1946						
C10 (250cc single)	1,300	2,000	2,900	3,900	5,200	6,500
C11 (250cc single)	1,300	2,000	2,900	3,900	5,200	6,500
B31 (350cc single)	1,300	2,000	2,900	3,900	5,200	6,500
B32 comp. (350cc single)	1,300	2,000	2,900	3,900	5,200	6,500
M20 (500cc single)	1,600	3,000	4,500	6,000	7,500	9,000
A7 (500cc twin)	2,000	3,000	4,500	6,000	8,000	10,000
M21 (600cc Single)	1,600	3,000	4,500	6,000	7,500	9,000
1947						
C10 (250cc single)	1,300	2,000	2,900	3,900	5,200	6,500
C11 (250cc single)	1,300	2,000	2,900	3,900	5,200	6,500
B31 (350cc single)	1,300	2,000	2,900	3,900	5,200	6,500
B32 comp. (350cc single)	1,300	2,000	2,900	3,900	5,200	6,500
A7 (500cc twin)	2,000	3,000	4,500	6,000	8,000	10,000
B33 (500cc single)	1,500	3,000	4,500	6,000	7,500	9,000
B34 Comp. (500cc single)	1,500	3,000	4,500	6,000	7,500	9,000
M20 (500cc single)	1,600	3,000	4,500	6,000	7,500	9,000
M21 (600cc Single)	1,600	3,000	4,500	6,000	7,500	9,000
1948						
C10 (250cc single)	1,300	2,000	2,900	3,900	5,200	6,500
B31 (350cc single)	1,300	2,000	2,900	3,900	5,200	6,500
B32 comp. (350cc single)	1,300	2,000	2,900	3,900	5,200	6,500
A7 (500cc twin)	2,000	3,000	4,500	6,000	8,000	10,000
B33 (500cc single)	1,500	3,000	4,500	6,000	7,500	9,000
B34 Comp. (500cc single)	1,500	3,000	4,500	6,000	7,500	9,000
M20 (500cc single)	1,600	3,000	4,500	6,000	7,500	9,000
M33 (500cc single)	1,100	2,000	3,500	5,000	6,500	8,000
M21 (600cc Single)	1,600	3,000	4,500	6,000	7,500	9,000
1949						
D1 Bantam (125cc single)	1,000	1,800	2,600	3,400	4,200	5,000
C10 (250cc single)	1,300	2,000	2,900	3,900	5,200	6,500
B31 (350cc single)	1,300	–2,000	–2,900	–3,900	5,200	6,500
B31 Plunger (350cc single)	1,000	1,500	3,000	4,500	6,000	7,500
B32 (350cc single)	–1,000	–1,500	–3,000	–4,500	6,000	7,500
B32 Comp. Plunger (350cc single)	–1,000	–1,500	–3,000	–4,500	6,000	7,500
B32GS Gold Star Plunger (350cc single) . .	2,000	3,000	4,500	6,000	8,500	11,000
A7 (500cc twin)	2,000	3,000	4,500	6,000	8,000	10,000
A7 Plunger (500cc twin)	2,000	3,000	4,500	6,000	8,000	10,000
A7S Star Plunger (500cc twin)	2,000	3,000	4,500	6,000	8,000	10,000
B33 (500cc single)	1,500	3,000	4,500	6,000	7,500	9,000
B33 Plunger (500cc single)	1,500	3,000	4,500	6,000	7,500	9,000
B34 Comp (500cc single)	1,500	3,000	4,500	6,000	7,500	9,000
B34 Comp Plunger (500cc single)	1,500	3,000	4,500	6,000	7,500	9,000
B34GS Gold Star (500cc single)	2,600	3,900	5,900	7,800	10,000	13,000
B34GS Gold Star Plunger (500cc single) . .	2,600	3,900	5,900	7,800	10,000	13,000
M20 (500cc single)	1,600	2,400	3,600	4,800	6,400	8,000
M33 (500cc single)	1,600	2,400	3,600	4,800	6,400	8,000
M21 (600cc single)	1,600	2,400	3,600	4,800	6,400	8,000
1950						
D1 Bantam w/WIPAC (125cc single)	600	–800	1,600	2,400	3,200	4,000
D1 Bantam w/Lucas (125cc single)	600	–800	1,600	2,400	3,200	4,000
D1 Bantam Plunger w/WIPAC (125cc single)	600	–800	1,600	2,400	3,200	4,000
D1 Bantam Plunger w/Lucas (125cc single) .	600	–800	1,600	2,400	3,200	4,000
C10 (250cc single)	–600	–800	1,600	2,400	3,200	4,000
C11 (250cc single)	–600	–800	1,600	2,400	3,200	4,000
B31 (350cc single)	1,000	2,000	3,000	4,000	5,000	6,000
B31 Plunger (350cc single)	1,000	1,500	2,500	4,000	5,500	7,000
B32 Comp (350cc single)	1,500	2,800	3,800	4,800	5,800	6,800
B32 Comp Plunger (350cc single)	1,500	2,800	3,800	4,800	5,800	6,800

	6	5	4	3	2	1
B32GS Gold Star (350cc single)	2,000	3,000	4,500	6,000	9,000	12,000
B32GS Gold Star Plunger (350cc single) . .	2,000	3,000	4,500	6,000	8,000	11,000
A7 (500cc twin)	2,000	3,000	4,500	6,000	8,000	10,000
A7Plunger (500cc twin)	2,000	3,000	4,500	6,000	8,000	10,000
A7S Star Plunger (500cc twin)	2,000	3,000	4,500	6,000	8,000	10,000
B33 (500cc single)	1,500	3,000	4,500	6,000	7,500	9,000
B33 Plunger (500cc single)	1,500	3,000	4,500	6,000	7,500	9,000
B34 Comp. (500cc single).	1,500	3,000	4,500	6,000	7,500	9,000
B34 Comp Plunger (500cc single).	1,500	3,000	4,500	6,000	7,500	9,000
B34GS Gold Star (500cc single)	2,600	3,900	5,900	7,800	10,000	13,000
B34GS Gold Star Plunger (500cc single) . .	2,600	3,900	5,900	7,800	10,000	13,000
M20 (500cc single)	1,600	2,400	3,600	4,800	6,400	8,000
M33 (500cc single)	**1,600**	**2,400**	**3,600**	**4,800**	**6,400**	**8,000**
M21 (600cc single)	1,600	2,400	3,600	4,800	6,400	8,000
1951						
D1 Bantam w/WIPAC (125cc single)	600	–800	**1,600**	**2,400**	**3,200**	**4,000**
D1 Bantam w/Lucas (125cc single)	600	–800	**1,600**	**2,400**	**3,200**	**4,000**
D1 Bantam Plunger w/WIPAC (125cc single)	600	–800	**1,600**	**2,400**	**3,200**	**4,000**
D1 Bantam Plunger w/Lucas (125cc single).	600	–800	**1,600**	**2,400**	**3,200**	**4,000**
D1 Bantam Plunger GPO (125cc single) . .	600	–800	**1,600**	**2,400**	**3,200**	**4,000**
C10 (250cc single)	600	–800	**1,600**	**2,400**	**3,200**	**4,000**
C10 Plunger (250cc single)	600	–800	**1,600**	**2,400**	**3,200**	**4,000**
C11 (250cc single)	600	–800	**1,600**	**2,400**	**3,200**	**4,000**
C11 Plunger (250cc single)	600	–800	**1,600**	**2,400**	**3,200**	**4,000**
B31 (350cc single)	1,000	2,000	3,000	4,000	5,000	6,000
B31 Plunger (350cc single)	1,000	1,500	2,500	4,000	5,500	7,000
B32 Comp (350cc single)	1,500	2,800	3,800	4,800	5,800	6,800
B32 Comp Plunger (350cc single).	1,500	2,800	3,800	4,800	5,800	6,800
B32GS Gold Star (350cc single)	2,000	3,000	4,500	6,000	9,000	12,000
B32GS Gold Star Plunger (350cc single) . .	2,200	3,300	5,000	6,600	8,800	11,000
A7 (500cc twin)	2,000	3,000	4,500	6,000	8,000	10,000
A7Plunger (500cc twin)	2,000	3,000	4,500	6,000	8,000	10,000
A7S Star Plunger (500cc twin)	2,000	3,000	4,500	6,000	8,000	10,000
B33 (500cc single)	1,500	3,000	4,500	6,000	7,500	9,000
B33 Plunger (500cc single)	1,500	3,000	4,500	6,000	7,500	9,000
B34 Comp. (500cc single).	1,500	3,000	4,500	6,000	7,500	9,000
B34 Comp Plunger (500cc single).	1,500	3,000	4,500	6,000	7,500	9,000
B34GS Gold Star (500cc single)	2,600	3,900	5,900	7,800	10,000	13,000
B34GS Gold Star Plunger (500cc single) . .	2,600	3,900	5,900	7,800	10,000	13,000
M20 (500cc single)	1,600	2,400	3,600	4,800	6,400	8,000
M20 Plunger (500cc single)	1,600	2,400	3,600	4,800	6,400	8,000
M33 (500cc single)	**1,600**	**2,400**	**3,600**	**4,800**	**6,400**	**8,000**
M33 Plunger (500cc single)	**1,600**	**2,400**	**3,600**	**4,800**	**6,400**	**8,000**
M21 (600cc single)	1,600	2,400	3,600	4,800	6,400	8,000
M21 Plunger (600cc single)	1,600	2,400	3,600	4,800	6,400	8,000
A10 Golden Flash (650cc twin)	2,000	3,000	4,500	6,000	8,000	10,000
A10 Golden Flash Plunger (650cc twin). .	2,000	3,000	4,500	6,000	8,000	10,000
1952						
D1 Bantam w/WIPAC (125cc single)	600	–800	**1,600**	**2,400**	**3,200**	**4,000**
D1 Bantam w/Lucas (125cc single)	600	–800	**1,600**	**2,400**	**3,200**	**4,000**
D1 Bantam Plunger w/WIPAC (125cc single)	600	–800	**1,600**	**2,400**	**3,200**	**4,000**
D1 Bantam Plunger w/Lucas (125cc single).	600	–800	**1,600**	**2,400**	**3,200**	**4,000**
D1 Bantam Plunger GPO (125cc single) . .	600	–800	**1,600**	**2,400**	**3,200**	**4,000**
C10 (250cc single)	600	–800	**1,600**	**2,400**	**3,200**	**4,000**
C10 Plunger (250cc single)	600	–800	**1,600**	**2,400**	**3,200**	**4,000**
C11 (250cc single)	600	–800	**1,600**	**2,400**	**3,200**	**4,000**
C11 Plunger (250cc single)	600	–800	**1,600**	**2,400**	**3,200**	**4,000**
B31 (350cc single)	1,000	2,000	3,000	4,000	5,000	6,000
B31 Plunger (350cc single)	1,000	1,500	2,500	4,000	5,500	7,000

	6	5	4	3	2	1
B32 Comp (350cc single)	1,500	2,800	3,800	4,800	5,800	6,800
B32 Comp Plunger (350cc single).	1,500	2,800	3,800	4,800	5,800	6,800
B32GS Gold Star (350cc single)	2,000	3,000	4,500	6,000	9,000	12,000
B32GS Gold Star Plunger (350cc single) . .	2,200	3,300	5,000	6,600	8,800	11,000
B32GS Gold Star Clubman (350cc single) .	2,700	4,100	6,100	9,000	12,000	15,000
B32GS Gold Star Clubman Plunger (350cc single)	2,700	4,100	6,100	9,000	12,000	15,000
A7 (500cc twin)	2,000	3,000	4,500	6,000	8,000	10,000
A7Plunger (500cc twin)	2,000	3,000	4,500	6,000	8,000	10,000
A7S Star Plunger (500cc twin)	2,000	3,000	4,500	6,000	8,000	10,000
B33 (500cc single)	1,500	3,000	4,500	6,000	7,500	9,000
B33 Plunger (500cc single)	1,500	3,000	4,500	6,000	7,500	9,000
B34 Comp. (500cc single).	1,200	2,000	4,000	6,000	7,500	9,000
B34 Comp Plunger (500cc single).	1,200	2,000	4,000	6,000	7,500	9,000
B34GS Gold Star (500cc single)	3,000	4,000	5,000	7,000	10,000	13,000
B34GS Gold Star Plunger (500cc single) . .	3,000	4,000	5,000	7,000	10,000	13,000
M20 (500cc single)	1,600	2,400	3,600	4,800	6,400	8,000
M20 Plunger (500cc single)	1,600	2,400	3,600	4,800	6,400	8,000
M33 (500cc single)	**1,600**	**2,400**	**3,600**	**4,800**	**6,400**	**8,000**
M33 Plunger (500cc single)	**1,600**	**2,400**	**3,600**	**4,800**	**6,400**	**8,000**
M21 (600cc single)	1,600	2,400	3,600	4,800	6,400	8,000
M21 Plunger (600cc single)	1,600	2,400	3,600	4,800	6,400	8,000
A10 Golden Flash (650cc twin)	2,000	3,000	4,500	6,000	8,000	10,000
A10 Golden Flash Plunger (650cc twin). . .	2,000	3,000	4,500	6,000	8,000	10,000
1953						
D1 Bantam w/WIPAC (125cc single)	600	–800	**1,600**	**2,400**	**3,200**	**4,000**
D1 Bantam w/Lucas (125cc single)	600	–800	**1,600**	**2,400**	**3,200**	**4,000**
D1 Bantam Plunger w/WIPAC (125cc single)	600	–800	**1,600**	**2,400**	**3,200**	**4,000**
D1 Bantam Plunger w/Lucas (125cc single).	600	–800	**1,600**	**2,400**	**3,200**	**4,000**
D1 Bantam Plunger GPO (125cc single) . .	600	–800	**1,600**	**2,400**	**3,200**	**4,000**
C10 (250cc single)	600	800	**1,600**	**2,400**	**3,200**	**4,000**
C10 Plunger (250cc single)	600	800	**1,600**	**2,400**	**3,200**	**4,000**
C11 (250cc single)	600	800	**1,600**	**2,400**	**3,200**	**4,000**
C11 Plunger (250cc single)	600	800	**1,600**	**2,400**	**3,200**	**4,000**
B31 (350cc single)	1,000	2,000	3,000	4,000	5,000	6,000
B31 Plunger (350cc single)	1,000	1,400	2,500	4,000	5,500	7,000
B32 Comp (350cc single)	1,500	2,800	3,800	4,800	5,800	6,800
B32 Comp Plunger (350cc single).	1,500	2,800	3,800	4,800	5,800	6,800
B32GS Gold Star (350cc single)	2,600	3,900	5,900	7,800	10,000	13,000
B32GS Gold Star Plunger (350cc single) . .	2,000	3,000	4,500	6,000	9,000	12,000
A7 (500cc twin)	2,000	3,000	4,500	6,000	8,000	10,000
A7 Plunger (500cc twin)	2,000	3,000	4,500	6,000	8,000	10,000
A7S Star Plunger (500cc twin)	2,000	3,000	4,500	6,000	8,000	10,000
B33 (500cc single)	1,500	3,000	4,500	6,000	7,500	9,000
B33 Plunger (500cc single)	1,500	3,000	4,500	6,000	7,500	9,000
B34 Comp (500cc single).	1,500	3,000	4,500	6,000	7,500	9,000
B34 Comp Plunger (500cc single).	1,500	3,000	4,500	6,000	7,500	9,000
B34GS Gold Star (500cc single)	3,000	4,000	6,000	8,000	11,000	14,000
B34GS Gold Star Plunger (500cc single) . .	3,000	4,000	6,000	8,000	11,000	14,000
M20 (500cc single)	1,600	2,400	3,600	4,800	6,400	8,000
M20 Plunger (500cc single)	1,600	2,400	3,600	4,800	6,400	8,000
M33 (500cc single)	**1,600**	**2,400**	**3,600**	**4,800**	**6,400**	**8,000**
M33 Plunger (500cc single)	**1,600**	**2,400**	**3,600**	**4,800**	**6,400**	**8,000**
M21 (600cc single)	1,600	2,400	3,600	4,800	6,400	8,000
M21 Plunger (600cc single)	1,600	2,400	3,600	4,800	6,400	8,000
A10 Golden Flash (650cc twin)	2,000	3,000	4,500	6,000	8,000	10,000
A10 Golden Flash Plunger (650cc twin). . .	2,000	3,000	4,500	6,000	8,000	10,000
A10SF Super Flash Plunger (650cc twin) . .	3,000	6,000	9,000	12,000	16,000	20,000

	6	5	4	3	2	1
1954						
D1 Bantam w/direct elec. (125cc single)	600	–800	**1,600**	**2,400**	**3,200**	4,000
D1 Bantam w/batt. (125cc single)	600	–800	**1,600**	**2,400**	**3,200**	4,000
D1 Bantam Plunger w/direc elec (125cc single)	600	–800	**1,600**	**2,400**	**3,200**	4,000
D1 Bantam Plunger w/batt. (125cc single)	600	–800	**1,600**	**2,400**	**3,200**	4,000
D1 Bantam Comp. Plunger (125cc single)	600	–800	**1,600**	**2,400**	**3,200**	4,000
D1 Bantam Plunger GPO (125cc single)	600	–800	**1,600**	**2,400**	**3,200**	4,000
D3 Bantam w/direct elec. (153cc single)	600	–800	**1,600**	**2,400**	**3,200**	4,000
D3 Bantam w/batt. (153cc single)	600	–800	**1,600**	**2,400**	**3,200**	4,000
D3 Bantam Plunger w/direct elec. (150cc single)	600	–800	**1,600**	**2,400**	**3,200**	4,000
D3 Bantam Plunger w/batt (150cc single)	600	–800	**1,600**	**2,400**	**3,200**	4,000
D3 Bantan Comp. Plunger (150cc single)	600	–800	**1,600**	**2,400**	**3,200**	4,000
C10L (250cc single)	600	800	**1,600**	**2,400**	**3,200**	4,000
C11G (250cc single)	600	800	**1,600**	**2,400**	**3,200**	4,000
C11G Plunger (250cc single)	600	800	**1,600**	**2,400**	**3,200**	4,000
C11G Rigid (250cc single)	600	800	**1,600**	**2,400**	**3,200**	4,000
B31 (350cc single)	1,000	2,000	3,000	4,000	5,000	6,000
B31 Plunger (350cc single)	1,000	1,400	2,500	4,000	5,500	7,000
B32 Comp (350cc single)	1,500	2,800	3,800	4,800	5,800	6,800
B32GS Gold Star (350cc single)	2,600	3,900	5,900	7,800	10,000	13,000
B32GS Gold Star New Clubman (350cc single)	3,000	4,000	6,000	8,000	11,000	14,000
A7Plunger (500cc twin)	2,000	3,000	4,500	6,000	8,000	10,000
A7 (500cc twin)	2,000	3,000	4,500	6,000	8,000	10,000
A7S Star Plunger (500cc twin)	2,000	3,000	4,500	6,000	8,000	10,000
A7SS Shooting Star (500cc twin)	2,000	3,000	4,500	6,000	8,000	10,000
B33 (500cc single)	1,500	3,000	4,500	6,000	7,500	9,000
B33 Plunger (500cc single)	1,500	3,000	4,500	6,000	7,500	9,000
B34 Comp. (500cc single)	1,500	3,000	4,500	6,000	7,500	9,000
B34GS Gold Star (500cc single)	3,000	5,000	8,000	10,000	13,000	16,000
B34GS Gold Star New Clubman (500cc single)	3,000	5,000	8,000	10,000	13,000	16,000
B34GS Gold Star Daytona (500cc single)	3,600	5,400	8,100	11,000	14,000	18,000
M20 (500cc single)	1,600	2,400	3,600	4,800	6,400	8,000
M20 Plunger (500cc single)	1,600	2,400	3,600	4,800	6,400	8,000
M33 (500cc single)	**1,600**	**2,400**	**3,600**	**4,800**	**6,400**	**8,000**
M33 Plunger (500cc single)	**1,600**	**2,400**	**3,600**	**4,800**	**6,400**	**8,000**
M21 (600cc single)	1,600	2,400	3,600	4,800	6,400	8,000
M21 Plunger (600cc single)	1,600	2,400	3,600	4,800	6,400	8,000
A10 Golden Flash Plunger (650cc twin)	2,000	3,000	4,500	6,000	8,000	10,000
A10SF Super Flash Plunger (650cc twin)	3,000	6,000	9,000	12,000	16,000	20,000
A10SF Super Flash (650cc twin)	3,000	6,000	9,000	12,000	16,000	20,000
A10R Road Rocket (650cc twin)	2,000	3,000	4,500	6,000	8,000	**11,000**
1955						
D1 Bantam w/direct elec. (125cc single)	600	800	**1,600**	**2,400**	**3,200**	4,000
D1 Bantam w/batt. (125cc single)	600	800	**1,600**	**2,400**	**3,200**	4,000
D3 Bantam w/direct elec. (153cc single)	600	800	**1,600**	**2,400**	**3,200**	4,000
D3 Bantam w/batt. (153cc single)	600	800	**1,600**	**2,400**	**3,200**	4,000
C10L (250cc single)	600	800	**1,600**	**2,400**	**3,200**	4,000
C11G (250cc single)	600	800	**1,600**	**2,400**	**3,200**	4,000
B31 (350cc single)	900	1,400	2,500	4,000	5,500	7,000
B32 Comp (350cc single)	1,400	2,000	3,100	4,100	5,400	6,800
B32GS Gold Star (350cc single)	2,600	3,900	5,900	7,800	10,000	13,000
B32GS Gold Star Clubman (350cc single)	3,000	4,000	6,000	8,000	11,000	14,000
A7 (500cc single)	2,000	3,000	4,500	6,000	8,000	10,000
A7SS Shooting Star (500cc twin)	2,000	3,000	4,500	6,000	8,000	10,000
B33 (500cc single)	1,500	3,000	4,500	6,000	7,500	9,000

	6	5	4	3	2	1
B34 Comp. (500cc single)	2,000	3,000	4,500	6,000	8,000	10,000
B34GS Gold Star (500cc single)	3,000	5,000	8,000	10,000	13,000	16,000
B34GS Gold Star New Clubman (500cc single)	3,000	5,000	8,000	10,000	13,000	16,000
M20 (500cc single)	1,600	2,400	3,600	4,800	6,400	8,000
M20 Plunger (500cc single)	1,600	2,400	3,600	4,800	6,400	8,000
M33 (500cc single)	**1,600**	**2,400**	**3,600**	**4,800**	**6,400**	**8,000**
M33 Plunger (500cc single)	**1,600**	**2,400**	**3,600**	**4,800**	**6,400**	**8,000**
M21 (600cc single)	1,600	2,400	3,600	4,800	6,400	8,000
M21 Plunger (600cc single)	1,600	2,400	3,600	4,800	6,400	8,000
A10 Golden Flash Plunger (650cc twin)	2,000	3,000	4,500	6,000	8,000	10,000
A10 Golden Flash (650cc twin)	2,000	3,000	4,500	6,000	8,000	10,000
A10R Road Rocket (650cc twin)	2,000	3,000	4,500	6,000	8,000	**11,000**
1956						
D1 Bantam w/direct elec. (125cc single)	600	800	**1,600**	**2,400**	**3,200**	**4,000**
D1 Bantam w/batt. (125cc single)	600	800	**1,600**	**2,400**	**3,200**	**4,000**
D3 Bantam w/direct elec. (153cc single)	600	800	**1,600**	**2,400**	**3,200**	**4,000**
D3 Bantam w/batt. (153cc single)	600	800	**1,600**	**2,400**	**3,200**	**4,000**
C10L (250cc single)	600	800	**1,600**	**2,400**	**3,200**	**4,000**
C11G (250cc single)	600	800	**1,600**	**2,400**	**3,200**	**4,000**
C12 (250cc single)	600	800	**1,600**	**2,400**	**3,200**	**4,000**
B31 (350cc single)	900	1,500	2,500	4,000	5,500	7,000
B32 Comp (350cc single)	1,500	2,800	3,800	4,800	5,800	6,800
B32GS Gold Star (350cc single)	2,600	3,900	5,900	7,800	10,000	13,000
A7 (500cc single)	2,000	3,000	4,500	6,000	8,000	10,000
A7SS Shooting Star (500cc twin)	2,000	3,000	4,500	6,000	8,000	10,000
B33 (500cc single)	1,500	3,000	4,500	6,000	7,500	9,000
B34 Comp. (500cc single)	1,500	3,000	4,500	6,000	9,000	12,000
DBD34 Gold Star (500cc single)	4,000	6,000	11,000	16,000	21,000	26,000
DBD34 Gold Star Rigid US (500cc single)	4,000	6,000	11,000	16,000	21,000	26,000
M33 (500cc single)	**1,600**	**2,400**	**3,600**	**4,800**	**6,400**	**8,000**
M33 Plunger (500cc single)	**1,600**	**2,400**	**3,600**	**4,800**	**6,400**	**8,000**
M21 (600cc single)	1,600	2,400	3,600	4,800	6,400	8,000
M21 Plunger (600cc single)	1,600	2,400	3,600	4,800	6,400	8,000
A10 Golden Flash Plunger (650cc twin)	2,000	3,000	4,500	6,000	8,000	10,000
A10 Golden Flash (650cc twin)	2,000	3,000	4,500	6,000	8,000	10,000
A10R Road Rocket (650cc twin)	2,000	3,000	4,500	6,000	8,000	**11,000**
1957						
Dandy (70cc single)	400	**700**	**1,400**	**2,100**	**2,800**	**3,500**
Dandy w/Lucas (70cc single)	400	**700**	**1,400**	**2,100**	**2,800**	**3,500**
D1 Bantam w/direct elec. (125cc single)	600	800	**1,600**	**2,400**	**3,200**	**4,000**
D1 Bantam w/batt. (125cc single)	600	800	**1,600**	**2,400**	**3,200**	**4,000**
D3 Bantam w/direct elec. (153cc single)	600	800	**1,600**	**2,400**	**3,200**	**4,000**
D3 Bantam w/batt. (153cc single)	600	800	**1,600**	**2,400**	**3,200**	**4,000**
C10L (250cc single)	600	800	**1,600**	**2,400**	**3,200**	**4,000**
C12 (250cc single)	600	800	**1,600**	**2,400**	**3,200**	**4,000**
B31 (350cc single)	900	1,500	2,500	4,000	5,500	7,000
B32 Comp (350cc single)	1,500	2,800	3,800	4,800	5,800	6,800
B32GS Gold Star (350cc single)	2,600	3,900	5,900	7,800	10,000	13,000
A7 (500cc single)	2,000	3,000	4,500	6,000	8,000	10,000
A7SS Shooting Star (500cc twin)	2,000	3,000	4,500	6,000	8,000	10,000
B33 (500cc single)	1,500	3,000	4,500	6,000	7,500	9,000
B34 Comp. (500cc single)	1,500	3,000	4,500	6,000	9,000	12,000
DBD34 Gold Star (500cc single)	4,000	6,000	11,000	16,000	21,000	26,000
DBD34 Gold Star Rigid US (500cc single)	4,000	6,000	11,000	16,000	21,000	26,000
M33 (500cc single)	**1,600**	**2,400**	**3,600**	**4,800**	**6,400**	**8,000**
M33 Plunger (500cc single)	**1,600**	**2,400**	**3,600**	**4,800**	**6,400**	**8,000**
M21 (600cc single)	1,600	2,400	3,600	4,800	6,400	8,000
M21 Plunger (600cc single)	1,600	2,400	3,600	4,800	6,400	8,000

	6	5	4	3	2	1
A10 Golden Flash Plunger (650cc twin) . . .	2,000	3,000	4,500	6,000	8,000	10,000
A10 Golden Flash (650cc twin)	2,000	3,000	4,500	6,000	8,000	10,000
A10R Road Rocket (650cc twin)	2,000	3,000	4,500	6,000	8,000	**11,000**
A10S Spitfire Scrambler (650cc twin)	2,000	4,000	7,000	10,000	**14,000**	**18,000**
1958						
Dandy (70cc single)	400	**700**	1,400	2,100	2,800	3,500
Dandy w/Lucas (70cc single)	400	**700**	1,400	2,100	2,800	3,500
D1 Bantam w/direct elec. (125cc single) . .	600	800	1,600	2,400	3,200	4,000
D1 Bantam w/batt. (125cc single)	600	800	1,600	2,400	3,200	4,000
D5 Bantam w/direct elec. (175cc single) . .	600	800	1,600	2,400	3,200	4,000
D5 Bantam w/batt. (175cc single)	600	800	1,600	2,400	3,200	4,000
C12 (250cc single)	600	800	1,600	2,400	3,200	4,000
B31 (350cc single)	900	1,500	2,500	4,000	5,500	7,000
A7 (500cc twin)	2,000	3,000	4,500	6,000	8,000	10,000
A7SS Shooting Star (500cc twin)	2,000	3,000	4,500	6,000	8,000	10,000
B33 (500cc single)	1,500	3,000	4,500	6,000	7,500	9,000
DBD34 Gold Star (500cc single)	4,000	6,000	11,000	16,000	21,000	26,000
M21 (600cc single)	1,600	2,400	3,600	4,800	6,400	8,000
M21 Plunger (600cc single)	1,600	2,400	3,600	4,800	6,400	8,000
A10 Golden Flash (650cc twin)	2,000	3,000	4,500	6,000	8,000	10,000
A10R Road Rocket (650cc twin)	2,000	3,000	4,500	6,000	8,000	**11,000**
A10S Spitfire Scrambler (650cc twin)	2,000	4,000	7,000	10,000	**14,000**	**18,000**
1959						
Dandy (70cc single)	400	**700**	1,400	2,100	2,800	3,500
Dandy w/Lucas (70cc single)	400	**700**	1,400	2,100	2,800	3,500
D1 Bantam w/direct elec. (125cc single) . .	600	800	1,600	2,400	3,200	4,000
D1 Bantam w/batt. (125cc single)	600	800	1,600	2,400	3,200	4,000
D7 Bantam w/direct elec. (175cc single) . .	600	800	1,600	2,400	3,200	4,000
D7 Bantam w/batt. (175cc single)	600	800	1,600	2,400	3,200	4,000
C15 Star (250cc single)	600	−800	1,600	2,400	3,200	4,000
C15 Scrambler (250cc single).	1,000	2,000	3,500	5,000	6,500	8,000
C15 Trails (250cc single)	**1,000**	**1,700**	2,400	3,100	2,800	4,500
B31 (350cc single)	1,600	2,400	3,600	4,800	6,400	8,000
B34GS Gold Star (350cc single)	2,000	3,000	5,000	7,000	10,000	13,000
A7 (500cc twin)	2,000	3,000	4,500	6,000	8,000	10,000
A7SS Shooting Star (500cc twin)	2,000	3,000	4,500	6,000	8,000	10,000
B33 (500cc single)	1,500	3,000	4,500	6,000	7,500	9,000
DBD34 Gold Star (500cc single)	4,000	6,000	11,000	16,000	21,000	26,000
DBD34 Gold Star Catalina (500cc single). .	3,800	6,000	10,000	14,000	18,000	22,000
M21 (600cc single)	1,600	2,400	3,600	4,800	6,400	8,000
M21 Plunger (600cc single)	1,600	2,400	3,600	4,800	6,400	8,000
A10 Golden Flash (650cc twin)	2,000	3,000	4,500	6,000	8,000	10,000
A10R Super Rocket (650cc twin)	2,000	**4,000**	7,000	10,000	**14,000**	**18,000**
A10S Spitfire Scrambler (650cc twin)	2,000	4,000	7,000	10,000	**14,000**	**18,000**
1960						
Dandy (70cc single)	400	700	1,400	2,100	2,800	3,500
Dandy w/Lucas (70cc single)	400	700	1,400	2,100	2,800	3,500
D1 Bantam w/direct elec. (125cc single) . .	600	800	1,600	2,400	3,200	4,000
D1 Bantam w/batt. (125cc single)	600	800	1,600	2,400	3,200	4,000
D7 Bantam w/direct elec. (175cc single) . .	600	800	1,600	2,400	3,200	4,000
D7 Bantam w/batt. (175cc single)	600	800	1,600	2,400	3,200	4,000
C15 Star (250cc single)	600	−800	1,600	2,400	3,200	4,000
C15 Scrambler (250cc single).	1,000	2,000	3,500	5,000	6,500	8,000
C15 Trails (250cc single)	**1,000**	**1,700**	2,400	3,100	2,800	4,500
A7 (500cc twin)	2,000	3,000	4,500	6,000	8,000	10,000
A7SS Shooting Star (500cc twin)	2,000	3,000	4,500	6,000	8,000	10,000
B33 (500cc single)	1,500	3,000	4,500	6,000	7,500	9,000
DBD34 Gold Star (500cc single)	4,000	6,000	11,000	16,000	21,000	26,000
DBD34 Gold Star Catalina (500cc single). .	3,800	6,000	10,000	14,000	18,000	22,000

	6	5	4	3	2	1
M21 (600cc single)	1,600	2,400	3,600	4,800	6,400	8,000
M21 Plunger (600cc single)	1,600	2,400	3,600	4,800	6,400	8,000
A10 Golden Flash (650cc twin)	2,000	3,000	4,500	6,000	8,000	10,000
A10R Super Rocket (650cc twin)	2,000	**4,000**	**7,000**	**10,000**	**14,000**	**18,000**
A10S Spitfire Scrambler (650cc twin)	2,000	4,000	7,000	10,000	14,000	18,000
1961						
Dandy (70cc single)	400	**700**	**1,400**	**2,100**	**2,800**	**3,500**
Dandy w/Lucas (70cc single)	400	**700**	**1,400**	**2,100**	**2,800**	**3,500**
D1 Bantam w/direct elec. (125cc single) . .	600	800	**1,600**	**2,400**	**3,200**	**4,000**
D1 Bantam w/batt. (125cc single)	600	800	**1,600**	**2,400**	**3,200**	**4,000**
D7 Bantam w/direct elec. (175cc single) . .	600	800	**1,600**	**2,400**	**3,200**	**4,000**
D7 Bantam w/batt. (175cc single)	600	800	**1,600**	**2,400**	**3,200**	**4,000**
C15 Star (250cc single)	600	−800	**1,600**	**2,400**	**3,200**	**4,000**
C15 SS80 Sports Start 80 (250cc single) . .	600	−800	**1,600**	**2,400**	**3,200**	**4,000**
C15 Scrambler (250cc single)	1,000	2,000	**3,500**	**5,000**	**6,500**	**8,000**
C15 Trails (250cc single)	**1,000**	**1,700**	**2,400**	**3,100**	−2,800	**4,500**
B40 Star (350cc single)	700	1,500	2,500	3,500	4,500	5,500
A7 (500cc twin)	2,000	3,000	4,500	6,000	8,000	10,000
A7 Shooting Star (500cc twin).	2,000	3,000	4,500	6,000	8,000	10,000
DBD34 Gold Star (500cc single)	4,000	6,000	11,000	16,000	21,000	26,000
DBD34 Gold Star Catalina (500cc single) . .	3,800	6,000	10,000	14,000	18,000	22,000
M21 (600cc single)	1,600	2,400	3,600	4,800	6,400	8,000
A10 Golden Flash (650cc twin)	2,000	3,000	4,500	6,000	8,000	10,000
A10R Super Rocket (650cc twin)	2,000	**4,000**	**7,000**	**10,000**	**14,000**	**18,000**
A10S Spitfire Scrambler (650cc twin)	2,000	4,000	7,000	10,000	14,000	18,000
1962						
Dandy (70cc single)	400	**700**	**1,400**	**2,100**	**2,800**	**3,500**
Dandy w/Lucas (70cc single)	400	**700**	**1,400**	**2,100**	**2,800**	**3,500**
D1 Bantam w/direct elec. (125cc single) . .	600	800	**1,600**	**2,400**	**3,200**	**4,000**
D1 Bantam w/batt. (125cc single)	600	800	**1,600**	**2,400**	**3,200**	**4,000**
D7 Bantam w/direct elec. (175cc single) . .	600	800	**1,600**	**2,400**	**3,200**	**4,000**
D7 Bantam w/batt. (175cc single)	600	800	**1,600**	**2,400**	**3,200**	**4,000**
C15 Star (250cc single)	600	−800	**1,600**	**2,400**	**3,200**	**4,000**
C15 SS80 Sports Start 80 (250cc single) . .	600	−800	**1,600**	**2,400**	**3,200**	**4,000**
C15 Scrambler (250cc single)	1,000	2,000	**3,500**	**5,000**	**6,500**	**8,000**
C15 Trails (250cc single)	**1,000**	**1,700**	**2,400**	**3,100**	−2,800	**4,500**
C15 Scrambler Special (250cc single) . . .	**1,000**	**1,700**	**2,400**	**3,100**	−2,800	**4,500**
C15 Trails Special (250cc single)	**1,000**	**1,700**	**2,400**	**3,100**	−2,800	**4,500**
B40 Star (350cc single)	700	1,500	2,500	3,500	4,500	5,500
B40 SS90 Sports Star 90 (350cc single) . .	700	1,500	2,500	3,500	4,500	5,500
A50 Star (500cc twin)	**2,000**	**3,500**	**5,000**	**6,500**	**7,000**	**8,500**
DBD34 Gold Star (500cc single)	4,000	6,000	11,000	16,000	21,000	26,000
DBD34 Gold Star Catalina (500cc single) . .	3,800	6,000	10,000	14,000	18,000	22,000
M21 (600cc single)	1,600	2,400	3,600	4,800	6,400	8,000
A10 Golden Flash (650cc twin)	2,000	3,000	4,500	6,000	8,000	10,000
A10R Super Rocket (650cc twin)	2,000	**4,000**	**7,000**	**10,000**	**14,000**	**18,000**
A10S Spitfire Scrambler (650cc twin)	2,000	4,000	7,000	10,000	14,000	18,000
A10RGS Rocket Gold Star (650cc twin). . .	4,000	8,000	13,000	18,000	23,000	28,000
A65 Star (650cc twin)	**2,000**	**3,500**	**5,000**	**6,500**	**7,000**	**8,500**
1963						
D1 Bantam w/direct elec. (125cc single) . .	600	800	**1,600**	**2,400**	**3,200**	**4,000**
D1 Bantam w/batt. (125cc single)	600	800	**1,600**	**2,400**	**3,200**	**4,000**
D7 Bantam w/direct elec. (175cc single) . .	600	800	**1,600**	**2,400**	**3,200**	**4,000**
D7 Bantam w/batt. (175cc single)	600	800	**1,600**	**2,400**	**3,200**	**4,000**
D7 Bantam US (175cc single).	600	800	**1,600**	**2,400**	**3,200**	**4,000**
D7 Bantam US w/batt. (175cc single)	600	800	**1,600**	**2,400**	**3,200**	**4,000**
D7 Bantam Police (175cc single)	600	800	**1,600**	**2,400**	**3,200**	**4,000**
D7 Bantam Trail (175cc single)	600	800	**1,600**	**2,400**	**3,200**	**4,000**
C15 Star (250cc single)	600	−800	**1,600**	**2,400**	**3,200**	**4,000**

	6	5	4	3	2	1
C15 Police (250cc single)	–600	–800	1,600	2,400	3,200	4,000
C15 SS80 Sports Start 80 (250cc single) . .	600	–800	1,600	2,400	3,200	4,000
C15 Scrambler (250cc single).	1,000	2,000	3,500	5,000	6,500	8,000
C15 Star US (250cc single)	–600	–800	1,600	2,400	3,200	4,000
C15 Starfire Roadster (250cc single)	–600	–800	1,600	2,400	3,200	4,000
C15 Trails (250cc single)	1,000	1,700	2,400	3,100	3,800	4,500
C15 Trials Pastoral (250cc single).	1,000	1,700	2,400	3,100	3,800	4,500
B40 Star (350cc single)	700	1,500	2,500	3,500	4,500	5,500
B40 SS90 Sports Star 90 (350cc single) . .	700	1,500	2,500	3,500	4,500	5,500
B40 Star US (350cc single)	700	1,500	2,500	3,500	4,500	5,500
A50 Star (500cc twin)	2,000	3,500	5,000	6,500	7,000	8,500
DBD34 Gold Star Clubman (500cc single) .	4,000	6,000	11,000	16,000	21,000	26,000
DBD34 Gold Star Catalina (500cc single) . .	3,800	6,000	10,000	14,000	18,000	22,000
M21 (600cc single)	1,600	2,400	3,600	4,800	6,400	8,000
A10 Golden Flash (650cc twin)	2,000	3,000	4,500	6,000	8,000	10,000
A10R Super Rocket (650cc twin)	2,000	4,000	7,000	10,000	14,000	18,000
A10S Spitfire Scrambler (650cc twin)	2,000	4,000	7,000	10,000	14,000	18,000
A10RGS Rocket Gold Star (650cc twin). . .	4,000	8,000	13,000	18,000	23,000	28,000
A65 Star (650cc twin)	2,000	3,500	5,000	6,500	7,000	8,500
1964						
Beagle (75cc single).	400	700	1,400	2,100	2,800	3,500
Starlite 75 (75cc single)	400	700	1,400	2,100	2,800	3,500
D1 Bantam Plunger GPO (125cc single) . .	600	800	1,600	2,400	3,200	4,000
D7 Bantam w/direct elec. (175cc single) . .	600	800	1,600	2,400	3,200	4,000
D7 Bantam w/batt. (175cc single)	600	800	1,600	2,400	3,200	4,000
D7 Bantam US (175cc single).	600	800	1,600	2,400	3,200	4,000
D7 Bantam US w/batt. (175cc single)	600	800	1,600	2,400	3,200	4,000
D7 Bantam Trail (175cc single)	600	800	1,600	2,400	3,200	4,000
C15 Star (250cc single)	600	–800	1,600	2,400	3,200	4,000
C15 SS80 Sports Start 80 (250cc single) . .	600	–800	1,600	2,400	3,200	4,000
C15 Police (250cc single)	–600	–800	1,600	2,400	3,200	4,000
C15 Star US (250cc single)	–600	–800	1,600	2,400	3,200	4,000
C15 Scrambler (250cc single).	1,000	2,000	3,500	5,000	6,500	8,000
C15 Starfire Roadster (250cc single)	1,000	1,700	2,400	3,100	3,800	4,500
C15 Trails (250cc single)	1,000	1,700	2,400	3,100	3,800	4,500
C15 Trials Pastoral (250cc single).	1,000	1,700	2,400	3,100	3,800	4,500
B40 Star (350cc single)	700	1,500	2,500	3,500	4,500	5,500
B40 Police (350cc single)	700	1,500	2,500	3,500	4,500	5,500
B40 Super Star US (350cc single).	700	1,500	2,500	3,500	4,500	5,500
B40 SS90 Sports Star 90 (350cc single) . .	700	1,500	2,500	3,500	4,500	5,500
B40 Enduro Star US (350cc single)	1,000	2,000	3,000	4,000	5,000	6,000
A50 Star (500cc twin)	2,000	3,500	5,000	6,500	7,000	8,500
A50C Cyclone (500cc twin)	2,000	3,500	5,000	6,500	8,000	9,500
A65 Star (650cc twin)	2,000	3,500	5,000	6,500	7,000	8,500
A65R Rocket (650cc twin)	2,000	3,500	5,000	6,500	8,000	9,500
A65T Thunderbolt Rocket (650cc twin) . . .	1,600	2,400	3,600	4,800	6,400	8,000
A65L Lightning Rocket (650cc twin).	1,500	3,000	6,000	9,000	12,000	15,000
A65SH Spitfire Hornet (650cc twin)	1,000	2,000	3,500	6,000	9,000	12,000
1965						
Beagle (75cc single).	400	700	1,400	2,100	2,800	3,500
Starlite 75 (75cc single)	400	700	1,400	2,100	2,800	3,500
D1 Bantam Plunger GPO (125cc single) . .	600	800	1,600	2,400	3,200	4,000
D7 Bantam w/direct elec. (175cc single) . .	600	800	1,600	2,400	3,200	4,000
D7 Bantam w/batt. (175cc single)	600	800	1,600	2,400	3,200	4,000
D7 Bantam Pastoral (175cc single)	600	800	1,600	2,400	3,200	4,000
D7 Bantam Trail Bonc (175cc single)	600	800	1,600	2,400	3,200	4,000
C15 Star (250cc single)	600	–800	1,600	2,400	3,200	4,000
C15 Star US (250cc single)	600	–800	1,600	2,400	3,200	4,000
C15 Police (250cc single)	600	–800	1,600	2,400	3,200	4,000

	6	5	4	3	2	1
C15 SS80 Sports Start 80 (250cc single) . .	600	−800	**1,600**	**2,400**	**3,200**	**4,000**
C15 Scrambler (250cc single)	1,000	2,000	**3,500**	**5,000**	**6,500**	**8,000**
C15 Starfire Roadster (250cc single)	−600	−800	1,600	**2,400**	**3,200**	**4,000**
C15 Trails (250cc single)	600	800	**1,600**	**2,400**	**3,200**	**4,000**
C15 Trails Cat (250cc single)	600	800	**1,600**	**2,400**	**3,200**	**4,000**
C15 Trials Pastoral (250cc single)	600	800	**1,600**	**2,400**	**3,200**	**4,000**
B40 Star (350cc single)	700	1,500	2,500	3,500	4,500	5,500
B40 Police (350cc single)	700	1,500	2,500	3,500	4,500	5,500
B40 SS90 Sports Star 90 (350cc single) . .	700	1,500	2,500	3,500	4,500	5,500
B40 Enduro Star US (350cc single)	1,000	2,000	3,000	4,000	5,000	6,000
B40 Sportsman US (350cc single)	700	1,500	2,500	3,500	4,500	5,500
A50 Star (500cc twin)	**2,000**	**3,500**	**5,000**	**6,500**	**7,000**	**8,500**
A50 Cyclone Comp UK (500cc twin)	**2,000**	**3,500**	**5,000**	**6,500**	**8,000**	**9,500**
A50 Cyclone UK (500cc twin)	**2,000**	**3,500**	**5,000**	**6,500**	**8,000**	**9,500**
A50C Cyclone (500cc twin)	**2,000**	**3,500**	**5,000**	**6,500**	**8,000**	**9,500**
A50CC Cyclone Comp (500cc twin)	**2,000**	**3,500**	**5,000**	**6,500**	**8,000**	**9,500**
A65 Star (650cc single)	**2,000**	**3,500**	**5,000**	**6,500**	**7,000**	**8,500**
A65 Lightning (650cc twin)	**2,000**	**3,500**	**5,000**	**6,500**	**7,000**	**8,500**
A65 Lightning Clubman (650cc twin)	1,500	3,000	4,500	6,500	9,500	12,500
A65L Lightning Rocket (650cc twin)	1,500	3,000	**6,000**	**9,000**	**12,000**	**15,000**
A65R Rocket (650cc twin)	**2,000**	**3,500**	**5,000**	**6,500**	**7,000**	**8,500**
A65SH Spitfire Hornet (650cc twin)	1,000	2,500	4,000	6,000	9,000	12,000
1966						
D7 Silver Bantam (175cc single)	−400	−700	**1,400**	**2,100**	**2,800**	**3,500**
D7 Bantam Deluxe (175cc single)	−400	−700	**1,400**	**2,100**	**2,800**	**3,500**
D7 Bantam Silver Deluxe (175cc single) . .	−400	−700	**1,400**	**2,100**	**2,800**	**3,500**
D7 Bantam GPO (175cc single)	−400	−700	**1,400**	**2,100**	**2,800**	**3,500**
C15 Star (250cc single)	−400	−700	1,400	**2,100**	**2,800**	**3,500**
C15 Sportsman (250cc single)	−400	−700	1,400	**2,100**	**2,800**	**3,500**
B40 Star (350cc single)	700	1,500	2,500	3,500	4,500	5,500
B40 Star Mod (350cc single)	700	1,500	2,500	3,500	4,500	5,500
B44 Victor Grand Prix (441cc single)	1,500	3,000	6,000	9,000	12,000	15,000
B44 Victor Enduro (441cc single)	1,000	2,000	4,000	5,500	6,000	7,500
A50R Royal Star (500cc twin)	**2,000**	**3,500**	**5,000**	**6,500**	**7,000**	**8,500**
A50W Wasp (500cc Twin)	900	1,500	3,000	4,500	6,500	8,500
A65T Thunderbolt (650cc twin)	**1,500**	**3,500**	**5,000**	**6,500**	**8,000**	**9,500**
A65L Lightning (650cc twin)	−1,000	2,500	**4,000**	**6,000**	**8,000**	**10,000**
A65LC Lightning Clubman (650cc twin) . . .	1,000	2,500	4,000	6,000	8,000	10,000
A65S Spitfire Mk II (650cc twin)	2,000	4,000	6,000	8,000	11,000	14,000
A65H Hornet (650cc twin)	1,000	2,000	4,000	6,000	**9,000**	**12,000**
1967						
D10 Bantam Silver (175cc single)	−400	−700	**1,400**	**2,100**	**2,800**	**3,500**
D10 Bantam GPO (175cc single)	−400	−700	**1,400**	**2,100**	**2,800**	**3,500**
D10 Bantam Supreme (175cc single)	−400	−700	**1,400**	**2,100**	**2,800**	**3,500**
D10 Bantam Sport (175cc single)	−400	−700	**1,400**	**2,100**	**2,800**	**3,500**
D10 Bushman (175cc single)	−400	−700	**1,400**	**2,100**	**2,800**	**3,500**
D10 Bushman Pastoral (175cc single) . . .	−400	−700	**1,400**	**2,100**	**2,800**	**3,500**
B25 Starfire US (250cc single)	800	1,500	2,000	2,500	3,000	4,000
C15 Star (250cc single)	−400	−700	1,400	**2,100**	**2,800**	**3,500**
C15 Police (250cc single)	−400	−700	1,400	**2,100**	**2,800**	**3,500**
C15 Sportsman (250cc single)	−400	−700	−1,400	**2,100**	**2,800**	**3,500**
C25 Barracuda (250cc single)	−400	−700	−1,400	**2,100**	**2,800**	**3,500**
B40 Star (350cc single)	700	1,500	2,500	3,500	4,500	5,500
B40 Military (350cc single)	**1,000**	**1,800**	**2,600**	**3,400**	**4,200**	**5,000**
B44 Victor Grand Prix (441cc single)	1,500	3,000	6,000	9,000	12,000	15,000
B44 Victor Enduro (441cc single)	1,000	2,000	4,000	5,500	6,000	7,500
B44 Victor Roadster (441cc single)	800	1,200	1,800	3,000	4,500	6,000
A50R Royal Star (500cc twin)	**2,000**	**3,500**	**5,000**	**6,500**	**7,000**	**8,500**
A50W Wasp (500cc Twin)	900	1,500	3,000	4,500	6,500	8,500

	6	5	4	3	2	1
A65T Thunderbolt (650cc twin)	1,500	3,500	5,000	6,500	8,000	9,500
A65L Lightning (650cc twin).	1,000	2,500	4,000	6,000	–8,000	–10,000
A65S Spitfire Mk II (650cc twin)	2,000	4,000	6,000	8,000	11,000	14,000
A65H Hornet (650cc twin)	1,000	2,000	4,000	6,000	8,000	10,000
1968						
D13 Bantam Supreme (175cc single)	–400	–700	1,400	2,100	2,800	3,500
D13 Bantam Sports (175cc single)	–400	–700	1,400	2,100	2,800	3,500
D13 Bantam Bushman (175cc single). . . .	–400	–700	1,400	2,100	2,800	3,500
D14/4 Bantam (175cc single)	–400	–700	1,400	2,100	2,800	3,500
D14/4 Sports (175cc single)	–400	–700	1,400	2,100	2,800	3,500
D14/4 Bantam Bushman (175cc single). . .	–400	–700	1,400	2,100	2,800	3,500
B25 Starfire US (250cc single)	800	1,500	2,000	2,500	3,000	4,000
B25 Fleetstar (250cc single).	600	1,000	1,700	2,400	3,100	3,800
B40 Military (350cc single)	700	1,100	1,600	2,400	3,200	4,000
B44 Shooting Star (441cc single)	1,000	2,000	3,000	4,000	5,000	6,000
B44 Victor Special (441cc single)	1,000	2,000	4,000	5,500	6,000	7,500
A50R Royal Star (500cc twin)	2,000	3,500	5,000	6,500	7,000	8,500
A50W Wasp (500cc Twin).	900	1,500	3,000	4,500	6,500	8,500
A65T Thunderbolt (650cc twin)	1,500	3,500	5,000	6,500	8,000	9,500
A65L Lightning (650cc twin).	1,000	2,500	4,000	6,000	–8,000	–10,000
A65F Firebird Scrambler (650cc twin). . . .	2,000	4,000	6,000	8,000	–1,000	–12,000
A65S Spitfire Mk IV (650cc twin)	2,000	4,000	6,000	8,000	11,000	–13,000
1969						
B175 Bantam (175cc single)	–400	–700	1,400	2,100	2,800	3,500
B175 Bantam Bushman (175cc single) . . .	–400	–700	1,400	2,100	2,800	3,500
B25 Starfire (250cc single)	800	1,500	2,000	2,500	3,000	4,000
B25FS Fleetstar (250cc single)	–400	–700	1,400	2,100	2,800	3,500
B40 Military (350cc single)	700	1,100	1,600	2,400	3,200	4,000
B40 Roughrider (350cc single)	700	1,100	1,600	2,400	3,200	4,000
B44SS Shooting Star (441cc single)	1,000	2,000	3,000	4,000	5,000	6,000
B44VS Victor Special (441cc single)	1,000	2,000	4,000	5,500	6,000	7,500
A50 Royal Star (500cc twin)	2,000	3,500	5,000	6,500	7,000	8,500
A65T Thunderbolt (650cc twin)	1,500	3,500	5,000	6,500	8,000	9,500
A65L Lightning (650cc twin).	1,000	2,500	4,000	6,000	–8,000	–10,000
A65F Firebird Scrambler (650cc twin). . . .	1,000	1,500	3,000	6,000	9,000	12,000
A75 Rocket III (750cc triple).	2,000	4,000	8,000	12,000	16,000	20,000
1970						
B175 Bantam (175cc single)	–400	–700	1,400	2,100	2,800	3,500
B175 Bantam Bushman (175cc single) . . .	–400	–700	1,400	2,100	2,800	3,500
B25 Starfire (250cc single)	800	1,500	2,000	2,500	3,000	4,000
B25FS Fleetstar (250cc single)	–400	–700	1,400	2,100	2,800	3,500
B40 Military (350cc single)	700	1,100	1,600	2,400	3,200	4,000
B44 Shooting Star (441cc single)	1,000	2,000	3,000	4,000	5,000	6,000
B44 Victor Special (441cc single)	1,000	2,000	4,000	5,500	6,000	7,500
A50 Royal Star (500cc twin).	2,000	3,500	5,000	6,500	7,000	8,500
A65T Thunderbolt (650cc twin)	1,500	3,500	5,000	6,500	8,000	9,500
A65L Lightning (650cc twin).	1,000	2,500	4,000	6,000	–8,000	–10,000
A65F Firebird Scrambler (650cc twin). . . .	1,000	1,500	3,000	6,000	9,000	12,000
A75 Rocket III (750cc triple).	2,000	4,000	8,000	12,000	16,000	20,000
1971						
B175 Bantam (175cc single)	–400	–700	1,400	2,100	2,800	3,500
B25 Victor Trail (250cc single)	700	1,100	1,600	2,100	2,800	3,500
B25FS Fleetstar (250cc single)	–400	–700	1,400	2,100	2,800	3,500
B25SS Gold Star 250 (250cc single)	–400	–700	1,400	2,100	2,800	3,500
B50 Motorcross (500cc single)	2,000	3,500	5,000	6,500	7,000	8,500
B50 Victor Trial (500cc single)	1,000	2,000	4,000	5,500	6,000	7,500
B50SS Gold Star 500 (500cc single)	1,000	2,000	4,000	5,500	6,000	7,500
A65 Thunderbolt (650cc twin)	1,000	2,000	4,000	5,500	6,000	7,500
A65 Lightning (650cc twin)	1,000	2,000	4,000	5,500	6,000	7,500

	6	5	4	3	2	1
A65 Firebird Scrambler (650cc twin)	1,000	2,000	4,000	5,500	6,000	7,500
A70 Lightning 750 (750cc twin)	3,000	6,000	10,000	16,000	22,000	28,500
A75 Rocket III (750cc triple).	2,000	4,000	8,000	14,000	20,000	26,000
1972						
Ariel 3 (48cc single)	200	400	800	1,200	1,600	2,000
B50 Motorcross (500cc single)	**2,000**	**3,500**	**5,000**	**6,500**	**7,000**	**8,500**
B50 Victor Trial (500cc single)	**1,000**	**2,000**	**4,000**	**5,500**	**6,000**	**7,500**
B50SS Gold Star 500 (500cc single)	**1,000**	**2,000**	**4,000**	**5,500**	**6,000**	**7,500**
A65 Thunderbolt (650cc twin)	1,000	2,000	**4,000**	5,500	6,000	7,500
A65 Lightning (650cc twin)	1,000	2,000	4,000	5,500	6,000	7,500
A75 Rocket III (750cc triple).	2,000	4,000	8,000	14,000	20,000	26,000
1973						
Ariel 3 (48cc single)	200	400	800	1,200	1,600	2,000
B50 Motorcross (500cc single)	**2,000**	**3,500**	**5,000**	**6,500**	**7,000**	**8,500**
T65 (660cc Twin)	900	1,500	3,000	4,500	6,500	8,500
1974						
Ariel 3 (48cc single)	200	400	800	1,200	1,600	2,000

BUELL

	6	5	4	3	2	1
1987						
RR1000 (1,000cc twin)	500	800	2,200	4,600	6,800	9,000
1988						
RR1000 (1,000cc twin)	600	900	2,400	4,900	7,300	9,900
1989						
RR1200 (1,200cc twin)	300	600	1,500	3,100	4,600	6,100
RS1200 (1,200cc twin)	300	500	1,400	2,900	4,400	5,900
1990						
RR1200 (1,200cc twin)	300	600	1,600	3,400	5,100	6,800
RS1200 (1,200cc twin)	300	600	1,600	3,200	4,800	5,400
1991						
RS1200 (1,200cc twin)	300	600	1,700	3,500	5,300	7,100
1992						
RS1200 (1,200cc twin)	300	700	1,800	3,700	5,800	6,900
RSS1200 (1,200cc twin)	300	600	1,700	3,500	5,200	6,900
1993						
RS1200 (1,200cc twin)	300	700	1,900	3,900	5,800	7,700
RSS1200 (1,200cc twin)	300	700	1,800	3,800	5,500	7,200
1995						
S2 Thunderbolt w/Fairing (1,203cc twin) . .	300	700	1,800	3,800	5,500	7,200
1996						
S1 Lightning w/Fairing (1,203cc twin)	300	700	1,800	3,800	5,500	7,200
S2 Thunderbolt w/Fairing (1,203cc twin) . .	300	700	1,900	3,900	5,800	7,700
S2T Thunderbolt (1,203cc twin)	300	700	1,900	3,900	5,800	7,700

BULTACO

	6	5	4	3	2	1
1962						
TSS (125cc).	1,500	3,000	5,000	8,000	11,000	14,000
1963						
Sherpa (200cc)	600	1,000	2,000	4,000	6,000	8,000
1964						
Matador (200cc).	1,000	2,000	3,000	4,000	5,000	6,000
Matisse (250cc)	600	1,000	2,000	4,000	6,000	8,000
1965						
Matisse (250cc)	600	1,000	2,000	4,000	6,000	8,000
1966						
Pursang (250cc).	3,000	4,400	5,400	6,500	9,300	12,000
Mercurio (200cc)	500	1,000	2,500	4,000	5,500	7,000
1968						
Lobito AK (100cc).	1,400	2,300	3,200	4,300	6,400	8,500
Lobito T (100cc).	1,400	2,300	3,200	4,300	6,400	8,500
Sherpa S (125cc)	2,000	2,800	3,400	4,100	5,900	7,500
Campera 4 Speed (175cc)	1,500	2,500	3,500	4,500	5,500	6,500

	6	5	4	3	2	1
Mercurio (175cc)	1,500	2,500	3,500	4,500	5,500	6,500
Sherpa S (175cc)	1,500	2,500	3,500	4,500	5,500	6,500
Mercurio (200cc)	600	1,100	1,400	1,600	2,300	3,000
Sherpa S (200cc)	800	1,300	1,900	2,400	3,400	4,400
El Tigre (250cc)	1,100	1,400	1,700	2,000	2,800	3,600
Matador (250cc)	500	1,000	1,700	2,300	3,400	4,500
Metralla (250cc)	2,500	3,200	3,900	4,700	6,900	8,000
Pursang (250cc)	3,000	4,400	5,400	6,500	9,300	12,000
Sherpa T (250cc)	700	1,700	2,800	4,000	5,800	7,500
Bandito (360cc)	1,600	2,200	2,700	3,200	4,600	5,800
Montadero (360cc)	900	1,500	2,700	3,900	5,300	6,500
1969						
Lobito 4 Speed (100cc)	1,400	2,300	3,200	4,300	6,400	8,500
Lobito AK (100cc)	1,400	2,300	3,200	4,300	6,400	8,500
Lobito (125cc)	700	1,100	2,200	3,300	4,000	4,800
Sherpa S (125cc)	1,500	2,800	4,200	5,800	9,000	12,000
Campera 4 Speed (175cc)	1,500	2,500	3,500	4,500	5,500	6,500
Sherpa S (175cc)	1,500	2,500	3,500	4,500	5,500	6,500
El Tigre (200cc)	800	1,300	1,900	2,400	3,400	4,400
Mercurio (200cc)	800	1,300	1,900	2,400	3,400	4,400
Sherpa S (200cc)	800	1,300	1,900	2,400	3,400	4,400
El Tigre (250cc)	1,000	1,400	1,700	2,000	2,800	3,600
Matador 5 Speed III (250cc)	500	1,000	1,700	2,300	3,400	4,500
Metralla (250cc)	1,400	2,300	3,200	4,200	6,100	7,500
Pursang (250cc)	3,000	4,400	5,400	6,500	9,300	12,000
Sherpa T (250cc)	1,000	1,700	2,800	4,000	5,800	7,500
El Bandito (360cc)	1,300	2,200	3,100	4,100	5,900	6,500
El Bandito TT (360cc)	1,300	2,200	3,100	4,100	5,900	6,500
Montadero (360cc)	900	1,500	2,700	3,900	5,300	6,500
1970						
Lobito (100cc)	1,400	2,300	3,200	4,300	6,400	8,500
Sherpa S (100cc)	500	800	1,000	1,100	1,500	2,000
Lobito (125cc)	700	1,100	2,200	3,300	4,000	4,800
Sherpa S (125cc)	1,500	2,800	4,200	5,800	9,000	12,000
TSS Water Cooled (125cc)	700	1,100	2,200	3,300	4,000	4,800
Campera MK II (175cc)	1,000	1,600	1,900	2,300	3,300	4,500
Sherpa S (175cc)	1,500	2,500	3,500	4,500	5,500	6,500
El Tigre (200cc)	800	1,300	1,900	2,400	3,400	4,400
Mercurio (200cc)	800	1,300	1,900	2,400	3,400	4,400
Sherpa S (200cc)	800	1,300	1,900	2,400	3,400	4,400
El Tigre (250cc)	1,000	1,400	1,700	2,000	2,800	3,600
Matador MK III (250cc)	500	1,000	1,600	2,200	3,400	4,500
Metralla MK III (250cc)	1,800	2,300	3,200	4,200	6,100	7,500
Pursang TT (250cc)	3,000	4,400	5,400	6,500	9,300	12,000
Sherpa T (250cc)	1,000	1,700	2,800	4,000	5,800	7,500
TSS Water Cooled (250cc)	1,000	1,700	2,800	4,000	5,800	7,500
Bandito (360cc)	1,000	1,600	2,400	3,300	5,100	6,500
Bandito TT (360cc)	1,300	1,900	2,700	3,900	5,600	8,000
Montadero (360cc)	900	1,500	2,700	3,900	5,300	6,500
TSS Air Cooled (360cc)	900	1,500	2,700	3,900	5,300	6,500
1971						
Lobito (100cc)	500	800	1,000	1,100	1,500	2,000
Sherpa S (100cc)	1,400	2,300	3,200	4,300	6,400	8,500
Lobito (125cc)	500	800	1,000	1,100	1,500	2,000
Sherpa S (125cc)	1,500	2,800	4,200	5,800	9,000	12,000
TSS Water Cooled (125cc)	700	1,100	2,200	3,300	4,000	4,800
Lobito (175cc)	1,000	1,600	1,900	2,300	3,300	4,500
Sherpa S (175cc)	1,000	1,600	1,900	2,300	3,300	4,500
Campera MK II (175cc)	1,500	2,500	3,500	4,500	5,500	6,500
Sherpa S (200cc)	800	1,300	1,900	2,400	3,400	4,400

	6	5	4	3	2	1
El Tigre (200cc)	800	1,300	1,900	2,400	3,400	4,400
Alpina (250cc)	800	1,400	2,400	3,400	4,900	6,400
Mercurio (200cc)	800	1,300	1,900	2,400	3,400	4,400
Matador SD (250cc)	500	1,000	1,600	2,200	3,400	4,500
Metralla (250cc)	1,800	2,300	3,200	4,200	6,100	7,500
Pursang A (250cc)	1,300	1,900	3,500	5,100	6,700	8,200
Pursang E (250cc)	1,300	1,900	3,500	5,100	6,700	8,200
Sherpa T 5 Speed (250cc)	1,000	1,700	2,800	4,000	5,800	7,500
El Tigre (250cc)	1,000	1,400	1,700	2,000	2,800	3,600
Matador MK III (250cc)	500	1,000	1,600	2,200	3,400	4,500
Pursang TT (250cc)	1,600	2,300	3,200	4,200	6,100	7,500
TSS Water Cooled (250cc)	1,000	1,700	2,800	4,000	5,800	7,500
Bandito (360cc)	1,500	2,200	3,200	4,100	5,900	7,500
Bandito TT (360cc)	1,300	1,900	2,700	3,900	5,600	8,000
Montadero (360cc)	900	1,500	2,700	3,900	5,300	6,500
TSS Air Cooled (360cc)	900	1,500	2,700	3,900	5,300	6,500
1972						
Tiron Mini Bike (100cc)	500	800	1,000	1,100	1,500	2,000
Lobito (125cc)	1,200	1,800	2,500	3,300	4,700	6,000
Pursang (125cc)	1,300	1,900	3,200	4,600	6,700	8,500
Sherpa T (125cc)	700	1,100	2,200	3,300	4,000	4,800
Lobito (175cc)	1,100	1,700	2,900	4,100	5,900	7,500
Alpina (250cc)	800	1,400	2,400	3,400	4,900	6,200
Matador SD MK IV (250cc)	1,000	1,700	3,000	4,500	6,000	7,500
Pursang Astro (250cc)	1,300	1,900	3,500	5,100	6,700	8,200
Pursang MK IX (250cc)	1,300	1,900	3,500	5,100	6,700	8,200
Sherpa T (250cc)	1,000	1,700	2,800	4,000	5,800	7,500
Montadero (360cc)	900	1,500	2,700	3,900	5,300	6,500
Pursang (360cc)	1,000	1,600	2,700	3,800	5,500	6,000
1973						
Tiron Mini Bike (100cc)	500	800	1,000	1,100	1,500	2,000
Alpina (125cc)	500	800	1,300	1,900	2,600	3,300
Pursang MK IX (125cc)	500	**900**	**1,800**	**2,700**	**3,600**	**4,500**
Alpina (175cc)	1,000	1,700	2,900	4,100	5,900	7,500
Pursang MK VII (175cc)	900	1,400	2,100	2,800	3,900	5,000
Pursang T (200cc)	1,000	1,500	2,300	3,200	4,600	6,000
Astro (250cc)	500	1,500	3,000	4,500	5,500	6,500
Alpina (250cc)	900	1,400	2,400	3,400	4,900	6,300
Matador SD MK IV (250cc)	1,000	1,700	3,000	4,500	6,000	7,500
Pursang MK IX (250cc)	1,100	1,600	2,700	3,800	5,500	7,000
Sherpa T (250cc)	1,000	1,700	2,800	4,000	5,800	7,500
Astro (350cc)	1,900	2,600	3,600	4,700	6,900	9,000
Alpina (350cc)	1,000	2,000	3,000	4,000	5,000	6,000
Sherpa T (350cc)	600	1,000	1,700	2,400	3,500	4,500
Pursang (360cc)	1,200	1,900	3,200	4,600	6,700	8,500
1974						
Tiron Mini Bike (100cc)	500	800	1,000	1,100	1,500	2,000
Alpina (125cc)	300	500	1,000	1,500	2,300	3,000
Pursang MK IX (125cc)	500	**900**	**1,800**	**2,700**	**3,600**	**4,500**
Alpina (175cc)	300	500	1,000	1,500	2,300	3,000
Pursang MK VI (175cc)	900	1,400	2,100	2,800	3,900	5,000
Pursang T (200cc)	1,000	1,500	2,300	3,200	4,600	6,000
Alpina (250cc)	500	800	1,300	1,800	2,500	3,200
Astro (250cc)	700	1,500	3,000	4,500	5,500	6,500
Matador SD MK IV (250cc)	1,000	1,700	3,000	4,500	6,000	7,500
Pursang MK IX (250cc)	500	1,000	1,500	2,000	3,000	4,000
Sherpa T (250cc)	1,000	1,700	2,800	4,000	5,800	7,500
Alpina (350cc)	1,000	2,000	3,000	4,000	5,000	6,000
Sherpa T (350cc)	600	1,000	1,700	2,400	3,500	4,500
El Bandito MX (360cc)	1,600	2,200	3,100	4,100	5,900	7,500

	6	5	4	3	2	1
Montadero MK II (360cc)	1,000	1,500	2,700	3,900	5,300	6,500
1975						
Pursang MK IX (125cc)	500	800	1,100	1,400	3,000	4,500
Pursang (200cc)	1,000	1,500	2,300	3,200	4,600	6,000
Alpina (250cc)	500	800	1,300	1,800	2,500	3,200
Astro (250cc)	700	1,500	3,000	4,500	5,500	6,500
Frontera MK IX (250cc)	**700**	**1,500**	**2,500**	**3,500**	**4,500**	**5,500**
Matador SD MK IV (250cc)	1,000	1,700	3,000	4,500	6,000	7,500
Pursang (250cc)	1,000	1,600	2,700	3,800	5,500	7,000
Sherpa T (250cc)	1,000	1,700	2,800	4,000	5,800	7,500
Alpina (350cc)	1,000	2,000	3,000	4,000	5,000	6,000
Astro (350cc)	1,500	2,100	2,900	3,700	5,600	7,500
Sherpa T (350cc)	600	1,000	1,700	2,400	3,500	4,500
Frontera MK IX (360cc)	500	1,000	2,000	3,000	4,000	5,000
Pursang (360cc)	1,200	1,900	3,200	4,600	6,700	8,500
1976						
Pursang MK IX (125cc)	500	700	1,100	1,400	1,900	2,200
Sherpa T (125cc)	400	600	900	1,100	1,600	2,100
Pursang MK IX (200cc)	900	1,500	2,300	3,200	4,600	5,500
Alpina (250cc)	500	800	1,300	1,800	2,500	3,200
Astro (250cc)	700	1,500	3,000	4,500	5,500	6,500
Frontera MK IX (250cc)	**700**	**1,500**	**2,500**	**3,500**	**4,500**	**5,500**
Pursang MK IX (250cc)	1,000	1,600	2,700	3,800	5,500	7,000
Sherpa T (250cc)	1,000	1,700	2,800	4,000	5,800	7,500
Alpina (350cc)	1,000	2,000	3,000	4,000	5,000	6,000
Astro (350cc)	1,500	2,100	2,900	3,900	5,600	7,500
Matador MK IX (350cc)	700	1,000	1,700	2,400	3,500	4,600
Sherpa T (350cc)	600	1,000	1,700	2,400	3,500	4,500
Frontera (360cc)	500	700	1,300	2,100	3,200	4,300
1977						
Pursang MK IX (125cc)	500	800	1,100	1,400	1,900	2,200
Sherpa T (125cc)	400	600	900	1,100	1,300	1,500
Pursang (200cc)	800	1,300	2,400	3,500	4,700	5,900
Alpina (250cc)	500	800	1,300	1,800	2,500	3,200
Astro (250cc)	800	1,500	3,000	4,500	5,500	6,500
Frontera (250cc)	**700**	**1,500**	**2,500**	**3,500**	**4,500**	**5,500**
Pursang MK IX (250cc)	1,000	1,600	2,700	3,800	5,500	7,000
Sherpa T (250cc)	1,000	1,700	2,800	4,000	5,800	7,500
Alpina (350cc)	1,000	2,000	3,000	4,000	5,000	6,000
Matador MK IX (350cc)	500	800	1,000	1,300	1,800	2,300
Sherpa T (350cc)	600	1,000	1,700	2,400	3,500	4,600
Frontera (370cc)	600	900	1,300	1,600	2,300	3,000
Pursang (370cc)	700	1,100	1,900	2,700	3,900	5,000
1978						
Streaker (125cc)	1,200	1,800	2,600	3,500	4,600	5,500
Pursang (200cc)	800	1,300	2,400	3,500	4,700	5,900
Alpina (250cc)	500	800	1,300	1,800	2,500	3,200
Astro (250cc)	800	1,500	3,000	4,500	5,500	6,500
Frontera MK IX (250cc)	**700**	**1,500**	**2,500**	**3,500**	**4,500**	**5,500**
Metralla (250cc)	700	1,000	1,700	2,400	3,500	4,500
Pursang (250cc)	1,000	1,600	2,700	3,800	5,500	7,000
Alpina (350cc)	1,000	2,000	3,000	4,000	5,000	6,000
Sherpa T (350cc)	600	1,000	1,700	2,400	3,500	4,600
Frontera MK IX (360cc)	700	1,100	1,700	2,300	3,200	4,100
Pursang (370cc)	700	1,100	1,900	2,700	3,900	5,000
1979						
Alpina (250cc)	500	800	1,300	1,800	2,500	3,200
Astro (250cc)	800	1,500	3,000	4,500	5,500	6,500
Frontera MK XI (250cc)	**700**	**1,500**	**2,500**	**3,500**	**4,500**	**5,500**
Pursang MK XII (250cc)	1,000	1,600	2,800	4,000	5,800	7,500

	6	5	4	3	2	1
Alpina (350cc)	1,000	2,000	3,000	4,000	5,000	6,000
Sherpa T (350cc)	600	1,000	1,700	2,400	3,500	4,600
Frontera MK XI (370cc)	1,000	2,000	3,500	5,000	6,000	7,500
Pursang MK XII Everts (370cc)	900	1,300	2,100	2,900	4,300	5,500
1980						
Astro (250cc)	800	1,200	2,000	2,900	4,300	5,700
Frontera MK XI (250cc)	1,900	2,600	3,300	4,000	5,500	7,000
Sherpa T (350cc)	600	1,000	1,700	2,500	3,500	4,500
1981						
Sherpa T (125cc)	600	1,000	1,600	2,300	2,900	3,500
Astro (250cc)	800	1,500	3,000	4,500	5,500	6,500
Pursang (250cc)	800	1,300	2,400	3,600	5,800	7,500
Sherpa T (250cc)	600	1,000	1,700	2,400	3,200	4,000
Sherpa T (350cc)	700	1,100	1,800	2,500	3,500	4,500
Astro (450cc)	900	1,400	2,100	3,000	4,400	5,800
Pursang (450cc)	1,000	1,500	2,600	3,800	6,000	8,000
1982						
Astro (200cc)	700	1,500	3,000	4,500	5,500	6,500
Sherpa T (200cc)	600	900	1,500	2,300	3,100	3,900
Frontera (250cc)	700	1,300	1,900	2,600	3,400	4,200
Pursang (250cc)	600	1,000	1,800	2,800	4,100	5,400
1983						
Sherpa T (125cc)	700	1,000	1,600	2,300	2,900	3,500
Astro (250cc)	800	1,500	3,000	4,500	5,500	6,500
Pursang (250cc)	800	1,300	2,400	3,600	5,800	7,500
Sherpa T (250cc)	700	1,000	1,600	2,400	3,200	4,000
Sherpa T (350cc)	800	1,100	1,800	2,500	3,500	4,500
Astro (450cc)	900	1,400	2,100	3,000	4,400	5,800
Pursang (450cc)	1,000	1,500	2,600	3,800	6,000	8,000
CAGIVA						
1981						
WMX 125	300	500	1,500	3,500	4,500	5,500
RXR 250	300	500	1,000	1,500	2,000	2,500
1984						
WMX 125	300	500	1,500	2,500	3,000	3,500
WRX 125	300	500	700	1,300	2,000	2,700
WRX 200	300	500	1,500	2,000	3,000	4,000
WMX 250	300	500	1,500	3,500	4,500	5,500
DG 350	300	500	1,000	1,500	2,500	3,500
MXR 500	300	500	1,500	3,500	4,500	5,500
1985						
WMX 125	300	500	700	1,300	2,000	2,700
Alazzurra 350	300	500	700	1,300	2,000	2,700
WMX 500	300	500	1,500	2,500	3,500	4,500
Elefant 650	300	500	1,600	2,000	3,000	4,000
Alazzurra 650	300	500	1,000	1,500	2,500	3,500
1986						
WMX 125	300	500	700	1,300	2,000	2,700
WMX 500	300	500	1,500	2,000	2,500	3,000
Alazzurra 650	300	500	700	1,300	1,800	2,300
Alazzurra 650SS	300	500	700	1,300	2,000	2,700
Elefant 650	500	800	1,500	2,000	3,000	4,000
F-1 Ducati	800	1,500	2,500	4,000	5,500	7,000
1987						
WMX 125	300	500	700	1,300	1,800	2,300
Alazzurra 650SS	300	500	700	1,300	2,000	2,700
Alazzurra Sport	300	500	700	1,300	1,800	2,300
Elefant 650	300	500	900	1,400	2,100	2,800
Elefant 650 SE	300	500	1,000	1,500	2,500	3,500
WMX 500	300	500	700	1,300	2,000	2,700

	6	5	4	3	2	1
1988						
WMX 125	300	500	700	1,300	1,600	2,000
WRK 125	300	500	700	1,300	1,800	2,300
WMX 250	300	500	700	1,300	2,000	2,700
1989						
WMX 125	300	500	700	1,300	1,800	2,300
WMX 250	300	500	700	1,300	2,000	2,700
CAN AM						
1965						
Bombardier	600	1,000	2,000	3,000	4,000	5,000
1974						
125 MX	1,000	1,600	2,200	2,900	4,500	6,000
125 TNT	600	900	1,300	1,700	2,500	3,300
175 MX	700	1,100	1,500	1,900	2,800	3,700
175 TNT	1,200	1,900	2,500	3,300	5,200	7,000
1975						
125 MX-2	1,000	1,400	1,900	2,600	4,000	5,400
125 TNT	600	900	1,300	1,700	2,600	3,500
175 MX-2	700	1,100	1,500	1,900	2,800	3,700
175 TNT	1,200	1,900	2,500	3,500	5,300	7,100
250 MX-2	1,900	2,600	3,600	4,800	7,500	9,500
250 TNT	1,700	2,300	3,100	4,200	6,500	7,800
1976						
175 OR	1,400	2,000	2,800	3,600	5,600	7,600
1977						
125 Qualifier	400	700	900	1,200	1,800	2,400
175 MX-3	500	800	1,100	1,400	2,200	3,000
175 Qualifier	1,400	2,100	2,800	3,700	5,700	7,700
175 TNT	1,200	1,900	2,500	3,300	5,300	7,300
250 MX-3	1,900	2,600	3,600	4,800	7,500	9,200
250 Qualifier	600	900	1,200	1,600	2,300	3,000
250 TNT	1,700	2,300	3,100	4,200	6,500	7,800
1978						
250 MX-4	1,000	1,500	1,900	2,500	3,500	4,500
370 MX	1,900	2,700	3,800	5,000	7,900	10,000
1979						
175 Qualifier	1,400	2,100	2,800	3,700	5,700	7,700
250 MX-5	800	1,200	1,700	2,200	3,500	4,800
250 Qualifier	600	900	1,200	1,600	2,300	3,000
370 MX-5	1,700	2,300	3,100	4,200	6,500	7,800
370 Qualifier	1,900	2,500	3,500	4,700	7,200	10,000
1980						
406	800	1,500	3,000	4,500	6,000	7,500
1982						
320 Trials	500	1,000	1,500	2,000	2,500	3,000
1987						
Trials	800	1,200	1,700	2,300	3,500	4,800
CCM						
1973						
Clews Bix Six 608	800	1,500	3,300	6,400	8,700	11,000
Clews Short Five 498	800	1,500	2,800	5,800	8,200	10,500
1974						
CCM 500	900	1,500	3,300	6,400	8,700	11,000
CCM 550	900	1,500	3,300	6,400	8,700	11,000
CCM 608	1,200	2,000	3,800	6,900	9,800	13,000
1975						
CCM Banks Replica 498	1,500	2,500	3,800	7,400	10,300	13,500
CCM 550	1,200	2,000	2,800	6,400	8,700	11,000
1979						
MX 4 Valve 498	1,200	2,000	3,300	5,300	7,600	10,000

	6	5	4	3	2	1
MX 2 Valve 572	1,200	2,000	2,800	5,300	7,100	9,000
1980						
CCM Honda MX 500	1,200	2,000	3,300	5,300	7,600	10,000
CCM MX 500	1,200	2,000	2,900	5,300	7,100	9,000
CCM MX 580	1,200	2,000	3,300	5,300	7,600	10,000
1981						
CCM MX 500	1,200	2,000	2,800	5,300	6,500	7,800
CCM MX 580	1,200	2,000	2,800	5,300	6,500	7,800
CCM MX 620	1,200	2,000	2,800	5,300	7,100	9,000
CUSHMAN						
1941						
Series 30	500	1,000	2,000	3,000	4,000	5,000
1942						
US Navy Patrol	600	1,300	2,100	2,900	3,700	4,500
1943						
Truckster	1,300	1,800	2,500	3,500	4,500	6,000
1944						
Military	600	1,300	2,100	2,900	3,700	4,500
Airborne	600	1,300	2,100	2,900	3,700	4,500
1945						
Model 53	600	1,300	2,100	2,900	3,700	4,500
1946						
RS52 Pacemaker	1,000	2,000	3,000	4,000	5,000	6,000
1947						
Husky	1,000	2,000	3,000	4,000	5,000	6,000
Scooter	1,000	2,000	3,000	4,000	5,000	6,000
RS52 Pacemaker	1,000	2,000	3,000	4,000	5,000	6,000
Road King	400	800	1,600	2,400	3,200	4,000
Civilian Airborne	1,000	2,000	3,000	4,000	5,000	6,000
1948						
Airborne	1,000	2,000	3,000	4,000	5,000	6,000
MC	1,000	2,000	3,000	4,000	5,000	6,000
Turtleback	1,500	2,000	2,600	3,200	4,000	5,000
Pacemaker	1,000	2,000	3,000	4,000	5,000	6,000
Road King	500	800	1,300	1,800	2,500	3,500
1949						
Eagle	1,000	2,000	3,000	4,000	5,000	6,000
Road King	500	800	1,300	1,800	2,500	3,500
1950						
711 Highlander	500	800	1,300	1,800	2,500	3,500
811	500	800	1,300	1,800	2,500	3,500
Eagle	1,000	2,000	3,000	4,000	5,000	6,000
Husky	1,000	2,000	3,000	4,000	5,000	6,000
1951						
Barrel Spring Eagle	1,000	2,000	3,000	4,000	5,000	6,000
1952						
Eagle	800	1,500	2,500	3,500	4,500	6,000
1953						
Series 60	1,000	2,000	3,000	4,000	5,000	6,000
780 Truckster	1,000	2,000	3,000	4,000	5,000	6,000
Highlander	400	800	1,600	2,400	3,200	4,000
1954						
Eagle	1,000	2,000	3,000	4,000	5,000	6,000
Model 762	1,000	2,000	3,000	4,000	5,000	6,000
1956						
Eagle	1,000	2,000	3,000	4,000	5,000	6,000
Husky	1,000	2,000	3,000	4,000	5,000	6,000
Truckster	500	800	1,300	1,800	2,500	3,500
1957						
Gator Road King	500	1,000	1,500	2,000	3,000	4,000
Highlander	500	1,000	2,000	3,000	4,000	5,000

	6	5	4	3	2	1
Eagle	1,000	2,000	3,000	4,000	5,000	6,000
1958						
720 Step Through	500	1,000	1,500	2,500	3,500	4,500
721 Highlander	500	1,000	2,000	3,000	4,000	5,000
Eagle	1,000	2,000	3,000	4,000	5,000	6,000
Pacemaker	1,000	2,000	3,000	4,000	5,000	6,000
1959						
Scooter	500	1,000	2,000	3,000	4,000	5,000
Eagle	1,000	2,000	3,000	4,000	5,000	6,000
Super Eagle	1,000	2,000	3,000	4,000	5,500	7,000
1960						
721 Highlander	500	1,000	2,000	3,000	4,000	5,000
Husky	1,000	2,000	3,000	4,000	5,000	6,000
Model 720	400	800	1,600	2,400	3,200	4,000
3 Wheeler	800	1,500	2,500	3,500	4,500	6,000
Eagle	1,000	2,000	3,000	4,000	5,000	6,000
Truckster	500	800	1,300	1,800	2,500	3,500
1961						
Trailster	400	800	1,600	2,400	3,200	4,000
Eagle	1,000	2,000	3,000	4,000	5,000	6,000
1962						
Scooter	800	1,400	2,000	3,000	4,000	5,000
Highlander	800	1,400	2,000	3,000	4,000	5,000
Truckster Runabout	1,000	2,000	3,000	4,000	5,000	6,000
Eagle	1,000	2,000	3,000	4,000	5,000	6,000
1963						
Eagle	1,000	2,000	3,000	4,000	5,000	6,000
Silver Eagle	1,000	2,000	3,000	4,000	5,000	6,000
Trailster	400	800	1,600	2,400	3,200	4,000
Trailster Husky	800	1,400	2,000	3,000	4,000	5,000
Highlander	400	800	1,600	2,400	3,200	4,000
MP	1,000	2,000	3,000	4,000	5,000	6,000
1964						
Eagle	1,000	2,000	3,000	4,000	5,000	6,000
Trailster	500	1,000	2,000	2,500	3,000	3,500
Silver Eagle	1,000	2,000	3,000	4,000	5,000	6,000
Super Silver Eagle	1,000	2,000	3,000	4,000	5,000	6,000
1965						
Silver Eagle	1,000	2,000	3,000	4,000	5,000	6,000
Super Eagle	1,000	2,000	3,000	4,000	5,000	6,000
Super Silver Eagle	1,000	2,000	3,000	4,000	5,000	6,000
1966						
Silver Eagle	1,000	2,000	3,000	4,000	5,000	6,000
1967						
Husky	600	1,200	2,500	4,000	5,500	7,000
1970						
Truckster	500	1,000	2,000	2,500	3,000	3,500
1972						
Truckster	500	1,000	2,000	2,500	3,000	3,500
1974						
Truckster	500	1,000	2,000	2,500	3,000	3,500
CZ						
1938						
Sport	1,500	2,200	4,400	6,600	9,900	14,000
1960						
360 Twin Port	1,000	2,000	4,000	6,000	8,000	10,000
1961						
250cc	1,000	2,000	4,000	6,000	8,000	10,000
1964						
250 Twin Pipe	3,500	6,000	8,100	11,000	16,000	21,000

	6	5	4	3	2	1
360 Twin Pipe.	4,000	6,500	9,100	12,000	18,000	24,000
1965						
250 Twin Pipe.	3,000	5,500	7,200	9,300	14,000	19,000
360 Twin Pipe.	3,500	6,000	8,100	11,000	16,000	21,000
1966						
250 Twin Pipe.	3,000	5,500	7,200	9,300	14,000	19,000
360 Twin Pipe.	3,500	6,000	8,100	11,000	16,000	21,000
1967						
250 Twin Pipe.	3,000	5,500	7,200	9,300	14,000	19,000
360 Twin Pipe.	3,500	6,000	8,100	11,000	16,000	21,000
1968						
250 Side Pipe.	2,000	2,700	4,200	6,100	9,000	12,500
360 Side Pipe.	2,500	3,300	4,600	6,400	9,600	13,000
1969						
250 Side Pipe.	1,800	2,500	3,900	5,700	8,500	12,500
360 Side Pipe.	2,400	3,000	4,200	6,100	9,000	12,000
1970						
250 Side Pipe.	1,800	2,500	3,900	5,700	8,500	12,500
360 Side Pipe.	2,400	3,000	4,200	6,100	9,000	12,000
1971						
125 Yellow Tank	1,800	2,500	3,900	5,700	8,500	11,500
250 Yellow Tank	1,400	2,000	3,500	5,400	8,000	11,000
400 Yellow Tank	1,800	2,500	3,900	5,700	8,500	11,500
1972						
125 Yellow Tank	1,800	2,500	3,900	5,700	8,500	11,500
250 Yellow Tank	1,400	2,000	3,500	5,400	8,000	11,000
400 Yellow Tank	1,800	2,500	3,900	5,700	8,500	11,500
1973						
125 White Tank.	1,400	2,000	3,500	5,400	8,000	11,000
250 Red Tank.	800	1,200	2,700	4,700	6,900	8,100
400 Blue Tank.	900	1,500	3,000	5,000	7,500	10,000
1974						
125 Red Frame	1,800	2,500	3,900	5,700	8,500	11,500
250 Red Frame	1,400	2,000	3,500	5,400	8,000	11,000
400 Red Frame	1,800	2,500	3,900	5,700	8,500	11,500
1975						
125 Falta	1,800	2,500	3,900	5,700	8,500	11,500
250 Falta	1,400	2,000	3,500	5,400	8,000	11,000
400 Falta	1,800	2,500	3,900	5,700	8,500	11,500
1976						
125 Falta	2,700	3,500	4,900	6,800	10,000	14,000
250 Falta	1,400	2,000	3,500	5,400	8,000	11,000
400 Falta	1,800	2,500	3,900	5,700	8,500	11,500
1978						
125 Red Tank.	300	500	1,000	1,800	2,700	3,600
1984						
250 #513	500	700	1,400	2,500	3,700	4,900
400 #514	500	700	1,600	2,900	4,200	5,500
1985						
250 #513	500	700	1,400	2,500	3,700	4,900
400 #514	500	700	1,600	2,900	4,200	5,500
DKW						
1930						
KM 175 (175cc).	500	700	1,100	1,400	1,900	2,400
Volksrad ES 200 (198cc)	500	800	1,100	1,500	2,000	2,500
ZiS (198cc)	600	900	1,300	1,700	2,300	2,900
Special 200/Luxus Special (192cc)	900	1,300	2,000	2,600	3,500	4,400
Luxux 200 (198cc).	600	900	1,300	1,700	2,300	2,800
Luxus 300 (293cc).	500	800	1,100	1,500	2,000	2,500
Luxus Sport 300 (293cc)	500	800	1,100	1,500	2,000	2,500

	6	5	4	3	2	1
Luxus 500 (494cc)	1,600	2,400	3,600	4,800	6,400	8,000
Supersport 500 (500cc)	1,600	2,400	3,600	4,800	6,400	8,000
1931						
KM 175 (175cc)	500	700	1,100	1,400	1,900	2,400
ZiS (198cc)	600	900	1,300	1,700	2,300	2,900
Volksrad ES 200 (198cc)	500	800	1,100	1,500	2,000	2,500
Block 200 (192cc)	400	700	1,000	1,300	1,800	2,200
Block 350 (345cc)	600	900	1,300	1,700	2,300	2,800
Special 200/Luxus Special (192cc)	900	1,300	2,000	2,600	3,500	4,400
Luxus 200 (198cc)	600	900	1,300	1,700	2,300	2,800
Luxus Sport 300 (293cc)	500	800	1,100	1,500	2,000	2,500
Supersport 500 (500cc)	1,600	2,400	3,600	4,800	6,400	8,000
Supersport 600 (586cc)	1,900	2,900	4,300	5,700	7,600	9,500
1932						
KM 175 (175cc)	500	700	1,100	1,400	1,900	2,400
TM 200 (192cc)	400	700	1,000	1,300	1,800	2,200
Block 200 (192cc)	400	700	1,000	1,300	1,800	2,200
Block 350 (345cc)	600	800	1,300	1,700	2,200	2,800
Luxus 200 (198cc)	600	900	1,300	1,700	2,300	2,800
Supersport 500 (500cc)	1,600	2,400	3,600	4,800	6,400	8,000
Supersport 600 (586cc)	1,900	2,900	4,300	5,700	7,600	9,500
1933						
KM 175 (175cc)	500	700	1,100	1,400	1,900	2,400
Block 175 (175cc)	500	700	1,100	1,400	1,900	2,400
SB 200 (192cc)	1,000	2,000	3,000	4,000	5,000	6,000
TM 200 (192cc)	400	700	1,000	1,300	1,800	2,200
BM 200 (199cc)	500	800	1,200	1,600	2,200	2,700
Sport 350 (345cc)	600	900	1,400	1,800	2,400	3,000
Block 500 (494cc)	1,000	1,500	2,300	3,000	4,000	5,000
1934						
RT 100 (98cc)	300	500	700	1,000	1,300	1,600
SB 200 (192cc)	1,000	2,000	3,000	4,000	5,000	6,000
KM 200 (200cc)	500	700	1,100	1,400	1,900	2,400
Sport 350 (345cc)	600	900	1,400	1,800	2,400	3,000
SB 500 (490cc)	1,100	1,700	2,600	4,000	6,000	8,000
1935						
RT 100 (98cc)	300	500	700	1,000	1,300	1,600
SB 200 (192cc)	1,000	2,000	3,000	4,000	5,000	6,000
KM 200 (200cc)	500	700	1,100	1,400	1,900	2,400
SB 500 (490cc)	1,100	1,700	2,600	4,000	6,000	8,000
1936						
RT 3 PS (97cc)	300	500	700	1,000	1,300	1,600
RT 100 (98cc)	300	500	700	1,000	1,300	1,600
SB 200 (192cc)	1,000	2,000	3,000	4,000	5,000	6,000
KS 200 (198cc)	400	600	900	1,100	1,500	1,900
KM 200 (200cc)	500	700	1,100	1,400	1,900	2,400
Sport 250 (247cc)	600	900	1,400	1,800	2,400	3,000
SB 500 (490cc)	1,100	1,700	2,600	4,000	6,000	8,000
1937						
RT 3 PS (97cc)	300	500	700	1,000	1,300	1,600
SB 200 (192cc)	1,000	2,000	3,000	4,000	5,000	6,000
KS 200 (198cc)	400	600	900	1,100	1,500	1,900
Sport 250 (247cc)	600	900	1,400	1,800	2,400	3,000
SB 500 (490cc)	1,100	1,700	2,600	4,000	6,000	8,000
1938						
RT 3 PS (97cc)	300	500	700	1,000	1,300	1,600
SB 200 (192cc)	1,000	2,000	3,000	4,000	5,000	6,000
KS 200 (198cc)	400	600	900	1,100	1,500	1,900
NZ 250 (245cc)	600	1,000	1,400	1,900	2,600	3,200
Sport 250 (247cc)	600	900	1,400	1,800	2,400	3,000

	6	5	4	3	2	1
NZ 350 (343cc)	1,000	2,000	**4,000**	**6,000**	**8,000**	**10,000**
SB 500 (490cc)	1,100	1,700	2,600	**4,000**	**6,000**	**8,000**
1939						
RT 3 PS (97cc)	300	500	700	1,000	1,300	1,600
RT 125 (123cc)	300	500	**800**	**1,200**	**1,600**	**2,000**
KS 200 (198cc)	400	600	900	1,100	1,500	1,900
NZ 250 (245cc)	600	1,000	1,400	1,900	2,600	3,200
NZ 350 (343cc)	1,000	2,000	**4,000**	**6,000**	**8,000**	**10,000**
NZ 500 (489cc)	1,000	1,500	2,300	3,000	4,000	5,000
SB 500 (490cc)	1,100	1,700	2,600	**4,000**	**6,000**	**8,000**
1940						
RT 3 PS (97cc)	300	500	700	1,000	1,300	1,600
RT 125 (123cc)	300	500	**800**	**1,200**	**1,600**	**2,000**
KS 200 (198cc)	400	600	900	1,100	1,500	1,900
NZ 250 (245cc)	600	1,000	1,400	1,900	2,600	3,200
NZ 350 (343cc)	1,000	2,000	**4,000**	**6,000**	**8,000**	**10,000**
NZ 500 (489cc)	1,000	1,500	2,300	3,000	4,000	5,000
1941						
RT 125 (123cc)	300	500	**800**	**1,200**	**1,600**	**2,000**
NZ 250 (245cc)	600	1,000	1,400	1,900	2,600	3,200
NZ 350 (343cc)	1,000	2,000	**4,000**	**6,000**	**8,000**	**10,000**
NZ 500 (489cc)	1,000	1,500	2,300	3,000	4,000	5,000
1942						
NZ 350 (343cc)	1,000	2,000	**4,000**	**6,000**	**8,000**	**10,000**
1943						
RT 125-1 (123cc)	300	500	700	1,000	1,300	1,600
NZ 350 (343cc)	1,000	2,000	**4,000**	**6,000**	**8,000**	**10,000**
1944						
RT 125-1 (123cc)	300	500	700	900	1,200	1,500
NZ 350-1 (343cc)	700	1,000	1,500	2,000	2,700	3,400
1945						
NZ 350-1 (343cc)	700	1,000	1,500	2,000	2,700	3,400
1949						
RT 125 W (123cc)	400	700	1,000	1,300	1,800	2,200
1950						
RT 125 W (123cc)	400	700	1,000	1,300	1,800	2,200
1951						
RT 125 W (123cc)	400	700	1,000	1,300	1,800	2,200
RT 200 (191cc)	500	800	1,100	1,500	2,000	2,500
1952						
RT 125/2 (123cc)	300	500	700	900	1,200	1,500
RT 125 W (123cc)	400	700	1,000	1,300	1,800	2,200
RT 200 (191cc)	500	800	1,100	1,500	2,000	2,500
RT 200 H (191cc)	400	600	900	1,100	1,500	1,900
RT 250 H (244cc)	400	700	1,000	1,300	1,800	2,200
1953						
RT 125/2 (123cc)	300	500	700	900	1,200	1,500
RT 200 H (191cc)	400	600	900	1,100	1,500	1,900
RT 250/1 (244cc)	400	600	1,000	1,300	1,700	2,100
RT 250/2 (244cc)	400	700	1,000	1,300	1,800	2,200
RT 250 H (244cc)	400	700	1,000	1,300	1,800	2,200
1954						
RT 125/2 (123cc)	300	500	700	900	1,200	1,500
RT 125/2 H (123cc)	400	600	900	1,100	1,500	1,900
RT 175 (174cc)	400	600	900	1,100	1,500	1,900
RT 200/2 (197cc)	400	700	1,000	1,300	1,800	2,200
RT 250 H (244cc)	400	700	1,000	1,300	1,800	2,200
1955						
RT 125/2 H (123cc)	400	600	900	1,100	1,500	1,900
RT 175 (174cc)	400	600	900	1,100	1,500	1,900

	6	5	4	3	2	1
RT 175 S (174cc)	300	500	700	900	1,200	1,500
RT 200/2 (197cc)	400	700	1,000	1,300	1,800	2,200
RT 200 S (197cc)	300	500	700	900	1,200	1,500
RT 250/2 (244cc)	400	700	1,000	1,300	1,800	2,200
RT 250 S (244cc)	500	800	1,100	1,500	2,000	2,500
RT 350 S (348cc)	900	1,400	2,100	2,800	3,800	4,700
1956						
RT 125/2 H (123cc)	400	600	900	1,100	1,500	1,900
RT 175 S (174cc)	300	500	700	900	1,200	1,500
RT 175 VS (174cc)	300	500	700	900	1,200	1,500
RT 200 S (197cc)	300	500	700	900	1,200	1,500
RT 200 VS (197cc)	300	500	700	900	1,200	1,500
RT 250 S (244cc)	500	800	1,100	1,500	2,000	2,500
RT 250 VS (244cc)	500	800	1,100	1,500	2,000	2,500
RT 350 S (348cc)	900	1,400	2,100	2,800	3,800	4,700
1957						
RT 125/2 H (123cc)	400	600	900	1,100	1,500	1,900
RT 175 VS (174cc)	300	500	700	900	1,200	1,500
RT 200 VS (197cc)	300	500	700	900	1,200	1,500
RT 250 VS (244cc)	500	800	1,100	1,500	2,000	2,500
1958						
RT 175 VS (174cc)	300	500	700	900	1,200	1,500
1964						
Hummel (155cc)	2,000	4,000	6,000	8,000	10,000	12,000
1965						
Hummel (155cc)	2,000	**4,000**	**6,000**	**8,000**	**10,000**	**12,000**
DOUGLAS						
1907 (30 made)						
Model A (350cc)	5,000	10,000	20,000	30,000	40,000	50,000
1908 (30 made)						
Model B (350cc)	5,000	10,000	20,000	30,000	40,000	50,000
1909 (280 made)						
Model C (350cc)	5,000	10,000	20,000	30,000	40,000	50,000
1910 (1022 made)						
Model D (350cc)	2,000	4,000	8,000	12,000	16,000	20,000
1911 (2534 made)						
Model D (350cc)	2,000	4,000	8,000	12,000	16,000	20,000
Model E (350cc)	2,000	4,000	8,000	12,000	16,000	20,000
Model F (350cc)	2,000	4,000	8,000	12,000	16,000	20,000
1912 (3100 made)						
Model G (350cc)	2,000	4,000	8,000	12,000	16,000	20,000
Model H (350cc)	2,000	4,000	8,000	12,000	16,000	20,000
Model J (350cc)	2,000	4,000	8,000	12,000	16,000	20,000
Model K (350cc)	2,000	4,000	8,000	12,000	16,000	20,000
Model L (350cc)	2,000	4,000	8,000	12,000	16,000	20,000
1913 (5560 made)						
Model N (350cc)	2,000	4,000	8,000	12,000	16,000	20,000
Model O (350cc)	2,000	4,000	8,000	12,000	16,000	20,000
Model P (350cc)	2,000	4,000	8,000	12,000	16,000	20,000
Model R (350cc)	2,000	4,000	8,000	12,000	16,000	20,000
Model S (350cc)	2,000	4,000	8,000	12,000	16,000	20,000
1914						
Model T (350cc)	2,000	4,000	8,000	12,000	16,000	20,000
Model U (350cc)	2,000	4,000	8,000	12,000	16,000	20,000
Model V (350cc)	2,000	4,000	8,000	12,000	16,000	20,000
Model W (350cc)	2,000	4,000	8,000	12,000	16,000	20,000
Model X (350cc)	2,000	4,000	8,000	12,000	16,000	20,000
Model A Twin (600cc)	2,500	5,000	10,000	15,000	20,000	25,000
Model B Twin (600cc)	2,500	5,000	10,000	15,000	20,000	25,000

	6	5	4	3	2	1
1915						
Model T (350cc)	2,000	4,000	8,000	12,000	16,000	20,000
Model U (350cc)	2,000	4,000	8,000	12,000	16,000	20,000
Model V (350cc)	2,000	4,000	8,000	12,000	16,000	20,000
Model W (350cc)	2,000	4,000	8,000	12,000	16,000	20,000
Model X (350cc)	2,000	4,000	8,000	12,000	16,000	20,000
Model WD (350cc)	2,000	4,000	8,000	12,000	16,000	20,000
Model A Twin (600cc)	2,500	5,000	10,000	15,000	20,000	25,000
Model B Twin (600cc)	2,500	5,000	10,000	15,000	20,000	25,000
1916						
Model U (350cc)	2,000	4,000	8,000	12,000	16,000	20,000
Model V (350cc)	2,000	4,000	8,000	12,000	16,000	20,000
Model W (350cc)	2,000	4,000	8,000	12,000	16,000	20,000
Model X (350cc)	2,000	4,000	8,000	12,000	16,000	20,000
Model WS (350cc)	2,000	4,000	8,000	12,000	16,000	20,000
Model A Twin (600cc)	2,500	5,000	10,000	15,000	20,000	25,000
Model B Twin (600cc)	2,500	5,000	10,000	15,000	20,000	25,000
1917						
Model A Twin (600cc)	2,500	5,000	10,000	15,000	20,000	25,000
Model B Twin (600cc)	2,500	5,000	10,000	15,000	20,000	25,000
350cc	2,000	4,000	8,000	12,000	16,000	20,000
1918						
Model U (350cc)	2,000	4,000	8,000	12,000	16,000	20,000
Model V (350cc)	2,000	4,000	8,000	12,000	16,000	20,000
Model W (350cc)	2,000	4,000	8,000	12,000	16,000	20,000
Model A Twin (600cc)	2,500	5,000	10,000	15,000	20,000	25,000
Model B Twin (600cc)	2,500	5,000	10,000	15,000	20,000	25,000
1919						
Model U (350cc)	2,000	4,000	8,000	12,000	16,000	20,000
Model V (350cc)	2,000	4,000	8,000	12,000	16,000	20,000
Model W (350cc)	2,000	4,000	8,000	12,000	16,000	20,000
Model A Twin (600cc)	2,500	5,000	10,000	15,000	20,000	25,000
Model B Twin (600cc)	2,500	5,000	10,000	15,000	20,000	25,000
1920						
Model WD (350cc)	3,000	6,000	9,000	12,000	15,000	18,000
Model W20 (350cc)	3,000	6,000	9,000	12,000	15,000	18,000
Model B20 Twin (600cc)	2,500	5,000	10,000	15,000	20,000	25,000
1921						
Model WD (350cc)	1,000	2,000	3,000	5,000	8,000	11,000
Model W21 (350cc)	1,000	2,000	3,000	5,000	8,000	11,000
Model B21 Twin (600cc)	2,500	5,000	10,000	15,000	20,000	25,000
Model S1 (500cc)	1,500	2,500	5,000	8,000	11,000	14,000
1922						
Model WD (350cc)	1,000	2,000	3,000	5,000	8,000	11,000
Model W21 (350cc)	1,000	2,000	3,000	5,000	8,000	11,000
Model B21 Twin (600cc)	2,500	5,000	10,000	15,000	20,000	25,000
Model S1 (500cc)	1,500	2,500	5,000	8,000	11,000	14,000
1923						
Model W (350cc)	1,000	2,000	3,000	5,000	8,000	11,000
Model 3SC (350cc)	1,000	2,000	3,000	5,000	8,000	11,000
Model RA (500cc)	1,500	2,500	5,000	8,000	11,000	14,000
Model B Twin (600cc)	2,500	5,000	10,000	15,000	20,000	25,000
Model S1 (500cc)	1,500	2,500	5,000	8,000	11,000	14,000
Model S2 (733cc)	2,000	4,000	8,000	12,000	16,000	20,000
1924						
Model SW (350cc)	3,000	6,000	9,000	12,000	15,000	18,000
Model TS (350cc)	1,000	2,000	3,000	5,000	8,000	11,000
Model RW (350cc)	3,000	6,000	9,000	12,000	15,000	18,000
Model CW (350cc)	1,000	2,000	3,000	5,000	8,000	11,000
Model RA (500cc)	1,500	2,500	5,000	8,000	11,000	14,000

	6	5	4	3	2	1
Model OB (600cc)	2,000	4,000	8,000	12,000	16,000	20,000
Model S2 (733cc)	2,000	4,000	8,000	12,000	16,000	20,000
1925						
Model TS25 (350cc)	1,000	2,000	3,000	5,000	8,000	11,000
Model CW25 (350cc)	1,000	2,000	3,000	5,000	8,000	11,000
Model RW (350cc)	1,500	2,500	5,000	8,000	11,000	14,000
Model RA (500cc)	1,500	2,500	5,000	8,000	11,000	14,000
Model OB (600cc)	2,000	4,000	8,000	12,000	16,000	20,000
1926						
Model TS26 (350cc)	1,000	2,000	3,000	5,000	8,000	11,000
Model CW26 (350cc)	1,000	2,000	3,000	5,000	8,000	11,000
Model EW (350cc)	2,000	4,000	8,000	12,000	16,000	20,000
Model IOM (350cc)	1,500	2,500	5,000	8,000	11,000	14,000
Model IOM-TT (600cc)	2,000	4,000	8,000	12,000	16,000	20,000
Model OC (600cc)	2,000	4,000	8,000	12,000	16,000	20,000
1927						
Model EW (350cc)	2,000	4,000	8,000	12,000	16,000	20,000
Model EW Sport (600cc)	2,000	4,000	8,000	12,000	16,000	20,000
Model IOM (350cc)	1,500	2,500	5,000	8,000	11,000	14,000
Model IOM-TT (600cc)	2,000	4,000	8,000	12,000	16,000	20,000
Model OC (600cc)	2,000	4,000	8,000	12,000	16,000	20,000
1928						
Model IOM (350cc)	1,500	2,500	5,000	8,000	11,000	14,000
Model IOM-TT (600cc)	2,000	4,000	8,000	12,000	16,000	20,000
Model EW (350cc)	2,000	4,000	8,000	12,000	16,000	20,000
Model EW Sport (600cc)	2,000	4,000	8,000	12,000	16,000	20,000
Model B28 (350cc)	1,500	2,500	5,000	8,000	11,000	14,000
Model G28 (500cc)	1,500	2,500	5,000	8,000	11,000	14,000
Model H29 (600cc)	2,000	4,000	8,000	12,000	16,000	20,000
Model DT5 (500cc)	1,500	2,500	5,000	8,000	11,000	14,000
Model DT6 (600cc)	2,000	4,000	8,000	12,000	16,000	20,000
Model SW5 (500cc)	1,500	2,500	5,000	8,000	11,000	14,000
Model SW6 (600cc)	2,000	4,000	8,000	12,000	16,000	20,000
1929						
Model IOM (350cc)	1,500	2,500	5,000	8,000	11,000	14,000
Model IOM-TT (600cc)	2,000	4,000	8,000	12,000	16,000	20,000
Model EW (350cc)	2,000	4,000	8,000	12,000	16,000	20,000
Model EW Sport (600cc)	2,000	4,000	8,000	12,000	16,000	20,000
Model B29 (350cc)	1,500	2,500	5,000	8,000	11,000	14,000
Model L29 (350cc)	1,500	2,500	5,000	8,000	11,000	14,000
Model G29 (600cc)	2,000	4,000	8,000	12,000	16,000	20,000
Model H29 (600cc)	2,000	4,000	8,000	12,000	16,000	20,000
Model DT5 (500cc)	1,500	2,500	5,000	8,000	11,000	14,000
Model DT6 (600cc)	2,000	4,000	8,000	12,000	16,000	20,000
Model SW5 (500cc)	1,500	2,500	5,000	8,000	11,000	14,000
Model SW6 (600cc)	2,000	4,000	8,000	12,000	16,000	20,000
1930						
Model H3 (350cc)	1,500	2,500	5,000	8,000	11,000	14,000
Model L3 (350cc)	1,500	2,500	5,000	8,000	11,000	14,000
Model S5 (500cc)	1,500	2,500	5,000	8,000	11,000	14,000
Model S6 (600cc)	2,000	4,000	8,000	12,000	16,000	20,000
Model T6 (750cc)	2,000	4,000	8,000	12,000	16,000	20,000
Model DT5 (500cc)	1,500	2,500	5,000	8,000	11,000	14,000
Model DT6 (600cc)	2,000	4,000	8,000	12,000	16,000	20,000
Model SW5 (500cc)	1,500	2,500	5,000	8,000	11,000	14,000
Model SW6 (600cc)	2,000	4,000	8,000	12,000	16,000	20,000
1931						
Model B31 (350cc)	1,500	3,000	6,000	9,000	12,000	15,000
Model DT5 (500cc)	1,500	2,500	5,000	8,000	11,000	14,000
Model DT6 (600cc)	2,000	4,000	8,000	12,000	16,000	20,000

	6	5	4	3	2	1
Model SW5 (500cc)	1,500	2,500	5,000	8,000	11,000	14,000
Model SW6 (600cc)	2,000	4,000	8,000	12,000	16,000	20,000
Model C31 (500cc)	1,500	2,500	5,000	8,000	11,000	14,000
Model E31 (600cc)	2,000	4,000	8,000	12,000	16,000	20,000
Model A31 (500cc)	2,500	5,500	7,500	9,500	12,000	14,000
Model F31 (500cc)	1,500	2,500	5,000	8,000	11,000	14,000
Model G31 (600cc)	2,000	4,000	8,000	12,000	16,000	20,000
1932						
Model B32 (350cc)	1,500	3,000	6,000	9,000	12,000	15,000
Model DT5 (500cc)	1,500	2,500	5,000	8,000	11,000	14,000
Model DT6 (600cc)	2,000	4,000	8,000	12,000	16,000	20,000
Model SW5 (500cc)	1,500	2,500	5,000	8,000	11,000	14,000
Model SW6 (600cc)	2,000	4,000	8,000	12,000	16,000	20,000
Model D32 (600cc)	2,000	4,000	8,000	12,000	16,000	20,000
Model E32 (600cc)	2,000	4,000	8,000	12,000	16,000	20,000
Model H32 (750cc)	2,000	4,000	8,000	12,000	16,000	20,000
Model A32 (500cc)	1,500	2,500	5,000	8,000	11,000	14,000
Model F32 (500cc)	1,500	2,500	5,000	8,000	11,000	14,000
Model G32 (600cc)	2,000	4,000	8,000	12,000	16,000	20,000
Model C32 (500cc)	1,500	2,500	5,000	8,000	11,000	14,000
Model K32 (500cc)	1,500	2,500	5,000	8,000	11,000	14,000
Model M32 (600cc)	2,000	4,000	8,000	12,000	16,000	20,000
1933						
Model D32 (600cc)	2,000	4,000	8,000	12,000	16,000	20,000
Model E32 (600cc)	2,000	4,000	8,000	12,000	16,000	20,000
Model H32 (750cc)	2,000	4,000	8,000	12,000	16,000	20,000
Model F33 (500cc)	1,500	2,500	5,000	8,000	11,000	14,000
Model G33 (600cc)	2,000	4,000	8,000	12,000	16,000	20,000
Model X (150cc)	1,000	2,000	3,000	4,000	5,000	6,000
1934						
Model X (150cc)	1,000	2,000	3,000	4,000	5,000	6,000
Model X1 (150cc)	1,000	2,000	3,000	4,000	5,000	6,000
Model Y (250cc)	1,000	2,000	3,000	4,000	5,000	6,000
Model Y1 (350cc)	1,500	3,000	6,000	9,000	12,000	15,000
Model Y2 (500cc)	1,500	2,500	5,000	8,000	11,000	14,000
Model Z (600cc)	2,000	4,000	8,000	12,000	16,000	20,000
Model Z1 (750cc)	2,000	4,000	8,000	12,000	16,000	20,000
Model OW (500cc)	2,000	4,000	8,000	12,000	16,000	20,000
Model OW1 (600cc)	2,000	4,000	8,000	12,000	16,000	20,000
1935						
Model X (150cc)	1,000	2,000	3,000	4,000	5,000	6,000
Model X1 (150cc)	1,000	2,000	3,000	4,000	5,000	6,000
Model Y (250cc)	1,000	2,000	3,000	4,000	5,000	6,000
Model 5Y1 (350cc)	1,500	3,000	6,000	9,000	12,000	15,000
Model 5Z (600cc)	2,000	4,000	8,000	12,000	16,000	20,000
Model 5Z1 (750cc)	2,000	4,000	8,000	12,000	16,000	20,000
Model OW (500cc)	2,000	4,000	8,000	12,000	16,000	20,000
Model OW1 (600cc)	2,000	4,000	8,000	12,000	16,000	20,000
Blue Chief (500cc)	2,000	4,000	8,000	12,000	16,000	20,000
Endeavor (500cc)	2,000	4,000	8,000	12,000	16,000	20,000
1936						
Aero (250cc)	1,000	2,000	3,000	4,000	5,000	6,000
Aero (500cc)	1,500	3,000	6,000	9,000	12,000	15,000
Aero (600cc)	2,000	4,000	8,000	12,000	16,000	20,000
Endeavor (500cc)	2,000	4,000	8,000	12,000	16,000	20,000
1937						
Aero (600cc)	2,000	4,000	8,000	12,000	16,000	20,000
1938						
Aero (600cc)	2,000	4,000	8,000	12,000	16,000	20,000
Model CL/38 (150cc)	1,000	2,000	3,000	4,000	5,000	6,000

	6	5	4	3	2	1
1946						
T35 (348cc)	1,000	2,000	3,000	4,000	5,000	6,000
1947						
T35 (348cc)	1,000	2,000	3,000	4,000	5,000	6,000
1948						
T35 (348cc)	1,000	2,000	3,000	4,000	5,000	6,000
Mark III (350cc)	1,000	2,000	3,000	4,000	5,000	6,000
Mark III Sport (350cc)	1,000	2,000	3,000	4,000	5,000	6,000
Model DV60 (600cc)	1,500	3,000	6,000	9,000	12,000	15,000
1949						
Mark III (350cc)	1,000	2,000	3,000	4,000	5,000	6,000
Mark III Sport (350cc)	1,000	2,000	3,000	4,000	5,000	6,000
Competition (350cc)	1,000	2,000	3,000	4,000	5,000	6,000
1950						
Mark IV (350cc)	1,000	2,000	3,000	4,000	5,000	6,000
Mark IV Sport (350cc)	1,000	2,000	3,000	4,000	5,000	6,000
Mark V (350cc)	1,000	2,000	3,000	4,000	5,000	6,000
Competition (350cc)	1,000	2,000	3,000	4,000	5,000	6,000
Plus 80 (350cc)	1,000	2,000	3,000	4,000	5,000	6,000
Plus 90 (350cc)	1,000	2,000	3,000	4,000	5,000	6,000
1951						
Competition (350cc)	1,000	2,000	3,000	4,000	5,000	6,000
Mark V (350cc)	1,000	2,000	3,000	4,000	5,000	6,000
Plus 80 (350cc)	1,000	2,000	3,000	4,000	5,000	6,000
Plus 90 (350cc)	1,000	2,000	3,000	4,000	5,000	6,000
1952						
Mark V (350cc)	1,000	2,000	3,000	4,000	5,000	6,000
Plus 90 (350cc)	1,000	2,000	3,000	4,000	5,000	6,000
1953						
Mark V (350cc)	1,000	2,000	3,000	4,000	5,000	6,000
Plus 90 (350cc)	1,000	2,000	3,000	4,000	5,000	6,000
1954						
Mark V (350cc)	1,000	2,000	3,000	4,000	5,000	6,000
Dragonfly Mark VI (350cc)	1,000	2,000	4,000	7,000	10,000	13,000
1955						
Dragonfly Mark VI (350cc)	1,000	2,000	4,000	7,000	10,000	13,000
1956						
Dragonfly Mark VI (350cc)	1,000	2,000	4,000	7,000	10,000	13,000
DUCATI						
1948						
Cucciolo (60cc)	5,000	10,000	20,000	30,000	40,000	50,000
1953						
98 Sport (98cc single)	1,200	1,800	2,700	3,600	4,800	6,000
1954						
98 Sport (98cc single)	1,200	1,800	2,700	3,600	4,800	6,000
98 Super Sport (98cc single)	1,300	2,000	2,900	3,900	5,200	6,500
1955						
98 Sport (98cc single)	1,200	1,800	2,700	3,600	4,800	6,000
98 Super Sport (98cc single)	1,300	2,000	2,900	3,900	5,200	6,500
Gran Sport (100cc single)	4,800	7,200	11,000	14,000	19,000	24,000
1956						
98 Sport (98cc single)	1,200	1,800	2,700	3,600	4,800	6,000
98 Super Sport (98cc single)	1,300	2,000	2,900	3,900	5,200	6,500
Gran Sport (100cc single)	4,800	7,200	11,000	14,000	19,000	24,000
1957						
98 Sport (98cc single)	1,200	1,800	2,700	3,600	4,800	6,000
Gran Sport (100cc single)	4,800	7,200	11,000	14,000	19,000	24,000
Grand Prix (125cc single)	5,200	7,800	18,000	16,000	21,000	26,000
1958						
98 Sport (98cc single)	1,200	1,800	2,700	3,600	4,800	6,000
Grand Prix (125cc single)	5,200	7,800	18,000	16,000	21,000	26,000

	6	5	4	3	2	1
125 F3 (125cc single)	2,400	3,600	5,400	7,200	9,600	12,000
175 F3 (175cc single)	3,400	5,100	7,700	10,000	14,000	17,000
1959						
Grand Prix (125cc single)	5,200	7,800	18,000	16,000	21,000	26,000
125 F3 (125cc single)	2,400	3,600	5,400	7,200	9,600	12,000
175 F3 (175cc single)	3,400	5,100	7,700	10,000	14,000	17,000
200 elite (200cc single)	1,000	1,500	2,300	3,000	4,000	5,000
1960						
Bronco (85cc single)	500	800	1,100	1,500	2,000	2,500
125 F3 (125cc single)	2,400	3,600	5,400	7,200	9,600	12,000
125 Grand Prix (125cc single)	5,200	7,800	18,000	16,000	21,000	26,000
173 F3 (175cc single)	3,400	5,100	7,700	10,000	14,000	17,000
200 Americano (200cc single)	700	1,100	1,600	2,100	2,800	3,500
200 elite (200cc single)	1,000	1,500	2,300	3,000	4,000	5,000
200 Motocross (200cc single)	1,000	1,500	2,300	3,000	4,000	5,000
220 Grand Prix (220cc single)	6,400	9,600	14,000	19,000	26,000	32,000
1961						
Bronco (85cc single)	500	800	1,100	1,500	2,000	2,500
Grand Prix (125cc single)	5,200	7,800	18,000	16,000	21,000	26,000
125 F3 (125cc single)	2,400	3,600	5,400	7,200	9,600	12,000
175 F3 (175cc single)	3,400	5,100	7,700	10,000	14,000	17,000
200 Americano (200cc single)	900	1,400	2,000	2,700	3,600	4,500
200 Elite (200cc single)	1,000	1,500	2,300	3,000	4,000	5,000
200 Motocross (200cc single)	1,000	1,500	2,300	3,000	4,000	5,000
Monza Tourer (250cc single)	800	1,200	1,800	2,400	3,200	4,000
250 F3 (250cc single)	3,400	5,100	7,700	10,000	14,000	17,000
1962						
48 Sport Falcon (48cc single)	600	1,000	1,400	1,900	2,600	3,200
Bronco (85cc single)	500	800	1,100	1,500	2,000	2,500
Diana (250cc single)	1,000	2,000	3,000	5,000	7,000	9,000
250 F3 (250cc single)	3,400	5,100	7,700	10,000	14,000	17,000
Monza Tourer (250cc single)	800	1,200	1,800	2,400	3,200	4,000
250 Scrambler (250cc single)	800	1,100	1,700	2,300	3,000	3,800
1963						
48 Sport Falcon (48cc single)	600	1,000	1,400	1,900	2,600	3,200
Bronco (85cc single)	500	800	1,100	1,500	2,000	2,500
Diana (250cc single)	1,000	2,000	3,000	5,000	7,000	9,000
Monza Tourer (250cc single)	800	1,200	1,800	2,400	3,200	4,000
250 Scrambler (250cc single)	700	1,100	1,600	2,100	2,800	3,500
1964						
48 SL (48cc single)	600	800	1,300	1,700	2,200	2,800
48 Sport Falcon (48cc single)	600	1,000	1,400	1,900	2,600	3,200
Cadet Falcon 100 (98cc single)	600	900	1,300	1,700	2,300	2,900
Mountaineer (98cc single)	600	900	1,400	1,800	2,400	3,000
Diana (250cc single)	1,100	2,000	3,000	5,000	7,000	9,000
Monza Tourer (250cc single)	800	1,200	1,800	2,400	3,200	4,000
250 GT (250cc single)	600	900	1,400	1,800	2,400	3,000
250 Mach 1 (250cc single)	1,100	1,700	2,500	3,300	4,400	5,500
1965						
48 SL (48cc single)	600	800	1,300	1,700	2,200	2,800
48 Sport Falcon (48cc single)	600	1,000	1,400	1,900	2,600	3,200
Cadet Falcon 100 (98cc single)	600	900	1,300	1,700	2,300	2,900
Mountaineer (98cc single)	600	900	1,400	1,800	2,400	3,000
Diana (250cc single)	1,100	2,000	3,000	5,000	7,000	9,000
Monza Tourer (250cc single)	800	1,200	1,800	2,400	3,200	4,000
250 GT (250cc single)	600	900	1,400	1,800	2,400	3,000
250 Mach 1 (250cc single)	1,100	1,700	2,500	3,300	4,400	5,500
1966						
50 SL (50cc single)	600	800	1,300	1,700	2,200	2,800
Cadet Falcon 100 (98cc single)	600	900	1,300	1,700	2,300	2,900

	6	5	4	3	2	1
Mountaineer (98cc single)	600	900	1,400	1,800	2,400	3,000
Monza Tourer (250cc single)	800	1,200	1,800	2,400	3,200	4,000
250 GT (250cc single)	600	900	1,400	1,800	2,400	3,000
250 Mach 1 (250cc single)	1,100	1,700	2,500	3,300	4,400	5,500
1967						
50 SL (50cc single)	600	800	1,300	1,700	2,200	2,800
Cadet Falcon 100 (98cc single)	600	900	1,300	1,700	2,300	2,900
Mountaineer (98cc single)	600	900	1,400	1,800	2,400	3,000
Monza (250cc single)	1,000	2,000	4,000	7,000	10,000	13,000
250 GT (250cc single)	600	900	1,400	1,800	2,400	3,000
250 Mach 1 (250cc single)	1,100	1,700	2,500	3,300	4,400	5,500
1968						
50 SL (50cc single)	600	800	1,300	1,700	2,200	2,800
160 Monza Junior (152cc single)	600	900	1,400	1,800	2,400	3,000
250 Mark 3 (250cc single)	800	1,200	1,800	2,600	4,000	5,000
250 Mark 3 Desmo (250cc single)	900	1,400	2,000	2,700	3,600	4,500
250 Street Scrambler (250cc single)	600	900	1,400	1,800	2,400	3,000
350 Mark 3 (340cc single)	900	2,000	3,000	4,000	5,000	6,000
350 Mark 3 Desmo (340cc single)	1,000	2,000	3,000	4,000	5,000	6,000
350 Street Scrambler (340cc single)	1,000	2,000	3,000	4,000	5,000	6,000
350 Sebring (340cc single)	600	900	1,400	1,800	2,400	3,000
1969						
50 Scrambler (50cc single)	500	700	1,100	1,400	1,900	2,400
50 SL (50cc single)	600	800	1,300	1,700	2,200	2,800
100 Scrambler (100cc single)	400	600	900	1,200	1,600	2,000
160 Monza Junior (152cc single)	600	900	1,400	1,800	2,400	3,000
250 Mark 3 (250cc single)	800	1,200	2,000	3,000	4,000	5,000
250 Mark 3 Desmo (250cc single)	900	1,400	2,000	2,700	3,600	4,500
250 Street Scrambler (250cc single)	600	900	1,400	1,800	2,400	3,000
350 Mark 3 (340cc single)	900	2,000	3,000	4,000	5,000	6,000
350 Mark 3 Desmo (340cc single)	1,000	2,000	3,000	4,000	5,000	6,000
350 Street Scrambler (340cc single)	1,000	2,000	3,000	4,000	5,000	6,000
350 Sebring (340cc single)	600	900	1,400	1,800	2,400	3,000
1970						
50 Scrambler (50cc single)	500	700	1,100	1,400	1,900	2,400
100 Scrambler (100cc single)	400	600	900	1,200	1,600	2,000
160 Monza Junior (152cc single)	600	900	1,400	1,800	2,400	3,000
250 Mark 3 (250cc single)	800	1,200	1,800	2,400	3,200	4,000
250 Mark 3 Desmo (250cc single)	900	1,400	2,000	2,700	3,600	4,500
250 Street Scrambler (250cc single)	600	900	1,400	1,800	2,400	3,000
350 Mark 3 (340cc single)	900	2,000	3,000	4,000	5,000	6,000
350 Mark 3 Desmo (340cc single)	1,000	2,000	3,000	4,000	5,000	6,000
350 Sebring (340cc single)	700	1,000	1,500	2,000	2,600	3,300
350 Street Scrambler (340cc single)	1,000	2,000	3,000	4,000	5,000	6,000
450 Mark 3 (436cc single)	900	1,400	2,100	2,800	3,800	4,700
450 Mark 3 Desmo (436cc single)	1,200	1,900	2,800	3,700	5,000	6,200
1971						
125 Scrambler (125cc single)	400	600	900	1,200	1,600	2,000
250 Mark 3 (250cc single)	800	1,200	1,800	2,400	3,200	4,000
250 Mark 3 Desmo (250cc single)	900	1,400	2,000	2,700	3,600	4,500
250 Street Scrambler (250cc single)	600	900	1,400	1,800	2,400	3,000
350 Mark 3 (340cc single)	900	2,000	3,000	4,000	5,000	6,000
350 Mark 3 Desmo (340cc single)	1,000	2,000	3,000	4,000	5,000	6,000
350 Sebring (340cc single)	600	900	1,400	1,800	2,400	3,000
350 Street Scrambler (340cc single)	1,000	2,000	3,000	4,000	5,000	6,000
450 Mark 3 (436cc single)	900	1,400	2,100	2,800	3,800	4,700
450 Mark 3 Desmo (436cc single)	1,200	1,900	2,800	3,700	5,000	6,200
750 GT (748cc V-twin)	**2,500**	**5,000**	**10,000**	**15,000**	**20,000**	**25,000**
1972						
250 Mark 3 (250cc single)	800	1,200	1,900	2,500	3,300	4,100

	6	5	4	3	2	1
250 Mark 3 Desmo (250cc single)	900	1,400	2,100	2,800	3,800	4,700
250 Street Scrambler (250cc single)	600	900	1,400	1,800	2,400	3,000
350 Mark 3 (340cc single)	900	2,000	3,000	4,000	5,000	6,000
350 Mark 3 Desmo (340cc single)	1,000	2,000	3,000	4,000	5,000	6,000
350 Desmo Silver Shotgun (340cc single). .	1,100	2,000	3,000	4,000	5,000	6,000
350 Sebring (340cc single)	600	900	1,400	1,800	2,400	3,000
350 Street Scrambler (340cc single)	1,000	2,000	3,000	4,000	5,000	6,000
450 Mark 3 (436cc single)	900	1,400	2,100	2,800	3,800	4,700
450 Mark 3 Desmo (436cc single)	1,200	1,900	2,800	3,700	5,000	6,200
750 GT (748cc V-twin)	**2,500**	**5,000**	**10,000**	**15,000**	**20,000**	**25,000**
750 Sport (748cc V-twin)	2,400	4,000	7,000	12,000	17,000	22,000
1973						
250 Mark 3 (250cc single)	800	1,200	1,900	2,500	3,300	4,100
250 Mark 3 Desmo (250cc single)	900	1,400	2,100	2,800	3,800	4,700
250 Street Scrambler (250cc single)	600	900	1,400	1,800	2,400	3,000
350 Mark 3 (340cc single)	900	2,000	3,000	4,000	5,000	6,000
350 Mark 3 Desmo (340cc single)	1,000	2,000	3,000	4,000	5,000	6,000
350 Street Scrambler (340cc single)	1,000	2,000	3,000	4,000	5,000	6,000
450 Mark 3 (436cc single)	900	1,400	2,100	2,800	3,800	4,700
450 Mark 3 Desmo (436cc single)	1,200	1,900	2,800	3,700	5,000	6,200
750 GT (748cc V-twin)	**2,500**	**5,000**	**10,000**	**15,000**	**20,000**	**25,000**
750 Sport (748cc V-twin)	2,400	4,000	7,000	12,000	17,000	22,000
750 SS Round Case (748cc V-twin).	**12,500**	**25,000**	**50,000**	**75,000**	**100K**	**125K**
1974						
250 Mark 3 (250cc single)	800	1,200	1,900	2,500	3,300	4,100
250 Mark 3 Desmo (250cc single)	900	1,400	2,100	2,800	3,800	4,700
250 Street Scrambler (250cc single)	600	900	1,400	1,800	2,400	3,000
350 Mark 3 (340cc single)	900	2,000	3,000	4,000	5,000	6,000
350 Mark 3 Desmo (340cc single)	1,000	2,000	3,000	4,000	5,000	6,000
350 Street Scrambler (340cc single)	1,000	2,000	3,000	4,000	5,000	6,000
450 Mark 3 (436cc single)	900	1,400	2,100	2,800	3,800	4,700
450 Mark 3 Desmo (436cc single)	1,200	1,900	2,800	3,700	5,000	6,200
750 GT (748cc V-twin)	**2,500**	**5,000**	**10,000**	**15,000**	**20,000**	**25,000**
750 Sport (748cc V-twin)	2,400	4,000	7,000	12,000	17,000	22,000
750 SS Round Case (748cc V-twin).	**12,500**	**25,000**	**50,000**	**75,000**	**100K**	**125K**
860 GT (864cc V-twin)	900	1,300	2,000	2,600	3,500	4,400
1975						
125 Regolarita (125cc single)	400	700	1,000	1,300	1,800	2,200
GTL 350 (350cc twin)	800	1,100	1,600	2,200	2,900	3,600
GTL 500 (496cc twin)	600	900	1,400	1,900	2,500	3,100
750 GT (748cc V-twin)	2,500	5,000	10,000	15,000	20,000	25,000
750 SS Square Case (748cc V-twin)	3,000	6,000	9,000	12,000	15,000	18,000
860 GT (864cc V-twin)	900	1,300	2,000	2,600	3,500	4,400
900 SS (864cc V-twin)	5,000	10,000	15,000	20,000	25,000	30,000
1976						
125 Regolarita (125cc single)	500	700	1,000	1,400	1,900	2,300
GTL 350 (350cc twin)	700	1,100	1,600	2,100	2,800	3,500
GTL 500 (496cc twin)	600	900	1,400	1,900	2,500	3,100
750 SS Square Case (748cc V-twin)	3,000	6,000	9,000	12,000	15,000	18,000
860 GT (864cc V-twin)	900	1,300	2,000	2,600	3,500	4,400
900 GTS (864cc V-twin).	1,200	1,800	2,700	3,600	4,800	6,000
900 SS (864cc V-twin)	5,000	10,000	15,000	20,000	25,000	30,000
1977						
125 Six Days (125cc single)	700	1,100	1,600	2,100	2,800	3,500
GTL 350 (350cc twin)	700	1,100	1,600	2,100	2,800	3,500
Sport Desmo 350 (350cc twin)	700	1,000	1,500	2,000	2,700	3,400
GTL 500 (496cc twin)	600	900	1,350	1,800	2,400	3,000
Sport Desmo 500 (496cc twin)	800	1,100	1,700	2,300	3,000	3,800
750 SS Square Case (748cc V-twin)	3,200	6,000	9,000	12,000	15,000	18,000
Darmah SD (864cc V-twin)	**1,000**	**2,000**	**3,500**	**5,000**	**6,500**	**8,000**

	6	5	4	3	2	1
900 GTS (864cc V-twin)	1,200	1,800	2,700	3,600	4,800	6,000
900 SS (864cc V-twin)	5,000	10,000	15,000	20,000	25,000	30,000
1978						
Sport Desmo 350 (350cc twin)	700	1,000	1,500	2,000	2,700	3,400
Sport Desmo 500 (496cc twin)	800	1,100	1,700	2,300	3,000	3,800
Darmah SD (864cc V-twin)	**1,000**	**2,000**	**3,500**	**5,000**	**6,500**	**8,000**
900 GTS (864cc V-twin)	1,200	1,800	2,700	3,600	4,800	6,000
900 SS (864cc V-twin)	5,000	10,000	15,000	20,000	25,000	30,000
1979						
GTV 350 (350cc twin)	600	1,000	1,400	1,900	2,600	3,200
Sport Desmo 350 (350cc twin)	700	1,000	1,500	2,000	2,700	3,400
GTV 500 (496cc twin)	700	1,100	1,600	2,100	2,800	3,500
Sport Desmo 500 (496cc twin)	800	1,100	1,700	2,300	3,000	3,800
500 SI Pantah (500cc V-twin)	800	1,100	1,700	2,300	3,000	3,800
Darmah SD (864cc V-twin)	1,000	**2,000**	**3,500**	**5,000**	**6,500**	**8,000**
Darmah SD Sport (864cc V-twin)	1,000	2,000	**3,500**	**5,000**	**6,500**	**8,000**
Darmah SS (864cc V-twin)	1,100	1,700	2,600	3,400	4,600	5,700
Mike Hailwood Replica (864cc V-twin)	2,400	4,000	8,000	12,000	16,000	20,000
900 SS (864cc V-twin)	5,000	10,000	15,000	20,000	25,000	30,000
1980						
GTV 350 (350cc twin)	600	1,000	1,400	1,900	2,600	3,200
Sport Desmo 350 (350cc twin)	700	1,000	1,500	2,000	2,700	3,400
GTV 500 (496cc twin)	700	1,100	1,600	2,100	2,800	3,500
Sport Desmo 500 (496cc twin)	800	1,100	1,700	2,300	3,000	3,800
500 SI Pantah (500cc V-twin)	800	1,100	1,700	2,300	3,000	3,800
Darmah SD (864cc V-twin)	1,000	**2,000**	**3,500**	**5,000**	**6,500**	**8,000**
Darmah SD Sport (864cc V-twin)	1,000	2,000	**3,500**	**5,000**	**6,500**	**8,000**
Darmah SS (864cc V-twin)	1,100	1,700	2,600	3,400	4,600	5,700
Mike Hailwood Replica (864cc V-twin)	2,400	4,000	8,000	12,000	16,000	20,000
900 SS (864cc V-twin)	5,000	10,000	15,000	20,000	25,000	30,000
1981						
Pantah (500cc twin)	1,500	2,000	3,000	4,800	6,500	7,500
Darmah (900cc twin)	1,500	2,500	4,000	6,000	7,500	9,000
Darmah SS (900cc twin)	2,000	3,000	4,500	5,900	7,900	9,000
Super Sport (900cc twin)	2,400	3,600	5,200	6,550	8,800	10,000
1982						
Pantah (500cc twin)	1,500	2,500	4,000	5,300	7,100	8,500
Darmah (900cc twin)	2,400	3,200	4,200	5,600	7,500	8,700
Darmah SS (900cc twin)	2,000	3,000	4,500	6,100	8,200	9,200
Super Sport (900cc twin)	2,200	3,400	5,000	6,700	9,000	12,000
1986						
F1-S Road Racer (750cc twin)	2,200	2,800	3,500	4,700	6,300	8,000
F1 Montjuich (750cc twin) (200)	3,500	7,000	1,400	21,000	28,000	35,000
1987						
Indiana (650cc twin)	1,100	1,600	2,200	2,900	3,600	4,300
Paso (750cc twin)	1,100	1,600	2,200	2,850	4,700	6,400
F1-B Road Racer (750cc twin)	1,400	2,400	3,800	5,000	6,700	7,500
Laguna Seca (750 cc twin) (200)	3,500	7,000	1,400	21,000	28,000	35,000
Desmo (750 cc twin) (134)	2,000	4,000	8,000	12,000	16,000	20,000
1988						
Paso (750cc twin)	1,200	1,800	2,300	3,000	4,800	6,700
Paso Limited (750cc twin)	1,200	1,800	2,400	3,100	5,100	7,200
F1-A Desmo (750cc twin)	2,000	4,000	8,000	12,000	16,000	20,000
F1-B Road Racer (750cc twin)	1,500	2,500	4,000	5,300	7,100	8,500
851 Tricolore (850cc twin)	4,000	8,000	16,000	24,000	32,000	40,000
1990						
750 Sport (750cc twin)	1,400	2,000	2,800	3,700	5,000	6,700
851 Sport (850cc twin)	**2,500**	**5,000**	**10,000**	**15,000**	**20,000**	**25,000**
906 Paso (900cc twin)	1,300	1,900	2,600	3,500	5,100	7,800

	6	5	4	3	2	1
1991						
851 Sport (850cc twin)	**2,500**	**5,000**	**10,000**	**15,000**	**20,000**	**25,000**
900 Super Sport (900cc twin)	1,600	2,200	3,000	3,900	5,900	7,900
907 Paso I.E. (900cc twin)	2,000	2,600	3,300	4,400	5,500	8,700
1992						
750SS (750cc twin)	1,500	2,100	2,700	3,600	5,400	7,400
851 Sport (850cc twin)	**2,500**	**5,000**	**10,000**	**15,000**	**20,000**	**25,000**
900 Super Sport (900cc twin)	1,900	2,500	3,200	4,200	6,300	8,500
907 Paso I.E. (900cc twin)	2,200	2,800	3,500	4,600	6,700	9,000
1993						
750SS (750cc twin)	1,700	2,300	2,900	3,800	5,500	7,500
888SPO (888cc twin)	2,500	4,200	6,300	8,400	10,500	13,000
900 Super Light (900cc twin)	2,000	3,400	5,200	7,000	8,800	11,000
900 Super Sport (900cc twin)	1,900	2,500	3,400	4,500	6,400	8,600
907 Paso I.E. (900cc twin)	2,300	2,900	3,700	5,000	7,000	9,300
M900 (900cc twin).	1,500	2,200	3,000	3,900	4,900	5,900
1994						
888 LTD (888cc twin)	800	1,200	2,100	4,300	6,300	9,100
900 CR (900cc twin)	200	500	1,400	2,900	4,300	5,700
900 SP (900cc twin)	300	600	1,600	3,300	4,900	6,500
E900 (900cc twin)	300	600	1,500	3,000	4,500	6,000
M900 (900cc twin)	1,500	2,200	3,000	3,900	4,900	5,900
916 (916cc twin)	600	900	2,600	5,300	7,800	10,300
1995						
E900 (900cc twin)	600	1,300	2,400	3,500	4,600	5,700
900 CR (900cc twin)	500	1,000	2,100	3,200	4,300	5,400
M900 (900cc twin)	600	1,200	2,300	3,400	4,500	5,600
900 SP (900cc twin)	700	1,300	2,500	3,700	4,900	6,100
916 (916cc twin)	800	1,600	3,300	5,000	6,700	8,000
1996						
900 CR (900cc twin)	500	1,000	2,100	3,200	4,300	5,400
M900 (900cc twin)	600	1,200	2,300	3,400	4,500	5,600
900 SP (900cc twin)	700	1,300	2,500	3,700	4,900	6,100
916 (916cc twin)	800	1,600	3,300	5,000	6,700	8,000
EXCELSIOR						
1907						
Single	15,000	20,000	26,000	35,000	45,000	55,000
1910						
Single	5,000	10,000	15,000	25,000	35,000	45,000
1911						
Single	10,000	20,000	30,000	40,000	50,000	60,000
Auto-Cycle	10,000	20,000	30,000	50,000	70,000	90,000
30.5 Twin	5,000	10,000	15,000	20,000	26,000	35,000
1913						
Big Valve Twin	15,000	25,000	35,000	50,000	60,000	70,000
Model 4C	15,000	20,000	25,000	30,000	35,000	40,000
1914						
Single	5,000	10,000	20,000	35,000	50,000	65,000
Short Coupled V-Twin	5,000	10,000	20,000	30,000	40,000	50,000
Twin	10,000	20,000	40,000	60,000	80,000	100K
Auto-Cycle	5,000	10,000	15,000	20,000	26,000	35,000
1915						
Twin	5,000	10,000	20,000	30,000	40,000	50,000
1916						
Super X Twin	25,000	35,000	45,000	55,000	70,000	90,000
1917						
Super X Twin	25,000	35,000	45,000	55,000	70,000	90,000
1918						
V-Twin	10,000	15,000	20,000	25,000	30,000	40,000

	6	5	4	3	2	1
1919						
Model 19	5,000	10,000	15,000	20,000	26,000	35,000
1920						
Big Valve Twin	5,000	10,000	20,000	30,000	40,000	50,000
1925						
Ladys Model.	3,000	6,000	10,000	15,000	20,000	25,000
1926						
Super X	4,000	8,000	16,000	24,000	32,000	40,000
1927						
Super X	4,000	8,000	16,000	24,000	32,000	40,000
1928						
Super X	4,000	8,000	16,000	24,000	32,000	40,000
1929						
Super X	10,000	20,000	35,000	50,000	65,000	80,000
1930						
Super X Streamliner.	10,000	20,000	35,000	50,000	65,000	80,000
1931						
Super X Super Sport	10,000	20,000	35,000	50,000	65,000	80,000
1938						
Manxman	3,000	6,000	10,000	15,000	20,000	25,000
1943						
Welbike	1,000	2,000	4,000	6,000	8,000	10,000
1956						
Courier (147cc)	300	600	1,200	1,800	2,400	3,000
GAS GAS						
1991						
Delta GT25 (238cc single).	100	200	400	700	1,000	1,300
Delta GT32 (327cc single).	100	200	400	700	1,000	1,300
1992						
Contact GT25 (238cc single)	100	200	400	800	1,100	1,400
Contact GT32 (327cc single)	100	200	400	800	1,100	1,400
1993						
Contact GT12 (124cc single)	100	200	500	800	1,100	1,600
Contact GT16 (143cc single)	100	200	400	900	1,200	1,500
Contact GT25 (238cc single)	100	200	500	900	1,300	1,700
Contact GT32 (327cc single)	100	200	500	900	1,300	1,700
1994						
Endurocross TT80 (80cc single).	100	300	500	700	900	1,300
Motocross TT80 (80cc single).	100	200	600	800	1,000	1,400
Endurocross TT125 (125cc single) . . .	100	200	400	800	1,200	1,700
Motocross TT125 (125cc single)	100	300	600	900	1,400	1,900
Contact GT16 (143cc single)	100	200	400	900	1,300	1,700
Contact GT25 JT (238cc single).	100	200	500	900	1,400	1,900
Endurocross TT250 (250cc single) . . .	100	200	600	1,100	1,700	2,300
Motocross TT250 (250cc single)	200	500	800	1,100	1,600	2,100
Contact GT32 JT (328cc single).	100	200	500	900	1,400	1,900
1995						
Endurocross TT80 (80cc single).	100	200	300	500	1,000	1,400
Cross CR125 (124cc single)	100	300	600	900	1,400	1,900
Endurocross TT124 (125cc single) . . .	100	300	600	800	1,300	1,800
Contact JT16 (144cc single).	100	300	600	900	1,300	1,800
Contact JT25 (238cc single).	100	300	600	900	1,300	1,800
Cross CR250 (249cc single)	200	500	800	1,100	1,700	2,300
Endurocross TT250 (250cc single) . . .	100	300	600	1,100	1,600	2,100
Contact JT32 (327cc single).	100	300	600	900	1,300	1,800
GREEVES						
1960						
Trials	1,500	3,000	4,000	5,000	6,000	7,000
24TCS.	300	600	1,200	1,800	2,400	3,000

	6	5	4	3	2	1
1962						
MC5.	1,000	2,000	3,000	4,000	5,000	6,000
1964						
Trials (250cc)	1,000	2,000	3,000	4,000	5,000	6,000
1965						
Challenger MX2 (246cc).	1,000	2,000	3,000	5,000	7,000	9,000
1966						
250cc	750	1,400	2,000	3,000	4,500	6,000
1967						
Challenger MX4 (362cc).	700	1,400	2,400	3,400	5,400	6,500
1969						
Ranger	1,500	3,000	4,000	5,000	6,000	7,000
1970						
250 Desert	1,200	1,700	2,300	3,100	4,800	6,500
250 Moto Cross	1,600	2,100	2,800	3,700	5,800	8,000
380 Desert	1,100	1,600	2,100	2,800	4,400	7,000
380 Moto Cross	2,100	2,900	3,900	5,200	8,100	10,000
1971						
250 Desert	1,200	1,700	2,300	3,100	4,800	6,500
250 Moto Cross	1,600	2,100	2,800	3,700	5,800	8,000
380 Desert	1,100	1,600	2,100	2,800	4,400	7,000
380 Moto Cross	2,100	2,900	3,900	5,200	8,100	10,000
1972						
250 Desert	1,200	1,700	2,300	3,100	4,800	6,500
250 Moto Cross	1,600	2,100	2,800	3,700	5,800	8,000
380 Desert	1,100	1,600	2,100	2,800	4,400	7,000
380 Moto Cross	2,100	2,900	3,900	5,200	8,100	10,000
1973						
250 Desert	1,200	1,700	2,300	3,100	4,800	6,500
250 Moto Cross	1,600	2,100	2,800	3,700	5,800	8,000
380 Desert	1,100	1,600	2,100	2,800	4,400	7,000
380 Moto Cross	2,100	2,900	3,900	5,200	8,100	10,000
1974						
250 Desert	1,200	1,700	2,300	3,100	4,800	6,500
250 Moto Cross	1,600	2,100	2,800	3,700	5,800	8,000
380 Desert	1,100	1,600	2,100	2,800	4,400	7,000
380 Moto Cross	2,100	2,900	3,900	5,200	8,100	10,000
1975						
250 Desert	1,200	1,700	2,300	3,100	4,800	6,500
250 Griffon	900	1,400	1,900	2,500	3,900	5,300
380 Desert	1,100	1,600	2,100	2,800	4,400	7,000
380 Griffon	1,400	2,000	3,500	5,000	6,500	8,000

HARLEY-DAVIDSON

	6	5	4	3	2	1
1903						
Single (24.74ci) (3)	3,000K	4,500K	6,000K	9,000K	12,000K	15,000K
1904						
Model 0 (24.74ci) (8)	1,000K	1,500K	2,000K	3,000K	4,000K	5,000K
1905						
Model 1 (24.74ci) (16).	500K	750K	1,000K	1,500K	2,000K	2,500K
1906						
Model 2 (24.74 ci) (50)	270K	360K	480K	720K	990K	1,200K
1907						
Model 3 (24.74ci) (150)	90,000	120K	160K	240K	330K	420K
1908						
Model 4 (26.8ci) (450)	29,000	39,000	52,000	79,000	113K	140K
1909						
5 Single (30ci) (864).	18,000	28,000	40,000	58,000	88,000	120K
5A Single (30ci) (54)	20,000	30,000	42,000	69,000	100K	130K
5B Single (30ci) (168).	18,000	28,000	40,000	58,000	88,000	120K
5C Single (35ci) (36)	20,000	30,000	42,000	69,000	100K	130K
5D Single (50ci) (27)	20,000	30,000	42,000	69,000	100K	130K

	6	5	4	3	2	1
1910						
6 Single (35ci) (2,302).	10,000	15,000	24,000	38,000	62,000	85,000
6A Single (35ci) (334)	10,000	15,000	24,000	38,000	62,000	85,000
6B Single (35ci) (443)	10,000	15,000	24,000	38,000	62,000	85,000
6C Single (35ci) (88)	10,000	15,000	24,000	38,000	62,000	85,000
1911						
7 Single (35ci).	9,000	14,000	21,000	31,000	47,000	60,000
7A Single (35ci)	9,000	14,000	21,000	31,000	47,000	60,000
7B Single (35ci)	9,000	14,000	21,000	31,000	47,000	60,000
7C Single (35ci)	9,000	14,000	21,000	31,000	47,000	60,000
7D Twin (49.48ci)	**25,000**	**50,000**	**100K**	**150K**	**200K**	**260K**
1912						
8 Single (35ci).	8,000	12,000	19,000	27,000	41,000	55,000
8A Single (35ci)	8,000	12,000	19,000	27,000	41,000	55,000
8D Twin (49.48ci)	12,000	19,000	33,000	48,000	70,000	90,000
X8 Twin (49.48ci)	11,000	15,000	21,000	31,000	47,000	60,000
X8A Single (35ci)	−10,000	−15,000	**30,000**	**45,000**	**60,000**	**75,000**
X8D Twin (49.48ci)	15,000	21,000	31,000	47,000	68,000	90,000
X8E Twin (61ci)	14,000	20,000	33,000	47,000	76,000	95,000
1913						
9A Single (35ci) (1,510)	7,000	11,000	16,000	24,000	38,000	50,000
9B Single (35ci) (4,601)	7,000	10,000	25,000	40,000	55,000	70,000
9E Twin (61ci) (6,732).	13,000	19,000	29,000	40,000	63,000	85,000
9F Twin (61ci) (49)	29,000	39,000	52,000	79,000	113K	140K
9G Delivery Twin (61ci)	13,000	19,000	29,000	40,000	63,000	85,000
1914						
10A Single (35ci) (316)	12,000	17,000	23,000	35,000	56,000	75,000
10B Single (35ci) (2,034)	8,000	15,000	25,000	35,000	45,000	55,000
10C Single (35ci) (877)	7,000	10,000	15,000	21,000	34,000	45,000
10E Twin (61ci) (5,055)	12,000	17,000	23,000	35,000	56,000	75,000
10F Twin (61ci) (7,956)	12,000	**20,000**	**40,000**	**60,000**	**80,000**	**105K**
10G Twin (61ci) (171)	29,000	39,000	52,000	79,000	113K	140K
1915						
11B Single (35ci) (670)	7,000	11,000	15,000	22,000	38,000	55,000
11C Single (35ci) (545)	7,000	11,000	15,000	22,000	38,000	55,000
11E Twin (61cici) (1,275)	9,000	12,000	18,000	27,000	43,000	60,000
11F Twin (61ci) (985)	10,000	**20,000**	**40,000**	**60,000**	**80,000**	**100K**
11G Twin (61ci) (93)	10,000	13,000	20,000	31,000	54,000	75,000
11H Twin (61ci) (140)	10,000	13,000	20,000	31,000	54,000	75,000
11J Twin (61ci) (1,719)	11,000	14,000	21,000	32,000	55,000	75,000
1916						
B Single (35ci) (292)	7,000	11,000	15,000	21,000	34,000	45,000
C Single (35ci) (862)	7,000	11,000	15,000	21,000	34,000	45,000
E Twin (61ci) (252)	9,000	12,000	17,000	28,000	45,000	60,000
F Twin (61ci) (9496).	10,000	13,000	19,000	31,000	48,000	65,000
J Twin (61ci) (5898)	10,000	14,000	19,000	31,000	48,000	65,000
1917						
B Single (35ci) (124)	4,000	6,000	7,000	12,000	23,000	35,000
C Single (35ci) (605)	4,000	6,000	7,000	12,000	23,000	35,000
E Twin (61ci) (68)	4,000	7,000	10,000	20,000	34,000	45,000
F Twin (61ci) (8,527)	4,000	7,000	10,000	20,000	34,000	45,000
J Twin (61ci) (9,180)	**5,000**	**10,000**	**20,000**	**35,000**	**50,000**	**65,000**
1918						
B Single (35ci) (19)	4,000	6,000	7,000	12,000	22,000	32,000
C Single (35ci) (251)	4,000	6,000	7,000	12,000	22,000	32,000
E Twin (61ci) (5).	4,000	7,000	10,000	20,000	34,000	45,000
F Twin (61ci) (11,764).	4,000	7,000	10,000	20,000	34,000	45,000
J Twin (61ci) (6,571)	4,000	7,000	10,000	20,000	34,000	45,000
1919						
F Twin (61ci) (5,064)	4,000	6,000	9,000	16,000	29,000	40,000

	6	5	4	3	2	1
J Twin (61ci) (9,941)	4,000	6,000	10,000	16,000	30,000	45,000
W Twin (35.64 ci)	4,000	6,000	10,000	16,000	30,000	45,000
1920						
WF (35.64ci twin) (4,459)	4,800	7,200	11,000	14,000	19,000	24,000
WJ (35.64ci twin) (810)	4,800	7,200	11,000	14,000	19,000	24,000
F (60.34ci V-twin) (7,579)	5,000	7,500	11,000	15,000	20,000	25,000
FS (60.34ci V-twin)	5,000	7,500	11,000	15,000	20,000	25,000
J (60.34ci V-twin) (14,192)	10,000	15,000	20,000	25,000	30,000	35,000
JS (60.34ci V-twin)	5,000	7,500	11,000	15,000	20,000	25,000
1921						
WF (35.64ci twin) (1,100)	4,400	6,600	9,900	13,000	18,000	22,000
WJ (35.64ci twin) (823)	4,400	6,600	9,900	13,000	18,000	22,000
CD (37ci single)	4,400	6,600	9,900	13,000	18,000	22,000
F (60.34ci V-twin) (2,413)	5,000	7,500	11,000	15,000	20,000	25,000
FS (60.34ci V-twin)	5,000	7,500	11,000	15,000	20,000	25,000
J (60.34ci V-twin) (4,526)	10,000	15,000	20,000	25,000	30,000	35,000
JS (60.34ci V-twin)	5,000	7,500	11,000	15,000	20,000	25,000
FD (74ci V-twin) (277).	5,100	7,600	15,000	20,000	25,000	30,000
FDS (74ci V-twin)	5,100	7,600	11,000	15,000	20,000	26,000
JD (74ci V-twin) (2,321)	6,000	10,000	14,000	18,000	23,000	28,000
JDS (74ci V-twin)	5,100	7,600	11,000	15,000	20,000	26,000
1922						
WF (35.64ci twin)	4,400	6,600	9,900	13,000	18,000	22,000
WJ (35.64ci twin) (455)	4,400	6,600	9,900	13,000	18,000	22,000
CD (37ci single) (39)	4,400	6,600	9,900	13,000	18,000	22,000
F (60.34ci V-twin) (1,824)	4,600	6,900	10,000	14,000	18,000	23,000
FS (60.34ci V-twin)	4,600	6,900	10,000	14,000	18,000	23,000
J (60.34ci V-twin) (3,183)	10,000	15,000	20,000	25,000	30,000	35,000
JS (60.34ci V-twin)	4,600	6,900	10,000	14,000	18,000	23,000
FD (74ci V-twin) (909).	5,000	7,500	11,000	15,000	20,000	25,000
FDS (74ci V-twin)	5,000	7,500	11,000	15,000	20,000	25,000
JD (74ci V-twin) (3,988)	6,000	10,000	14,000	18,000	23,000	28,000
JDS (74ci V-twin)	5,000	7,500	11,000	15,000	20,000	25,000
1923						
WF (35.64ci twin) (614)	4,400	6,600	9,900	13,000	18,000	22,000
WJ (35.64ci twin) (481)	4,400	6,600	9,900	13,000	18,000	22,000
F (60.34ci V-twin) (2,822)	4,600	6,900	10,000	14,000	18,000	23,000
FS (60.34ci V-twin)	4,600	6,900	10,000	14,000	18,000	23,000
J (60.34ci V-twin) (4,802)	10,000	15,000	20,000	25,000	30,000	35,000
JS (60.34ci V-twin)	5,000	7,500	12,500	15,000	20,000	25,000
FD (74ci V-twin) (869).	5,000	7,500	11,000	15,000	20,000	25,000
FDS (74ci V-twin)	5,000	7,500	11,000	15,000	20,000	25,000
JD (74ci V-twin) (7,458)	6,000	10,000	14,000	18,000	23,000	28,000
JDS (74ci V-twin)	5,000	7,500	11,000	15,000	20,000	25,000
1924						
FE (60.34ci V-twin)	3,800	5,700	8,600	11,000	15,000	19,000
FES (60.34ci V-twin)	3,800	5,700	8,600	11,000	15,000	19,000
JE (60.34ci V-twin)	4,200	6,300	11,000	15,000	19,000	23,000
JES (60.34ci V-twin).	4,200	6,300	9,500	13,000	17,000	21,000
FD (74ci V-twin)	4,000	6,000	9,000	12,000	16,000	20,000
FDS (74ci V-twin)	4,000	6,000	9,000	12,000	16,000	20,000
FDCA (74ci V-twin)	4,000	6,000	9,000	12,000	16,000	20,000
FDSCA (74ci V-twin)	4,000	6,000	9,000	12,000	16,000	20,000
FDCB (74ci V-twin)	4,000	6,000	9,000	12,000	16,000	20,000
JD (74ci V-twin)	4,600	6,900	10,000	14,000	18,000	23,000
JDS (74ci V-twin)	4,600	6,900	10,000	14,000	18,000	23,000
JDCA (74ci V-twin)	4,600	6,900	10,000	14,000	18,000	23,000
JDSCA (74ci V-twin)	4,600	6,900	10,000	14,000	18,000	23,000
JDCB (74ci V-twin)	4,600	6,900	10,000	14,000	18,000	23,000

	6	5	4	3	2	1
1925						
FE (60.34ci V-twin)	3,800	5,700	8,600	11,000	15,000	19,000
FES (60.34ci V-twin)	3,800	5,700	8,600	11,000	15,000	19,000
JE (60.34ci V-twin)	4,200	6,300	9,500	13,000	17,000	21,000
JES 60.34ci V-twin)	4,200	6,300	9,500	13,000	17,000	21,000
FDCB (74ci V-twin)	4,000	6,000	9,000	12,000	16,000	20,000
FDCBS (74ci V-twin)	4,000	6,000	9,000	12,000	16,000	20,000
JDCB (74ci V-twin)	**5,000**	**7,000**	**14,000**	**21,000**	**28,000**	**35,000**
JDCBS (74ci/V-twin)	4,600	6,900	10,000	14,000	18,000	23,000
1926						
A (21.35ci single)	3,200	4,800	7,200	9,600	13,000	16,000
B (21.35ci single)	–3,000	**6,000**	**9,000**	**12,000**	**15,000**	18,000
AA (21.35ci single)	4,000	6,000	9,000	12,000	16,000	20,000
BA (21.35ci single)	4,000	6,000	9,000	12,000	16,000	20,000
S (21.35ci single)	4,400	6,600	9,900	13,000	18,000	22,000
J (60.34ci V-twin)	4,600	6,900	10,000	14,000	18,000	23,000
JS (60.34ci V-twin)	4,600	6,900	10,000	14,000	18,000	23,000
JD (74ci V-twin)	4,600	6,900	10,000	14,000	18,000	23,000
JDS (74ci V-twin)	4,600	6,900	10,000	14,000	18,000	23,000
1927						
A (21.35ci single)	3,200	4,800	7,200	9,600	13,000	16,000
B (21.35ci single)	–3,000	**6,000**	**9,000**	**12,000**	**15,000**	**18,000**
AA (21.35ci single)	3,900	5,900	8,800	12,000	16,000	20,000
BA (21.35ci single)	4,000	6,000	9,000	12,000	16,000	20,000
S (21.35ci single)	4,400	6,600	9,900	13,000	18,000	22,000
J (60.34ci V-twin)	4,600	6,900	10,000	14,000	18,000	23,000
JS (60.34ci V-twin)	4,600	6,900	10,000	14,000	18,000	23,000
JD (74ci V-twin)	4,600	6,900	10,000	14,000	18,000	23,000
JDS (74ci V-twin)	4,600	6,900	10,000	14,000	18,000	23,000
1928						
B (21.35ci single)	3,000	**6,000**	**9,000**	**12,000**	**15,000**	**18,000**
BA (21.35ci single)	3,800	5,700	**10,000**	**15,000**	**20,000**	**25,000**
J (60.34ci V-twin)	4,600	6,900	10,000	14,000	18,000	23,000
JS (60.34ci V-twin)	4,600	6,900	10,000	14,000	18,000	23,000
JL (60.34ci V-twin)	5,000	7,500	11,000	15,000	20,000	25,000
JH (60.34ci V-twin)	8,400	13,000	19,000	25,000	34,000	42,000
JD (74ci V-twin)	4,600	6,900	10,000	14,000	18,000	23,000
JDS (74ci V-twin)	4,600	6,900	10,000	14,000	18,000	23,000
JDL (74ci V-twin)	5,000	7,500	11,000	15,000	20,000	25,000
JDH (74ci V-twin)	**10,000**	**20,000**	**40,000**	**60,000**	**80,000**	–10,000
1929						
B (21.35ci single)	3,000	4,500	6,800	9,000	12,000	15,000
BA (21.35ci single)	3,800	5,700	8,600	11,000	15,000	19,000
C (30.50ci single)	3,400	5,100	7,700	10,000	14,000	17,000
D (45ci V-twin)	3,800	**7,000**	**14,000**	**21,000**	**28,000**	**35,000**
DL (45ci V-twin)	4,000	6,000	10,000	15,000	20,000	25,000
J (60.34ci V-twin)	4,600	6,900	10,000	14,000	18,000	23,000
JS (60.34ci V-twin)	4,600	6,900	10,000	14,000	18,000	23,000
JH 60.34ci V-twin)	8,400	13,000	19,000	25,000	34,000	42,000
JD 74ci V-twin)	4,600	6,900	10,000	14,000	18,000	23,000
JDS (74ci V-twin)	4,600	6,900	10,000	14,000	18,000	23,000
JDH (74ci V-twin)	10,000	20,000	30,000	40,000	50,000	60,000
1930						
B (21.35ci single)	**3,000**	**6,000**	**9,000**	**12,000**	**15,000**	**18,000**
C (30.50ci single)	2,800	4,200	6,300	8,400	11,000	14,000
D (45ci V-twin)	3,800	5,700	8,600	11,000	15,000	19,000
DS (45ci V-twin)	3,800	5,700	8,600	11,000	15,000	19,000
DL (45ci V-twin)	4,000	6,000	10,000	15,000	20,000	25,000
DLD (45ci V-twin)	4,000	6,000	9,000	12,000	16,000	20,000
V (74ci V-twin)	4,400	**8,000**	**16,000**	**24,000**	**32,000**	**40,000**

	6	5	4	3	2	1
VL (74ci V-twin)	5,000	10,000	15,000	21,000	28,000	35,000
VS (74ci V-twin)	4,400	6,600	9,900	13,000	18,000	22,000
VC (74ci V-twin)	4,400	6,600	9,900	13,000	18,000	22,000
1931						
C (30.50ci single)	2,800	4,200	6,300	8,400	11,000	14,000
D (45ci V-twin)	3,400	5,100	7,700	10,000	14,000	17,000
DS (45ci V-twin)	3,400	5,100	7,700	10,000	14,000	17,000
DL (45ci V-twin)	3,600	5,400	10,000	15,000	20,000	25,000
DLD (45ci V-twin)	3,700	5,600	8,300	11,000	15,000	19,000
V (74ci V-twin)	4,400	6,600	9,900	13,000	18,000	22,000
VS (74ci V-twin)	4,400	6,600	9,900	13,000	18,000	22,000
VL (74ci V-twin)	4,800	7,200	**14,000**	**21,000**	**28,000**	**35,000**
VC (74ci V-twin)	4,000	6,000	9,000	12,000	16,000	20,000
1932						
B (21.35ci single)	**3,000**	**6,000**	**9,000**	**12,000**	**15,000**	**18,000**
C (30.50ci single)	2,800	4,200	6,300	8,400	11,000	14,000
R (45ci V-twin)	2,600	3,900	5,900	7,800	10,000	13,000
RS (45ci V-twin)	2,600	3,900	5,900	7,800	10,000	13,000
RL (45ci V-twin)	2,700	4,100	6,100	8,100	11,000	14,000
RLD (45ci V-twin)	3,000	4,500	6,800	9,000	12,000	15,000
G Servi-Car (45ci V-twin)	2,000	4,000	8,000	12,000	16,000	20,000
GA Servi-Car (45ci V-twin)	2,000	4,000	8,000	12,000	16,000	20,000
GD Servi-Car (45ci V-twin)	2,000	4,000	8,000	12,000	16,000	20,000
GE Servi-Car (45ci V-twin)	2,000	4,000	8,000	12,000	16,000	20,000
V (74ci V-twin)	4,400	6,600	9,900	13,000	18,000	22,000
VS (74ci V-twin)	4,400	6,600	9,900	13,000	18,000	22,000
VL (74ci V-twin)	4,800	7,200	**14,000**	**21,000**	**28,000**	**35,000**
VC (74ci V-twin)	4,000	6,000	9,000	12,000	16,000	20,000
1933						
B (21.35ci single)	**3,000**	**6,000**	**9,000**	**12,000**	**15,000**	**18,000**
C (30.50ci single)	2,800	4,200	6,300	8,400	11,000	14,000
CB (30.50ci single)	2,800	4,200	6,300	8,400	11,000	14,000
R (45ci V-twin)	2,800	4,200	6,300	8,400	11,000	14,000
RS (45ci V-twin)	2,800	4,200	6,300	8,400	11,000	14,000
RL (45ci V-twin)	3,000	4,500	6,800	9,000	12,000	15,000
RLD (45ci V-twin)	3,000	4,500	6,800	9,000	12,000	15,000
G Servi-Car (45ci V-twin)	2,000	4,000	8,000	12,000	16,000	20,000
GA Servi-Car (45ci V-twin)	2,000	4,000	8,000	12,000	16,000	20,000
GD Servi-Car (45ci V-twin)	2,000	4,000	8,000	12,000	16,000	20,000
GDT Servi-Car (45ci V-twin)	2,000	4,000	8,000	12,000	16,000	20,000
GE Servi-Car (45ci V-twin)	2,000	4,000	8,000	12,000	16,000	20,000
V (74ci V-twin)	4,400	6,600	9,900	13,000	18,000	22,000
VS (74ci V-twin)	4,400	6,600	9,900	13,000	18,000	22,000
VL (74ci V-twin)	4,800	7,200	11,000	14,000	19,000	24,000
VLD (74ci V-twin)	4,900	7,400	11,000	15,000	20,000	25,000
VC (74ci V-twin)	4,200	6,300	9,500	13,000	17,000	21,000
1934						
B (21.35ci single)	**3,000**	**6,000**	**9,000**	**12,000**	**15,000**	**18,000**
C (30.50ci single)	2,800	4,200	6,300	8,400	11,000	14,000
CB (30.50ci single)	2,800	4,200	6,300	8,400	11,000	14,000
R (45ci V-twin)	2,800	4,200	6,300	8,400	11,000	14,000
RL (45ci V-twin)	3,000	4,500	6,800	9,000	12,000	15,000
RLD (45ci V-twin)	3,300	5,000	7,400	9,900	13,000	17,000
G Servi-Car (45ci V-twin)	2,000	4,000	8,000	12,000	16,000	20,000
GA Servi-Car (45ci V-twin)	2,000	4,000	8,000	12,000	16,000	20,000
GD Servi-Car (45ci V-twin)	2,000	4,000	8,000	12,000	16,000	20,000
GDT Servi-Car (74ci V-twin)	2,000	4,000	8,000	12,000	16,000	20,000
GE Servi-Car (74ci V-twin)	2,000	4,000	8,000	12,000	16,000	20,000
VLD (74ci V-twin)	4,400	6,600	9,900	13,000	18,000	22,000
VD (74ci V-twin)	3,800	5,700	8,600	11,000	15,000	19,000

	6	5	4	3	2	1
VDS (74ci V-twin)	3,800	5,700	8,600	11,000	15,000	19,000
VFDS (74ci V-twin)	4,000	6,000	**10,000**	**14,000**	**18,000**	**22,000**
1935						
R (45ci V-twin)	2,600	3,900	5,900	7,800	10,000	13,000
RL (45ci V-twin)	3,000	4,500	6,800	9,000	12,000	15,000
RS (45ci V-twin)	2,600	3,900	5,900	7,800	10,000	13,000
RLD (45ci V-twin)	3,000	4,500	6,800	9,000	12,000	15,000
RLDR (45ci V-twin)	3,200	4,800	7,200	9,600	13,000	16,000
G Servi-Car (45ci V-twin)	2,000	4,000	8,000	12,000	16,000	20,000
GA Servi-Car (45ci V-twin)	2,000	4,000	8,000	12,000	16,000	20,000
GD Servi-Car (45ci V-twin)	2,000	4,000	8,000	12,000	16,000	20,000
GDT Servi-Car (45ci V-twin)	2,000	4,000	8,000	12,000	16,000	20,000
GE Servi-Car (45ci V-twin)	2,000	4,000	8,000	12,000	16,000	20,000
VD (74ci V-twin)	3,800	5,700	8,600	11,000	15,000	19,000
VDS (74ci V-twin)	3,800	5,700	8,600	11,000	15,000	19,000
VLD (74ci V-twin)	4,400	6,600	9,900	13,000	18,000	22,000
VLDJ (74ci V-twin)	5,000	7,500	11,000	15,000	20,000	25,000
VLDD (80ci V-twin)	5,000	7,500	11,000	15,000	20,000	25,000
VLDS (80ci V-twin)	5,000	7,500	11,000	15,000	20,000	25,000
1936						
R (45ci V-twin)	2,600	3,900	5,900	7,800	10,000	13,000
RL (45ci V-twin)	3,000	4,500	6,800	9,000	12,000	15,000
RLD (45ci V-twin)	3,200	4,800	7,200	9,600	13,000	16,000
RLDR (45ci V-twin)	3,200	4,800	7,200	9,600	13,000	16,000
RS (45ci V-twin)	2,600	3,900	5,900	7,800	10,000	13,000
G Servi-Car (45ci V-twin)	2,000	4,000	8,000	12,000	16,000	20,000
GA Servi-Car (45ci V-twin)	2,000	4,000	8,000	12,000	16,000	20,000
GD Servi-Car (45ci V-twin)	2,000	4,000	8,000	12,000	16,000	20,000
GDT Servi-Car (45ci V-twin)	2,000	4,000	8,000	12,000	16,000	20,000
GE Servi-Car (45ci V-twin)	2,000	4,000	8,000	12,000	16,000	20,000
E (61ci V-twin)	9,400	14,000	21,000	28,000	38,000	47,000
ES (61ci V-twin)	9,400	14,000	21,000	28,000	38,000	47,000
EL (61ci V-twin)	**15,000**	**25,000**	**45,000**	**85,000**	**125K**	**165K**
VD (74ci V-twin)	4,000	6,000	9,000	12,000	16,000	20,000
VDS (74ci V-twin)	4,000	6,000	9,000	12,000	16,000	20,000
VLD (74ci V-twin)	4,500	6,800	10,000	14,000	18,000	23,000
VLH (80ci V-twin)	4,800	7,200	11,000	14,000	19,000	24,000
VHS (80ci V-twin)	4,800	7,200	11,000	14,000	19,000	24,000
1937						
W (45ci V-twin)	2,400	3,600	5,400	7,200	9,600	12,000
WS (45ci V-twin)	2,400	3,600	5,400	7,200	9,600	12,000
WL (45ci V-twin)	2,700	4,100	6,100	8,100	11,000	14,000
WLD (45ci V-twin)	3,000	4,500	**8,000**	**12,000**	**16,000**	**20,000**
WLDR (45ci V-twin)	3,400	5,100	**8,000**	**12,000**	**16,000**	**20,000**
G Servi-Car (45ci V-twin)	2,000	4,000	8,000	12,000	16,000	20,000
GA Servi-Car (45ci V-twin)	2,000	4,000	8,000	12,000	16,000	20,000
GD Servi-Car (45ci V-twin)	2,000	4,000	8,000	12,000	16,000	20,000
GDT Servi-Car (45ci V-twin)	2,000	4,000	8,000	12,000	16,000	20,000
GE Servi-Car (45ci V-twin)	2,000	4,000	8,000	12,000	16,000	20,000
E (61ci V-twin)	8,000	12,000	18,000	24,000	32,000	40,000
ES (61ci V-twin)	8,000	12,000	18,000	24,000	32,000	40,000
EL (61ci V-twin)	**10,000**	**20,000**	**30,000**	**40,000**	**50,000**	**60,000**
U (74ci V-twin)	4,400	6,600	9,900	13,000	18,000	22,000
US (74ci V-twin)	4,400	6,600	9,900	13,000	18,000	22,000
UL (74ci V-twin)	5,100	10,000	15,000	20,000	25,000	30,000
UH (80ci V-twin)	4,400	6,600	9,900	13,000	18,000	22,000
UHS (80ci V-twin)	4,400	6,600	9,900	13,000	18,000	22,000
ULH (80ci V-twin)	5,000	**8,000**	**12,000**	**18,000**	**24,000**	**30,000**
1938						
WL (45ci V-twin)	3,000	4,500	6,800	9,000	12,000	15,000

	6	5	4	3	2	1
WLD (45ci V-twin).	3,400	5,100	**8,000**	**12,000**	**16,000**	**20,000**
WLDR (45ci V-twin).	3,400	5,100	**8,000**	**12,000**	**16,000**	**20,000**
G Servi-Car (45ci V-twin)	2,000	4,000	8,000	12,000	16,000	20,000
GA Servi-Car (45ci V-twin)	2,000	4,000	8,000	12,000	16,000	20,000
GD Servi-Car (45ci V-twin)	2,000	4,000	8,000	12,000	16,000	20,000
GDT Servi-Car (45ci V-twin).	2,000	4,000	8,000	12,000	16,000	20,000
EL (61ci V-twin)	**10,000**	**20,000**	**30,000**	**40,000**	**50,000**	**60,000**
ES (61ci V-twin)	8,000	12,000	18,000	24,000	32,000	40,000
U (74ci V-twin)	4,000	6,000	9,000	12,000	16,000	20,000
US (74ci V-twin)	4,000	6,000	9,000	12,000	16,000	20,000
UL (74ci V-twin)	4,200	6,300	9,500	13,000	17,000	21,000
UH (80ci V-twin)	4,000	6,000	9,000	12,000	16,000	20,000
UHS (80ci V-twin)	4,000	6,000	9,000	12,000	16,000	20,000
ULH (80ci V-twin)	**5,000**	**8,000**	**12,000**	**18,000**	**24,000**	**30,000**
1939						
WL (45ci V-twin).	3,200	4,700	7,100	9,500	13,000	16,000
WLD (45ci V-twin).	3,400	5,100	**8,000**	**12,000**	**16,000**	**20,000**
WLDR (45ci V-twin).	3,500	5,300	**8,000**	**12,000**	**16,000**	**20,000**
G Servi-Car (45ci V-twin)	2,000	4,000	8,000	12,000	16,000	20,000
GA Servi-Car (45ci V-twin)	2,000	4,000	8,000	12,000	16,000	20,000
GD Servi-Car (45ci V-twin)	2,000	4,000	8,000	12,000	16,000	20,000
GDT Servi-Car (45ci V-twin).	2,000	4,000	8,000	12,000	16,000	20,000
EL (61ci V-twin)	**10,000**	**20,000**	**30,000**	**40,000**	**50,000**	**60,000**
ES (61ci V-twin)	8,000	12,000	18,000	24,000	32,000	40,000
U (74ci V-twin)	4,000	6,000	9,000	12,000	16,000	20,000
US (74ci V-twin)	4,000	6,000	9,000	12,000	16,000	20,000
UL (74ci V-twin)	4,400	6,600	9,900	13,000	18,000	22,000
UH (80ci V-twin)	4,000	6,000	9,000	12,000	16,000	20,000
UHS (80ci V-twin)	4,000	6,000	9,000	12,000	16,000	20,000
ULH (80ci V-twin)	**5,000**	**8,000**	**12,000**	**18,000**	**24,000**	**30,000**
1940						
WL (45ci V-twin).	3,200	4,700	7,100	9,500	13,000	16,000
WLD (45ci V-twin).	3,400	5,100	7,700	10,000	14,000	17,000
WLDR (45ci V-twin).	3,700	5,600	8,300	11,000	15,000	19,000
G Servi-Car (45ci V-twin)	2,000	4,000	8,000	12,000	16,000	20,000
GA Servi-Car (45ci V-twin)	2,000	4,000	8,000	12,000	16,000	20,000
GD Servi-Car (45ci V-twin)	2,000	4,000	8,000	12,000	16,000	20,000
GDT Servi-Car (45ci V-twin).	2,000	4,000	8,000	12,000	16,000	20,000
EL (61ci V-twin)	**10,000**	**20,000**	**30,000**	**40,000**	**50,000**	**60,000**
ES (61ci V-twin)	8,000	12,000	18,000	24,000	32,000	40,000
U (74ci V-twin)	4,000	6,000	9,000	12,000	16,000	20,000
UL (74ci V-twin)	4,200	6,300	10,000	14,000	17,000	22,000
US (74ci V-twin)	4,000	6,000	9,000	12,000	16,000	20,000
UH (80ci V-twin)	3,800	5,700	8,600	11,000	15,000	19,000
ULH (80ci V-twin)	4,200	6,300	9,500	13,000	17,000	21,000
UHS (80ci V-twin)	3,800	5,700	8,600	11,000	15,000	19,000
1941						
WL (45ci V-twin).	3,000	4,500	7,100	9,500	13,000	16,000
WLA (45ci V-twin).	3,400	5,100	7,700	10,000	14,000	17,000
WLD (45ci V-twin).	3,400	5,100	7,700	10,000	14,000	17,000
WLDR (45ci V-twin).	3,600	5,400	8,100	11,000	14,000	18,000
G Servi-Car (45ci V-twin)	2,000	4,000	8,000	12,000	16,000	20,000
GA Servi-Car (45ci V-twin)	2,000	4,000	8,000	12,000	16,000	20,000
GD Servi-Car (45ci V-twin)	2,000	4,000	8,000	12,000	16,000	20,000
GDT Servi-Car (45ci V-twin).	2,000	4,000	8,000	12,000	16,000	20,000
EL (61ci V-twin)	**10,000**	**20,000**	**30,000**	**40,000**	**50,000**	**60,000**
ES (61ci V-twin)	7,600	11,000	17,000	23,000	30,000	38,000
U (74ci V-twin)	4,000	7,000	10,000	12,000	16,000	20,000
UL (74ci V-twin)	4,200	6,300	10,000	14,000	17,000	22,000
US (74ci V-twin)	4,000	6,000	9,000	12,000	16,000	20,000

	6	5	4	3	2	1
FL (74ci V-twin)	5,800	8,700	13,000	17,000	23,000	29,000
FS (74ci V-twin)	5,500	83,000	12,000	17,000	22,000	28,000
UH (80ci V-twin)	3,800	5,700	8,600	11,000	15,000	19,000
ULH (80ci V-twin)	4,200	6,300	9,500	13,000	17,000	21,000
UHS (80ci V-twin)	3,800	5,700	8,600	11,000	15,000	19,000
1942						
WL (45ci V-twin)	3,200	4,700	7,100	9,500	13,000	16,000
WLA (45ci V-twin)	5,000	8,000	12,000	16,000	20,000	25,000
WLC (45ci V-twin)	3,000	5,100	7,700	10,000	14,000	17,000
WLD (45ci V-twin)	3,400	5,100	7,700	10,000	14,000	17,000
G Servi-Car (45ci V-twin)	2,000	4,000	8,000	12,000	16,000	20,000
GA Servi-Car (45ci V-twin)	2,000	4,000	8,000	12,000	16,000	20,000
XA (45ci V-twin)	4,000	8,000	**16,000**	**24,000**	**32,000**	**40,000**
E (61ci V-twin)	6,800	10,000	15,000	20,000	27,000	34,000
EL (61ci V-twin)	7,000	11,000	16,000	21,000	28,000	35,000
U (74ci V-twin)	3,800	5,700	8,600	11,000	15,000	19,000
UL (74ci V-twin)	4,000	6,000	10,000	14,000	17,000	22,000
F (74ci V-twin)	5,400	8,100	12,000	16,000	22,000	27,000
FL (74ci V-twin)	5,800	8,700	13,000	17,000	23,000	29,000
1943						
WLA (45ci V-twin)	3,400	5,100	7,700	10,000	14,000	17,000
WLC (45ci V-twin)	3,400	5,100	7,700	10,000	14,000	17,000
G Servi-Car (45ci V-twin)	2,000	4,000	8,000	12,000	16,000	20,000
GA Servi-Car (45ci V-twin)	2,000	4,000	8,000	12,000	16,000	20,000
XA (45ci V-twin)	4,000	8,000	**16,000**	**24,000**	**32,000**	**40,000**
E (61ci V-twin)	6,800	10,000	15,000	20,000	27,000	34,000
EL (61ci V-twin)	7,000	11,000	16,000	21,000	28,000	35,000
U (74ci V-twin)	3,800	5,700	8,600	11,000	15,000	19,000
UL (74ci V-twin)	4,000	6,000	10,000	14,000	17,000	22,000
F (74ci V-twin)	5,400	8,100	12,000	16,000	22,000	27,000
FL (74ci V-twin)	5,800	8,700	13,000	17,000	23,000	29,000
1944						
WLA (45ci V-twin)	3,400	5,100	7,700	10,000	14,000	17,000
WLC (45ci V-twin)	3,400	5,100	7,700	10,000	14,000	17,000
G Servi-Car (45ci V-twin)	2,000	4,000	8,000	12,000	16,000	20,000
GA Servi-Car (45ci V-twin)	2,000	4,000	8,000	12,000	16,000	20,000
E (61ci V-twin)	6,500	9,800	15,000	20,000	26,000	33,000
EL (61ci V-twin)	6,800	10,000	15,000	20,000	27,000	34,000
U (74ci V-twin)	3,600	5,400	8,100	11,000	14,000	18,000
UL (74ci V-twin)	4,000	6,000	10,000	14,000	17,000	22,000
F (74ci V-twin)	5,400	8,100	12,000	16,000	22,000	27,000
FL (74ci V-twin)	5,800	8,700	13,000	17,000	23,000	29,000
1945						
WL (45ci V-twin)	3,200	4,800	7,200	9,600	13,000	16,000
WLA (45ci V-twin)	3,400	5,100	7,700	10,000	14,000	17,000
G Servi-Car (45ci V-twin)	2,200	4,000	8,000	12,000	16,000	20,000
GA Servi-Car (45ci V-twin)	2,200	4,000	8,000	12,000	16,000	20,000
E (61ci V-twin)	6,400	9,600	14,000	19,000	26,000	32,000
EL (61ci V-twin)	6,600	9,900	15,000	20,000	26,000	33,000
ES (61ci V-twin)	6,400	9,600	14,000	19,000	26,000	32,000
U (74ci V-twin)	3,600	5,400	8,100	11,000	14,000	18,000
UL (74ci V-twin)	4,000	6,000	10,000	14,000	17,000	22,000
US (74ci V-twin)	3,600	5,400	8,100	11,000	14,000	18,000
F (74ci V-twin)	5,300	8,000	12,000	16,000	21,000	27,000
FL (74ci V-twin)	5,800	8,700	13,050	17,450	23,200	29,000
FS (74ci V-twin)	5,300	8,000	12,000	16,000	21,000	27,000
1946						
WL (45ci V-twin)	3,400	5,100	7,700	10,000	14,000	17,000
G Servi-Car (45ci V-twin)	2,400	3,600	5,400	7,200	9,600	12,000
GA Servi-Car (45ci V-twin)	2,400	3,600	5,400	7,200	9,600	12,000

	6	5	4	3	2	1
E (61ci V-twin)	6,000	9,000	13,500	18,000	24,000	30,000
EL (61ci V-twin)	6,400	9,600	14,000	19,000	26,000	32,000
ES (61ci V-twin)	6,000	9,000	13,500	18,000	24,000	30,000
U (74ci V-twin)	5,000	7,000	9,000	13,000	16,000	20,000
UL (74ci V-twin)	4,000	6,000	10,000	14,000	17,000	22,000
US (74ci V-twin)	3,600	5,400	8,100	11,000	14,000	18,000
F (74ci V-twin)	5,300	8,000	12,000	16,000	21,000	27,000
FL (74ci V-twin)	5,800	8,700	13,050	17,400	23,200	29,000
FS (74ci V-twin)	5,300	8,000	12,000	16,000	21,000	27,000
1947						
WL (45ci V-twin)	3,400	5,100	7,700	10,000	14,000	17,000
G Servi-Car (45ci V-twin)	2,400	3,600	5,400	7,200	9,600	12,000
GA Servi-Car (45ci V-twin)	2,400	3,600	5,400	7,200	9,600	12,000
E (61ci V-twin)	5,600	8,400	13,000	17,000	22,000	28,000
EL (61ci V-twin)	5,900	8,900	13,000	18,000	24,000	30,000
ES (61ci V-twin)	5,600	8,400	13,000	17,000	22,000	28,000
U (74ci V-twin)	3,600	5,400	8,100	11,000	14,000	18,000
UL (74ci V-twin)	3,600	5,400	10,000	14,000	17,000	22,000
US (74ci V-twin)	3,600	5,400	8,100	11,000	14,000	18,000
F (74ci V-twin)	5,200	7,800	12,000	16,000	21,000	26,000
FL (74ci V-twin)	5,600	8,400	13,000	17,000	22,000	28,000
FS (74ci V-twin)	5,200	7,800	12,000	16,000	21,000	26,000
1948						
S Hummer (125cc single)	1,500	3,000	4,500	6,000	7,500	9,000
WL (45ci V-twin)	3,300	5,000	7,400	9,900	13,000	17,000
G Servi-Car (45ci V-twin)	2,400	3,600	5,400	7,200	9,600	12,000
GA Servi-Car (45ci V-twin)	2,400	3,600	5,400	7,200	9,600	12,000
E (61ci V-twin)	4,100	6,200	9,200	12,000	16,000	21,000
EL (61ci V-twin)	4,200	6,300	**13,000**	**18,000**	**24,000**	**30,000**
ES (61ci V-twin)	4,100	6,200	9,200	12,000	16,000	21,000
U (74ci V-twin)	3,200	4,800	7,200	9,600	13,000	16,000
UL (74ci V-twin)	3,500	5,200	10,000	14,000	17,000	22,000
US (74ci V-twin)	3,200	4,800	7,200	9,600	13,000	16,000
F (74ci V-twin)	5,200	7,800	12,000	16,000	21,000	26,000
FL (74ci V-twin)	5,600	8,400	13,000	17,000	22,000	28,000
FS (74ci V-twin)	5,200	7,800	12,000	16,000	21,000	26,000
1949						
S Hummer (125cc single)	1,500	3,000	4,500	6,000	7,500	9,000
WL (45ci V-twin)	3,300	5,000	7,400	9,900	13,000	17,000
G Servi-Car (45ci V-twin)	2,600	3,900	5,900	7,800	10,000	13,000
GA Servi-Car (45ci V-twin)	2,600	3,900	5,900	7,800	10,000	13,000
E (61ci V-twin)	3,800	5,700	8,600	11,000	15,000	19,000
EL (61ci V-twin)	4,200	6,300	**13,000**	**18,000**	**24,000**	**30,000**
ES (61ci V-twin)	3,800	5,700	8,600	11,000	15,000	19,000
EP (61ci V-twin)	4,000	5,900	8,900	12,000	16,000	20,000
ELP (61ci V-twin)	4,100	6,200	9,200	12,000	16,000	21,000
F Hydra-Glide (74ci V-twin)	4,200	6,300	9,500	13,000	17,000	21,000
FL Hydra-Glide (74ci V-twin)	4,700	7,100	11,000	**16,000**	**24,000**	**30,000**
FS Hydra-Glide (74ci V-twin)	4,200	6,300	9,500	13,000	17,000	21,000
FP Hydra-Glide (74ci V-twin)	4,300	6,500	9,700	13,000	17,000	22,000
FLP Hydra-Glide (74ci V-twin)	4,800	7,200	11,000	14,000	19,000	24,000
1950						
S Hummer (125cc single)	1,500	3,000	4,500	6,000	7,500	9,000
WL (45ci V-twin)	3,300	5,000	7,400	9,900	13,000	17,000
G Servi-Car (45ci V-twin)	2,600	3,900	7,000	10,000	13,000	16,000
GA Servi-Car (45ci V-twin)	2,600	3,900	5,900	7,800	10,000	13,000
E (61ci V-twin)	4,200	6,300	9,500	13,000	17,000	21,000
EL (61ci V-twin)	4,200	6,300	9,500	13,000	17,000	21,000
ES (61ci V-twin)	4,200	6,300	9,500	13,000	17,000	21,000
F Hydra-Glide (74ci V-twin)	4,200	6,300	9,500	13,000	17,000	21,000

	6	5	4	3	2	1
FL Hydra-Glide (74ci V-twin)	4,500	6,800	10,000	15,000	20,000	25,000
FS Hydra-Glide (74ci V-twin)	4,200	6,300	9,500	13,000	17,000	21,000
1951						
S Hummer (125cc single)	**1,500**	**3,000**	**4,500**	**6,000**	**7,500**	**9,000**
WL (45ci V-twin).	3,300	5,000	7,400	9,900	13,000	17,000
G Servi-Car (45ci V-twin)	2,600	3,900	5,900	7,800	10,000	13,000
GA Servi-Car (45ci V-twin)	2,600	3,900	5,900	7,800	10,000	13,000
EL (61ci V-twin)	4,200	6,300	9,500	13,000	17,000	21,000
ELS (61ci V-twin)	4,200	6,300	9,500	13,000	17,000	21,000
FL Hydra-Glide (74ci V-twin)	**4,500**	**6,800**	**10,000**	**15,000**	**20,000**	**25,000**
FLS Hydra-Glide (74ci V-twin).	4,300	6,500	9,700	13,000	17,000	22,000
1952						
S Hummer (125cc single)	900	1,400	2,000	2,700	3,600	4,500
K (45ci V-twin).	2,900	4,400	**8,000**	**12,000**	**16,000**	**20,000**
G Servi-Car (45ci V-twin)	2,600	3,900	5,900	7,800	10,000	13,000
GA Servi-Car (45ci V-twin)	2,600	3,900	5,900	7,800	10,000	13,000
EL (61ci V-twin)	4,200	6,300	10,000	15,000	20,000	25,000
ELF (61ci V-twin)	4,200	6,300	10,000	15,000	20,000	25,000
ELS (61ci V-twin)	4,200	6,300	9,500	13,000	17,000	21,000
FL Hydra-Glide (74ci V-twin)	4,200	6,300	9,500	13,000	17,000	21,000
FLF Hydra-Glide (74ci V-twin).	4,300	6,500	9,700	13,000	17,000	22,000
FLS Hydra-Glide (74ci V-twin)	4,200	6,300	9,500	13,000	17,000	21,000
1953						
ST Hummer (165cc single)	1,000	1,500	2,300	3,000	4,000	5,000
K (45ci V-twin).	2,900	4,400	**8,000**	**12,000**	**16,000**	**20,000**
G Servi-Car (45ci V-twin)	2,600	3,900	5,900	7,800	10,000	13,000
GA Servi-Car (45ci V-twin)	2,600	3,900	5,900	7,800	10,000	13,000
FL Hydra-Glide (74ci V-twin)	4,200	6,300	9,500	13,000	17,000	21,000
FLF Hydra-Glide (74ci V-twin)	4,100	6,100	9,100	12,000	16,000	20,000
FLE Hydra-Glide (74ci V-twin).	4,200	6,300	9,500	13,000	17,000	21,000
FLEF Hydra-Glide (74ci V-twin)	4,100	6,100	9,100	12,000	16,000	20,000
1954						
ST Hummer (165cc single)	1,000	2,000	3,000	4,000	5,000	6,000
STU Hummer (165cc single)	1,000	2,000	3,000	4,000	5,000	6,000
G Servi-Car (45ci V-twin)	2,600	3,900	5,900	7,800	10,000	13,000
GA Servi-Car (45ci V-twin)	2,600	3,900	5,900	7,800	10,000	13,000
KH (55ci V-twin).	4,000	6,000	8,000	**12,000**	**16,000**	**20,000**
FL Hydra-Glide (74ci V-twin)	4,600	6,900	10,000	14,000	18,000	23,000
FLF Hydra-Glide (74ci V-twin).	4,200	6,300	9,500	13,000	17,000	21,000
FLE Hydra-Glide (74ci V-twin)	4,600	6,900	10,000	14,000	18,000	23,000
FLEF Hydra-Glide (74ci V-twin)	4,200	6,300	9,500	13,000	17,000	21,000
1955						
B Hummer (125cc single)	900	1,400	2,000	2,700	3,600	4,500
ST Hummer (165cc single)	1,000	1,500	2,300	3,000	4,000	5,000
STU Hummer (165cc single)	1,000	1,500	2,300	3,000	4,000	5,000
G Servi-Car (45ci V-twin)	2,600	3,900	5,900	7,800	10,000	13,000
GA Servi-Car (45ci V-twin)	2,600	3,900	5,900	7,800	10,000	13,000
KH (55ci V-twin).	2,800	4,200	6,300	8,400	11,000	14,000
KHK (55ci V-twin)	3,000	4,500	6,800	9,000	12,000	15,000
FL Hydra-Glide (74ci V-twin)	4,000	6,000	9,000	12,000	16,000	20,000
FLE Hydra-Glide (74ci V-twin)	4,000	6,000	9,000	12,000	16,000	20,000
FLEF Hydra-Glide (74ci V-twin)	3,800	5,700	8,600	11,000	15,000	19,000
FLF Hydra-Glide (74ci V-twin)	3,800	5,700	8,600	11,000	15,000	19,000
FLH Hydra-Glide (74ci V-twin)	4,100	**7,000**	**11,000**	**15,000**	**19,000**	**23,000**
FLHF Hydra-Glide (74ci V-twin)	4,000	**7,000**	**11,000**	**15,000**	**19,000**	**23,000**
1956						
B Hummer (125cc single)	900	1,400	2,000	2,700	3,600	4,500
ST Hummer (165cc single)	1,000	1,500	2,300	3,000	4,000	5,000
STU Hummer (165cc single)	1,000	1,500	2,300	3,000	4,000	5,000
G Servi-Car (45ci V-twin)	2,600	3,900	5,900	7,800	10,000	13,000

	6	5	4	3	2	1
GA Servi-Car (45ci V-twin)	2,600	3,900	5,900	7,800	10,000	13,000
KH (55ci V-twin)	2,800	4,200	6,300	8,400	11,000	14,000
KHK (55ci V-twin)	3,000	5,000	7,000	10,000	13,000	16,000
FL Hydra-Glide (74ci V-twin)	4,000	6,000	9,000	12,000	16,000	20,000
FLE Hydra-Glide (74ci V-twin)	4,000	6,000	9,000	12,000	16,000	20,000
FLEF Hydra-Glide (74ci V-twin)	3,800	5,700	8,600	11,000	15,000	19,000
FLF Hydra-Glide (74ci V-twin)	3,800	5,700	8,600	11,000	15,000	19,000
FLH Hydra-Glide (74ci V-twin)	4,100	**7,000**	**11,000**	**15,000**	**19,000**	**23,000**
FLHF Hydra-Glide (74ci V-twin)	4,000	**7,000**	**11,000**	**15,000**	**19,000**	**23,000**
1957						
B Hummer (125cc single)	900	1,400	2,000	2,700	3,600	4,500
ST Hummer (165cc single)	1,000	1,500	2,300	3,000	4,000	5,000
STU Hummer (165cc single)	1,000	1,500	2,300	3,000	4,000	5,000
G Servi-Car (45ci V-twin)	2,600	3,900	5,900	7,800	10,000	13,000
GA Servi-Car (45ci V-twin)	2,600	3,900	5,900	7,800	10,000	13,000
XL Sportster (55ci V-twin)	3,000	6,000	12,000	18,000	24,000	30,000
FL Hydra-Glide (74ci V-twin)	4,200	6,300	9,500	13,000	17,000	21,000
FLF Hydra-Glide (74ci V-twin)	4,000	6,000	9,000	12,000	16,000	20,000
FLH Hydra-Glide (74ci V-twin)	4,200	**7,000**	**11,000**	**15,000**	**19,000**	**23,000**
FLHF Hydra-Glide (74ci V-twin)	4,000	**7,000**	**11,000**	**15,000**	**19,000**	**23,000**
1958						
B Hummer (125cc single)	800	1,200	1,800	2,400	3,200	4,000
ST Hummer (165cc single)	800	1,200	1,800	2,400	3,200	4,000
STU Hummer (165cc single)	800	1,200	1,800	2,400	3,200	4,000
G Servi-Car (45ci V-twin)	2,600	3,900	5,900	7,800	10,000	13,000
GA Servi-Car (45ci V-twin)	2,600	3,900	5,900	7,800	10,000	13,000
XL Sportster (55ci V-twin)	2,000	5,000	7,000	9,000	11,000	13,000
XLH Sportster (55ci V-twin)	2,500	5,000	7,000	9,000	11,000	13,000
XLC Sportster (55ci V-twin)	2,200	5,000	7,000	9,000	11,000	13,000
XLCH Sportster (55ci V-twin)	2,300	5,000	7,000	9,000	11,000	13,000
FL Duo-Glide (74ci V-twin)	3,500	6,000	9,000	12,000	15,000	18,000
FLF Duo-Glide (74ci V-twin)	4,000	6,000	9,000	12,000	16,000	20,000
FLH Duo-Glide (74ci V-twin)	4,200	6,300	9,500	13,000	17,000	21,000
FLHF Duo-Glide (74ci V-twin)	4,000	6,000	9,000	12,000	16,000	20,000
1959						
B Hummer (125cc single)	900	1,300	1,900	2,600	3,400	4,300
ST Hummer (165cc single)	800	1,200	1,800	2,300	3,100	3,900
STU Hummer (165cc single)	800	1,200	1,800	2,300	3,100	3,900
G Servi-Car (45ci V-twin)	2,600	3,900	5,900	7,800	10,000	13,000
GA Servi-Car (45ci V-twin)	2,600	3,900	5,900	7,800	10,000	13,000
XL Sportster (55ci V-twin)	2,000	3,000	4,500	6,000	8,000	10,000
XLH Sportster (55ci V-twin)	2,200	5,000	7,000	9,000	11,000	13,000
XLCH Sportster (55ci V-twin)	2,300	5,000	7,000	9,000	11,000	13,000
FL Duo-Glide (74ci V-twin)	3,500	6,000	9,000	12,000	15,000	18,000
FLF Duo-Glide (74ci V-twin)	4,000	6,000	9,000	12,000	16,000	20,000
FLH Duo-Glide (74ci V-twin)	4,200	6,300	9,500	13,000	17,000	21,000
FLHF Duo-Glide (74ci V-twin)	4,000	6,000	9,000	12,000	16,000	20,000
1960						
A Topper (165cc single)	1,000	1,500	2,300	3,000	4,000	5,000
AU Topper (165cc single)	900	1,400	2,000	2,700	3,600	4,500
BT Pacer (165cc single)	500	800	1,100	1,500	2,000	2,500
BTU Pacer (165cc single)	500	800	1,100	1,500	2,000	2,500
G Servi-Car (45ci V-twin)	2,400	3,600	5,400	7,200	9,600	12,000
GA Servi-Car (45ci V-twin)	2,400	3,600	5,400	7,200	9,600	12,000
XLH Sportster (55ci V-twin)	2,200	5,000	7,000	9,000	11,000	13,000
XLCH Sportster (55ci V-twin)	2,300	5,000	7,000	9,000	11,000	13,000
FL Duo-Glide (74ci V-twin)	4,200	6,300	9,500	13,000	17,000	21,000
FLF Duo-Glide (74ci V-twin)	4,000	6,000	9,000	12,000	16,000	20,000
FLH Duo-Glide (74ci V-twin)	4,200	6,300	9,500	13,000	17,000	21,000
FLHF Duo-Glide (74ci V-twin)	4,000	6,000	9,000	12,000	16,000	20,000

	6	5	4	3	2	1
1961						
AH Topper (165cc single)	1,000	1,500	3,500	4,000	5,500	7,000
AU Topper (165cc single)	900	1,400	2,000	2,700	3,600	4,500
BT Pacer (165cc single)	700	1,000	1,500	2,000	3,000	4,000
BTU Pacer (165cc single)	700	1,000	1,500	2,000	3,000	4,000
C Sprint (250cc single)	700	1,100	1,600	2,100	2,800	3,500
G Servi-Car (45ci V-twin)	2,500	4,000	6,000	9,000	12,000	15,000
GA Servi-Car (45ci V-twin)	2,400	3,600	5,400	7,200	9,600	12,000
XLH Sportster (55ci V-twin)	2,200	5,000	7,000	9,000	11,000	13,000
XLCH Sportster (55ci V-twin)	2,200	5,000	7,000	9,000	11,000	13,000
FL Duo-Glide (74ci V-twin)	4,200	6,300	9,500	13,000	17,000	21,000
FLF Duo-Glide (74ci V-twin)	4,000	6,000	9,000	12,000	16,000	20,000
FLH Duo-Glide (74ci V-twin)	4,200	6,300	9,500	13,000	17,000	21,000
FLHF Duo-Glide (74ci V-twin)	4,000	6,000	9,000	12,000	16,000	20,000
1962						
AH Topper (165cc single)	1,000	1,500	3,500	4,000	5,500	7,000
AU Topper (165cc single)	900	1,400	2,000	2,700	3,600	4,500
BTF Ranger (165cc single)	600	900	1,400	1,800	2,400	3,000
BTU Pacer (165cc single)	700	1,000	1,500	2,000	2,700	3,400
BT Pacer (175cc single)	700	1,000	1,500	2,000	2,700	3,400
BTH Scat (175cc single)	700	1,100	1,600	2,100	2,800	3,500
C Sprint (250cc single)	700	1,100	1,700	2,200	3,000	3,700
CH Sprint (250cc single)	800	1,200	1,800	2,300	3,100	3,900
G Servi-Car (45ci V-twin)	2,400	3,600	5,400	7,200	9,600	12,000
GA Servi-Car (45ci V-twin)	2,400	3,600	5,400	7,200	9,600	12,000
XLH Sportster (55ci V-twin)	2,400	5,000	7,000	9,000	11,000	13,000
XLCH Sportster (55ci V-twin)	2,400	5,000	7,000	9,000	11,000	13,000
FL Duo-Glide (74ci V-twin)	4,200	6,300	9,500	13,000	17,000	21,000
FLF Duo-Glide (74ci V-twin)	4,000	6,000	9,000	12,000	16,000	20,000
FLH Duo-Glide (74ci V-twin)	4,200	6,300	9,500	13,000	17,000	21,000
FLHF Duo-Glide (74ci V-twin)	4,000	6,000	9,000	12,000	16,000	20,000
1963						
AH Topper (165cc single)	1,000	1,500	3,500	4,000	5,500	7,000
AU Topper (165cc single)	900	1,400	2,000	3,000	4,000	6,000
BT Pacer (175cc single)	700	1,000	1,500	2,500	3,500	5,000
BTU Pacer (165cc single)	700	1,000	1,500	2,500	3,500	5,000
BTH Scat (175cc single)	700	1,100	1,600	2,100	2,800	3,500
C Sprint (250cc single)	700	1,100	1,700	2,200	3,000	3,700
CH Sprint (250cc single)	800	1,200	1,800	2,300	3,100	3,900
G Servi-Car (45ci V-twin)	2,400	3,600	5,400	7,200	9,600	12,000
GA Servi-Car (45ci V-twin)	2,400	3,600	5,400	7,200	9,600	12,000
XLH Sportster (55ci V-twin)	2,400	5,000	7,000	9,000	11,000	13,000
XLCH Sportster (55ci V-twin)	2,400	5,000	7,000	9,000	11,000	13,000
FL Duo-Glide (74ci V-twin)	4,200	6,300	9,500	13,000	17,000	21,000
FLF Duo-Glide (74ci V-twin)	4,000	6,000	9,000	12,000	16,000	20,000
FLH Duo-Glide (74ci V-twin)	4,200	6,300	9,500	13,000	17,000	21,000
FLHF Duo-Glide (74ci V-twin)	4,000	6,000	9,000	12,000	16,000	20,000
1964						
AH Topper (165cc single)	1,000	1,500	3,500	4,000	5,500	7,000
AU Topper (165cc single)	1,000	1,500	3,500	4,000	5,500	7,000
BT Pacer (175cc single)	700	1,000	1,500	2,500	3,500	5,000
BTU Pacer (165cc single)	700	1,000	1,500	2,500	3,500	5,000
BTH Scat (175cc single)	700	1,100	1,600	2,100	2,800	3,500
C Sprint (250cc single)	800	1,100	1,700	2,300	3,000	3,800
CH Sprint (250cc single)	800	1,200	1,800	2,400	3,200	4,000
GE Servi-Car (45ci V-twin)	2,200	3,300	5,000	6,600	9,000	12,000
XLH Sportster (55ci V-twin)	2,400	5,000	7,000	9,000	11,000	13,000
XLCH Sportster (55ci V-twin)	2,400	5,000	7,000	9,000	11,000	13,000
FL Duo-Glide (74ci V-twin)	4,200	6,300	9,500	13,000	17,000	21,000
FLF Duo-Glide (74ci V-twin)	4,000	6,000	9,000	12,000	16,000	20,000

	6	5	4	3	2	1
FLH Duo-Glide (74ci V-twin)	4,200	6,300	9,500	13,000	17,000	21,000
FLHF Duo-Glide (74ci V-twin).	4,000	6,000	9,000	12,000	16,000	20,000
1965						
M50 (50cc single)	1,000	2,000	3,000	4,000	5,000	6,000
AH Topper (165cc single)	1,000	1,500	3,500	4,000	5,500	7,000
BT Pacer (175cc single).	700	1,000	2,500	3,000	3,500	4,000
BTH Scat (175cc single)	700	1,100	1,600	2,100	2,800	3,500
C Sprint (250cc single)	800	1,200	1,800	2,400	3,200	4,000
CH Sprint (250cc single)	800	1,200	1,800	2,400	3,200	4,000
GE Servi-Car (45ci V-twin)	2,200	3,300	5,000	6,600	9,000	12,000
XLH Sportster (55ci V-twin)	2,400	5,000	7,000	9,000	11,000	13,000
XLCH Sportster (55ci V-twin)	2,400	5,000	7,000	9,000	11,000	13,000
FLB Electra-Glide (74ci V-twin)	4,200	6,300	9,500	13,000	17,000	21,000
FLFB Electra-Glide (74ci V-twin)	4,000	6,000	9,000	12,000	16,000	20,000
FLHB Electra-Glide (74ci V-twin)	4,200	6,300	9,500	13,000	17,000	21,000
FLHFB Electra-Glide (74ci V-twin)	4,000	6,000	9,000	12,000	16,000	20,000
1966						
M50 (50cc single)	1,000	2,000	3,000	4,000	5,000	6,000
MS (50cc single)	600	900	1,400	1,900	2,500	3,100
BTH Bobcat (175cc single)	600	900	1,400	1,800	2,400	3,000
C Sprint (250cc single)	800	1,200	1,800	2,400	3,200	4,000
CH Sprint (250cc single)	800	1,200	1,800	2,400	3,200	4,000
GE Servi-Car (45ci V-twin)	2,200	3,300	5,000	6,600	9,000	12,000
XLH Sportster (55ci V-twin)	2,200	5,000	7,000	9,000	11,000	13,000
XLCH Sportster (55ci V-twin)	2,200	5,000	7,000	9,000	11,000	13,000
FLB Electra-Glide (74ci V-twin)	3,400	5,100	7,700	10,000	14,000	17,000
FLFB Electra-Glide (74ci V-twin)	3,300	5,000	7,400	9,900	13,000	16,000
FLHB Electra-Glide (74ci V-twin)	3,400	5,100	7,700	10,000	14,000	17,000
FLHFB Electra-Glide (74ci V-twin)	3,300	5,000	7,400	9,900	13,000	16,000
1967						
M (65cc single)	600	1,000	1,600	2,400	3,200	4,000
MS (65cc single)	600	900	1,400	1,900	2,500	3,100
SS Sprint (250cc single).	800	1,300	1,900	2,500	3,400	4,200
CH Sprint (250cc single)	800	1,200	1,800	2,400	3,200	4,000
GE Servi-Car (45ci V-twin)	2,200	3,300	5,000	6,600	9,000	12,000
XLH Sportster (55ci V-twin)	2,200	5,000	7,000	9,000	11,000	13,000
XLCH Sportster (55ci V-twin)	2,200	5,000	7,000	9,000	11,000	13,000
FLB Electra-Glide (74ci V-twin)	3,400	5,100	7,700	10,000	14,000	17,000
FLFB Electra-Glide (74ci V-twin)	3,300	5,000	7,400	9,900	13,000	16,000
FLHB Electra-Glide (74ci V-twin)	3,400	5,100	7,700	10,000	14,000	17,000
FLHFB Electra-Glide (74ci V-twin)	3,300	5,000	7,400	9,900	13,000	16,000
1968						
M (65cc single)	600	1,000	1,600	2,400	3,200	4,000
MS (65cc single)	600	900	1,400	1,900	2,500	3,100
ML Rapido (125cc single)	700	1,000	1,500	2,000	2,700	3,400
SS Sprint (250cc single).	800	1,300	1,900	2,500	3,400	4,200
CH Sprint (250cc single)	800	1,200	1,800	2,400	3,200	4,000
GE Servi-Car (45ci V-twin)	2,100	3,200	4,700	6,300	9,000	12,000
XLH Sportster (55ci V-twin)	1,900	2,900	4,300	5,700	7,600	10,000
XLCH Sportster (55ci V-twin)	2,200	3,300	5,000	6,600	8,800	11,000
FLB Electra-Glide (74ci V-twin)	3,200	4,700	7,100	9,500	13,000	16,000
FLFB Electra-Glide (74ci V-twin)	3,000	4,500	6,800	9,000	12,000	15,000
FLHB Electra-Glide (74ci V-twin)	3,200	4,700	8,000	11,000	15,000	18,000
FLHFB Electra-Glide (74ci V-twin)	3,000	4,500	6,800	9,000	12,000	15,000
1969						
M (65cc single)	600	1,000	1,600	2,400	3,200	4,000
MS (65cc single)	600	900	1,400	1,800	2,400	3,000
ML Rapido (125cc single)	700	1,000	1,500	2,000	2,600	3,300
MLS Rapido Scrambler (125cc single) . . .	700	1,000	1,500	2,000	2,700	3,400
SS Sprint (350cc single).	800	1,200	1,800	2,400	3,200	4,000

	6	5	4	3	2	1
ERS Sprint (350cc single)	800	1,300	2,000	3,000	4,000	5,000
GE Servi-Car (45ci V-twin)	2,000	3,000	4,500	6,000	9,000	12,000
XLH Sportster (55ci V-twin)	1,900	3,000	5,000	7,000	9,000	11,000
XLCH Sportster (55ci V-twin)	2,200	3,300	4,950	6,600	8,800	11,000
FLB Electra-Glide (74ci V-twin)	3,200	4,700	7,100	9,500	13,000	16,000
FLFB Electra-Glide (74ci V-twin)	3,000	4,500	6,800	9,000	12,000	15,000
FLHB Electra-Glide (74ci V-twin)	3,200	4,700	7,100	9,500	13,000	16,000
FLHFB Electra-Glide (74ci V-twin)	3,000	4,500	6,800	9,000	12,000	15,000
1970						
MS Leggero (65cc single)	600	900	1,300	1,700	2,300	2,900
MSR Baja 100 (100cc single)	−600	−800	**1,600**	**2,400**	**3,200**	**4,000**
MLS Scrambler (125cc single)	700	1,000	1,600	2,100	2,800	3,500
SS Sprint (350cc single)	800	1,200	1,800	2,400	3,200	4,000
ERS Sprint (350cc single)	800	1,200	1,900	2,500	3,300	4,100
GE Servi-Car (45ci V-twin)	2,000	3,000	4,500	6,000	**9,000**	**12,000**
XLH Sportster (55ci V-twin)	1,800	2,700	4,050	5,400	7,200	9,000
XLCH Sportster (55ci V-twin)	2,000	3,000	4,500	6,000	8,000	10,000
FLB Electra-Glide (74ci V-twin)	2,900	4,400	6,500	8,700	12,000	15,000
FLFB Electra-Glide (74ci V-twin)	2,800	4,200	6,300	8,400	11,200	14,000
FLHB Electra-Glide (74ci V-twin)	2,900	4,400	6,500	9,200	12,000	15,000
FLHFB Electra-Glide (74ci V-twin)	2,800	4,200	6,300	8,400	11,200	14,000
1971						
MS (65cc single)	600	800	1,200	1,600	2,200	2,700
MSR Baja 100 (100cc single)	600	800	**1,600**	**2,400**	**3,200**	**4,000**
MLS Scrambler (125cc single)	600	800	1,300	1,700	2,200	2,800
SS Sprint (350cc single)	800	1,100	1,700	2,300	3,000	3,800
SX Sprint (350cc single)	800	1,200	**2,000**	**3,000**	**4,000**	**5,000**
ERS Sprint (350cc single)	800	1,200	1,800	2,400	3,200	4,000
GE Servi-Car (45ci V-twin)	2,000	3,000	4,500	6,000	**9,000**	**12,000**
XLH Sportster (55ci V-twin)	1,600	2,400	**4,000**	**6,000**	**8,000**	**10,000**
XLCH Sportster (55ci V-twin)	1,600	2,400	4,000	6,000	8,000	10,000
FX Electra-Glide (74ci V-twin)	2,500	3,800	5,600	7,500	10,000	13,000
FLP Electra-Glide (74ci V-twin)	2,900	4,400	6,500	8,700	12,000	15,000
FLPF Electra-Glide (74ci V-twin)	2,800	4,200	6,300	8,400	11,200	14,000
FLH Electra-Glide (74ci V-twin)	2,900	4,400	6,500	8,700	12,000	15,000
FLHF Electra-Glide (74ci V-twin)	2,800	4,200	6,300	8,400	11,200	14,000
1972						
MC (65cc single)	600	800	1,200	1,600	2,200	2,700
MS (65cc single)	600	800	1,200	1,600	2,200	2,700
MSR Baja 100 (100cc single)	600	800	**1,600**	**2,400**	**3,200**	**4,000**
MLS Scrambler (125cc single)	600	800	1,300	1,700	2,200	2,800
SS Sprint (350cc single)	800	1,100	1,700	2,300	3,000	3,800
SX Sprint (350cc single)	800	1,200	2,000	3,000	4,000	5,000
ERS Sprint (350cc single)	800	1,200	1,800	2,400	3,200	4,000
GE Servi-Car (45ci V-twin)	2,000	3,000	4,500	6,000	9,000	12,000
XLH Sportster (61ci V-twin)	1,600	2,400	4,000	6,000	8,000	11,000
XLCH Sportster (61ci V-twin)	1,600	2,400	4,000	6,000	8,000	10,000
FX Super Glide (74ci V-twin)	2,400	3,600	5,400	7,200	9,600	12,000
FLP Electra-Glide (74ci V-twin)	2,600	3,900	5,900	7,800	10,000	13,000
FLPF Electra-Glide (74ci V-twin)	2,500	3,800	5,600	7,500	10,000	13,000
FLH Electra-Glide (74ci V-twin)	2,600	3,900	5,900	7,800	10,000	13,000
FLHF Electra-Glide (74ci V-twin)	2,500	3,800	5,600	7,500	10,000	13,000
1973						
X (90cc single)	**350**	**700**	**1,400**	**2,100**	**2,800**	**3,500**
Z (90cc single)	300	600	900	1,200	1,500	1,800
MSR Baja 100 (100cc single)	**600**	**800**	**1,600**	**2,400**	**3,200**	**4,000**
TX (125cc single)	400	600	1,000	1,300	1,700	2,100
S Sprint (350cc single)	600	1,000	1,400	1,900	2,600	3,200
SX Sprint (350cc single)	**800**	**1,200**	**2,000**	**3,000**	**4,000**	**5,000**
GE Servi-Car (45ci V-twin)	2,000	3,000	4,500	6,000	**9,000**	**12,000**

	6	5	4	3	2	1
XLH Sportster (61ci V-twin)	1,600	2,400	3,600	4,800	6,400	8,000
XLCH Sportster (61ci V-twin)	1,600	2,400	3,600	4,800	6,400	8,000
FX Super Glide (74ci V-twin)	2,200	3,300	5,000	6,600	8,800	11,000
FL Electra-Glide (74ci V-twin)	2,500	3,800	5,600	7,500	10,000	13,000
FLH Electra-Glide (74ci V-twin)	2,500	3,800	5,600	7,500	10,000	13,000
1974						
X (90cc single)	**350**	**700**	**1,400**	**2,100**	**2,800**	**3,500**
Z (90cc single)	300	600	900	1,200	1,500	1,800
SR (100cc single)	500	700	**1,200**	**1,800**	**2,400**	**3,000**
SX (125cc single)	400	600	**1,400**	**2,100**	**2,800**	**3,500**
SX (175cc single)	400	700	1,000	1,300	1,800	2,200
SS Sprint (350cc single).	600	1,000	1,400	1,900	2,600	3,200
SX Sprint (350cc single).	**800**	**1,200**	**2,000**	**3,000**	**4,000**	**5,000**
XLH Sportster (61ci V-twin)	1,400	2,100	3,200	4,200	5,600	7,000
XLCH Sportster (61ci V-twin)	1,400	2,100	3,200	4,200	5,600	7,000
FX Super Glide (74ci V-twin)	2,200	3,300	5,000	6,600	8,800	11,000
FXE Super Glide (74ci V-twin)	2,200	3,300	5,000	6,600	8,800	11,000
FLH Electra-Glide (74ci V-twin)	2,300	3,500	5,200	6,900	9,200	12,000
FLHF Electra-Glide (74ci V-twin)	2,300	3,500	5,200	6,900	9,200	12,000
FLP Electra-Glide (74ci V-twin)	2,400	3,600	5,400	7,200	9,600	12,000
1975						
X (90cc single)	**350**	**700**	**1,400**	**2,100**	**2,800**	**3,500**
Z (90cc single)	300	600	900	1,200	1,500	1,800
SXT (125cc single)	400	700	**1,400**	**2,100**	**2,800**	**3,500**
SX (175cc single)	400	600	1,000	1,300	1,700	2,100
SX (250cc single)	500	700	1,400	2,100	2,800	3,500
SS Sprint (250cc single)	500	700	1,100	1,400	1,900	2,400
XLH Sportster (61ci V-twin)	1,400	2,100	3,200	4,200	5,600	7,000
XLCH Sportster (61ci V-twin)	1,400	2,100	3,200	4,200	5,600	7,000
FX Super Glide (74ci V-twin)	2,200	3,300	5,000	6,600	8,800	11,000
FXE Super Glide (74ci V-twin)	2,200	3,300	5,000	6,600	8,800	11,000
FLH Electra-Glide (74ci V-twin)	2,300	3,500	5,200	6,900	9,200	12,000
FLHF Electra-Glide (74ci V-twin)	2,300	3,500	6,000	8,000	11,000	13,000
FLP Electra-Glide (74ci V-twin)	2,400	3,600	5,400	7,200	9,600	12,000
1976						
SS (125cc single)	400	600	1,000	1,300	1,700	2,100
SXT (125cc single)	400	**700**	**1,400**	**2,100**	**2,800**	**3,500**
SS (175cc single)	400	600	1,000	1,300	1,700	2,100
SX (175cc single)	400	600	1,000	1,300	1,700	2,100
SS (250cc single)	500	800	1,200	1,600	2,200	2,700
SX (250cc single)	500	800	1,400	2,100	2,800	3,500
XLH Sportster (61ci V-twin)	1,300	2,000	2,900	3,900	5,200	6,500
XLCH Sportster (61ci V-twin)	1,300	2,000	2,900	3,900	5,200	6,500
FX Super Glide (74ci V-twin)	2,200	3,300	5,000	6,600	8,800	11,000
FXE Super Glide (74ci V-twin)	2,200	3,300	5,000	6,600	8,800	11,000
FLH Electra-Glide (74ci V-twin)	2,400	3,600	5,400	7,200	9,600	12,000
1977						
SS (125cc single)	400	600	900	1,200	1,600	2,000
SXT (125cc single)	400	**700**	**1,400**	**2,100**	**2,800**	**3,500**
SS (175cc single)	400	600	900	1,200	1,600	2,000
SS (250cc single)	500	800	1,200	1,600	2,200	2,700
SX (250cc single)	500	800	1,400	2,100	2,800	3,500
XLH Sportster (61ci V-twin)	1,300	2,000	2,900	3,900	5,200	6,500
XLT Sportster (61ci V-twin)	1,300	2,000	2,900	3,900	5,200	6,500
XLCH Sportster (61ci V-twin)	1,300	2,000	2,900	3,900	5,200	6,500
XLCR Sportster (61ci V-twin)	3,000	6,000	9,000	12,000	15,000	18,000
FX Super Glide (74ci V-twin)	2,000	3,000	4,500	6,000	8,000	10,000
FXE Super Glide (74ci V-twin)	2,000	3,000	4,500	6,000	8,000	10,000
FXS Low Rider (74ci V-twin)	2,200	3,300	4,500	6,000	8,000	10,000
FLH Electra-Glide (74ci V-twin)	2,400	3,600	5,400	7,200	9,600	12,000

	6	5	4	3	2	1
FLHS Electra-Glide (74ci V-twin)	2,500	3,800	5,600	7,500	10,000	13,000
1978						
SS (125cc single)	400	600	1,000	1,300	1,700	2,100
XLH Sportster (61ci V-twin)	1,300	2,000	2,900	3,900	5,200	6,500
XLH Sportster (61ci V-twin,75th Anniversary)	1,300	2,000	2,900	3,900	5,200	6,500
XLT Sportster (61ci V-twin)	1,300	2,000	2,900	3,900	5,200	6,500
XLCH Sportster (61ci V-twin)	1,300	2,000	2,900	3,900	5,200	6,500
XLCR Sportster (61ci V-twin)	3,000	6,000	9,000	12,000	15,000	18,000
FX Super Glide (74ci V-twin)	2,000	3,000	4,500	6,000	8,000	10,000
FXE Super Glide (74ci V-twin)	2,000	3,000	4,500	6,000	8,000	10,000
FXS Low Rider (74ci V-twin)	2,200	3,300	5,000	6,600	8,800	11,000
FLH Electra-Glide (74ci V-twin, 75th						
Anniversary)	2,300	3,500	5,200	6,900	9,200	12,000
FLH-80 Electra-Glide (80ci V-twin)	2,000	3,000	4,500	6,000	8,000	10,000
1979						
XLS Sportster (61ci V-twin)	1,300	2,000	2,900	3,900	5,200	6,500
XLH Sportster (61ci V-twin)	1,300	2,000	2,900	3,900	5,200	6,500
XLCH Sportster (61ci V-twin)	1,300	2,000	2,900	3,900	5,200	6,500
FXE Super Glide (74ci V-twin)	2,000	3,000	4,500	6,000	8,000	10,000
FXS-74 Super Glide (74ci V-twin).	2,000	3,000	4,500	6,000	8,000	10,000
FXS-80 Super Glide (80ci V-twin).	2,000	3,000	4,500	6,000	8,000	10,000
FXEF-74 Fat Bob (74ci V-twin)	2,300	3,500	5,200	6,900	9,200	12,000
FXEF-80 Fat Bob (80ci V-twin)	2,300	3,500	5,200	6,900	9,200	12,000
FLH-74 Electra Glide (74ci V-twin)	2,000	3,000	4,500	6,000	8,000	10,000
FXH-80 Electra Glide (80ci V-twin)	2,100	3,200	4,700	6,300	8,400	11,000
FLHC Electra Glide (80ci V-twin)	2,100	3,200	4,700	6,300	8,400	11,000
FLHCE Electra Glide (80ci V-twin)	2,100	3,200	4,700	6,300	8,400	11,000
FLHP-74 Electra Glide (74ci V-twin).	2,200	3,300	5,000	6,600	8,800	11,000
FLH-80 Electra-Glide (80ci V-twin)	2,200	3,300	5,000	6,600	8,800	11,000
1980						
XLS Sportster (61ci V-twin)	1,300	2,000	2,900	3,900	5,200	6,500
XLH Sportster (61ci V-twin)	1,300	2,000	2,900	3,900	5,200	6,500
FXB-80 Super Glide Sturgis (80ci V-twin) . .	2,600	3,900	5,900	7,800	10,000	13,000
FXS-74 Super Glide (74ci V-twin)	2,200	3,300	5,000	6,600	8,800	11,000
FXEF-80 Fat Bob (80ci V-twin)	2,300	3,500	5,200	6,900	9,200	12,000
FXS-74 Low Rider (74ci V-twin)	2,000	3,000	4,500	6,000	8,000	10,000
FXS-80 Low Rider (80ci V-twin)	2,000	3,000	4,500	6,000	8,000	10,000
FXWG-80 Wide Glide (80ci V-twin)	2,100	3,200	4,700	6,300	8,400	11,000
FLH-74 Electra Glide (74ci V-twin)	2,000	3,000	4,500	6,000	8,000	10,000
FLH-80 Electra Glide (80ci V-twin)	2,100	3,200	4,700	6,300	8,400	11,000
FLHC-80 Electra Glide Classic (50ci V-twin)	2,100	3,200	4,700	6,300	8,400	11,000
FLHCE-80 Electra Glide Classic (80ci V-twin)	2,100	3,200	4,700	6,300	8,400	11,000
FLHP-74 Electra Glide (74ci V-twin).	2,200	3,300	5,000	6,600	8,800	11,000
FLHP-80 Electra-Glide (80ci V-twin)	2,200	3,300	5,000	6,600	8,800	11,000
FLT Tour Glide (80ci V-twin)	2,000	3,000	4,500	6,000	8,000	10,000
1981						
XLS Sportster (61ci V-twin)	2,300	3,500	5,200	6,900	9,200	12,000
XLH Sportster (61ci V-twin)	1,300	2,000	2,900	3,900	5,200	6,500
FXB Super Glide Sturgis (80ci V-twin) . . .	2,100	3,200	4,700	6,300	8,400	11,000
FXE Super Glide (80ci V-twin)	2,200	3,300	5,000	6,600	8,800	11,000
FXEF Fat Bob (80ci V-twin)	2,300	3,500	5,200	6,900	9,200	12,000
FXWG Wide Glide (80ci V-twin)	2,100	3,200	4,700	6,300	8,400	11,000
FLH Electra Glide (80ci V-twin)	2,200	3,300	5,000	6,600	8,800	11,000
FLH Electra Glide Heritage (80ci V-twin) . .	2,200	3,300	5,000	6,600	8,800	11,000
FLHC Electra Glide Classic (80ci V-twin) . .	2,200	3,300	5,000	6,600	8,800	11,000
FLHCE Electra Glide Classic (80ci V-twin) .	2,200	3,300	5,000	6,600	8,800	11,000
FLHP Electra-Glide (80ci V-twin)	2,200	3,300	5,000	6,600	8,800	11,000
FLT Tour Glide (80ci V-twin)	2,000	3,000	4,500	6,000	8,000	10,000
FLT Tour Glide Classic (80ci V-twin)	2,000	3,000	4,500	6,000	8,000	10,000

	6	5	4	3	2	1
1982						
XLH Sportster (61ci V-twin)	1,300	2,000	2,900	3,900	5,200	6,500
XLHA Sportster (61ci V-twin, 25th Anniv)	1,500	2,200	3,300	4,400	5,800	7,300
XLS Sportster (61ci V-twin)	1,300	2,000	2,900	3,900	5,200	6,500
XLSA Sportster (61ci V-twin, 25th Anniv) . .	1,500	2,200	3,300	4,400	5,800	7,300
FLH Electra Glide (80ci V-twin)	2,200	3,300	5,000	6,600	8,800	11,000
FLHC Electra Glide Classic (80ci V-twin) . .	2,200	3,300	5,000	6,600	8,800	11,000
FLT Tour Glide (80ci V-twin)	2,000	3,000	4,500	6,000	8,000	10,000
FLT Tour Glide Classic (80ci V-twin)	2,000	3,000	4,500	6,000	8,000	10,000
FXB Super Glide "Sturgis" (80ci V-twin). . .	2,800	4,200	6,300	8,400	11,000	14,000
FXE Super Glide (80ci V-twin)	2,200	3,300	5,000	6,600	8,800	11,000
FXR Super Glide II (80ci V-twin)	2,200	3,300	5,000	6,600	8,800	11,000
FXRS Super Glide II (80ci V-twin)	2,200	3,300	5,000	6,600	8,800	11,000
FXS Low Rider (80ci V-twin)	2,300	3,500	5,200	6,900	9,200	12,000
FXWG Wide Glide (80ci V-twin).	2,300	3,500	5,200	6,900	9,200	12,000
1983						
XLH Sportster (61ci V-twin)	1,300	2,000	2,900	3,900	5,200	6,500
XLS Sportster (61ci V-twin)	1,300	2,000	2,900	3,900	5,200	6,500
XLX Sportster (61ci V-twin)	1,300	2,000	2,900	3,900	5,200	6,500
XR-1000 Sportster (61ci V-twin).	3,000	5,000	8,000	10,000	13,000	16,000
FLH Electra Glide (80ci V-twin)	2,200	3,300	5,000	6,600	8,800	11,000
FLHT Electra Glide (80ci V-twin)	2,200	3,300	5,000	6,600	8,800	11,000
FLHTC Electra Glide Classic (80ci V-twin) .	2,200	3,300	5,000	6,600	8,800	11,000
FLT Tour Glide (80ci V-twin)	2,000	3,000	4,500	6,000	8,000	10,000
FLTC Tour Glide Classic (80ci V-twin) . . .	2,000	3,000	4,500	6,000	8,000	10,000
FXDG Super Glide (80ci V-twin)	2,200	3,300	5,000	6,600	8,800	11,000
FXE Super Glide (80ci V-twin)	2,200	3,300	5,000	6,600	8,800	11,000
FXR Super Glide II (80ci V-twin)	2,200	3,300	5,000	6,600	8,800	11,000
FXRS Super Glide II (80ci V-twin).	2,200	3,300	5,000	6,600	8,800	11,000
FXRT Super Glide II Touring (80ci V-twin). .	2,200	3,300	5,000	6,600	8,800	11,000
FXSB Low Rider (80ci V-twin)	2,300	3,500	5,200	6,900	9,200	12,000
FXWG Wide Glide (80ci V-twin).	2,300	3,500	5,200	6,900	9,200	12,000
1984						
XLH Sportster (61ci V-twin)	1,300	2,000	2,900	3,900	5,200	6,500
XLS Sportster (61ci V-twin)	1,300	2,000	2,900	3,900	5,200	6,500
XLX Sportster (61ci V-twin)	1,300	2,000	2,900	3,900	5,200	6,500
XR-1000 Sportster (61ci V-twin).	3,000	5,000	8,000	10,000	13,000	16,000
FLH Electra Glide (80ci V-twin)	2,200	3,300	5,000	6,600	8,800	11,000
FLHT "Last Edition" (80ci V-twin)	2,700	4,100	6,100	8,100	11,000	14,000
FLHTC Electra Glide Classic (80ci V-twin) .	2,200	3,300	5,000	6,600	8,800	11,000
FLTC Tour Glide Classic (80ci V-twin) . . .	2,000	3,000	4,500	6,000	8,000	10,000
FXE Super Glide (80ci V-twin)	2,200	3,300	5,000	6,600	8,800	11,000
FXRDG Disc Glide (80ci V-twin)	2,400	3,600	5,400	7,200	9,600	12,000
FXRP Super Glide (80ci V-twin)	2,200	3,300	5,000	6,600	8,800	11,000
FXRS Low Glide (80ci V-twin)	2,300	3,500	5,200	6,900	9,200	12,000
FXRT Sport Glide (80ci V-twin)	2,400	3,600	5,400	7,200	9,600	12,000
FXSB Low Rider (80ci V-twin)	2,300	3,500	5,200	6,900	9,200	12,000
FXST Softail (80ci V-twin)	2,700	4,100	6,100	8,100	11,000	14,000
FXWG Wide Glide (80ci V-twin).	2,300	3,500	5,200	6,900	9,200	12,000
1985						
XLH Sportster (61ci V-twin)	1,300	2,000	2,900	3,900	5,200	6,500
XLS Sportster (61ci V-twin)	1,300	2,000	2,900	3,900	5,200	6,500
XLX Sportster (61ci V-twin)	1,300	2,000	2,900	3,900	5,200	6,500
FLHTC Electra Glide Classic (80ci V-twin) .	2,000	3,000	4,500	6,000	8,000	10,000
FLTC Tour Glide Classic (80ci V-twin) . . .	2,000	3,000	4,500	6,000	8,000	10,000
FXEF Fat Bob (80ci V-twin)	2,300	3,500	5,200	6,900	9,200	12,000
FXRC Low Glide Custom (80ci V-twin) . . .	2,500	3,800	5,600	7,500	10,000	13,000
FXRP Super Glide (80ci V-twin)	2,200	3,300	5,500	6,600	8,800	11,000
FXRS Low Glide (80ci V-twin).	2,400	3,600	5,400	7,200	9,600	12,000
FXRT Sport Glide (80ci V-twin)	2,400	3,600	5,400	7,200	9,600	12,000

	6	5	4	3	2	1
FXSB Low Rider (80ci V-twin).	2,300	3,500	5,200	6,900	9,200	12,000
FXST Softail (80ci V-twin).	2,700	4,100	6,100	8,100	11,000	14,000
FXWG Wide Glide (80ci V-twin).	2,300	3,500	5,200	6,900	9,200	12,000
1986						
XLH-883 Sportster (883cc V-twin).	1,300	2,000	2,900	3,900	5,200	6,500
XLH-1100 Sportster (1100cc V-twin) . .	1,800	2,700	4,100	5,400	7,200	9,000
FLHT Electra Glide (80ci V-twin)	2,000	3,000	4,500	6,000	8,000	10,000
FLHTC Electra Glide Classic (80ci V-twin) .	2,000	3,000	4,500	6,000	8,000	10,000
FLTC Tour Glide Classic (80ci V-twin) . .	2,000	3,000	4,500	6,000	8,000	10,000
FXR Super Glide (80ci V-twin)	2,200	3,300	5,000	6,600	8,800	11,000
FXRD Sport Glide Deluxe (80ci V-twin) . . .	2,200	3,300	5,000	6,600	8,800	11,000
FXRP Super Glide (80ci V-twin).	2,200	3,300	5,000	6,600	8,800	11,000
FXRS Low Rider (80ci V-twin)	2,400	3,600	5,400	7,200	9,600	12,000
FXRT Sport Glide (80ci V-twin)	2,200	3,300	5,000	6,600	8,800	11,000
FXST Softail (80ci V-twin).	2,700	4,100	6,100	8,100	11,000	14,000
FXSTC Softail Custom (80ci V-twin) . . .	2,700	4,100	6,100	8,100	11,000	14,000
FXSTH Softail Heritage (80ci V-twin)	2,700	4,100	6,100	8,100	11,000	14,000
1987						
XLH-883 Sportster (883cc V-twin).	1,300	2,000	2,900	3,900	5,200	6,500
XLH-1100 Sportster (1100cc V-twin)	1,700	2,600	3,800	5,100	6,800	8,500
XLH-1100 Sportster (1100cc V-twin, 30th Anniv)	2,100	3,500	4,700	6,300	8,400	11,000
FLHS Electra Glide Sport (80ci V-twin) . . .	2,000	3,000	4,500	6,000	8,000	10,000
FLHTC Electra Glide Classic (80ci V-twin) .	2,000	3,000	4,500	6,000	8,000	10,000
FLST Heritage Softail (80ci V-twin)	2,300	3,500	5,200	6,900	9,200	12,000
FLSTC Heritage Softail Special (80ci V-twin)	2,300	3,500	5,200	6,900	9,200	12,000
FLTC Tour Glide Classic (80ci V-twin) . . .	2,000	3,000	4,500	6,000	8,000	10,000
FXLR Low Rider Custom (80ci V-twin) . . .	2,400	3,600	5,400	7,200	9,600	12,000
FXLR Low Rider Custom (80ci V-twin, 10th Anniv.)	2,700	4,100	6,100	8,100	11,000	14,000
FXR Super Glide (80ci V-twin)	2,200	3,300	5,000	6,600	8,800	11,000
FXRP Super Glide (80ci V-twin).	2,200	3,300	5,000	6,600	8,800	11,000
FXRS Low Rider (80ci V-twin)	2,400	3,600	5,400	7,200	9,600	12,000
FXRS-SP Low Rider Sport (80ci V-twin) . .	2,600	3,800	5,700	7,700	10,000	13,000
FXRT Sport Glide (80ci V-twin)	2,200	3,300	5,000	6,600	8,800	11,000
FXST Softail (80ci V-twin).	2,700	4,100	6,100	8,100	11,000	14,000
FXSTC Softail Custom (80ci V-twin)	2,700	4,100	6,100	8,100	11,000	14,000
1988						
XLH-883 Sportster (883cc V-twin).	1,300	2,000	2,900	3,900	5,200	6,500
XLH-883 Sportster Hugger (883cc V-twin). .	1,400	2,100	3,200	4,200	5,600	7,000
XLH-883 Sportster Deluxe (883cc V-twin). .	1,400	2,100	3,200	4,200	5,600	7,000
XLH-1200 Sportster (1200cc V-twin)	2,000	3,000	4,000	5,000	7,000	8,000
FLHS Electra Glide Sport (80ci V-twin) . .	2,000	3,000	4,500	6,000	8,000	10,000
FLHTC Electra Glide Classic (80ci V-twin) .	2,000	3,000	4,500	6,000	8,000	10,000
FLHTC Electra Glide Classic (80ci V-twin, 85th Anniv.)	2,600	3,900	5,900	7,800	10,000	13,000
FLST Heritage Softail (80ci V-twin)	2,300	3,500	5,200	6,900	9,200	12,000
FLSTC Heritage Softail Custom (80ci V-twin)	2,300	3,500	5,200	6,900	9,200	12,000
FLTC Tour Glide Classic (80ci V-twin) . . .	2,200	3,300	5,000	6,600	8,800	11,000
FLTC Tour Glide Classic (80ci V-twin, 85th Anniv.)	2,600	6,900	5,900	7,800	10,000	13,000
FXLR Low Rider Custom (80ci V-twin) . . .	2,400	3,600	5,400	7,200	9,600	12,000
FXR Super Glide (80ci V-twin)	2,200	3,300	5,000	6,600	8,800	11,000
FXRP Super Glide (80ci V-twin).	2,200	3,300	5,000	6,600	8,800	11,000
FXRS Low Rider (80ci V-twin).	2,400	3,600	5,400	7,200	9,600	12,000
FXRS Low Rider (80ci V-twin, 85th Anniv) .	2,700	4,100	6,100	8,100	11,000	14,000
FXRS-SP Low Rider Sport (80ci V-twin) . .	2,400	3,800	5,700	7,700	10,000	13,000
FXRT Sport Glide (80ci V-twin)	2,200	3,300	5,000	6,600	8,800	11,000
FXST Softail (80ci V-twin).	2,700	4,100	6,100	8,100	11,000	14,000
FXST Softail (80ci V-twin, 85th Anniv.) . . .	2,900	4,400	6,500	8,700	12,000	15,000

	6	5	4	3	2	1
FXSTC Softail Custom (80ci V-twin)	2,700	4,100	6,100	8,100	11,000	14,000
1989						
XLH-883 Sportster (883cc V-twin).	1,300	2,000	2,900	3,900	5,200	6,500
XLH-883 Sportster Hugger (883cc V-twin) .	1,400	2,100	3,200	4,200	5,600	7,000
XLH-883 Sportster Deluxe (883cc V-twin). .	1,400	2,100	3,200	4,200	5,600	7,000
XLH-1200 Sportster (1200cc V-twin)	2,000	3,000	4,000	5,000	7,000	8,000
FLHS Electra Glide Sport (80ci V-twin) . . .	2,200	3,300	5,000	6,600	8,800	11,000
FLHTC Electra Glide Classic (80ci V-twin) .	2,200	3,300	5,000	6,600	8,800	11,000
FLHTCU Electra Glide Ultra Classic (80ci V-twin)	2,800	4,200	6,300	8,400	11,000	14,000
FLST Heritage Softail (80ci V-twin)	2,300	3,500	5,200	6,900	9,200	12,000
FLSTC Heritage Softail Custom (80ci V-twin)	2,300	3,500	5,200	6,900	9,200	12,000
FLTC Tour Glide Classic (80ci V-twin) . . .	2,300	3,500	5,200	6,900	9,200	12,000
FLTCU Tour Glide Ultra Classic (80ci V-twin)	2,800	4,200	6,300	8,400	11,000	14,000
FXLR Low Rider Custom (80ci V-twin) . . .	2,400	3,600	5,400	7,200	9,600	12,000
FXR Super Glide (80ci V-twin)	2,200	3,300	5,000	6,600	8,800	11,000
FXRP Super Glide (80ci V-twin).	2,200	3,300	5,000	6,600	8,800	11,000
FXRS Low Rider (80ci V-twin)	2,500	3,800	5,600	7,500	10,000	13,000
FXRS-C Low Rider Convertible (80ci V-twin)	2,500	3,800	5,600	7,500	10,000	13,000
FXRS-SP Low Rider Sport (80ci V-twin) . .	2,500	3,800	5,600	7,500	10,000	13,000
FXRT Sport Glide (80ci V-twin)	2,200	3,300	5,000	6,600	8,800	11,000
FXST Softail (80ci V-twin).	2,600	3,900	5,900	7,800	10,000	13,000
FXSTC Softail Custom (80ci V-twin)	2,700	4,100	6,100	8,100	11,000	14,000
FXSTS Springer Softail (80ci V-twin)	2,700	4,100	6,100	8,100	11,000	14,000
1990						
XLH-883 Sportster (883cc V-twin).	1,300	2,000	2,900	3,900	5,200	6,500
XLH-883 Sportster Hugger (883cc V-twin) .	1,400	2,100	3,200	4,200	5,600	7,000
XLH-883 Sportster Deluxe (883cc V-twin). .	1,400	2,100	3,200	4,200	5,600	7,000
XLH-1200 Sportster (1200cc V-twin)	2,000	3,000	4,000	5,000	7,000	8,000
FLHS Electra Glide Sport (80ci V-twin) . . .	2,200	3,300	5,000	6,600	8,800	11,000
FLHTC Electra Glide Classic (80ci V-twin) .	2,200	3,300	5,000	6,600	8,800	11,000
FLHTCU Electra Glide Ultra Classic (80ci V-twin)	2,800	4,200	6,300	8,400	11,000	14,000
FLST Heritage Softail (80ci V-twin)	2,300	3,500	5,200	6,900	9,200	12,000
FLSTC Heritage Softail Custom (80ci V-twin)	2,300	3,500	5,200	6,900	9,200	12,000
FLSTF Fat Boy (80ci V-twin)	2,600	3,900	5,900	7,800	10,000	13,000
FLTC Tour Glide Classic (80ci V-twin) . . .	2,500	3,800	5,600	7,500	10,000	13,000
FLTCU Tour Glide Ultra Classic (80ci V-twin)	2,800	4,200	6,300	8,400	11,000	14,000
FXLR Low Rider Custom (80ci V-twin) . . .	2,400	3,600	5,400	7,200	9,600	12,000
FXR Super Glide (80ci V-twin)	2,200	3,300	5,000	6,600	8,800	11,000
FXRP Super Glide (80ci V-twin).	2,200	3,300	5,000	6,600	8,800	11,000
FXRS Low Rider (80ci V-twin).	2,500	3,800	5,600	7,500	10,000	13,000
FXRS-C Low Rider Convertible (80ci V-twin)	2,500	3,800	5,600	7,500	10,000	13,000
FXRS-SP Low Rider Sport (80ci V-twin) . .	2,500	3,800	5,600	7,500	10,000	13,000
FXRT Sport Glide (80ci V-twin)	2,200	3,300	5,000	6,600	8,800	11,000
FXST Softail (80ci V-twin).	2,600	3,900	5,900	7,800	10,000	13,000
FXSTC Softail Custom (80ci V-twin)	2,700	4,100	6,100	8,100	11,000	14,000
FXSTS Springer Softail (80ci V-twin)	2,700	4,100	6,100	8,100	11,000	14,000
1991						
XLH-883 Sportster (883cc V-twin).	1,300	2,000	2,900	3,900	5,200	6,500
XLH-883 Sportster Hugger (883cc V-twin) .	1,400	2,100	3,200	4,200	5,600	7,000
XLH-883 Sportster Deluxe (883cc V-twin). .	1,400	2,100	3,200	4,200	5,600	7,000
XLH-1200 Sportster (1200cc V-twin)	2,000	3,000	4,000	5,000	7,000	8,000
FXR Super Glide (80ci V-twin)	2,200	3,300	5,000	6,600	8,800	11,000
FXRS Low Rider (80ci V-twin)	2,500	3,800	5,600	7,500	10,000	13,000
FXRS-SP Low Rider Sport (80ci V-twin) . .	2,500	3,800	5,600	7,500	10,000	13,000
FXLR Low Rider Custom (80ci V-twin) . . .	2,400	3,600	5,400	7,200	9,600	12,000
FXRS-C Low Rider Convertible (80ci V-twin)	2,500	3,800	5,600	7,500	10,000	13,000

	6	5	4	3	2	1
FXSTC Softail Custom (80ci V-twin)	2,700	4,100	6,100	8,100	11,000	14,000
FLSTF Fat Boy (80ci V-twin)	2,600	3,900	5,900	7,800	11,000	13,000
FXSTS Springer Softail (80ci V-twin)	2,700	4,100	6,100	8,100	11,000	14,000
FLSTC Heritage Softail Custom (80ci V-twin)	2,300	3,500	5,200	6,900	9,200	12,000
FXDB Dyna Sturgis (80ci V-twin)	3,000	5,000	7,000	8,900	12,000	14,000
FLHS Electra Glide Sport (80ci V-twin) . . .	2,200	3,300	5,000	6,600	8,800	11,000
FXRT Sport Glide (80ci V-twin)	2,200	3,300	5,000	6,600	8,800	11,000
FLTC Tour Glide Classic (80ci V-twin) . . .	2,200	3,300	5,000	6,600	8,800	11,000
FLHTC Electra Glide Classic (80ci V-twin) .	2,200	3,300	5,000	6,600	8,800	11,000
FLTCU Tour Glide Ultra Classic (80ci V-twin)						
	2,800	4,200	6,300	8,400	11,000	14,000
FLHTCU Electra Glide Ultra Classic (80ci V-twin)	2,800	4,200	6,300	8,400	11,000	14,000
1992						
XLH-883 Sportster (883cc V-twin).	1,300	2,000	2,900	3,900	5,200	6,500
XLH-883 Sportster Hugger (883cc V-twin) .	1,400	2,100	3,200	4,200	5,600	7,000
XLH-883 Sportster Deluxe (883cc V-twin). .	1,400	2,100	3,200	4,200	5,600	7,000
XLH-1200 Sportster (1200cc V-twin)	2,000	3,000	4,000	5,000	7,000	8,000
FXR Super Glide (80ci V-twin)	2,200	3,300	5,000	6,600	8,800	11,000
FXRS Low Rider (80ci V-twin).	2,500	3,800	5,600	7,500	10,000	13,000
FXRS-SP Low Rider Sport (80ci V-twin) . .	2,500	3,800	5,600	7,500	10,000	13,000
FXLR Low Rider Custom (80ci V-twin) . . .	2,400	3,600	5,400	7,200	9,600	12,000
FXRS-C Low Rider Convertible (80ci V-twin)	2,500	3,800	5,600	7,500	10,000	13,000
FXSTC Softail Custom (80ci V-twin)	2,700	4,100	6,100	8,100	11,000	14,000
FXDC Dyna Custom (80ci V-twin).	2,700	4,100	6,100	8,100	11,000	14,000
FLSTF Fat Boy (80ci V-twin)	2,600	3,900	5,900	7,800	11,000	13,000
FXSTS Springer Softail (80ci V-twin)	2,700	4,100	6,100	8,100	11,000	14,000
FXDB Dyna Daytona (80ci V-twin)	3,000	5,000	7,000	9,200	12,000	14,000
FLSTC Heritage Softail Custom (80ci V-twin)	2,300	3,500	5,200	6,900	9,200	12,000
FXRT Sport Glide (80ci V-twin)	2,200	3,300	5,000	6,600	8,800	11,000
FLHTC Electra Glide Classic (80ci V-twin) .	2,200	3,300	5,000	6,600	8,800	11,000
FLTCU Tour Glide Ultra Classic (80ci V-twin)						
	2,800	4,200	6,300	8,400	11,000	14,000
FLHTCU Electra Glide Ultra Classic (80ci V-twin)	2,800	4,200	6,300	8,400	11,000	14,000
1993						
XLH-883 Sportster (883cc V-twin).	1,500	2,200	3,200	4,400	5,500	6,600
XLH-883 Sportster Hugger (883cc V-twin) .	1,800	2,500	3,500	4,800	5,600	6,700
XLH-883 Sportster Deluxe (883cc V-twin). .	1,900	2,600	3,600	4,900	5,700	6,800
XLH-1200 Sportster (1200cc V-twin)	2,000	2,600	4,100	5,500	6,200	7,000
XLH-1200 Sportster Annversary (1200cc V-twin)	2,000	2,600	4,300	5,800	6,300	7,500
FXR Super Glide (80ci V-twin)	2,100	3,200	5,100	7,100	9,600	12,000
FXRS-SP Low Rider Sport (80ci V-twin) . .	2,200	3,300	5,300	7,500	10,100	13,000
FXLR Low Rider Custom (80ci V-twin) . . .	2,300	3,400	5,400	7,600	10,300	13,000
FXDL Dyna Low Rider (80ci V-twin).	2,400	3,500	5,500	7,700	10,500	13,000
FXRS Low Rider Convertible (80ci V-twin) .	2,500	3,600	5,600	7,800	10,600	13,000
FXLR Low Rider Custom Annivesary(80ci V-twin)	2,300	3,400	5,400	7,700	10,500	13,000
FXSTC Softail Custom (80ci V-twin)	2,500	4,100	6,200	8,600	11,700	14,000
FXDWG Dyna Wide Glide (80ci V-twin) . . .	2,400	4,000	6,000	8,200	11,200	14,000
FXSTS Springer Softail (80ci V-twin)	2,500	4,100	6,200	8,600	11,700	14,000
FLSTF Fat Boy (80ci V-twin)	2,600	4,200	6,300	8,800	12,000	15,000
FLSTC Heritage Softail Custom (80ci V-twin)	2,600	4,200	6,300	8,800	12,000	15,000
FXDWG Dyna Wide Glide Anniversary (80ci V-twin)	2,400	4,000	6,000	8,300	11,300	14,000
FLSTN Heritage Nostalgia (80ci V-twin). . .	4,200	6,300	8,400	11,000	14,600	17,000
FLHS Electra Glide Sport (80ci V-twin) . . .	2,200	3,300	5,300	7,500	12,200	15,000
FLHTC Electra Glide Classic (80ci V-twin) .	2,400	4,000	6,000	8,200	11,200	14,000

	6	5	4	3	2	1
FLHTC Electra Glide Classic Anniversary (80ci V-twin)	2,500	4,100	6,100	8,300	11,300	14,000
FLTCU Tour Glide Ultra Classic (80ci V-twin)	2,400	4,000	6,000	8,200	11,200	14,000
FLHTCU Electra Glide Ultra Classic (80ci V-twin)	2,500	4,100	6,100	8,300	11,300	14,000
FLTCU Tour Glide Ultra Classic Anniv (80ci V-twin)	2,500	4,100	6,100	8,300	11,300	14,000
FLHTCU Electra Glide Ultra Classic Anniv (80ci V-twin)	2,500	4,100	6,200	8,400	11,400	14,000
1994						
XL-883 Sportster (883cc V-twin)	1,500	2,200	3,200	4,400	5,500	6,600
XL-883 Sportster Hugger (883cc V-twin)	1,800	2,500	3,500	4,800	5,600	6,700
XL-883 Sportster Deluxe (883cc V-twin)	1,900	2,600	3,600	4,900	5,700	6,800
XL-1200 Sportster (1200cc V-twin)	2,000	2,600	4,100	5,500	6,200	7,000
FLHR Road King (80ci V-twin)	800	1,200	3,500	7,200	10,500	13,000
FLHTC Electra Glide Classic (80ci V-twin)	2,400	4,000	6,000	8,200	11,200	14,000
FLHTCU Electra Glide Ultra Classic (80ci V-twin)	2,500	4,100	6,100	8,300	11,300	14,000
FLSTC Heritage Softail (80ci V-twin)	2,500	4,100	6,200	8,600	11,700	14,000
FLSTF Fat Boy (80ci V-twin)	2,600	4,200	6,300	8,800	12,000	15,000
FLSTN Heritage Nostalgia (80ci V-twin)	4,200	6,300	8,400	11,000	14,600	17,000
FLTCU Tour Glide Ultra Classic (80ci V-twin)	2,500	4,100	6,100	8,300	11,300	14,000
FXDL Dyna Low Rider (80ci V-twin)	2,400	3,500	5,500	7,700	10,500	13,000
FXDS Convertible Low Rider (80ci V-twin)	2,000	3,000	4,700	7,200	9,700	12,500
FXDWG Dyna Wide Glide (80ci V-twin)	2,400	4,000	6,000	8,200	11,200	14,000
FXLR Low Rider (80ci V-twin)	2,300	3,400	5,400	7,700	10,500	13,000
FXR Super Glide (80ci V-twin)	2,100	3,200	5,100	7,100	9,600	12,000
FXSTC Softail (80ci V-twin)	2,500	4,100	6,200	8,600	11,700	14,000
FXSTS Springer Softail (80ci V-twin)	2,500	4,100	6,200	8,600	11,700	14,000
1995						
XL-883 Sportster (883cc V-twin)	900	2,100	3,300	4,500	5,700	7,000
XL-883 Sportster Hugger (883cc V-twin)	1,000	2,300	3,600	4,900	5,900	7,000
XL-883 Sportster Deluxe (883cc V-twin)	1,100	2,400	3,700	5,000	5,300	7,000
XL-1200 Sportster (1200cc V-twin)	1,200	2,700	4,200	5,700	6,600	7,500
FXD Dyna Super Glide (80ci V-twin)	1,200	2,200	4,200	6,400	8,600	10,800
FXDL Dyna Low Rider (80ci V-twin)	1,200	2,400	5,400	8,400	11,400	14,500
FXDS Convertible Dyna Low Rider (80ci V-twin)	1,100	2,100	4,800	7,500	10,200	13,000
FXSTC Softail Custom (80ci V-twin)	1,500	3,300	6,300	9,300	12,700	16,000
FXSTS Springer Softail (80ci V-twin)	1,500	3,300	6,300	9,300	12,600	16,000
FXDWG Dyna Wide Glide (80ci V-twin)	1,500	3,000	5,900	8,900	12,100	14,500
FLSTF Fat Boy Softail (80ci V-twin)	1,700	3,500	6,500	9,500	12,900	16,000
FLSTN Heritage Softail Special (80ci V-twin)	2,000	4,000	7,200	10,200	13,700	16,500
FXSTSB Bad Boy Softail (80ci V0twin)	1,800	3,500	7,000	10,000	13,400	16,500
FLSTC Heritage Softail (80ci V-twin)	1,800	3,500	6,500	9,500	12,900	16,000
FLHT Electra Glide (80ci V-twin)	1,200	2,500	5,000	8,000	10,900	14,000
FLHR Electra Road King (80ci V-twin)	1,500	3,000	6,000	9,000	12,000	15,000
FLHTC Classic (80ci V-twin)	1,500	3,000	6,000	8,900	12,100	15,000
FLTCU Tour Glide Ultra Classic (80ci V-twin)	1,500	3,000	6,000	9,000	12,200	15,000
FLHTCU Electra Glide Ultra Classic (80ci V-twin)	1,500	3,000	6,000	9,100	12,300	15,000
FLHTCUI Anniversary (80ci V-twin)	1,500	3,100	6,200	9,600	13,100	15,500
1996						
XL-883 Sportster (883cc V-twin)	900	1,200	1,500	3,000	4,000	5,100
XL-883 Sportster Hugger (883cc V-twin)	900	1,400	2,100	3,300	4,500	5,800
XL-1200 Sportster (1200cc V-twin)	1,200	2,700	4,200	5,700	6,600	7,500
XL-1200 Sportster Sport (1200cc V-twin)	1,200	2,700	4,200	5,700	6,600	7,700

	6	5	4	3	2	1
XL-1200 Sportster Custom (1200cc V-twin) .	1,200	2,700	4,200	5,700	6,600	7,900
FXD Dyna Super Glide (80ci V-twin)	1,200	2,200	4,200	6,400	8,600	10,200
FXDL Dyna Low Rider (80ci V-twin).	1,200	2,400	5,400	8,400	11,400	13,000
FXDS Convertible Dyna Low Rider (80ci V-						
twin)	1,100	2,100	4,800	7,500	10,200	13,300
FXSTC Softail Custom (80ci V-twin)	1,500	3,300	6,300	8,500	11,000	13,600
FLSTF Fat Boy Softail (80ci V-twin)	1,700	3,500	6,000	8,500	11,000	13,900
FXDWG Dyna Wide Glide (80ci V-twin) . . .	1,500	3,000	5,000	8,000	11,000	14,000
FXSTS Springer Softail (80ci V-twin)	1,500	3,000	5,000	8,000	11,000	14,000
FXSTSB Bad Boy Softail (80ci V0twin) . . .	1,500	3,000	5,000	8,000	11,000	14,400
FLSTC Heritage Softail Classic (80ci V-twin)	1,500	3,000	5,000	8,000	11,000	14,400
FLSTN Heritage Softail Special (80ci V-twin)	1,500	3,000	5,000	8,000	11,000	14,700
FLHT Electra Glide (80ci V-twin)	1,000	1,500	3,000	6,000	9,000	12,200
FLHR Road King (80ci V-twin)	1,500	3,000	5,000	8,000	11,000	14,000
FLHTC Classic (80ci V-twin)	1,500	3,000	5,000	8,000	11,000	14,400
FLHRI Road King (80ci V-twin)	1,500	3,000	5,000	8,000	11,000	14,800
FLHTCI Classic (80 ci V-twin)	1,500	3,000	6,000	9,000	12,000	15,200
FLHTCU Ultra Classic (80ci V-twin).	1,500	3,000	6,000	9,200	12,500	16,600
FLTCUI Ultra TG Classic (80ci V-twin) . . .	2,000	4,000	7,000	10,000	13,000	17,400
FLHTCUI Ultra Classic (80ci V-twin)	2,000	4,000	7,000	10,000	13,000	17,400

HENDERSON

	6	5	4	3	2	1
1919						
Model Z (72 cid, inline 4-cyl))	15,000	25,000	35,000	45,000	55,000	65,000
1920						
Model K (80-cid, inline 4-cyl)	11,000	16,000	24,000	32,000	43,000	54,000
1921						
Model K (80-cid, inline 4-cyl)	11,000	16,000	24,000	32,000	43,000	54,000
1922						
DeLuxe (80-cid, inline 4-cyl).	11,000	16,000	24,000	32,000	42,000	53,000
1923						
DeLuxe (80-cid, inline 4-cyl).	11,000	16,000	24,000	32,000	42,000	53,000
1924						
DeLuxe (80-cid, inline 4-cyl).	11,000	16,000	24,000	32,000	42,000	53,000
1925						
DeLuxe (80-cid, inline 4-cyl).	11,000	16,000	24,000	32,000	42,000	53,000
1926						
DeLuxe (80-cid, inline 4-cyl).	11,000	16,000	24,000	32,000	42,000	53,000
1927						
DeLuxe (80-cid, inline 4-cyl).	11,000	20,000	30,000	35,000	45,000	55,000
1928						
DeLuxe (80-cid, inline 4-cyl).	11,000	20,000	30,000	35,000	45,000	55,000
1929						
Streamline KJ (80-cid, inline 4-cyl)	11,000	20,000	30,000	40,000	50,000	60,000
1930						
Streamline KJ (80-cid, inline 4-cyl)	11,000	20,000	30,000	40,000	50,000	60,000
Streamline KI (high comp.)	12,000	17,000	26,000	35,000	46,000	58,000
1931						
Streamline KJ (80-cid, inline 4-cyl)	11,000	20,000	30,000	40,000	50,000	60,000
Streamline KI (high comp.)	12,000	17,000	26,000	35,000	46,000	58,000

HERCULES

	6	5	4	3	2	1
1974						
Hercules Wankel 2000	2,000	3,500	4,500	5,500	6,500	7,500
1975						
Hercules Wankel 2000	2,000	3,500	4,500	5,500	6,500	7,500
1977						
Hercules Wankel 2000	**2,000**	**3,500**	**4,500**	**5,500**	**6,500**	**7,500**

	6	5	4	3	2	1
HIAWATHA						
1946						
Doodlebug Model A	1,000	1,800	2,500	3,500	4,500	5,500
1947						
Doodlebug Model B	1,000	1,800	2,500	3,500	4,500	5,500
1948						
Doodlebug Super 8	1,000	1,800	2,500	3,500	4,500	5,500
HILDEBRAND and WOLFMULLER						
1894						
First known motorcycle in world	25,000	50,000	100K	125K	150K	175K
HODAKA						
1964						
ACE 90 (90cc single)	400	500	800	1,200	1,600	2,000
1965						
ACE 90 (90cc single)	400	500	800	1,200	1,600	2,000
1966						
ACE 90 (90cc single)	400	500	800	1,200	1,600	2,000
1967						
ACE 90 (90cc single)	400	500	800	1,200	1,600	2,000
1968						
ACE 100 (100cc single)	400	500	1,000	**1,500**	**2,000**	**2,500**
1969						
ACE 100A (100cc single)	400	500	800	1,100	1,400	1,800
ACE 100 Super Rat (100cc single)	800	1,200	1,800	2,300	3,100	3,900
1970						
ACE 100B (100cc single)	400	500	800	1,200	1,500	1,900
ACE 100 Super Rat (100cc single)	800	1,300	1,900	2,400	3,200	4,000
1971						
ACE 100B+ (100cc single)	500	700	1,100	1,400	1,900	2,400
ACE 100 Super Rat (100cc single)	800	1,200	1,900	2,500	3,300	4,100
1972						
ACE 100B+ (100cc single)	500	700	1,100	1,400	1,900	2,400
ACE 100 Super Rat (100cc single)	800	1,200	1,900	2,500	3,300	4,100
125 Wombat (125cc single)	500	800	1,200	1,600	2,100	2,600
1973						
100 Dirt Squirt (100cc single)	500	700	1,100	1,400	1,900	2,400
125 Combat Wombat (125cc single)	600	900	1,300	1,700	2,300	2,900
125 Combat Wombat (125cc single)	500	800	1,200	1,600	2,100	2,600
1974						
100 Dirt Squirt (100cc single)	500	700	1,100	1,400	1,900	2,400
100 Road Toad (100cc single)	500	800	1,100	1,500	2,000	2,500
100 Super Rat (100cc single)	800	1,200	1,800	2,300	3,100	3,900
125 Super Combat (125cc single)	900	1,400	2,000	2,700	3,600	4,500
1975						
100 Dirt Squirt (100cc single)	500	800	1,100	1,500	2,000	2,500
100 Road Toad (100cc single)	500	1,000	1,500	2,000	2,500	3,000
1976						
100 Road Toad (100cc single)	500	800	1,100	1,500	2,000	2,500
125 Wombat (125cc single)	600	900	1,300	1,700	2,300	2,900
250 ED (250cc single)	600	1,000	1,400	1,900	2,600	3,200
250 SL (250cc single)	600	900	1,300	1,700	2,300	2,900
1977						
Dirt Squirt 80 (80cc single)	600	900	1,300	1,700	2,300	2,900
175 SL (175cc single)	700	1,100	1,600	2,100	2,800	3,500
250 SL (250cc single)	600	900	1,300	1,700	2,300	2,900
1978						
Dirt Squirt 80 (80cc single)	600	900	1,300	1,700	2,300	2,900
175 SL (175cc single)	700	1,100	1,600	2,100	2,800	3,500
250 SL 70A (250cc single)	600	900	1,300	1,700	2,300	2,900

	6	5	4	3	2	1
HONDA						
1951						
Dream (98cc)	5,000	10,000	20,000	30,000	40,000	50,000
1955						
Dream 250 (250 cc)	2,000	4,000	8,000	12,000	16,000	20,000
1957						
Dream 250 (250 cc)	2,000	4,000	8,000	12,000	16,000	20,000
1958						
Benly JC 58 (125 cc)	3,500	7,000	11,000	15,000	19,000	23,000
1959						
C100 Super Cub (49cc single)	600	900	1,400	1,800	2,400	3,000
CA92 Benly Touring 125 (124cc twin)	800	1,200	1,800	2,400	3,200	4,000
CB92 Benly Super Sport 125 (124cc twin) .	2,400	3,600	5,400	7,200	9,600	12,000
CA95 Benly Touring 150 Early (154cc twin) .	800	1,200	1,800	2,400	3,200	4,000
CA71 Dream Touring 250 (247 cc twin) . . .	1,300	2,000	2,900	3,900	5,200	6,500
CE71 Dream Sport 250 (247cc twin)	2,400	3,600	5,400	7,200	9,600	12,000
C76 Dream Touring 300 (305cc twin) . . .	1,300	2,000	2,900	3,900	5,200	6,500
CA76 Dream Touring 300 (305cc twin) . . .	1,300	1,900	2,900	3,800	5,100	6,400
1960						
C100 Super Cub (49cc single)	600	900	1,400	1,800	2,400	3,000
C102 Super Cub (49cc single)	600	900	1,400	1,800	2,400	3,000
C110 Super Sports Cub (49cc single)	600	900	1,400	1,800	2,400	3,000
CB92 Benly Super Sport 125 (124cc twin) .	2,400	3,600	5,400	7,200	9,600	12,000
CA95 Benly Touring 150 Early (154cc twin) .	800	1,200	1,800	2,400	3,200	4,000
CA71 Dream Touring 250 (247cc twin) . . .	1,300	1,950	2,900	3,900	5,200	6,500
CA72 Dream Touring 250 Early (247cc twin)	1,000	1,500	2,300	3,000	4,000	5,000
CE71 Dream Sport 250 (247cc twin)	2,200	3,300	5,000	6,600	8,800	11,000
C76 Dream Touring 300 (305cc twin) . . .	1,300	2,000	2,900	3,900	5,200	6,500
CA76 Dream Touring 300 (305cc twin) . . .	1,200	1,800	2,700	3,600	4,800	6,000
CA77 Dream Touring 305 Early (305cc twin)	900	1,400	2,000	2,700	3,600	4,500
CS76 Dream Sport 300 (305cc twin)	2,200	3,300	5,000	6,600	8,800	11,000
CSA76 Dream Sport 300 (305cc twin) . . .	1,800	2,700	4,100	5,400	7,200	9,000
CSA77 Dream Sport 305 (305cc twin) . . .	1,000	1,500	2,300	3,000	4,000	5,000
1961						
C100 Super Cub (49cc single)	600	900	1,400	1,800	2,400	3,000
C102 Super Cub (49cc single)	600	900	1,400	1,800	2,400	3,000
CA100T Trail 50 (49cc single)	600	900	1,400	1,800	2,400	3,000
C110 Super Sports Cub (49cc single)	600	900	1,400	1,800	2,400	3,000
CB92R Benly SS Racer 125 (124cc twin) . .	4,400	6,600	9,900	13,200	17,600	22,000
CA95 Benly Touring 150 Early (154cc twin) .	800	1,200	1,800	2,400	3,200	4,000
CA72 Dream Touring 250 (247cc twin) . . .	1,000	2,000	3,000	4,000	5,000	6,000
CA72 Dream Touring 250 Early (247cc twin)	1,000	2,000	3,000	4,000	5,000	6,000
CB72 Hawk 250 (247cc twin)	1,000	1,800	2,600	3,400	4,200	5,000
C77 Dream Touring 305 (305cc twin)	800	1,200	2,000	3,000	4,000	5,000
CA77 Dream Touring 305 Early (305cc twin)	900	1,300	2,000	3,000	4,000	5,000
CB77 Super Hawk 305 (305cc twin)	900	1,500	3,000	4,000	5,000	6,000
CSA77 Dream Sport 305 (305cc twin) . . .	1,000	1,500	2,300	3,000	4,000	5,000
1962						
C100 Super Cub (49cc single)	600	900	1,400	1,800	2,400	3,000
C102 Super Cub (49cc single)	600	900	1,400	1,800	2,400	3,000
C110 Super Sports Cub (49cc single)	600	900	1,400	1,800	2,400	3,000
CA100 Honda 50 (49cc single)	600	900	1,400	1,800	2,400	3,000
CA100T Trail 50 (49cc single)	600	900	1,400	1,800	2,400	3,000
CA102 Honda 50 (49cc single)	600	900	1,400	1,800	2,400	3,000
C110 Sport 50 (49cc single)	600	900	1,400	1,800	2,400	3,000
CA105T Trail 55 (55cc single)	500	800	1,100	1,500	2,000	2,500
CB92R Benly SS Racer 125 (124cc twin) .	4,400	6,600	9,900	13,200	17,600	22,000
CA95 Benly Touring 150 Early (154cc twin) .	800	1,200	1,800	2,400	3,200	4,000
CA72 Dream Touring 250 Early (247cc twin)	1,000	2,000	3,000	4,000	5,000	6,000
CB72 Hawk 250 (247cc twin)	1,000	1,500	2,300	3,000	4,000	5,000

	6	5	4	3	2	1
CL72 Scrambler 250 (247cc twin)	1,000	1,500	2,000	2,500	3,500	4,500
C77 Dream Touring 305 (305cc twin)	800	1,200	1,900	2,500	3,300	4,100
CA77 Dream Touring 305 Early (305cc twin)	900	1,300	1,900	2,600	3,400	4,250
CB77 Super Hawk 305 (305cc twin).	900	1,500	3,000	4,000	5,000	6,000
CSA77 Dream Sport 305 (305cc twin) . . .	1,000	1,500	2,300	3,000	4,000	5,000
1963						
CA100 Honda 50 (49cc single)	500	800	1,100	1,500	2,000	2,500
CA102 Honda 50 (49cc single)	500	800	1,100	1,500	2,000	2,500
CA110 Sport 50 (49cc single)	600	900	1,400	1,800	2,400	3,000
CA105T Trail 55 (55cc single).	500	750	1,400	1,500	2,000	2,500
C105T Trail 55 (55cc single)	500	750	1,400	1,500	2,000	2,500
CA200 Honda 90 (89cc single)	500	700	1,100	1,400	1,900	2,400
CA95 Benly Touring 150 Early (154cc twin).	800	1,200	1,800	2,400	3,200	4,000
CA95 Benly Touring 150 Late (154cc twin) .	800	1,200	1,800	2,400	3,200	4,000
CA72 Dream Touring 250 Early (247cc twin)	1,000	2,000	3,000	4,000	5,000	6,000
CA72 Dream Touring 250 Late (247cc twin)	1,000	2,000	3,000	4,000	5,000	6,000
CB72 Hawk 250 (247cc twin).	1,000	1,800	2,600	3,400	4,200	5,000
CL72 Scrambler 250 (247cc twin)	1,000	1,500	2,000	2,500	3,500	4,500
C77 Dream Touring 305 (305cc twin)	800	1,200	2,000	3,000	4,000	5,000
CA77 Dream Touring 305 Early (305cc twin)	900	1,300	2,000	3,000	4,000	5,000
CA77 Dream Touring 305 Late (305cc twin)	900	1,300	2,000	3,000	4,000	5,000
CB77 Super Hawk 305 (305cc twin).	900	1,500	3,000	4,000	5,000	6,000
CSA77 Dream Sport 305 (305cc twin) . . .	1,000	1,500	2,300	3,000	4,000	5,000
1964						
CA100 Honda 50 (49cc single)	500	800	1,100	1,500	2,000	2,500
CA102 Honda 50 (49cc single)	500	800	1,100	1,500	2,000	2,500
CA110 Sport 50 (49cc single)	500	800	1,100	1,500	2,000	2,500
C105T Trail 55 (55cc single)	500	700	1,100	1,400	1,900	2,400
C200 Honda 90 (87cc single)	500	700	1,100	1,400	1,900	2,400
CA200 Honda 90 (87cc single)	500	700	1,100	1,400	1,900	2,400
CT200 Trail 90 (87cc single)	–400	700	**1,400**	**2,100**	**2,800**	**3,500**
S90 Super 90 (89cc single)	400	600	**1,200**	**1,800**	**2,400**	**3,000**
CA95 Benly Touring 150 Late (154cc twin) .	800	1,400	2,000	2,600	3,000	4,000
CA72 Dream Touring 250 Late (247cc twin)	1,000	2,000	3,000	4,000	5,000	6,000
CB72 Hawk 250 (247cc twin).	1,000	1,800	2,600	3,400	4,200	5,000
CL72 Scrambler 250 (247cc twin)	1,000	1,500	2,000	2,500	3,500	4,500
C77 Dream Touring 305 (305cc twin)	800	1,200	2,000	3,000	4,000	5,000
CA77 Dream Touring 305 Late (305cc twin)	800	1,200	2,000	3,000	4,000	5,000
CB77 Super Hawk 305 (305cc twin).	600	1,500	3,000	4,000	5,000	6,000
1965						
CA100 Honda 50 (49cc single)	500	800	900	1,200	1,600	2,000
CA102 Honda 50 (49cc single)	500	800	1,100	1,500	2,000	2,500
CA110 Sport 50 (49cc single)	500	800	1,100	1,500	2,000	2,500
CZ100 (49cc single).	800	1,200	2,000	3,000	4,000	5,000
C105T Trail 55 (55cc single)	500	700	1,100	1,400	1,900	2,400
S65 Sport 65 (63cc single)	400	**700**	**1,400**	**2,100**	**2,800**	**3,500**
CA200 Honda 90 (87cc single)	500	700	1,100	1,400	1,900	2,400
CT200 Trail 90 (87cc single)	400	**700**	**1,400**	**2,100**	**2,800**	**3,500**
S90 Super 90 (89cc single)	400	600	**1,200**	**1,800**	**2,400**	**3,000**
CA95 Benly Touring 150 Late (154cc twin) .	800	1,400	2,000	2,600	3,000	4,000
CB160 Sport 160 (161cc twin)	1,000	2,000	3,000	4,000	5,000	6,000
CA72 Dream Touring 250 Late (247cc twin)	1,000	2,000	3,000	4,000	5,000	6,000
CB72 Hawk 250 (247cc twin).	1,000	1,800	2,600	3,400	4,200	5,000
CL72 Scrambler 250 (247cc twin)	1,000	1,500	2,000	2,500	3,500	4,500
CA77 Dream Touring 305 Late (305cc twin)	800	1,200	2,000	3,000	4,000	5,000
CB77 Super Hawk 305 (305cc twin).	600	1,500	3,000	4,000	5,000	6,000
CL77 Scrambler 305 (305cc twin).	1,500	2,500	3,500	4,500	5,500	6,500
CB450 Super Sport 450 (444cc twin)	**1,500**	**3,000**	**5,000**	**7,000**	**9,000**	**11,000**
1966						
CA100 Honda 50 (49cc single)	400	600	900	1,200	1,600	2,000

	6	5	4	3	2	1
CA102 Honda 50 (49cc single)	400	600	900	1,200	1,600	2,000
CA110 Sport 50 (49cc single)	400	600	900	1,200	1,600	2,000
S65 Sport 65 (63cc single)	400	**700**	**1,400**	**2,100**	**2,800**	**3,500**
CA200 Honda 90 (87cc single)	400	600	1,000	1,300	1,800	2,200
CT200 Trail 90 (87cc single)	400	**700**	**1,400**	**2,100**	**2,800**	**3,500**
CM91 Honda 90 (89cc single).	400	600	900	1,200	1,600	2,000
CT90 Trail 90 (89cc single)	400	600	900	1,200	1,600	2,000
S90 Super 90 (89cc single)	400	600	**1,200**	**1,800**	**2,400**	**3,000**
CA95 Benly Touring 150 Late (154cc twin) .	800	1,400	2,000	2,600	3,000	4,000
CA160 Touring 160 (161cc twin)	400	600	900	1,500	2,000	2,500
CB160 Sport 160 (161cc twin)	1,000	2,000	3,000	4,000	5,000	6,000
CL160 Scrambler 160 (161cc twin)	1,000	2,000	3,000	4,000	5,000	6,000
CA72 Dream Touring 250 Late (247cc twin)	1,000	2,000	3,000	4,000	5,000	6,000
CB72 Hawk 250 (247cc twin).	1,000	1,800	2,600	3,400	4,200	5,000
CA77 Dream Touring 305 Late (305cc twin)	800	1,200	1,900	2,500	3,300	4,100
CB77 Super Hawk 305 (305cc twin).	600	1,000	3,000	4,000	5,000	6,000
CL77 Scrambler 305 (305cc twin).	1,500	2,500	3,500	4,500	5,500	6,500
CB450 Super Sport 450 (444cc twin)	**1,500**	**3,000**	**5,000**	**7,000**	**9,000**	**11,000**
1967						
CA100 Honda 50 (49cc single)	400	600	900	1,200	1,600	2,000
CA102 Honda 50 (49cc single)	400	600	900	1,200	1,600	2,000
CA110 Sport 50 (49cc single)	400	600	900	1,200	1,600	2,000
S65 Sport 65 (63cc single)	400	**700**	**1,400**	**2,100**	**2,800**	**3,500**
CL90 Scrambler 90 (89cc single)	400	500	700	1,000	1,400	1,700
CM91 Honda 90 (89cc single).	400	600	900	1,100	1,500	1,900
CT90 Trail 90 (89cc single)	400	600	900	1,200	1,600	2,000
S90 Super 90 (89cc single)	400	600	**1,200**	**1,800**	**2,400**	**3,000**
CL125A Scrambler 125 (124cc twin)	400	**700**	**1,400**	**2,100**	**2,800**	**3,500**
SS125A Super Sport 125 (124cc twin) . . .	400	500	800	1,100	1,400	1,800
CA160 Touring 160 (161cc twin)	400	600	1,000	1,500	2,000	2,500
CB160 Sport 160 (161cc twin)	1,000	2,000	3,000	4,000	5,000	6,000
CL160 Scrambler 160 (161cc twin)	1,000	2,000	3,000	4,000	5,000	6,000
CL160D Scrambler 160D (161cc twin) . . .	1,000	2,000	3,000	4,000	5,000	6,000
C200 (200cc single)	500	1,000	1,500	2,000	2,500	3,000
CA77 Dream Touring 305 Late (305cc twin)	800	1,200	1,900	2,500	3,300	4,100
CB77 Super Hawk 305 (305cc twin).	800	1,200	3,000	4,000	5,000	6,000
CL77 Scrambler 305 (305cc twin).	1,500	2,500	3,500	4,500	5,500	6,500
CB450 Super Sport 450 (444cc twin)	1,000	2,000	3,500	5,000	6,500	8,000
CB450D Super Sport 450D (444cc twin) . .	800	1,200	1,800	2,400	3,200	4,000
CL450 Scrambler 450 (444cc twin)	500	1,000	2,000	3,000	4,000	5,000
1968						
CA100 Honda 50 (49cc single)	400	600	900	1,100	1,500	1,900
CA102 Honda 50 (49cc single)	400	600	900	1,100	1,500	1,900
CA110 Sport 50 (49cc single)	400	600	900	1,200	1,600	2,000
S65 Sport 65 (63cc single)	400	**700**	**1,400**	**2,100**	**2,800**	**3,500**
CL90 Scrambler 90 (89cc single)	400	600	900	1,200	1,600	2,000
CL90L Scrambler 90 (89cc single)	400	500	700	1,000	1,400	1,700
CM91 Honda 90 (89cc single).	400	600	900	1,100	1,500	1,900
CT90 Trail 90 (89cc single)	300	500	800	1,000	1,400	1,700
CZ50M (90cc single)	400	600	900	1,200	1,600	2,000
S90 Super 90 (89cc single)	400	600	**1,200**	**1,800**	**2,400**	**3,000**
CL125A Scrambler 125 (124cc twin)	400	**700**	**1,400**	**2,100**	**2,800**	**3,500**
SS125A Super Sport 125 (124cc twin) . . .	420	630	950	1,260	1,680	2,100
CA160 Touring 160 (161cc twin)	400	600	900	1,100	1,500	1,900
CB160 Sport 160 (161cc twin)	800	1,800	2,600	3,400	4,200	5,000
CL160D Scrambler 160D (161cc twin) . . .	1,000	2,000	3,000	4,000	5,000	6,000
CA175 Touring 175 (174cc twin)	400	500	800	1,100	1,400	1,800
CL175 Scrambler 175 (174cc twin)	–300	**600**	**1,200**	**1,800**	**2,400**	**3,000**
CA77 Dream Touring 305 Late (305cc twin)	800	1,200	1,800	2,400	3,200	4,000

	6	5	4	3	2	1
CB77 Super Hawk 305 (305cc twin).	900	1,400	3,000	4,000	5,000	6,000
CL77 Scrambler 305 (305cc twin).	1,500	2,500	3,500	4,500	5,500	6,500
CB350 Super Sport 350 (325cc twin)	700	1,100	1,700	2,200	3,000	3,700
CL350 Scrambler 350 (325cc twin)	700	1,100	1,700	2,400	3,200	4,000
CB450 Super Sport 450 (444cc twin)	800	1,200	1,900	2,500	3,300	4,100
CB450K1 Super Sport 450 (444cc twin). . .	800	1,300	1,900	2,500	3,400	4,200
CL450K1 Scrambler 450 (444cc twin). . . .	500	1,000	2,000	3,000	4,000	5,000
1969						
Z50 AK1 Mini Trail (49cc single)	**800**	**1,500**	**2,500**	**3,500**	**4,500**	**5,500**
CA100 Honda 50 (49cc single)	400	500	800	1,100	1,400	1,800
CA102 Honda 50 (49cc single)	400	500	800	1,100	1,400	1,800
CA110 Sport 50 (49cc single)	400	600	900	1,200	1,600	2,000
S65 Sport 65 (63cc single)	400	**700**	**1,400**	2,100	2,800	3,500
CL70 Scrambler 70 (72cc single)	400	600	900	1,200	1,600	2,000
CL90 Scrambler 90 (89cc single)	400	600	900	1,200	1,600	2,000
CL90L Scrambler 90 (89cc single)	300	500	800	1,000	1,400	1,700
CM91 Honda 90 (89cc single).	400	600	900	1,100	1,500	1,900
CT90K1 Trail 90 (89cc single).	300	500	800	1,000	1,400	1,700
S90 Super 90 (89cc single)	400	600	**1,200**	**1,800**	**2,400**	**3,000**
SL90 Motosport 90 (89cc single)	400	600	900	1,100	1,500	1,900
CL125A Scrambler 125 (124cc twin)	400	**700**	**1,400**	2,100	2,800	3,500
SS125A Super Sport 125 (124cc twin) . . .	400	600	1,000	1,300	1,700	2,100
CA160 Touring 160 (161cc twin)	400	600	800	1,100	1,500	1,900
CB160 Sport 160 (161cc twin)	800	1,800	2,600	3,400	4,200	5,000
CA175 Touring 175 (174cc twin)	300	500	800	1,000	1,400	1,700
CA175K3 Touring 175 (174cc twin).	400	600	900	1,200	1,600	2,000
CB175K3 Super Sport 175 Early (174cc twin)	400	600	1,000	1,500	2,000	2,500
CB175K3 Super Sport 175 Late (174cc twin)	400	600	1,000	1,500	2,000	2,500
CD175 (174cc twin)	500	1,000	2,000	3,000	4,000	5,000
CL175 Scrambler 175 (174cc twin)	–300	**600**	**1,200**	**1,800**	**2,400**	**3,000**
CL175K3 Scrambler 175 (174cc twin). . . .	–300	**600**	**1,200**	**1,800**	**2,400**	**3,000**
CA77 Dream Touring 305 Late (305cc twin)	700	1,100	1,700	2,200	3,000	3,700
CB350 Super Sport 350 (325cc twin)	700	1,100	1,600	2,100	2,800	3,500
CB350K1 Super Sport (325cc twin)	700	1,100	1,600	2,100	2,800	3,500
CL350 Scrambler 350 (325cc twin)	700	1,100	1,700	**2,400**	**3,200**	**4,000**
CL350K1 Scrambler 350 (325cc twin). . . .	700	–1,000	–1,600	**2,400**	**3,200**	**4,000**
SL350 Motosport 350 (325cc twin)	400	700	1,000	1,300	1,800	2,200
CB450K1 Super Sport 450 (444cc twin). . .	900	1,400	2,000	2,700	3,600	4,500
CB450K2 Super Sport 450 (444cc twin). . .	800	1,200	1,800	2,400	3,200	4,100
CL450K1 Scrambler 450 (444cc twin)	500	1,000	2,000	3,000	4,000	5,000
CL450K2 Scrambler 450 (444cc twin). . . .	500	1,000	2,000	3,000	4,000	5,000
CB750 Four Sandcast (736cc four)	5,000	10,000	15,000	21,000	28,000	35,000
CB750 Four Diecast (736cc four)	1,800	2,600	3,800	**6,000**	**9,000**	**12,000**
1970						
CA100 Honda 50 (49cc single)	200	400	500	700	1,000	1,200
C70M Honda 70 (72cc single).	300	500	600	900	1,200	1,500
CL70K1 Scrambler 70 (72cc single).	300	400	600	800	1,000	1,300
CT70HK0 (72cc single)	400	700	1,000	2,000	3,000	4,000
CL90L Scrambler 90 (89cc single)	300	500	700	900	1,200	1,500
CT90K2 Trail 90 (89cc single).	300	500	700	900	1,200	1,500
CB100 Super Sport 100 (99cc single). . . .	300	400	600	800	1,000	1,300
C100 Scrambler 100 (99cc single)	200	300	500	700	900	1,100
SL100 Motosport 100 (99cc single)	200	300	500	700	900	1,100
CA175K3 Touring 175 (174cc twin)	300	400	600	800	1,100	1,400
CB175K4 Super Sport 175 (174cc twin). . .	300	500	1,000	1,500	2,000	2,500
CL175K3 Scrambler 175 (174cc twin). . . .	300	**600**	**1,200**	**1,800**	**2,400**	**3,000**
CL175K4 Scrambler 175 (174cc twin). . . .	300	**600**	**1,200**	**1,800**	**2,400**	**3,000**
SL175 Motosport 175 (174cc twin)	400	500	800	1,100	1,400	1,800
CB350K2 Super Sport350 (325cc twin) . . .	600	900	1,300	1,700	2,300	2,900

	6	5	4	3	2	1
CL350K2 Scrambler 350 (325cc twin). . . .	600	**1,000**	**1,600**	**2,400**	**3,200**	**4,000**
SL350 Motosport 350 (325cc twin)	600	800	1,400	2,000	2,800	3,500
SL350K1 Motosport 350 (325cc twin)	600	800	1,300	1,700	2,200	2,800
CB450K3 Super Sport 450 (444cc twin). . .	600	1,000	1,400	1,900	2,600	3,200
CL450K3 Scrambler 450 (444cc twin). . . .	500	1,000	2,000	3,000	4,000	5,000
CB750K0 750 Four (736cc four).	1,800	2,600	3,800	**6,000**	9,000	12,000
1971						
Z50 AK1 Mini Trail (49cc single)	**800**	**1,500**	**2,500**	**3,500**	**4,500**	**5,500**
C70M Honda 70 (72cc single).	300	500	600	900	1,200	1,500
CL70K2 Scrambler 70 (72cc single).	200	300	400	600	800	1,000
SL70 Motosport 70 (72cc single)	200	300	500	600	800	1,100
SL70K1 Motosport 70 (72cc single)	200	300	500	600	800	1,000
CT90K3 Trail 90 (89cc single)	300	400	500	800	1,100	1,400
CB100K1 Super Sport 100 (99cc single) . .	200	400	500	700	1,000	1,200
CL100K1 Scrambler 100 (99cc single) . . .	300	400	600	800	1,000	1,300
CL100S Scrambler 100S (99cc single) . . .	300	400	600	800	1,000	1,300
SL100K1 Motosport 100 (99cc single) . . .	300	400	600	800	1,000	1,300
SL125 Motosport 125 (122cc single)	300	400	600	800	1,100	1,400
CB175K5 Super Sport 175 (174cc twin). . .	300	500	1,000	1,500	2,000	2,500
CL175K5 Scrambler 175 (174cc twin). . . .	300	**600**	**1,200**	**1,800**	**2,400**	**3,000**
SL175K1 Motosport 175 (174cc twin). . . .	300	400	600	800	1,100	1,400
CB350K3 Super Sport 350 (325cc twin). . .	600	800	1,200	1,600	2,500	3,000
CL350K3 Scrambler 350 (325cc twin). . . .	600	**1,000**	**1,600**	**2,400**	**3,200**	**4,000**
SL350K1 Motosport 350 (325cc twin)	600	800	1,400	2,100	2,800	3,500
CB450K4 Super Sport 450 (444cc twin). . .	600	1,000	1,400	1,900	2,600	3,200
CL450K2 Scrambler 450 (444cc twin). . . .	500	1,000	2,000	3,000	4,000	5,000
CB500 500 Four (498cc four)	700	1,100	1,600	2,400	3,200	4,000
CB750K1 750 Four (736cc four).	1,800	2,600	3,800	5,000	**7,000**	**9,000**
1972						
C70K1 Honda 70 (72cc single)	200	300	400	600	800	1,000
CL70K3 Scrambler 70 (72cc single).	200	300	400	600	800	1,000
SL70 Motosport 70 (72cc single)	200	300	400	600	800	1,000
SL70K1 Motosport 70 (72cc single)	200	300	400	600	800	1,000
CT90K4 Trail 90 (89cc single)	300	500	1,000	1,500	2,000	2,500
CB100K2 Super Sport 100 (99cc single) . .	300	500	600	900	1,200	1,500
CL100K2 Scrambler 100 (99cc single) . . .	200	300	500	700	900	1,100
CL100S2 Scrambler 100S (99cc single). . .	200	400	500	700	900	1,200
SL100K2 Motosport 100 (99cc single) . . .	200	400	500	700	900	1,200
SL125K1 Motosport 125 (122cc single) . . .	200	400	600	800	1,100	1,400
CB175K6 Super Sport 175 (174cc twin) . . .	200	500	1,000	1,500	2,000	2,500
CL175K6 Scrambler 175 (174cc twin)	**300**	**600**	**1,200**	**1,800**	**2,400**	**3,000**
SL175K1 Motosport 175 (174cc twin)	200	400	500	700	900	1,200
XL250 Motosport 250 (248cc single)	400	600	800	1,000	1,300	1,600
CB350K4 Super Sport 350 (325cc twin) . . .	400	500	1,000	1,500	2,000	2,500
CL350K4 Scrambler 350 (325cc twin). . . .	**600**	**1,000**	**1,600**	**2,400**	**3,200**	**4,000**
SL350K2 Motosport 350 (325cc twin)	400	500	800	1,100	1,400	1,800
CB350F (347cc four)	500	700	1,100	1,500	2,000	3,000
CB450K5 Super Sport 450 (444cc twin). . .	400	600	900	1,200	1,600	2,000
CL450K5 Scrambler 450 (444cc twin). . . .	500	1,000	2,000	3,000	4,000	5,000
CB500K1 500 Four (498cc four).	600	1,000	1,600	2,400	3,200	4,000
CB750K2 750 Four (736cc four).	1,800	2,600	3,800	5,000	**7,000**	**9,000**
1973						
C70K1 Honda 70 (72cc single)	200	300	400	600	800	1,000
CL70K3 Scrambler 70 (72cc single).	200	300	400	600	800	1,000
CT70K2 (72cc single)	400	700	1,000	2,000	3,000	4,000
XR75 (72cc single)	200	300	400	600	800	1,000
CT90K4 Trail 90 (89cc single).	300	400	800	1,200	1,600	2,000
CL100S3 Scrambler 100S (99cc single). . .	200	300	500	600	800	1,000
SL100K3 Motosport 100 (99cc single) . . .	200	300	500	600	800	1,000
CB125S (122cc single)	300	500	800	1,200	1,600	2,000

	6	5	4	3	2	1
CL125S Scrambler 125 (122cc single) . . .	200	300	500	700	900	1,100
SL125K2 Motosport 125 (122cc single) . . .	200	500	800	1,200	1,600	2,000
TL 125 Trails 125 (122cc single)	200	300	500	700	900	1,100
XL175 (173cc single)	300	600	900	1,200	1,600	2,000
CB175K7 Super Sport 175 (174cc twin). . .	200	400	500	700	1,000	1,200
CL175K7 Scrambler 175 (174cc twin). . . .	**300**	**600**	**1,200**	**1,800**	**2,400**	**3,000**
CR250M Elsinore (248cc single)	500	**1,000**	**2,500**	4,000	5,500	7,000
XL250 Motosport 250 (248cc single)	300	500	1,000	1,500	2,000	2,500
CB350G Super Sport 350 (325cc twin) . . .	400	500	800	1,100	1,400	1,800
CB350K4 Super Sport 350 (325cc twin). . .	400	500	1,000	1,500	2,000	2,500
CL350K5 Scrambler 350 (325cc twin). . . .	600	**1,000**	**1,600**	2,400	3,200	**4,000**
SL350K2 Motosport 350 (325cc twin)	400	600	1,000	1,500	2,000	2,500
CB350F (347cc four)	400	700	1,000	1,500	2,000	3,000
CB450K6 Super Sport 450 (444cc twin). . .	700	1,000	1,500	2,000	2,500	3,000
CL450K5 Scrambler 450 (444cc twin). . . .	500	1,000	2,000	3,000	4,000	5,000
CB500K2 500 Four (498cc four).	600	900	1,600	2,400	3,200	4,000
CB750K3 750 Four (736cc four).	1,600	2,400	3,500	5,000	6,800	8,500
1974						
MR50 Elsinore (49cc single)	200	300	500	700	900	1,100
XL70 (72cc single)	200	400	500	700	1,000	1,200
XR75K1 (72cc single).	200	300	600	900	1,200	1,500
CT90K5 Trail 90 (89cc single).	200	400	800	1,200	1,600	2,000
XL100 Motosport 100 (99cc single)	200	400	500	700	1,000	1,200
CB125S1 Scrambler 125 (122cc single). . .	300	500	800	1,200	1,600	2,000
CL125S1 Scrambler 125 (122cc single). . .	300	500	700	900	1,100	1,300
TL125K1 Trails 125 (122cc single)	200	300	500	700	900	1,100
XL125 (122cc single)	200	400	500	700	1,000	1,200
CR125M Elsinore (123cc single)	300	500	1,000	1,500	2,000	2,500
MT125 Elsinore (123cc single)	300	400	800	1,200	1,600	2,000
XL175K1 (173cc single).	300	600	900	1,200	1,600	2,000
CB200 (198cc twin)	200	400	500	700	1,000	1,200
CL200 Scrambler (198cc twin)	200	400	500	700	1,000	1,200
CR250M Elsinore (248cc single)	**1,000**	**2,000**	**3,000**	**4,000**	**5,000**	**6,000**
MT250 Elsinore (248cc single)	300	400	700	900	1,200	1,500
XL250K1 Motosport (248cc single)	300	500	1,000	1,500	2,000	2,500
CB350F1 (347cc four).	400	600	1,200	1,800	2,400	3,000
XL350 (348cc single)	400	500	800	1,100	1,400	1,800
CB360 (356cc twin)	400	500	1,000	1,500	2,000	2,500
CB360G (356cc twin)	400	500	800	1,100	1,400	1,800
CL360 Scrambler 360 (356cc twin)	400	500	1,000	1,500	2,000	2,500
CB450K7 Super Sport 450 (444cc twin). . .	700	1,000	1,500	2,000	2,500	3,000
CL450K6 Scrambler 450 (444cc twin). . . .	500	1,000	2,000	3,000	4,000	5,000
CB500 500 Four (498cc four)	400	800	1,600	2,400	3,200	4,000
CB750K4 750 Four (736cc four).	1,600	2,400	3,500	4,800	6,500	8,000
1975						
MR50K1 Elsinore (49cc single)	200	300	500	700	900	1,100
ST70 (72cc single)	300	500	1,000	1,900	2,800	3,700
XL70K1 (72cc single)	200	400	500	700	900	1,200
XR75K2 (72cc single)	200	300	400	600	800	1,000
CT90K6 Trail 90 (89cc single).	200	400	800	1,200	1,600	2,000
CB125S2 (122cc single).	200	400	600	900	1,200	1,500
TL125K2 Trails 125 (122cc single)	200	400	600	900	1,200	1,500
XL125K1 (122cc single)	200	400	500	700	1,000	1,200
CR125M1 Elsinore (123cc single).	300	500	1,000	1,500	2,000	2,500
MT125K1 Elsinore (123cc single)	300	400	800	1,200	1,600	2,000
MR175 (171cc single).	300	400	600	800	1,100	1,400
CB200T (198cc twin)	300	400	600	800	1,100	1,400
CR250M1 Elsinore (248cc single).	**1,000**	**2,000**	**3,000**	**4,000**	**5,000**	**6,000**
MT250K1 Elsinore (248cc single)	300	400	700	900	1,200	1,500
TL250 Trails 250 (248cc single).	400	600	1,000	2,000	3,000	4,000

	6	5	4	3	2	1
XL250K2 (248cc single).	300	500	700	900	1,200	1,500
XL350K1 (348cc single).	400	500	800	1,200	1,600	2,000
CB360T (356cc twin)	300	500	1,000	1,500	2,000	2,500
CL360K1 Scrambler 360 (356cc twin).	300	500	800	1,000	1,400	1,700
CB400F Super Sport 400 Four (408cc four).	1,000	1,800	2,600	3,400	4,200	5,000
CB500T 500 Twin (498cc twin)	500	1,000	1,600	2,400	3,200	4,000
CB550F Super Sport 550 (544cc four) . . .	–500	1,000	**1,600**	2,400	**3,200**	4,000
CB550K1 550 Four (544cc four).	800	**1,500**	**2,500**	3,500	**4,500**	**5,500**
CB750F 750 Super Sport (736cc four) . . .	900	1,400	2,000	2,700	3,600	4,500
CB750K5 750 Four (736cc four). . .	1,200	2,000	3,000	4,200	5,500	7,000
GL1000 Gold Wing (999cc four).	**1,500**	**3,000**	**4,500**	**6,000**	**8,000**	10,000
1976						
XL70 (72cc single)	200	300	500	700	900	1,100
XR75 (72cc single)	200	300	400	600	800	1,000
CT90 Trail 90 (89cc single)	200	400	800	1,200	1,600	2,000
XL100 (99cc single)	200	300	500	700	900	1,100
CR125M Elsinore (123cc single)	300	500	1,000	1,500	2,000	2,500
MT125 Elsinore (123cc single)	300	400	800	1,200	1,600	2,000
CB125S (124cc single)	200	300	500	700	900	1,100
TL1215S Trails 125 (124cc single)	200	300	500	700	900	1,100
XL125 (124cc single)	200	400	500	700	1,000	1,200
MR175 Elsinore (171cc single)	300	400	600	800	1,100	1,400
XL175 (171cc single)	300	400	600	800	1,000	1,300
CB200T (198cc twin)	300	400	600	800	1,000	1,300
CR250M Elsinore (248cc single)	**1,000**	**2,000**	**3,000**	**4,000**	**5,000**	**6,000**
MR250 Elsinore (248cc single)	300	500	700	900	1,200	1,500
MT250 Elsinore (248cc single)	300	400	700	900	1,200	1,500
TL250 Trails 250 (248cc single).	400	600	1,000	2,000	3,000	4,000
XL250 (248cc single)	300	500	1,000	1,500	2,000	2,500
XL350 (348cc single)	600	900	1,200	1,500	2,000	2,500
CB360T (356cc twin)	300	500	800	1,000	1,400	1,700
CJ360T (356cc twin)	300	500	800	1,000	1,400	1,700
CB400F Super Sport 400 Four (408cc four).	1,000	1,800	2,600	3,400	4,200	5,000
CB500T 500 Twin (498cc twin)	500	1,000	1,500	2,000	2,500	3,500
CB550F Super Sport 550 (544cc four) . . .	**500**	**1,000**	**1,600**	2,400	**3,200**	4,000
CB550K 550 Four K (544cc four)	600	**1,500**	**2,500**	3,500	**4,500**	**5,500**
CB750F 750 Hondamatic (736cc four) . . .	–600	–1,000	2,000	**3,000**	**4,000**	5,000
CB750F 750 Super Sport (736cc four) . . .	**900**	**1,800**	**2,600**	3,400	**4,200**	5,000
CB750K 750 Four K (736cc four)	1,200	2,000	3,000	4,200	5,500	7,000
GL1000 Gold Wing (999cc four).	1,000	1,500	2,000	3,000	4,000	5,000
GL1000LTD Gold Wing Limited Edition						
(999cc four)	1,000	1,500	2,000	3,000	4,000	5,000
1977						
XR75 (72cc single)	200	300	400	600	800	1,000
XL75 (75cc single)	200	300	500	700	900	1,100
CT90 Trail 90 (89cc single)	200	400	800	1,200	1,600	2,000
XL100 (99cc single).	200	300	500	700	900	1,100
CR125M Elsinore (123cc single)	300	500	1,000	1,500	2,000	2,500
CT125 Trail 125 (123cc single)	200	400	500	700	1,000	1,200
MT125R Elsinore (123cc single)	200	400	800	1,200	1,600	2,000
XL125 (124cc single)	200	400	500	700	1,000	1,200
MR175 Elsinore (171cc single)	300	400	600	800	1,100	1,400
XL175 (171cc single)	200	400	500	700	1,000	1,200
XL350 (348cc single)	300	500	700	1,000	1,300	1,600
CJ360T (356cc twin)	300	500	800	1,000	1,400	1,700
CB400F Super Sport 400 Four (408cc four).	1,000	1,800	2,600	3,400	4,200	5,000
CB550F Super Sport 550 (544cc four) . . .	**500**	**1,000**	**1,600**	**2,400**	**3,200**	4,000
CB550K 550 Four K (544cc four)	400	**700**	**1,400**	2,100	**2,800**	3,500
CB750A 750 Hondamatic (736cc four) . . .	600	**1,000**	**2,000**	**3,000**	**4,000**	**5,000**

	6	5	4	3	2	1
CB750F 750 Super Sport (736cc four) . . .	900	1,800	2,600	3,400	4,200	5,000
CB750K 750 Four K (736cc four)	900	1,800	2,600	3,400	4,200	5,000
GL1000 Gold Wing (999cc four).	700	1,000	1,500	2,500	4,000	5,000
1978						
XR75 (72cc single)	200	300	400	600	800	1,000
XL75 (75cc single)	200	300	500	600	800	1,000
CT90 Trail 90 (89cc single)	200	400	800	1,200	1,600	2,000
XL100 (99cc single)	200	300	500	700	900	1,100
CB125S (122cc single)	200	300	500	700	900	1,100
CR125M Elsinore (123cc single)	300	500	1,000	1,500	2,000	2,500
MT125R Elsinore (123cc single)	200	400	800	1,200	1,600	2,000
XL125 (124cc single)	200	400	500	700	1,000	1,200
XL175 (173cc single)	200	400	500	700	1,000	1,200
CM185T Twinstar (181cc twin)	200	400	500	700	1,000	1,200
CR250R Elsinore (247cc single)	900	1,500	2,000	2,500	3,500	5,000
XL250S (249cc single)	300	500	700	900	1,200	1,500
XL350 (348cc single)	300	500	700	1,000	1,300	1,600
CB400A Hawk Hondamatic (395cc twin) . .	400	600	900	1,200	1,600	2,000
CB400TI Hawk I (395cc twin)	300	500	700	1,000	1,300	1,600
CB400TII Hawk II (395cc twin)	300	500	800	1,000	1,300	1,700
CX500 (496cc V-twin).	300	500	700	1,000	1,300	1,700
CB550K 550 Four K (544cc four)	400	700	1,400	2,100	2,800	3,500
CB750A 750 Hondamatic (736cc four) . .	600	1,000	2,000	3,000	4,000	5,000
CB750F 750 Super Sport (736cc four) . . .	900	1,800	2,600	3,400	4,200	5,000
CB750K 750 Four K (736cc four)	900	1,800	2,600	3,400	4,200	5,000
GL1000 Gold Wing (999cc four).	600	1,000	1,400	1,900	2,600	3,200
1979						
XL75 (75cc single)	200	300	400	500	700	900
XR80 (80cc single)	200	300	400	600	800	1,000
CT90 Trail 90 (89cc single)	200	400	800	1,200	1,600	2,000
XL100S (99cc single)	200	300	400	600	800	1,000
CB125S (122cc single)	200	300	500	700	900	1,100
CR125R Elsinore (124cc single)	300	500	1,000	1,500	2,000	2,500
XL125S (124cc single)	200	300	500	700	900	1,100
XL185S (180cc single)	200	400	500	700	1,000	1,200
XR185 (180cc single)	200	400	500	700	1,000	1,200
CM185T Twinstar (181cc twin)	200	400	500	700	1,000	1,200
CR250R Elsinore (247cc single)	900	1,500	2,000	2,500	3,500	5,000
XL250S (249cc single)	300	400	600	800	1,100	1,400
XR250 (249cc single)	300	500	700	1,000	1,300	1,600
CB400TI Hawk I (395cc twin)	300	500	700	1,000	1,300	1,600
CB400TII Hawk II (395cc twin)	300	500	800	1,000	1,300	1,700
CM400A Hondamatic (395cc twin)	400	600	900	1,200	1,600	2,000
CM400T (395cc twin)	400	600	1,000	1,300	1,700	2,100
CX500 (496cc V-twin).	300	500	800	1,000	1,400	1,700
CX500C Custom (496cc V-twin)	300	500	800	1,000	1,400	1,700
XL500S (498cc single)	300	500	700	1,000	1,300	1,600
XR500 (498cc single)	300	500	700	1,000	1,300	1,600
CB650 (627cc four)	300	500	800	1,000	1,400	1,700
CB750F 750 Super Sport (736cc four) . . .	900	1,800	2,600	3,400	4,200	5,000
CB750K 750 Four K (736cc four)	900	1,800	2,600	3,400	4,200	5,000
CB750K Limited Edition (749cc four) . . .	600	900	1,400	1,800	2,400	3,000
GL1000 Gold Wing (999cc four).	600	1,000	2,000	4,000	6,000	8,000
CBX Super Sport (1047cc six)	2,000	2,800	4,300	6,000	9,000	12,000
1980						
C70 Passport (72cc single)	200	300	400	600	900	1,200
CR80R Elsinore (80cc single)	200	300	400	600	800	1,000
XL80S (80cc single)	200	300	400	600	800	1,000
XR80 (80cc single)	200	300	400	600	800	1,000
XL100S (99cc single)	200	300	400	600	800	1,000

	6	5	4	3	2	1
CT110 Trail 110 (105cc single)	200	300	500	600	800	1,000
CB125S (124cc single)	200	300	500	700	900	1,100
CR125R Elsinore (124cc single)	300	500	1,000	1,500	2,000	2,500
XL125S (124cc single)	200	300	500	700	900	1,100
XL185S (180cc single)	200	400	500	700	1,000	1,200
CM200T Twinstar (194cc twin)	200	400	500	700	1,000	1,200
XR200 (195cc single)	300	400	800	1,100	1,400	
CR250R Elsinore (247cc single) . . .	400	600	1,000	2,000	3,500	5,000
XL250S (249cc single)	300	400	600	800	1,100	1,400
XR250 (249cc single)	300	500	700	1,000	1,300	1,600
CB400T Hawk (395cc twin)	300	500	700	1,000	1,300	1,600
CM400A Hondamatic (395cc twin) . .	400	600	900	1,100	1,500	1,900
CM400E (395cc twin)	400	600	900	1,200	1,600	2,000
CM400T (395cc twin)	400	600	900	1,200	1,600	2,000
CX500C Custom (496cc V-twin)	300	500	800	1,000	1,400	1,700
CX500D Deluxe (496cc V-twin)	300	500	800	1,000	1,400	1,700
XL500S (498cc single)	300	500	700	900	1,200	1,500
XR500 (498cc single)	300	500	700	900	1,200	1,500
CB650 (627cc four)	300	500	800	1,000	1,400	1,700
CB650C 650 Custom (627cc four)	300	500	700	1,000	1,300	1,600
CB750C 750 Custom (749cc four) . . .	500	800	1,100	1,500	2,000	2,500
CB750F 750 Super Sport (736cc four) . . .	600	1,000	**1,600**	**2,400**	**3,200**	**4,000**
CB750K 750 Four K (736cc four) . . .	500	800	1,100	1,500	2,000	2,500
CB900C 900 Custom (902cc four) . . .	500	800	1,100	1,500	2,000	2,500
CBX Super Sport (1047cc six)	2,000	2,800	4,300	5,700	7,500	9,500
GL1100 Gold Wing (1085cc four)	700	1,100	1,600	2,100	2,800	3,500
GL1100I Gold Wing Interstate (1085cc four)	800	1,300	1,900	2,500	3,400	4,200
1981						
Z50R (49cc single)	200	300	400	600	900	1,200
C70 Passport (72cc single)	200	300	400	600	900	1,200
C80R Elsinore (80cc single)	200	300	400	600	800	1,000
XL80S (80cc single)	200	300	400	600	800	1,000
XR80 (80cc single)	200	300	400	600	800	1,000
XL100S (99cc single)	200	300	400	600	800	1,000
XR100 (99cc single)	200	300	500	700	900	1,100
CT110 Trail 110 (105cc single)	200	300	500	600	800	1,000
CR125R Elsinore (123cc single)	300	400	600	800	1,100	1,400
CB125S (124cc single)	200	300	500	700	900	1,100
XL125S (124cc single)	200	300	500	700	900	1,100
XL185S (180cc single)	200	400	500	700	1,000	1,200
CM200T Twinstar (194cc twin)	200	400	500	700	1,000	1,200
XR200 (195cc single)	300	400	600	800	1,100	1,400
XR200R (195cc single)	300	500	800	1,000	1,400	1,700
CR250R Elsinore (246cc single)	400	600	900	1,200	1,600	2,000
XL250S (249cc single)	300	400	600	800	1,100	1,400
XR250R (249cc single)	400	600	900	1,100	1,500	1,900
CB400T Hawk (395cc twin)	400	500	800	1,100	1,400	1,800
CM400A Hondamatic (395cc twin) . .	400	600	900	1,200	1,600	2,000
CM400C Custom (395cc twin)	400	600	900	1,200	1,600	2,000
CM400E (395cc twin)	400	600	900	1,200	1,600	2,000
CM400T (395cc twin)	400	600	900	1,200	1,600	2,000
CR480R Elsinore (431cc single)	400	700	1,000	1,300	1,800	2,200
CX500C Custom (496cc V-twin)	400	500	800	1,100	1,400	1,800
CX500D Deluxe (496cc V-twin)	400	500	800	1,100	1,400	1,800
GL500 Silver Wing (496cc V-twin). . . .	600	900	1,350	1,800	2,400	3,000
GL500I Silver Wing Interstate (496cc V-twin)	600	900	1,350	1,800	2,400	3,000
XL500S (498cc single)	400	600	900	1,200	1,600	2,000
XR500R (498cc single)	500	800	1,100	1,500	2,000	2,500
CB650 (627cc four)	300	500	800	1,000	1,400	1,700
CB650C 650 Custom (627cc four)	300	500	700	1,000	1,300	1,600

	6	5	4	3	2	1
CB750C 750 Custom (749cc four)	400	600	900	1,200	1,600	2,000
CB750F 750 Super Sport (749cc four) . . .	**600**	**1,000**	**1,600**	**2,400**	**3,200**	**4,000**
CB750K 750 Four K (749cc four)	500	800	1,100	1,500	2,000	2,500
CB900C 900 Custom (902cc four)	600	800	1,300	1,700	2,200	2,800
CB900F 900 Super Sport (902cc four) . . .	600	900	1,400	1,800	2,400	3,000
CBX Super Sport (1,047cc six)	2,000	3,000	4,500	5,500	7,000	9,000
GL1100 Gold Wing (1,085cc four).	700	1,100	1,600	2,100	2,800	3,500
GL1100I Gold Wing Interstate (1,085cc four)	900	1,300	1,900	2,500	2,400	4,200
1982						
MB5 (49cc single).	400	600	800	1,000	1,200	1,500
C70 Passport (72cc single)	200	300	400	600	900	1,200
C80R Elsinore (80cc single).	200	300	400	600	800	1,000
XL80S (80cc single).	200	300	400	600	800	1,000
XR80 (80cc single)	200	300	400	600	800	1,000
XL100S (99cc single)	200	300	400	600	800	1,000
XR100 (99cc single).	200	300	500	700	900	1,100
CT110 Trail 110 (105cc single)	200	300	500	600	800	1,000
CR125R Elsinore (123cc single)	300	400	600	800	1,100	1,400
CB125S (124cc single)	200	300	500	700	900	1,100
XL125S (124cc single)	200	300	500	700	900	1,100
XL185S (180cc single)	200	300	500	700	1,000	1,200
CM200T Twinstar (194cc twin)	200	400	500	700	1,000	1,200
XR200 (195cc single)	300	400	600	800	1,100	1,400
XR200R (195cc single)	300	500	700	900	1,200	1,500
CM250C 250 Custom (234cc twin)	300	500	700	900	1,200	1,500
CR250R (246cc single)	400	600	900	1,200	1,600	2,000
XL250R (249cc single)	400	600	900	1,100	1,500	1,900
XR250R (249cc single)	400	600	900	1,200	1,500	1,900
CB450SC Nighthawk 450 (447cc twin) . . .	400	600	900	1,200	1,600	2,000
CB450T Hawk (447cc twin).	400	500	800	1,100	1,400	1,800
CM450A Hondamatic (447cc twin)	400	600	900	1,200	1,600	2,000
CM450C Custom (447cc twin)	400	600	900	1,200	1,600	2,000
CM450E (447cc twin)	400	600	900	1,100	1,500	1,900
CR480R (431cc single)	400	600	1,000	1,300	1,700	2,100
CX500C Custom (496cc V-twin)	400	500	800	1,100	1,400	1,800
GL500 Silver Wing (496cc V-twin).	600	900	1,400	1,800	2,400	3,000
GL500I Silver Wing Interstate (496cc V-twin)	600	900	1,400	1,800	2,400	3,000
CX500TC 500 Turbo (497cc turbo V-twin) .	1,200	1,800	2,700	3,600	4,800	6,000
FT500 Ascot (498cc single)	900	1,400	2,000	2,700	3,600	4,500
XL500R (498cc single)	400	600	900	1,200	1,600	2,000
XR500R (498cc single)	500	800	1,100	1,500	2,000	2,500
CB650 (627cc four)	500	800	1,100	1,500	2,000	2,500
CB650SC Nighthawk 650 (627cc four) . . .	800	1,100	1,700	2,300	3,000	3,800
VF750C V45 Magna (748cc V-four).	600	1,000	1,400	1,900	2,600	3,200
VF750S V45 Sabre (748cc V-four)	600	1,000	1,400	1,900	2,600	3,200
CB750C 750 Custom (749cc four)	400	600	900	1,200	1,600	2,000
CB750F 750 Super Sport (749cc four) . . .	**600**	**1,000**	**1,600**	**2,400**	**3,200**	**4,000**
CB750K 750 Four K (749cc four)	500	800	1,100	1,500	2,000	2,500
CB750SC Nighthawk 750 (749cc four) . . .	1,000	1,500	2,300	3,000	4,000	5,000
CB900C 900 Custom (902cc four)	600	800	1,300	1,700	2,200	2,800
CB900F 900 Super Sport (902cc four) . . .	600	900	1,400	1,800	2,400	3,000
CBX Super Sport (1,047cc six)	2,000	3,000	4,500	6,000	8,000	10,000
GL1100 Gold Wing (1,085cc four).	700	1,100	1,600	2,100	2,800	3,500
GL1100 Gold Wing Aspencade (1,085cc four)						
	900	1,400	2,100	2,800	2,700	4,600
GL1100I Gold Wing Interstate (1,085cc four)	800	1,300	1,900	2,500	3,400	4,200
1983						
CR60R (58cc single)	200	300	500	600	800	1,000
C70 Passport (72cc single)	200	300	400	600	900	1,200
C80R Elsinore (80cc single).	200	300	400	600	800	1,000

	6	5	4	3	2	1
XL80S (80cc single).	200	300	400	600	800	1,000
XR80 (80cc single)	200	300	400	600	800	1,000
XL100S (99cc single)	200	300	400	600	800	1,000
XR100 (99cc single).	200	300	500	700	900	1,100
CT110 Trail 110 (105cc single)	200	300	500	600	800	1,000
CR125R (123cc single)	300	400	600	800	1,100	1,400
XL185S (180cc single)	200	400	500	700	1,000	1,200
XL200R (195cc single)	300	400	600	800	1,100	1,400
XR200 (195cc single)	300	500	700	900	1,200	1,500
XR200R (195cc single)	400	600	900	1,100	1,500	1,900
CM250C 250 Custom (234cc twin)	300	500	700	900	1,200	1,500
CR250R (246cc single)	400	600	900	1,200	1,600	2,000
XL250R (249cc single)	400	600	900	1,100	1,500	1,900
XR350R (339cc single)	400	700	1,000	1,300	1,800	2,200
CB450SC Nighthawk 450 (447cc twin) . . .	400	600	900	1,200	1,600	2,000
CM450A Hondamatic (447cc twin)	500	700	1,000	1,500	2,000	2,500
CM450E (447cc twin)	400	600	900	1,100	1,500	1,900
CR480R (431cc single)	400	600	1,000	1,300	1,700	2,100
VT500C Shadow 500 (491cc V-twin)	400	600	900	1,200	1,600	2,000
FT500 Ascot (498cc single)	900	1,000	1,500	2,000	3,000	4,000
XR500R (498cc single)	500	800	1,100	1,500	2,000	2,500
CB550SC Nighthawk 550 (572cc four) . . .	600	900	1,400	1,900	2,500	3,100
CBX550F2 (550cc four) . . .	500	1,000	1,500	2,000	2,500	3,000
XL600R (589cc single)	400	600	1,000	1,300	1,700	2,100
CB650SC Nighthawk 650 (627cc four) . . .	700	1,100	1,600	2,100	2,800	3,500
CX650C Custom (674cc V-twin)	600	1,000	1,400	1,900	2,600	3,200
CX650T 650 Turbo (674cc turbo V-twin) . .	1,100	2,200	3,300	4,400	5,500	6,500
GL650 Silver Wing (674cc V-twin) . . .	700	1,100	1,600	2,100	2,800	3,500
GL650I Silver Wing Interstate (674cc V-twin)	700	1,100	1,600	2,100	2,800	3,500
VF750C V45 Magna (748cc V-four).	600	1,000	1,400	1,900	2,600	3,200
VF750F V45 Interceptor (748cc V-four) . . .	900	1,500	2,500	3,500	4,500	5,500
VF750S V45 Sabre (748cc V-four)	700	1,000	1,500	2,000	2,700	3,400
VT750C Shadow 750 (749cc V-four)	700	1,000	1,500	2,000	2,700	3,400
CB750SC Nighthawk 750 (749cc four) . . .	1,000	1,400	2,200	2,900	3,800	4,800
CB1000C 1000 Custom (973cc four)	600	1,500	2,500	3,500	4,500	5,500
CB1100F Super Sport (1,067cc four)	900	1,400	2,100	2,800	3,800	4,700
GL1100 Gold Wing (1,085cc four).	700	1,100	1,600	2,100	2,800	3,500
GL1100A Gold Wing Aspencade (1,085cc four)	900	1,400	2,100	2,800	3,400	4,600
GL1100I Gold Wing Interstate (1,085cc four)	900	1,400	2,100	2,800	3,800	4,700
VF1100 V65 Magna (1,098cc V-four)	700	1,100	1,600	2,100	2,800	3,500
1984						
CR60R (58cc single)	200	300	500	600	800	1,000
CR80R (80cc single)	200	300	500	700	900	1,100
XL80S (80cc single).	200	300	500	600	800	1,000
XR80 (80cc single)	200	300	500	600	800	1,000
XL100S (99cc single)	200	300	500	600	800	1,000
XR100 (99cc single).	200	300	500	600	800	1,000
CT110 Trail 110 (105cc single)	200	300	500	600	800	1,000
CR125R (123cc single)	300	400	600	800	1,100	1,400
CB125S (124cc single)	200	400	500	700	1,000	1,200
XL125S (124cc single)	200	400	500	700	1,000	1,200
XL200R (195cc single)	300	400	600	800	1,100	1,400
XR200 (195cc single)	300	500	700	900	1,200	1,500
XR200R (195cc single)	400	600	900	1,100	1,500	1,900
CR250R (246cc single)	400	600	900	1,200	1,600	2,000
XL250R (249cc single)	400	600	900	1,100	1,500	1,900
XR250R (249cc single)	400	700	1,000	1,300	1,800	2,200
XL350R (339cc single)	400	700	1,000	1,300	1,800	2,200
XR350R (339cc single)	400	700	1,000	1,300	1,800	2,200

	6	5	4	3	2	1
CR500R (491cc single)	500	800	1,200	1,600	2,100	2,600
VT500C Shadow 500 (491cc V-twin)	400	600	900	1,200	1,600	2,000
VT500FT Ascott (491cc V-twin)	900	1,400	2,000	2,700	3,600	4,500
VF500C V30 Magna (498cc V-four).	600	800	1,300	1,700	2,200	2,800
VF500F 500 Interceptor (498cc V-four) . . .	600	900	1,400	1,900	2,500	3,100
XR500R (498cc single)	500	700	1,000	1,400	1,800	2,300
XL600R (589cc single)	500	**1,000**	**2,500**	**4,000**	**5,500**	**7,000**
CB650SC Nighthawk 650 (655cc four) . . .	700	1,100	1,600	2,100	2,800	3,500
VT700C Shadow (694cc V-twin)	700	1,000	1,500	2,000	2,700	3,400
CB700SC Nighthawk S (696cc V-four) . . .	800	1,200	1,800	2,400	3,200	4,000
VF700C Magna (699cc V-four)	600	900	1,400	1,800	2,400	3,000
VF700F Interceptor (699cc V-four)	600	1,000	1,400	1,900	2,600	3,200
VF700S Sabre (699cc V-four).	600	900	1,400	1,800	2,400	3,000
VF750F V45 Interceptor (748cc V-four) . . .	900	1,300	2,000	2,600	3,500	4,400
VF1000S 1000 Interceptor (998cc V-four). .	1,000	1,500	2,300	3,000	4,000	5,000
VF1100 V65 Magna (1,098cc V-four). . . .	700	1,100	1,600	2,100	2,800	3,500
VF1100S V65 Sabre (1,098cc V-four). . . .	800	1,200	1,800	2,300	3,100	3,900
GL1200 Gold Wing (1,182cc four).	800	1,100	1,700	2,300	3,000	3,800
GL1200A Gold Wing Aspencade (1,182cc four)	900	1,400	2,100	2,800	3,800	4,700
GL1200I Gold Wing Interstate (1,182cc four)	800	1,300	1,900	2,500	3,400	4,200
1985						
XL80S (80cc single).	200	300	500	600	800	1,000
XR80 (80cc single)	200	300	500	600	800	1,000
CR80R (80cc single)	200	300	500	600	800	1,000
XL100S (99cc single)	200	300	500	600	800	1,000
XR100R (99cc single).	200	300	500	600	800	1,000
CB125S (124cc single)	200	300	500	600	800	1,000
CR125R (123cc single)	300	400	600	800	1,100	1,400
XL125S (124cc single)	200	400	500	700	1,000	1,200
XR200R (195cc single)	300	400	600	800	1,100	1,400
CMX250C Rebel 250 (234cc twin)	300	500	700	900	1,200	1,500
CR250R (246cc single)	400	600	900	1,200	1,600	2,000
XL250R (249cc single)	400	600	900	1,100	1,500	1,900
XR250R (249cc single)	400	600	1,000	1,300	1,700	2,100
XL350R (339cc single)	400	600	1,000	1,300	1,700	2,100
XR350R (339cc single)	500	700	1,100	1,400	1,900	2,400
CB450SC Nighthawk 450 (447cc twin) . . .	400	600	1,000	1,300	1,700	2,100
CR500R (491cc single)	500	700	1,100	1,400	1,900	2,400
VF500C V30 Magna (498cc V-four).	600	800	1,300	1,700	2,200	2,800
VF500F 500 Interceptor (498cc V-four) . . .	600	900	1,400	1,900	2,500	3,100
XL600R (589cc single)	500	700	1,000	1,400	1,800	2,300
XR600R (591cc single)	500	**1,000**	**2,500**	**4,000**	**5,500**	**7,000**
CB650SC Nighthawk 650 (655cc four) . . .	700	1,100	1,600	2,100	2,800	3,500
CB700SC Nighthawk S (696cc V-four) . . .	800	1,100	1,700	2,300	3,000	3,800
VT700C Shadow (694cc V-twin)	700	1,000	1,500	2,000	2,700	3,400
VF700C Magna (699cc V-four)	600	900	1,400	1,900	2,500	3,100
VF700F Interceptor (699cc V-four)	700	1,000	1,500	2,000	2,600	3,300
VF700S Sabre (699cc V-four).	600	900	1,400	2,100	2,800	3,500
VF1000R (998cc V-four)	1,500	2,500	3,500	4,500	5,500	6,500
VF1100 V65 Magna (1,098cc V-four). . . .	700	1,100	1,600	2,100	2,800	3,500
VF1100S V65 Sabre (1,098cc V-four). . . .	800	1,200	1,800	2,300	3,100	3,900
VT1100C Shadow 1100 (1,099cc V-twin) . .	900	1,300	1,900	2,500	3,400	4,200
GL1200A Gold Wing Aspencade (1,182cc four)	1,000	1,400	2,200	2,900	3,800	4,800
GL1200I Gold Wing Interstate (1,182cc four)	800	1,300	1,900	2,500	3,400	4,200
GL1200 Gold Wing Ltd Edition (1,182cc four)	900	1,400	2,100	2,800	3,700	4,600
1986						
XR80 (80cc single)	200	300	500	600	800	1,000
CR80R (83cc single)	200	300	500	600	800	1,000

	6	5	4	3	2	1
XR100R (99cc single)	200	300	500	600	800	1,000
CT110 Trail 110 (105cc single)	200	300	500	600	800	1,000
CR125R (124cc single)	200	400	500	700	1,000	1,200
TLR200 Reflex (195cc single)	200	300	800	1,200	1,600	2,000
XR200R (195cc single)	200	400	500	700	1,000	1,200
TR200 Fat Cat (199cc single)	200	400	700	1,000	1,500	2,000
CMX250C Rebel 250 (234cc twin)	300	400	700	1,000	1,500	2,000
CMX250CD Rebel 250 (234cc twin)	300	500	700	900	1,200	1,600
CR250R (246cc single)	400	500	800	1,100	1,400	1,800
XL250R (249cc single)	400	500	800	1,100	1,400	1,800
XR250R (249cc single)	400	500	800	1,100	1,400	1,800
CB450SC Nighthawk 450 (447cc twin)	400	600	900	1,200	1,600	2,000
CMX450C Rebel 450 (447cc twin)	300	500	800	1,000	1,400	1,700
CR500R (491cc single)	400	700	1,000	1,300	1,800	2,200
VF500F 500 Interceptor (498cc V-four)	600	900	1,400	1,900	2,500	3,100
XL600R (589cc single)	500	700	1,000	1,400	1,800	2,300
XR600R (591cc single)	500	**1,000**	**2,500**	**4,000**	**5,500**	**7,000**
VT700C Shadow (694cc V-twin)	700	1,100	1,600	2,100	2,800	3,500
CB700SC Nighthawk S (696cc V-four)	800	1,200	1,800	2,300	3,100	3,900
VFR700F Interceptor (699cc V-four)	700	1,000	1,500	2,000	2,700	3,400
VFR700F2 Interceptor (699cc V-four)	800	1,100	1,700	2,300	3,000	3,800
VF700C Magna (699cc V-four)	600	900	1,400	1,900	2,500	3,100
VFR750F Interceptor (748cc V-four)	800	1,200	2,200	3,100	3,800	4,500
VF1000R (998cc V-four)	1,500	2,500	3,500	4,500	5,500	6,500
VF1100 V65 Magna (1,098cc V-four)	700	1,000	1,500	2,000	2,700	3,400
VT1100C Shadow 1100 (1,099cc V-twin)	800	1,200	1,900	2,500	3,300	4,100
GL1200A Gold Wing Aspencade (1,182cc four)	900	1,400	2,100	2,800	3,700	4,600
GL1200I Gold Wing Interstate (1,182cc four)	800	1,200	1,800	2,400	3,200	4,000
GL1200SEI Gold Wing Aspencade (1,182cc four)	1,000	1,500	2,200	2,900	3,900	4,900
1987						
XR80 (80cc single)	200	300	500	600	800	1,000
CR80R (83cc single)	200	300	500	600	800	1,000
XR100R (99cc single)	200	300	500	600	800	1,000
CR125R (124cc single)	200	300	500	600	800	1,000
TLR200 Reflex (195cc single)	200	600	800	1,000	1,200	1,400
XR200R (195cc single)	200	400	500	700	1,000	1,200
TR200 Fat Cat (199cc single)	200	400	500	700	1,000	1,200
CMX250C Rebel 250 (234cc twin)	300	400	600	800	1,100	1,400
CR250R (246cc single)	400	500	800	1,100	1,400	1,800
XL250R (249cc single)	400	500	800	1,100	1,400	1,800
XR250R (249cc single)	400	500	800	1,100	1,400	1,800
CMX450C Rebel 450 (447cc twin)	300	500	800	1,000	1,400	1,700
CR500R (491cc single)	400	600	1,000	1,300	1,700	2,100
XL600R (589cc single)	500	700	1,000	1,400	1,800	2,300
XR600R (591cc single)	500	**1,000**	**2,500**	**4,000**	**5,500**	**7,000**
CBR600F Hurricane 600 (598cc four)	600	900	1,400	1,800	2,400	3,000
VT700C Shadow (694cc V-twin)	700	1,000	1,500	2,000	2,600	3,300
VFR700F2 Interceptor (699cc V-four)	700	1,100	1,700	2,200	3,000	3,700
VF700C Magna (699cc V-four)	600	1,000	1,400	2,100	2,800	3,500
CBR1000F 1000 Hurricane (998cc four)	800	1,200	1,800	2,400	3,200	4,000
VT1100C Shadow 1100 (1,099cc V-twin)	800	1,200	1,800	2,400	3,200	4,000
GL1200A Gold Wing Aspencade (1,182cc four)	900	1,400	2,100	2,800	3,700	4,600
GL1200I Gold Wing Interstate (1,182cc four)	800	1,200	1,800	2,400	3,200	4,000
1988						
XR80 (80cc single)	200	300	500	600	800	1,000
CR80R (83cc single)	200	300	500	600	800	1,000
XR100R (99cc single)	200	300	500	600	800	1,000

	6	5	4	3	2	1
CR125R (124cc single)	200	300	500	600	800	1,000
NX125 (124cc single)	200	300	500	600	800	1,000
XR200R (195cc single)	200	300	400	500	700	900
CR250R (246cc single)	200	400	500	700	1,000	1,200
NX250 (249cc single)	200	300	500	700	900	1,100
VTR250 Interceptor VTR (249cc twin). . .	300	500	700	900	1,200	1,500
XR250R (249cc single)	300	500	700	1,000	1,300	1,600
CR500R (491cc single)	300	500	700	1,000	1,300	1,600
VT600C Shadow VLX (598cc four)	700	1,100	1,600	2,100	2,800	3,500
XR600R (591cc single)	500	**1,000**	**2,500**	**4,000**	**5,500**	**7,000**
CBR600F Hurricane 600 (598cc four). . . .	600	900	1,400	1,800	2,400	3,000
NX650 (644cc single)	400	700	1,000	1,300	1,800	2,200
NT650 Hawk GT (647cc V-twin).	500	800	1,200	1,600	2,200	2,700
VF750C V45 Magna (748cc V-four).	600	1,000	1,400	1,900	2,600	3,200
VT800C Shadow (800cc V-twin)	1,000	1,500	2,300	3,000	4,000	5,000
CBR1000F 1000 Hurricane (998cc four) . .	800	1,200	1,900	2,500	3,300	4,100
VT1100C Shadow 1100 (1,099cc V-twin) . .	800	1,200	1,800	2,400	3,200	4,000
GL1500 Gold Wing (1,520cc six)	1,200	1,800	2,700	3,600	4,800	6,000
1989						
CR80R (83cc single)	200	300	500	600	800	1,000
XR100R (99cc single).	200	300	500	600	800	1,000
NX125 (124cc single)	200	300	500	600	800	1,000
CR125R (125cc single)	200	300	500	600	800	1,000
CR250R (246cc single)	200	400	500	700	1,000	1,200
NX250 (249cc single)	200	400	500	700	1,000	1,200
VTR250 VTR (249cc twin).	300	500	700	900	1,200	1,500
XR250R (249cc single)	300	500	700	900	1,200	1,500
CB400F CB1 (399cc four).	400	600	1,000	1,300	1,700	2,100
CR500R (491cc single)	300	500	800	1,000	1,400	1,700
GB500 Tourist Trophy (499cc single)	1,400	2,100	**4,000**	**6,000**	**8,000**	**10,000**
VT600C Shadow VLX (598cc four)	700	1,100	1,600	2,100	2,800	3,500
XL600V TransAlp (583cc V-twin)	1,000	1,500	2,300	3,000	4,000	5,000
XR600R (591cc single)	500	**1,000**	**2,500**	**4,000**	**5,500**	**7,000**
CBR600F (598cc four)	600	900	1,400	1,800	2,400	3,000
NX650 (644cc single)	400	700	1,000	1,300	1,800	2,200
NT650 Hawk GT (647cc V-twin).	500	800	1,200	1,600	2,500	3,000
PC800 Pacific Coast (800cc V-twin)	800	1,200	1,800	2,400	3,200	4,000
VT1100C Shadow 1100 (1,099cc V-twin) . .	800	1,200	1,800	2,400	3,200	4,000
GL1500 Gold Wing (1,520cc six)	1,200	1,800	2,700	3,600	4,800	6,000
1990						
NS50F (49cc single).	200	300	400	500	600	800
XR80 (80cc single)	200	300	500	600	800	1,000
CR80R (83cc single)	200	300	500	600	800	1,000
XR100R (99cc single).	200	300	500	600	800	1,000
NX125 (124cc single)	200	300	500	600	800	1,000
CR125R (125cc single)	200	300	500	600	800	1,000
XR200R (195cc single)	300	400	500	700	1,000	1,200
CR250R (246cc single)	300	400	500	700	1,000	1,200
NX250 (249cc single)	300	400	500	700	1,000	1,200
VTR250 VTR (249cc twin).	300	500	700	900	1,200	1,500
XR250R (249cc single)	300	500	700	900	1,200	1,500
CB400F CB1 (399cc four).	400	600	1,000	1,300	1,700	2,100
CR500R (491cc single)	300	500	800	1,000	1,400	1,700
GB500 Tourist Trophy (499cc single)	1,400	2,100	**4,000**	**6,000**	**8,000**	**10,000**
XL600V TransAlp (583cc V-twin)	1,000	1,500	2,300	3,000	4,000	5,000
XR600R (591cc single)	500	**1,000**	**2,500**	**4,000**	**5,500**	**7,000**
CBR600F (598cc four)	600	900	1,400	1,800	2,400	3,000
NT650 Hawk GT (647cc V-twin).	500	800	1,200	1,600	2,200	2,700
VFR750F VFR (748cc V-four).	700	1,000	1,500	2,500	3,500	4,500
VFR750R RC30 (748cc V-four)	1,700	2,600	3,800	5,100	6,800	8,500

	6	5	4	3	2	1
PC800 Pacific Coast (800cc V-twin).	800	1,200	1,800	2,400	3,200	4,000
CBR1000F (998cc four).	800	1,200	2,000	3,000	4,000	5,000
VT1100C Shadow 1100 (1,099cc V-twin). .	800	1,200	1,800	2,400	3,200	4,000
GL1500 Gold Wing (1,520cc six).	1,200	1,800	2,700	3,600	4,800	6,000
GL1500SE Gold Wing SE (1,520cc six). . .	1,300	2,000	2,900	3,900	5,200	6,500
1991						
ZR50R Mini (50cc single)	200	300	400	700	800	900
CT70 (70cc single)	200	400	600	1,000	1,100	1,300
XR80R (80cc single)	200	300	500	600	800	1,000
CR80R (83cc single)	200	300	500	600	800	1,000
EZ90 Cub (90cc single)	200	400	600	900	1,000	1,200
XR100R (99cc single)	200	300	500	600	800	1,000
CR125R (125cc single)	200	300	500	600	800	1,000
XR200R (195cc single)	200	400	500	700	1,000	1,200
CR250R (246cc single)	200	400	500	700	1,000	1,200
XR250 (249cc single)	300	400	600	800	1,100	1,400
XR250R (249cc single)	300	500	700	900	1,200	1,500
CB250 Nighthawk (250cc twin)	500	700	1,000	1,400	1,700	2,200
CR500R (491cc single)	300	500	800	1,000	1,400	1,700
XR600R (591cc single)	500	**1,000**	**2,500**	**4,000**	**5,500**	**7,000**
VT600C Shadow VLX (598cc four)	600	1,000	1,600	2,200	2,800	3,400
CBR600F2 (598cc four)	600	900	1,400	1,800	2,400	3,000
NT650 Hawk GT (647cc V-twin).	500	800	1,200	1,600	2,200	2,700
VFR750F (748cc V-four)	700	1,000	1,500	2,500	3,500	4,500
CB750 Nighthawk (750cc four)	700	1,100	1,700	2,300	2,900	3,500
CBR1000F (998cc four)	800	1,200	2,000	3,000	4,000	5,000
ST1100 (1,100cc four)	1,200	1,900	2,800	3,800	4,700	5,500
GL1500I Gold Wing Interstate (1,520cc six).	2,000	3,000	4,000	5,300	6,000	6,500
GL1500A Gold Wing Aspencade (1,520cc						
six).	2,200	3,200	4,300	5,700	6,200	6,800
GL1500SE Gold Wing SE (1,520cc six). . .	2,300	3,300	5,000	6,500	7,000	7,500
1992						
ZR50R Mini (50cc single)	200	300	400	700	800	900
CT70 (70cc single)	200	400	600	1,000	1,100	1,300
CR80R (83cc single)	200	300	500	600	800	1,000
EZ90 Cub (90cc single)	200	400	600	900	1,000	1,200
XR100R (99cc single)	200	300	500	600	800	1,000
CR125R (125cc single)	200	300	500	600	800	1,000
CR250R (246cc single)	200	400	500	700	1,000	1,200
XR250 (249cc single)	300	400	600	800	1,100	1,400
XR250L (249cc single)	300	500	700	900	1,200	1,500
CB250 Nighthawk (250cc twin)	500	700	1,000	1,400	1,700	2,200
CR500R (491cc single)	300	500	800	1,000	1,400	1,700
XR600R (591cc single)	500	**1,000**	**2,500**	**4,000**	**5,500**	**7,000**
VT600C Shadow VLX (598cc twin)	600	1,000	1,600	2,200	2,800	3,400
CBR600F2 (598cc four)	600	900	1,400	1,800	2,400	3,000
VFR750F (748cc V-four)	700	1,000	1,500	2,500	3,500	4,500
CB750 Nighthawk (750cc four)	700	1,100	1,700	2,300	2,900	3,500
VT1100CL Shadow (1,100cc twin)	1,000	1,600	2,200	3,000	3,800	4,600
ST1100 (1,100cc four)	1,200	1,900	2,800	3,800	4,700	5,500
ST1100AL ABS (1,100cc four)	1,300	2,000	2,900	3,900	4,800	5,600
GL1500I Gold Wing Interstate (1,520cc six).	2,100	3,100	4,100	5,500	6,100	6,600
GL1500A Gold Wing Aspencade (1,520cc						
six).	2,300	3,300	4,500	5,900	6,300	6,900
GL1500SE Gold Wing SE (1,520cc six). . .	2,400	3,500	5,100	6,700	7,200	7,700
1993						
ZR50R Mini (50cc single)	200	300	400	700	800	900
CT70 (70cc single)	200	400	600	1,000	1,100	1,300
ZR80R (80cc single)	300	500	600	700	900	1,100
CR80R (83cc single)	200	300	500	600	800	1,100

	6	5	4	3	2	1
EZ90 Cub (90cc single)	200	400	600	900	1,000	1,200
XR100R (99cc single)	200	300	500	600	800	1,000
CR125R (125cc single)	200	300	500	600	800	1,000
XR200R (200cc single)	300	600	1,000	1,400	1,800	2,200
CR250R (246cc single)	200	400	500	700	1,000	1,200
XR250L (249cc single)	300	500	700	900	1,200	1,500
XR250R (249cc single)	300	500	700	900	1,200	1,500
CB250 Nighthawk (250cc twin)	500	700	1,000	1,400	1,700	2,200
CR500R (491cc single)	300	500	800	1,000	1,400	1,700
XR600R (591cc single)	500	**1,000**	**2,500**	**4,000**	**5,500**	**7,000**
VT600C Shadow VLX (598cc twin)	600	1,000	1,600	2,200	2,800	3,400
VT600CD Shadow VLX Deluxe (598cc twin)	700	1,200	1,800	2,400	3,000	3,600
CBR600F2 (598cc four)	600	900	1,400	1,800	2,400	3,000
XR650L (650cc single)	500	800	1,100	1,300	1,500	1,800
VFR750F (748cc V-four)	700	1,000	1,500	2,500	3,500	4,500
CB750 Nighthawk (750cc four)	700	1,100	1,700	2,300	2,900	3,500
CBR900RR (900cc four)	1,400	2,000	2,900	3,800	4,700	5,600
CBR1000F (1000cc four)	1,200	1,800	2,500	3,400	4,300	5,200
VT1100CL Shadow (1,100cc twin)	1,000	1,600	2,200	3,000	3,800	4,600
ST1100 (1,100cc four)	1,200	1,900	2,800	3,800	4,700	5,500
ST1100AL ABS (1,100cc four)	1,300	2,000	2,900	3,900	4,800	5,600
GL1500I2 Gold Wing Interstate (1,520cc six)	2,100	3,100	4,100	5,500	6,100	6,600
GL1500A2 Gold Wing Aspencade (1,520cc six)	2,300	3,300	4,500	5,900	6,300	6,900
GL1500SE Gold Wing SE (1,520cc six) . . .	2,400	3,500	5,100	6,700	7,200	7,700
1994						
ZR50R Mini (50cc single)	200	300	400	700	800	900
CT70 (70cc single)	200	400	600	1,000	1,100	1,300
ZR80R (80cc single)	300	500	600	700	900	1,100
CR80R (83cc single)	200	300	500	600	800	1,100
EZ90 Cub (90cc single)	200	400	600	900	1,000	1,200
XR100R (99cc single)	200	300	500	600	800	1,000
CR125R (125cc single)	200	300	500	600	800	1,000
XR200R (200cc single)	300	600	1,000	1,400	1,800	2,200
CR250R (246cc single)	200	400	500	700	1,000	1,200
XR250L (249cc single)	300	500	700	900	1,200	1,500
XR250R (249cc single)	300	500	700	900	1,200	1,500
CB250 Nighthawk (250cc twin)	500	700	1,000	1,400	1,700	2,200
CR500R (491cc single)	300	500	800	1,000	1,400	1,700
XR600R (591cc single)	500	**1,000**	**2,500**	**4,000**	**5,500**	**7,000**
VT600C Shadow VLX (598cc twin)	600	1,000	1,600	2,200	2,800	3,400
VT600CD Shadow VLX Deluxe (598cc twin)	700	1,200	1,800	2,400	3,000	3,600
CBR600F2 (598cc four)	600	900	1,400	1,800	2,400	3,000
XR650L (650cc single)	500	800	1,100	1,300	1,500	1,800
VF750C Magna (750cc four)	500	900	1,800	2,600	3,400	4,200
VFR750F (748cc V-four)	700	1,000	1,500	2,500	3,500	4,500
RV750R RC45 (750cc four)	2,500	5,000	7,100	9,100	11,675	14,000
PC800 Pacific Coast (800cc V-twin)	500	1,000	1,900	2,800	3,700	4,600
CBR900RR (900cc four)	1,400	2,000	2,900	3,800	4,700	5,600
CB1000 (1000cc four)	500	1,000	1,800	2,700	3,500	4,300
CBR1000F (1000cc four)	1,200	1,800	2,500	3,400	4,300	5,200
VT1100CL Shadow (1,100cc twin)	1,000	1,600	2,200	3,000	3,800	4,600
ST1100 (1,100cc four)	1,200	1,900	2,800	3,800	4,700	5,500
ST1100A ABS-TCS (1,100cc four)	1,300	2,000	2,900	3,900	4,800	5,600
GL1500I Gold Wing Interstate (1,520cc six) .	2,100	3,100	4,100	5,500	6,100	6,600
GL1500A Gold Wing Aspencade (1,520cc six)	2,300	3,300	4,500	5,900	6,300	6,900
GL1500SE2 Gold Wing SE (1,520cc six) . .	2,400	3,500	5,100	6,700	7,200	7,700
1995						
ZR50R Mini (50cc single)	200	300	400	700	800	900

	6	5	4	3	2	1
ZR80R (80cc single)	300	500	600	700	900	1,100
CR80R (80cc single)	200	300	500	600	800	1,100
EZ90 Cub (90cc single)	200	400	600	900	1,000	1,200
XR100R (99cc single)	200	300	500	600	800	1,000
CR125R (125cc single)	200	300	500	600	800	1,000
XR200R (200cc single)	300	600	1,000	1,400	1,800	2,200
CR250R (246cc single)	200	400	500	700	1,000	1,200
XR250L (249cc single)	300	500	700	900	1,200	1,500
XR250R (249cc single)	300	500	700	900	1,200	1,500
CB250 Nighthawk (250cc twin)	500	700	1,000	1,400	1,700	2,200
CR500R (491cc twin)	300	500	800	1,000	1,400	1,700
XR600R (591cc single)	500	**1,000**	**2,500**	**4,000**	**5,500**	**7,000**
VT600C Shadow VLX (598cc twin)	600	1,000	1,600	2,200	2,800	3,400
VT600CD Shadow VLX Deluxe (598cc twin)	700	1,200	1,800	2,400	3,000	3,600
CBR600F3 (598cc four)	600	900	1,400	1,800	2,400	3,000
XR650L (650cc single)	500	800	1,100	1,300	1,500	1,800
VFR750F (748cc V-four)	700	1,000	1,500	2,500	3,500	4,500
CB750 Nighthawk (750cc four)	500	800	1,400	2,000	2,700	3,400
VF750C Magna (750cc four)	500	900	1,800	2,600	3,400	4,200
VF750CD Magna Deluxe (750cc four) . . .	700	1,400	2,000	2,700	3,600	4,500
PC800 Pacific Coast (800cc V-twin). . . .	500	1,000	1,900	2,800	3,700	4,600
CBR900RR (900cc four).	1,400	2,000	2,900	3,800	4,700	5,600
CB1000 (1000cc four).	500	1,000	1,800	2,700	3,500	4,300
CBR1000F (1000cc four)	1,200	1,800	2,500	3,400	4,300	5,200
VT1100 Shadow (1,100cc twin)	1,000	1,600	2,200	3,000	3,800	4,600
VT11A Shadow American Classic (1,100 cc twin)	600	1,200	2,200	3,200	4,200	5,200
ST1100 (1,100cc four)	1,200	1,900	2,800	3,800	4,700	5,500
ST1100A ABS-TCS (1,100cc four)	1,300	2,000	2,900	3,900	4,800	5,600
GL1500I Gold Wing Interstate (1,520cc six).	2,100	3,100	4,100	5,500	6,100	6,600
GL1500A Gold Wing Aspencade (1,520cc six).	2,300	3,300	4,500	5,900	6,300	6,900
GL1500SE Gold Wing SE (1,520cc six). . .	2,400	3,500	5,100	6,700	7,200	7,700
1996						
Z50R Mini (50cc single)	200	300	400	700	800	900
CR80R (80cc single)	200	300	500	600	800	1,100
CR80RB Expert Mini (80cc single)	200	300	500	600	900	1,200
ZR80R (80cc single)	300	500	600	700	900	1,100
EZ90 Cub (90cc single)	200	400	600	900	1,000	1,200
XR100R (99cc single)	200	300	500	600	800	1,000
CR125R (125cc single)	200	300	500	600	800	1,000
XR200R (200cc single)	300	600	1,000	1,400	1,800	2,200
CMX250C Rebel 250 (234cc twin)	500	700	1,000	1,400	1,700	2,200
CR250R (246cc single)	200	400	500	700	1,000	1,200
XR250R (249cc single)	300	500	700	900	1,200	1,500
XR250L (249cc single)	300	500	700	900	1,200	1,500
CB250 Nighthawk (250cc twin)	500	700	1,000	1,400	1,700	2,200
XR400R (400cc single)	300	600	900	1,200	1,500	2,100
CR500R (491cc single)	300	500	800	1,000	1,400	1,700
XR600R (591cc single)	500	**1,000**	**2,500**	**4,000**	**5,500**	**7,000**
VT600C Shadow VLX (598cc twin)	600	1,000	1,600	2,200	2,800	3,400
VT600CD Shadow VLX Deluxe (598cc twin)	700	1,200	1,800	2,400	3,000	3,600
CBR600F3 (598cc four).	600	900	1,400	1,800	2,400	3,000
CBR600SJR (600cc four)	500	800	1,600	2,400	3,200	4,000
XR650L (650cc single)	500	800	1,100	1,300	1,500	1,800
CB750 Nighthawk (750cc four)	500	800	1,400	2,000	2,700	3,400
VF750C Magna (750cc four)	500	900	1,800	2,600	3,400	4,200
VF750CD Magna Deluxe (750cc four) . . .	700	1,400	2,000	2,700	3,600	4,500
VFR750F (750cc four).	700	1,400	2,600	3,400	4,200	5,000
PC800 Pacific Coast (800cc V-twin). . . .	500	1,000	1,900	2,800	3,700	4,600

	6	5	4	3	2	1
CBR900RR (900cc four)	1,400	2,000	2,900	3,800	4,700	5,600
CBR1000F (1,000cc four).	1,000	2,000	3,000	4,000	5,000	6,000
VT1100B Shadow (1,100cc twin)	1,000	1,600	2,200	3,000	3,800	4,600
VT1100A1 Shadow American Classic (1,100 cc twin).	600	1,200	2,200	3,200	4,200	5,200
ST1100 (1,100cc four)	900	1,900	2,800	3,800	4,700	5,500
ST1100 ABS (1,100cc four)	1,000	2,000	3,000	4,000	5,000	6,000
GL1500I Gold Wing Interstate (1,520cc six).	2,100	3,100	4,100	5,500	6,100	6,600
GL1500A Gold Wing Aspencade (1,520cc six).	2,300	3,300	4,500	5,900	6,300	6,900
GL1500SE Gold Wing SE (1,520cc six). . .	2,400	3,500	5,100	6,700	7,200	7,700

HUSABERG

1990						
501E (501cc single).	100	200	300	500	700	900
1991						
350E (349cc single).	100	200	300	600	900	1,200
501E (504cc single).	100	200	300	600	900	1,200
1992						
350E (349cc single).	100	200	400	700	1,000	1,300
499C (499cc single).	100	200	300	600	900	1,200
501E (501cc single).	100	200	400	800	1,100	1,400
600C (595cc single).	100	200	300	600	900	1,200
1993						
350E (349cc single).	100	200	500	900	1,300	1,700
499C (499cc single).	100	200	400	700	1,000	1,300
501E (501cc single).	100	200	500	900	1,400	1,900
600C (595cc single).	100	200	400	700	1,000	1,300
600E (595cc single).	100	200	500	1,000	1,400	1,800
1994						
350E (349cc single).	100	200	600	1,100	1,600	2,100
501C (501cc single).	100	200	400	900	1,200	1,500
501E (501cc single).	100	200	600	1,100	1,700	2,300
600C (595cc single).	100	200	400	900	1,200	1,500
600E (595cc single).	100	200	600	1,100	1,700	2,300
1995						
FE350 (349cc single)	100	200	400	900	1,500	2,100
FC501 (501cc single)	100	300	600	1,100	1,700	2,300
FE501 (501cc single)	100	300	600	1,100	1,600	2,100
FC600 (595cc single)	100	300	600	1,200	1,800	2,400
FE600 (595cc single)	100	200	500	1,000	1,600	2,200

HUSQVARNA

1928						
Model 180 (550cc twin)	4,000	8,000	16,000	24,000	32,000	40,000
1938						
Model 301 (98cc single).	2,000	4,000	6,000	8,000	10,000	12,000
1957						
Novolette(125cc)	1,300	2,000	2,800	3,600	5,300	7,000
1958						
Corona	600	900	1,200	1,600	2,100	3,000
1966						
Moto Cross (250cc single).	2,400	3,800	5,400	7,000	10,000	14,000
Moto Cross (360cc single).	2,600	4,000	6,000	10,000	15,000	21,000
1967						
Moto Cross (250cc single).	1,300	2,000	2,800	3,600	5,300	7,000
Viking (360cc single)	1,300	2,000	2,800	3,600	5,300	7,000
1968						
Commando T (250cc single)	1,300	2,000	2,800	3,600	5,300	7,000
Moto Cross (250cc single).	1,300	2,000	2,800	3,600	5,300	7,000
Sportsman Enduro (360cc single).	1,300	2,000	2,800	3,600	5,300	7,000
Viking (360cc single)	1,300	2,000	2,800	3,600	5,300	7,000

	6	5	4	3	2	1
1969						
Moto Cross (250cc single)	1,300	2,000	2,800	3,600	5,300	7,000
Sportsman Enduro T (250cc single)	1,300	2,000	2,800	3,600	5,300	7,000
Moto Cross (360cc single)	1,300	2,000	2,800	3,600	5,300	7,000
Sportsman Enduro (360cc single)	1,300	2,000	2,800	3,600	5,300	7,000
Moto Cross (400cc single)	1,500	2,200	3,000	4,000	5,500	7,500
1970						
Moto Cross (250cc single)	1,300	2,000	2,800	3,600	5,300	7,000
Sportsman (360cc single)	1,300	2,000	2,800	3,600	5,300	7,000
Viking (360cc single)	1,300	2,000	2,800	3,600	5,300	7,000
Moto Cross (400cc single)	1,500	2,200	3,000	4,000	5,500	7,500
1971						
Moto Cross 4 Speed (250cc single)	1,300	2,000	2,800	3,600	5,300	7,000
Moto Cross 6 Speed (250cc single)	1,300	2,000	2,800	3,600	5,300	7,000
Moto Cross 8 Speed (250cc single)	1,300	2,000	2,800	3,600	5,300	7,000
Enduro C 4 Speed (360cc single)	1,300	2,000	2,800	3,600	5,300	7,000
Enduro C 8 Speed (360cc single)	1,300	2,000	2,800	3,600	5,300	7,000
Moto Cross 4 Speed (360cc single)	1,300	2,000	2,800	3,600	5,300	7,000
Moto Cross 8 Speed (360cc single)	1,300	2,000	2,800	3,600	5,300	7,000
Moto Cross 4 Speed (400cc single)	1,200	1,800	2,400	3,600	4,800	6,000
Moto Cross 8 Speed (400cc single)	1,200	1,800	2,400	3,600	4,800	6,000
1972						
CR (125cc single)	800	1,200	1,700	2,300	3,300	4,300
WR (125cc single)	800	1,200	1,700	2,300	3,300	4,300
CR (250cc single)	500	800	1,100	1,900	2,700	3,500
WR (250cc single)	500	1,000	2,000	3,000	4,000	5,000
Enduro (360cc single)	900	1,400	2,000	2,600	3,700	4,800
CR (400cc single)	800	1,200	1,800	2,300	3,300	4,300
CR (450cc single)	600	900	1,200	1,500	2,100	2,700
WR (450cc single)	600	900	1,200	2,000	3,000	4,000
DM (450cc single)	600	900	1,200	1,500	2,100	2,700
1973						
CR (125cc single)	800	1,200	1,700	2,300	3,300	4,300
WR (125cc single)	800	1,200	1,700	2,300	3,300	4,300
CR (250cc single)	900	1,400	2,100	2,800	3,800	4,800
WR (250cc single)	900	1,400	2,100	2,800	3,800	4,800
WR RT (250cc single)	600	900	1,200	1,500	2,100	2,700
WR RT (360cc single)	900	1,400	2,000	2,600	3,700	4,800
CR (400cc single)	800	1,200	1,800	2,300	3,300	4,300
CR (450cc single)	600	900	1,200	1,500	2,100	2,700
WR (450cc single)	600	900	1,200	1,500	2,100	2,700
1974						
CR (125cc single)	1,300	2,000	2,800	3,600	5,300	7,000
SC (125cc single)	1,300	2,000	2,800	3,600	5,300	7,000
WR (175cc single)	1,300	2,000	2,800	3,600	5,300	7,000
CR (250cc single)	1,300	2,000	2,800	3,600	5,300	7,000
WR (250cc single)	500	1,500	2,000	3,000	4,000	5,000
RT SK (360cc single)	1,300	2,000	2,800	3,600	5,300	7,000
CR (400cc single)	1,300	2,000	2,800	3,600	5,300	7,000
WR (400cc single)	1,300	2,000	2,800	3,600	5,300	7,000
SC (400cc single)	1,300	2,000	2,800	3,600	5,300	7,000
CR (450cc single)	500	1,500	2,000	3,000	4,000	5,000
WR (450cc single)	500	1,500	2,000	3,000	4,000	5,000
1975						
CC GP (175cc single)	900	1,400	2,000	2,500	3,700	4,900
CR GP (250cc single)	900	1,400	2,100	2,800	3,800	4,800
WR (250cc single)	600	900	1,200	1,500	2,100	2,700
CR GP (360cc single)	900	1,400	2,000	2,600	3,700	4,800
WR (400cc single)	700	1,000	1,300	1,700	2,400	3,100
CR (460cc single)	800	1,200	1,800	2,400	3,300	4,500

	6	5	4	3	2	1
1976						
CR (125cc single)	800	1,200	1,700	2,300	3,300	4,300
CC GP (175cc single)	900	1,400	2,000	2,500	3,700	4,900
CR (250cc single)	900	1,400	2,100	2,800	3,800	4,800
WR (250cc single).	600	900	1,200	1,500	2,100	2,700
Automatic (360cc single)	900	1,400	2,000	2,600	3,700	4,800
CR (360cc single)	1,600	2,200	3,000	4,000	5,800	7,500
WR (360cc single)	900	1,400	2,000	2,600	3,700	4,800
1977						
CR (125cc single)	800	1,200	1,700	2,300	3,300	4,300
CR (250cc single)	900	1,400	2,100	2,800	3,800	4,800
WR (250cc single).	600	900	1,200	1,500	2,100	2,700
Automatic (360cc single)	900	1,400	2,000	2,600	3,700	4,800
WR (360cc single)	900	1,400	2,000	2,600	3,700	4,800
CR (390cc single)	900	1,400	2,000	2,600	3,700	4,800
1978						
CR (125cc single)	800	1,200	1,700	2,300	3,300	4,300
CR (250cc single)	900	1,400	2,100	2,800	3,800	4,800
OR (250cc single)	900	1,400	2,100	2,800	3,800	4,800
WR (250cc single).	600	900	1,200	1,500	2,100	2,700
CR (390cc single)	1,300	2,000	2,800	3,600	5,300	7,000
OR (390cc single)	800	1,200	1,700	2,300	3,300	4,300
WR (390cc single)	800	1,200	1,700	2,300	3,300	4,300
1979						
CR (125cc single)	800	1,200	1,700	2,300	3,300	4,300
WR (125cc single)	800	1,200	1,700	2,300	3,300	4,300
CR (250cc single)	600	900	1,200	1,500	2,100	2,700
OR (250cc single)	900	1,400	2,100	2,800	3,800	4,800
WR (250cc single).	600	900	1,200	1,500	2,100	2,700
ACC (390cc single)	1,000	1,600	2,200	2,900	4,100	5,300
CR (390cc single)	1,300	2,000	2,800	3,600	5,300	7,000
OR (390cc single)	800	1,200	1,700	2,300	3,300	4,300
WR (390cc single)	800	1,200	1,700	2,300	3,300	4,300
1980						
CR (125cc single)	800	1,200	1,700	2,300	3,300	4,300
CR (250cc single)	400	600	800	1,000	1,400	2,000
OR (250cc single)	900	1,400	2,100	2,800	3,800	4,800
WR (250cc single).	600	900	1,200	1,500	2,100	2,700
ACC (390cc single)	1,100	1,700	2,400	3,100	4,500	5,900
CR (390cc single)	1,300	2,000	2,800	3,600	5,300	7,000
OR (390cc single)	800	1,200	1,700	2,300	3,300	4,300
WR (390cc single)	800	1,200	1,700	2,300	3,300	4,300
1981						
CR (125cc single)	800	1,200	1,700	2,300	3,300	4,300
WR (125cc single)	800	1,200	1,700	2,300	3,300	4,300
CR (250cc single)	800	1,200	1,600	2,000	2,400	3,000
WR (250cc single).	800	1,200	1,600	2,000	2,400	3,000
XC (250cc single)	900	1,400	2,100	2,800	3,800	4,800
AE 4 Speed Automatic (420cc single) . . .	900	1,400	2,100	2,800	3,800	4,800
AXC 4 Speed Automatic (420cc single) . . .	900	1,400	2,100	2,800	3,800	4,800
CR (430cc single)	900	1,400	2,100	2,800	3,800	4,800
WR (430cc single)	900	1,400	2,100	2,800	3,800	4,800
XC (430cc single)	900	1,400	2,100	2,800	3,800	4,800
1982						
CR (125cc single)	800	1,200	1,600	2,000	2,400	3,000
WR (125cc single).	800	1,200	1,600	2,000	2,400	3,000
XC (125cc single)	800	1,200	1,600	2,000	2,400	3,000
CR (250cc single)	800	1,200	1,600	2,000	2,400	3,000
WR (250cc single)	800	1,200	1,600	2,000	2,400	3,000
XC (250cc single)	900	1,400	2,100	2,800	3,800	4,800

	6	5	4	3	2	1
Automatic (420cc single)	900	1,400	2,100	2,800	3,800	4,800
CR (430cc single)	900	1,400	2,100	2,800	3,800	4,800
WR (430cc single).	900	1,400	2,100	2,800	3,800	4,800
XC (430cc single)	900	1,400	2,100	2,800	3,800	4,800
CR (500cc single)	800	1,200	1,600	2,000	2,400	3,000
1983						
CR (125cc single)	800	1,200	1,600	2,000	2,400	3,000
WR (125cc single).	800	1,200	1,600	2,000	2,400	3,000
XC (125cc single)	800	1,200	1,600	2,000	2,400	3,000
WR (175cc single).	800	1,200	1,600	2,000	2,400	3,000
XC (175cc single)	800	1,200	1,600	2,000	2,400	3,000
CR (250cc single)	800	1,200	1,600	2,000	2,400	3,000
WR (250cc single).	800	1,200	1,600	2,000	2,400	3,000
XC (250cc single)	900	1,400	2,100	2,800	3,800	4,800
WR (430cc single).	800	1,200	1,600	2,000	2,400	3,000
CR (500cc single)	800	1,200	1,600	2,000	2,400	3,000
TC (500cc single)	800	1,200	1,600	2,000	2,400	3,000
XC (500cc single)	800	1,200	1,600	2,000	2,400	3,000
1984						
CR (125cc single)	800	1,200	1,600	2,000	2,400	3,000
WR (125cc single).	800	1,200	1,600	2,000	2,400	3,000
XC (125cc single)	800	1,200	1,600	2,000	2,400	3,000
CR (250cc single)	800	1,200	1,600	2,000	2,400	3,000
WR (250cc single).	800	1,200	1,600	2,000	2,400	3,000
XC (250cc single)	900	1,400	2,100	2,800	3,800	4,800
WR (400cc single).	700	1,000	1,300	1,700	2,400	3,100
AE Automatic (500cc single)	800	1,200	1,600	2,000	2,400	3,000
CR (500cc single)	800	1,200	1,600	2,000	2,400	3,000
WR (500cc single).	800	1,200	1,600	2,000	2,400	3,000
XC (500cc single)	800	1,200	1,600	2,000	2,400	3,000
1985						
CR (125cc single)	300	600	1,000	1,400	1,800	2,200
XC (125cc single)	300	600	1,000	1,400	1,800	2,200
WR (125cc single).	300	700	1,300	1,900	2,600	3,300
CR (250cc single)	400	800	1,400	2,000	2,600	3,300
XC (250cc single)	300	700	1,300	2,000	2,600	3,200
WR (250cc single).	800	1,200	1,600	2,000	2,400	3,000
WR (400cc single).	700	1,000	1,300	1,700	2,400	3,100
AE Automatic (500cc single)	300	700	1,300	2,000	2,800	3,600
TC (500cc single)	300	700	1,300	2,000	2,700	3,500
CR (500cc single)	800	1,200	1,600	2,000	2,400	3,000
XC (500cc single)	300	700	1,400	2,100	2,800	3,500
TX (510cc single)	300	700	1,300	2,000	2,800	3,600
TE (510cc single)	500	900	1,600	2,300	3,000	3,700
1986						
CR (125cc single)	300	600	1,000	1,400	1,800	2,200
XC (125cc single)	300	600	1,000	1,400	1,800	2,200
WR (125cc single).	300	700	1,300	1,900	2,600	3,300
CR (250cc single)	400	800	1,400	2,000	2,600	3,300
XC (250cc single)	300	700	1,300	2,000	2,600	3,200
WR (250cc single).	800	1,200	1,600	2,000	2,400	3,000
WR (400cc single).	700	1,000	1,300	1,700	2,400	3,100
XC (400cc single)	300	700	1,300	2,000	2,800	3,600
AE Automatic (500cc single)	300	700	1,300	2,000	2,800	3,600
TC (500cc single)	300	700	1,300	2,000	2,700	3,500
CR (500cc single)	800	1,200	1,600	2,000	2,400	3,000
XC (500cc single)	300	700	1,400	2,100	2,800	3,500
TX (510cc single)	300	700	1,300	2,000	2,800	3,600
TE (510cc single)	500	900	1,600	2,300	3,000	3,700

	6	5	4	3	2	1
1987						
CR (250cc single)	400	800	1,400	2,000	2,600	3,300
XC (250cc single)	300	700	1,300	2,000	2,600	3,200
WR (250cc single)	300	700	1,300	1,900	2,600	3,300
CR (430cc single)	300	700	1,300	2,000	2,700	3,400
XC (430cc single)	300	700	1,300	2,000	2,700	3,400
WR (430cc single)	300	700	1,300	2,000	2,700	3,400
AE Automatic (430cc single)	300	700	1,300	2,000	2,800	3,600
XC (500cc single)	300	700	1,400	2,100	2,800	3,500
TC (510cc single)	300	700	1,300	2,000	2,700	3,500
TX (510cc single)	300	700	1,300	2,000	2,800	3,600
TE (510cc single)	500	900	1,600	2,300	3,000	3,700
1988						
WRK (125cc single)	400	800	1,200	1,600	2,000	2,200
XC (250cc single)	400	1,000	1,600	2,300	3,000	3,700
WR (250cc single)	800	1,200	1,600	2,200	3,000	3,800
CR (430cc single)	500	1,100	1,600	2,400	3,200	4,000
XC (430cc single)	900	1,400	2,100	2,800	3,400	4,100
WR (430cc single)	500	1,000	1,600	2,400	3,200	4,000
AE Automatic (430cc single)	800	1,200	1,600	2,200	3,200	4,200
TC (510cc single)	500	1,000	2,000	3,000	4,000	5,000
TX (510cc single)	900	1,400	2,100	2,800	3,800	5,000
TE (510cc single)	900	1,400	2,100	2,800	3,800	5,000
1990						
WMX (125cc single)	300	700	1,400	2,100	2,800	3,500
WMX (250cc single)	500	1,000	1,800	2,600	3,400	4,200
WMX (510cc single)	600	1,200	2,000	2,800	3,600	4,400
WXE (125cc single)	600	1,200	2,000	2,800	3,600	4,400
WXE (250cc single)	700	1,400	2,200	3,200	4,200	5,200
WXE (510cc single)	800	1,500	2,500	3,500	4,500	5,500
1991						
WMX (125cc single)	300	700	1,400	2,100	2,800	3,500
WXE (125cc single)	600	1,200	2,000	2,800	3,600	4,400
WMX (250cc single)	500	1,000	1,800	2,600	3,400	4,200
WXE (250cc single)	700	1,400	2,200	3,200	4,200	5,200
WXE (260cc single)	800	1,500	2,500	3,500	4,500	5,500
WXE (350cc single)	900	1,700	2,700	3,700	4,700	5,700
WMX (610cc single)	800	1,500	2,300	3,100	3,900	4,700
WXE (610cc single)	1,000	2,000	3,000	4,000	5,000	6,000
1992						
WXC (125cc single)	400	800	1,600	2,400	3,200	4,000
WXE (125cc single)	600	1,200	2,000	2,800	3,600	4,400
WXC (250cc single)	600	1,200	2,100	3,000	3,900	4,800
WXE (250cc single)	700	1,400	2,200	3,200	4,200	5,200
WXC (350cc single)	600	1,200	2,100	3,100	4,100	5,100
WXE (350cc single)	800	1,500	2,500	3,500	4,500	5,500
WXC (360cc single)	700	1,400	2,400	3,400	4,400	5,400
WXE (360cc single)	900	1,700	2,700	3,700	4,700	5,700
WXC (610cc single)	900	1,800	2,800	3,800	4,800	5,800
WXE (610cc single)	1,000	2,000	3,000	4,000	5,000	6,000
1993						
WXC (250cc single)	600	1,200	2,100	3,000	3,900	4,800
WXC (350cc single)	600	1,200	2,100	3,100	4,100	5,100
WXC (360cc single)	700	1,400	2,400	3,400	4,400	5,400
WXC (610cc single)	900	1,800	2,800	3,800	4,800	5,800
1994						
WXC (125cc single)	400	800	1,600	2,400	3,200	4,000
WXE (125cc single)	600	1,200	2,000	2,800	3,600	4,400
WXC (250cc single)	600	1,200	2,100	3,000	3,900	4,800
WXE (250cc single)	700	1,400	2,200	3,200	4,200	5,200

	6	5	4	3	2	1
WXC (350cc single)	600	1,200	2,100	3,100	4,100	5,100
WXE (350cc single)	700	1,500	2,500	3,500	4,500	5,500
WXC (360cc single)	700	1,400	2,400	3,400	4,400	5,400
WXE (360cc single)	900	1,700	2,700	3,700	4,700	5,700
WXC (610cc single)	900	1,800	2,800	3,800	4,800	5,800
WXE (610cc single)	1,000	2,000	3,000	4,000	5,000	6,000
1995						
WXE (125cc single)	600	1,200	2,000	2,800	3,600	4,400
WXE (250cc single)	700	1,400	2,200	3,200	4,200	5,200
WXE (350cc single)	800	1,500	2,500	3,500	4,500	5,500
WXE (360cc single)	900	1,700	2,700	3,700	4,700	5,700
WXE (610cc single)	1,000	2,000	3,000	4,000	5,000	6,000
1996						
WXC (125cc single)	400	800	1,800	2,600	3,400	4,200
WXE (125cc single)	600	1,200	2,000	2,800	3,600	4,400
WXC (250cc single)	600	1,000	2,000	3,000	4,000	5,000
WXE (250cc single)	700	1,400	2,200	3,200	4,200	5,200
WXC (360cc single)	700	1,400	2,400	3,400	4,400	5,400
WXE (360cc single)	900	1,700	2,700	3,700	4,700	5,700
WXC (410cc single)	900	1,700	2,700	3,700	4,700	5,700
WXE (410cc single)	900	1,800	2,800	3,800	4,800	5,800
WXC (610cc single)	900	1,900	3,000	4,100	5,200	6,300
WXE (610cc single)	1,000	2,500	3,500	4,500	5,500	6,500

INDIAN						
1901						
Single 1.75hp (3)	60,000	75,000	90,000	105K	120K	135K
1902						
Single 1.75hp (143)	60,000	75,000	90,000	105K	120K	135K
1903						
Single 1.75hp (376)	60,000	75,000	90,000	105K	120K	135K
1904						
Single 1.75hp (596)	60,000	75,000	90,000	105K	120K	135K
1905						
Single 2.25hp (1,181)	6,000	11,000	19,000	33,000	55,000	75,000
1906						
Single 2.5hp (1,698)	6,000	10,000	18,000	30,000	53,000	70,000
1907						
Single 2.25hp (2,176)	6,000	10,000	15,000	28,000	49,000	70,000
Twin 3.5hp (incl. above)	8,000	15,000	26,000	47,000	75,000	95,000
1908						
Single 3.5hp (3,257)	6,000	8,000	13,000	24,000	42,000	60,000
Twin 5hp (incl. above)	7,000	12,000	21,000	38,000	59,000	80,000
1909						
Single 2hp (4,771)	5,000	7,000	12,000	21,000	40,000	60,000
Single 3.5hp (incl. above)	5,000	8,000	13,000	22,000	41,000	60,000
Single 4hp (incl. above)	6,000	9,000	14,000	24,000	42,000	60,000
Twin 5hp (incl. above)	8,000	14,000	21,000	33,000	54,000	70,000
Twin 7hp (incl. above)	9,000	15,000	22,000	34,000	57,000	80,000
1910 (Model B)						
Single 2.75hp (6,137)	5,000	7,000	11,000	19,000	35,000	50,000
Single 4hp (incl. above)	5,000	8,000	13,000	23,000	39,000	55,000
Twin 5hp (incl. above)	7,000	13,000	20,000	31,000	50,000	70,000
Twin 7hp (incl. above)	8,000	14,000	21,000	32,000	52,000	70,000
1911 (Model C)						
Single 2.75hp (9,763)	5,000	7,000	10,000	19,000	33,000	45,000
Single 4hp (incl. above)	5,000	7,000	12,000	20,000	36,000	50,000
Twin 5hp (incl. above)	6,000	12,000	18,000	29,000	48,000	65,000
Twin 7hp (incl. above)	7,000	13,000	19,000	30,000	50,000	70,000
1912 (Model D)						
Single 4hp (19,500)	5,000	15,000	25,000	35,000	50,000	65,000

	6	5	4	3	2	1
Twin 7hp (incl. above)	6,000	11,000	17,000	28,000	48,000	65,000
1913 (Model E)						
Single 4hp (32,000)	4,000	7,000	10,000	19,000	33,000	50,000
Twin 7hp (incl. above).	6,000	10,000	16,000	26,000	41,000	55,000
1914 (Model F)						
Hendee Special 7hp (25,000)	14,000	18,000	49,000	59,000	74,000	90,000
Single 4hp (incl. above).	5,000	7,000	10,000	17,000	32,000	45,000
Twin 7hp (incl. above).	6,000	9,000	15,000	25,000	38,000	50,000
1915						
Hendee Special 7hp (21,000)	14,000	18,000	49,000	59,000	74,000	90,000
Single 4hp (incl. above)	4,000	6,000	10,000	17,000	32,000	45,000
Twin 7hp (incl. above).	6,000	9,000	14,000	24,000	42,000	60,000
1916						
Model K Featherweight 2.5hp (22,000) . . .	6,000	9,000	14,000	24,000	42,000	60,000
Single 4hp (incl. above).	3,000	5,000	8,000	15,000	27,000	40,000
Powerplus (33ci single) (incl. above)	4,000	7,000	11,000	17,000	31,000	45,000
Twin 7hp (incl. above).	5,000	8,000	13,000	20,000	34,000	50,000
Powerplus (61ci twin) (incl. above)	10,000	20,000	30,000	40,000	50,000	60,000
1917						
Single 4hp (20,500)	3,000	5,000	8,000	14,000	26,000	40,000
Powerplus (33ci single) (incl. above)	4,000	7,000	11,000	16,000	29,000	40,000
Twin 2.5hp (incl. above).	4,000	7,000	11,000	17,000	27,000	40,000
Twin 7hp (incl. above).	5,000	8,000	12,000	19,000	32,000	45,000
Model O Light (15.7ci twin) (incl. above) . .	4,000	6,000	10,000	15,000	22,000	30,000
Powerplus (61ci twin) (incl. above)	10,000	20,000	30,000	40,000	50,000	60,000
1918						
Single 4hp (22,000)	3,000	5,000	8,000	14,000	25,000	35,000
Powerplus (33ci single) (incl. above)	4,000	7,000	10,000	15,000	27,000	40,000
Twin 2.5hp (incl. above).	4,000	7,000	10,000	16,000	26,000	35,000
Twin 7hp (incl. above).	5,000	8,000	11,000	18,000	30,000	45,000
Model O Light (15.7ci twin) (incl. above) . .	4,000	6,000	9,000	14,000	21,000	30,000
Powerplus (61ci twin) (incl. above)	10,000	20,000	30,000	40,000	50,000	60,000
1919						
Single 4hp (21,500)	3,000	5,000	8,000	14,000	25,000	35,000
Powerplus (33ci single) (incl. above)	4,000	7,000	10,000	15,000	27,000	40,000
Twin 2.5hp (incl. above).	4,000	7,000	10,000	16,000	25,000	35,000
Twin 7hp (incl. above).	5,000	8,000	11,000	18,000	30,000	45,000
Twin Big Valve 8hp (incl. above)	7,000	12,000	20,000	30,000	40,000	50,000
Model O Light (15.7ci twin) (incl. above) . .	4,000	6,000	9,000	14,000	21,000	30,000
Powerplus (61ci twin) (incl. above)	10,000	20,000	30,000	40,000	50,000	60,000
1920						
Powerplus (33-cid single)	5,000	7,000	11,000	15,000	20,000	25,000
Scout (37-cid V-twin)	8,000	15,000	20,000	25,000	35,000	45,000
Powerplus (61-cid V-twin)	6,000	9,000	13,000	17,000	23,000	29,000
1921						
Powerplus (33-cid single)	5,000	7,000	11,000	15,000	20,000	25,000
Scout (37-cid V-twin)	8,000	15,000	20,000	25,000	35,000	45,000
Powerplus (61-cid V-twin)	6,000	8,000	13,000	17,000	23,000	28,000
1922						
Powerplus (33-cid single)	4,000	7,000	10,000	13,000	18,000	23,000
Scout (37-cid V-twin)	8,000	15,000	20,000	25,000	35,000	45,000
Powerplus (61-cid V-twin)	6,000	8,000	13,000	17,000	23,000	28,000
Chief (61-cid V-twin).	9,000	13,000	20,000	26,000	35,000	43,000
1923						
Powerplus (33-cid single)	4,000	6,500	1,000	13,000	17,000	22,000
Scout (37-cid V-twin)	6,000	9,000	13,000	17,000	23,000	30,000
Powerplus (61-cid V-twin)	5,000	8,000	12,000	16,000	22,000	28,000
Chief (61-cid V-twin).	8,000	13,000	19,000	25,000	34,000	43,000
Big Chief (74-cid V-twin)	9,000	13,000	20,000	26,000	35,000	44,000

	6	5	4	3	2	1
1924						
Powerplus (33-cid single)	4,000	6,000	10,000	13,000	17,000	22,000
Scout (37-cid V-twin)	5,000	8,000	12,000	16,000	21,000	27,000
Powerplus (61-cid V-twin)	5,000	8,000	12,000	16,000	21,000	27,000
Chief (61-cid V-twin).	8,000	13,000	19,000	25,000	34,000	43,000
Big Chief (74-cid V-twin)	9,000	13,000	19,000	25,000	34,000	44,000
1925						
Prince (21-cid single)	4,000	5,000	8,000	11,000	14,000	18,000
Scout (37-cid V-twin)	5,000	7,000	11,000	14,000	19,000	24,000
Chief (61-cid V-twin).	8,000	12,000	18,000	25,000	33,000	42,000
Big Chief (74-cid V-twin)	9,000	13,000	19,000	25,000	34,000	44,000
1926						
Prince (21-cid single)	5,000	7,000	11,000	14,000	19,000	24,000
Scout (37-cid V-twin)	5,000	7,000	11,000	14,000	19,000	24,000
Chief (61-cid V-twin).	8,000	12,000	18,000	25,000	33,000	42,000
Big Chief (74-cid V-twin)	9,000	13,000	19,000	25,000	34,000	44,000
1927						
Prince (21-cid single)	3,000	5,000	8,000	10,000	14,000	17,000
Scout (37-cid V-twin)	4,000	6,000	9,000	13,000	17,000	21,000
Scout (45-cid V-twin)	5,000	7,000	10,000	14,000	18,000	23,000
Chief (61-cid V-twin).	8,000	12,000	18,000	24,000	32,000	40,000
Big Chief (74-cid V-twin)	9,000	13,000	19,000	26,000	34,000	44,000
Indian Ace (78-cid, inline 4-cyl)	10,000	20,000	30,000	40,000	50,000	60,000
1928						
Prince (21-cid single)	3,000	5,000	8,000	10,000	14,000	17,000
101 Scout (37-cid V-twin)	4,000	7,000	12,000	17,000	20,000	25,000
101 Scout (45-cid V-twin)	5,000	7,000	12,000	18,000	24,000	30,000
Chief (61-cid V-twin).	8,000	12,000	18,000	24,000	32,000	40,000
Big Chief (74-cid V-twin)	9,000	13,000	19,000	26,000	35,000	44,000
Indian Ace (78-cid, inline 4-cyl)	10,000	20,000	30,000	40,000	50,000	60,000
1929						
101 Scout (37-cid V-twin)	4,000	7,000	10,000	13,000	18,000	22,000
101 Scout (45-cid V-twin)	5,000	7,000	11,000	15,000	20,000	25,000
Chief (74-cid V-twin).	8,000	12,000	17,000	23,000	31,000	39,000
Model 401 (78-cid, inline 4-cyl)	15,000	30,000	40,000	50,000	60,000	70,000
Model 402 (78-cid, inline 4-cyl)	15,000	30,000	40,000	50,000	60,000	70,000
1930						
101 Scout (37-cid V-twin)	4,000	7,000	10,000	13,000	18,000	22,000
101 Scout (45-cid V-twin)	5,000	7,000	11,000	15,000	20,000	25,000
Chief (74-cid V-twin).	8,000	11,000	17,000	23,000	30,000	38,000
Model 402 (78-cid, inline 4-cyl)	15,000	30,000	40,000	50,000	60,000	70,000
1931						
101 Scout (37-cid V-twin) (4,557)	4,000	7,000	10,000	13,000	18,000	22,000
101 Scout (45-cid V-twin) (incl. above) . . .	5,000	8,000	11,000	15,000	20,000	25,000
Chief (74-cid V-twin) (incl. above)	8,000	11,000	17,000	23,000	30,000	38,000
Model 402 (78-cid, inline 4-cyl) (incl. above)	15,000	30,000	40,000	50,000	60,000	70,000
1932						
Scout Pony (30-cid, V-twin) (2,360)	3,000	5,000	7,000	10,000	13,000	16,000
Scout (45-cid V-twin) (incl. above).	4,000	6,000	9,000	13,000	17,000	21,000
Chief (74-cid V-twin) (incl. above).	8,000	11,000	17,000	23,000	30,000	39,000
Model 403 (78-cid, inline 4-cyl) (incl. above)	1,000	20,000	30,000	40,000	50,000	60,000
1933						
Junior Scout (30.5-cid V-twin) (1,667)	3,000	5,000	7,000	10,000	13,000	16,000
Standard Scout (45-cid V-twin) (incl. above)	4,000	6,000	9,000	12,000	16,000	20,000
Motoplane (45-cid V-twin) (incl. above) . . .	20,000	30,000	40,000	50,000	60,000	70,000
Chief (74-cid V-twin) (incl. above).	8,000	11,000	17,000	23,000	30,000	38,000
Model 403 (78-cid, inline 4-cyl) (incl. above)	10,000	20,000	30,000	40,000	50,000	60,000
1934						
Junior Scout (30.5-cid V-twin) (2,809)	3,000	5,000	7,000	10,000	13,000	16,000
Standard Scout (45-cid V-twin) (incl. above)	4,000	6,000	9,000	11,000	15,000	19,000

	6	5	4	3	2	1
Sport Scout (45-cid V-twin) (incl. above) . .	5,000	7,000	14,000	21,000	28,000	35,000
Chief (74-cid V-twin) (incl. above).	8,000	11,000	17,000	23,000	30,000	38,000
Model 434 (78-cid, inline 4-cyl) (incl. above)	10,000	20,000	30,000	40,000	50,000	60,000
1935						
Junior Scout (30.5-cid V-twin) (3,703). . . .	3,000	5,000	7,000	10,000	13,000	16,000
Standard Scout (45-cid V-twin) (incl. above)	4,000	6,000	9,000	11,000	15,000	19,000
Sport Scout (45-cid V-twin) (incl. above) . .	5,000	7,000	14,000	21,000	28,000	35,000
Chief (74-cid V-twin) (incl. above).	8,000	11,000	17,000	23,000	30,000	38,000
Model 435 (78-cid, inline 4-cyl) (incl. above)	10,000	20,000	30,000	40,000	50,000	60,000
1936						
Junior Scout (30.5-cid V-twin) (5,028). . . .	3,000	5,000	7,000	9,000	12,000	15,000
Scout 45 (45-cid V-twin) (incl. above)	4,000	5,000	8,000	11,000	14,000	18,000
Sport Scout (45-cid V-twin) (incl. above) . .	5,000	7,000	14,000	21,000	28,000	35,000
Chief (74-cid V-twin) (incl. above).	7,000	11,000	17,000	22,000	30,000	38,000
Model 436 (78-cid, inline 4-cyl) (incl. above)	10,000	20,000	30,000	40,000	50,000	60,000
1937						
Junior Scout (30.5-cid V-twin) (6,037). . . .	3,000	6,000	9,000	12,000	15,000	18,000
Scout 45 (45-cid V-twin) (incl. above)	4,000	5,000	8,000	11,000	14,000	18,000
Sport Scout (45-cid V-twin) (incl. above) . .	5,000	7,000	14,000	21,000	28,000	35,000
Chief (74-cid V-twin) (incl. above).	7,000	11,000	17,000	22,000	30,000	38,000
Model 437 (78-cid, inline 4-cyl) (incl. above)	10,000	20,000	30,000	40,000	50,000	60,000
1938						
Junior Scout (30.5-cid V-twin) (3,650). . . .	5,000	7,000	9,000	12,000	15,000	18,000
Sport Scout (45-cid V-twin) (incl. above) . .	5,000	7,000	14,000	21,000	28,000	35,000
Chief (74-cid V-twin) (incl. above).	8,000	12,000	18,000	25,000	33,000	41,000
Model 438 (78-cid, inline 4-cyl) (incl. above)	11,000	20,000	30,000	40,000	50,000	60,000
1939						
Junior Scout (30.5-cid V-twin) (3,012). . . .	4,000	6,000	9,000	12,000	16,000	20,000
Sport Scout (45-cid V-twin) (incl. above) . .	5,000	7,000	14,000	21,000	28,000	35,000
Chief (74-cid V-twin) (incl. above).	8,000	11,000	17,000	23,000	30,000	38,000
Model 439 (78-cid, inline 4-cyl) (incl. above)	10,000	20,000	30,000	40,000	50,000	60,000
1940						
Thirty-fifty (30.5-cid V-twin) (10,431)	3,000	5,000	7,000	9,000	12,000	15,000
Sport Scout (45-cid V-twin) (incl. above) . .	6,000	8,000	14,000	21,000	28,000	35,000
Chief (74-cid V-twin) (incl. above).	8,000	12,000	18,000	23,000	31,000	40,000
Model 440 (78-cid, inline 4-cyl) (incl. above)	11,000	20,000	30,000	40,000	50,000	60,000
1941						
Thirty-fifty (30.5-cid V-twin) (8,739)	3,000	4,000	6,000	8,000	11,000	14,000
Model 741 (30.5-cid V-twin, military) (incl. above)	3,000	**5,000**	**8,000**	**11,000**	**14,000**	**17,000**
Sport Scout (45-cid V-twin) (incl. above) . .	6,000	8,000	14,000	21,000	28,000	35,000
Model 640-B(45-cid V-twin, military) (incl. above)	3,000	5,000	7,000	10,000	13,000	16,000
Model 841 (45-cid V-twin, shaft-drive, military) (incl. above).	5,000	10,000	**16,000**	**24,000**	**32,000**	**40,000**
Chief (74-cid V-twin) (incl. above).	8,000	12,000	18,000	23,000	31,000	39,000
Model 441 (78-cid, inline 4-cyl) (incl. above)	11,000	20,000	30,000	40,000	50,000	60,000
1942						
Model 741 (30.5-cid V-twin, military) (16,647)	3,000	**5,000**	**8,000**	**11,000**	**14,000**	**17,000**
Model 640-B(45-cid V-twin, military) (incl. above)	3,000	5,000	7,000	10,000	13,000	16,000
Model 841 (45-cid V-twin, shaft-drive, military) (incl. above).	5,000	10,000	**16,000**	**24,000**	**32,000**	**40,000**
Chief (74-cid V-twin) (incl. above).	8,000	12,000	18,000	23,000	31,000	39,000
Chief (74-cid V-twin, military) (incl. above) .	8,000	12,000	18,000	23,000	31,000	39,000
Model 442 (78-cid, inline 4-cyl) (incl. above)	15,000	25,000	35,000	45,000	55,000	65,000
1943						
Model 640-B(45-cid V-twin, military) (16,456)	3,000	5,000	7,000	10,000	13,000	16,000
Model 841 (45-cid V-twin, shaft-drive, military) (incl. above).	5,000	10,000	**16,000**	**24,000**	**32,000**	**40,000**

	6	5	4	3	2	1
Chief (74-cid V-twin, military) (incl. above) .	7,000	10,000	15,000	20,000	27,000	34,000
1944						
Chief (74-cid V-twin, military) (17,006) . . .	6,000	10,000	14,000	19,000	26,000	32,000
1945						
Chief (74-cid V-twin) (2,070)	7,000	11,000	16,000	21,000	28,000	35,000
Chief (74-cid V-twin, military) (incl. above) .	6,000	10,000	14,000	19,000	26,000	32,000
1946						
Chief (74-cid V-twin) (3,621)	7,000	11,000	13,000	16,000	20,000	25,000
1947						
Chief (74-cid V-twin) (11,849)	7,000	11,000	13,000	16,000	20,000	25,000
Chief Roadmaster (74-cid V-twin) (incl. above)	7,000	11,000	16,000	22,000	25,000	30,000
1948						
Chief (74-cid V-twin) (9,000)	7,000	11,000	16,000	19,000	25,000	32,000
Chief Roadmaster (74-cid V-twin)	7,000	11,000	16,000	22,000	25,000	30,000
1949						
Arrow (13-cid single) (incl. above).	2,000	3,000	5,000	10,000	15,000	20,000
Warrior (30.5-cid vertical twin) (incl. above) .	2,000	3,000	6,000	8,000	10,000	12,000
Scout (27-cid vertical twin) (incl. above). . .	2,000	3,000	5,000	8,000	12,000	15,000
Papoose Scooter	500	700	1,000	1,500	2,500	3,500
1950						
Arrow (13-cid single) (2,000)	2,000	3,000	4,000	6,000	8,000	10,000
Scout (27-cid vertical twin) (incl. above). . .	2,000	3,000	4,000	6,000	8,000	10,000
Warrior (30.5-cid vertical twin) (incl. above) .	2,000	3,000	6,000	8,000	10,000	12,000
Warrior TT (30.5-cid vertical twin) (incl. above)	2,000	3,000	6,000	8,000	10,000	12,000
Chief (80-cid V-twin) (incl. above)	8,000	12,000	19,000	25,000	33,000	41,000
1951						
Brave (15-cid single) (500)	1,000	2,000	3,000	4,000	7,000	9,000
Warrior (30.5-cid vertical twin) (incl. above) .	2,000	3,000	6,000	8,000	10,000	12,000
Warrior TT (30.5-cid vertical twin) (incl. above)	2,000	3,000	6,000	8,000	10,000	12,000
Chief (80-cid V-twin) (incl. above)	8,000	12,000	19,000	25,000	30,000	35,000
1952						
Brave (15-cid single) (500)	1,000	2,000	3,000	4,000	7,000	9,000
Warrior (30.5-cid vertical twin) (incl. above) .	2,000	3,000	6,000	8,000	10,000	12,000
Warrior TT (30.5-cid vertical twin) (incl. above)	2,000	3,000	6,000	8,000	10,000	12,000
Chief (80-cid V-twin) (incl. above)	8,000	12,000	19,000	25,000	33,000	42,000
1953						
Brave (15-cid single) (2,000)	1,000	2,000	3,000	4,000	7,000	9,000
Chief (80-cid V-twin) (incl. above)	9,000	13,000	20,000	26,000	35,000	44,000

JAWA						
1936						
Special	1,500	2,500	3,800	5,300	7,000	9,000
1938						
Robot 100	500	1,000	1,500	2,000	2,500	3,000
1948						
Perek	1,500	3,000	4,500	6,000	7,500	9,000
1955						
Speedway	1,000	2,000	3,000	4,000	5,000	6,000
1957						
175	400	600	1,000	2,000	3,500	5,000
1960						
355	400	600	1,000	2,000	3,500	5,000
1965						
350	500	1,000	2,000	3,000	4,000	5,000
1967						
Junior (250cc)	1,500	3,000	4,200	5,400	6,600	8,000
CZ 590	500	1,000	1,500	2,000	2,500	3,000

	6	5	4	3	2	1
1969						
Speedway	1,500	3,000	4,200	5,400	6,600	8,000
1970						
Speedway	1,500	3,000	4,200	5,400	6,600	8,000
1972						
250 Twin	400	600	1,000	2,000	3,500	5,000
DT 500 Speedway.	500	1,000	1,500	2,000	2,500	3,000
1973						
125 MX Desert	1,000	1,700	2,300	3,100	4,800	6,500
175 Trial.	600	1,000	1,300	1,700	2,600	3,500
250 MX	700	1,200	1,600	2,100	3,400	4,700
400 MX	1,500	2,200	3,000	4,000	6,300	8,600
1974						
125 MX Desert	1,000	1,700	2,300	3,100	4,800	6,500
125 Sport	300	600	800	1,000	1,500	2,000
175 Sport 4 Speed	1,000	1,600	2,200	3,000	4,600	6,200
175 Sport 6 Speed	1,100	1,800	2,400	3,300	4,900	6,800
250 MX Desert	700	1,200	1,700	2,200	3,500	4,800
400 MX Desert	1,500	2,000	2,800	3,700	5,800	8,000
1975						
125 Moto Cross	1,100	1,800	2,500	3,300	5,100	7,000
125 Street	1,000	1,600	2,200	2,900	4,500	6,100
250 Enduro	700	1,200	1,700	2,200	3,500	4,800
250 GP Moto Cross	800	1,300	1,800	2,400	3,800	5,000
250 MX Desert	700	1,200	1,700	2,200	3,500	4,800
400 GP Moto Cross	800	1,300	1,800	2,400	3,800	5,000
400 MX Desert	1,500	2,000	2,800	3,700	5,800	8,000
1976						
250 Enduro	1,100	1,800	2,500	3,300	5,100	7,000
250 Falta GP-C	1,300	2,000	2,700	3,600	5,600	7,600
350 TSII-C	1,700	2,200	3,000	3,800	5,000	6,500
400 Falta GP-C	1,500	2,000	2,800	3,700	5,800	8,000
1977						
175 Enduro	700	1,200	1,700	2,200	3,400	4,600
250 Enduro	1,100	1,800	2,500	3,300	5,100	7,000
250 MX	800	1,300	1,900	2,400	3,800	5,200
1979						
125 MX	900	1,500	2,100	2,800	4,200	5,500
1980						
500 Jawa 894.1	1,100	1,800	2,500	3,300	5,100	7,000
1994						
TS 350 Twin Sport (344cc)	200	500	1,000	1,500	2,000	2,500
JEFFERSON						
1913						
Twin	10,000	20,000	40,000	50,000	60,000	70,000
1914						
Twin	10,000	20,000	40,000	50,000	60,000	70,000
KAWASAKI						
1963						
B8 (125cc single)	700	1,100	1,600	2,100	2,800	3,500
B8T (125cc single)	700	1,100	1,600	2,100	2,800	3,500
1964						
B8 (125cc single)	600	1,000	1,400	1,900	2,600	3,200
B8T (125cc single)	600	1,000	1,400	1,900	2,600	3,200
SG (250cc single)	700	1,100	1,700	2,200	3,000	3,700
1965						
J1 (85cc single)	400	600	900	1,200	1,600	2,000
J1T (85cc single)	400	600	900	1,200	1,600	2,000
B8 (125cc single)	600	900	1,400	1,800	2,400	3,000
B8T (125cc single)	600	900	1,400	1,800	2,400	3,000

	6	5	4	3	2	1
B8S (125cc single)	600	900	1,400	1,900	2,500	3,100
SG (250cc single)	700	1,100	1,700	2,200	3,000	3,700
1966						
M10 (50cc single)	300	500	700	900	1,200	1,500
M11 (50cc single)	300	500	700	900	1,200	1,500
J1 (85cc single)	400	600	800	1,100	1,500	1,900
J1T (85cc single)	400	600	800	1,100	1,500	1,900
J1R (85cc single)	400	600	900	1,200	1,600	2,000
D1 (100cc single)	300	500	800	1,000	1,400	1,700
C1 (120cc single)	400	600	900	1,200	1,600	2,000
C1D (120 cc single)	400	600	900	1,200	1,600	2,000
B1 (125cc single)	400	600	900	1,200	1,600	2,000
B1T (125cc single)	400	600	900	1,200	1,600	2,000
B1TL (125cc single)	400	600	900	1,200	1,600	2,000
B8 (125cc single)	400	700	1,000	1,300	1,800	2,200
B8T (125cc single)	400	700	1,000	1,300	1,800	2,200
B8S (125cc single)	500	700	1,100	1,400	1,900	2,400
F1 (175cc single)	400	700	1,000	1,300	1,800	2,200
F1TR (175cc single)	500	700	1,000	1,400	1,800	2,300
F2 (175cc single)	500	700	1,000	1,400	1,800	2,300
SG (250cc single)	600	900	1,350	1,800	2,400	3,000
W1 (624cc twin)	1,500	2,300	3,600	4,900	6,600	8,500
1967						
M10 (50cc single)	300	500	700	900	1,200	1,500
M11 (50cc single)	300	500	700	900	1,200	1,500
J1D (85cc single)	400	500	800	1,100	1,400	1,800
J1TL (85cc single)	400	500	800	1,100	1,400	1,800
J1TRL (85cc single)	400	600	900	1,200	1,600	2,000
G1M (90cc single)	300	500	800	1,000	1,400	1,700
D1 (100cc single)	300	500	800	1,000	1,400	1,700
C1DL (120 cc single)	400	600	900	1,200	1,600	2,000
C1L (120cc single)	400	600	900	1,200	1,600	2,000
C2SS Roadrunner (120cc single)	400	500	800	1,100	1,400	1,800
C2TR Roadrunner (120cc single)	400	600	900	1,200	1,600	2,000
B1 (125cc single)	400	600	900	1,200	1,600	2,000
B1T (125cc single)	400	600	900	1,200	1,600	2,000
B1TL (125cc single)	400	600	900	1,200	1,600	2,000
F2 (175cc single)	500	700	1,000	1,400	1,800	2,300
F2TR (175cc single)	500	700	1,000	1,400	1,800	2,300
A1 Samurai (247cc twin)	700	1,000	1,600	2,100	2,700	3,300
A1R (247cc twin)	2,000	3,000	4,500	6,000	8,000	10,000
A1SS Samurai (247cc twin)	700	1,000	1,600	2,100	2,700	3,300
SG (250cc single)	600	900	1,400	1,800	2,400	3,000
A7 Avenger (338cc twin)	800	1,200	1,700	2,300	3,000	3,700
A7SS Avenger (338cc twin)	800	1,200	1,700	2,300	3,000	3,700
W1 (624cc twin)	1,500	2,300	3,600	4,900	6,600	8,500
1968						
M10 (50cc single)	300	500	700	900	1,200	1,500
M11 (50cc single)	300	500	700	900	1,200	1,500
J1L (85cc single)	300	500	700	1,000	1,300	1,600
G1L (90cc single)	300	500	700	1,000	1,300	1,600
G1M (90cc single)	300	500	700	1,000	1,300	1,600
D1 (100cc single)	400	500	800	1,100	1,400	1,800
C2SS Roadrunner (120cc single)	400	500	800	1,100	1,400	1,800
C2TR Roadrunner (120cc single)	400	600	900	1,200	1,600	2,000
B1L (125cc single)	400	600	900	1,200	1,600	2,000
B1T (125cc single)	400	600	900	1,200	1,600	2,000
B1TL (125cc single)	400	600	900	1,200	1,600	2,000
F2 (175cc single)	400	600	1,000	1,300	1,700	2,100
F3 Bushwacker (175cc single)	500	700	1,000	1,400	1,800	2,300

	6	5	4	3	2	1
A1 Samurai (247cc twin)	700	1,000	1,600	2,100	2,700	3,300
A1R (247cc twin)	2,000	3,000	4,500	6,000	8,000	10,000
A1SS Samurai (247cc twin)	700	1,000	1,600	2,100	2,700	3,300
F21M (250cc single).	600	900	2,000	4,000	6,000	8,000
SG (250cc single).	600	900	1,400	1,800	2,400	3,000
A7 Avenger (338cc twin)	800	1,200	1,700	2,300	3,000	3,700
A7SS Avenger (338cc twin)	800	1,200	1,700	2,300	3,000	3,700
W1 (624cc twin)	1,200	2,200	3,400	5,000	6,000	7,000
W1SS (624cc twin)	1,200	2,200	3,400	5,000	6,000	7,000
W2SS Commander (624cc twin)	1,200	2,200	3,400	5,000	6,000	7,000
1969						
M10 (50cc single)	200	400	500	700	1,000	1,200
M11 (50cc single)	200	400	500	700	1,000	1,200
GA1 (90cc single)	300	400	600	800	1,100	1,400
GA2 (90cc single)	300	400	600	800	1,100	1,400
GA3 Street Scrambler (90cc single).	300	400	600	800	1,100	1,400
G1DL (90cc single)	300	500	700	1,000	1,300	1,600
G1TRL (90cc single)	300	500	700	1,000	1,300	1,600
G3SS (90cc single)	300	500	700	1,000	1,300	1,600
G3TR Bushmaster (90cc single)	300	500	700	1,000	1,300	1,600
B1L (125cc single)	300	500	700	900	1,200	1,600
B1T (125cc single)	300	500	700	900	1,200	1,600
B1TL (125cc single)	300	500	700	900	1,200	1,600
F2 (175cc single)	400	600	1,000	1,300	1,700	2,100
F3 Bushwacker (175cc single)	600	900	1,400	1,800	2,400	3,000
A1 Samurai (247cc twin)	700	1,000	1,600	2,100	2,700	3,300
A1SS Samurai (247cc twin)	700	1,000	1,600	2,100	2,700	3,300
F4 Sidewinder (250cc single)	400	700	1,000	1,300	1,800	2,200
F21M (250cc single).	700	1,100	2,000	4,000	6,000	8,000
SG (250cc single)	400	700	1,000	1,300	1,800	2,200
A7 Avenger (338cc twin)	800	1,200	1,700	2,300	3,000	3,700
A7SS Avenger (338cc twin)	800	1,200	1,700	2,300	3,000	3,700
H1 Mach III (498cc triple)	1,500	3,000	**6,000**	**9,000**	**12,000**	**15,000**
H1R Roadracer (498cc triple)	5,200	7,800	12,000	16,000	21,000	26,000
W1SS (624cc twin)	1,200	2,200	3,400	5,000	6,000	7,000
W2SS Commander (624cc twin)	1,200	2,200	3,400	5,000	6,000	7,000
W2TT Commander (624cc twin)	2,600	4,000	6,000	8,000	11,000	13,000
1970						
GA1 (90cc single)	300	400	600	800	1,100	1,400
GA2 (90cc single)	300	400	600	800	1,100	1,400
GA3 Street Scrambler (90cc single).	300	400	600	800	1,100	1,400
G3SS (90cc single)	300	500	700	1,000	1,300	1,600
G3TR Bushmaster (90cc single)	300	500	700	1,000	1,300	1,600
G4TR Trail Boss (100cc single)	300	500	800	1,000	1,400	1,700
G31M Centurian (100cc single)	1,500	2,500	3,500	4,500	5,500	6,500
B1LA (125cc single)	300	500	700	900	1,200	1,500
F3 Bushwacker (175cc single)	600	900	1,400	1,800	2,400	3,000
A1A Samurai (247cc twin).	700	1,000	1,600	2,100	2,700	3,300
A1SSA Samurai (247cc twin)	700	1,000	1,600	2,100	2,700	3,300
F4 Sidewinder (250cc single)	400	600	900	1,200	1,600	2,000
F21M (250cc single).	700	1,100	2,000	4,000	6,000	8,000
A7A Avenger (338cc twin).	700	1,000	1,600	2,100	2,700	3,300
A7SSA Avenger (338 cc twin)	700	1,000	1,600	2,100	2,700	3,300
F5 Big Horn (350cc single)	400	600	1,000	1,300	1,700	2,100
H1 Mach III (498cc triple)	1,500	2,300	3,500	5,000	6,500	8,000
H1R Roadracer (498cc triple)	5,200	7,800	12,000	16,000	21,000	26,000
W1SS (624cc twin)	1,200	2,200	3,400	5,000	6,000	7,000
W2SS Commander (624cc twin)	1,200	2,200	3,400	5,000	6,000	7,000

	6	5	4	3	2	1
1971						
GA1A (90cc single)	300	400	600	800	1,100	1,400
GA2A (90cc single)	300	400	600	800	1,100	1,400
G3SS (90cc single)	300	500	700	1,000	1,300	1,600
GA5A (100cc single)	300	500	700	1,000	1,300	1,600
G3TRA (100cc single).	300	500	700	1,000	1,300	1,600
G4TRA Trail Boss (100cc single)	300	500	800	1,000	1,400	1,700
G31M Centurian (100cc single)	1,500	2,500	3,500	4,500	5,500	6,500
F6 (125cc single)	300	500	700	1,000	1,300	1,600
F7 (175cc single)	300	500	800	1,000	1,400	1,700
A1B Samurai (247cc twin).	600	900	1,400	1,800	2,400	3,000
A1SSB Samurai (247cc twin)	600	900	1,400	1,800	2,400	3,000
F8 (250cc single)	500	700	1,100	1,400	1,900	2,400
A7B Avenger (338cc twin).	500	800	1,200	1,600	2,100	2,700
A7SSB Avenger (338 cc twin).	500	800	1,200	1,600	2,100	2,700
F5B Big Horn (350cc single)	400	500	800	1,100	1,400	1,800
H1 Mach III (498cc triple)	1,400	2,100	3,500	5,000	6,500	8,000
H1R Roadracer (498cc triple)	5,200	7,800	12,000	16,000	21,000	26,000
W1SS (624cc twin)	1,200	2,200	3,400	5,000	6,000	7,000
1972						
GA1A (90cc single)	300	400	600	800	1,000	1,300
GA2A (90cc single)	300	400	600	800	1,000	1,300
G3SS (90cc single)	200	400	500	700	1,000	1,200
GA5A (100cc single)	300	400	600	800	1,100	1,400
G4TRB Trail Boss (100cc single)	300	400	600	800	1,100	1,400
G5 (100cc single)	200	400	500	700	1,000	1,200
B1LA (125cc single).	200	400	500	700	1,000	1,200
F6A (125cc single)	300	400	600	800	1,000	1,300
F7A (175cc single)	300	500	700	900	1,200	1,500
S1 Mach I (249cc triple)	800	1,200	1,600	2,500	3,200	4,000
F8A Bison (250cc single)	400	600	900	1,200	1,600	2,000
F11 (250cc single).	400	500	800	1,100	1,400	1,800
F9 Big Horn (350cc single)	300	500	700	1,000	1,300	1,600
S2 Mach II (350cc triple)	400	600	3,000	4,000	5,000	6,000
H1B Mach III (498cc triple)	1,000	2,000	**3,500**	**5,000**	**6,500**	**8,000**
H2 Mach IV (750cc triple)	2,500	4,000	6,000	**9,000**	**12,000**	**16,000**
1973						
GA1A (90cc single)	200	400	500	700	1,000	1,200
GA2A (90cc single)	200	400	500	700	1,000	1,200
G3SS (90cc single)	200	400	500	700	1,000	1,200
GA5A (100cc single)	300	400	600	800	1,000	1,300
G4TRC Trail Boss (100cc single)	300	400	600	800	1,100	1,400
G7S (100cc single)	200	400	500	700	1,000	1,200
G7T (100cc single)	200	400	500	700	1,000	1,200
B1LA (125cc single).	200	400	500	700	1,000	1,200
F6B (125cc single)	300	400	600	800	1,000	1,300
F7B (175cc single)	300	400	600	800	1,000	1,300
S1A Mach I (249cc triple)	800	1,200	1,600	2,500	3,200	4,000
F11 (250cc single)	400	600	900	1,100	1,500	1,900
F9A Big Horn (350cc single)	400	600	900	1,200	1,600	2,000
S2A Mach II (350cc triple).	500	700	1,000	1,500	2,000	2,500
F12MX (450cc single)	300	500	800	1,000	1,400	1,700
H1D Mach III (498cc triple)	1,000	2,000	**3,500**	**5,000**	**6,500**	**8,000**
H2A Mach IV (750cc triple)	**2,500**	**4,000**	6,000	**9,000**	**12,000**	**16,000**
Z2 (750cc four)	2,000	5,000	10,000	15,000	20,000	25,000
Z1 (903cc four) (20,000).	4,000	5,000	8,000	12,000	15,000	18,000
1974						
GA1A (90cc single)	200	300	500	700	900	1,100
GA2A (90cc single)	200	300	500	700	900	1,100
G2S (90cc single)	200	400	500	700	1,000	1,200

	6	5	4	3	2	1
G2T (90cc single)	200	400	500	700	1,000	1,200
G3SS (90cc single)	200	400	500	700	1,000	1,200
GA5A (100cc single)	300	400	600	800	1,000	1,300
G4TRD Trail Boss (100cc single)	300	400	600	800	1,100	1,400
G5B (100cc single)	200	500	800	1,200	1,600	2,000
G7S (100cc single)	200	400	500	700	1,000	1,200
G7T (100cc single)	200	400	500	700	1,000	1,200
B1LA (125cc single)	300	400	600	800	1,000	1,300
KS125 (125cc single)	200	300	500	700	900	1,100
S1B Mach I (249cc triple)	800	1,200	1,600	2,500	3,200	4,000
F11A (250cc single)	400	600	900	1,100	1,500	1,900
KX250 (250cc single)	400	600	900	1,200	1,600	2,000
F9B Big Horn (350cc single)	400	600	900	1,200	1,600	2,000
KZ400D (400cc twin)	400	600	900	1,100	1,500	1,900
S3 (400cc triple)	800	1,200	1,600	2,500	3,200	4,000
KX450 (450cc single)	400	600	900	1,100	1,600	2,100
H1E Mach III (498cc triple)	1,000	2,000	3,000	4,000	5,000	6,000
H2B Mach IV (750cc triple)	1,500	2,000	4,000	7,000	9,000	12,000
Z2A (750cc four)	1,500	4,000	8,000	12,000	16,000	20,000
Z1A (903cc four) (27,500)	2,800	4,200	6,600	8,200	12,000	14,000
1975						
GA1A (90cc single)	200	300	400	500	700	900
G2T (90cc single)	200	300	400	500	700	900
G3SSE (100cc single)	200	300	500	600	800	1,000
G3T (100cc single)	200	300	500	600	800	1,000
G4TRE Trail Boss (100cc single)	200	300	500	600	800	1,000
G5C (100cc single)	200	300	500	700	900	1,100
G7SA (100cc single)	200	300	500	700	900	1,100
G7TA (100cc single)	200	300	500	700	900	1,100
B1LA (125cc single)	200	400	500	700	1,000	1,200
KD125 (125cc single)	200	300	500	600	800	1,000
KS125A (125cc single)	200	300	500	600	800	1,000
KX125A (125cc single)	200	300	500	700	900	1,100
KD175-A1 (175cc single)	200	400	500	700	1,000	1,200
KD250B1-Mach 1 (249cc triple)	800	1,200	1,600	2,500	3,200	4,000
KT250 (250cc single)	500	700	1,000	1,500	2,000	2,500
KX250-A3 (250cc single)	300	400	600	800	1,000	1,300
KZ400D (398cc twin)	300	400	600	800	1,000	1,300
KZ400S (398cc twin)	300	500	700	900	1,200	1,500
KH400-A3 (400cc triple)	800	1,200	1,600	2,500	3,200	4,000
KX400 (400cc single)	300	500	800	1,000	1,400	1,700
KH500-AB Mach III (498cc triple)	1,000	2,000	3,000	4,000	5,000	6,000
H2C (750cc triple)	1,500	**3,000**	**6,000**	**9,000**	**12,000**	**15,000**
Z2B (750cc four)	1,500	4,000	8,000	12,000	16,000	20,000
Z1B (903cc four) (38,200)	2,700	4,000	6,000	8,000	11,000	13,000
1976						
G2T (90cc single)	200	300	400	500	700	900
G3T (100cc single)	200	300	400	500	700	900
G7TA (100cc single)	200	300	500	600	800	1,000
KE100-A5 (100cc single)	200	300	500	700	900	1,200
KH100-B7 (100cc single)	200	300	500	700	900	1,100
B1LA (125cc single)	200	300	500	700	900	1,100
KD125 (125cc single)	200	300	500	600	800	1,000
KE125-A3 (125cc single)	200	300	500	600	800	1,000
KX125-A3 (125cc single)	200	300	500	600	800	1,000
KD175-A1 (175cc single)	200	400	500	700	1,000	1,200
KE175-B1 (175cc single)	200	400	500	700	1,000	1,200
KH250-A5 (249cc triple)	800	1,200	1,600	2,500	3,200	4,000
KT250 (250cc single)	300	500	1,000	1,500	2,000	2,500
KX250-A3 (250cc single)	200	400	500	700	1,000	1,200

	6	5	4	3	2	1
KX400 (398cc single)	300	500	800	1,000	1,400	1,700
KX400-A2 (398cc single)	300	400	600	800	1,000	1,300
KZ400D3 (398cc twin)	300	500	700	900	1,200	1,600
KZ400S2 (398cc twin)	300	500	700	900	1,200	1,600
KH500-A8 (498cc triple)	700	1,000	2,000	3,000	4,000	5,000
KZ750-B1 (750cc twin)	400	600	900	1,200	1,600	2,000
Z750-A4 (750cc four)	1,500	4,000	8,000	12,000	16,000	20,000
KZ900-A4 (903cc four)	1,000	2,000	4,000	5,500	7,000	8,500
KZ900-B1LTD (903cc four)	1,200	2,000	3,000	4,500	6,000	7,000
1977						
KC90-C1 (90cc single)	200	300	400	500	700	900
KE100-A6 (100cc single)	200	300	500	700	900	1,200
KH100-A2 (100cc single)	200	300	500	600	800	1,000
KH100-B8 (100cc single)	200	300	500	600	800	1,000
KH100-C1 (100cc single)	200	300	500	600	800	1,000
KH100-E1ES (100cc single)	200	300	500	600	800	1,000
KC125-A6 (125cc single)	200	300	500	600	800	1,000
KD125-A2 (125cc single)	200	300	500	600	800	1,000
KE125-A4 (125cc single)	200	300	500	600	800	1,000
KH125-A1 (125cc single)	200	300	500	600	800	1,000
KD175-A1 (175cc single)	200	300	500	700	900	1,100
KE175-B2 (175cc single)	200	300	500	700	900	1,100
KZ200 (200cc single)	200	300	500	600	800	1,000
KH250-B2 Mach 1 (249cc triple) . . .	600	900	1,200	2,000	2,700	3,500
KE250-B1 (250cc single)	300	400	600	800	1,000	1,300
KH400-A4 (398cc triple)	600	900	1,200	2,000	2,700	3,500
KZ400-A1 (398cc twin)	300	500	700	900	1,200	1,600
KZ400-D4 (398cc twin)	300	500	700	900	1,200	1,600
KZ400-S3 (398cc twin)	200	400	500	700	1,000	1,200
KZ650 (652cc four)	500	700	1,000	1,400	1,800	2,200
KZ650-B1 (652cc four)	500	700	1,000	1,400	1,800	2,200
KZ750-B2 (750cc twin)	400	500	800	1,100	1,400	1,800
Z750-A5 (750cc four)	1,500	4,000	8,000	12,000	16,000	20,000
KZ900-A5 (903cc four)	1,000	**2,000**	**3,000**	**4,000**	**5,000**	**6,000**
KZ1000-A1 (1,015cc four)	1,000	2,000	4,000	5,500	7,000	8,500
KZ1000-B1LTD (1,015cc four)	1,000	1,500	2,200	**3,000**	**4,000**	**5,000**
1978						
KE100-A7 (100cc single)	200	300	500	700	900	1,200
KD125-A2 (125cc single)	200	300	500	600	800	1,000
KE125-A5 (125cc single)	200	300	500	700	900	1,100
KH125-A2 (125cc single)	200	300	500	600	800	1,000
KX125-A3 (125cc single)	200	300	500	600	800	1,000
KD175-A1 (175cc single)	200	300	500	700	900	1,100
KE175-B3 (175cc single)	200	300	500	700	900	1,100
KE250-B2 (250cc single)	300	400	600	800	1,000	1,300
KL250-A1 (250cc single)	200	300	500	700	900	1,100
KX250 (250cc single)	200	300	500	700	900	1,100
KH400-A5 (398cc triple)	500	700	1,000	1,400	1,800	2,200
KZ400-A2 (398cc twin)	300	500	700	900	1,200	1,600
KZ400-B1 (398cc twin)	300	500	700	900	1,200	1,500
KZ400-C1 (398cc twin)	200	400	500	700	1,000	1,200
KZ650-B2 (652cc four)	400	600	900	1,200	1,600	2,000
KZ650-C2 (652cc four)	400	600	900	1,100	1,600	2,100
KZ650-D1SR (652cc four)	500	600	700	1,200	1,800	2,400
KZ750-B3 (750cc twin)	400	500	800	1,100	1,400	1,800
Z750-D1 (750cc four)	1,500	4,000	8,000	12,000	16,000	20,000
KZ1000-A2 (1,015cc four)	1,000	1,500	3,000	4,000	**6,000**	**8,000**
KZ1000-D1Z1R (1,015cc four)	1,000	2,000	4,000	6,000	8,000	10,000
KZ1000-D1Z1R Turbo (1,015cc four) . . .	1,500	3,000	6,000	9,000	12,000	15,000

	6	5	4	3	2	1
1979						
KE100-A8 (100cc single)	200	300	500	700	900	1,200
KM100-A4 (100cc single)	200	300	500	700	900	1,100
KD125-A2 (125cc single)	200	300	500	600	800	1,000
KE125-A6 (125cc single)	200	300	500	600	800	1,000
KX125-A3 (125cc single)	200	300	500	600	800	1,000
KD175-A4 (175cc single)	200	300	500	600	800	1,000
KZ200-A2 (200cc single)	200	300	500	600	800	1,000
KE250-B3 (250cc single)	200	300	500	700	900	1,100
KL250-A2 (250cc single)	200	300	500	700	900	1,100
KX250 (250cc single)	300	400	600	800	1,000	1,300
KDX400 (398cc single)	300	400	600	800	1,100	1,400
KZ400-B2 (398cc twin)	300	500	700	900	1,200	1,500
KZ650-B3 (652cc four)	400	600	900	1,200	1,600	2,000
KZ650-C3 (652cc four)	400	600	900	1,100	1,600	2,100
KZ650-D2 (652cc four)	500	700	1,100	1,400	1,900	2,400
KZ750-B4 (750cc twin)	200	300	500	700	900	1,100
KZ1000-A3 (1,015cc four)	500	700	1,100	1,400	1,900	2,400
KZ1000-B3LTD (1,015cc four)	600	900	1,400	1,800	2,240	3,000
KZ1000-E1 (1,015cc four)	600	800	1,300	1,700	2,300	2,800
KZ1300-A1 (1,286cc six)	700	1,000	1,500	3,000	4,000	5,000
1980						
KE100-A9 (100cc single)	200	300	400	700	900	1,200
KE125-A7 (125cc single)	200	300	400	500	700	900
KX125-A6 (125cc single)	200	300	400	500	700	900
KDX175-A1 (175cc single)	200	300	500	600	800	1,000
KD175-D2 (175cc single)	200	300	500	600	800	1,000
KZ250-A1 (249cc single)	300	400	600	800	1,100	1,400
KDX250-A1 (250cc single)	200	300	500	700	900	1,100
KL250-A3 (250cc single)	200	300	500	700	900	1,100
KLX250-A2 (250cc single)	200	300	500	700	900	1,100
KX250-A6 (250cc single)	200	300	500	700	900	1,100
KDX400-A2 (398cc single)	300	400	600	800	1,100	1,400
KX400 (398cc single)	300	500	700	900	1,200	1,500
KX420-A1 (420cc single)	300	500	700	900	1,200	1,500
KZ440-A1 (443cc twin)	300	500	700	1,000	1,300	1,600
KZ440-B1 (443cc twin)	300	500	700	1,000	1,300	1,600
KZ440-D1 (443cc twin)	300	500	700	1,000	1,300	1,600
KZ550-A1 (553cc four)	200	300	400	500	700	900
KZ550-C1 (553cc four)	200	300	400	500	700	900
KZ650-E1LTD (652cc four)	200	300	500	600	800	1,000
KZ650-F1 (652cc four)	200	300	500	600	800	1,000
KZ750-E1 (739cc four)	200	400	500	700	1,000	1,200
KZ750-G1LTD (739cc four)	200	400	500	700	1,000	1,200
KZ750-H1 (739cc four)	200	400	500	700	1,000	1,200
KZ1000-B3LTD (1,015cc four)	600	800	1,500	2,000	2,500	3,000
KZ1000-D3Z1R (1,015cc four)	600	800	1,300	1,700	2,300	2,800
KZ1000-E3 Shaft (1,015cc four)	600	900	1,400	1,900	2,500	3,100
KZ1000-G1 Classic (1,015cc four)	600	900	1,300	2,000	3,000	4,000
KZ1300-A2 (1,286cc six)	700	1,000	1,500	3,000	4,000	5,000
KZ1300-B2 (1,286cc six)	700	1,000	1,500	3,000	4,000	5,000
1981						
KZ250-D2 CSR (250cc single)	200	300	500	800	1,000	1,300
KZ305-A1 CSR (305cc twin)	200	400	600	900	1,200	1,500
KZ440-B2 STD (440cc twin)	300	500	800	1,000	1,300	1,600
KZ440-A2 LTD (440cc twin)	300	500	800	1,200	1,500	1,900
KZ440-D2 LTD (440cc twin)	300	500	800	1,100	1,500	1,900
KZ550-A2 STD (550cc four)	300	500	800	1,300	1,800	2,300
KZ550-C2 LTD (550cc four)	300	500	800	1,300	1,800	2,400
KZ550-D1 GPZ (550cc four)	500	700	1,100	1,600	2,100	2,600

	6	5	4	3	2	1
KZ650-H1 CSR (650cc four)	500	700	1,000	1,400	1,800	2,200
KZ750-E2 STD (750cc four)	500	800	1,100	1,700	2,300	2,900
KZ750-H2 LTD (750cc four)	400	600	1,000	1,600	2,300	3,000
KZ1000-M1 CSR (1,000cc four)	600	900	1,300	2,100	2,900	3,700
KZ1000-K1 LTD (1,000cc four)	800	1,100	1,600	2,200	3,000	3,900
KZ1100-M1 (1,100cc four)	600	800	1,200	2,000	2,800	3,700
KZ1100-J1 STD (1,100cc four)	600	900	1,300	2,100	2,900	3,800
KZ1100-A1 (1,100cc four)	600	900	1,300	2,200	3,100	4,000
KZ1100-B1 GP (1,100cc four)	1,100	1,400	1,900	2,800	3,600	4,400
KZ1300-A3 (1,300cc six)	1,100	1,400	1,900	3,000	4,000	5,000
1982						
AR50-A1 Mini GP (50cc single)	200	300	500	600	700	800
AR80-A1 Mini GP (80cc single)	200	300	500	600	800	900
KZ250-L1 CSR (250cc single)	200	300	600	800	1,100	1,400
KZ305-A2 CSR (305cc twin)	200	400	700	900	1,200	1,500
KZ305-B1 CSR (305cc twin)	200	400	700	1,000	1,300	1,600
KZ440-G1 Sports (440cc twin)	300	500	800	1,100	1,400	1,800
KZ440-A3 LTD (440cc twin)	300	500	900	1,200	1,500	1,900
KZ440-D4 LTD (440cc twin)	300	500	800	1,200	1,600	2,000
KZ550-A3 Sports (550cc four)	300	500	800	1,300	1,800	2,400
KZ550-C3 LTD (550cc four)	300	500	800	1,400	1,900	2,500
KZ550-H1 GPZ (550cc four)	500	700	1,100	1,600	2,100	2,700
KZ650-H2 CSR (650cc four)	500	700	1,100	1,400	1,800	2,200
KZ750-E3 Sports (750cc four)	500	800	1,100	1,700	2,300	3,000
KZ750-H3 LTD (750cc four)	400	600	1,000	1,700	2,400	3,100
KZ750-M1 CSR Twin (750cc twin)	400	600	1,000	1,400	1,800	2,300
KZ750-R1 GPZ (750cc twin)	700	1,000	1,400	2,000	2,600	3,300
KZ750-N1 Spectre (750cc four)	500	700	1,100	1,800	2,600	3,400
KZ1000-M2 CSR (1,000cc four)	500	700	1,000	1,800	2,600	3,500
KZ1000-J2 Sports (1,000cc four)	700	1,000	1,400	2,100	2,900	3,700
KZ1000-K2 LTD (1,000cc four)	1,000	1,300	1,800	2,500	3,200	3,900
KZ1000-R1 (1,000cc four)	2,000	2,400	3,100	3,400	4,000	4,400
KZ1100-A2 Sports (1,100cc four)	700	1,000	1,300	2,100	3,100	4,100
KZ1100-D1 Spectre (1,100cc four)	700	1,000	1,500	2,400	3,300	4,300
KZ1100-B2 GPZ (1,100cc four)	1,100	1,400	2,000	2,800	3,600	4,400
KZ1300-A4 Sports (1,300cc six)	1,200	1,600	2,100	3,100	4,100	5,200
1983						
KZ250-W1 LTD (250cc single)	300	500	700	1,000	1,500	2,000
EX305-B1 GPZ (305cc twin)	200	400	700	1,000	1,300	1,800
KZ440-D5 LTD (440cc twin)	500	700	1,000	1,500	2,000	2,500
KZ550-A4 Sports (550cc four)	400	600	800	1,300	1,800	2,400
KZ550-C4 LTD (550cc four)	300	500	800	1,300	1,900	2,500
KZ550-M1 LTD (550cc four)	400	700	900	1,400	2,000	2,600
KZ550-F1 Spectre (550cc four)	400	600	900	1,500	2,100	2,700
KZ550-H2 GPZ (550cc four)	500	700	1,100	1,600	2,200	2,800
KZ650-H3 CSR (650cc four)	500	700	1,100	1,500	2,000	2,500
KZ750-K1 LTD (750cc four)	400	600	1,000	1,400	1,900	2,400
KZ750-H4 LTD (750cc four)	500	700	1,000	1,700	2,400	3,100
KZ750-L3 Sports (750cc four)	500	700	1,100	1,700	2,400	3,100
KZ750-F1 LTD (750cc four)	500	700	1,100	1,700	2,400	3,200
KZ750-N2 Spectre (750cc four)	500	700	1,100	1,800	2,600	3,400
ZX750-A1 GPZ (750cc four)	700	1,000	1,400	2,000	2,700	3,400
KZ1000-R2 Replica (1000cc four)	2,000	2,400	3,200	3,500	3,800	4,200
KZ1100-A3 (1,100cc four)	600	900	1,400	2,300	3,200	4,100
KZ1100-L1 LTD (1,100cc four)	700	1,000	1,500	2,300	3,200	4,100
KZ1100-D2 Spectre (1,100cc four)	800	1,000	1,600	2,500	3,400	4,300
ZX1100-A1 GPZ (1,100cc four)	1,100	1,500	2,000	2,800	3,600	4,500
ZN1300-A Voyager (1,300cc six)	1,900	2,300	3,050	4,200	5,600	7,000

	6	5	4	3	2	1
1984						
KZ550-F2 LTD (550cc four)	400	600	900	1,500	2,100	2,800
ZX550-A1 GPZ (550cc four).	500	800	1,100	1,700	2,300	2,900
KZ700-A1 Sports (700cc four).	500	800	1,100	1,800	2,400	3,000
ZN700-A1 LTD (700cc four).	800	1,100	1,500	2,100	2,600	3,100
ZX750-A2 GPZ (750cc four).	700	1,000	1,400	2,200	2,900	3,700
ZX750-E1 Turbo (750cc four)	1,300	1,700	2,300	3,500	4,200	4,800
ZX900-A1 Ninja (900cc four)	800	1,100	1,600	2,500	3,400	4,400
KZ1000-P3 Police (1,000cc four).	800	1,100	1,500	2,500	3,500	4,500
ZN1100-B1 LTD (1,100cc four).	700	1,000	1,400	2,400	3,400	4,400
ZX1100-A2 GPZ (1,100cc four)	1,100	1,500	2,000	2,800	3,900	4,800
ZN1300-A2 Voyager (1,300cc six)	1,000	1,300	3,100	4,200	5,600	7,000
1985						
KX60-B1 (60cc single)	200	400	600	700	800	900
KDX80-C2 (80cc single).	200	400	500	600	700	800
KX80-E3 (80cc single).	200	400	700	800	900	1,100
KX125-D1 (125cc single)	300	500	800	1,200	1,600	2,000
KDX200-A3 (200cc single)	300	500	800	1,100	1,400	1,800
KL250-D2 KLR (250cc single).	300	500	800	1,200	1,600	2,000
KX250-D1 (250cc single)	400	600	900	1,500	2,000	2,500
EN450-A1 454 LTD (450cc twin)	700	900	1,200	1,400	1,700	2,000
KX500-B1 (500cc single)	400	600	900	1,500	2,100	2,700
ZX550-A2 GPZ (550cc four).	500	800	1,400	2,100	2,800	3,500
KL600-B1 KLR (600cc single)	400	600	900	1,500	2,000	2,500
ZX600-A1 Ninja R (600cc four)	600	900	1,300	2,000	2,600	3,300
ZN700-A2 LTD (700cc four).	700	1,100	1,500	2,000	2,600	3,100
VN700-A1 Vulcan (700cc twin)	800	1,100	1,600	2,100	2,700	3,300
ZX750-A3 GPZ (750cc four).	700	1,000	1,400	2,100	2,800	3,500
ZX750-E2 Turbo (750cc four)	1,400	2,000	2,800	3,500	4,000	5,000
XL900-A1 Eliminator (900cc four).	1,300	1,700	2,400	3,100	3,800	4,500
ZX900-A2 Ninja (900cc four)	900	1,200	1,600	2,600	3,600	4,600
ZN1100-B2 LTD (1,100cc four).	700	1,000	1,400	2,400	3,400	4,550
ZN1300-A3 Voyager (1,300cc six)	1,000	1,300	3,100	4,200	5,600	7,000
1986						
KX60-B2 Mini (60cc single)	200	400	600	700	800	900
KD80-M7 (80cc single)	200	300	400	500	600	700
KDX80-C3 Mini (80cc single)	200	400	600	700	800	900
KX80-G1 Mini (80cc single)	200	400	700	800	1,000	1,100
KE100-B5 (100cc single)	200	400	700	800	900	1,000
KX125-E1 (125cc single)	400	600	900	1,300	1,700	2,100
KDX200-C1 (200cc single)	300	500	800	1,100	1,500	1,900
EX250-E1 Ninja (250cc twin)	500	800	1,100	1,500	1,900	2,300
KL250-D3 KLR (250cc single).	400	600	900	1,300	1,700	2,100
KX250-D2 (250cc single)	500	700	1,000	1,500	2,000	2,600
EN450-A2 454 LTD (450cc twin)	600	900	1,300	1,600	1,900	2,200
KX500-B2 (500cc single)	500	700	1,000	1,600	2,200	2,800
KL600-B2 KLR (560cc single).	400	600	1,000	1,500	2,000	2,600
ZL600-A1 (600cc four)	700	1,000	1,400	2,100	2,800	3,500
ZX600-A2 Ninja R (600cc four)	700	1,000	1,400	2,100	2,800	3,600
VN750-A2 Vulcan (750cc twin)	1,100	1,500	2,100	2,500	3,000	3,500
ZL900-A2 Eliminator (900cc four)	1,400	1,800	2,400	3,000	3,500	4,500
ZX900-A3 Ninja (900cc four)	900	1,300	1,700	2,800	3,800	4,800
ZX1000-A1 Ninja R (1,000cc four)	1,200	1,600	2,100	3,200	4,200	5,200
ZG1000-A1 Concours (1,000cc four) . . .	1,200	1,600	2,100	3,300	4,400	5,700
ZG1200-A1 Voyager XII (1,200cc four) . . .	1,900	2,400	3,200	4,200	5,600	7,000
ZN1300-A4 Voyager (1,300cc six)	1,900	2,400	3,200	4,200	5,600	7,000
1987						
KX60-B3 (60cc single)	200	400	700	800	900	1,000
KD80-M8 (80cc single)	200	400	600	700	800	900
KDX80-C4 (80cc single).	200	400	700	800	900	1,000

	6	5	4	3	2	1
KX80-G2 (80cc single)	300	500	700	900	1,000	1,200
KX80-J2 (80cc single).	300	500	800	900	1,100	1,300
KE100-B6 (100cc single)	200	400	700	800	900	1,000
KX125-E2 (125cc single)	400	600	1,000	1,400	1,800	2,300
KDX200-C2 (200cc single)	300	500	900	1,300	1,700	2,100
EX250-E2 Ninja (250cc twin)	500	800	1,200	1,600	2,000	2,400
KL250D4 KLR (250cc single)	400	600	1,000	1,400	1,800	2,300
KX250-E1 (250cc single)	500	700	1,100	1,700	2,300	2,900
KZ305-B2 LTD (305cc twin).	500	800	1,000	1,300	1,600	1,900
EN450-A3 454 LTD (450cc twin)	600	900	1,300	1,700	2,100	2,500
EX500-A1 (500cc four)	600	900	1,300	1,800	2,300	2,900
KX500-C1 (500cc single)	500	700	1,100	1,700	2,300	3,000
ZL600-A2 (600cc four)	700	1,000	1,400	2,100	2,800	3,500
ZX600-A3 Ninja R (600cc four)	700	1,000	1,500	2,200	3,000	3,800
ZX600-B1 Ninja RX (600cc four)	700	1,000	1,500	2,300	3,100	4,000
KL650-A1 KLR (650cc single).	500	700	1,000	1,700	2,300	3,000
VN750-A3 Vulcan (750cc twin)	1,200	1,600	2,100	2,600	3,200	3,800
ZX750-F1 Ninja R (750cc four)	900	1,200	1,700	2,700	3,800	4,800
ZG1000-A2 Concours (1,000cc four) . . .	1,200	1,600	2,200	3,500	4,900	6,300
ZL1000-A1 (1,000cc four).	1,400	1,900	2,500	3,300	4,100	4,900
ZX1000-A2 Ninja R (1,000cc four)	1,300	1,700	2,200	3,300	4,500	5,700
ZG1200-B1 Voyager XII (1,200cc four) . . .	1,900	2,400	3,200	4,200	5,600	7,000
ZN1300-A5 Voyager (1,300cc six) . . .	1,900	2,400	3,200	4,300	5,700	7,200
VN1500-A1 Vulcan 88 (1,500cc twin)	1,300	1,700	2,300	3,400	4,700	5,900
VN1500-B1 Vulcan 88SE (1,500cc twin) . .	1,300	1,700	2,300	3,400	4,700	5,900
1988						
KX60-B4 (60cc single)	200	400	700	900	1,000	1,200
KD80-N1 (80cc single)	200	400	700	800	900	1,000
KDX80-C5 Mini (80cc single)	200	400	700	900	1,000	1,200
KX80-L1 (80cc single).	300	500	800	1,000	1,200	1,400
KX80-N1 (80cc single)	300	500	800	1,000	1,200	1,500
KE100-B7 (100cc single)	300	500	800	900	1,000	1,100
KX125-F1 (125cc single)	500	700	1,000	1,500	2,000	2,500
KDX200-C3 (200cc single)	400	600	900	1,300	1,800	2,200
EL250-B2 Eliminator (250cc twin). . . .	500	800	1,100	1,500	2,000	2,400
EX250-F2 Ninja R (250c twin).	600	800	1,200	1,800	2,300	2,800
KL250-D5 KLR (250cc single)	500	700	1,000	1,500	2,000	2,500
KX250-F1 (250cc single)	500	800	1,200	1,800	2,400	3,100
KZ305-B3 LTD (305cc twin).	500	700	1,000	1,300	1,600	1,900
EN450-A4 454 LTD (450cc twin).	600	900	1,300	1,800	2,200	2,600
EX500-A2 (500cc twin)	600	900	1,300	1,900	2,500	3,100
KX500-D1 (500cc single)	500	800	1,200	1,800	2,500	3,200
ZX600-C1 Ninja R (600cc four)	900	1,200	1,700	2,400	3,200	4,000
KL650-A2 KLR (650cc single).	500	800	1,100	1,700	2,400	3,100
VN750-A4 Vulcan (750cc twin)	1,200	1,600	2,200	2,800	3,400	4,000
ZX750-F2 Ninja R (750cc four)	1,000	1,300	1,800	3,000	4,000	5,000
ZX1000-B1 Ninja ZX10 (1,000cc four) . . .	1,300	1,800	2,400	3,600	4,800	6,000
ZG1000-A3 Concours (1,000cc four)	1,300	1,700	2,300	3,800	5,300	6,600
ZG1200-B2 Voyager XII (1,200cc four) . . .	2,000	2,500	3,300	4,600	5,900	7,200
ZN1300-A6 Voyager (1,300cc six)	2,000	2,500	3,300	4,700	6,000	7,400
VN1500-A2 Vulcan 88 (1,500cc twin)	1,300	1,800	2,400	3,700	4,900	6,200
VN1500-B2 Vulcan 88SE (1,500cc twin) . .	1,300	1,800	2,400	3,700	4,900	6,200
1989						
KX60 (60cc single)	300	500	800	1,000	1,200	1,500
KD80-N2 (80cc single)	200	400	500	900	1,000	1,200
KD80X Mini (80cc single)	200	400	700	900	1,000	1,200
KX80-L2 (80cc single).	300	500	800	1,200	1,500	1,800
KX80-N2 (80cc single)	300	500	800	1,200	1,500	1,900
KE100-B8 (100cc single)	300	500	800	1,000	1,100	1,300
KX125-G1 (125cc single)	500	800	1,100	1,800	2,400	3,000

	6	5	4	3	2	1
KDX200-E1 (200cc single)	400	600	1,000	1,500	2,100	2,700
EL250-B3 Eliminator (250cc twin)	500	800	1,200	1,700	2,200	2,700
EX250-F3 (250cc twin)	600	900	1,300	1,900	2,600	3,300
KL250-D6 KLR (250cc single).	500	700	1,100	1,600	2,200	2,800
KX250-G1 (250cc single)	600	900	1,300	2,000	2,800	3,600
EN450-A45 454 LTD (450cc twin).	600	900	1,300	1,900	2,500	3,100
EX500-A3 (500cc twin)	700	1,000	1,300	1,900	2,600	3,300
KX500-E1 (500cc single)	600	900	1,300	2,100	2,900	3,800
ZX600-C2 Ninja R (600cc four)	900	1,300	1,700	2,600	3,500	4,400
KL650-A3 KLR (650cc single)	500	800	1,200	1,900	2,700	3,500
VN750-A5 Vulcan (750cc twin)	1,300	1,700	2,200	2,900	3,600	4,300
ZX750-F3 Ninja R (750cc four)	1,000	1,400	1,900	3,000	4,100	5,200
ZX750-H1 Ninja ZX7 (750cc four). . . .	1,500	1,900	2,500	3,800	5,000	6,200
ZX1000-B2 Ninja ZX10 (1,000cc four) . .	1,500	1,900	2,500	3,800	5,000	6,200
ZG1200 Voyager XII (1,200cc four)	2,100	2,600	3,500	4,700	6,000	7,400
VN1500-A3 Vulcan 88 (1,500cc twin) . . .	1,500	1,900	2,500	3,800	5,000	6,300
1990						
KX60-B6 (60cc single)	300	500	800	1,100	1,300	1,600
KX80-L3 (80cc single).	300	500	1,200	1,500	1,500	1,900
KX80-N3 (80cc single).	400	600	900	1,200	1,600	2,000
KE100-B9 (100cc single)	300	500	800	1,000	1,100	1,300
KX125-H1 (125cc single)	500	800	1,200	1,900	2,500	3,200
KDX200-E2 (200cc single)	500	700	1,100	1,600	2,200	2,800
EX250-F4 Ninja R (250cc twin)	600	900	1,300	2,000	2,700	3,400
KL250-D7 KLR (250cc single).	500	800	1,200	1,700	2,300	2,900
KR-1S (249cc twin)	500	700	1,100	1,600	2,200	2,800
KX250-H1 (250cc single)	700	1,000	1,400	2,200	3,000	3,900
EN450-A6 454 LTD (450cc twin)	700	1,000	1,400	1,900	2,500	3,100
EX500-A4 (500cc twin)	700	1,100	1,500	2,200	2,800	3,400
EN500-A1 Vulcan (500cc twin)	900	1,300	1,800	2,400	3,000	3,700
KX500-E2 (500cc single)	700	1,000	1,400	2,200	3,100	4,000
ZR550-B1 Zephyr (550cc four)	900	1,200	1,700	2,400	3,200	4,000
ZX600-C3 Ninja R (600cc four)	900	1,300	1,800	2,500	3,300	4,500
ZX600-D1 Ninja ZX6 (600cc four).	1,200	1,700	2,300	3,300	4,400	5,500
KL650-A4 KLR (650cc single)	600	900	1,300	2,000	2,800	3,600
KL650-B2 Tengai (650cc single)	600	900	1,300	2,200	3,000	3,900
VN750-A6 Vulcan (750cc twin)	1,200	1,700	2,300	3,000	3,700	4,500
ZX750-F4 Ninja R (750cc four)	1,100	1,500	2,000	3,100	4,200	5,400
ZX750-H2 Ninja ZX7 (750cc four). . . .	1,500	2,000	2,700	4,000	5,200	6,400
KZ1000 Police (1,000cc four)	900	1,300	1,800	3,000	4,000	5,000
ZG1000-A5 Concours (1,000cc four) . . .	1,300	1,800	2,400	3,900	5,400	6,800
ZX1000-B3 Ninja ZX10 (1,000cc four) . .	1,500	2,000	2,700	4,000	5,300	6,600
ZX1100-C1 Ninja ZX11 (1,100cc four) . .	1,800	2,300	3,000	4,500	6,000	7,600
ZG1200 Voyager XII (1,200cc four)	2,000	2,700	3,500	4,700	6,000	7,600
VN1500-B4 Vulcan 88SE (1,500cc twin) . .	1,300	1,900	2,600	3,900	5,200	6,400
VN1500A4 Vulcan 88 (1,500cc twin)	1,300	1,900	2,600	3,900	5,200	6,500
1991						
KX60-B7 (60cc single)	300	500	900	1,100	1,300	1,600
KX80-R1 (80cc single)	400	600	900	1,400	1,700	2,000
KX80-T1 (80cc single).	400	650	900	1,300	1,700	2,100
KE100-B10 (100cc single).	400	600	900	1,000	1,200	1,400
KX125-H2 (125cc single)	600	900	1,300	2,000	2,700	3,300
KDX200-E3 (200cc single)	500	800	1,100	1,700	2,300	2,900
EL250-E1 250HS (250cc twin)	500	800	1,200	1,800	2,400	3,000
KDX250-D1 (250cc single)	500	800	1,200	2,100	3,000	4,000
KL250-D8 KLR (250cc single).	600	900	1,300	1,800	2,300	2,900
KX250-H2 (250cc single)	700	1,000	1,500	2,300	3,100	4,000
EX500-A5 (500cc twin)	800	1,100	1,600	2,200	2,800	3,500
EN500-A2 Vulcan (500cc twin)	1,000	1,400	1,900	2,500	3,100	3,700
KX500-E3 (500cc single)	700	1,100	1,500	2,400	3,200	4,000

	6	5	4	3	2	1
ZR550-B2 Zephyr (550cc four)	1,000	1,300	1,800	2,500	3,200	4,000
ZX600-C4 Ninja R (600cc four)	1,000	1,400	1,900	2,800	3,800	4,700
ZX600-D2 Ninja ZX6 (600cc four)	1,300	1,800	2,400	3,500	4,600	5,600
KL650-A5 KLR (650cc single)	700	1,000	1,400	2,100	2,800	3,600
VN750-A7 Vulcan (750cc twin)	1,300	1,800	2,400	3,100	3,800	4,600
ZR750-C1 Zephyr (750cc four)	1,000	1,300	1,900	2,800	3,700	4,700
ZX750-J1 Ninja ZX7 (750cc four)	1,600	2,100	2,800	4,200	5,600	7,000
ZX750-K1 Ninja ZX7R (750cc four)	1,800	2,300	3,100	5,000	7,000	9,000
KZ1000 Police (1,000cc four)	1,100	1,500	2,000	3,000	4,000	5,000
ZG1000-A6 Concours (1,000cc four)	1,300	1,800	2,500	3,900	5,300	6,900
ZX1100-C2 Ninja ZX11 (1,100cc four) . . .	1,900	2,400	3,200	4,800	6,400	8,000
ZG1200 Voyager XII (1,200cc four)	2,000	2,700	3,600	5,000	6,300	7,700
VN1500-A5 Vulcan 88 (1,500cc twin) . . .	1,500	2,000	2,700	3,900	5,400	6,600
1992						
KX60-B8 (60cc single)	400	600	900	1,100	1,400	1,700
KX80-R2 (80cc single)	400	600	1,000	1,300	1,700	2,100
KX80-T2 (80cc single).	400	600	1,000	1,400	1,800	2,200
KE100-B11 (100cc single).	400	600	900	1,100	1,200	1,400
KX125-J1 (125cc single)	700	1,000	1,400	2,100	2,700	3,400
KDX200-E4 (200cc single)	500	800	1,200	1,800	2,400	3,000
EX250-F6 Ninja R (250cc twin)	700	1,000	1,400	2,000	2,500	3,000
KDX250-D2 (250cc single)	600	900	1,300	2,100	3,000	4,000
KL250-D9 KLR (250cc single).	700	1,000	1,400	1,900	2,400	3,000
KX250-J1 (250cc single)	800	1,100	1,500	2,400	3,200	4,200
EX500-A6 (500cc twin)	800	1,200	1,700	2,300	2,900	3,500
EN500-A3 Vulcan (500cc twin)	1,000	1,400	1,900	2,600	3,200	3,800
KX500-E4 (500cc single)	800	1,100	1,600	2,400	3,300	4,200
ZX600-C5 Ninja R (600cc four)	1,100	1,500	2,100	3,000	3,900	4,700
ZX600-D3 Ninja ZX6 (600cc four)	1,400	1,900	2,500	3,500	4,500	5,600
KL650-A6 KLR (650cc single).	800	1,100	1,500	2,200	2,900	3,700
VN750-A8 Vulcan (750cc twin)	1,300	1,800	2,400	3,200	3,900	4,800
ZR750-C2 Zephyr (750cc four)	1,000	1,400	2,000	2,900	3,900	4,800
ZX750-J2 Ninja ZX7 (750cc four)	1,800	2,200	3,000	4,300	5,600	7,000
ZX750-K2 Ninja ZX7R (750cc four)	1,900	2,500	3,300	5,300	7,300	9,400
KZ1000 Police (1,000cc four)	1,100	1,600	2,100	3,000	4,000	5,000
ZG1000-A7 Concours (1,000cc four)	1,400	1,900	2,500	4,000	5,500	7,100
ZX1100-C3 Ninja ZX11 (1,100cc four) . . .	1,900	2,500	3,000	4,000	5,000	7,000
ZG1200 Voyager XII (1,200cc four)	2,200	2,800	3,700	5,100	6,500	8,000
VN1500-A6 Vulcan 88 (1,500cc twin) . . .	1,500	2,000	2,700	4,000	5,300	6,700
1993						
KX60-B9 (60cc single)	400	600	900	1,100	1,400	1,700
KX80-R3 (80cc single)	400	600	1,000	1,300	1,700	2,100
KX80-T3 Big Wheel (80cc single).	400	600	1,000	1,400	1,800	2,200
KE100-B12 (100cc single).	400	600	900	1,100	1,200	1,400
KX125-J2 (125cc single)	700	1,000	1,400	2,100	2,700	3,400
KDX200-E5 (200cc single)	500	800	1,200	1,800	2,400	3,000
EX250-F7 Ninja R (250cc twin)	700	1,000	1,400	2,000	2,500	3,000
KDX250-D3(250cc single).	600	900	1,300	2,100	3,000	4,000
KL250-D10 KLR (250cc single).	700	1,000	1,400	1,900	2,400	3,000
KX250-J2 (250cc single)	800	1,100	1,500	2,400	3,200	4,200
EN500-A4 Vulcan (500cc twin)	1,000	1,400	1,900	2,600	3,200	3,800
EX500-A7 (500cc twin)	800	1,200	1,700	2,300	2,900	3,500
KX500-E5 (500cc single)	800	1,100	1,600	2,400	3,300	4,200
ZX600-C6 Ninja R (600cc four)	1,100	1,500	2,100	3,000	3,900	4,700
ZX600-D4 Ninja ZX6 (600cc four)	1,400	1,900	2,500	3,500	4,500	5,600
ZX600-E1 Ninja ZX6 (600cc four)	1,400	1,900	2,500	3,500	4,500	5,600
KLX650-A1 (650cc single).	800	1,100	1,500	2,200	2,900	3,700
KL650-A7 KLR (650cc single).	800	1,100	1,500	2,200	2,900	3,700
KLX650-C1 (650cc single).	800	1,100	1,500	2,200	2,900	3,700
VN750-A9 Vulcan (750cc twin)	1,300	1,800	2,400	3,200	3,900	4,800

	6	5	4	3	2	1
ZX750-L1 Ninja ZX7 (750cc four)	1,800	2,200	3,000	4,300	5,600	7,000
ZX750-M1 Ninja ZX7R (750cc four)	1,900	2,500	3,300	5,300	7,300	9,400
KZ1000 Police (1,000cc four)	1,100	1,600	2,100	3,000	4,000	5,000
ZG1000-A8 Concours (1,000cc four)	1,400	1,900	2,500	4,000	5,500	7,100
ZR1100-A2 ZR1100 (1,100cc four)	1,300	1,800	2,400	3,200	3,900	4,800
ZX1100-C4 Ninja ZX11 (1,100cc four) . . .	1,900	2,500	3,000	4,000	5,000	7,000
ZX1100-D1 Ninja ZX11 (1,100cc four) . . .	1,900	2,500	3,000	4,000	5,000	7,000
ZG1200 Voyager XII (1,200cc four)	2,200	2,800	3,700	5,100	6,500	8,000
VN1500-A7 Vulcan 88 (1,500cc twin)	1,500	2,000	2,700	4,000	5,300	6,700
1994						
KX60-B10 (60cc single)	400	600	900	1,100	1,400	1,700
KX80-R4 (80cc single)	400	600	1,000	1,300	1,700	2,100
KX80-T4 Big Wheel (80cc single)	400	600	1,000	1,400	1,800	2,200
KE100-B13 (100cc single)	400	600	900	1,100	1,200	1,400
KX125-K1 (125cc single)	700	1,000	1,400	2,100	2,700	3,400
KDX200-E6 (200cc single)	500	800	1,200	1,800	2,400	3,000
EX250-F8 Ninja R (250cc twin)	700	1,000	1,400	2,000	2,500	3,000
KDX250-D4(250cc single).	600	900	1,300	2,100	3,000	4,000
KL250-D11 KLR (250cc single)	700	1,000	1,400	1,900	2,400	3,000
KLX250-D2 (250cc single)	500	900	1,300	1,800	2,300	2,800
KX250-K2 (250cc single)	800	1,100	1,500	2,400	3,200	4,200
EN500-A5 Vulcan (500cc twin)	1,000	1,400	1,900	2,600	3,200	3,800
EX500-D1 Ninja (500cc twin)	700	1,000	1,700	2,200	2,700	3,200
KX500-E6 (500cc single)	800	1,100	1,600	2,400	3,300	4,200
ZX600-C7 Ninja R (600cc four)	1,100	1,500	2,100	3,000	3,900	4,700
ZX600-E2 Ninja ZX6 (600cc four)	1,400	1,900	2,500	3,500	4,500	5,600
KLX650-A2 (650cc single).	800	1,100	1,500	2,200	2,900	3,700
KL650-A8 KLR (650cc single).	800	1,100	1,500	2,200	2,900	3,700
KLX650-C2 (650cc single)	800	1,100	1,500	2,200	2,900	3,700
VN750-A10 Vulcan (750cc twin).	1,300	1,800	2,400	3,200	3,900	4,800
ZX750-L2 Ninja ZX7 (750cc four)	1,800	2,200	3,000	4,300	5,600	7,000
ZX750-M2 Ninja ZX7R (750cc four)	1,900	2,500	3,300	5,300	7,300	9,400
ZX900-B1 Ninja (900cc four)	1,000	2,000	2,900	3,800	4,700	6,000
KZ1000 Police (1,000cc four)	1,100	1,600	2,100	3,000	4,000	5,000
ZG1000-A9 Concours (1,000cc four)	1,400	1,900	2,500	4,000	5,500	7,100
ZX1100-D2 Ninja ZX11 (1,100cc four) . . .	1,900	2,500	3,000	4,000	5,000	7,000
ZG1200 Voyager XII (1,200cc four)	2,200	2,800	3,700	5,100	6,500	8,000
VN1500-A8 Vulcan 88 (1,500cc twin)	1,500	2,000	2,700	4,000	5,300	6,700
1995						
KX60-B11 (60cc single)	200	400	800	1,200	1,600	2,000
KX80-R5 (80cc single)	300	700	1,100	1,600	2,100	2,600
KX100-B5 (100cc single)	400	800	1,200	1,800	2,400	3,000
KE100-B14 (100cc single).	200	400	600	1,000	1,400	1,800
KX125-K2 (125cc single)	400	700	1,400	2,400	3,400	4,400
KDH200-H1 (200cc single)	400	800	1,600	2,400	3,200	4,000
KLX250-D3 (250cc single)	800	1,700	2,500	3,300	4,100	4,900
KX250-K2 (250cc single)	600	1,200	2,200	3,200	4,200	5,200
KL250-D12 KLR (250cc single)	300	600	1,300	2,100	2,900	3,700
EX250-F9 Ninja R (250cc twin)	500	1,100	1,700	2,300	2,900	3,500
KX500-E7 (500cc single)	500	1,100	2,100	3,100	4,100	5,100
EN500-A6 Vulcan (500cc twin)	700	1,400	2,200	3,000	3,800	4,600
EX500-D2 Ninja (500cc twin)	700	1,400	2,200	3,000	3,800	4,600
ZX600-C8 Ninja R (600cc four)	900	2,000	2,900	3,800	4,700	5,600
ZX600-E3 Ninja ZX6 (600cc four)	1,000	2,500	3,700	4,900	6,000	7,100
ZX600-F1 Ninja ZX6R (600cc four)	1,000	2,000	3,500	5,000	6,500	7,900
KLX650-A3 (650cc single)	600	1,200	2,200	3,200	4,200	5,200
KL650-A9 KLR (650cc single).	600	1,300	2,100	2,900	3,700	4,500
KLX650-C3 (650cc single)	800	1,600	2,500	3,400	4,300	5,400
VN750-A11 Vulcan (750cc twin).	600	1,200	2,500	3,500	5,100	6,100
ZX750-L3 Ninja ZX7 (750cc four)	1,100	2,600	4,100	5,600	7,100	8,600

	6	5	4	3	2	1
ZX750 Ninja ZX7R (750cc four)	1,500	3,000	4,500	6,000	7,500	9,000
VN800-A1 Vulcan (800cc twin)	800	1,500	2,800	4,100	5,400	6,700
ZX900-B2 Ninja ZX9R (900cc four)	800	1,600	3,600	5,600	7,600	9,600
KZ1000P Police (1,000cc four)	600	1,200	2,500	4,000	5,500	7,000
ZG1000-A10 Concours (1,000cc four). . . .	1,500	3,000	4,500	6,000	7,500	9,000
ZX1100-E1 GPZ (1,100cc four)	1,000	2,000	3,500	5,000	6,500	8,000
ZX1100-D3 Ninja ZX11 (1,100cc four) . . .	1,000	2,000	4,000	6,000	8,000	10,000
ZG1200-B9 Voyager XII (1,200cc four) . . .	1,000	2,000	4,000	6,500	9,000	11,500
VN1500-A9 Vulcan 88 (1,500cc twin)	800	1,500	2,800	4,300	6,700	8,200
1996						
KX60-B12 (60cc single)	200	400	800	1,200	1,600	2,000
KX80-R6 (80cc single)	300	700	1,100	1,600	2,100	2,600
KE100-B15 (100cc single).	200	400	600	1,000	1,400	1,800
KX100-B6 (100cc single)	400	800	1,200	1,800	2,400	3,000
KX125-K3 (125cc single)	400	700	1,400	2,400	3,400	4,400
KDH200-H2 (200cc four)	400	800	1,600	2,400	3,200	4,000
EX250-F10 Ninja R (250cc twin)	500	1,100	1,700	2,300	2,900	3,500
KL250-D13 KLR (250cc single)	300	600	1,300	2,100	2,900	3,700
KLX250-D4 (250cc single)	800	1,700	2,500	3,300	4,100	4,900
KLX250R (250cc single).	800	1,700	2,500	3,300	4,100	4,900
KX250-K3 (250cc single)	600	1,200	2,200	3,200	4,200	5,200
EX500-D3 Ninja (500cc four)	700	1,400	2,200	3,000	3,800	4,600
EN500-A7 Vulcan (500cc twin)	700	1,400	2,200	3,000	3,800	4,600
EN500-C1 Vulcan LTD (500cc twin).	700	1,400	2,200	3,000	3,800	4,800
KX500-E8 (500cc single)	500	1,100	2,100	3,100	4,100	5,100
ZX600-C9 Ninja R (600cc four)	900	2,000	2,900	3,800	4,700	5,600
ZL600-B2 Eliminator (600cc four)	900	2,000	3,000	4,000	5,000	6,000
ZX600-E4 Ninja ZX6 (600cc four)	1,000	2,500	3,700	4,900	6,000	7,100
ZX600-F2 Ninja ZX6R (600cc four)	1,000	2,000	3,500	5,000	6,500	7,900
KLX650-D1 (650cc single)	700	1,500	2,500	3,500	4,500	5,500
KLX650R (650cc single).	700	1,500	2,500	3,500	4,500	5,500
KL650-A10 KLR (650cc single)	600	1,300	2,100	2,900	3,700	4,500
KLX650-C4 (650cc single)	800	1,600	2,500	3,400	4,300	5,400
VN750-A12 Vulcan (750cc twin)	600	1,200	2,500	3,500	5,100	6,100
ZX750-P1 Ninja ZX7R (750cc four)	1,500	3,000	4,500	6,000	7,500	9,000
ZX750-N1 Ninja ZX7RR (750cc four)	1,500	3,000	4,500	6,000	8,000	10,000
VN800-A2 Vulcan (800cc twin)	800	1,500	2,800	4,100	5,400	6,700
ZX900-B3 Ninja ZX9R (900cc four)	800	1,600	3,600	5,600	7,600	9,600
KZ1000P Police (1,000cc four)	600	1,200	2,500	4,000	5,500	7,000
ZX1100-E2 GPZ (1,100cc four)	1,000	2,000	3,500	5,000	6,500	8,000
ZX1100-F1 GPZ ABS (1,100cc four)	1,000	2,000	3,500	500	7,000	85,000
ZX1100-D4 Ninja ZX11 (1,100cc four) . . .	1,000	2,000	4,000	6,000	8,000	10,000
ZG1200-B10 Voyager XII (1,200cc four) . .	1,000	2,000	4,000	6,500	9,000	11,500
VN1500-A10 Vulcan 88 (1,500cc twin) . . .	800	1,500	2,800	4,300	6,700	8,200
VN1500-C3 Vulcan L (1,500cc twin)	800	1,600	2,900	4,400	6,800	8,600
VN1500-D1 Vulcan Classic (1,500cc twin) .	900	1,700	3,000	4,500	7,000	9,000

KTM

	6	5	4	3	2	1
1947						
Cross Country 125	800	1,300	1,800	2,400	3,800	5,200
1976						
Cross Country 125	800	1,300	1,800	2,300	3,700	5,100
ISDT Enduro 125	800	1,300	1,800	2,300	3,700	5,100
Moto Cross 125	800	1,300	1,800	2,300	3,700	5,100
Cross Country 175	1,000	1,600	2,200	2,800	4,500	6,200
ISDT Enduro 175	1,000	1,600	2,200	2,800	4,500	6,200
Moto Cross 175	1,000	1,600	2,200	2,800	4,500	6,200
Cross Country 250	800	1,300	1,800	2,300	3,500	4,700
ISDT Enduro 250	800	1,300	1,800	2,300	3,500	4,700
Moto Cross 250	800	1,300	1,800	2,300	3,500	4,700

	6	5	4	3	2	1
Cross Country 400	700	1,400	2,100	2,800	3,500	4,800
ISDT Enduro 400	700	1,400	2,100	2,800	3,500	4,800
Moto Cross 400	700	1,400	2,100	2,800	3,500	4,800
1977						
Cross Country 125	800	1,300	1,800	2,300	3,700	5,100
ISDT Enduro 125	800	1,300	1,800	2,300	3,700	5,100
Moto Cross 125	800	1,300	1,800	2,300	3,700	5,100
Cross Country 175	1,000	1,600	2,200	2,800	4,500	6,200
SD Enduro 175	1,000	1,600	2,200	2,800	4,500	6,200
Moto Cross 175	1,000	1,600	2,200	2,800	4,500	6,200
Cross Country 250	800	1,300	1,800	2,300	3,500	4,700
Moto Cross 250	800	1,300	1,800	2,300	3,500	4,700
SD Enduro 250	800	1,300	1,800	2,300	3,500	4,700
Cross Country 400	700	1,400	2,100	2,800	3,500	4,800
Moto Cross 400	700	1,400	2,100	2,800	3,500	4,800
SD Enduro 400	700	1,400	2,100	2,800	3,500	4,800
1978						
MC5 125	800	1,200	1,600	2,200	3,400	4,600
MC5 175	1,000	1,600	2,200	2,800	4,500	6,200
MC5 250	800	1,300	1,800	2,300	3,500	4,700
MC5 400	1,300	2,000	2,700	3,500	5,500	7,500
1979						
LC 125	800	1,200	1,600	2,200	3,400	4,600
WR 175	1,000	1,600	2,200	2,800	4,500	6,200
MX 250	800	1,300	1,800	2,300	3,500	4,700
MX 400	700	1,400	2,100	2,800	3,500	4,800
MX 420	700	1,400	2,100	2,800	3,500	4,800
1980						
LC 125	800	1,200	1,600	2,200	3,400	4,600
WR 175	1,000	1,600	2,200	2,800	4,500	6,200
MX 250	800	1,300	1,800	2,300	3,500	4,700
MX 420	700	1,400	2,100	2,800	3,500	4,800
1981						
LC 125	800	1,200	1,600	2,200	3,400	4,600
RV/WR 125	800	1,200	1,600	2,200	3,400	4,600
WR 175	1,000	1,600	2,200	2,800	4,500	6,200
MX 250	800	1,300	1,800	2,300	3,500	4,700
WR 250	800	1,300	1,800	2,300	3,500	4,700
WR 390	700	1,400	2,100	2,800	3,500	4,800
MX 420	700	1,400	2,100	2,800	3,500	4,800
MX 495	800	1,400	2,100	3,000	4,000	5,000
1982						
LC/MX 125	800	1,200	1,600	2,200	3,400	4,600
WR 125	800	1,200	1,600	2,200	3,400	4,600
MX 250	800	1,300	1,800	2,300	3,500	4,700
WR 250	800	1,300	1,800	2,300	3,500	4,700
WR 400	700	1,400	2,100	2,800	3,500	4,800
MX 495	800	1,400	2,100	3,000	4,000	5,000
1983						
MX 125	800	1,200	1,600	2,200	3,400	4,600
MXC 125	800	1,200	1,600	2,200	3,400	4,600
GS 250	800	1,300	1,800	2,300	3,500	4,700
MX 250	800	1,300	1,800	2,300	3,500	4,700
MXC 250	800	1,300	1,800	2,300	3,500	4,700
GS 400	700	1,400	2,100	2,800	3,500	4,800
MX 495	800	1,400	2,100	3,000	4,000	5,000
GS 504	800	1,400	2,100	3,000	4,000	5,000
MX 504	800	1,400	2,100	3,000	4,000	5,000
1984						
MX 125	800	1,200	1,600	2,200	3,400	4,600

	6	5	4	3	2	1
MXC 125	800	1,200	1,600	2,200	3,400	4,600
MX 250	800	1,300	1,800	2,300	3,500	4,700
MXC 250	800	1,300	1,800	2,300	3,500	4,700
MXC 420	700	1,400	2,100	2,800	3,500	4,800
MX 495	800	1,400	2,100	3,000	4,000	5,000
MXC 495	800	1,400	2,100	3,000	4,000	5,000
560	800	1,400	2,100	3,000	4,000	5,000
1985						
MX 125 (123cc single)	200	400	600	900	1,200	1,500
MXC 125 (123cc single).	200	300	500	800	1,100	1,400
MX 250 (247cc single)	200	400	600	900	1,200	1,500
MXC 250 (247cc single).	200	400	600	900	1,200	1,500
MXC 350 (350cc single).	200	400	600	900	1,200	1,500
MX 500 (488cc single)	200	400	600	1,000	1,400	1,800
MXC 500 (488cc single).	200	400	600	900	1,200	1,500
MXC 600 (560cc single).	200	400	600	900	1,200	1,500
1986						
MX 80 (80cc single).	200	300	500	800	1,100	1,400
MX 125 (125cc single)	200	400	600	900	1,200	1,500
MXC 125 (125cc single).	200	300	500	800	1,100	1,400
MX 250 (250cc single)	200	400	700	1,000	1,300	1,600
MXC 250 (250cc single).	200	400	600	900	1,200	1,500
MXC 350 (350cc single).	200	400	600	900	1,200	1,500
MX 500 (500cc single)	200	400	700	1,000	1,300	1,600
MXC 500 (500cc single).	200	400	600	900	1,200	1,500
1987						
MX 80 (82cc single)	200	300	500	800	1,100	1,400
MX 125 (124cc single)	200	400	700	1,000	1,300	1,600
MX 250 (247cc single)	300	500	800	1,100	1,400	1,700
D/CC 250 (247cc single)	200	400	600	1,000	1,400	1,800
D/CC 350 (349cc single)	200	400	600	1,000	1,400	1,800
MX 500 (497cc single)	300	500	800	1,100	1,400	1,700
1988						
MX 80 (83cc single)	200	300	500	800	1,100	1,400
MX 125 (125cc single)	200	400	700	1,100	1,500	1,900
D/CC 125 (125cc single)	200	400	600	900	1,200	1,500
MX 250 (246cc single)	300	500	800	1,100	1,400	1,700
D/CC 250 (246cc single)	200	400	700	1,000	1,300	1,600
D/CC 350 (345cc single)	200	400	700	1,000	1,300	1,600
MX 500 (485cc single)	300	600	900	1,200	1,500	1,800
MX 600 (553cc single)	300	600	900	1,300	1,700	2,100
D/CC 600 (553cc single)	300	500	800	1,100	1,400	1,700
1989						
MX 125 (125cc single)	300	500	800	1,100	1,400	1,700
EXC 125 (125cc single).	700	1,400	2,100	2,800	3,500	4,200
MX 250 (250cc single)	300	600	900	1,300	1,700	2,100
DXC 250 (250cc single).	200	400	700	1,100	1,500	1,900
EXC 250 (250cc single).	300	500	800	1,100	1,400	1,700
MX 350 (350cc single)	300	600	900	1,300	1,700	2,100
EXC 350 (350cc single).	900	1,900	2,700	3,500	4,300	5,100
MX 500 (500cc single)	300	600	900	1,300	1,700	2,100
DXC 500 (500cc single).	300	500	800	1,100	1,400	1,700
MX 600 (600cc single)	400	700	1,000	1,400	1,800	2,200
EXC 600 (600cc single).	300	600	900	1,200	1,500	1,800
1990						
MX 85 (83cc single).	200	400	600	900	1,200	1,500
MX 125 (125cc single)	300	600	900	1,200	1,500	1,800
DXC 125 (125cc single).	200	400	700	1,000	1,300	1,600
EXC 125 (125cc single).	700	1,400	2,100	2,800	3,500	4,200
MX 250 (249cc single)	400	700	1,000	1,400	1,800	2,200

	6	5	4	3	2	1
DXC 250 (249cc single)	300	500	800	1,200	1,600	2,000
EXC 250 (249cc single)	900	1,900	2,700	3,500	4,300	5,100
MX 300 (297cc single)	900	1,900	2,700	3,500	4,300	5,100
DXC 300 (297cc single)	300	500	800	1,200	1,600	2,000
EXC 300 (297cc single)	900	1,900	2,700	3,500	4,300	5,100
EXC 350 (345cc single)	300	600	900	1,200	1,500	1,800
MX 500 (498cc single)	400	700	1,000	1,500	2,000	2,500
DXC 540 (534cc single)	300	500	800	1,200	1,600	2,000
MX 600 (553cc single)	400	700	1,100	1,500	1,900	2,300
DXC 600 (553cc single)	300	600	900	1,300	1,700	2,100
1991						
MX 125 (125cc single)	400	700	1,000	1,400	1,800	2,200
EXC 125 (125cc single)	700	1,400	2,100	2,800	3,500	4,200
MX 250 (249cc single)	400	700	1,100	1,600	2,100	2,600
DXC 250 (249cc single)	300	600	900	1,300	1,700	2,100
EXC 250 (249cc single)	900	1,900	2,700	3,500	4,300	5,100
MX 300 (297cc single)	900	1,900	2,700	3,500	4,300	5,100
DXC 300 (297cc single)	300	600	900	1,300	1,700	2,100
TXC 300 (297cc single)	300	600	900	1,300	1,700	2,100
EXC 300 (297cc single)	900	1,900	2,700	3,500	4,300	5,100
MX 500 (498cc single)	400	700	1,100	1,600	2,100	2,600
DXC 540 (548cc single)	300	600	900	1,300	1,700	2,100
LC4 600 (553cc single)	400	700	1,000	1,400	1,800	2,200
1992						
SX 125 (125cc single)	700	1,400	2,100	2,800	3,500	4,200
EXC 125 (125cc single)	700	1,400	2,100	2,800	3,500	4,200
SX 250 (249cc single)	400	800	1,200	1,700	2,200	2,700
DXC 250 (249cc single)	400	700	1,000	1,400	1,800	2,200
EXC 250 (249cc single)	900	1,900	2,700	3,500	4,300	5,100
SX 300 (297cc single)	400	800	1,200	1,700	2,200	2,700
DXC 300 (297cc single)	400	700	1,000	1,400	1,800	2,200
TXC 300 (297cc single)	400	700	1,000	1,400	1,800	2,200
EXC 300 (297cc single)	900	1,900	2,700	3,500	4,300	5,100
SX 500 (498cc single)	400	800	1,200	1,700	2,200	2,700
DXC 540 (548cc single)	400	700	1,000	1,400	1,800	2,200
LC4 600 (553cc single)	400	700	1,100	1,500	1,900	2,300
1993						
SX 125 (125cc single)	700	1,400	2,100	2,800	3,500	4,200
EXC 125 (125cc single)	700	1,400	2,100	2,800	3,500	4,200
SX 250 (249cc single)	800	1,600	2,400	3,400	4,200	5,000
EXC 250 (249cc single)	900	1,900	2,700	3,500	4,300	5,100
MXC 300 (297cc single)	900	1,900	2,700	3,500	4,300	5,100
EXC 300 (297cc single)	900	1,900	2,700	3,500	4,300	5,100
LC4 EXC 400 (400cc single)	1,000	2,100	3,100	4,100	5,100	6,100
MXC 550 (548cc single)	800	1,600	2,500	3,400	4,300	5,200
LC4 EXC 600 (600cc single)	900	1,800	2,900	3,900	4,900	5,900
1994						
SX 125 (125cc single)	700	1,400	2,100	2,800	3,500	4,200
EXC 125 (125cc single)	700	1,400	2,100	2,800	3,500	4,200
SX 250 (249cc single)	800	1,600	2,400	3,400	4,200	5,000
EXC 250 (249cc single)	900	1,900	2,700	3,500	4,300	5,100
MXC 300 (297cc single)	900	1,900	2,700	3,500	4,300	5,100
EXC 300 (297cc single)	900	1,900	2,700	3,500	4,300	5,100
LC4 RXC 400 (398cc single)	1,000	2,100	3,100	4,100	5,100	6,100
LC4 EXC 400 (398cc single)	600	1,200	2,200	3,400	4,600	5,800
MXC 440 (435cc single)	800	1,600	2,500	3,400	4,300	5,200
EXC 440 (435cc single)	800	1,600	2,500	3,400	4,300	5,300
MXC 550 (548cc single)	800	1,600	2,500	3,400	4,300	5,200
LC4 RXC 620 (609cc single)	700	1,400	2,600	3,800	5,000	6,200
LC4 EXC 620 (609cc single)	900	1,800	2,900	3,900	4,900	5,900

	6	5	4	3	2	1
1995						
SX 125 (125cc single)	700	1,400	2,100	2,800	3,500	4,200
EXC 125 (125cc single)	700	1,400	2,100	2,800	3,500	4,200
SX 250 (249cc single)	800	1,600	2,400	3,400	4,200	5,000
EXC 250 (249cc single)	900	1,900	2,700	3,500	4,300	5,100
MXC 300 (297cc single)	900	1,900	2,700	3,500	4,300	5,100
EXC 300 (297cc single)	900	1,900	2,700	3,500	4,300	5,100
LC4 RXC 400 (398cc single)	1,000	2,100	3,100	4,100	5,100	6,100
LC4 EXC 400 (398cc single)	600	1,200	2,200	3,400	4,600	5,800
MXC 440 (435cc single)	800	1,600	2,500	3,400	4,300	5,200
EXC 440 (435cc single)	800	1,600	2,500	3,400	4,300	5,300
MXC 550 (548cc single)	800	1,600	2,500	3,400	4,300	5,200
LC4 RXC 620 (609cc single)	700	1,400	2,600	3,800	5,000	6,200
LC4 EXC 620 (609cc single)	900	1,800	2,900	3,900	4,900	5,900
1996						
SX 50 (50cc single)	300	500	700	900	1,100	1,300
SXR 50 (50cc single)	300	500	700	900	1,200	1,500
SX3 50 (50cc single)	300	500	800	1,100	1,400	1,700
SXR Pro (50cc single)	300	600	900	1,200	1,500	1,800
EXC 125 (125cc single)	700	1,400	2,100	2,800	3,500	4,200
SX 125 (125cc single)	700	1,400	2,100	2,800	3,500	4,200
EXC 250 (249cc single)	900	1,900	2,700	3,500	4,300	5,100
SX 250 (249cc single)	800	1,600	2,400	3,400	4,200	5,000
EXC 300 (297cc single)	900	1,900	2,700	3,500	4,300	5,100
MXC 300 (297cc single)	500	1,000	2,000	3,400	4,500	5,600
EXC 360 (354cc single)	900	1,900	2,900	3,900	4,900	5,900
MXC 360 (354cc single)	600	1,400	2,500	3,600	4,700	5,800
SX 360 (354cc single)	500	900	1,900	3,200	4,500	5,700
EXC 400 (398cc single)	900	1,800	2,900	4,000	5,100	6,200
RXC 400 (398cc single)	900	1,700	2,900	4,100	5,300	6,500
MXC 550 (548cc single)	800	1,600	2,500	3,400	4,300	5,200
EXC 620 (609cc single)	900	1,700	2,900	4,100	5,300	6,500
SX 620 (609cc single)	500	1,000	2,000	3,500	5,000	6,500
RXC 620 (609cc single)	1,000	2,000	3,000	4,200	5,500	6,800
Duke 620 (609cc single)	1,200	2,300	4,300	5,700	7,000	8,300
LAVERDA						
1954						
175cc	1,600	2,400	3,600	4,800	6,400	8,000
1957						
Turismo (100cc)	400	800	1,600	2,400	3,200	4,000
1969						
American Eagle (750cc twin)	1,300	2,000	2,900	3,900	5,200	6,500
1970						
American Eagle (750cc twin)	1,300	2,000	2,900	3,900	5,200	6,500
750 S (750cc twin)	1,400	2,100	3,200	4,200	5,600	7,000
1971						
GT750 (750cc twin)	1,400	2,100	3,200	4,200	5,600	7,000
SFC750 Racer (750cc twin)	2,000	3,000	4,500	6,000	8,000	10,000
1972						
GT750 (750cc twin)	1,400	2,100	3,200	4,200	5,600	7,000
SF750 (750cc twin)	1,500	2,300	3,400	6,000	9,000	12,000
SFC750 Racer (750cc twin)	2,000	3,000	4,500	6,000	8,000	10,000
1973						
GT750 (750cc twin)	1,400	2,100	3,200	4,200	5,600	7,000
SF750 (750cc twin)	1,500	2,300	3,400	6,000	9,000	12,000
SFC750 Racer (750cc twin)	2,000	3,000	4,500	6,000	8,000	10,000
3C (1,000cc triple)	1,600	2,400	3,600	6,000	9,000	12,000
1974						
GT750 (750cc twin)	1,400	2,100	3,200	4,200	5,600	7,000
SF750 (750cc twin)	1,500	2,300	3,400	6,000	9,000	12,000

	6	5	4	3	2	1
SFC750 Racer (750cc twin)	2,000	3,000	4,500	6,000	8,000	10,000
3C (1,000cc triple)	1,600	2,400	3,600	6,000	9,000	12,000
1975						
GTL750 (750cc twin)	1,300	2,000	2,900	3,900	5,200	6,500
SF750 (750cc twin)	1,500	2,300	3,400	6,000	9,000	12,000
SFC750 Racer (750cc twin)	2,000	3,000	4,500	6,000	8,000	10,000
3C (1,000cc triple)	1,600	2,400	3,600	6,000	9,000	12,000
1976						
GTL750 (750cc twin)	1,300	2,000	2,900	3,900	5,200	6,500
SF750 (750cc twin)	1,500	2,300	3,400	6,000	9,000	12,000
SFC750 Racer (750cc twin)	2,000	3,000	4,500	6,000	8,000	10,000
3CL (1,000cc triple)	1,600	2,400	3,600	4,800	6,400	8,000
Jota (1,000cc triple)	2,500	4,000	5,000	7,000	10,000	12,000
1977						
Alpino (500cc twin)	1,200	1,800	2,700	3,600	4,800	6,000
GTL750 (750cc twin)	1,300	2,000	2,900	3,900	5,200	6,500
SF750 (750cc twin)	1,500	2,300	3,400	6,000	9,000	12,000
3CL (1,000cc triple)	1,600	2,400	3,600	4,800	6,400	8,000
Jota (1,000cc triple)	2,500	4,000	5,000	7,000	10,000	12,000
1200 (1,116cc triple)	1,600	2,400	3,600	4,800	6,400	8,000
1978						
Alpino (500cc twin)	1,200	1,800	2,700	3,600	4,800	6,000
Montjuic (500cc twin)	1,200	1,800	2,700	3,600	4,800	6,000
GTL750 (750cc twin)	1,300	2,000	2,900	3,900	5,200	6,500
3CL (1,000cc triple)	1,600	2,400	3,600	4,800	6,400	8,000
Jarama (1,000cc triple)	1,600	2,400	3,600	4,800	6,400	8,000
Jota (1,000cc triple)	2,500	4,000	5,000	7,000	10,000	12,000
1200 (1,116cc triple)	1,600	2,400	3,600	4,800	6,400	8,000
1979						
Alpino (500cc twin)	1,200	1,800	2,700	3,600	4,800	6,000
Montjuic (500cc twin)	1,200	1,800	2,700	3,600	4,800	6,000
GTL750 (750cc twin)	1,300	2,000	2,900	3,900	5,200	6,500
3CL (1,000cc triple)	1,600	2,400	3,600	4,800	6,400	8,000
Jota (1,000cc triple)	2,500	4,000	5,000	7,000	10,000	12,000
1200 (1,116cc triple)	1,600	2,400	3,600	4,800	6,400	8,000
1980						
Alpino (500cc twin)	1,200	1,800	2,700	3,600	4,800	6,000
Montjuic (500cc twin)	1,200	1,800	2,700	3,600	4,800	6,000
GTL750 (750cc twin)	1,300	2,000	2,900	3,900	5,200	6,500
3CL (1,000cc triple)	1,600	2,400	3,600	4,800	6,400	8,000
Jota (1,000cc triple)	2,500	4,000	5,000	7,000	10,000	12,000
1200 (1,116cc triple)	1,600	2,400	3,600	4,800	6,400	8,000
1981						
Alpino (500cc twin)	1,200	1,800	2,700	3,600	4,800	6,000
Montjuic (500cc twin)	1,200	1,800	2,700	3,600	4,800	6,000
GTL750 (750cc twin)	1,300	2,000	2,900	3,900	5,200	6,500
3CL (1,000cc triple)	1,600	2,400	3,600	4,800	6,400	8,000
Jota (1,000cc triple)	2,500	4,000	5,000	7,000	10,000	12,000
Jota 120 (1,116cc triple)	2,000	3,000	4,500	6,000	8,000	10,000
1200 (1,116cc triple)	1,600	2,400	3,600	4,800	6,400	8,000
1982						
Alpino (500cc twin)	1,200	1,800	2,700	3,600	4,800	6,000
Montjuic (500cc twin)	1,200	1,800	2,700	3,600	4,800	6,000
Jota 120 (1,116cc triple)	2,500	4,000	5,000	7,000	10,000	12,000
RGS (1,000cc triple)	1,600	2,500	4,000	6,000	7,500	9,000
SFC (1,000cc triple)	1,600	2,400	3,600	4,800	6,400	8,000
1983						
RGS (1,000cc triple)	1,600	2,500	4,000	6,000	7,500	9,000
SFC (1,000cc triple)	1,600	2,400	3,600	4,800	6,400	8,000

	6	5	4	3	2	1
1984						
RGS (1,000cc triple).	1,600	2,500	4,000	6,000	7,500	9,000
SFC (1,000cc triple).	1,600	2,400	3,600	4,800	6,400	8,000
1985						
RGS (1,000cc triple).	1,600	2,500	4,000	6,000	7,500	9,000
SFC (1,000cc triple).	1,600	2,400	3,600	4,800	6,400	8,000
MAICO						
1955						
Typhoon.	400	800	1,600	2,400	3,200	4,000
1964						
Blizzard (250cc).	500	1,000	1,500	2,000	2,500	3,000
1967						
390	900	1,600	3,200	4,300	6,800	8,300
1968						
360 X3	900	1,600	3,200	4,300	6,800	8,300
1969						
360 X4A.	900	1,600	3,200	4,300	6,800	8,300
1970						
250 T5.	800	1,300	2,500	3,700	6,300	8,900
400 X5	900	1,500	2,800	4,000	6,600	9,200
1971						
250 K	800	1,300	2,500	3,900	6,300	8,700
400 K	900	1,500	2,800	4,000	6,600	9,200
501 K	1,500	3,000	4,500	6,500	9,800	12,000
1972						
125 K	900	1,500	2,000	2,700	4,200	5,700
250 K	900	1,500	2,000	2,700	4,200	5,700
400 K	800	1,300	2,500	3,700	6,300	8,900
501 K	1,500	3,000	4,500	6,500	9,800	12,000
1973						
125 K	900	1,500	2,000	2,700	4,200	5,700
250 R	1,000	2,000	3,400	4,900	7,300	9,700
400 R	1,100	2,200	3,700	5,100	7,400	9,700
450 R	1,300	2,500	3,900	5,300	7,700	10,100
1974						
125 K	1,000	2,000	3,400	4,900	7,300	9,700
250 R	1,000	2,000	3,400	4,900	7,300	9,700
400 R	1,400	2,700	3,700	5,100	7,800	10,500
450 R	1,300	2,500	3,900	5,300	8,300	11,300
1975						
125 MC U	900	1,500	2,000	2,700	4,200	5,700
250 GS K Enduro	600	1,000	1,400	1,800	5,400	9,000
250 MC U	1,000	1,700	2,300	3,000	6,500	10,000
400 GS K Enduro	900	1,500	2,200	2,800	5,500	9,200
400 MC U	1,300	2,600	3,600	5,100	7,300	9,500
450 GS K Enduro	900	1,500	2,200	2,700	5,500	9,300
450 MC K	1,000	2,000	3,400	4,900	7,300	9,700
450 MC U	1,000	2,000	3,400	4,900	7,300	9,700
1976						
250 AW	800	1,300	2,500	3,700	6,300	8,900
250 WR Enduro	600	1,000	1,800	2,400	4,900	7,400
400 AW	900	1,500	2,500	3,700	6,300	8,900
400 WR Enduro	600	1,100	2,000	2,800	5,400	8,000
450 AW	1,000	1,700	2,800	4,000	6,600	9,200
450 WR Enduro	700	1,200	2,100	3,800	5,600	8,000
1977						
125 AW	1,000	2,000	3,000	4,600	6,800	9,000
250 AW	1,000	18,000	3,000	4,600	6,800	9,000
250 WR Enduro	900	1,400	1,700	2,400	4,400	6,400
400 AW	1,000	2,000	3,700	5,100	7,300	9,500

	6	5	4	3	2	1
400 WR Enduro	600	1,000	1,800	2,400	4,900	7,400
450 AW	1,100	2,200	3,800	5,600	7,800	10,000
450 WR Enduro	800	1,300	2,200	2,700	5,900	8,100
1978						
125 Magnum	700	1,200	2,200	2,700	5,900	8,300
250 Magnum	700	1,200	2,200	2,700	5,900	8,300
250 Magnum Enduro	600	1,000	1,800	2,400	4,900	7,400
400 Magnum	700	1,300	2,200	2,700	5,900	8,300
400 Magnum Enduro	600	1,100	1,800	2,600	5,400	8,200
450 Magnum	700	1,300	2,200	2,700	5,900	8,300
450 Magnum Enduro	600	1,100	1,800	2,600	5,400	8,200
1979						
125 Magnum	800	1,200	2,200	2,800	6,000	9,400
250 Magnum Enduro	600	900	1,700	2,400	4,400	6,400
250 Magnum II	800	1,200	2,200	3,200	6,000	8,800
400 Magnum Enduro	600	1,000	1,800	2,400	4,900	7,400
400 Magnum II	800	1,300	2,000	3,200	6,000	8,800
450 Magnum Enduro	600	1,000	1,800	2,400	4,900	7,400
450 Magnum II	800	1,300	2,500	3,700	6,300	8,900
1980						
250 Enduro	600	900	1,500	2,400	4,400	6,400
250 M1	700	1,200	2,300	2,800	5,600	8,400
400 Enduro	600	1,000	1,900	2,600	4,900	7,200
400 M1	700	1,300	2,200	2,800	5,900	9,000
450 Enduro	600	1,100	1,800	2,600	5,400	8,200
450 M1	700	1,300	2,200	2,800	5,900	9,000
1981						
250 Mega 2	1,300	2,100	3,600	5,000	7,800	10,600
250 Mega E	1,300	2,100	3,600	5,000	7,800	10,600
400 Mega 2	1,400	2,900	3,800	5,300	8,300	11,300
400 Mega E	1,400	2,900	3,800	5,300	8,300	11,300
490 Mega 2	1,500	2,500	4,000	5,800	8,800	11,800
490 Mega E	1,500	2,500	4,000	5,800	8,800	11,800
1982						
250 Alpha E	700	1,200	1,800	2,600	5,400	8,200
250 Alpha I MX	700	1,200	1,800	2,600	5,400	8,200
490 Alpha E	900	1,500	2,800	4,000	6,600	9,200
490 Alpha I MX	900	1,500	2,800	4,000	6,600	9,200
1983						
250 Spider	1,200	2,100	3,600	5,000	7,800	10,600
250 Spider E	1,200	2,100	3,600	5,000	7,800	10,600
490 Spider	1,400	2,300	3,800	5,300	8,300	11,300
490 Spider E	1,400	2,300	3,800	5,300	8,300	11,300
1992						
250 GS (250cc single)	300	600	800	1,100	1,600	2,100
250 MC (250cc single)	200	500	700	900	1,400	1,900
320 GS (320cc single)	200	500	700	900	1,400	1,900
320 MC (320cc single)	300	700	900	1,300	1,700	2,100
440 GS (440cc single)	200	500	700	900	1,400	1,900
440 MC (440cc single)	200	500	800	1,100	1,600	2,100
500 GS (500cc single)	200	500	700	900	1,400	1,900
500 MC (500cc single)	300	600	900	1,100	1,600	2,100
1993						
250 GS (250cc single)	300	600	700	900	1,400	1,900
250 MC (250cc single)	200	500	700	900	1,500	2,100
320 GS (320cc single)	300	600	900	1,200	1,700	2,200
320 MC (320cc single)	200	500	700	900	1,500	2,100
440 GS (440cc single)	300	700	900	1,300	1,700	2,100
440 MC (440cc single)	200	500	700	900	1,400	1,900
500 GS (500cc single)	300	700	1,000	1,400	2,000	2,600

	6	5	4	3	2	1
500 MC (500cc single)	300	600	900	1,200	1,700	2,200
1994						
250 GS (250cc single).	300	600	900	1,200	1,700	2,200
250 MC (250cc single)	300	600	700	900	1,500	2,100
320 GS (320cc single).	300	600	900	1,200	1,700	2,200
320 MC (320cc single).	300	600	800	1,000	1,600	2,200
440 GS (440cc single).	500	800	1,400	2,100	2,700	3,300
440 MC (440cc single)	300	600	900	1,200	1,700	2,200
500 GS (500cc single).	300	700	1,000	1,400	2,000	2,600
500 MC (500cc single)	300	600	900	1,200	1,700	2,200
545 GS (545cc single)	400	700	1,200	1,600	2,100	2,600
545 MC (545cc single)	300	600	900	1,200	1,700	2,200
1996						
RC250 (250cc single)	300	700	1,100	1,500	2,100	2,700
RE250 (250cc single)	300	600	1,000	1,400	1,900	2,400
RC320 (320cc single)	300	700	1,100	1,500	2,100	2,700
RE320 (320cc single)	300	600	1,000	1,400	1,900	2,400
RC440 (440cc single)	300	700	1,100	1,500	2,100	2,700
RE440 (440cc single)	300	600	1,000	1,400	1,900	2,400
RC500 (500cc single)	300	700	1,100	1,600	2,100	2,700
RE500 (500cc single)	300	600	1,000	1,400	1,900	2,400
MATCHLESS						
1933						
Silver Hawk (592cc).	5,000	10,000	20,000	30,000	40,000	50,000
1934						
Silver Hawk (592cc).	5,000	10,000	20,000	30,000	40,000	50,000
1935						
G3C.	1,000	2,000	4,000	6,000	8,000	10,000
1936						
G3C.	1,000	2,000	4,000	6,000	8,000	10,000
1937						
Model X	**5,000**	**10,000**	**15,000**	**20,000**	**25,000**	**30,000**
1938						
Model X	**5,000**	**10,000**	**15,000**	**20,000**	**25,000**	**30,000**
1939						
Model X	5,000	10,000	15,000	20,000	25,000	30,000
1941						
G3L (350cc single)	1,000	2,000	4,000	6,000	8,000	10,000
1945						
G3L (350cc single)	1,200	1,700	2,500	3,900	6,500	9,000
G80 Clubman (500cc single)	1,500	1,900	**3,000**	**6,000**	**9,000**	**12,000**
1946						
G3L (350cc single)	1,200	1,700	2,500	3,900	6,500	9,000
G80 Clubman (500cc single)	1,500	1,900	**3,000**	**6,000**	**9,000**	**12,000**
1947						
G3L (350cc single)	1,200	1,700	2,500	3,900	6,500	9,000
G80 Clubman (500cc single)	1,500	1,900	**3,000**	**6,000**	**9,000**	**12,000**
1948						
G3L (350cc single)	1,200	1,700	2,500	3,900	6,300	8,500
G3LC Competition (350cc single)	1,500	1,900	2,700	4,300	7,000	9,500
G80 Clubman (500cc single)	1,500	1,900	2,700	**4,300**	**7,000**	**9,500**
G80C Competition (500cc single)	−1,500	−1,900	−3,000	**6,000**	**9,000**	**12,000**
1949						
G3L (350cc single)	1,200	1,800	2,500	4,000	5,500	7,000
G3LC (350cc single)	1,200	1,800	2,500	4,000	5,500	7,000
G3LS (350cc single).	1,200	1,800	2,500	4,000	5,500	7,000
G9 (500cc twin)	1,200	2,000	4,000	6,000	8,000	10,000
G9CSR (500cc twin)	1,200	2,000	4,000	6,000	8,000	**11,000**
G80 (500cc single)	1,300	2,000	3,500	5,000	7,500	9,000
G80C (500cc single)	1,400	2,000	3,500	5,500	7,500	9,500

	6	5	4	3	2	1
1950						
G3L (350cc single)	1,200	1,800	2,700	3,600	4,800	6,000
G3LC (350cc single)	1,300	1,900	2,900	3,800	5,100	6,400
G3LCS (350cc single)	1,300	1,900	2,900	3,800	5,100	6,400
G3LS (350cc single)	1,200	1,800	2,700	3,600	4,800	6,000
G9 (500cc twin)	1,200	2,000	4,000	6,000	8,000	10,000
G9CSR (500cc twin)	1,200	2,000	4,000	6,000	8,000	**11,000**
G80 (500cc single)	1,300	2,000	3,500	5,000	7,500	9,000
G80C (500cc single)	1,300	2,000	3,500	5,000	7,500	9,000
G80C (500cc single)	1,300	2,000	3,500	5,000	7,500	9,000
G80CS (500cc single)	2,000	4,000	6,000	8,000	10,000	12,000
G80S (500cc single)	1,300	2,000	3,500	5,000	7,500	9,000
1951						
G3L (350cc single)	1,200	1,800	2,700	3,600	4,800	6,000
G3LC (350cc single)	1,300	1,900	2,900	3,800	5,100	6,400
G3LCS (350cc single)	1,300	1,900	2,900	3,800	5,100	6,400
G3LS (350cc single)	1,200	1,800	2,700	3,600	4,800	6,000
G9 (500cc twin)	1,200	2,000	4,000	6,000	8,000	10,000
G9CSR (500cc twin)	1,200	2,000	4,000	6,000	8,000	**11,000**
G80 (500cc single)	1,300	2,000	3,500	5,000	7,500	9,000
G80C (500cc single)	1,300	2,000	3,500	5,000	7,500	9,000
G80CS (500cc single)	2,000	4,000	6,000	8,000	10,000	12,000
G80S (500cc single)	1,300	2,000	3,500	5,000	7,500	9,000
1952						
G3L (350cc single)	1,200	1,800	2,800	3,700	4,900	6,100
G3LC (350cc single)	1,300	2,000	3,000	4,000	5,300	6,600
G3LCS (350cc single)	1,400	2,000	3,100	4,100	5,400	6,800
G3LS (350cc single)	1,200	1,800	2,800	3,700	4,900	6,100
G9 (500cc twin)	1,200	2,000	4,000	6,000	8,000	10,000
G9CSR (500cc twin)	1,200	2,000	4,000	6,000	8,000	**11,000**
G80 (500cc single)	1,300	2,000	3,500	5,000	7,500	9,000
G80C (500cc single)	1,300	2,000	3,500	5,000	7,500	9,000
G80CS (500cc single)	2,000	4,000	6,000	8,000	10,000	12,000
G80S (500cc single)	1,300	2,000	3,500	5,000	7,500	9,000
1953						
G3L (350cc single)	1,200	1,800	2,800	3,700	4,900	6,100
G3LC (350cc single)	1,300	2,000	3,000	4,000	5,300	6,600
G3LCS (350cc single)	1,400	2,100	3,200	4,200	5,600	7,000
G3LS (350cc single)	1,200	1,800	2,800	3,700	4,900	6,100
G9 (500cc twin)	1,200	2,000	4,000	6,000	8,000	10,000
G9CSR (500cc twin)	1,200	2,000	4,000	6,000	8,000	**11,000**
G45 (500cc twin)	6,000	10,000	20,000	30,000	40,000	50,000
G80 (500cc single)	1,300	2,000	3,500	5,000	7,500	9,000
G80C (500cc single)	1,300	2,000	3,500	5,000	7,500	9,000
G80CS (500cc single)	2,000	4,000	6,000	8,000	10,000	12,000
G80S (500cc single)	1,300	2,000	3,500	5,000	7,500	9,000
1954						
G3L (350cc single)	1,200	1,800	2,800	3,700	4,900	6,100
G3LC (350cc single)	1,300	2,000	3,000	4,000	5,300	6,600
G3LCS (350cc single)	1,400	2,100	3,200	4,200	5,600	7,000
G3LS (350cc single)	1,200	1,800	2,800	3,700	4,900	6,100
G9 (500cc twin)	1,300	2,000	3,500	5,000	7,500	9,000
G9CSR (500cc twin)	1,200	2,000	4,000	6,000	8,000	**11,000**
G45 (500cc twin)	6,000	10,000	20,000	30,000	40,000	50,000
G80 (500cc single)	1,300	2,000	3,500	5,000	7,500	9,000
G80C (500cc single)	1,300	2,000	3,500	5,000	7,500	9,000
G80CS (500cc single)	2,000	4,000	6,000	8,000	10,000	12,000
G80S (500cc single)	1,300	2,000	3,500	5,000	7,500	9,000
G9B (545cc twin)	1,300	2,000	3,500	5,000	7,500	9,000
G9BCSR (545cc twin)	1,200	2,000	4,000	6,000	8,000	**11,000**

	6	5	4	3	2	1
1955						
G3L (350cc single)	1,200	1,800	2,800	3,700	4,900	6,100
G3LC (350cc single)	1,300	2,000	2,900	3,900	5,200	6,500
G3LCS (350cc single)	1,400	2,100	3,200	4,200	5,600	7,000
G3LS (350cc single)	1,200	1,800	2,800	3,700	4,900	6,100
G9 (500cc twin)	1,300	2,000	3,500	5,000	7,500	9,000
G9CSR (500cc twin)	1,200	2,000	4,000	6,000	8,000	**11,000**
G45 (500cc twin)	6,000	10,000	20,000	30,000	40,000	50,000
G80 (500cc single)	1,300	2,000	3,500	5,000	6,500	8,000
G80C (500cc single)	1,300	2,000	3,500	5,000	7,500	9,000
G80CS (500cc single)	2,000	4,000	6,000	8,000	10,000	12,000
G80S (500cc single)	1,300	2,000	3,500	5,000	7,500	9,000
G9B (545cc twin)	1,300	2,000	3,500	5,000	7,500	9,000
G9BCSR (545cc twin)	1,200	2,000	4,000	6,000	8,000	**11,000**
1956						
G3LCS (350cc single)	1,400	2,100	3,200	4,200	5,600	7,000
G3LS (350cc single)	1,300	2,000	2,900	3,900	5,200	6,500
G9 (500cc twin)	1,300	2,000	3,500	5,000	7,500	9,000
G9CSR (500cc twin)	1,200	2,000	4,000	6,000	8,000	**11,000**
G45 (500cc twin)	6,000	10,000	20,000	30,000	40,000	50,000
G80CS (500cc single)	2,000	4,000	6,000	8,000	10,000	12,000
G80S (500cc single)	1,300	2,000	3,500	5,000	7,500	9,000
G11 (600cc twin)	1,300	2,000	3,500	5,000	7,500	9,000
G11CSR (600cc twin)	1,200	2,000	4,000	6,000	8,000	**11,000**
1957						
G3LCS (350cc single)	1,400	2,100	3,200	4,200	5,600	7,000
G3LS (350cc single)	1,300	2,000	2,900	3,900	5,200	6,500
G9 (500cc twin)	1,300	2,000	3,500	5,000	7,500	9,000
G9CSR (500cc twin)	1,400	−2,000	4,000	6,000	8,000	10,000
G45 (500cc twin)	6,000	10,000	20,000	30,000	40,000	50,000
G80CS (500cc single)	2,000	4,000	6,000	8,000	10,000	12,000
G80R/R Dirt Tracker (500cc single)	2,400	3,600	5,400	7,200	9,600	12,000
G80S (500cc single)	1,300	2,000	3,500	5,000	7,500	9,000
G11 (600cc twin)	1,300	2,000	3,500	5,000	7,500	9,000
G11CSR (600cc twin)	1,500	2,700	3,000	5,000	8,000	11,000
1958						
G2 (250cc single)	−500	−800	**1,600**	**2,400**	**3,200**	**4,000**
G3LCS (350cc single)	1,400	2,100	3,200	4,200	5,600	7,000
G3LS (350cc single)	1,200	1,900	2,800	3,700	5,000	6,200
G9 (500cc twin)	1,300	2,000	3,500	5,000	7,500	9,000
G9CSR (500cc twin)	1,200	2,000	4,000	6,000	8,000	10,000
G45 (500cc twin)	6,000	10,000	20,000	30,000	40,000	50,000
G80CS (500cc single)	2,000	4,000	6,000	8,000	10,000	12,000
G80S (500cc single)	1,300	2,000	3,500	5,000	7,500	9,000
G11 (600cc twin)	1,300	2,000	3,500	5,000	7,500	9,000
G11CS (600cc twin)	1,200	2,000	4,000	6,000	8,000	10,000
G11 CSR (600cc twin)	1,200	2,000	4,000	6,000	8,000	**11,000**
1959						
G2 (250cc single)	−500	−800	**1,600**	**2,400**	**3,200**	**4,000**
G2CS (250cc single)	**1,000**	**1,700**	**2,400**	**3,100**	**3,800**	**4,500**
G3 (350cc single)	1,200	1,900	2,800	3,700	5,000	6,200
G3C (350cc single)	1,400	2,100	3,200	4,200	5,600	7,000
G3CS (350cc single)	1,400	2,100	3,200	4,300	5,700	7,100
G9 (500cc twin)	1,300	2,000	3,500	5,000	7,500	9,000
G9CS (500cc twin)	1,200	2,000	4,000	6,000	8,000	10,000
G9CSR (500cc twin)	1,200	2,000	4,000	6,000	8,000	10,000
G45 (500cc twin)	6,000	10,000	20,000	30,000	40,000	50,000
G50 (500cc single)	7,000	11,000	16,000	21,000	28,000	35,000
G80CS (500cc single)	2,000	4,000	6,000	8,000	10,000	12,000
G80S (500cc single)	1,300	2,000	3,500	5,000	7,500	9,000

	6	5	4	3	2	1
G80 Typhoon (600cc single)	2,000	3,000	4,500	6,000	9,000	12,000
G12 Deluxe (650cc twin)	1,300	2,000	3,500	5,000	7,500	9,000
G12 (650cc twin)	1,300	2,000	3,500	5,000	7,500	9,000
G12CS (650cc twin)	1,300	2,000	3,500	5,000	7,500	9,000
G12CSR (650cc twin)	1,200	2,000	4,000	6,000	8,000	–1,100
1960						
G2 (250cc single)	–500	–800	**1,600**	**2,400**	**3,200**	**4,000**
G2CS (250cc single)	**1,000**	**1,700**	**2,400**	**3,100**	**3,800**	**4,500**
G3 (350cc single)	1,200	1,900	2,800	3,700	5,000	6,200
G3C (350cc single)	1,400	2,100	3,200	4,200	5,600	7,000
G5 (350cc single)	1,100	1,700	2,500	3,300	4,400	5,500
G9 (500cc twin)	1,200	2,000	3,500	5,000	6,500	8,000
G9CSR (500cc twin)	1,300	2,000	3,500	5,000	7,500	9,000
G50 (500cc single)	7,000	11,000	16,000	21,000	28,000	35,000
G80 (500cc single)	1,300	2,000	3,500	5,000	7,500	9,000
G80CS (500cc single)	2,000	4,000	6,000	8,000	10,000	12,000
G80 Typhoon (600cc single)	–1,500	3,000	**5,000**	**8,000**	**11,000**	**14,000**
G12 (650cc twin)	1,200	2,000	3,500	5,000	6,500	8,000
G12 Deluxe (650cc twin)	1,300	2,000	3,500	5,000	7,500	9,000
G12CS (650cc twin)	1,300	2,000	3,500	5,000	7,500	9,000
G12CSR (650cc twin)	1,200	2,000	4,000	6,000	8,000	**11,000**
1961						
G2 (250cc single)	–500	–800	**1,600**	**2,400**	**3,200**	**4,000**
G2CS (250cc single)	**1,000**	**1,700**	**2,400**	**3,100**	**3,800**	**4,500**
G2S (250cc single)	–500	–800	**1,600**	**2,400**	**3,200**	**4,000**
G3 (350cc single)	1,200	1,900	2,800	3,700	5,000	6,200
G3C (350cc single)	1,400	2,100	3,200	4,200	5,600	7,000
G5 (350cc single)	1,100	1,700	2,500	3,300	4,400	5,500
G9 (500cc twin)	1,200	2,000	3,500	5,000	6,500	8,000
G9CSR (500cc twin)	1,300	2,000	3,500	5,000	7,500	9,000
G50 (500cc single)	7,000	11,000	16,000	21,000	28,000	35,000
G80 (500cc single)	1,300	2,000	3,500	5,000	7,500	9,000
G80CS (500cc single)	2,000	4,000	6,000	8,000	10,000	12,000
G80 Typhoon (600cc single)	–1,500	3,000	**5,000**	**8,000**	**11,000**	**14,000**
G12 (650cc twin)	1,200	2,000	3,500	5,000	6,500	8,000
G12 Deluxe (650cc twin)	1,300	2,000	3,500	5,000	7,500	9,000
G12CSR (650cc twin)	1,200	2,000	4,000	6,000	8,000	**11,000**
1962						
G2 (250cc single)	–500	–800	**1,600**	**2,400**	**3,200**	**4,000**
G2CS (250cc single)	**1,000**	**1,700**	**2,400**	**3,100**	**3,800**	**4,500**
G2CSR (250cc single)	–500	–800	1,600	**2,400**	**3,200**	**4,000**
G2S (250cc single)	–500	–800	**1,600**	**2,400**	**3,200**	**4,000**
G3 (350cc single)	1,200	1,900	2,800	3,700	5,000	6,200
G3C (350cc single)	1,400	2,100	3,200	4,200	5,600	7,000
G3S (350cc single)	1,200	1,900	2,800	3,700	5,000	6,200
G5 (350cc single)	1,100	1,600	2,400	3,200	4,300	5,400
G50 (500cc single)	7,000	11,000	16,000	21,000	28,000	35,000
G80 (500cc single)	1,300	2,000	**3,000**	**4,500**	**6,000**	**7,500**
G80CS (500cc single)	**2,000**	**4,000**	6,000	8,000	10,000	12,000
G80 Typhoon (600cc single)	–1,500	3,000	**5,000**	**8,000**	**11,000**	**14,000**
G12 (650cc twin)	1,200	**2,000**	3,500	5,000	6,500	8,000
G12CSR (650cc twin)	1,200	**2,000**	4,000	6,000	8,000	11,000
1963						
G2 (250cc single)	–500	–800	**1,600**	**2,400**	**3,200**	**4,000**
G2CSR (250cc single)	**1,000**	**1,700**	**2,400**	**3,100**	**3,800**	**4,500**
G3 (350cc single)	1,200	1,900	2,800	3,700	5,000	6,200
G3C (350cc single)	1,400	2,100	3,200	4,200	5,600	7,000
G50 (500cc single)	7,000	11,000	16,000	21,000	28,000	35,000
G80 (500cc single)	1,300	2,000	**4,000**	**5,500**	**7,000**	**8,500**

	6	5	4	3	2	1
G80CS (500cc single)	2,000	4,000	6,000	8,000	10,000	12,000
G80 Typhoon (600cc single)	−1,500	3,000	5,000	8,000	11,000	14,000
G12 (650cc twin)	1,200	2,000	3,500	5,000	6,500	8,000
G12CSR (650cc twin)	1,500	3,000	4,500	6,000	7,500	9,000
G15 (750cc twin)	1,500	3,000	4,500	6,000	7,500	9,000
G15CSR (750cc twin)	2,000	3,000	4,500	6,000	8,000	10,000
1964						
G2CSR (250cc single)	1,000	1,700	2,400	3,100	3,800	4,500
G3 (350cc single)	1,200	1,900	2,800	3,700	5,000	6,200
G3C (350cc single)	1,300	2,000	3,000	4,000	5,400	6,700
G80 (500cc single)	1,300	2,000	4,000	5,500	7,000	8,500
G80CS (500cc single)	2,000	4,000	6,000	8,000	10,000	12,000
G80 Typhoon (600cc single)	−1,500	3,000	5,000	8,000	11,000	14,000
G12 (650cc twin)	1,200	2,000	3,500	5,000	6,500	8,000
G12CSR (650cc twin)	1,500	3,000	4,500	6,000	7,500	9,000
G15 (750cc twin)	1,100	1,700	2,500	4,000	6,000	8,000
G15CSR (750cc twin)	2,000	3,000	4,500	6,000	8,000	10,000
1965						
G2CSR (250cc single)	1,000	1,700	2,400	3,100	3,800	4,500
G3 (350cc single)	1,200	1,800	2,700	3,600	4,800	6,000
G80 (500cc single)	1,300	2,000	4,000	5,500	7,000	8,500
G80CS (500cc single)	2,000	4,000	6,000	8,000	10,000	12,000
G80 Typhoon (600cc single)	−1,500	3,000	5,000	8,000	11,000	14,000
G12 (650cc twin)	1,200	2,000	3,500	5,000	6,500	8,000
G12CSR (650cc twin)	1,500	3,000	4,500	6,000	7,500	9,000
G15 (750cc twin)	1,100	1,700	2,500	4,000	6,000	8,000
G15CSR (750cc twin)	2,000	3,000	4,500	6,000	8,000	10,000
1966						
G2CSR (250cc single)	1,000	1,700	2,400	3,100	3,800	4,500
G3 (350cc single)	1,200	1,800	2,700	3,600	4,800	6,000
G80 (500cc single)	1,300	2,000	4,000	5,500	7,000	8,500
G85CS (500cc single)	2,000	5,000	8,000	11,000	14,000	18,000
G80 Typhoon (600cc single)	−1,500	3,000	5,000	8,000	11,000	14,000
G12 (650cc twin)	1,200	2,000	3,500	5,000	6,500	8,000
G12CSR (650cc twin)	1,500	3,000	4,500	6,000	7,500	9,000
G15 (750cc twin)	1,100	1,700	2,500	4,000	6,000	8,000
G15CSR (750cc twin)	2,000	3,000	4,500	6,000	8,000	10,000
P11 (750cc twin)	−1,500	3,000	6,000	9,000	12,000	15,000
1967						
G85CS (500cc single)	2,000	5,000	8,000	11,000	14,000	18,000
G15 (750cc twin)	2,000	3,000	4,500	6,000	8,000	10,000
G15CSR (750cc twin)	2,000	4,000	6,000	8,000	10,000	12,000
1968						
G85CS (500cc single)	2,000	5,000	8,000	11,000	14,000	18,000
G15 (750cc twin)	1,500	3,000	4,500	6,000	7,500	9,000
G15CSR (750cc twin)	−1,200	2,000	4,000	6,000	8,000	11,000
1969						
G85CS (500cc single)	2,000	5,000	8,000	11,000	14,000	18,000
G15 (750cc twin)	1,500	3,000	4,500	6,000	7,500	9,000
G15CSR (750cc twin)	−1,200	2,000	4,000	6,000	8,000	11,000

MONTESA						
1963						
Impala (175cc)	1,000	2,000	3,000	4,000	5,000	6,000
1967						
La Cros 250	700	1,200	1,600	2,200	3,400	4,600
1968						
Cappra 250	1,300	2,000	2,700	3,600	5,500	7,400
Impala Special 250	1,300	2,000	2,700	3,600	5,500	7,400
La Cros 250	700	1,200	1,600	2,200	3,400	4,600

	6	5	4	3	2	
Scorpion 250	1,300	2,000	2,700	3,600	5,500	7,.
Cappra 360	1,600	2,400	3,300	4,400	6,900	8,40
1969						
Cota 247	900	1,400	2,200	3,000	4,000	6,200
Cappra 5 Speed 250	1,300	2,000	2,700	3,600	5,500	7,400
Cappra 250GP	1,300	2,000	2,700	3,600	5,500	7,400
Cappra 360GP	1,600	2,400	3,300	4,400	6,900	8,400
Cappra 53M	2,000	3,500	5,000	7,500	8,000	9,500
1970						
Cota 247	900	1,400	2,200	3,000	4,000	6,200
Cappra 5 Speed 250	1,300	2,000	2,700	3,600	5,500	7,400
Cappra 250GP	1,300	2,000	2,700	3,600	5,500	7,400
Cappra 360GP	1,600	2,400	3,300	4,400	6,900	8,400
1971						
Cappra 125MX	900	1,400	1,900	2,600	3,900	5,200
Texas T175	900	1,400	1,900	2,600	3,900	5,200
Texas XLT175	900	1,400	1,900	2,600	3,900	5,200
Cota 247	900	1,400	2,200	3,000	4,000	6,200
Cappra 5 Speed 250	1,300	2,000	2,700	3,600	5,500	7,400
King Scorpion 250	1,300	2,000	2,700	3,600	5,500	7,400
Cappra 250GP	1,300	2,000	2,700	3,600	5,500	7,400
Cappra 360GP	1,600	2,400	3,300	4,400	6,900	8,400
1972						
Cota 125	900	1,400	1,900	2,600	3,900	5,200
Capra 125MX	900	1,400	1,900	2,600	3,900	5,200
Cota 247	900	1,400	2,200	3,000	4,000	6,200
King Scorpion 250	1,300	2,000	2,700	3,600	5,500	7,400
Cappra 250MX	1,300	2,000	2,700	3,600	5,500	7,400
Cota25 50	600	1,100	1,600	2,100	3,300	4,500
1973						
Cota 125	900	1,400	1,900	2,600	3,900	5,200
Cappra 125MX	900	1,400	1,900	2,600	3,900	5,200
Cota 247	900	1,400	2,200	3,000	4,000	6,200
King Scorpion 250	1,300	2,000	2,700	3,600	5,500	7,400
Cappra 250MX	1,300	2,000	2,700	3,600	5,500	7,400
Cappra 250VR	600	1,200	1,600	2,200	3,400	4,600
Cota25 50	600	1,100	1,600	2,100	3,300	4,500
1974						
Cota 123	900	1,400	1,900	2,600	4,000	5,400
Cota 123T	900	1,500	2,000	2,700	4,100	5,500
Cota 247	900	1,400	2,200	3,000	4,000	6,200
Cota 247T	900	1,400	2,200	3,000	4,000	6,200
Enduro 250	1,300	2,000	2,700	3,600	5,500	7,400
King Scorpion 250	1,300	2,000	2,700	3,600	5,500	7,400
Rapita 250	1,300	2,000	2,700	3,600	5,500	7,400
Cappra 250VR	600	1,200	1,600	2,200	3,400	4,600
Cota 50	600	1,100	1,600	2,100	3,300	4,500
Cota25 50	600	1,100	1,600	2,100	3,300	4,500
1975						
Cota 123	900	1,400	1,900	2,600	4,000	5,400
Cota 123T	900	1,500	2,000	2,700	4,100	5,500
Cappra 125	1,100	1,800	2,500	3,200	5,100	7,000
Cota 247	900	1,400	2,200	3,000	4,000	6,200
Cota 247T	900	1,400	2,200	3,000	4,000	6,200
Enduro 250	1,300	2,000	2,700	3,600	5,500	7,400
King Scorpion 250	1,300	2,000	2,700	3,600	5,500	7,400
Rapita 250	1,300	2,000	2,700	3,600	5,500	7,400
Cappra 250VR	600	1,200	1,600	2,200	3,400	4,600
Cota 50	600	1,100	1,600	2,100	3,300	4,500
Cota25 50	600	1,100	1,600	2,100	3,300	4,500

	6	5	4	3	2	1
⌐T.	900	1,400	1,900	2,600	4,000	5,400
⌐T.	900	1,500	2,000	2,700	4,100	5,500
a 125	1,100	1,800	2,500	3,200	5,100	7,000
⌐172	900	1,400	1,900	2,600	3,900	5,200
⌐ota 247	900	1,400	2,200	3,000	4,000	6,200
Cota 247T.	900	1,400	2,200	3,000	4,000	6,200
Cappra 250	1,300	2,000	2,700	3,600	5,500	7,400
Enduro 250	1,300	2,000	2,700	3,600	5,500	7,400
Cota 348	900	1,400	1,900	2,500	3,900	5,300
Cappra 360	900	1,400	1,900	2,500	3,900	5,300
Cota 25C 50.	600	1,100	1,600	2,100	3,300	4,500
1977						
Cota 123	900	1,400	1,900	2,600	4,000	5,400
Enduro 125	1,100	1,600	2,100	2,800	4,500	6,200
Cappra 125VB	1,100	1,600	2,100	2,800	4,500	6,200
Cota 247	900	1,400	2,200	3,000	4,000	6,200
Cota 247T.	900	1,400	2,200	3,000	4,000	6,200
Cappra 250VB	1,500	2,200	2,900	3,900	5,900	7,900
Cota 25C 50.	600	1,100	1,600	2,100	3,300	4,500
1978						
Cota 123	900	1,400	1,900	2,600	4,000	5,400
Enduro 125H	1,100	1,600	2,100	2,800	4,500	6,200
Cappra 125VB	1,100	1,600	2,100	2,800	4,500	6,200
Cota 247	900	1,400	2,200	3,000	4,000	6,200
Enduro 250HG	1,500	2,200	2,900	3,900	5,900	7,900
Cappra 250VB	1,500	2,200	2,900	3,900	5,900	7,900
Cota 348	900	1,400	1,900	2,500	3,900	5,300
Cota 348T.	900	1,400	1,900	2,500	3,900	5,300
Enduro 360H	900	1,400	1,900	2,500	3,900	5,300
Cappra 360VB	900	1,400	1,900	2,500	3,900	5,300
Cota 49	400	700	900	1,200	1,700	2,200
1979						
Cappra 125VF.	1,100	1,600	2,100	2,800	4,500	6,200
Cota 247C.	900	1,400	2,200	3,000	4,000	6,200
Cappra 250VF.	1,500	2,200	2,900	3,900	5,900	7,900
Cota 348T.	900	1,400	1,900	2,500	3,900	5,300
Cota 349	400	700	900	1,200	1,700	2,200
Enduro 360H	900	1,400	1,900	2,500	3,900	5,300
Cappra 414VF.	400	800	1,300	1,800	2,200	2,600
Cota 49	400	700	900	1,200	1,700	2,200
1980						
Cappra 125VF.	1,100	1,600	2,100	2,800	4,500	6,200
Cota 247C.	900	1,400	2,200	3,000	4,000	6,200
Cappra 250VF.	1,500	2,200	2,900	3,900	5,900	7,900
Cota 348T.	900	1,400	1,900	2,500	3,900	5,300
Cota 349	400	700	900	1,200	1,700	2,200
Enduro 360H	900	1,400	1,900	2,500	3,900	5,300
Cappra 414VF.	400	800	1,300	1,800	2,200	2,600
Cota 49	400	700	900	1,200	1,700	2,200
1981						
Cappra 125VF.	1,100	1,600	2,100	2,800	4,500	6,200
Cappra 250VF.	1,500	2,200	2,900	3,900	5,900	7,900
Cappra 414VF.	400	800	1,300	1,800	2,200	2,600
Cota 123	400	700	900	1,200	1,700	2,200
Cota 200	400	700	900	1,200	1,700	2,200
Cota 247	400	700	900	1,200	1,700	2,200
Cota 248	400	700	900	1,200	1,700	2,200
Cota 348T.	1,000	1,600	2,100	2,800	4,400	6,000
Cota 349	400	700	900	1,200	1,700	2,200

	6	5	4	3	2	
Enduro 250H6	400	700	900	1,200	1,700	2,
Enduro 360H6	400	700	900	1,200	1,700	2,
1982						
Cappra 250VG	1,500	2,200	2,900	3,900	5,900	7,90
Cappra 414VG	400	800	1,300	1,800	2,200	2,600
Cota 123	400	700	900	1,200	1,700	2,200
Cota 200	400	700	900	1,200	1,700	2,200
Cota 349	400	700	900	1,200	1,700	2,200
Enduro 250H6	400	700	900	1,200	1,700	2,200
Enduro 360H7	400	700	900	1,200	1,700	2,200
1983						
Cappra 250VG	1,500	2,200	2,900	3,900	5,900	7,900
Cota 123	400	700	900	1,200	1,700	2,200
Cota 200	400	700	900	1,200	1,700	2,200
Cota 349	400	700	900	1,200	1,700	2,200
Enduro 250H6	400	700	900	1,200	1,700	2,200
Enduro 360H7	400	700	900	1,200	1,700	2,200
1984						
Cota 200	100	200	300	400	500	600
Cota 242	100	200	300	400	500	600
Cota 350	100	200	300	400	500	600
Enduro 250 H7	100	200	400	600	800	1,000
Enduro 360 H7	100	200	400	600	800	1,000
1985						
Cota 242	100	200	300	400	500	600
Cota 330	100	200	300	400	500	600
Cota 348	100	200	300	400	500	600
Enduro 250 H7	100	200	400	600	800	1,000
Enduro 360 H7	100	200	400	600	800	1,000
1986						
Cota 123 (125cc single)	100	200	300	400	500	600
Cota 242 (240cc single)	100	200	300	400	500	600
Cota 304 (240cc single)	100	200	300	400	500	600
Cota 330 (330 cc single)	100	200	300	400	500	600
1987						
Cota 242 (240cc single)	100	200	300	400	500	600
Cota 304 (240cc single)	100	200	300	400	500	600
Cota 335 (330cc single)	100	200	300	400	500	600
1988						
Cota 307 (240cc single)	100	200	300	500	700	1,000
1989						
Cota 307 (240cc single)	100	200	300	500	700	1,000
Cota 309 (260cc single)	100	200	300	500	700	1,000
1990						
Cota 309 (260cc single)	100	200	300	500	700	1,000
1991						
Cota 310 (260cc single)	100	200	300	600	900	1,200
1993						
Cota 311 (260cc single)	100	200	400	800	1,100	1,400
1994						
Cota 314 (260cc single)	100	200	500	1,000	1,500	2,000
1995						
Cota 314R (260cc single)	200	400	800	1,300	1,800	2,300
MOTO GUZZI						
1922						
Normale 500 (498cc single)	6,000	9,000	14,000	18,000	24,000	30,000
1923						
Normale 500 (498cc single)	6,000	9,000	14,000	18,000	24,000	30,000
1924						
Normale 500 (498cc single)	6,000	9,000	14,000	18,000	24,000	30,000

	6	5	4	3	2	1
. . . .	10,000	20,000	30,000	40,000	50,000	60,000
(498cc single)	2,400	3,600	5,400	7,200	9,600	15,000
(cc)	3,000	6,000	12,000	18,000	24,000	30,000
2						
(175cc single)	1,200	1,800	2,700	3,600	4,800	6,000
ort 15 (498cc single) . . .	2,400	3,600	5,400	7,200	9,600	12,000
1933						
Model 157	2,400	3,600	5,400	7,200	9,600	12,000
P175 (175cc single)	1,200	1,800	2,700	3,600	4,800	6,000
Sport 15 (498cc single) . . .	2,400	3,600	5,400	7,200	9,600	12,000
1934						
PE250 (238cc single)	1,500	2,300	**4,000**	**6,000**	**8,000**	**10,000**
Sport 15 (498cc single) . . .	2,400	3,600	5,400	7,200	9,600	12,000
1935						
PE250 (238cc single)	1,500	2,300	**4,000**	**6,000**	**8,000**	**10,000**
Sport 15 (498cc single) . . .	2,400	3,600	5,400	7,200	9,600	12,000
GTW500 (499cc single)	2,000	3,000	4,500	6,000	8,000	12,000
1936						
PE250 (238cc single)	1,500	2,300	**4,000**	**6,000**	**8,000**	**10,000**
Sport 15 (498cc single) . . .	2,400	3,600	5,400	7,200	9,600	12,000
GTW500 (499cc single)	2,000	3,000	4,500	6,000	8,000	12,000
1937						
PE250 (238cc single)	1,200	1,800	**4,000**	**6,000**	**8,000**	**10,000**
Sport 15 (498cc single) . . .	2,000	3,000	4,500	6,000	8,000	10,000
GTW500 (499cc single)	2,000	3,000	4,500	6,000	8,000	10,000
1938						
PE250 (238cc single)	1,200	1,800	**4,000**	**6,000**	**8,000**	**10,000**
Condor 500 Sport (498cc single)	2,000	3,000	4,500	6,000	8,000	10,000
Sport 15 (498cc single) . . .	1,800	2,700	4,100	5,400	7,200	9,000
GTW500 (499cc single)	1,600	2,400	3,600	4,800	6,400	8,000
1939						
PE250 (238cc single)	1,200	1,800	**4,000**	**6,000**	**8,000**	**10,000**
Condor 500 Sport (498cc single)	1,900	2,900	4,300	5,700	7,600	9,500
Sport 15 (498cc single) . . .	1,800	2,700	4,100	5,400	7,200	9,000
GTW500 (499cc single)	1,600	2,400	3,600	4,800	6,400	8,000
Alce (500cc)	1,600	2,400	3,600	4,800	6,400	8,000
1940						
GTW500 (499cc single)	1,600	2,400	3,600	4,800	6,400	8,000
1941						
GTW500 (499cc single)	1,600	2,400	3,600	4,800	6,400	8,000
1942						
GTW500 (499cc single)	1,600	2,400	3,600	4,800	6,400	8,000
1943						
GTW500 (499cc single)	1,600	2,400	3,600	4,800	6,400	8,000
Super Alce (500cc single)	2,500	5,000	7,500	10,000	12,500	15,000
1944						
GTW500 (499cc single)	1,600	2,400	3,600	4,800	6,400	8,000
Super Alce (500cc single)	2,500	5,000	7,500	10,000	12,500	15,000
1945						
GTW500 (499cc single)	1,600	2,400	3,600	4,800	6,400	8,000
Super Alce (500cc single)	2,500	5,000	7,500	10,000	12,500	15,000
1946						
Guzzino 65 (64cc single)	400	600	900	1,200	1,600	2,000
Airone 250 Turismo (247cc single) . . .	1,300	2,000	2,900	3,900	5,200	6,500
GTV500 Alloy (499cc single)	2,400	3,600	5,400	7,200	9,600	12,000
GTW500 (499cc single)	1,600	2,400	3,600	4,800	6,400	12,000
GTW500 Competition (499cc single)	2,000	3,000	4,500	6,000	8,000	10,000
Super Alce (500cc single)	2,500	5,000	7,500	10,000	12,500	15,000

	6	5	4	3	2	1
1947						
Guzzino 65 (64cc single)	400	600	900	1,200	1,600	2,000
Airone 250 Turismo (247cc single)	1,300	2,000	2,900	3,900	5,200	6,500
GTV500 Alloy (499cc single)	2,400	3,600	5,400	7,200	9,600	12,000
GTW500 (499cc single)	1,600	2,400	3,600	4,800	6,400	12,000
Super Alce (500cc single)	2,500	5,000	7,500	10,000	12,500	15,000
1948						
Guzzino 65 (64cc single)	400	600	900	1,200	1,600	2,000
Airone 250 Turismo (247cc single)	1,300	2,000	2,900	3,900	5,200	6,500
GTV500 Alloy (499cc single)	2,400	3,600	5,400	7,200	9,600	12,000
GTW500 (499cc single)	1,600	2,400	3,600	4,800	6,400	12,000
Super Alce (500cc single)	2,500	5,000	7,500	10,000	12,500	15,000
1949						
Airone 250 Sport (247cc single)	1,500	3,000	4,500	6,000	**8,000**	**10,000**
Airone 250 Turismo (247cc single)	1,300	2,000	2,900	3,900	5,200	6,500
GTV500 Alloy (499cc single)	2,400	3,600	5,400	7,200	10,000	13,000
GTW500 (499cc single)	1,600	2,400	3,600	4,800	6,400	12,000
Super Alce (500cc single)	2,500	5,000	7,500	10,000	12,500	15,000
1950						
Guzzino 65 (64cc single)	400	600	900	1,200	1,600	2,000
Airone 250 Sport (247cc single)	1,500	3,000	4,500	6,000	**8,000**	**10,000**
Airone 250 Turismo (247cc single)	1,300	2,000	2,900	3,900	5,200	6,500
Astore 500 (497cc single)	1,700	2,600	3,800	5,100	6,800	8,500
Falcone 500 Sport (498cc single)	3,000	6,000	12,000	18,000	24,000	30,000
Falcone 500 Tourismo (498cc single)	3,000	6,000	12,000	18,000	24,000	30,000
Super Alce (500cc single)	2,500	5,000	7,500	10,000	12,500	15,000
1951						
Guzzino 65 (64cc single)	400	600	900	1,200	1,600	2,000
Airone 250 Sport (247cc single)	1,500	3,000	4,500	6,000	**8,000**	**10,000**
Airone 250 Turismo (247cc single)	1,300	2,000	2,900	3,900	5,200	6,500
Astore 500 (497cc single)	1,700	2,600	3,800	5,100	6,800	8,500
Falcone 500 Sport (498cc single)	**2,000**	**4,000**	8,000	12,000	16,000	20,000
Falcone 500 Tourismo (498cc single)	**2,000**	**4,000**	8,000	12,000	16,000	20,000
Super Alce (500cc single)	2,500	5,000	7,500	10,000	12,500	15,000
1952						
Airone 250 Sport (247cc single)	1,500	3,000	4,500	6,000	**8,000**	**10,000**
Airone 250 Turismo (247cc single)	1,300	2,000	2,900	3,900	5,200	6,500
Astore 500 (497cc single)	1,700	2,600	3,800	5,100	6,800	8,500
Falcone 500 Sport (498cc single)	**2,000**	**4,000**	8,000	12,000	16,000	20,000
Falcone 500 Tourismo (498cc single)	**2,000**	**4,000**	8,000	12,000	16,000	20,000
Super Alce (500cc single)	2,500	5,000	7,500	10,000	12,500	15,000
1953						
Guzzino 65 (64cc single)	400	600	900	1,200	1,600	2,000
Motoleggera (65cc single)	1,000	2,000	3,000	4,000	5,000	6,000
Airone 250 Sport (247cc single)	1,500	3,000	4,500	6,000	**8,000**	**10,000**
Airone 250 Turismo (247cc single)	1,300	2,000	2,900	3,900	5,200	6,500
Astore 500 (497cc single)	1,700	2,600	3,800	5,100	6,800	8,500
Falcone 500 Sport (498cc single)	**2,000**	**4,000**	8,000	12,000	16,000	20,000
Falcone 500 Tourismp (498cc single)	**2,000**	**4,000**	8,000	12,000	16,000	20,000
Super Alce (500cc single)	2,500	5,000	7,500	10,000	12,500	15,000
1954						
Guzzino 65 (64cc single)	400	600	900	1,200	1,600	2,000
Zigolo 100 (98cc single)	600	800	1,300	1,700	2,200	2,800
Airone 250 Sport (247cc single)	1,500	3,000	4,500	6,000	**8,000**	**10,000**
Airone 250 Turismo (247cc single)	1,300	2,000	2,900	3,900	5,200	6,500
Astore 500 (497cc single)	1,700	2,600	3,800	5,100	6,800	8,500
Falcone 500 Sport (498cc single)	**2,000**	**4,000**	8,000	12,000	16,000	20,000
Falcone 500 Tourismo (498cc single)	**2,000**	**4,000**	8,000	12,000	16,000	20,000
Super Alce (500cc single)	2,500	5,000	7,500	10,000	12,500	15,000

	6	5	4	3	2	1
1955						
Cardellino 65 (64cc single)	400	600	900	1,200	1,600	2,000
Zigolo 100 (98cc single).	600	800	1,300	1,700	2,200	2,800
Airone 250 Sport (247cc single).	1,500	3,000	4,500	6,000	**8,000**	**10,000**
Airone 250 Turismo (247cc single)	1,300	2,000	2,900	3,900	5,200	6,500
Falcone 500 Sport (498cc single)	**2,000**	**4,000**	**8,000**	**12,000**	**16,000**	**20,000**
Falcone 500 Tourismo (498cc single) . . .	**2,000**	**4,000**	**8,000**	**12,000**	**16,000**	**20,000**
Super Alce (500cc single)	2,500	5,000	7,500	10,000	12,500	15,000
1956						
Cardellino 65 (64cc single)	400	600	900	1,200	1,600	2,000
Zigolo 100 (98cc single).	600	800	1,300	1,700	2,200	2,800
Lodola 175 (174cc single).	700	1,100	1,600	2,200	2,900	3,600
Airone 250 Sport (247cc single).	1,500	3,000	4,500	6,000	**8,000**	**10,000**
Airone 250 Turismo (247cc single)	1,300	2,000	2,900	3,900	5,200	6,500
Falcone 500 Sport (498cc single)	**2,000**	**4,000**	**8,000**	**12,000**	**16,000**	**20,000**
Falcone 500 Tourismo (498cc single) . . .	**2,000**	**4,000**	**8,000**	**12,000**	**16,000**	**20,000**
1957						
Cardellino 65 (64cc single)	400	600	900	1,200	1,600	2,000
Zigolo 100 (98cc single).	600	800	1,300	1,700	2,200	2,800
Lodola 175 (174cc single).	700	1,100	1,600	2,200	2,900	3,600
Airone 250 Sport (247cc single).	1,500	3,000	4,500	6,000	**8,000**	**10,000**
Airone 250 Turismo (247cc single)	1,300	2,000	2,900	3,900	5,200	6,500
Falcone 500 Sport (498cc single)	**2,000**	**4,000**	**8,000**	**12,000**	**16,000**	**20,000**
Falcone 500 Tourismo (498cc single)	**2,000**	**4,000**	**8,000**	**12,000**	**16,000**	**20,000**
1958						
Cardellino 65 (64cc single)	400	600	900	1,200	1,600	2,000
Zigolo 100 (98cc single).	600	800	1,300	1,700	2,200	2,800
Lodola 175 (174cc single).	700	1,100	2,000	3,000	4,000	5,000
Falcone 500 Sport (498cc single)	**2,000**	**4,000**	**8,000**	**12,000**	**16,000**	**20,000**
Falcone 500 Tourismo (498cc single)	**2,000**	**4,000**	**8,000**	**12,000**	**16,000**	**20,000**
1959						
Cardellino 75 (73cc single)	500	800	1,100	1,500	2,000	2,500
Zigolo 110 (110cc single)	600	900	1,350	1,800	2,400	3,000
Lodola 235 (235cc single)	1,300	2,000	2,900	3,900	5,200	6,500
Falcone 500 Sport (498cc single)	1,900	2,900	4,300	5,700	7,600	9,500
Falcone 500 Tourismo (498cc single)	1,600	2,400	3,600	4,800	6,400	8,000
1960						
Cardellino 75 (73cc single)	500	800	1,100	1,500	2,000	2,500
Zigolo 110 (110cc single)	600	900	1,350	1,800	2,400	3,000
Lodola 175 Regolarita (175cc single) . . .	1,600	2,400	3,600	4,800	6,400	8,000
Lodola 235 (235cc single)	1,200	1,800	2,700	3,600	4,800	6,000
Lodola 235 Regolarita (235cc single) . . .	1,700	2,600	3,800	5,100	6,800	8,500
Falcone 500 Sport (498cc single)	1,900	2,900	4,300	5,700	7,600	9,500
Falcone 500 Tourismo (498cc single)	1,600	2,400	3,600	4,800	6,400	8,000
1961						
Cardellino 75 (73cc single)	400	600	900	1,200	1,600	2,000
Zigolo 110 (110cc single)	600	900	1,400	1,800	2,400	3,000
Stornello Sport (125cc single)	700	1,000	1,500	**2,100**	**2,800**	**3,500**
Lodola 175 Regolarita (175cc single) . . .	1,600	2,400	3,600	4,800	6,400	8,000
Lodola 235 (235cc single)	1,200	1,800	2,700	3,600	4,800	6,000
Lodola 235 Regolarita (235cc single) . . .	1,700	2,600	3,800	5,100	6,800	8,500
Falcone 500 Sport (498cc single)	1,900	2,900	4,300	5,700	7,600	9,500
Falcone 500 Tourismo (498cc single)	1,600	2,400	3,600	4,800	6,400	8,000
1962						
Cardellino 75 (73cc single)	400	600	900	1,200	1,600	2,000
Zigolo 110 (110cc single)	600	900	1,400	1,800	2,400	3,000
Stornello Sport (125cc single)	700	1,000	1,500	**2,100**	**2,800**	**3,500**
Lodola 235 (235cc single)	1,200	1,800	2,700	3,600	4,800	6,000
Falcone 500 Sport (498cc single)	1,900	2,900	4,300	5,700	7,600	9,500
Falcone 500 Tourismo (498cc single)	1,600	2,400	3,600	4,800	6,400	8,000

	6	5	4	3	2	1
1963						
Cardellino 75 (73cc single)	400	600	900	1,200	1,600	2,000
Zigolo 110 (110cc single)	600	900	1,400	1,800	2,400	3,000
Lodola 235 (235cc single).	1,200	1,800	2,700	3,600	4,800	6,000
Falcone 500 Sport (498cc single)	1,900	2,900	4,300	5,700	7,600	9,500
Falcone 500 Tourismo (498cc single) . . .	1,600	2,400	3,600	4,800	6,400	8,000
1964						
Cardellino 85 (83cc single)	400	600	900	1,200	1,600	2,000
Zigolo 110 (110cc single)	600	900	1,400	1,800	2,400	3,000
Stornello Sport (125cc single).	700	1,000	1,500	2,000	2,600	3,300
Lodola 235 (235cc single).	1,200	1,800	2,700	3,600	4,800	6,000
Falcone 500 Sport (498cc single)	1,900	2,900	4,300	5,700	7,600	9,500
Falcone 500 Tourismo (498cc single) . . .	1,600	2,400	3,600	4,800	6,400	8,000
1965						
Cardellino 85 (83cc single)	400	600	900	1,200	1,600	2,000
Zigolo 110 (110cc single)	600	900	1,400	1,800	2,400	3,000
Stornello Sport (125cc single).	700	1,000	1,500	2,000	2,600	3,300
Lodola 235 (235cc single).	1,200	1,800	2,700	3,600	4,800	6,000
1966						
Zigolo 110 (110cc single)	600	900	1,400	1,800	2,400	3,000
Stornello Sport (125cc single).	700	1,000	1,500	2,000	2,600	3,300
Lodola 235 (235cc single).	1,200	1,800	2,700	3,600	4,800	6,000
1967						
Zigolo 110 (110cc single)	600	900	1,400	1,800	2,400	3,000
Stornello 125 American (123cc single) . . .	700	1,000	1,500	2,000	2,600	3,300
Stornello 125 Sport (123cc single)	700	1,000	1,500	2,000	2,600	3,300
1968						
Zigolo 110 (110cc single)	600	900	1,400	1,800	2,400	3,000
Stornello 125 American (123cc single) . . .	700	1,000	1,500	2,000	2,600	3,300
Stornello 125 Sport (123cc single)	700	1,000	1,500	2,000	2,600	3,300
V7 700 (703cc twin)	1,500	3,000	4,500	6,000	7,500	9,000
1969						
Stornello 125 American (123cc single) . . .	700	1,000	1,500	2,000	2,600	3,300
Falcone 500 Nuovo (498cc single)	1,100	1,700	2,500	3,400	4,500	5,600
V7 700 (703cc twin)	1,500	2,300	3,400	4,500	6,000	7,500
V7 750 Ambassador (757cc twin)	1,800	2,700	4,100	5,400	7,200	9,000
1970						
Stornello 125 American (123cc single) . . .	700	1,000	1,500	2,000	2,600	3,300
Falcone 500 Nuovo (498cc single)	1,100	1,700	2,500	3,400	4,500	5,600
V7 750 Ambassador (757cc twin)	1,800	2,700	4,100	5,400	7,200	9,000
1971						
Stornello 125 American (123cc single) . . .	700	1,000	1,500	2,000	2,600	3,300
Falcone 500 Nuovo (498cc single)	1,100	1,700	2,500	3,400	4,500	5,600
V7 750 Police (750cc twin)	2,000	3,000	4,500	6,000	8,000	10,000
V7 750 Ambassador (757cc twin)	1,800	2,700	4,100	5,400	7,200	9,000
1972						
Stornello 125 American (123cc single) . . .	700	1,000	1,500	2,000	2,600	3,300
Falcone 500 Nuovo (498cc single)	1,100	1,700	2,500	3,400	4,500	5,600
V7 750 Police (750cc twin)	2,000	3,000	4,500	6,000	8,000	10,000
V7 750 Sport (748cc twin).	2,100	3,200	5,000	7,000	9,000	11,000
Eldorado 850GT (844cc twin)	2,100	3,200	4,700	6,000	8,000	10,000
V850 California (844cc twin)	2,400	3,600	5,400	7,200	9,600	12,000
1973						
Stornello 125 American (123cc single) . . .	700	1,000	1,500	2,000	2,600	3,300
Falcone 500 Nuovo (498cc single)	1,200	1,800	2,700	3,600	4,800	6,000
850 Eldorado LAPD (844cc twin)	2,200	3,300	5,000	6,600	8,800	11,000
V7 750 Sport (748cc twin).	2,100	3,200	5,000	7,000	9,000	11,000
Eldorado 850GT (844cc twin)	2,100	3,200	4,700	6,300	8,400	11,000
V850 California (844cc twin)	2,400	3,600	5,400	7,200	9,600	12,000

	6	5	4	3	2	1
1974						
Stornello 125 American (123cc single) . . .	700	1,000	1,500	2,000	2,600	3,300
V7 750 Sport (748cc twin).	2,100	3,200	5,000	7,000	9,000	11,000
850T (844cc twin)	1,300	2,000	2,900	3,900	5,200	6,500
Eldorado 850GT (844cc twin)	2,100	3,200	4,700	6,300	8,400	11,000
V850 California (844cc twin)	2,400	3,600	5,400	7,200	9,600	12,000
1975						
850T (844cc twin)	1,300	2,000	2,900	3,900	5,200	6,500
1976						
850T3 (844cc twin)	1,700	2,600	3,800	5,100	6,800	8,500
LeMans I 850 (844cc twin)	2,400	**4,000**	**8,000**	**12,000**	**16,000**	**20,000**
V1000 Convert (948cc twin).	1,200	1,800	2,700	3,600	4,800	6,000
1977						
850T3 (844cc twin)	1,700	2,600	3,800	5,100	6,800	8,500
LeMans I 850 (844cc twin)	2,400	**4,000**	**8,000**	**12,000**	**16,000**	**20,000**
V1000 Convert (948cc twin).	1,200	1,800	2,700	3,600	4,800	6,000
1978						
V50 (490cc twin)	600	900	1,350	1,800	2,400	3,000
850T3 (844cc twin)	1,700	2,600	3,800	5,100	6,800	8,500
LeMans I 850 (844cc twin)	2,400	**4,000**	**8,000**	**12,000**	**16,000**	**20,000**
1000SP (948cc twin)	1,300	2,000	2,900	3,900	5,200	6,500
V1000 Convert (948cc twin).	1,200	1,800	2,700	3,600	4,800	6,000
1979						
V50 II (490cc twin)	600	900	1,350	1,800	2,400	3,000
V50 (490cc twin)	600	900	1,350	1,800	2,400	3,000
1000 G5 (948cc twin)	1,300	2,000	2,900	3,900	5,200	6,500
1000SP (948cc twin)	1,300	2,000	2,900	3,900	5,200	6,500
V1000 Convert (948cc twin).	1,200	1,800	2,700	3,600	4,800	6,000
1980						
V50 II (490cc twin)	600	900	1,350	1,800	2,400	3,000
V50 Monza (490cc twin).	1,000	1,400	2,200	2,900	3,800	4,800
1000 G5 (948cc twin)	1,300	2,000	2,900	3,900	5,200	6,500
1000SP (948cc twin)	1,300	2,000	2,900	3,900	5,200	6,500
LeMans CX100 (998cc twin)	1,700	2,550	3,830	5,100	6,800	8,500
1981						
V50MKIII (490cc twin)	800	1,200	1,700	2,300	2,800	3,300
500 Monza (490cc twin).	900	1,100	1,800	2,400	2,900	3,400
1000 LAPD (1000cc twin)	1,000	1,200	1,900	2,500	3,000	3,500
1000SP (1000cc twin)	1,400	1,900	2,400	3,700	4,100	4,500
CX100 LeMans (1000cc twin)	2,100	2,700	3,300	4,300	4,900	5,500
1982						
V50MKIII (490cc twin)	800	1,200	1,700	2,300	2,800	3,300
500 Monza (490cc twin).	900	1,100	1,800	2,400	2,900	3,400
1000 LAPD (1000cc twin)	1,000	1,200	1,900	2,500	3,000	3,500
1000SP (1000cc twin)	1,400	1,900	2,400	3,700	4,500	5,000
CX100 LeMans (1000cc twin).	2,100	2,700	3,300	4,300	4,900	5,500
1000 Convertible (1000cc twin)	1,200	1,800	2,500	3,900	4,900	6,000
G5 California (1000cc twin)	1,200	1,800	2,500	3,900	4,900	6,000
1983						
LeMans III (850cc twin)	1,300	2,000	2,700	4,200	5,100	6,200
SP/NT (1000cc twin)	1,400	1,900	2,400	3,700	4,500	5,000
California II (1000cc twin)	1,200	1,800	2,500	3,900	4,900	6,000
1984						
V650SP (650cc twin)	600	800	1,500	2,500	3,500	4,500
850T5 (850cc twin)	700	900	1,300	1,800	2,300	4,500
LeMans III (850cc twin)	1,000	1,800	2,700	3,600	4,500	5,400
SP/NT (1000cc twin)	800	1,600	2,400	3,200	4,000	4,800
California II (1000cc twin)	900	1,600	2,500	3,400	4,300	5,200
California II Automatic (950cc twin)	900	1,600	2,500	3,400	4,300	5,200

	6	5	4	3	2	1
1985						
Lario (650cc twin)	600	800	1,000	1,400	1,800	2,200
LeMans (950cc twin)	1,000	1,800	2,700	3,600	4,500	5,400
California II (950cc twin)	900	1,700	2,600	3,500	4,400	5,300
California II Automatic (950cc twin)	900	1,700	2,600	3,500	4,400	5,300
1986						
V65TT (650cc twin)	500	700	1,000	1,500	3,500	5,000
Lario (650cc twin)	600	800	1,000	1,400	1,800	2,200
1000 SP II (950cc twin)	900	1,600	2,400	3,200	4,000	4,800
California II (950cc twin)	1,000	1,900	2,800	3,700	4,600	5,500
California II Automatic (950cc twin)	1,000	1,900	2,800	3,700	4,600	5,500
1987						
LeMans 1000 (950cc twin)	1,100	2,100	3,100	4,100	5,100	6,100
Lemans SE 1000 (950cc twin)	1,300	2,300	3,300	4,300	5,300	6,300
1000 SP II (950cc twin)	1,200	2,200	3,200	4,200	5,200	6,200
1989						
Mille GT (950cc twin)	1,000	2,000	2,900	3,800	4,700	5,600
California III (950cc twin)	1,000	2,000	3,000	4,000	5,000	6,000
LeMans V (950cc twin)	1,200	2,300	3,400	4,500	5,600	6,500
California III Touring (950cc twin)	1,100	2,200	3,200	4,300	5,400	6,300
1990						
Mille GT (950cc twin)	1,100	2,100	3,100	4,100	5,100	6,100
California III (950cc twin)	1,200	2,200	3,200	4,200	5,200	6,200
LeMans V (950cc twin)	1,300	2,400	3,600	4,800	5,800	6,600
California III Touring (950cc twin)	1,300	2,400	3,500	4,600	5,700	6,500
1991						
1000S (950cc twin)	1,200	2,400	3,500	4,600	5,700	6,500
1000SP III (950cc twin)	1,900	2,800	3,800	5,000	6,000	7,000
1992						
1000S (950cc twin)	1,900	2,800	3,800	5,000	6,000	7,000
1000SP III (950cc twin)	2,000	3,000	4,000	5,300	6,600	7,500
1993						
1000S (950cc twin)	1,900	2,800	3,800	5,000	6,000	7,000
1000SP III (950cc twin)	2,000	3,000	4,000	5,300	6,600	7,500
California (950cc twin).	2,000	3,000	4,000	5,300	6,600	7,500
Daytona 1000 FI (1000cc twin)	2,200	3,300	4,400	5,700	7,400	9,000
1994						
California (1,064cc twin).	2,000	3,900	5,400	6,900	7,500	8,900
Sport (1,064cc twin).	2,000	3,900	5,400	6,900	7,500	8,900
1995						
California (1,064cc twin).	1,900	3,300	4,700	6,100	7,500	8,900
Sport (1,064cc twin).	1,900	3,400	4,900	6,400	7,900	9,400
California IE (1,064 twin)	1,900	3,400	5,000	6,600	8,200	9,800
Sport IE (1,064 twin)	1,900	3,500	5,100	6,700	8,400	10,400
1996						
California (1,064cc twin).	1,900	3,300	4,700	6,100	7,500	8,900
California I (1,064 twin)	1,900	3,400	5,000	6,600	8,200	9,800
Sport (1,064cc twin).	1,900	3,400	4,900	6,400	7,900	9,400
MOTO MORINI						
1953						
Model 175N (175cc).	1,000	2,000	3,000	4,000	5,000	6,000
1954						
Turismo (175cc).	1,000	2,000	3,000	4,000	5,000	6,000
1956						
Cardellino	500	1,000	2,000	3,500	5,000	6,500
Cosaro	500	1,000	2,000	3,500	5,000	6,500
1957						
Tresette (175cc).	1,000	2,000	3,000	4,000	5,000	6,000
1959						
Corsa (175cc).	1,000	2,000	3,000	4,500	6,500	8,400

	6	5	4	3	2	1
1961						
Tresette (175cc)	1,000	2,000	3,000	4,000	5,000	6,000
1962						
Bronco (100cc)	200	300	500	800	1,000	1,500
1964						
Apache (100cc)	200	300	500	800	1,100	1,500
1974						
3.5 (350cc)	500	1,000	2,500	4,000	5,500	7,000
1975						
Standard (350cc twin)	300	600	1,000	1,500	2,000	2,500
Sport (350cc)	500	1,000	2,000	4,000	6,000	8,000
Strada (350cc)	1,000	2,000	3,000	4,000	5,000	6,000
1976						
Sport (350cc)	1,000	2,000	3,000	4,000	5,000	6,000
1977						
Standard (350cc twin)	200	300	500	800	1,100	1,500
café (350cc twin)	200	400	600	1,000	1,400	1,800
Sport (350cc)	1,000	2,000	3,000	4,000	5,000	6,000
1978						
Strada (350 cc twin)	200	300	500	900	1,300	1,700
café (350cc twin)	200	400	700	1,000	1,300	1,600
Sport (350cc)	1,000	2,000	3,000	4,000	5,000	6,000
500 (500cc)	500	1,000	2,500	4,000	5,500	7,000
1979						
Standard (125cc single)	200	300	400	700	1,000	1,300
Standard (250cc twin)	200	300	500	800	1,100	1,400
Standard (350cc twin)	200	400	600	900	1,200	1,500
café (350cc twin)	200	400	700	1,100	1,400	1,700
Standard GT (350cc twin)	200	400	600	1,000	1,400	1,800
Sport GT (350cc twin)	200	400	600	1,000	1,400	1,800
500 (500cc)	500	1,000	2,500	4,000	5,500	7,000
1980						
Standard (350cc twin)	200	400	600	900	1,200	1,500
café Sport (350cc twin)	200	400	700	1,100	1,400	1,700
Standard (500cc twin)	200	400	700	1,000	1,300	1,600
café Sport (500cc twin)	1,000	2,000	3,000	4,000	5,000	6,000
1981						
Standard (125cc single)	200	300	500	800	1,100	1,400
Standard (250cc twin)	200	400	600	900	1,200	1,500
Standard (350cc twin)	200	400	600	1,000	1,400	1,800
café Sport (350cc twin)	200	500	800	1,100	1,400	1,700
Standard (500cc twin)	200	400	700	1,000	1,300	1,600
café Sport (500cc twin)	1,000	2,000	3,000	4,000	5,000	6,000
1982						
Single (125cc single)	200	300	500	800	1,100	1,400
V-twin (250cc twin)	200	400	600	1,000	1,400	1,800
Strada (350 cc twin)	200	400	700	1,000	1,300	1,600
Sport (350cc twin)	200	500	800	1,200	1,600	2,000
Standard (500cc twin)	200	400	700	1,100	1,400	1,700
Sport (500cc twin)	200	500	900	1,200	1,500	1,900
1983						
Standard (125cc single)	200	300	500	800	1,100	1,400
Standard (250cc twin)	200	400	700	1,000	1,300	1,600
Strada (350 cc twin)	200	400	700	1,100	1,500	1,900
Sport (350cc twin)	200	500	900	1,200	1,500	1,800
Standard (500cc twin)	200	500	800	1,100	1,400	1,700
Sport (500cc twin)	200	500	900	1,300	1,700	2,100
1984						
Standard (125cc single)	200	300	500	800	1,100	1,400
Standard Twin (250cc twin)	200	400	700	1,000	1,300	1,600
Strada (350 cc twin)	200	500	800	1,100	1,400	1,700

	6	5	4	3	2	1
Sport (350cc twin)	200	500	900	1,300	1,700	2,100
K2 (350cc twin)	200	500	900	1,300	1,700	2,100
Strada (500cc twin)	200	500	800	1,200	1,600	2,000
Sport Special (500cc twin)	200	500	900	1,300	1,700	2,100
K2 (500cc twin)	200	500	900	1,300	1,700	2,100
1985						
Kangura (350cc twin)	200	400	600	900	1,200	1,500
Camel (500cc twin)	300	600	1,000	1,500	2,000	2,500
K2 (350cc twin)	200	500	900	1,300	1,700	2,100
1986						
Kangura (350cc twin)	200	400	600	1,000	1,400	1,800
Camel (500cc twin)	300	600	1,000	1,500	2,000	2,500
K2 (350cc twin)	300	600	1,000	1,400	1,800	2,200
Excalibur (500cc twin)	300	600	1,000	1,400	1,800	2,200
1987						
Kangura (350cc twin)	200	500	700	1,000	1,300	1,600
Camel (500cc twin)	300	600	1,000	1,500	2,000	2,500
Excalibur (500cc twin)	300	600	1,000	1,500	2,000	2,500
1988						
Coguro (500cc twin)	200	500	800	1,100	1,400	1,700
Dart (350cc twin)	200	500	700	1,000	1,300	1,600
New Yorker (500cc twin)	200	500	800	1,100	1,400	1,700
1990						
Coguro (500cc twin)	200	500	800	1,200	1,600	2,000
Dart (350cc twin)	200	500	800	1,100	1,400	1,700
New Yorker (500cc twin)	300	600	900	1,300	1,700	2,100
1991						
Coguro (500cc twin)	300	600	900	1,300	1,700	2,100
Dart (350cc twin)	200	500	800	1,200	1,600	2,000
New Yorker (500cc twin)	300	600	1,000	1,400	1,800	2,200
1992						
Coguro (500cc twin)	300	600	1,000	1,400	1,800	2,200
Dart (350cc twin)	300	600	900	1,300	1,700	2,100
New Yorker (500cc twin)	300	600	1,000	1,400	1,800	2,200
1993						
Coguro (500cc twin)	300	600	1,000	1,400	1,800	2,200
Dart (350cc twin)	300	600	900	1,300	1,700	2,100
New Yorker (500cc twin)	300	600	1,000	1,400	1,800	2,200
1994						
New Yorker (500cc twin)	300	700	1,100	1,500	1,900	2,300
1995						
New Yorker (500cc twin)	300	700	1,100	1,500	1,900	2,300

MOTOR-PIPER

	6	5	4	3	2	1
1940						
Motopipe 108MC	100	200	300	400	500	600
Motopipe 208MC	100	200	300	400	500	600
1941						
Motopipe 108MC	100	200	300	400	500	600
Motopipe 208MC	100	200	300	400	500	600
Motopipe 250MC	100	200	300	400	600	700
1942						
Motopipe 108MC	100	200	300	400	500	600
Motopipe 208MC	100	200	300	400	500	600
Motopipe 250MC	100	200	300	400	600	700
1943						
Motopipe 108MC	100	200	300	400	500	600
Motopipe 208MC	100	200	300	400	500	600
Motopipe 250MC	100	200	300	400	600	700
Piper 80M	100	200	300	400	500	600

	6	5	4	3	2	1
1944						
Motopipe 108MC	100	200	300	400	500	600
Motopipe 208MC	100	200	300	400	500	600
Motopipe 250MC	100	200	300	400	600	700
Piper 80M	100	200	300	400	500	600
1945						
Motopipe 108MC	100	200	300	400	500	600
Motopipe 208MC	100	200	300	400	500	600
Motopipe 250MC	100	200	300	400	600	700
Piper 80M	100	200	300	400	500	600
1946						
Motopipe 108MC	100	200	300	400	500	600
Motopipe 208MC	100	200	300	400	500	600
Motopipe 250MC	100	200	300	400	600	700
Piper 80M	100	200	300	400	500	600
1947						
Motopipe 108MC	100	200	300	400	500	600
Motopipe 208MC	100	200	300	400	500	600
Motopipe 250MC	100	200	300	400	600	700
Piper 350M	100	200	400	500	800	1,100
Piper 80M	100	200	300	400	500	600
1948						
Motopipe 108MC	100	200	300	400	500	600
Motopipe 208MC	100	200	300	400	500	600
Motopipe 250MC	100	200	300	400	600	700
Piper 350M	100	200	400	500	800	1,100
Piper 80M	100	200	300	400	500	600
1949						
Moto 108M	100	200	300	400	500	600
Moto 208M	100	200	300	400	500	600
Moto 250M	100	200	400	600	800	1,000
Pipe 350M	100	300	500	700	1,000	1,300
Pipe 80M	100	200	300	400	500	600
1950						
Moto 108M	100	200	300	400	500	600
Moto 208M	100	200	300	400	500	600
Moto 250M	100	200	400	600	800	1,000
Pipe 350M	100	300	500	700	1,000	1,300
Pipe 80M	100	200	300	400	500	600
1951						
Moto 108M	100	200	300	400	500	600
Moto 208M	100	200	300	400	500	600
Moto 250M	100	200	400	600	800	1,000
Pipe 350M	100	300	500	700	1,000	1,300
Pipe 80M	100	200	300	400	500	600
1952						
Moto 108M	100	200	300	400	500	600
Moto 208M	100	200	300	400	500	600
Moto 250M	200	300	600	900	1,200	1,500
Pipe 350M	200	400	800	1,000	1,800	2,400
Pipe 80M	100	200	300	400	500	600
1953						
Moto 108M	100	200	300	400	500	600
Moto 208M	100	200	300	400	500	600
Moto 250M	200	400	800	1,000	1,800	2,600
Pipe 350M	300	600	1,000	1,400	2,000	2,600
Pipe 80M	100	200	300	400	500	600
1954						
Moto 108M	100	200	400	600	900	1,200
Moto 208M	100	300	500	600	900	1,200

	6	5	4	3	2	1
Moto 250M	200	400	800	1,000	1,800	2,400
Pipe 350M	300	600	1,000	1,400	2,000	2,600
Pipe 80M	100	200	300	400	500	600
1955						
Moto 108M	100	200	400	600	1,500	2,400
Moto 208M	200	400	800	1,000	1,900	2,800
Moto 250M	1,300	2,000	2,800	3,600	5,900	8,200
Pipe 350M	600	1,000	1,700	2,900	5,000	7,100
Pipe 80M	100	200	300	400	500	600

MUNCH

	6	5	4	3	2	1
1969						
Mammut 1200 TTS	20,000	35,000	50,000	60,000	70,000	100K
1970						
Mammut 1200 TTS	20,000	35,000	50,000	60,000	70,000	100K
1971						
Mammut 1200 TTS	20,000	35,000	50,000	60,000	70,000	100K
1972						
Mammut 1200 TTS	20,000	35,000	50,000	60,000	70,000	100K
1973						
Mammut 1200 TTS	20,000	35,000	50,000	60,000	70,000	100K

MUSTANG

	6	5	4	3	2	1
1945						
Model 2	1,900	2,600	3,200	4,400	7,200	10,000
1946						
Colt	1,000	2,000	3,500	5,000	7,500	10,000
Model 2	1,900	2,600	3,200	4,400	7,200	10,000
Solo	500	1,000	2,000	4,000	6,000	8,000
1947						
Model 2	1,900	2,600	3,200	4,400	7,200	10,000
1948						
Model 2	1,900	2,600	3,200	4,400	7,200	10,000
Pony	1,800	2,500	4,000	6,000	8,000	10,500
1949						
Pony	1,800	2,500	4,000	6,000	8,000	10,500
1950						
Bronco	1,900	2,600	3,200	4,400	7,200	10,000
Pony	1,800	2,500	4,000	6,000	8,000	10,500
Trail Machine	300	500	600	800	1,600	2,400
3 Wheel Delivery Cycle	3,000	6,000	9,000	12,000	16,000	20,000
1951						
Pony	1,800	2,500	4,000	6,000	8,000	10,500
Trail Machine	300	500	600	800	1,600	2,400
1952						
Pony	1,800	2,500	4,000	6,000	8,000	10,500
Trail Machine	300	500	600	800	1,600	2,400
1953						
Pony	1,800	2,500	3,700	4,400	6,700	9,000
Trail Machine	300	500	600	800	1,600	2,400
1954						
Pony	1,800	2,500	3,700	4,400	6,700	9,000
Trail Machine	300	500	600	800	1,600	2,400
1955						
Pony	1,800	2,500	3,700	4,400	6,700	9,000
Trail Machine	300	500	600	800	1,600	2,400
3 Wheel Delivery Cycle	3,000	6,000	9,000	12,000	16,000	20,000
1956						
Colt	500	1,000	2,500	4,000	5,500	7,000
Pony	1,800	2,500	3,700	4,400	6,700	9,000
Trail Machine	300	500	600	800	1,600	2,400
3 Wheel Delivery Cycle	3,000	6,000	9,000	12,000	16,000	20,000

	6	5	4	3	2	1
M-Eight	2,000	3,100	4,200	5,300	8,300	11,300
1957						
M-Eight	2,000	3,100	4,200	5,300	8,300	11,300
Pony.	1,800	2,500	3,700	4,400	6,700	9,000
Trail Machine	300	500	600	800	1,600	2,400
3 Wheel Delivery Cycle	3,000	6,000	9,000	12,000	16,000	20,000
1958						
M-Eight	2,000	3,100	4,200	5,300	8,300	11,300
Pony.	1,800	2,500	3,700	4,400	6,700	9,000
Trail Machine	300	500	600	800	1,600	2,400
3 Wheel Delivery Cycle	3,000	6,000	9,000	12,000	16,000	20,000
1959						
Bronco	1,800	2,900	4,200	5,300	7,800	10,300
M-Eight	2,000	3,100	4,200	5,300	8,300	11,300
Pony.	1,800	2,500	3,700	4,400	6,700	9,000
Stallion	2,100	3,600	5,100	6,800	9,400	12,000
Trail Machine	300	500	600	800	1,600	2,400
3 Wheel Delivery Cycle	3,000	4,500	5,400	7,300	10,500	14,000
1960						
Bronco	1,800	2,900	4,200	5,300	7,800	10,300
Pony.	1,800	2,500	3,700	4,400	6,700	9,000
Stallion	2,100	3,600	5,100	6,800	9,400	12,000
Thoroughbred.	2,100	3,600	5,200	7,000	10,200	13,500
Trail Machine	300	500	600	800	1,600	2,400
3 Wheel Delivery Cycle	3,000	4,500	5,400	7,300	10,500	14,000
1961						
Bronco	1,800	2,900	4,200	5,300	7,800	10,300
Pony.	1,800	2,500	3,700	4,400	6,700	9,000
Stallion	2,100	3,600	5,100	6,800	9,400	12,000
Thoroughbred.	2,100	3,600	5,200	7,000	10,200	13,500
3 Wheel Delivery Cycle	3,000	4,500	5,400	7,300	10,500	14,000
1962						
Bronco	1,800	2,900	4,200	5,300	7,800	10,300
Stallion	2,100	3,600	5,100	6,800	9,400	12,000
Thoroughbred.	2,100	3,600	5,200	7,000	10,200	13,500
3 Wheel Delivery Cycle	3,000	4,500	5,400	7,300	10,500	14,000
1963						
Stallion	2,100	3,600	5,100	6,800	9,400	12,000
Thoroughbred.	2,100	3,600	5,200	7,000	10,200	13,500
3 Wheel Delivery Cycle	3,000	4,500	5,400	7,300	10,500	14,000
1964						
Stallion	2,100	3,600	5,100	6,800	9,400	12,000
Thoroughbred.	2,100	3,600	5,200	7,000	10,200	13,500
1965						
Stallion	2,100	3,600	5,100	6,800	9,400	12,000
Thoroughbred.	2,100	3,600	5,200	7,000	10,200	13,500
MV AGUSTA						
1947						
S3 Velocita (83cc).	**5,000**	**10,000**	**15,000**	**20,000**	**25,000**	**30,000**
1948						
2 Tempi 3 Velocita (125cc)	5,000	10,000	15,000	20,000	25,000	30,000
1950						
CSL Scooter (123cc)	1,000	2,000	3,000	4,000	5,000	6,000
CGT Scooter (150cc)	1,000	2,000	3,000	4,000	5,000	6,000
Turismo C Serbatoio Cromato (125cc)	600	1,200	2,500	4,000	6,000	8,000
1951						
Turismo C (125cc).	1,000	2,000	3,000	4,000	5,000	6,000
1952						
Sport E (125cc)	1,000	2,000	3,000	4,000	5,000	6,000
CGT Scooter (150cc)	1,000	1,800	2,600	3,400	4,200	5,000

	6	5	4	3	2	1
Sport Super Lusso (150cc)	2,000	4,000	8,000	12,000	16,000	20,000
1953						
TEL (125cc)	600	1,200	2,500	4,000	6,000	8,000
Sport E Lusso	600	1,200	2,500	4,000	6,000	8,000
Ovunque	1,000	2,000	3,000	4,000	5,000	6,000
1954						
Rapido Sport (125cc)	1,000	2,000	3,000	4,000	5,000	6,000
Pullman 1A Serie	1,000	1,800	2,600	3,400	4,200	5,000
CST 1A Serie (175cc)	1,000	2,000	4,000	6,000	9,000	12,000
CS Disco Volante (175cc)	2,000	4,000	8,000	12,000	16,000	20,000
CSS Disco Volante (175cc)	2,000	4,000	8,000	12,000	16,000	20,000
1955						
TR (125cc)	1,000	1,800	2,600	3,400	4,200	5,000
1956						
Ciclomotore (48cc)	1,000	1,800	2,600	3,400	4,200	5,000
CSTL	600	1,200	2,500	4,000	6,000	8,000
Disco Volante (175cc)	2,000	4,000	8,000	12,000	16,000	20,000
Pullman 2A Serie	1,000	1,800	2,600	3,400	4,200	5,000
Superpullman	600	1,200	2,500	4,000	6,000	8,000
CSS/5V Squalo (175cc)	4,000	8,000	16,000	24,000	32,000	40,000
1957						
125TR (125cc)	1,000	2,000	3,000	4,000	5,000	6,000
Turismo CSTE AB (175cc)	600	1,200	2,500	4,000	6,000	8,000
Turismo Monoalbero CSGT	600	1,200	2,500	4,000	6,000	8,000
Grand Prix Sport (250cc)	1,000	2,000	4,000	6,000	8,000	10,000
1958						
Lusso America	1,000	2,000	3,000	4,000	5,000	6,000
Turismo Rapido America TRA (125cc) . . .	1,000	1,800	2,600	3,400	4,200	5,000
CS Disco Volante (175cc)	2,500	5,000	10,000	15,000	20,000	25,000
1959						
Ottantatre Turismo (83cc)	600	1,200	2,500	3,500	5,000	7,000
125	1,000	2,000	4,000	6,000	8,000	10,000
TRA (125cc single)	1,000	1,800	2,600	3,400	4,200	5,000
Raid (250cc)	2,500	5,000	10,000	15,000	20,000	25,000
1960						
TREL Centomila (125cc)	600	1,200	2,500	4,000	6,000	8,000
Chicco Scooter (155cc)	1,000	2,000	3,000	4,000	5,000	6,000
Tevere (235cc)	600	1,200	2,500	4,000	6,000	8,000
1961						
Checca Gran Turismo (99cc)	1,000	1,800	2,600	3,400	4,200	5,000
125	1,000	2,000	3,000	4,000	5,000	6,000
Centauro 2A Serie (150cc)	2,000	4,000	5,500	7,000	8,500	10,000
Raid Militare (300cc)	2,000	4,000	5,500	7,000	8,500	10,000
1962						
Liberty Sport (48cc)	1,000	2,000	3,000	4,000	5,000	6,000
GP	600	1,200	2,500	3,500	5,000	7,000
Centomile	600	1,200	2,500	3,500	5,000	7,000
Checca GTL (124cc)	600	1,200	2,500	4,000	6,000	8,000
1963						
Sport GT (99cc)	2,000	4,000	6,000	8,000	10,000	12,000
RS (150cc)	600	1,200	2,500	4,000	6,000	8,000
1964						
Liberty (50cc)	1,000	2,000	3,000	4,000	5,000	6,000
Germano Sport 1A Serie	1,000	2,000	3,000	4,000	5,000	6,000
Germano Turismo G	600	1,200	2,500	4,000	6,000	8,000
Gran Turismo Lusso (125cc)	2,000	4,000	5,500	7,000	8,500	10,000
1965						
RS (150cc)	600	1,200	2,500	4,000	6,000	8,000
1966						
Ciclomotore Germano Turismo 2A (48cc) . .	1,000	2,000	3,000	4,000	5,000	6,000
Liberty Turismo 2A Versione (50cc)	600	1,200	2,500	3,500	5,000	7,000

	6	5	4	3	2	1
Germano Sport 2A Serie	1,000	1,800	2,600	3,400	4,200	5,000
1967						
Regolarita 1A Serie (125cc)	2,000	4,000	5,500	7,000	8,500	10,000
1968						
Roadster Four (600cc)	4,000	8,000	16,000	24,000	32,000	40,000
1969						
250B (250cc)	2,000	4,000	5,500	7,000	8,500	10,000
Bicilindrico B Scrambler (250cc).	1,500	3,000	6,000	9,000	12,000	15,000
1971						
GTL-S Sport (125cc)	1,000	2,000	3,000	4,000	5,000	6,000
Sport 4C75 1A Serie (750cc)	10,000	20,000	30,000	40,000	50,000	60,000
B Twin Sports 1A Serie (350cc)	3,000	6,000	9,000	12,000	15,000	18,000
1972						
GTL-S Carenata (125cc)	2,000	4,000	8,000	12,000	16,000	20,000
Elettronica S (350cc twin)	1,500	3,000	5,000	8,000	10,000	12,000
Scrambler (350cc).	1,500	3,000	6,000	9,000	12,000	15,000
4C75 2A Serie (750cc)	10,000	20,000	35,000	50,000	65,000	80,000
1973						
750 GT (750cc)	10,000	20,000	35,000	50,000	65,000	80,000
1974						
Elettronica S (350cc twin)	1,500	3,000	5,000	8,000	10,000	12,000
1975						
Sport	2,000	4,000	6,000	8,000	10,000	12,000
Sport E (125cc)	600	1,200	2,500	4,000	6,000	8,000
Sport Ipotesi (350cc)	2,000	4,000	5,500	7,000	8,500	10,000
750S America (750cc).	5,000	10,000	20,000	30,000	40,000	50,000
1976						
125 Sport	200	400	800	1,200	1,600	2,000
Ipotesi GT (350cc).	2,000	4,000	**8,000**	**12,000**	**16,000**	**20,000**
750S America (750cc).	5,000	10,000	20,000	30,000	40,000	50,000
1977						
850SS	5,000	10,000	20,000	35,000	50,000	65,000

NORTON

	6	5	4	3	2	1
1928						
Model 16HM.	2,500	5,000	7,500	10,500	12,500	15,000
1929						
Model 18 (490cc single)	2,500	5,000	7,500	10,500	12,500	15,000
CS1 (490cc single)	4,000	8,000	16,000	24,000	32,000	40,000
1930						
CJ (348cc single)	1,900	2,900	4,300	5,700	7,600	9,500
CS1 (490cc single)	3,000	**5,000**	**10,000**	**15,000**	**20,000**	**25,000**
ES2 (490cc single)	1,800	2,700	4,100	5,400	7,200	9,000
Model 16H (490cc single)	2,100	3,200	4,700	6,300	8,400	11,000
Model 18 (490cc single).	2,100	3,200	6,000	9,000	12,000	15,000
Model 19 (588cc single)	2,100	3,200	6,000	8,000	10,000	12,000
Model 20 (490cc single)	2,000	4,000	8,000	12,000	16,000	20,000
Big 4 (633cc single)	**1,500**	**2,500**	**4,000**	**5,500**	**7,000**	**8,500**
1931						
CJ (348cc single)	1,900	2,900	4,300	5,700	7,600	9,500
CS1 (490cc single)	3,000	**5,000**	**10,000**	**15,000**	**20,000**	**25,000**
ES2 (490cc single)	1,800	2,700	4,100	5,400	7,200	9,000
Model 16H (490cc single)	2,100	3,200	4,700	6,300	8,400	11,000
Model 18 (490cc single)	2,100	3,200	6,000	9,000	12,000	15,000
Model 19 (588cc single)	2,100	3,200	6,000	8,000	10,000	12,000
Big 4 (633cc single)	**1,500**	**2,500**	**4,000**	**5,500**	**7,000**	**8,500**
1932						
CJ (348cc single)	1,900	2,900	4,300	5,700	7,600	9,500
Model 40 International (348cc single)	3,000	4,500	6,800	9,000	12,000	15,000
Model 30 International (490cc single)	3,000	4,500	7,000	11,000	15,000	19,000
ES2 (490cc single)	1,800	2,700	4,100	5,400	7,200	9,000

	6	5	4	3	2	1
Model 16H (490cc single)	2,100	3,200	4,700	6,300	8,400	11,000
Model 18 (490cc single).	2,100	3,200	6,000	9,000	12,000	15,000
Model 19 (588cc single)	2,100	3,200	6,000	8,000	10,000	12,000
Big 4 (633cc single)	**1,500**	**2,500**	**4,000**	**5,500**	**7,000**	**8,500**
1933						
CJ (348cc single)	1,900	2,900	4,300	5,700	7,600	9,500
Model 50 (348cc single).	1,900	2,900	4,300	5,700	7,600	9,500
Model 40 International (348cc single) . . .	3,000	4,500	6,800	9,000	12,000	15,000
Model 30 International (490cc single)	3,000	4,500	7,000	11,000	15,000	19,000
ES2 (490cc single)	1,800	2,700	4,100	5,400	7,200	9,000
Model 16H (490cc single)	2,100	3,200	4,700	6,300	8,400	11,000
Model 18 (490cc single).	2,100	3,200	6,000	9,000	12,000	15,000
Model 19 (588cc single)	2,100	3,200	6,000	8,000	10,000	12,000
Big 4 (633cc single)	**1,500**	**2,500**	**4,000**	**5,500**	**7,000**	**8,500**
1934						
CJ (348cc single)	1,900	2,900	4,300	5,700	7,600	9,500
Model 50 (348cc single).	1,900	2,900	4,300	5,700	7,600	9,500
Model 40 International (348cc single)	3,000	4,500	6,800	9,000	12,000	15,000
Model 30 International (490cc single)	3,000	4,500	7,000	11,000	15,000	19,000
ES2 (490cc single)	1,800	2,700	4,100	5,400	7,200	9,000
Model 16H (490cc single)	2,100	3,200	4,700	6,300	8,400	11,000
Model 18 (490cc single).	1,500	2,000	4,000	6,000	9,000	12,000
Model 19 (588cc single)	2,100	3,200	6,000	8,000	10,000	12,000
Big 4 (633cc single)	**1,500**	**2,500**	**4,000**	**5,500**	**7,000**	**8,500**
1935						
CJ (348cc single)	1,900	2,900	4,300	5,700	7,600	9,500
Model 50 (348cc single).	1,900	2,900	4,300	5,700	7,600	9,500
Model 40 International (348cc single)	3,000	4,500	6,800	9,000	12,000	15,000
Model 30 International (490cc single)	3,000	4,500	8,000	12,000	16,000	20,000
ES2 (490cc single)	2,000	3,000	5,000	7,000	9,000	12,000
Model 16H (490cc single)	2,100	3,200	4,700	6,300	8,400	11,000
Model 18 (490cc single).	1,500	2,000	4,000	6,000	9,000	12,000
Model 19 (588cc single)	2,100	3,200	6,000	8,000	10,000	12,000
Big 4 (633cc single)	**1,500**	**2,500**	**4,000**	**5,500**	**7,000**	**8,500**
1936						
CJ (348cc single)	1,900	2,900	4,300	5,700	7,600	9,500
Model 50 (348cc single).	1,900	2,900	4,300	5,700	7,600	9,500
Model 40 International (348cc single)	4,000	5,000	8,000	10,000	13,000	16,000
Model 30 International (490cc single)	3,000	4,500	8,000	12,000	16,000	20,000
ES2 (490cc single)	1,800	2,700	4,100	5,400	7,200	9,000
Model 16H (490cc single)	2,000	3,000	4,500	6,000	8,000	10,000
Model 18 (490cc single).	1,500	2,000	4,000	6,000	9,000	12,000
Model 19 (588cc single)	2,000	3,000	6,000	8,000	10,000	12,000
Big 4 (633cc single)	**1,500**	**2,500**	**4,000**	**5,500**	**7,000**	**8,500**
1937						
CJ (348cc single)	1,900	2,900	4,300	5,700	7,600	9,500
Model 50 (348cc single).	1,900	2,900	4,300	5,700	7,600	9,500
Model 40 International (348cc single)	3,000	4,500	6,800	9,000	12,000	15,000
Model 30 International (490cc single)	3,000	4,500	8,000	12,000	16,000	20,000
ES2 (490cc single)	1,800	2,700	4,100	5,400	7,200	9,000
Model 16H (490cc single)	2,000	3,000	4,500	6,000	8,000	10,000
Model 18 (490cc single).	1,500	2,000	4,000	6,000	9,000	12,000
Model 19 (588cc single)	2,000	3,000	6,000	8,000	10,000	12,000
Big 4 (633cc single)	**1,500**	**2,500**	**4,000**	**5,500**	**7,000**	**8,500**
1938						
CJ (348cc single)	1,900	2,900	4,300	5,700	7,600	9,500
Model 50 (348cc single).	1,900	2,900	4,300	5,700	7,600	9,500
Model 40 International (348cc single)	3,000	4,500	6,800	9,000	12,000	15,000
Model 30 International (490cc single)	3,000	4,500	8,000	12,000	16,000	20,000
ES2 (490cc single)	1,800	2,700	4,100	5,400	7,200	9,000

	6	5	4	3	2	1
Model 16H (490cc single)	2,000	3,000	4,500	6,000	8,000	10,000
Model 18 (490cc single)	1,500	2,000	4,000	6,000	9,000	12,000
Model 19 (588cc single)	2,000	3,000	6,000	8,000	10,000	12,000
Big 4 (633cc single)	**1,500**	**2,500**	**4,000**	**5,500**	**7,000**	**8,500**
1939						
CJ (348cc single)	1,700	2,600	3,800	5,100	6,800	8,500
Model 50 (348cc single)	1,700	2,600	3,800	5,100	6,800	8,500
Model 40 International (348cc single)	3,000	4,500	6,800	9,000	12,000	15,000
Model 30 International (490cc single)	3,000	4,500	8,000	12,000	16,000	20,000
ES2 (490cc single)	1,800	2,700	4,100	5,400	7,200	9,000
Model 16H (490cc single)	1,800	2,700	4,100	5,400	7,200	9,000
Model 18 (490cc single)	1,500	2,000	4,000	6,000	9,000	12,000
Model 19 (588cc single)	1,800	2,700	6,000	8,000	10,000	12,000
Big 4 (633cc single)	**1,500**	**2,500**	**4,000**	**5,500**	**7,000**	**8,500**
1940						
WD/Model 16H (490cc single)	**1,500**	**2,500**	**4,000**	**5,500**	**7,000**	**8,500**
WD/Big 4 (633cc single)	**1,500**	**2,500**	**4,000**	**5,500**	**7,000**	**8,500**
1941						
WD/Model 16H (490cc single)	**1,500**	**2,500**	**4,000**	**5,500**	**7,000**	**8,500**
WD/Big 4 (633cc single)	**1,500**	**2,500**	**4,000**	**5,500**	**7,000**	**8,500**
1942						
WD/Model 16H (490cc single)	**1,500**	**2,500**	**4,000**	**5,500**	**7,000**	**8,500**
WD/Big 4 (633cc single)	**1,500**	**2,500**	**4,000**	**5,500**	**7,000**	**8,500**
1943						
WD/Model 16H (490cc single)	**1,500**	**2,500**	**4,000**	**5,500**	**7,000**	**8,500**
WD/Big 4 (633cc single)	**1,500**	**2,500**	**4,000**	**5,500**	**7,000**	**8,500**
1944						
WD/Model 16H (490cc single)	**1,500**	**2,500**	**4,000**	**5,500**	**7,000**	**8,500**
WD/Big 4 (633cc single)	**1,500**	**2,500**	**4,000**	**5,500**	**7,000**	**8,500**
1945						
WD/Model 16H (490cc single)	**1,500**	**2,500**	**4,000**	**5,500**	**7,000**	**8,500**
WD/Big 4 (633cc single)	**1,500**	**2,500**	**4,000**	**5,500**	**7,000**	**8,500**
1946						
Manx 40M (348cc single)	5,000	10,000	15,000	20,000	25,000	30,000
Model 40 International (348cc single)	2,800	4,200	6,300	8,400	11,000	14,000
Model 16H (490cc single)	1,500	3,000	4,500	6,000	7,500	9,000
Model 18 (490cc single)	−1,500	**2,500**	**4,000**	**5,500**	**7,000**	**8,500**
Model 30 International (490cc single)	3,000	4,500	8,000	12,000	16,000	20,000
Manx 30M (498cc single)	5,200	7,800	12,000	16,000	25,000	35,000
Model 19R (596cc single)	**1,500**	**2,500**	**4,000**	**5,500**	**7,000**	**8,500**
Model 19S (596cc single)	**1,500**	**2,500**	**4,000**	**5,500**	**7,000**	**8,500**
Big 4 (633cc single)	**1,500**	**2,500**	**4,000**	**5,500**	**7,000**	**8,500**
1947						
Manx 40M (348cc single)	5,000	10,000	15,000	20,000	25,000	30,000
Model 40 International (348cc single)	2,600	3,900	5,900	7,800	10,000	13,000
Model 50 (348cc single)	1,000	1,500	**2,500**	**4,000**	**5,500**	**7,000**
Trials (348cc single)	1,000	1,500	**2,500**	**4,000**	**5,500**	**7,000**
Model 16H (490cc single)	1,500	**2,500**	**4,000**	**5,500**	**7,000**	**8,500**
Model 18 (490cc single)	−1,500	**2,500**	**4,000**	**5,500**	**7,000**	**8,500**
Model 30 International (490cc single)	3,000	4,500	8,000	12,000	16,000	20,000
ES2 (490cc single)	1,500	3,000	4,500	6,000	9,000	12,000
Trials (498cc single)	1,000	1,500	**2,500**	**4,000**	**5,500**	**7,000**
Manx 30M (498cc single)	5,200	7,800	12,000	16,000	25,000	35,000
Model 19R (596cc single)	**1,500**	**2,500**	**4,000**	**5,500**	**7,000**	**8,500**
Model 19S (596cc single)	**1,500**	**2,500**	**4,000**	**5,500**	**7,000**	**8,500**
Big 4 (633cc single)	**1,500**	**2,500**	**4,000**	**5,500**	**7,000**	**8,500**
1948						
Manx 40M (348cc single)	5,000	10,000	15,000	20,000	25,000	30,000
Model 40 International (348cc single)	2,600	3,900	5,900	7,800	10,000	13,000
Model 50 (348cc single)	1,000	1,500	**2,500**	**4,000**	**5,500**	**7,000**

	6	5	4	3	2	1
Model 16H (490cc single)	1,500	2,300	3,400	4,500	6,000	7,500
Model 18 (490cc single)	−1,500	2,500	4,000	5,500	7,000	8,500
Model 30 International (490cc single)	3,000	4,500	8,000	12,000	16,000	20,000
ES2 (490cc single)	1,500	3,000	4,500	6,000	9,000	12,000
Manx 30M (498cc single)	5,200	7,800	12,000	16,000	25,000	35,000
Model 19R (596cc single)	1,500	2,500	4,000	5,500	7,000	8,500
Model 19S (596cc single)	1,500	2,500	4,000	5,500	7,000	8,500
Big 4 (597cc single)	1,500	2,500	4,000	5,500	7,000	8,500
1949						
Manx 40M (348cc single)	5,000	10,000	15,000	20,000	25,000	30,000
Model 40 International (348cc single)	2,600	3,900	5,900	7,800	10,000	13,000
Model 50 (348cc single)	1,500	2,300	3,400	4,500	6,000	7,500
ES2 (490cc single)	1,500	3,000	4,500	6,000	9,000	12,000
Model 16H (490cc single)	1,500	2,500	4,000	5,500	7,000	8,500
Model 18 (490cc single)	−1,500	2,500	4,000	5,500	7,000	8,500
Model 30 International (490cc single)	3,000	4,500	8,000	12,000	16,000	20,000
Model 500T (490cc single)	1,500	2,300	4,000	6,000	8,000	10,000
Dominator Model 7 (497cc twin)	1,500	3,000	4,500	6,000	9,000	12,000
Manx 30M (498cc single)	5,200	7,800	12,000	16,000	25,000	35,000
Model 19R (596cc single)	1,500	3,000	4,500	6,000	7,500	9,000
Model 19S (596cc single)	1,500	3,000	4,500	6,000	7,500	9,000
Big 4 (597cc single)	1,500	3,000	4,500	6,000	7,500	9,000
1950						
Manx 40M (348cc single)	5,000	10,000	15,000	20,000	25,000	30,000
Model 40 International (348cc single)	2,600	3,900	5,900	7,800	10,000	13,000
Model 50 (348cc single)	1,500	2,300	3,400	4,500	6,000	7,500
ES2 (490cc single)	1,500	3,000	4,500	6,000	9,000	12,000
Model 16H (490cc single)	1,500	2,500	4,000	5,500	7,000	8,500
Model 18 (490cc single)	−1,500	2,500	4,000	5,500	7,000	8,500
Model 30 International (490cc single)	3,000	4,500	8,000	12,000	16,000	20,000
Model 500T (490cc single)	1,500	2,300	4,000	6,000	8,000	10,000
Dominator Model 7 (497cc twin)	1,500	3,000	4,500	6,000	9,000	12,000
Manx 30M (498cc single)	5,200	7,800	12,000	16,000	25,000	35,000
Model 19R (596cc single)	1,500	3,000	4,500	6,000	7,500	9,000
Model 19S (596cc single)	1,500	3,000	4,500	6,000	7,500	9,000
Big 4 (597cc single)	1,500	3,000	4,500	6,000	7,500	9,000
1951						
Manx 40M (348cc single)	5,000	10,000	15,000	20,000	25,000	30,000
Model 40 International (348cc single)	2,600	3,900	5,900	7,800	11,000	13,000
Model 50 (348cc single)	1,500	2,300	3,400	4,500	6,000	7,500
ES2 (490cc single)	1,500	3,000	4,500	6,000	9,000	12,000
Model 16H (490cc single)	1,500	2,500	4,000	5,500	7,000	8,500
Model 18 (490cc single)	−1,500	2,500	4,000	5,500	7,000	8,500
Model 30 International (490cc single)	3,000	5,000	7,000	10,000	15,000	20,000
Model 500T (490cc single)	1,500	2,300	4,000	6,000	8,000	10,000
Dominator Model 7 (497cc twin)	1,500	3,000	4,500	6,000	9,000	12,000
Manx 30M (498cc single)	5,200	7,800	12,000	16,000	25,000	35,000
Model 19R (596cc single)	1,500	3,000	4,500	6,000	7,500	9,000
Model 19S (596cc single)	1,500	3,000	4,500	6,000	7,500	9,000
Big 4 (597cc single)	1,500	3,000	4,500	6,000	7,500	9,000
1952						
Manx 40M (348cc single)	5,000	10,000	15,000	20,000	25,000	30,000
Model 40 International (348cc single)	2,600	3,900	5,900	7,800	10,000	13,000
Model 50 (348cc single)	1,500	2,300	3,400	4,500	6,000	7,500
ES2 (490cc single)	1,500	3,000	4,500	6,000	9,000	12,000
Model 16H (490cc single)	1,500	2,500	4,000	5,500	7,000	8,500
Model 18 (490cc single)	−1,500	2,500	4,000	5,500	7,000	8,500
Model 30 International (490cc single)	3,000	5,000	7,000	10,000	15,000	20,000
Model 500T (490cc single)	1,500	2,300	4,000	6,000	8,000	10,000
Dominator Model 7 (497cc twin)	1,500	3,000	4,500	6,000	9,000	12,000

	6	5	4	3	2	1
Dominator Model 88 (497cc twin)	1,500	3,000	4,500	6,000	9,000	12,000
Manx 30M (498cc single)	5,400	8,100	12,000	16,000	25,000	35,000
Model 19R (596cc single)	1,500	3,000	4,500	6,000	7,500	9,000
Model 19S (596cc single)	1,500	3,000	4,500	6,000	7,500	9,000
Big 4 (597cc single)	1,500	3,000	4,500	6,000	7,500	9,000
1953						
Manx 40M (348cc single)	5,000	10,000	15,000	20,000	25,000	30,000
Model 40 International (348cc single)	2,600	3,900	5,900	7,800	10,000	13,000
Model 50 (348cc single)	**1,500**	**2,300**	**3,400**	**4,500**	**6,000**	**7,500**
ES2 (490cc single)	1,500	3,000	4,500	6,000	9,000	12,000
Model 16H (490cc single)	1,500	2,500	4,000	5,500	7,000	8,500
Model 18 (490cc single)	−1,500	2,500	4,000	5,500	7,000	8,500
Model 30 International (490cc single)	3,000	5,000	7,000	10,000	15,000	20,000
Model 500T (490cc single)	1,500	2,300	4,000	6,000	8,000	10,000
Dominator Model 7 (497cc twin)	1,500	3,000	4,500	6,000	9,000	12,000
Dominator Model 88 (497cc twin)	1,500	3,000	4,500	6,000	9,000	12,000
Manx 30M (498cc single)	5,400	8,100	12,000	16,000	25,000	35,000
Model 19R (596cc single)	1,500	3,000	4,500	6,000	7,500	9,000
Model 19S (596cc single)	1,500	3,000	4,500	6,000	7,500	9,000
Big 4 (597cc single)	1,500	3,000	4,500	6,000	7,500	9,000
1954						
Manx 40M (348cc single)	5,000	10,000	15,000	20,000	25,000	30,000
Model 40 International (348cc single)	2,600	3,900	5,900	7,800	10,000	13,000
Model 50 (348cc single)	**1,500**	**2,300**	**3,400**	**4,500**	**6,000**	**7,500**
ES2 (490cc single)	1,500	3,000	4,500	6,000	9,000	12,000
Model 16H (490cc single)	1,500	2,500	4,000	5,500	7,000	8,500
Model 18 (490cc single)	−1,500	2,500	4,000	5,500	7,000	8,500
Model 30 International (490cc single)	3,000	5,000	7,000	10,000	15,000	20,000
Model 500T (490cc single)	1,500	2,300	4,000	6,000	8,000	10,000
Dominator Model 7 (497cc twin)	1,500	3,000	4,500	6,000	9,000	12,000
Dominator Model 88 (497cc twin)	1,500	3,000	4,500	6,000	9,000	12,000
Manx 30M (498cc single)	6,200	9,300	14,000	19,000	25,000	35,000
Model 19R (596cc single)	1,500	3,000	4,500	6,000	7,500	9,000
Model 19S (596cc single)	1,500	3,000	4,500	6,000	7,500	9,000
Big 4 (597cc single)	1,500	3,000	4,500	6,000	7,500	9,000
1955						
Manx 40M (348cc single)	5,000	10,000	15,000	20,000	25,000	30,000
Model 40 International (348cc single)	2,600	3,900	5,900	7,800	10,000	13,000
Model 50 (348cc single)	**1,500**	**2,300**	**3,400**	**4,500**	**6,000**	**7,500**
ES2 (490cc single)	1,500	3,000	4,500	6,000	9,000	12,000
Model 30 International (490cc single)	3,000	5,000	7,000	10,000	15,000	20,000
Dominator Model 7 (497cc twin)	1,500	3,000	4,500	6,000	9,000	12,000
Dominator Model 88 (497cc twin)	1,500	3,000	4,500	6,000	9,000	12,000
Manx 30M (498cc single)	6,200	9,300	15,000	22,000	26,000	35,000
Model 19R (596cc single)	1,500	3,000	4,500	6,000	7,500	9,000
Model 19S (596cc single)	1,500	3,000	4,500	6,000	7,500	9,000
1956						
Manx 40M (348cc single)	5,000	10,000	15,000	20,000	25,000	30,000
Model 40 International (348cc single)	2,600	3,900	5,900	7,800	10,000	13,000
Model 50 (348cc single)	**1,500**	**2,300**	**3,400**	**4,500**	**6,000**	**7,500**
ES2 (490cc single)	1,500	3,000	4,500	6,000	7,500	9,000
Model 30 International (490cc single)	3,000	5,000	7,000	10,000	15,000	20,000
Dominator Model 88 (497cc twin)	1,500	3,000	4,500	6,000	9,000	12,000
Manx 30M (498cc single)	6,200	9,300	14,000	19,000	25,000	35,000
Model 19S (596cc single)	1,500	3,000	4,500	6,000	7,500	9,000
Dominator Model 99 (596cc twin)	1,500	3,000	4,500	6,000	9,000	12,000
1957						
Manx 40M (348cc single)	5,000	10,000	15,000	20,000	25,000	30,000
Model 40 International (348cc single)	2,600	3,900	5,900	7,800	10,000	13,000
Model 50 (348cc single)	**1,500**	**2,300**	**3,400**	**4,500**	**6,000**	**7,500**

	6	5	4	3	2	1
ES2 (490cc single)	1,500	3,000	4,500	6,000	9,000	12,000
Model 30 International (490cc single)	3,000	5,000	7,000	10,000	15,000	20,000
Dominator Model 88 (497cc twin)	1,500	3,000	4,500	6,000	9,000	12,000
Manx 30M (498cc single)	6,200	9,300	14,000	19,000	25,000	35,000
Dominator Model 77 (596cc twin)	1,500	3,000	4,500	6,000	9,000	12,000
Dominator Model 99 (596cc twin)	1,500	3,000	4,500	6,000	9,000	12,000
Model 19S (596cc single)	1,500	3,000	4,500	6,000	7,500	9,000
1958						
Manx 40M (348cc single)	5,000	10,000	15,000	20,000	25,000	30,000
Model 50 (348cc single).	**1,500**	**2,300**	**3,400**	**4,500**	**6,000**	**7,500**
ES2 (490cc single)	**1,500**	**2,500**	**4,000**	**5,500**	**7,000**	**8,500**
Dominator Model 88 (497cc twin)	1,500	3,000	4,500	6,000	9,000	12,000
Manx 30M (498cc single)	6,300	9,500	14,000	19,000	25,000	35,000
Dominator Model 77 (596cc twin)	1,500	3,000	4,500	6,000	9,000	12,000
Dominator Model 99 (596cc twin)	1,500	3,000	4,500	6,000	9,000	12,000
Model 19S (596cc single)	1,500	3,000	4,500	6,000	7,500	9,000
Nomad (596cc twin).	**2,000**	**4,000**	**7,000**	**10,000**	**13,000**	**16,000**
1959						
Jubilee Deluxe (249cc twin)	1,000	1,500	**2,500**	**4,000**	**5,500**	**7,000**
Manx 40M (348cc single)	5,000	10,000	15,000	20,000	25,000	30,000
Model 50 (348cc single).	**1,500**	**2,300**	**3,400**	**4,500**	**6,000**	**7,500**
ES2 (490cc single)	1,500	3,000	4,500	6,000	7,500	9,000
Dominator Model 88 (497cc twin)	1,500	3,000	4,500	6,000	9,000	12,000
Manx 30M (498cc single)	6,300	9,500	14,000	19,000	25,000	35,000
Dominator Model 99 (596cc twin)	1,500	3,000	4,500	6,000	9,000	12,000
Nomad (596cc twin).	**2,000**	**4,000**	**7,000**	**10,000**	**13,000**	**16,000**
1960						
Jubilee Deluxe (249cc twin)	1,000	1,500	**2,500**	**4,000**	**5,500**	**7,000**
Manx 40M (348cc single)	5,000	10,000	15,000	20,000	25,000	30,000
Model 50 (348cc single).	**1,500**	**2,300**	**3,400**	**4,500**	**6,000**	**7,500**
ES2 (490cc single)	1,500	3,000	4,500	6,000	7,500	9,000
Dominator Model 88 (497cc twin)	1,500	3,000	4,500	6,000	9,000	12,000
Dominator Model 88 Deluxe (497cc twin) . .	1,500	3,000	4,500	6,000	9,000	12,000
Manx 30M (498cc single)	6,300	9,500	14,000	19,000	25,000	35,000
Dominator Model 99 (596cc twin)	1,500	3,000	4,500	6,000	9,000	12,000
Dominator Model 99 Deluxe (596cc twin) . .	1,500	3,000	4,500	6,000	9,000	12,000
Nomad (596cc twin).	**2,000**	**4,000**	**7,000**	**10,000**	**13,000**	**16,000**
Manxman (646cc twin)	1,800	3,000	4,500	6,000	8,500	11,000
1961						
Jubilee Deluxe (249cc twin)	1,000	1,500	**2,500**	**4,000**	**5,500**	**7,000**
Jubilee Standard (249cc twin).	1,000	1,500	**2,500**	**4,000**	**5,500**	**7,000**
Manx 40M (348cc single)	5,000	10,000	15,000	20,000	25,000	30,000
Model 50 (348cc single).	**1,500**	**2,300**	**3,400**	**4,500**	**6,000**	**7,500**
Navigator (349cc twin)	1,000	1,500	**2,500**	**4,000**	**5,500**	**7,000**
Navigator Deluxe (349cc twin)	1,000	1,500	**2,500**	**4,000**	**5,500**	**7,000**
ES2 (490cc single)	1,600	3,000	4,500	6,000	7,500	9,000
Dominator Model 88 (497cc twin)	1,500	3,000	4,500	6,000	9,000	12,000
Dominator Model 88 Deluxe (497cc twin) . .	1,500	3,000	4,500	6,000	9,000	12,000
Dominator Model 88SS (497cc twin)	1,500	3,000	4,500	6,000	9,000	12,000
Manx 30M (498cc single)	6,400	9,600	14,000	19,000	26,000	35,000
Dominator Model 99 (596cc twin)	1,500	3,000	4,500	6,000	9,000	12,000
Dominator Model 99 Deluxe (596cc twin) . .	1,500	3,000	4,500	6,000	9,000	12,000
Dominator Model 99SS (596cc twin)	1,500	3,000	4,500	6,000	9,000	12,000
Manxman (646cc twin)	1,800	3,000	4,500	6,000	8,500	11,000
1962						
Jubilee Deluxe (249cc twin)	1,000	1,500	**2,500**	**4,000**	**5,500**	**7,000**
Jubilee Standard (249cc twin)	1,000	1,500	**2,500**	**4,000**	**5,500**	**7,000**
Manx 40M (348cc single) (691 from 1946-63)	5,000	10,000	15,000	20,000	25,000	30,000
Model 50 (348cc single).	**1,500**	**2,300**	**3,400**	**4,500**	**6,000**	**7,500**
Navigator (349cc twin)	1,000	1,500	**2,500**	**4,000**	**5,500**	**7,000**

	6	5	4	3	2	1
Navigator Deluxe (349cc twin)	1,000	1,500	**2,500**	**4,000**	5,500	7,000
ES2 (490cc single)	1,600	3,000	4,000	6,000	8,000	10,000
Dominator Model 88 (497cc twin)	1,500	3,000	4,500	6,000	9,000	12,000
Dominator Model 88 Deluxe (497cc twin) . .	1,500	3,000	4,500	6,000	9,000	12,000
Dominator Model 88SS (497cc twin)	1,500	3,000	4,500	6,000	9,000	12,000
Manx 30M (498cc single)	6,800	10,000	15,000	20,000	27,000	35,000
Dominator Model 99 (596cc twin)	1,500	3,000	4,500	6,000	9,000	12,000
Dominator Model 99 Deluxe (596cc twin) . .	1,500	3,000	4,500	6,000	9,000	12,000
Dominator Model 99SS (596cc twin)	1,500	3,000	4,500	6,000	9,000	12,000
Model 650SS (646cc twin)	1,800	3,000	4,500	6,000	8,500	11,000
Atlas (745cc twin)	−1,500	**3,000**	**4,500**	6,000	**9,000**	**12,000**
1963						
Jubilee Deluxe (249cc twin)	1,000	1,500	**2,500**	**4,000**	5,500	7,000
Jubilee Standard (249cc twin)	1,000	1,500	**2,500**	**4,000**	5,500	7,000
Manx 40M (348cc single)	5,000	10,000	15,000	20,000	25,000	30,000
Model 50 (348cc single)	**1,500**	**2,300**	**3,400**	**4,500**	**6,000**	**7,500**
Navigator (349cc twin)	1,000	1,500	**2,500**	**4,000**	5,500	7,000
Navigator Deluxe (349cc twin)	1,000	1,500	**2,500**	**4,000**	5,500	7,000
Electra (400cc twin)	1,000	1,500	**2,500**	**4,000**	5,500	7,000
ES2 (490cc single)	−1,500	**3,000**	**4,500**	**6,000**	7,500	9,000
Dominator Model 88 (497cc twin)	1,500	3,000	4,500	6,000	9,000	12,000
Dominator Model 88SS (497cc twin)	1,500	3,000	4,500	6,000	9,000	12,000
Manx 30M (498cc single) (1202 from 1946-63)	6,800	10,000	15,000	20,000	27,000	35,000
Model 650SS (646cc twin)	1,400	2,100	4,000	6,000	8,000	10,000
Atlas (745cc twin)	−1,500	**3,000**	**4,500**	6,000	**9,000**	**12,000**
1964						
Jubilee Standard (249cc twin)	1,000	1,500	**2,500**	**4,000**	5,500	7,000
Model 50MK II (348cc single)	**1,500**	**2,300**	**3,400**	**4,500**	**6,000**	**7,500**
Navigator (349cc twin)	1,000	1,500	**2,500**	**4,000**	5,500	7,000
Electra (400cc twin)	1,000	1,500	**2,500**	**4,000**	5,500	7,000
Dominator Model 88SS (497cc twin)	1,500	3,000	4,500	6,000	9,000	12,000
Model 650SS (646cc twin)	1,400	2,100	4,000	6,000	8,000	10,000
Atlas (745cc twin)	**1,500**	**3,000**	**4,500**	**6,000**	**9,000**	**12,000**
Atlas Scrambler (750cc twin)	−1,500	**3,000**	**4,500**	6,000	**9,000**	**12,000**
N15CS (750cc twin)	−1,500	**3,000**	**4,500**	6,000	**9,000**	**12,000**
1965						
Jubilee Standard (249cc twin)	1,000	1,500	**2,500**	**4,000**	5,500	7,000
Model 50MK II (348cc single)	**1,500**	**2,300**	**3,400**	**4,500**	**6,000**	**7,500**
Navigator (349cc twin)	1,000	1,500	**2,500**	**4,000**	5,500	7,000
Electra (400cc twin)	1,000	1,500	**2,500**	**4,000**	5,500	7,000
ES2 MK II (490cc single)	1,300	2,000	3,500	5,000	6,500	8,000
Dominator Model 88SS (497cc twin)	1,500	3,000	4,500	6,000	9,000	12,000
Model 650SS (646cc twin)	1,400	2,100	4,000	6,000	8,000	10,000
Atlas (745cc twin)	−1,500	**3,000**	**4,500**	6,000	**9,000**	**12,000**
NC15S (750cc twin)	−1,500	**3,000**	**4,500**	6,000	**9,000**	**12,000**
1966						
Jubilee Standard (249cc twin)	1,000	1,500	**2,500**	**4,000**	5,500	7,000
Model 50MK II (348cc single)	**1,500**	**2,300**	**3,400**	**4,500**	**6,000**	**7,500**
ES2 MK II (490cc single)	−1,000	**2,500**	**4,000**	5,500	7,000	8,500
Dominator Model 88SS (497cc twin)	1,700	3,000	5,000	7,000	9,000	11,000
Model 650SS (646cc twin)	1,400	2,100	4,000	6,000	8,000	10,000
Atlas (745cc twin)	−1,500	**3,000**	**4,500**	6,000	**9,000**	**12,000**
NC15S (750cc twin)	−1,500	**3,000**	**4,500**	6,000	**9,000**	**12,000**
1967						
Model 650SS (646cc twin)	1,400	2,100	4,000	6,000	8,000	10,000
Atlas (745cc twin)	−1,500	**3,000**	**4,500**	6,000	**9,000**	**12,000**
Commando (745cc twin)	**1,500**	**2,500**	**4,000**	7,000	10,000	13,000
NC15S (750cc twin)	−1,500	**3,000**	**4,500**	6,000	**9,000**	**12,000**

	6	5	4	3	2	1
P11 (750cc twin)	1,500	3,000	6,000	9,000	12,000	15,000
1968						
Model 650SS (646cc twin)	1,400	2,100	4,000	6,000	8,000	10,000
Atlas (745cc twin)	−1,500	3,000	4,500	6,000	9,000	12,000
Commando (745cc twin)	1,500	2,500	4,000	7,000	10,000	13,000
P11 (750cc twin)	1,500	3,000	6,000	9,000	12,000	15,000
1969						
Commando 750R (745cc twin)	1,500	3,000	6,000	10,000	14,000	18,000
Commando 750S (745cc twin)	1,500	2,500	5,000	8,000	11,000	14,000
Commando Fastback (745cc twin)	1,500	2,500	5,000	8,000	11,000	14,000
Mercury (750cc twin)	−1,500	−2,500	4,000	6,000	9,000	12,000
Ranger (750cc twin).	1,500	3,000	6,000	9,000	12,000	15,000
1970						
Commando 750 Roadster (745cc twin) . . .	1,600	2,800	4,000	7,000	10,000	13,000
Commando 750S (745cc twin)	1,500	2,500	5,000	8,000	11,000	14,000
Commando 750SS (745cc twin).	−1,500	−2,500	5,000	8,000	11,000	14,000
Commando Fastback (745cc twin)	1,500	2,500	5,000	8,000	11,000	14,000
Mercury (750cc twin)	−1,500	−2,500	4,000	6,000	9,000	12,000
1971						
Commando 750 Production Racer (745cc twin)	2,800	−4,000	7,000	10,000	13,000	16,000
Commando 750 Roadster (745cc twin) . . .	−1,600	−2,800	−4,000	−7,000	−10,000	13,000
Commando 750S (745cc twin)	−1,500	−2,500	5,000	8,000	11,000	14,000
Commando 750SS (745cc twin)	1,500	2,500	5,000	8,000	11,000	14,000
Commando Fastback (745cc twin)	−1,500	−2,500	5,000	8,000	11,000	14,000
Commando Fastback LR (745cc twin) . . .	1,500	2,500	5,000	8,000	11,000	14,000
Commando Hi-Rider (745cc twin)	1,600	2,800	4,000	7,000	10,000	13,000
1972						
Commando Hi-Rider (745cc twin)	−1,500	−2,500	−5,000	−8,000	−11,000	−14,000
Commando 750 Interstate Combat (745cc twin)	2,600	3,900	5,900	7,800	11,000	13,000
Commando 750 Production Racer (745cc twin)	2,800	−4,000	7,000	10,000	13,000	16,000
Commando 750 Roadster (745cc twin) . . .	−1,600	−2,800	−4,000	7,000	10,000	13,000
Commando Fastback (745cc twin)	1,500	2,500	5,000	8,000	11,000	14,000
Commando Fastback LR (745cc twin) . . .	1,500	2,500	5,000	8,000	11,000	14,000
1973						
Commando Hi-Rider (745cc twin)	−1,500	−2,500	−5,000	−8,000	−11,000	−14,000
Commando 750 Interstate (745cc twin) . . .	2,600	3,900	5,900	7,800	11,000	13,000
Commando 750 Production Racer (745cc twin)	2,800	−4,000	7,000	10,000	13,000	16,000
Commando 750 Roadster (745cc twin) . . .	1,600	2,800	4,000	7,000	10,000	13,000
Commando Fastback (745cc twin)	1,500	2,500	5,000	8,000	11,000	14,000
Commando 850 Hi-Rider (828cc twin) . . .	−1,500	−2,500	5,000	8,000	11,000	14,000
Commando 850 Interstate (828cc twin) . . .	1,500	2,500	5,000	8,000	11,000	14,000
Commando 850 Roadster (828cc twin) . . .	−1,500	−2,500	−5,000	8,000	11,000	14,000
1974						
Commando 850 Hi-Rider (828cc twin) . . .	−1,500	−2,500	−5,000	−8,000	−11,000	−14,000
Commando 850 Interstate (828cc twin) . . .	1,500	2,500	5,000	8,000	11,000	14,000
Commando 850 John Player (828cc twin). .	−1,500	−2,500	−5,000	−8,000	−11,000	−14,000
Commando 850 Roadster (828cc twin) . . .	−1,500	−2,500	−5,000	8,000	11,000	14,000
1975						
Commando 850 Hi-Rider (828cc twin) . . .	2,400	3,600	6,000	9,000	12,000	15,000
Commando 850 Interstate (828cc twin) . . .	2,400	−3,600	−6,000	9,000	12,000	15,000
Commando 850 John Player (828cc twin). .	3,400	5,100	7,700	10,000	14,000	17,000
Commando MK III (828cc twin)	2,400	−3,600	6,000	9,000	12,000	15,000
Commando 850 Roadster (828cc twin) . . .	2,400	−3,600	6,000	9,000	12,000	15,000
1976						
Commando 850 Roadster (828cc twin) . . .	2,400	−3,600	6,000	9,000	12,000	15,000

	6	5	4	3	2	1
Commando MK III (828cc twin)	2,400	–3,600	6,000	9,000	12,000	15,000
1977						
Commando 850 Roadster (828cc twin) . . .	**2,400**	**–3,600**	**6,000**	**9,000**	**12,000**	**15,000**
Commando MK III (828cc twin)	**2,400**	**–3,600**	**6,000**	**9,000**	**12,000**	**15,000**

OSSA

	6	5	4	3	2	1
1966						
Turismo 160.	600	900	2,700	5,000	7,400	10,000
1967						
Sport 175	600	900	2,700	4,600	6,900	9,200
Pioneer 230	500	800	2,300	4,300	6,400	8,500
Stiletto 230	700	1,200	3,100	5,400	8,000	10,600
Wildfire 230	800	1,300	3,400	6,100	9,000	12,000
1968						
Pioneer 230	500	800	2,300	4,300	6,400	8,500
Plonker 230	700	1,100	3,200	5,700	8,500	11,200
Stiletto 230	600	1,000	2,800	4,700	6,900	9,100
Wildfire 230	800	1,300	3,400	6,100	9,000	12,000
1969						
Sport 175	500	800	2,200	4,700	6,900	9,100
Stiletto 175	500	800	2,700	5,000	7,400	9,800
Pioneer 230	600	1,000	2,800	5,000	7,400	9,800
Plonker 230	900	1,400	3,700	6,400	9,600	13,000
Pioneer 250	700	1,000	2,800	5,000	7,400	9,800
Plonker 250	800	1,300	3,600	6,400	9,600	13,000
Stiletto 250	700	1,200	3,200	5,700	8,400	12,000
Wildfire 250	400	600	3,300	6,300	9,300	12,300
1970						
Pioneer 175	400	600	1,300	2,500	3,700	4,900
Stiletto 175	500	700	1,600	2,900	4,200	5,500
Dick Mann Replica 250	2,000	4,000	6,100	8,700	13,700	19,000
Pioneer 250	400	600	1,600	3,000	4,500	6,000
Plonker 250	1,000	1,500	3,800	6,400	9,600	13,000
Stiletto 250	900	1,400	3,400	5,700	8,500	11,300
Wildfire 250	1,100	1,600	3,800	6,500	9,700	13,000
1971						
Stiletto 125	1,300	1,800	4,300	7,200	10,600	14,000
Pioneer 175	500	700	1,400	2,500	3,800	5,100
Stiletto 175	500	700	1,600	2,900	4,200	5,500
Dick Mann Replica 250	1,500	2,500	5,300	8,700	12,700	17,000
Pioneer 250	500	800	1,700	3,100	4,700	6,300
Stiletto 250 MX	900	1,400	3,300	5,700	8,500	11,300
Stiletto 250 TT.	1,000	1,500	3,600	6,100	9,000	12,000
Wildfire 250	1,100	1,600	4,000	6,800	10,100	13,500
1972						
Pioneer 175	400	600	1,300	2,400	3,600	4,800
Stiletto 175	500	700	1,600	2,900	4,200	5,500
Mick Andrews Replica 250	500	700	1,600	2,900	4,200	5,500
Pioneer 250	500	800	1,700	3,000	4,500	6,000
Stiletto 250 MX	900	1,400	3,300	5,700	8,500	11,300
Stiletto 250 TT.	1,200	1,700	3,700	6,100	9,000	12,000
1973						
Pioneer 175	400	700	1,400	2,500	3,700	4,900
Six Days Replica 175	500	800	1,900	3,400	5,100	6,800
Stiletto 175	400	700	1,600	2,900	4,200	5,500
Explorer 250.	400	700	1,500	2,700	4,000	5,300
Mick Andrews Replica 250	400	700	1,600	2,900	4,200	5,500
Pioneer 250	500	800	1,700	3,000	4,500	6,000
Six Days Replica 250	500	800	1,700	3,200	4,500	5,800
Stiletto 250 MX	1,100	1,700	3,700	6,100	9,000	12,000
Stiletto 250 TT.	1,200	1,800	3,900	6,400	9,600	13,000

	6	5	4	3	2	1
1974						
Phantom 125	1,500	2,500	4,100	6,100	9,000	12,000
Phantom 175	700	1,000	2,400	4,300	6,400	8,500
Six Days Replica 175	500	800	1,900	3,400	5,100	6,800
Explorer 250	400	600	1,300	2,700	4,000	5,300
Mick Andrews Replica 250	500	800	1,700	3,100	4,700	6,300
Phantom 250	1,000	1,500	3,600	6,100	9,000	12,000
Pioneer 250	500	800	1,700	3,000	4,500	6,000
Six Days Replica 250	400	600	1,700	3,000	4,500	6,000
Stiletto 250 MX	1,100	1,700	3,500	5,700	8,500	11,300
Stiletto 250 TT	1,200	1,800	4,700	6,100	9,000	12,000
1975						
Phantom 125	1,500	2,500	4,100	6,100	9,000	12,000
Phantom 175	700	1,100	2,500	4,300	6,400	8,500
Desert Phantom 250	600	900	2,200	3,900	5,900	7,900
Explorer 250	400	600	1,400	2,700	4,000	5,300
Phantom 250	900	1,500	3,600	6,100	9,000	12,000
Phantom GP1 250	900	1,400	3,200	5,400	8,000	10,600
Plonker/Mick Andrews Replica 250	500	800	1,800	3,200	4,700	6,200
Super Pioneer 250	400	700	1,600	3,000	4,500	6,000
1976						
Super Pioneer 175	400	600	1,300	2,500	3,800	5,100
Desert Phantom 250	900	1,500	2,600	4,200	6,200	8,200
Explorer 250	400	600	1,400	2,700	4,000	5,300
Phantom GP2 250	1,500	2,100	4,200	6,800	10,100	13,400
Super Pioneer 250	500	800	1,800	3,200	4,700	6,200
BLT/Mick Andrews Repica 350	1,800	2,800	5,500	8,700	12,700	17,000
Mick Andrews Replica 350	1,800	2,800	5,500	8,700	12,700	17,000
Mountaineer 350	600	900	2,000	3,600	5,300	7,000
Plonker 350	600	900	1,900	3,400	5,100	5,800
Yankee SS 500	3,000	5,500	10,400	15,900	23,300	31,000
1977						
Desert Phantom 250	800	1,300	2,500	4,200	6,200	8,200
Phantom GP3 250	1,500	2,300	4,900	7,900	11,700	15,500
Short Track STI 250	2,000	3,500	5,800	8,700	12,700	17,000
Super Pioneer 250	700	1,000	1,900	3,300	4,900	6,500
BLT/Mick Andrews Repica 350	1,500	2,500	5,300	8,700	12,700	17,000
Mick Andrews Replica 350	600	900	1,900	3,400	5,100	6,800
Mountaineer 350	700	1,100	2,200	3,700	5,500	6,300
Mountaineer BLT 350	3,000	5,000	6,900	9,300	13,800	18,300
Yankee SS 500	2,000	3,500	9,400	15,900	23,300	31,000
1978						
Super Pioneer 250	600	900	1,800	3,200	4,700	6,200
Mick Andrews Replica 350	600	900	1,900	3,400	5,100	6,800
STI 250	2,000	3,500	5,700	8,300	12,200	16,100
Mountaineer 350	600	900	2,000	3,700	5,500	7,300
Mountaineer BLT 350	3,000	4,700	6,300	8,300	12,200	16,100
Six Days	1,500	2,500	4,900	7,900	11,700	15,500
1980						
TR-80 Orange 250	700	1,000	2,400	4,200	6,200	8,400
TR-80 Yellow Gripper 350	700	1,100	2,500	4,400	6,600	8,800
1981						
TR-80 Orange 250	700	1,000	2,400	4,200	6,200	8,400
TR-80 Yellow Gripper 350	700	1,100	2,500	4,400	6,600	8,800
1982						
TR-80 Orange 250	700	1,100	2,500	4,400	6,600	8,800
TR-80 Yellow Gripper 350	700	1,000	2,400	4,200	6,200	8,400
1983						
TR-80 Orange 250	700	1,100	2,500	4,400	6,600	8,800
TR-80 Yellow Gripper 350	700	1,000	2,400	4,200	6,200	8,400

	6	5	4	3	2	1
PANTHER						
1935						
250 (250cc single).	2,000	4,000	8,000	10,000	13,000	16,000
1937						
Model 20 (250cc single).	1,600	2,400	4,000	6,000	7,500	9,000
Model 100 (600cc single)	1,600	2,400	4,000	6,000	8,000	10,000
1939						
Model 100 (600cc single)	1,600	2,400	4,000	6,000	8,000	10,000
1946						
Model 100 (600cc single)	1,600	2,400	4,000	6,000	**8,000**	**10,000**
1947						
Model 65 (250cc single).	800	1,200	1,800	2,400	3,200	4,000
Model 75 (350cc single).	900	1,400	2,000	2,700	3,600	4,500
Model 100 (600cc single)	1,600	2,400	4,000	6,000	**8,000**	**10,000**
1948						
Model 65 (250cc single).	800	1,200	1,800	2,400	3,200	4,000
Model 75 (350cc single).	900	1,400	2,000	2,700	3,600	4,500
Model 100 (600cc single)	1,600	2,400	4,000	6,000	**8,000**	**10,000**
1949						
Model 65 (250cc single).	800	1,200	1,800	2,400	3,200	4,000
Model 75 (350cc single).	900	1,400	2,000	2,700	3,600	4,500
Model 100 (600cc single)	1,600	2,400	4,000	6,000	**8,000**	**10,000**
1950						
Model 65 (250cc single).	800	1,200	1,800	2,400	3,200	4,000
Model 75 (350cc single).	900	1,400	2,000	2,700	3,600	4,500
Model 100 (600cc single)	1,600	2,400	4,000	6,000	**8,000**	**10,000**
1951						
Model 65 (250cc single).	800	1,200	1,800	2,400	3,200	4,000
Model 75 (350cc single).	900	1,400	2,000	2,700	3,600	4,500
Model 100 (600cc single)	1,600	2,400	4,000	6,000	**8,000**	**10,000**
1952						
Model 65 (250cc single).	800	1,200	1,800	2,400	3,200	4,000
Model 75 (350cc single).	900	1,400	2,000	2,700	3,600	4,500
Model 100 (600cc single)	1,600	2,400	4,000	6,000	**8,000**	**10,000**
1953						
Model 65 (250cc single).	800	1,200	1,800	2,400	3,200	4,000
Model 75 (350cc single).	900	1,400	2,000	2,700	3,600	4,500
Model 100 (600cc single)	1,600	2,400	4,000	6,000	**8,000**	**10,000**
1954						
Model 65 (250cc single).	800	1,200	1,800	2,400	3,200	4,000
Model 75 (350cc single).	900	1,400	2,000	2,700	3,600	4,500
Model 100 (600cc single)	1,600	2,400	4,000	6,000	**8,000**	**10,000**
1955						
Model 65 (250cc single).	800	1,200	1,800	2,400	3,200	4,000
Model 75 (350cc single).	900	1,400	2,000	2,700	3,600	4,500
Model 100 (600cc single)	1,600	2,400	4,000	6,000	**8,000**	**10,000**
1956						
Model 65 (250cc single).	800	1,200	1,800	2,400	3,200	4,000
Model 75 (350cc single).	900	1,400	2,000	2,700	3,600	4,500
Model 100 (600cc single)	1,600	2,400	4,000	6,000	**8,000**	**10,000**
1957						
Model 65 (250cc single).	800	1,200	1,800	2,400	3,200	4,000
Model 75 (350cc single).	900	1,400	2,000	2,700	3,600	4,500
Model 100 (600cc single)	1,600	2,400	4,000	6,000	**8,000**	**10,000**
1958						
Model 65 (250cc single).	800	1,200	1,800	2,400	3,200	4,000
Model 75 (350cc single).	900	1,400	2,000	2,700	3,600	4,500
Model 100 (600cc single)	1,600	2,400	4,000	6,000	**8,000**	**10,000**
1959						
Model 65 (250cc single).	800	1,200	1,800	2,400	3,200	4,000

	6	5	4	3	2	1
Model 75 (350cc single)	900	1,400	2,000	2,700	3,600	4,500
Model 100 (600cc single)	1,600	2,400	4,000	6,000	**8,000**	**10,000**
Model 120 (650cc single)	1,600	2,400	3,600	4,800	6,400	8,000
1960						
Model 65 (250cc single)	800	1,200	1,800	2,400	3,200	4,000
Model 75 (350cc single)	900	1,400	2,000	2,700	3,600	4,500
Model 100 (600cc single)	1,600	2,400	4,000	6,000	**8,000**	**10,000**
Model 120 (650cc single)	1,600	2,400	3,600	4,800	6,400	8,000
1961						
Model 65 (250cc single)	800	1,200	1,800	2,400	3,200	4,000
Model 75 (350cc single)	900	1,400	2,000	2,700	3,600	4,500
Model 100 (600cc single)	1,600	2,400	4,000	6,000	**8,000**	**10,000**
Model 120 (650cc single)	1,600	2,400	3,600	4,800	6,400	8,000
1962						
Model 65 (250cc single)	800	1,200	1,800	2,400	3,200	4,000
Model 75 (350cc single)	900	1,400	2,000	2,700	3,600	4,500
Model 100 (600cc single)	1,600	2,400	4,000	6,000	**8,000**	**10,000**
Model 120 (650cc single)	1,600	2,400	3,600	4,800	6,400	8,000
1963						
Model 100 (600cc single)	1,600	2,400	4,000	6,000	**8,000**	**10,000**
Model 120 (650cc single)	1,600	2,400	3,600	4,800	6,400	8,000
1964						
Model 120 (650cc single)	1,600	2,400	3,600	4,800	6,400	8,000
1965						
Model 120 (650cc single)	1,600	2,400	3,600	4,800	6,400	8,000

PENTON						
1968						
125 (125cc)	500	1,000	2,000	4,000	6,000	8,000
1969						
Berkshire (100cc)	1,000	2,000	3,000	4,000	5,000	6,000
Six Day (125cc)	1,000	2,000	3,000	4,000	5,000	6,000
1970						
Wassell Enduro (125cc)	400	800	1,600	2,400	3,200	4,000
café MX	600	1,000	1,600	2,200	3,700	5,250
Berkshire (100cc)	1,000	2,000	3,000	4,000	5,000	6,000
1971						
Six Day (125cc)	500	1,000	1,500	3,000	4,000	5,000
1972						
Berkshire (100cc)	200	400	600	1,400	2,600	3,800
Berkshire Enduro (100cc)	200	400	600	1,400	2,600	3,800
Six Day (125cc)	500	1,000	1,500	3,000	4,000	5,000
Six Day Enduro (125cc)	200	400	600	1,400	2,600	3,800
Jack Piner (175cc)	300	600	900	1,600	2,900	4,200
Jack Piner Enduro (175cc)	300	600	900	1,600	3,100	4,600
Mudlark (125cc)	1,000	2,000	3,000	4,000	5,000	6,000
1973						
Berkshire (100cc)	200	400	700	1,200	2,600	4,000
Berkshire Enduro (100cc)	200	400	700	1,300	2,800	4,300
Six Day (125cc)	500	1,000	1,500	3,000	4,000	5,000
Six Day Enduro (125cc)	500	1,000	1,500	3,000	4,000	5,000
Jack Piner (175cc)	300	500	800	1,600	2,900	4,200
Jack Piner Enduro (175cc)	300	500	800	1,600	3,100	4,600
Hare Scrambler (250cc)	300	500	800	1,600	3,100	4,600
Hare Scrambler Enduro (250cc)	300	500	900	1,600	3,300	5,000
Mudlark (125cc)	1,000	2,000	3,000	4,000	5,000	6,000
1974						
Berkshire (97cc)	200	400	700	1,200	2,600	4,000
Berkshire Enduro (97cc)	200	400	700	1,300	2,800	4,300
Six Day (122cc)	500	1,000	2,000	3,500	5,000	6,500
Six Day D (122cc)	500	1,000	2,000	3,500	5,000	6,500

	6	5	4	3	2	1
Jack Piner (171cc)	300	500	800	1,600	3,000	4,400
Jack Piner D (171cc)	300	500	900	1,700	3,100	4,700
Jack Piner SS (171cc)	300	500	900	1,700	3,100	4,700
Hare Scrambler (246cc)	500	1,000	2,000	3,500	5,000	6,500
Hare Scrambler D (246cc)	500	1,000	2,000	3,500	5,000	6,500
Mint (400cc)	400	600	900	1,900	3,800	5,700
Mint D (400cc)	400	600	900	2,000	4,000	6,000
1975						
Berkshire D (97cc)	200	400	700	1,300	2,800	4,300
Six Day (122cc)	300	500	800	1,200	3,000	4,800
Six Day D (122cc)	300	500	800	1,600	3,300	4,800
Jack Piner (171cc)	200	400	800	1,400	2,900	4,400
Jack Piner D (171cc)	200	400	800	1,500	3,100	4,700
Jack Piner SS (171cc)	200	400	800	1,600	3,300	5,000
Hare Scrambler (246cc)	200	400	800	1,500	3,100	4,700
Hare Scrambler D (246cc)	300	500	800	1,600	3,300	5,000
Mint (357cc)	300	500	800	1,900	3,900	5,900
Mint D (357cc)	400	600	900	2,000	4,000	6,000
1976						
Six Day (122cc)	300	500	800	1,200	3,000	4,800
Six Day D (122cc)	300	500	800	1,600	3,300	5,000
Jack Piner (171cc)	200	400	800	1,400	2,900	4,400
Jack Piner D (171cc)	200	400	800	1,500	3,100	4,700
Jack Piner SS (171cc)	200	400	800	1,600	3,300	5,000
Hare Scrambler (246cc)	200	400	800	1,500	3,100	4,700
Hare Scrambler D (246cc)	300	500	800	1,600	3,300	5,000
Mint (357cc)	300	500	800	1,900	3,900	5,900
Mint D (357cc)	400	600	900	2,000	4,000	6,000
1977						
GS6 (250cc)	300	500	800	1,600	3,300	5,000
POPE						
1911						
Single	2,500	5,000	10,000	15,000	20,000	25,000
1912						
Single	3,000	6,000	9,000	12,000	16,000	20,000
Twin	25,000	40,000	55,000	70,000	85,000	100K
1913						
Twin	25,000	40,000	55,000	70,000	85,000	100K
1915						
OHV V-Twin	25,000	40,000	55,000	70,000	85,000	100K
1916						
Twin	25,000	40,000	55,000	70,000	85,000	100K
1918						
18L	10,000	20,000	40,000	60,000	80,000	100K
RICKMAN						
1969						
Metisse	3,000	5,000	7,000	8,500	10,000	12,000
1972						
Rickman Hodaka 100	600	1,100	2,400	4,800	6,500	8,200
Rickman 125E	300	500	1,100	2,100	3,300	4,500
Rickman 125MX	300	500	1,900	3,200	4,400	5,600
Rickman 250MX	300	500	1,900	3,700	4,900	6,100
1973						
Rickman 125MX	300	500	1,400	2,700	3,800	4,900
Rickman 125SD	300	500	1,100	2,100	3,300	4,500
Rickman 250MX	300	500	1,900	3,700	4,900	6,100
1974						
Rickman 125MX	300	500	1,400	2,700	3,800	4,900
Rickman 125SD	300	500	1,100	2,100	3,300	4,500
Rickman 250MXVR	300	500	1,900	3,700	4,900	6,100

	6	5	4	3	2	1
Rickman CR Kawasaki 900	2,000	4,000	8,000	12,000	16,000	20,000
1975						
Rickman 125MX.	300	500	1,400	2,700	3,800	4,900
Rickman 125SD.	300	500	1,100	2,100	3,300	4,500
Rickman 250MXVR	300	500	1,900	3,700	4,900	6,100
Rickman CR Honda 750	2,000	4,000	8,000	12,000	16,000	20,000
1978						
Rickman 750 2A.	800	1,500	2,800	6,900	9,200	12,000
1979						
Rickman 1-1 Honda 750	800	1,500	2,900	6,400	8,200	10,500
Rickman CR Honda 750	800	1,500	2,800	6,900	9,300	12,000
Rickman 1-1 Kawasaki 1000	800	1,500	2,800	6,400	8,700	10,000
Rickman CR Kawasaki 1000	800	1,500	2,800	6,900	9,800	12,500
1980						
Rickman 1-1 Honda 750	800	1,500	2,900	6,400	8,200	10,500
Rickman CR Honda 750	800	1,500	2,800	6,900	9,300	12,000
Rickman 1-1 Kawasaki 1000	800	1,500	2,800	6,400	8,700	10,000
Rickman CR Kawasaki 1000	800	1,500	2,800	6,900	9,800	12,500
1981						
Rickman CRE Honda	800	1,500	2,800	6,900	8,700	10,500
Rickman CRE Kawasaki	800	1,500	2,800	6,900	9,300	12,000
1982						
Rickman CRE Honda	800	1,500	2,800	6,900	9,300	12,000
Rickman CRE Kawasaki	800	1,500	2,800	6,900	8,200	9,500
Rickman CRE Suzuki	800	1,500	2,800	5,300	7,600	10,000
Rickman CRE Honda	800	1,500	2,800	–6,400	–8,700	–10,000
Rickman CRE Kawasaki	800	1,500	2,800	–6,400	–7,600	–8,800
Rickman CRE Suzuki	800	1,500	2,800	**5,800**	**8,200**	**10,800**

ROYAL ENFIELD

	6	5	4	3	2	1
1910						
V-Twin (425cc twin)	4,000	8,000	16,000	24,000	32,000	40,000
1911						
Model 160.	3,000	6,000	12,000	18,000	24,000	30,000
V-Twin.	4,000	8,000	16,000	24,000	32,000	40,000
1912						
V-Twin.	4,000	8,000	16,000	24,000	32,000	40,000
1913						
V-Twin (600cc twin)	4,000	8,000	16,000	24,000	32,000	40,000
1914						
Single (225cc single)	2,000	4,000	8,000	12,000	16,000	20,000
V-Twin (425cc twin)	3,000	6,000	12,000	18,000	24,000	30,000
V-Twin (600cc twin)	4,000	8,000	16,000	24,000	32,000	40,000
1915						
Single (225cc single)	–2,000	–4,000	–8,000	–12,000	–16,000	–20,000
V-Twin (425cc twin)	4,000	8,000	16,000	24,000	32,000	40,000
Inline 3 Cylinder (675 cc triple)	10,000	20,000	40,000	60,000	80,000	100K
1916						
Single (225cc single)	–2,000	–4,000	–8,000	–12,000	–16,000	–20,000
V-Twin (425cc twin)	4,000	8,000	16,000	24,000	32,000	40,000
1917						
RE 2 Stroke	2,000	4,000	–6,000	–8,000	–10,000	–12,000
Single (225cc single)	–2,000	–4,000	–8,000	–12,000	–16,000	–20,000
V-Twin (425cc twin)	4,000	8,000	16,000	24,000	32,000	40,000
1918						
Single (225cc single)	–2,000	–4,000	–8,000	–12,000	–16,000	–20,000
V-Twin (425cc twin)	4,000	8,000	16,000	24,000	32,000	40,000
1919						
Single (225cc single)	–2,000	–4,000	–8,000	–12,000	–16,000	–20,000
V-Twin (425cc twin)	4,000	8,000	16,000	24,000	32,000	40,000

	6	5	4	3	2	1
1920						
Single (225cc single)	–2,000	–4,000	–8,000	–12,000	–16,000	–20,000
V-Twin (976cc twin)	4,000	8,000	16,000	24,000	32,000	40,000
1921						
Single (225cc single)	–1,500	–3,000	–6,000	–9,000	–12,000	–15,000
V-Twin (976cc twin)	4,000	8,000	16,000	24,000	32,000	40,000
1922						
Single (225cc single)	–1,500	–3,000	–6,000	–9,000	–12,000	–15,000
V-Twin (976cc twin)	4,000	8,000	16,000	24,000	32,000	40,000
1923						
Single (225cc single)	–1,500	–3,000	–6,000	–9,000	–12,000	–15,000
V-Twin (976cc twin)	4,000	8,000	16,000	24,000	32,000	40,000
1924						
Single (225cc single)	–1,500	–3,000	–6,000	–9,000	–12,000	–15,000
Single (350cc single)	–1,500	–3,000	–6,000	–9,000	–12,000	–15,000
V-Twin (976cc twin)	4,000	8,000	16,000	24,000	32,000	40,000
1925						
Single (225cc single)	–1,500	–3,000	–6,000	–9,000	–12,000	–15,000
V-Twin (976cc twin)	4,000	8,000	16,000	24,000	32,000	40,000
1926						
Single (225cc single)	–1,500	–3,000	–6,000	–9,000	–12,000	–15,000
201A	–1,500	–3,000	–6,000	–9,000	–12,000	–15,000
V-Twin (976cc twin)	4,000	8,000	16,000	24,000	32,000	40,000
1927						
Single (488cc single)	–1,500	–3,000	–6,000	–9,000	–12,000	–15,000
V-Twin (976cc twin)	4,000	8,000	16,000	24,000	32,000	40,000
1928						
Single (225cc single)	–1,500	–3,000	–6,000	–9,000	–12,000	–15,000
V-Twin (976cc twin)	4,000	8,000	16,000	24,000	32,000	40,000
1929						
350SV	2,000	4,000	–6,000	–8,000	–10,000	–12,000
Twinport (488cc single)	–1,500	–3,000	–6,000	–9,000	–12,000	–15,000
V-Twin (976cc twin)	4,000	8,000	16,000	24,000	32,000	40,000
1930						
Single (225cc single)	–1,500	–3,000	–6,000	–9,000	–12,000	–15,000
V-Twin (976cc twin)	4,000	8,000	16,000	24,000	32,000	40,000
1931						
Single	–1,500	–3,000	–6,000	–9,000	–12,000	–15,000
V-Twin (976cc twin)	4,000	8,000	16,000	24,000	32,000	40,000
1932						
Bullet	–1,500	–3,000	–6,000	–9,000	–12,000	–15,000
Model K (976cc twin)	4,000	8,000	16,000	24,000	32,000	40,000
1933						
Bullet	–1,500	–3,000	–6,000	–9,000	–12,000	–15,000
Model K (976cc twin)	4,000	8,000	16,000	24,000	32,000	40,000
1934						
Bullet	–1,500	–3,000	–6,000	–9,000	–12,000	–15,000
Model K (976cc twin)	4,000	8,000	16,000	24,000	32,000	40,000
1935						
T (148cc single)	1,000	2,000	3,000	4,000	**5,500**	7,000
A (225cc single)	1,000	**2,000**	3,500	5,000	6,500	8,000
Bullet (250cc single)	1,000	**2,000**	3,500	5,000	6,500	8,000
Bullet (350cc single)	1,000	**2,000**	3,500	5,000	6,500	8,000
Bullet (500cc single)	–1,000	–2,000	–4,000	6,000	**8,000**	10,000
1936						
T (148cc single)	1,000	2,000	3,000	4,000	**5,500**	7,000
A (225cc single)	1,000	**2,000**	3,500	5,000	6,500	8,000
Bullet (250cc single)	1,000	**2,000**	3,500	5,000	6,500	8,000
Bullet (350cc single)	1,000	**2,000**	3,500	5,000	6,500	8,000
Bullet (500cc single)	–1,000	–2,000	–4,000	6,000	**8,000**	10,000

	6	5	4	3	2	1
1937						
T (148cc single)	1,000	2,000	3,000	4,000	5,500	7,000
A (225cc single)	1,000	2,000	3,500	5,000	6,500	8,000
Bullet (250cc single)	1,000	2,000	3,500	5,000	6,500	8,000
Bullet (350cc single)	1,000	2,000	3,500	5,000	6,500	8,000
Bullet (500cc single)	−1,000	−2,000	−4,000	6,000	8,000	10,000
V-Twin (1,140cc twin)	3,500	7,000	13,000	19,000	25,000	31,000
1938						
T (148cc single)	1,000	2,000	3,000	4,000	5,500	7,000
A (225cc single)	1,000	2,000	3,500	5,000	6,500	8,000
Bullet (250cc single)	1,000	2,000	3,500	5,000	6,500	8,000
Bullet (350cc single)	1,000	2,000	3,500	5,000	6,500	8,000
Bullet (500cc single)	−1,000	−2,000	−4,000	6,000	8,000	10,000
K (1,140cc twin)	3,500	7,000	13,000	19,000	25,000	31,000
1939						
T (148cc single)	1,000	2,000	3,000	4,000	5,500	7,000
A (225cc single)	1,000	2,000	3,500	5,000	6,500	8,000
Bullet (250cc single)	1,000	2,000	3,500	5,000	6,500	8,000
Bullet (350cc single)	1,000	2,000	3,500	5,000	6,500	8,000
Bullet (500cc single)	−1,000	−2,000	−4,000	6,000	8,000	10,000
K (1,140cc twin)	3,500	7,000	13,000	19,000	25,000	31,000
1940						
A (225cc single)	1,000	2,000	3,500	5,000	6,500	8,000
Bullet (250cc single)	1,000	2,000	3,500	5,000	6,500	8,000
Bullet (350cc single)	1,000	2,000	3,500	5,000	6,500	8,000
Bullet (500cc single)	−1,000	−2,000	−4,000	6,000	8,000	10,000
K (1,140cc twin)	3,500	7,000	13,000	19,000	25,000	31,000
1941						
WP Models (350cc single)	1,000	2,500	4,000	5,500	7,000	8,500
1942						
WP Models (350cc single)	1,000	2,500	4,000	5,500	7,000	8,500
1943						
WP Models (350cc single)	1,000	2,500	4,000	5,500	7,000	8,500
1944						
WP Models (350cc single)	1,000	2,500	4,000	5,500	7,000	8,500
1945						
WP Models (350cc single)	1,000	2,500	4,000	5,500	7,000	8,500
1946						
RE (125cc single)	1,000	1,800	2,600	3,400	4,200	5,000
G (350cc single)	1,000	2,500	4,000	5,500	7,000	8,500
J (500cc twin)	2,000	3,500	5,000	6,500	8,000	9,500
1947						
RE (125cc single)	1,000	1,800	2,600	3,400	4,200	5,000
G (350cc single)	1,000	2,500	4,000	5,500	7,000	8,500
J (500cc twin)	2,000	3,500	5,000	6,500	8,000	9,500
1948						
RE (125cc single)	1,000	1,800	2,600	3,400	4,200	5,000
G (350cc single)	1,000	2,500	4,000	5,500	7,000	8,500
J (500cc twin)	2,000	3,500	5,000	6,500	8,000	9,500
J2 (500cc twin)	2,000	3,500	5,000	6,500	8,000	9,500
1949						
RE (125cc single)	1,000	1,800	2,600	3,400	4,200	5,000
G (350cc single)	1,000	2,500	4,000	5,500	7,000	8,500
Bullet (350cc single)	1,000	2,500	4,000	5,500	7,000	8,500
Bullet (500cc single)	1,000	2,500	4,000	5,500	7,000	8,500
J (500cc twin)	2,000	3,500	5,000	6,500	8,000	9,500
J2 (500cc twin)	2,000	3,500	5,000	6,500	8,000	9,500
1950						
RE (125cc single)	1,000	1,800	2,600	3,400	4,200	5,000

	6	5	4	3	2	1
G (350cc single)	1,000	2,500	4,000	5,500	7,000	8,500
Bullet (350cc single)	1,000	2,500	4,000	5,500	7,000	8,500
Bullet (500cc single)	1,000	2,500	4,000	5,500	7,000	8,500
J (500cc twin)	2,000	3,500	5,000	6,500	8,000	9,500
J2 (500cc twin)	2,000	3,500	5,000	6,500	8,000	9,500
1951						
RE (125cc single)	1,000	1,800	2,600	3,400	4,200	5,000
RE2 (125cc single)	1,000	1,800	2,600	3,400	4,200	5,000
G (350cc single)	1,000	2,500	4,000	5,500	7,000	8,500
Bullet (350cc single)	1,000	2,500	4,000	5,500	7,000	8,500
Bullet (500cc single)	2,000	3,500	5,000	6,500	8,000	9,500
J (500cc twin)	2,000	3,500	5,000	6,500	8,000	9,500
J2 (500cc twin)	2,000	3,500	5,000	6,500	8,000	9,500
1952						
RE (125cc single)	1,000	1,800	2,600	3,400	4,200	5,000
RE2 (125cc single)	1,000	1,800	2,600	3,400	4,200	5,000
G (350cc single)	1,000	2,500	4,000	5,500	7,000	8,500
Bullet (350cc single)	1,000	2,500	4,000	5,500	7,000	8,500
Bullet (500cc single)	2,000	3,500	5,000	6,500	8,000	9,500
J (500cc twin)	2,000	3,500	5,000	6,500	8,000	9,500
J2 (500cc twin)	2,000	3,500	5,000	6,500	8,000	9,500
1953						
RE2 (125cc single)	1,000	1,800	2,600	3,400	4,200	5,000
Ensign (148cc single)	900	1,400	1,900	2,900	3,500	4,100
Bullet (350cc single)	1,000	2,500	4,000	5,500	7,000	8,500
G (350cc single)	1,000	2,500	4,000	5,500	7,000	8,500
Trials (350cc single)	−1,500	3,000	4,500	6,000	7,500	9,000
Bullet (500cc single)	2,000	3,500	5,000	6,500	8,000	9,500
J (500cc twin)	2,000	3,500	5,000	6,500	8,000	9,500
J2 (500cc twin)	2,000	3,500	5,000	6,500	8,000	9,500
Meteor (700cc twin)	−1,000	2,000	4,000	6,000	8,000	10,000
1954						
RE2 (125cc single)	1,000	1,800	2,600	3,400	4,200	5,000
Ensign (148cc single)	900	1,400	1,900	2,900	3,500	4,100
Clipper (250cc single)	1,000	1,700	2,400	3,100	3,800	4,500
S (250cc single)	1,000	1,700	2,400	3,100	3,800	4,500
Bullet (350cc single)	1,000	2,500	4,000	5,500	7,000	8,500
G (350cc single)	1,000	2,500	4,000	5,500	7,000	8,500
Trials (350cc single)	−1,500	3,000	4,500	6,000	7,500	9,000
Bullet (500cc single)	2,000	3,500	5,000	6,500	8,000	9,500
J (500cc twin)	2,000	3,500	5,000	6,500	8,000	9,500
J2 (500cc twin)	2,000	3,500	5,000	6,500	8,000	9,500
Meteor (700cc twin)	−1,000	2,000	4,000	6,000	8,000	10,000
1955						
Ensign (148cc single)	900	1,400	1,900	2,900	3,500	4,100
Clipper (250cc single)	1,000	1,700	2,400	3,100	3,800	4,500
S (250cc single)	1,000	1,700	2,400	3,100	3,800	4,500
Bullet (350cc single)	1,000	2,500	4,000	5,500	7,000	8,500
Trials (350cc single)	−1,500	3,000	4,500	6,000	7,500	9,000
Bullet (500cc single)	2,000	3,500	5,000	6,500	8,000	9,500
J (500cc twin)	2,000	3,500	5,000	6,500	8,000	9,500
J2 (500cc twin)	2,000	3,500	5,000	6,500	8,000	9,500
Meteor (700cc twin)	−1,000	2,000	4,000	6,000	8,000	10,000
1956						
Ensign (148cc single)	900	1,400	1,900	2,900	3,500	4,100
Ensign II (150cc single)	900	1,400	1,900	2,900	3,500	4,100
Clipper (250cc single)	1,000	1,700	2,400	3,100	3,800	4,500
Crusader (250cc single)	1,000	1,800	2,600	3,400	4,200	5,000
Bullet (350cc single)	1,000	2,500	4,000	5,500	7,000	8,500

	6	5	4	3	2	1
Trials (350cc single).	−1,500	3,000	4,500	6,000	7,500	9,000
Bullet (500cc single).	2,000	3,500	5,000	6,500	8,000	9,500
J2 (500cc twin)	2,000	3,500	5,000	6,500	8,000	9,500
Meteor (700cc twin)	−1,000	2,000	4,000	6,000	8,000	10,000
Super Meteor (700cc twin)	−1,000	2,000	4,000	6,000	8,000	10,000
1957						
Ensign II (150cc single)	900	1,400	1,900	2,900	3,500	4,100
Clipper (250cc single)	1,000	2,000	3,000	3,900	4,800	5,500
Crusader (250cc single)	1,000	2,000	3,000	3,900	4,800	5,500
Bullet (350cc single).	1,000	−1,500	−3,000	4,500	6,000	7,500
Trials (350cc single).	1,000	2,500	4,000	5,500	7,000	8,500
Bullet (500cc single).	1,000	−1,500	−3,000	4,500	6,000	7,500
J2 (500cc twin)	1,000	2,500	4,000	5,500	7,000	8,500
Meteor (700cc twin)	−1,000	2,000	4,000	6,000	8,000	10,000
Super Meteor (700cc twin)	−1,000	2,000	4,000	6,000	8,000	10,000
1958						
Ensign II (150cc single)	900	1,400	1,900	2,900	3,500	4,100
Ensign III (150cc single).	900	1,400	1,900	2,900	3,500	4,100
Crusader (250cc single)	1,000	2,000	3,000	3,900	4,800	5,500
Bullet (350cc single).	1,000	−1,500	−3,000	4,500	6,000	7,500
Clipper (350cc single)	1,000	1,800	2,600	3,400	4,200	5,000
Trials (350cc single).	1,000	2,500	4,000	5,500	7,000	8,500
Bullet (500cc single).	1,000	−1,500	−3,000	4,500	6,000	7,500
J2 (500cc twin)	1,000	2,500	4,000	5,500	7,000	8,500
Meteor (700cc twin)	−1,000	2,000	4,000	6,000	8,000	10,000
Meteor Air Flow (700cc twin)	1,000	2,000	4,000	6,000	8,000	11,000
Super Meteor (700cc twin)	−1,000	2,000	4,000	6,000	8,000	10,000
1959						
Ensign III (150cc single).	900	1,400	1,900	2,900	3,500	4,100
Prince (150cc single)	900	1,400	1,900	2,900	3,500	4,100
Crusader (250cc single)	1,000	2,000	3,000	3,900	4,800	5,500
Bullet (350cc single).	1,000	−1,500	−3,000	4,500	6,000	7,500
Clipper (350cc single)	1,000	1,800	2,600	3,400	4,200	5,000
Trials (350cc single).	1,000	2,500	4,000	5,500	7,000	8,500
Bullet (500cc single).	1,000	−1,500	−3,000	4,500	6,000	7,500
J2 (500cc twin)	1,000	2,500	4,000	5,500	7,000	8,500
Constellation (700cc twin)	2,000	3,500	5,000	6,500	8,000	9,500
Meteor (700cc twin)	−1,000	2,000	4,000	6,000	8,000	10,000
Meteor Air Flow (700cc twin)	1,000	2,000	4,000	6,000	8,000	11,000
Meteor Deluxe (700cc twin)	−1,000	2,000	4,000	6,000	8,000	10,000
Super Meteor (700cc twin)	−1,000	2,000	4,000	6,000	8,000	10,000
1960						
Ensign III (150cc single).	1,000	1,800	2,600	3,400	4,200	5,000
Prince (150cc single)	1,000	2,000	3,000	3,900	4,800	5,500
Crusader (250cc single)	1,000	2,000	3,000	3,900	4,800	5,500
Bullet (350cc single).	1,000	−1,500	−3,000	4,500	6,000	7,500
Clipper (350cc single)	1,000	−1,500	−3,000	4,500	6,000	7,500
Trials (350cc single).	1,000	2,500	4,000	5,500	7,000	8,500
Big Head Bullet (500cc single)	2,000	4,000	7,000	10,000	13,000	16,000
Fury (US) (500cc single)	2,000	4,000	7,000	10,000	13,000	16,000
J2 (500cc twin)	1,000	2,500	4,000	5,500	7,000	8,500
Meteor Minor (500cc twin).	1,000	2,500	4,000	5,500	7,000	8,500
Constellation (700cc twin)	2,000	3,500	5,000	6,500	8,000	9,500
Meteor (700cc twin)	2,000	3,500	5,000	6,500	8,000	9,500
Meteor Air Flow (700cc twin)	1,000	2,000	4,000	6,000	8,000	11,000
Meteor Deluxe (700cc twin)	−1,000	2,000	4,000	6,000	8,000	10,000
Super Meteor (700cc twin)	−1,000	2,000	4,000	6,000	8,000	10,000
1961						
Prince (150cc single)	1,000	2,000	3,000	3,900	4,800	5,500

	6	5	4	3	2	1
Crusader (250cc single).	1,000	2,000	3,000	3,900	4,800	5,500
Bullet (350cc single).	1,000	−1,500	−3,000	4,500	6,000	7,500
Clipper (350cc single).	1,000	−1,500	−3,000	4,500	6,000	7,500
Trials (350cc single).	1,000	2,500	4,000	5,500	7,000	8,500
Big Head Bullet (500cc single)	2,000	4,000	7,000	10,000	13,000	16,000
Fury (US) (500cc single)	2,000	4,000	7,000	10,000	13,000	16,000
J2 (500cc twin)	1,000	2,500	4,000	5,500	7,000	8,500
Constellation (700cc twin).	2,000	3,500	5,000	6,500	8,000	9,500
Meteor Deluxe (700cc twin)	−1,000	2,000	4,000	6,000	8,000	10,000
Super Meteor (700cc twin)	−1,000	2,000	4,000	6,000	8,000	10,000
1962						
Crusader (250cc single).	1,000	2,000	3,000	3,900	4,800	5,500
Super 5 (250cc single)	−1,000	−1,500	3,000	4,500	6,000	7,500
Bullet (350cc single).	1,000	−1,500	−3,000	4,500	6,000	7,500
Clipper (350cc single).	1,000	−1,500	−3,000	4,500	6,000	7,500
Big Head Bullet (500cc single)	2,000	4,000	7,000	10,000	13,000	16,000
Fury (US) (500cc single)	2,000	4,000	7,000	10,000	13,000	16,000
Constellation (700cc twin).	2,000	3,500	5,000	6,500	8,000	9,500
Meteor Deluxe (700cc twin)	−1,000	2,000	4,000	6,000	8,000	10,000
Super Meteor (700cc twin)	−1,000	2,000	4,000	6,000	8,000	10,000
1963						
Continental (250cc single).	1,000	2,000	3,000	4,000	5,000	6,000
Super 5 (250cc single)	−1,000	−1,500	3,000	4,500	6,000	7,500
Bullet (350cc single).	1,000	−1,500	−3,000	4,500	6,000	7,500
Clipper (350cc single).	1,000	−1,500	−3,000	4,500	6,000	7,500
Big Head Bullet (500cc single)	2,000	4,000	7,000	10,000	13,000	16,000
Fury (US) (500cc single)	2,000	4,000	7,000	10,000	13,000	16,000
Interceptor (750cc twin)	1,500	2,500	4,500	7,500	10,500	13,500
1964						
Continental (250cc single).	1,000	2,000	3,000	4,000	5,000	6,000
GT (250cc single)	1,000	2,000	3,000	3,900	4,800	5,500
Olympic (250cc single)	1,000	2,000	3,000	3,900	4,800	5,500
Super 5 (250cc single)	−1,000	−1,500	3,000	4,500	6,000	7,500
Turbo Twin (250cc single)	−1,000	−2,000	3,500	5,000	6,500	8,000
Interceptor (750cc twin)	1,500	2,500	4,500	7,500	10,500	13,500
1965						
Continental (250cc single).	1,000	2,000	3,000	4,000	5,000	6,000
Crusader (250cc single).	1,000	2,000	3,000	3,900	4,800	5,500
GT (250cc single)	1,000	2,000	3,000	3,900	4,800	5,500
Olympic (250cc single)	1,000	2,000	3,000	3,900	4,800	5,500
Turbo Twin (250cc single).	−1,000	−2,000	3,500	5,000	6,500	8,000
Interceptor (750cc twin)	1,500	2,500	4,500	7,500	10,500	13,500
1966						
Crusader Sports (250cc single)	1,000	1,800	2,600	3,400	4,200	5,000
GT (250cc single)	−1,000	−1,500	3,000	4,500	6,000	7,500
Turbo Twin (250cc single).	−1,000	−2,000	3,500	5,000	6,500	8,000
Interceptor (750cc twin)	1,500	2,500	4,500	7,500	10,500	13,500
1967						
Crusader Sports (250cc single)	1,000	2,000	3,000	3,900	4,800	5,500
Interceptor (750cc twin)	1,500	2,500	4,500	7,500	10,500	13,500
1968						
Interceptor (750cc twin)	1,200	2,500	4,500	6,500	8,500	10,500
Interceptor II (750cc twin)	−1,500	2,500	4,500	7,500	10,500	13,500
1969						
Interceptor II (750cc twin)	−1,500	2,500	4,500	7,500	10,500	13,500
1970						
Interceptor II (750cc twin)	−1,500	2,500	4,500	7,500	10,500	13,500
1971						
Interceptor II (750cc twin)	−1,500	2,500	4,500	7,500	10,500	13,500

	6	5	4	3	2	1
SUNBEAM						
1916						
500	2,500	5,000	10,000	15,000	20,000	25,000
3.5 HP	3,000	6,000	9,000	12,000	16,000	20,000
1918						
Twin Jap	4,000	8,000	16,000	24,000	32,000	40,000
1924						
Model 5	7,000	10,000	12,500	15,000	18,000	21,000
Model 80 (347cc single)	7,000	10,000	12,500	15,000	18,000	21,000
Longstroke (500cc)	2,000	4,000	8,000	12,000	16,000	20,000
1925						
Longstroke (500cc)	2,000	4,000	8,000	12,000	16,000	20,000
1927						
Model 9	5,000	10,000	15,000	20,000	25,000	30,000
1928						
Model 6	7,000	10,000	12,500	15,000	18,000	21,000
1929						
Model 2	3,500	5,000	7,000	8,800	11,000	14,000
1930						
Model 8 (348cc single)	3,500	5,000	7,000	8,800	11,000	14,000
Model 9 (493cc twin)	3,500	5,000	7,000	8,800	11,000	14,000
1931						
Model 9 (493cc twin)	3,500	5,000	7,000	8,800	11,000	14,000
1932						
Model 6	3,500	5,000	7,000	8,800	11,000	14,000
1933						
Model 90	6,000	9,000	12,000	15,000	18,000	21,000
1935						
Model 16	3,000	4,000	6,000	8,000	10,000	13,000
1937						
Light Solo (500cc)	7,000	10,000	12,500	15,000	18,000	21,000
Model 8	3,500	5,000	7,000	8,800	11,000	14,000
Model 9 (493cc twin)	3,500	5,000	7,000	8,800	11,000	14,000
1938						
250 (250cc)	1,000	2,000	4,000	6,000	8,000	10,000
Light Solo (500cc)	1,000	2,000	4,000	6,000	8,000	10,000
Lion (600cc)	2,000	4,000	6,000	8,000	10,000	12,000
1939						
B25 (497cc twin)	2,000	4,000	6,000	8,000	10,000	12,000
1947						
S7 (487cc twin, shaft drive)	3,000	4,000	6,000	8,000	10,000	13,000
1948						
S7 (487cc twin, shaft drive)	3,000	4,000	6,000	8,000	10,000	13,000
1949						
S7 (487cc twin, shaft drive)	3,000	4,000	6,000	8,000	10,000	13,000
1950						
S7 Deluxe (487cc twin, shaft drive)	3,000	4,000	6,000	8,000	10,000	13,000
S8 (487cc twin, shaft drive)	3,000	4,000	6,000	8,000	10,000	13,000
1951						
S7 Deluxe (487cc twin, shaft drive)	3,000	4,000	6,000	8,000	10,000	13,000
S8 (487cc twin, shaft drive)	3,000	4,000	6,000	8,000	10,000	13,000
1952						
S7 Deluxe (487cc twin, shaft drive)	3,000	4,000	6,000	8,000	10,000	13,000
S8 (487cc twin, shaft drive)	3,000	4,000	6,000	8,000	10,000	13,000
1953						
S7 Deluxe (487cc twin, shaft drive)	3,000	4,000	6,000	8,000	10,000	13,000
S8 (487cc twin, shaft drive)	3,000	4,000	6,000	8,000	10,000	13,000
1954						
S7 Deluxe (487cc twin, shaft drive)	3,000	4,000	6,000	8,000	10,000	13,000
S8 (487cc twin, shaft drive)	3,000	4,000	6,000	8,000	10,000	13,000

	6	5	4	3	2	1
1955						
S7 Deluxe (487cc twin, shaft drive)	3,000	4,000	6,000	8,000	10,000	13,000
S8 (487cc twin, shaft drive)	3,000	4,000	6,000	8,000	10,000	13,000
1956						
S7 Deluxe (487cc twin, shaft drive)	3,000	4,000	6,000	8,000	10,000	13,000
S8 (487cc twin, shaft drive)	3,000	4,000	6,000	8,000	10,000	13,000
SUZUKI						
1963						
RM63 (50cc single)	11,000	17,000	25,000	33,000	44,000	55,000
RT63 (124cc twin).	10,000	15,000	22,500	30,000	40,000	50,000
S31 (124cc twin)	200	300	500	700	900	1,100
S250 Colleda (248cc twin)	300	500	700	900	1,200	1,500
TC250 El Camino (248cc twin)	300	500	700	900	1,200	1,500
1964						
M12 Sports 50 (50cc single).	200	300	500	700	900	1,100
K10 (80cc single)	200	300	500	700	900	1,100
K11 Sports 80 (79cc single).	200	300	500	700	900	1,100
T10 (246cc twin)	300	500	700	900	1,200	1,500
1965						
K10 (80cc single)	200	300	500	700	900	1,100
K11 Sports 80 (79cc single).	200	300	400	500	700	900
Hillbilly K15 (80cc single)	300	500	700	1,000	1,300	1,600
B100 (118cc single)	200	300	400	500	700	900
S10 (124cc twin)	200	300	500	700	900	1,100
S32 (149cc twin)	200	400	500	700	1,000	1,200
T20 (247cc twin)	800	1,800	2,600	3,400	4,200	5,000
X-6 Super Six (247cc twin)	300	500	700	1,000	1,300	1,600
1966						
M15 (49cc single)	200	300	400	500	700	900
K11 P Challenger (79cc single)	200	300	400	500	700	900
A100 (98cc single)	200	300	400	500	700	900
B120 (118cc single)	200	400	500	700	1,000	1,200
S32 II (149cc twin)	200	400	500	700	1,000	1,200
T20 (247cc twin)	800	1,800	2,600	3,400	4,200	5,000
1967						
RK67 Racer (50cc twin)	9,000	14,000	20,000	27,000	36,000	45,000
K10 P Corsair (79cc single)	200	300	400	500	700	900
K11 P Challenger (79cc single)	200	300	400	500	700	900
K15 P Hillbilly (79cc single)	300	600	900	1,200	1,500	1,800
A90 (86cc single)	200	300	500	600	800	1,000
A100 Charger (98cc single)	200	300	500	600	800	1,000
AS100 Sierra (98cc single)	200	300	500	600	800	1,000
B100P Magnum (118cc single)	200	300	500	600	800	1,100
BP105 P Bearcat (118cc single).	200	300	500	600	800	1,100
B120 (118cc single)	200	300	500	600	800	1,100
TC120 (118cc single)	200	300	500	600	800	1,100
T125 (124cc single)	200	400	500	700	1,000	1,200
T200 (196cc single)	200	400	500	700	1,000	1,200
TC200 Stingray (196cc single)	200	400	500	700	1,000	1,200
T20 Super Six (247cc twin)	800	1,800	2,600	3,400	4,200	5,000
T21 Super (247cc twin)	300	500	700	900	1,200	1,500
TC250 Hustler (247cc twin)	700	1,100	1,600	2,100	2,800	3,500
1968						
AC90 (86 single)	200	300	500	600	800	1,100
KT120 Trail (118cc single)	200	300	400	500	700	900
T200 (196cc single)	200	400	500	700	1,000	1,200
TC200 Stingray (196cc single)	200	400	500	700	1,000	1,200
TC250 (247cc twin)	300	500	700	900	1,200	1,500
TM250 (249cc single)	400	700	1,000	1,300	1,800	2,200
T305 (305cc twin)	500	800	1,100	1,500	2,000	2,500

	6	5	4	3	2	1
TC305 (305cc twin)	500	800	1,400	2,100	2,800	3,500
T500 Cobra (492cc twin)	600	900	1,600	2,400	3,200	4,000
1969						
AS50 (49cc single)	200	400	700	1,000	1,500	2,000
A95 (69cc single)	300	500	700	1,000	1,300	1,600
T90 Wolf (89cc twin)	300	500	700	1,000	1,300	1,600
T125 Stinger (124cc twin)	300	500	1,000	1,500	2,000	2,500
T250 Hustler (247cc twin)	400	700	1,000	1,300	1,800	2,200
TS250 (247cc twin)	400	600	900	1,200	1,600	2,000
T305 Raider (305cc twin)	500	700	1,100	1,440	1,900	2,400
T350 Rebel (315cc twin)	500	800	1,200	1,600	2,100	2,600
T500 II Titan (492cc twin)	700	1,000	1,600	2,000	3,000	4,000
TR500 (500cc twin)	600	900	1,600	2,400	3,200	4,000
1970						
AC50 Maverick (49cc single)	200	400	500	700	1,000	1,200
TC90 Blazer (89cc single).	300	500	700	1,000	1,300	1,600
TS90 Honcho (89cc single)	300	500	700	1,000	1,300	1,600
TC120 II Cat (118cc single)	300	500	700	1,000	1,300	1,600
T125 II Stinger (124cc twin)	300	500	1,000	1,500	2,000	2,500
TS250 II Savage (246cc single).	400	600	900	1,200	1,600	2,000
T250 II Hustler (247cc twin)	400	700	1,000	1,300	1,800	2,200
T350 II Rebel (315cc twin)	500	800	1,200	1,600	2,100	2,600
T500 II Titan (492cc twin)	700	1,000	1,600	2,000	3,000	4,000
1971						
TS50R (49cc single).	300	500	700	900	1,200	1,500
TC90R (89cc single)	300	500	700	1,000	1,300	1,600
TS90R (89cc single).	300	500	700	1,000	1,300	1,600
TC120R (188cc single)	300	500	800	1,000	1,400	1,700
TS125R (123cc single)	300	500	800	1,000	1,400	1,700
TS185R (183cc single)	400	600	900	1,100	1,500	1,900
T250R (246cc single)	400	600	900	1,200	1,600	2,000
TS250R (247cc twin)	500	700	1,000	1,400	1,800	2,300
T350R (315cc twin)	500	800	1,200	1,600	2,100	2,600
T500R Titan (492cc twin)	700	1,000	1,600	2,000	3,000	4,000
1972						
T50J Gaucho (49cc single)	300	400	600	800	1,000	1,300
TC90J Blazer (89cc single)	300	500	700	1,000	1,300	1,600
TS125J (123cc single)	300	500	800	1,000	1,400	1,700
TS185J Sierra (183cc single)	400	500	800	1,100	1,400	1,800
TS250J Savage (246cc single)	400	600	900	1,100	1,500	1,900
T250J Hustler (247cc twin)	400	600	1,000	1,300	1,700	2,100
GT380J Sebring (371cc triple)	600	900	1,200	1,500	2,000	2,500
TS400J (396cc twin)	400	600	1,000	1,300	1,700	2,100
TS500J Titan (492cc twin).	600	900	1,400	1,800	2,400	3,000
GT550J Indy (543cc triple)	500	800	1,200	1,600	2,100	2,600
GT750J LeMans (739cc triple)	1,500	2,000	3,500	5,000	6,500	8,000
1973						
T50K Gaucho (49cc single)	200	400	500	700	900	1,200
TC100K Blazer (97cc single)	200	400	500	700	1,000	1,200
TS100K Honcho (97cc single).	200	400	500	700	1,000	1,200
TS125K Duster (123cc single)	300	500	800	1,000	1,400	1,700
TS185K Sierra (183cc single)	400	500	800	1,100	1,400	1,800
GT185K Adventurer (184cc twin)	400	500	800	1,100	1,400	1,800
T250K Hustler (247cc twin)	400	700	1,000	1,300	1,800	2,200
TS250K Savage (246cc single)	400	600	900	1,100	1,500	1,900
GT380K Sebring (371cc triple)	600	900	1,200	1,500	2,000	2,500
TS400K (396cc twin)	400	600	1,000	1,300	1,700	2,100
TS500K Titan (492cc twin)	600	900	1,400	1,800	2,400	3,000
GT550K Indy (543cc triple)	500	800	1,200	1,600	2,100	2,600
GT750K LeMans (739cc triple)	1,000	2,000	3,500	5,000	6,500	8,000

	6	5	4	3	2	1
1974						
T50L Gaucho (49cc single)	200	400	500	700	900	1,200
TC100L Blazer (97cc single)	200	400	500	700	1,000	1,200
TS100L Honcho (97cc single)	200	400	500	700	1,000	1,200
TS125L Duster (123cc single)	300	500	700	1,000	1,300	1,600
TC185L Ranger (183cc single)	300	500	800	1,000	1,400	1,700
TS185L Sierra (183cc single)	300	500	800	1,000	1,400	1,700
GT185L Adventurer (184cc twin)	400	500	800	1,100	1,400	1,800
T250L Hustler (247cc twin)	400	700	1,000	1,300	1,800	2,200
TS250L Savage (246cc single)	400	600	900	1,100	1,500	1,900
GT380L Sebring (371cc triple)	600	900	1,200	1,500	2,000	2,500
TS400L (396cc twin)	400	600	1,000	1,300	1,700	2,100
TS500L Titan (492cc twin)	600	900	1,400	1,800	2,400	3,000
GT550L Indy (543cc triple)	500	800	1,200	1,600	2,100	2,600
GT750L LeMans (739cc triple)	1,000	2,000	3,500	5,000	6,500	8,000
1975						
TC100M Blazer (97cc single)	200	400	500	700	1,000	1,200
TS100M Honcho (97cc single)	200	400	500	700	1,000	1,200
TS125M Duster (123cc single)	300	500	700	1,000	1,300	1,600
TC185M Ranger (183cc single)	300	500	800	1,000	1,400	1,700
TS185M Sierra (183cc single)	400	600	1,000	1,300	1,700	2,100
GT185M Adventurer (184cc twin)	400	500	800	1,100	1,400	1,800
T250M Hustler (247cc twin)	400	700	1,000	1,300	1,800	2,200
TS250M Savage (246cc single)	400	500	800	1,200	1,600	2,000
GT380M Sebring (371cc triple)	600	900	1,200	1,500	2,000	2,500
TS400M (396cc twin)	400	600	1,000	1,300	1,700	2,100
TS500M Titan (492cc twin)	600	900	1,400	1,800	2,400	3,000
RE5M (497cc single rotary)	1,700	2,300	3,500	5,000	7,500	9,000
GT550M Indy (543cc triple)	500	800	1,200	1,600	2,100	2,600
GT750M LeMans (739cc triple)	1,000	2,000	3,500	5,000	6,500	8,000
1976						
TC100A Blazer (97cc single)	200	400	500	700	1,000	1,200
TS100A Honcho (97cc single)	200	400	500	700	1,000	1,200
TS125A Duster (123cc single)	300	500	700	1,000	1,300	1,600
TC185A Ranger (183cc single)	300	500	800	1,000	1,400	1,700
TS185A Sierra (183cc single)	300	500	800	1,200	1,600	2,000
GT185A Adventurer (184cc twin)	400	500	800	1,100	1,400	1,800
T250A Hustler (247cc twin)	400	700	1,000	1,300	1,800	2,200
TS250A Savage (246cc single)	400	500	800	1,100	1,400	1,800
RM370A Cyclone	500	1,200	2,700	3,600	5,500	7,400
GT380A Sebring (371cc triple)	600	900	1,200	1,500	2,000	2,500
TS400A (396cc twin)	400	600	1,000	1,300	1,700	2,100
TS500A Titan (492cc twin)	600	900	1,400	1,800	2,400	3,000
RE5A (497cc single rotary)	1,200	1,800	2,600	3,600	4,700	6,000
GT550A Indy (543cc triple)	500	800	1,200	1,600	2,100	2,600
GT750A LeMans (739cc triple)	1,000	2,000	3,500	5,000	6,500	8,000
1977						
TC100B Blazer (97cc single)	200	300	500	700	900	1,100
TS100B Honcho (97cc single)	200	300	500	700	900	1,100
TS125B (123cc single)	300	400	600	800	1,100	1,400
TC185B Ranger (183cc single)	300	500	800	1,000	1,400	1,700
TS185B Sierra (183cc single)	300	500	800	1,200	1,600	2,000
GT185B Adventurer (184cc twin)	400	500	800	1,100	1,400	1,800
GT250 (250cc twin)	400	700	1,000	1,300	1,800	2,200
T250B Hustler (247cc twin)	400	700	1,000	1,300	1,800	2,200
TS250B Savage (246cc single)	400	500	800	1,100	1,400	1,800
GT380B Sebring (371cc triple)	600	900	1,200	1,500	2,000	2,500
TS400B Apache (396cc twin)	400	600	900	1,200	1,600	2,000
GS400B (398cc four)	300	500	800	1,000	1,400	1,700
GS400XB (398cc four)	400	600	900	1,100	1,500	1,900

	6	5	4	3	2	1
T500B Titan (492cc twin)	500	800	1,300	1,700	2,300	2,800
GT550B Indy (543cc triple)	400	600	1,000	1,300	1,700	2,100
GS550B (549cc four)	400	600	900	1,100	1,500	1,900
GT750B LeMans (739cc triple)	1,000	2,000	3,500	5,000	6,500	8,000
GS750B (748cc four)	900	1,300	2,000	2,600	3,500	4,400
1978						
TS100C (97cc single)	200	300	500	700	900	1,100
TS125C (123cc single)	200	400	500	700	1,000	1,200
TS185C (183cc single)	300	500	700	900	1,200	1,500
TS250C (246cc single)	400	500	800	1,100	1,400	1,800
DR370C (370cc single)	400	500	800	1,100	1,400	1,800
SP370C (370cc single)	400	500	800	1,100	1,400	1,800
GS400C (398cc four)	300	500	800	1,000	1,400	1,700
GS400XC (398cc four)	400	600	900	1,100	1,500	1,900
GS550C (549cc four)	400	700	1,000	1,300	1,800	2,200
GS550EC (549cc four)	400	700	1,000	1,300	1,800	2,200
GS750C (748cc four)	600	900	1,300	1,700	2,300	2,900
GS750EC (748cc four)	600	900	1,300	1,700	2,300	2,900
GS1000C (997cc four)	600	900	1,400	1,800	2,400	3,000
1979						
TS100N (97cc single)	200	300	400	500	700	900
TS125N (123cc single)	200	300	500	600	800	1,000
TS185N (183cc single)	200	300	500	700	900	1,100
TS250N (246cc single)	300	500	800	1,000	1,400	1,700
DR370N (370cc single)	300	500	700	1,000	1,300	1,600
SP370N (370cc single)	300	500	700	1,000	1,300	1,600
GS425EN (423cc twin)	300	400	600	800	1,100	1,400
GS425LN (423cc twin)	300	400	600	800	1,100	1,400
GS425N (423cc twin)	300	400	600	800	1,100	1,400
GS550EN (549cc four)	400	600	900	1,200	1,600	2,000
GS550LN (549cc four)	400	600	900	1,200	1,600	2,000
GS550N (549cc four)	400	600	900	1,200	1,600	2,000
GS750EN (748cc four)	400	700	1,000	1,300	1,800	2,200
GS750LN (748cc four)	400	700	1,000	1,300	1,800	2,200
GS750N (748cc four)	400	700	1,000	1,300	1,800	2,200
GS850GN (843cc four)	500	700	1,000	1,400	1,800	2,300
GS1000EN (997cc four).	600	900	1,400	1,800	2,400	3,000
GS1000LN (997cc four).	600	900	1,400	1,800	2,400	3,000
GS1000N (997cc four).	600	900	1,400	1,800	2,400	3,000
GS1000SN (997cc four).	700	1,100	1,600	2,100	2,800	3,500
1980						
DR50T (49cc single)	200	300	400	500	700	900
RM50T (49cc single)	200	300	400	500	700	900
TS100T (97cc single)	200	300	400	500	700	900
RM100T (99cc single).	200	300	400	500	700	900
TS125T (123cc single)	200	300	500	600	800	1,000
RM125T (124cc single)	200	300	500	600	800	1,000
PE175T (172cc single)	200	300	500	600	800	1,100
RS175T (174cc single)	200	300	500	600	800	1,100
TS185T (183cc single)	200	400	500	700	1,000	1,200
PE250T (246cc single)	200	400	500	700	1,000	1,200
RM250T (246cc single)	200	400	500	700	1,000	1,200
RS250T (246cc single)	300	400	600	800	1,100	1,400
TS250T (246cc single)	300	400	600	800	1,100	1,400
GS250TT (247cc twin)	300	450	680	900	1,200	1,500
GN400TT (396cc single)	300	400	600	800	1,100	1,400
GN400XT (396cc single)	300	400	600	800	1,100	1,400
DR400T (399cc single)	300	500	700	900	1,200	1,500
RM400T (396cc single)	300	500	800	1,000	1,400	1,700
GS450ET (448cc twin)	300	500	700	900	1,200	1,500

	6	5	4	3	2	1
GS450LT (448cc twin)	300	500	700	900	1,200	1,500
GS450ST (448cc twin)	300	500	700	900	1,200	1,500
GS550ET (549cc four)	300	500	800	1,000	1,400	1,700
GS550LT (549cc four)	300	500	800	1,000	1,400	1,700
GS750ET (748cc four)	400	600	900	1,100	1,500	1,900
GS750LT (748cc four).	400	600	900	1,100	1,500	1,900
GS850GLT (843cc four).	400	600	900	1,200	1,600	2,000
GS1000ET (997cc four)	600	900	1,400	1,800	2,400	3,000
GS1000GLT (997cc four)	600	900	1,400	1,800	2,400	3,000
GS1000GT (997cc four).	600	900	1,400	1,800	2,400	3,000
GS1000ST (997cc four).	700	1,000	1,500	2,000	2,700	3,400
GS1100ET (1,074cc four)	700	1,000	15,000	2,000	2,600	3,300
GS1100LT (1,074cc four)	700	1,000	15,000	2,000	2,600	3,300
1981						
GS250T (250cc twin)	300	500	700	800	1,000	1,100
GN400X (400cc single)	300	500	700	800	900	1,000
GN400T (400cc single)	300	500	700	800	1,000	1,100
GS450E (450cc twin)	300	500	900	1,200	1,500	1,800
GS450T (450cc twin)	300	500	900	1,200	1,500	1,800
GS450L (450cc twin)	300	500	900	1,200	1,500	1,800
GS450S (450cc twin)	400	600	900	1,300	1,600	1,900
GS550T (550cc four)	400	600	900	1,400	1,700	2,000
GS550L (550cc four)	400	600	1,000	1,400	1,900	2,400
GS650E (650cc four)	400	600	900	1,500	2,000	2,600
GS650G (650cc four)	400	600	900	1,500	2,100	2,700
GS650GL (650cc four)	400	700	1,100	1,600	2,200	2,800
GS750E (750cc four)	400	700	1,100	1,700	2,300	3,000
GS750L (750cc four)	500	700	1,100	1,600	2,200	2,800
GS850G (850cc four)	500	800	1,100	1,700	2,300	3,000
GS850GL (850cc four)	500	800	1,100	1,900	2,500	3,500
GS1000G (1,000cc four)	600	900	1,300	2,000	3,000	4,000
GS1100GL (1,000cc four)	650	950	1,300	2,000	3,000	4,000
GS1100E (1,100cc four)	800	1,200	2,000	3,000	4,000	5,000
1982						
GN125 (125cc single)	200	400	700	800	900	1,000
GN250 (250cc single)	300	500	800	1,000	1,200	1,400
TS 250 ER (250cc single)	300	500	800	1,000	1,200	1,400
GS300L (300cc twin)	300	500	800	1,000	1,300	1,500
GN400T (400cc single)	300	500	800	1,000	1,300	1,600
GS450TX (450cc twin)	400	600	900	1,200	1,400	1,600
GS450T (450cc twin)	400	600	900	1,300	1,500	1,900
GS450E (450cc twin)	300	500	800	1,300	1,500	1,900
GS450L (450cc twin)	400	600	900	1,200	1,500	1,900
GS450GA Automatic (450cc twin).	400	600	900	1,300	1,600	2,000
GS550L (550cc four)	500	700	1,000	1,500	2,000	2,500
GS550M (550cc four)	500	700	1,000	1,500	2,100	2,600
GS650E (650cc four)	400	600	900	1,500	2,100	2,600
GS650G (650cc four)	400	600	900	1,600	2,200	2,800
GS650GL (650cc four)	500	700	1,000	1,600	2,200	2,900
GS750E (750cc four)	500	700	1,100	1,700	2,400	3,100
GS750T (750cc four)	500	700	1,100	1,600	2,300	3,000
GS850G (850cc four)	600	800	1,200	1,900	2,700	3,500
GS850GL (850cc four)	600	800	1,200	2,000	2,800	3,600
GS1000S Katana (1,000cc four)	1,000	1,300	2,000	3,000	4,000	6,000
GS1100E (1,100cc four).	1,000	**1,800**	**2,600**	**3,400**	**4,200**	**5,000**
GS1100G (1,100cc four)	700	1,000	1,500	2,300	3,200	4,000
GS1100GL (1,100cc four).	700	1,000	1,500	2,300	3,200	4,000
GS1100GK (1,100cc four).	700	1,000	1,500	2,800	4,000	5,000

	6	5	4	3	2	1
1983						
GN125 (125cc single)	200	400	700	800	1,000	1,100
GN250 (250cc single)	300	500	800	1,000	1,300	1,500
GS300L (300cc twin)	300	500	800	1,100	1,300	1,600
GS450TX (450cc twin)	500	700	1,000	1,300	1,600	1,800
GS450E (450cc twin)	400	600	900	1,350	1,700	2,000
GS450L (450cc twin)	400	600	1,000	1,400	1,750	2,000
GS450GA (450cc twin)	500	700	1,000	1,400	1,800	2,100
GS550L Impulse (570cc four)	500	700	1,000	1,600	2,100	2,600
GS550E (570cc four)	500	700	1,000	1,650	2,200	2,800
GS550ES (570cc four)	500	700	1,100	1,800	2,500	3,000
GR650X Tempter (650cc twin)	500	800	1,100	1,400	1,700	2,100
GR650 Tempter (650cc twin)	500	800	1,100	1,500	1,900	2,400
GS650G (670cc twin)	500	700	1,000	1,600	2,300	2,900
GS650M Katana (670cc four)	400	600	1,000	1,600	2,300	2,900
GS650GL (670cc four)	500	800	1,100	1,700	2,400	3,000
XN85 Turbo (670cc four)	1,200	1,600	2,100	2,900	3,700	4,700
GS750T (750cc four)	500	800	1,200	1,800	2,400	3,000
GS750E (750cc four)	600	900	1,200	1,900	2,600	3,300
GS750ES (750cc four)	600	900	1,300	2,000	2,800	3,500
GS750S Katana (750cc four)	600	900	1,300	2,000	2,800	3,500
GS850G (850cc four)	600	900	1,300	2,100	2,900	3,600
GS850GL (850cc four)	600	900	1,300	2,100	2,900	3,600
GS1100E (1,075cc four)	1,000	**1,800**	2,600	3,400	4,200	5,000
GS1100G (1,075cc four)	700	1,000	1,500	2,300	3,200	4,100
GS1100GL (1,075cc four)	700	1,000	1,500	2,300	3,200	4,100
GS1100ES (1,075cc four)	1,000	1,300	1,800	2,500	3,400	4,300
GS1100S Katana (1,075cc four)	700	1,000	1,500	2,500	3,500	4,500
GS1100GK (1,075cc four)	800	1,100	1,500	2,900	4,000	5,000
1984						
GS550ES (575cc four)	500	700	1,100	1,600	2,500	3,100
GS1150ES (1,150cc four)	1,200	1,600	2,200	3,000	3,900	4,800
GS1100GK (1,075cc four)	800	1,100	1,500	3,200	4,300	5,500
1985						
JR50 Mini (50cc single)	200	300	500	600	700	800
DS80 Mini (80cc single)	200	400	600	700	800	900
RM80 (80cc single)	200	400	700	800	900	1,000
RM125 (125cc single)	300	500	800	1,200	1,500	1,900
DR200 (200cc single)	300	500	800	900	1,100	1,100
RM250 (250cc single)	400	600	900	1,400	1,900	2,500
DR250 (250cc single)	300	500	800	1,200	1,500	1,700
SP250 (250cc single)	300	500	800	1,200	1,500	1,700
GN250 (250cc single)	300	500	800	1,000	1,200	1,400
GS300L (300cc twin)	300	500	800	1,100	1,300	1,500
GS450L (450cc twin)	400	700	1,000	1,200	1,500	1,800
GS450GA (450cc twin)	400	700	1,000	1,400	1,800	2,200
GS550L (570cc four)	400	700	1,000	1,500	2,000	2,500
GS550E (570cc four)	400	700	1,000	1,500	2,100	2,600
GS550ES (570cc four)	400	700	1,100	1,700	2,400	3,100
SP600 (600cc single)	400	600	900	1,400	1,900	2,400
GS700E (700cc four)	700	1,000	1,400	1,800	2,400	3,100
GS700ES (700cc four)	700	1,000	1,400	1,900	2,600	3,300
GV700GL Madura (700cc four)	900	1,200	1,700	2,400	3,000	3,500
GS1150E (1,135cc four)	1,200	1,600	2,100	2,800	3,600	4,400
GS1150ES (1,135cc four)	1,300	1,700	2,300	3,000	3,900	4,800
GV1200GL Madura (1,165 four)	900	1,200	1,700	2,600	3,600	4,500
1986						
JR50 Mini (50cc single)	200	300	400	500	600	700
DS80 Mini (80cc single)	200	400	500	600	700	800
RM80 (80cc single)	200	400	700	800	1,000	1,100

	6	5	4	3	2	1
DR100 (100cc single)	200	400	700	800	900	1,100
DR125 (125cc single)	300	500	800	900	1,100	1,300
RM125 (125cc single)	400	600	900	1,300	1,700	2,100
SP125 (125cc single)	300	500	800	900	1,100	1,300
DR200 (200cc single)	300	500	800	1,100	1,300	1,600
SP200 (200cc single)	300	500	800	1,200	1,400	1,600
RM250 (250cc single)	400	600	1,000	1,500	2,000	2,600
GS450L (450cc twin)	400	700	1,000	1,300	1,600	1,900
GS550L (570cc four)	400	700	1,100	1,600	2,200	2,700
GS550ES (570cc four)	400	700	1,100	1,700	2,300	2,900
LS650F Savage (650cc single)	700	1,000	1,500	1,600	1,800	2,000
LS650P Savage (650cc single)	700	1,000	1,500	1,600	1,800	2,000
VS700GLF Intruder (700cc twin)	800	1,100	1,500	2,200	2,800	3,400
VS700GLEF Intruder (700cc twin).	800	1,100	1,600	2,300	2,900	3,600
GSX-R750 (750cc four)	1,300	1,700	2,300	3,100	3,800	4,500
GSX-R750P Ltd Edition (750cc four)	1,400	1,800	2,500	3,800	5,200	6,500
GSX-R1100 (1,050cc four)	1,500	1,900	2,500	3,500	4,500	5,400
GS1150E (1,135cc four).	1,200	1,600	2,200	3,000	3,700	4,600
GV1200GL Madura (1,165cc four)	1,000	1,300	1,800	2,700	3,700	4,650
GV1400GT Cavalcade (1,360cc four). . . .	1,500	2,000	2,600	4,000	5,100	6,300
GV1400GD Cavalcade LX (1,360cc four) . .	1,500	2,000	2,700	4,000	5,100	6,300
GV1400GC Cavalcade LXE (1,360cc four) .	1,700	2,200	2,900	4,000	5,100	6,300
1987						
JR50 Mini (50cc single)	200	300	400	500	600	700
RB50 Mini GSX-R50 (50cc single)	400	500	600	700	800	1,000
DS80 Mini (80cc single)	200	400	600	700	800	900
RM80 (80cc single)	300	500	800	900	1,100	1,300
DR100 (100cc single)	200	400	700	900	1,100	1,200
DR125 (125cc single)	300	500	800	1,000	1,200	1,400
RM125 (125cc single)	400	600	1,000	1,400	1,900	2,400
SP125 (125cc single)	300	500	800	1,100	1,300	1,500
DR200 (200cc single)	400	600	900	1,200	1,400	1,700
SP200 (200cc single)	300	600	900	1,200	1,500	1,800
RM250 (250cc single)	400	700	1,000	1,600	2,300	2,900
GS450L (450cc twin)	400	700	1,000	1,300	1,600	2,000
LS650 Savage (650cc single)	800	1,100	1,500	1,800	2,000	2,300
VS700GLF Intruder (700cc twin)	800	1,100	1,600	2,200	2,900	3,700
VS700GLEF Intruder (700cc twin).	800	1,200	1,600	2,300	3,000	3,800
GSX-R750 (750cc four)	1,500	1,800	2,500	3,200	4,000	4,900
GSX-R1100 (1,050cc four)	1,500	2,000	2,700	3,700	4,800	5,900
VS1400GLF Intruder (1,360cc twin).	1,300	1,700	2,200	3,500	4,700	5,900
GV1400GD Cavalcade LX (1,360cc four) . .	1,600	2,000	2,700	3,900	5,000	6,500
GV1400GC Cavalcade LXE (1,360cc four) .	1,700	2,200	3,000	4,000	5,100	6,500
1988						
JR50 Mini (50cc single)	200	300	400	500	600	700
DS80 Mini (80cc single)	200	400	700	800	900	1,000
RM80 (80cc single)	300	500	800	1,000	1,200	1,400
DR100 (100cc single)	200	400	700	900	1,100	1,300
DR125 (125cc single)	300	500	800	1,100	1,300	1,500
RM125 (125cc single)	400	700	1,000	1,500	2,000	2,500
SP125 (125cc single)	400	600	900	1,100	1,300	1,600
DR200 (200cc single)	400	600	900	1,300	1,600	1,900
SP200 (200cc single)	400	600	1,000	1,300	1,600	1,900
GN250 (250cc single)	400	600	900	1,200	1,500	1,800
RM250 (250cc single)	500	800	1,100	1,800	2,400	3,100
GS450L (450cc twin)	500	700	1,100	1,400	1,800	2,200
GSX600F Katana (600cc four)	1,000	1,400	1,900	2,500	3,300	4,000
LS650P Savage (650cc single)	800	1,100	1,600	1,900	2,200	2,500
VS750GLP Intruder (750cc twin)	1,100	1,500	2,000	2,600	3,200	4,000
GSX-R750 (750cc four)	1,500	1,900	2,600	3,400	4,300	5,200

	6	5	4	3	2	1
GSX-R1100 (1,050cc four)	1,600	2,100	2,800	3,800	4,900	6,200
GSX1100F Katana (1,125cc four).	1,300	1,700	2,300	3,700	4,800	6,000
VS1400GLP Intruder (1,360cc twin). . . .	1,300	1,700	2,300	3,700	4,800	6,000
GV1400GD Cavalcade LX (1,360cc four) . .	1,700	2,100	2,800	4,000	5,100	6,500
1989						
JR50 Mini (50cc single)	200	300	500	600	700	800
DS80 Mini (80cc single)	200	400	700	1,000	1,100	1,200
RM80 (80cc single)	300	500	800	1,200	1,500	1,800
DR100 (100cc single)	300	500	800	1,000	1,250	1,500
RM125 (125cc single).	500	800	1,100	1,800	2,400	3,000
RM250 (250cc single).	500	800	1,200	2,000	2,800	3,700
RMX250 (250cc single)	500	800	1,100	2,000	2,900	3,900
GS500E (500cc twin)	600	900	1,400	1,900	2,500	3,000
GSX600F Katana (600cc four)	1,100	1,500	2,000	2,700	3,500	4,400
VS750GLP Intruder (750cc twin)	1,100	1,500	2,100	2,700	3,500	4,300
GSX750F Katana (750cc four)	1,200	1,600	2,200	3,000	4,000	5,300
GSX-R750 (750cc four)	1,700	2,000	2,700	3,600	4,600	5,800
GSX1100F Katana (1,100cc four).	1,400	1,800	2,500	3,500	5,000	6,400
GSX-R1100 (1,100cc four)	1,800	2,200	3,000	4,300	5,400	6,600
VS1400GLP Intruder (1,400cc twin). . . .	1,300	1,700	2,300	3,600	5,200	6,500
GV1400GD Cavalcade LX (1,360cc four) . .	1,800	2,200	2,900	4,000	5,200	6,500
1990						
JR50 Mini (50cc single)	200	300	500	600	700	800
DS80 Mini (80cc single)	300	500	800	1,000	1,150	1,300
RM80 (80cc single)	400	600	900	1,300	1,700	2,000
DR100 (100cc single)	300	500	800	1,100	1,300	1,500
RM125 (125cc single).	500	800	1,200	1,800	2,500	3,300
DR250 (250cc single)	500	800	1,100	1,800	2,400	3,000
DR250S (250cc single)	500	800	1,200	1,800	2,400	3,000
RM250 (250cc single).	600	900	1,300	2,000	3,000	3,900
RMX250 (250cc single)	500	800	1,200	2,000	3,000	4,000
DR350 (350cc single)	500	800	1,100	1,900	2,500	3,300
DR350S (350cc single)	500	800	1,200	1,900	2,500	3,300
GS500E (500cc twin)	700	1,000	1,400	1,900	2,500	3,100
DR650S (650cc single)	600	900	1,300	2,000	2,700	3,600
GSX600F Katana (600cc four)	1,100	1,500	2,100	2,800	3,700	4,600
VS750GLP Intruder (750cc twin)	1,200	1,600	2,100	2,800	3,700	4,500
GSX750F Katana (750cc four)	1,400	1,800	2,400	3,300	4,400	5,500
GSX-R750 (750cc four)	1,800	2,200	2,900	4,000	5,000	6,200
VX800 Marauder (800cc twin)	1,000	1,350	1,800	2,800	3,700	4,600
GSX1100F Katana (1,100cc four).	1,600	1,900	2,600	4,300	5,400	6,600
GSX-R1100 (1,100cc four)	1,900	2,400	3,100	4,300	5,500	7,000
VS1400GLP Intruder (1,400cc twin). . . .	1,400	1,800	2,400	4,000	5,000	6,000
1991						
JR50 Mini (50cc single)	200	400	500	600	700	800
DS80 Mini (80cc single)	300	500	800	1,000	1,100	1,300
RM80 (80cc single)	400	600	900	1,300	1,700	2,100
GN125E (125cc single)	400	600	1,000	1,200	1,500	1,800
RM125 (125cc single).	700	900	1,300	2,000	2,700	3,400
DR250 (250cc single)	500	800	1,200	1,800	2,500	3,100
RM250 (250cc single).	700	1,000	1,400	2,200	3,100	4,000
RMX250 (250cc single)	600	900	1,300	2,100	3,100	4,100
DR350 (350cc single)	600	900	1,200	1,900	2,600	3,400
DR250S (250cc single)	600	900	1,300	1,900	2,500	3,100
DR350S (350cc single)	600	900	1,300	2,000	2,700	3,400
GSF400 Bandit (400cc four).	900	1,200	1,700	2,400	3,100	3,700
GS500E (500cc twin)	800	1,100	1,500	2,000	2,500	3,150
GSX600F Katana (600cc four)	1,200	1,600	2,200	3,000	3,800	4,700
DR650S (650cc single)	700	1,000	1,400	2,200	3,000	3,700
VS750GLP Intruder (750cc twin)	1,200	1,600	2,200	3,000	3,800	4,600

	6	5	4	3	2	1
GSX750F Katana (750cc four)	1,600	1,900	2,500	3,300	4,400	5,600
GSX-R750 (750cc four)	1,900	2,300	3,100	4,200	5,300	6,500
VX800 Maurauder (800cc twin)	1,000	1,400	1,900	2,700	3,700	4,700
GSX1100G (1,100cc four).	1,600	2,000	2,700	4,000	5,000	6,000
GSX1100F Katana (1,100cc four).	1,700	2,100	2,800	4,400	5,500	6,800
GSX-R1100 (1,100cc four)	1,900	2,500	3,300	4,500	5,600	7,300
VS1400GLP Intruder (1,400cc twin). . . .	1,400	1,900	2,500	4,100	5,100	6,200
1992						
JR50 Mini (50cc single)	200	400	600	700	800	900
DS80 Mini (80cc single)	300	500	800	1,000	1,200	1,400
RM80 (80cc single)	400	600	1,000	1,400	1,800	2,200
GN125E (125cc single)	500	700	1,000	1,300	1,600	1,900
RM125 (125cc single).	700	1,000	1,400	2,100	2,800	3,500
DR250 (250cc single)	600	900	1,300	1,900	2,500	3,200
DR250S (250cc single)	700	1,000	1,400	2,000	2,600	3,200
RM250 (250cc single)	800	1,100	1,500	2,300	3,200	4,100
RMX250 (250cc single)	700	1,000	1,400	2,200	3,200	4,200
DR350 (350cc single)	600	900	1,300	2,000	2,700	3,500
DR350S (350cc single)	700	1,000	1,400	2,100	2,800	3,500
GSF400 Bandit (400cc four).	1,000	1,300	1,800	2,500	3,200	3,900
GS500E (500cc twin)	800	1,100	1,500	2,100	2,700	3,250
GSX600F Katana (600cc four)	1,300	1,700	2,200	3,000	3,900	4,800
GSX-R600 (600cc four)	1,600	2,000	2,700	3,900	5,000	6,200
DR650S (650cc single)	800	1,100	1,500	2,200	3,000	3,800
GSX750F Katana (750cc four)	1,600	2,000	2,700	3,800	4,800	5,800
GSX-R750 (750cc four)	1,900	2,500	3,300	4,400	5,500	6,700
VS800FLP Intruder (800cc twin)	1,400	1,800	2,500	3,200	4,000	4,800
VX800 Maurauder (800cc twin)	1,100	1,500	2,000	2,900	3,800	4,800
GSX1100G (1,100cc four).	1,700	2,100	2,900	4,000	5,000	6,200
GSX1100F Katana (1,100cc four).	1,700	2,200	2,900	4,400	5,500	7,000
GSX-R1100 (1,100cc four)	2,000	2,700	3,500	4,600	5,700	7,500
VS1400GLP Intruder (1,400cc twin). . . .	1,600	2,000	2,700	4,100	5,200	6,400
1993						
JR50 Mini (50cc single)	200	400	600	700	800	900
DS80 Mini (80cc single)	300	500	800	1,000	1,200	1,400
RM80 (80cc single)	400	600	1,000	1,400	1,800	2,200
GN125E (125cc single)	500	700	1,000	1,300	1,600	1,900
RM125 (125cc single).	700	1,000	1,400	2,100	2,800	3,500
DR250 (250cc single)	600	900	1,300	1,900	2,500	3,200
DR250SE (250cc single)	700	1,000	1,400	2,000	2,600	3,200
RM250 (250cc single)	800	1,100	1,500	2,300	3,200	4,100
RMX250 (250cc single)	700	1,000	1,400	2,200	3,200	4,200
DR350 (350cc single)	600	900	1,300	2,000	2,700	3,500
DR350S (350cc single)	700	1,000	1,400	2,100	2,800	3,500
GSF400 Bandit (400cc four).	1,000	1,300	1,800	2,500	3,200	3,900
GS500E (500cc twin)	800	1,100	1,500	2,100	2,700	3,250
GSX600F Katana (600cc four)	1,300	1,700	2,200	3,000	3,900	4,800
GSX-R600W (600cc four)	1,600	2,000	2,700	3,900	5,000	6,200
DR650S (650cc single)	600	900	1,200	1,700	2,300	3,000
GSX750F Katana (750cc four)	1,600	2,000	2,700	3,800	4,800	5,800
GSX-R750W (750cc four)	1,900	2,500	3,300	4,400	5,500	6,700
VX800 Maurauder (800cc twin)	1,100	1,500	2,000	2,900	3,800	4,800
VS800GL Intruder (800cc twin)	1,400	1,800	2,500	3,200	4,000	4,800
GSX1100G (1,100cc four).	1,700	2,100	2,900	4,000	5,000	6,200
GSX1100F Katana (1,100cc four).	1,700	2,200	2,900	4,400	5,500	7,000
GSX-R1100W (1,100cc four)	2,000	2,700	3,500	4,600	5,700	7,500
VS1400GLP Intruder (1,400cc twin). . . .	1,600	2,000	2,700	4,100	5,200	6,400
1994						
JR50 Mini (50cc single)	200	400	600	700	800	900
DS80 Mini (80cc single)	300	500	800	1,000	1,200	1,400

	6	5	4	3	2	1
RM80 (80cc single)	400	600	1,000	1,400	1,800	2,200
DR125SE (125cc single)	400	600	1,000	1,400	1,800	2,200
GN125E (125cc single)	500	700	1,000	1,300	1,600	1,900
RM125 (125cc single)	700	1,000	1,400	2,100	2,800	3,500
DR250SE (250cc single)	700	1,000	1,400	2,000	2,600	3,200
RM250 (250cc single)	800	1,100	1,500	2,300	3,200	4,100
RMX250 (250cc single)	700	1,000	1,400	2,200	3,200	4,200
DR350 (350cc single)	600	900	1,300	2,000	2,700	3,500
DR350SE (350cc single)	700	1,000	1,400	2,100	2,800	3,500
GS500E (500cc twin)	800	1,100	1,500	2,100	2,700	3,250
GSX600F Katana (600cc four)	800	1,700	2,700	3,700	4,700	5,700
RF600R (600cc four)	700	1,200	1,900	2,600	3,300	4,000
DR650SE (650cc single)	600	900	1,200	1,700	2,300	3,000
GSX750F Katana (750cc four)	1,000	2,000	3,200	4,400	5,600	6,800
GSX-R750W (750cc four)	1,400	2,900	4,300	5,700	7,100	8,500
VS800GL Intruder (800cc twin)	800	1,900	2,900	3,900	4,900	5,900
RF900R (900cc four)	1,400	2,900	4,300	5,700	7,100	8,500
GSX-R1100W (1,100cc four)	2,000	2,700	3,500	4,600	5,700	7,500
VS1400GLP Intruder (1,400cc twin)	1,600	2,000	2,700	4,100	5,200	6,400
1995						
JR50 Mini (50cc single)	200	400	600	700	800	900
DS80 Mini (80cc single)	300	500	800	1,000	1,200	1,400
RM80 (80cc single)	400	600	1,000	1,400	1,800	2,200
DR125SE (125cc single)	400	600	1,000	1,400	1,800	2,200
GN125E (125cc single)	500	700	1,000	1,300	1,600	1,900
RM125 (125cc single)	700	1,000	1,400	2,100	2,800	3,500
DR250SE (250cc single)	700	1,000	1,400	2,000	2,600	3,200
RM250 (250cc single)	800	1,100	1,500	2,300	3,200	4,100
RMX250 (250cc single)	700	1,000	1,400	2,200	3,200	4,200
DR350 (350cc single)	600	900	1,300	2,000	2,700	3,500
DR350SE (350cc single)	700	1,000	1,400	2,100	2,800	3,500
GS500E (500cc twin)	800	1,100	1,500	2,100	2,700	3,250
GSX600F Katana (600cc four)	800	1,700	2,700	3,700	4,700	5,700
RF600R (600cc four)	700	1,200	1,900	2,600	3,300	4,000
DR650SE (650cc single)	600	900	1,200	1,700	2,300	3,000
LS650P Savage (650cc single)	500	800	1,600	2,400	3,200	4,000
GSX750F Katana (750cc four)	1,000	2,000	3,200	4,400	5,600	6,800
GSX-R750W (750cc four)	1,400	2,900	4,300	5,700	7,100	8,500
VS800GL Intruder (800cc twin)	800	1,900	2,900	3,900	4,900	5,900
RF900R (900cc four)	1,400	2,900	4,300	5,700	7,100	8,500
GSX-R1100W (1,100cc four)	2,000	2,700	3,500	4,600	5,700	7,500
VS1400GLP Intruder (1,400cc twin)	1,600	2,000	2,700	4,100	5,200	6,400
1996						
JR50 Mini (50cc single)	200	400	600	700	800	900
DS80 Mini (80cc single)	300	500	800	1,000	1,200	1,400
RM80 (80cc single)	400	600	1,000	1,400	1,800	2,200
RM125 (125cc single)	700	1,000	1,400	2,100	2,800	3,500
DR125SE (125cc single)	400	600	1,000	1,400	1,800	2,200
GN125E (125cc single)	500	700	1,000	1,300	1,600	1,900
DR200SE (200cc single)	300	600	1,200	1,800	2,400	3,000
RM250 (250cc single)	800	1,100	1,500	2,300	3,200	4,100
RMX250 (250cc single)	700	1,000	1,400	2,200	3,200	4,200
DR350 (350cc single)	600	900	1,300	2,000	2,700	3,500
DR350SE (350cc single)	700	1,000	1,400	2,100	2,800	3,500
GS500E (500cc twin)	800	1,100	1,500	2,100	2,700	3,250
GSF600S Bandit S (600cc four)	800	1,600	2,600	3,600	4,600	5,600
GSX600F Katana (600cc four)	800	1,700	2,700	3,700	4,700	5,700
RF600R (600cc four)	700	1,200	1,900	2,600	3,300	4,000
DR650SE (650cc single)	600	900	1,200	1,700	2,300	3,000
LS650P Savage (650cc single)	500	800	1,600	2,400	3,200	4,000

	6	5	4	3	2	1
GSX750F Katana (750cc four)	1,000	2,000	3,200	4,400	5,600	6,800
GSX-R750 (750cc four)	1,400	2,900	4,300	5,700	7,100	8,500
VS800GL Intruder (800cc twin)	800	1,900	2,900	3,900	4,900	5,900
RF900R (900cc four)	1,400	2,900	4,300	5,700	7,100	8,500
GSX-R1100W (1,100cc four)	2,000	2,700	3,500	4,600	5,700	7,500
VS1400GLP Intruder (1,400cc twin). . . .	1,600	2,000	2,700	4,100	5,200	6,400

SWM

1978
	6	5	4	3	2	1
RS125 GS.	200	500	1,100	1,900	2,900	3,900
RS125 MC	200	500	1,400	2,400	3,900	5,400
RS175 GS.	200	500	100	1,900	2,900	3,900
RS250 GS.	200	500	1,400	2,400	3,900	5,400
RS250 MC	200	500	1,400	2,900	4,400	5,700
320 TL.	200	500	1,400	1,900	2,900	3,900

1979
SWM 50.	200	500	1,000	1,300	1,800	2,300
RS125 GS.	200	500	1,400	1,900	2,900	3,900
RS125 MC	200	500	1,400	2,400	3,400	4,400
RS175 GS.	200	500	1,400	1,900	2,900	3,900
RS175 MC	200	500	1,400	1,900	2,900	3,900
RS250 GS.	200	500	1,400	2,900	3,900	4,900
RS250 MC	200	500	1,400	2,900	4,400	5,700
320 TL.	200	500	1,400	1,900	2,900	3,900
RS350 GS.	200	500	1,400	2,400	3,400	4,400

1980
50 Automatic	200	300	700	900	1,500	2,100
50 Cross Boy	200	300	700	900	1,500	2,100
125 Enduro	200	500	1,400	2,400	3,400	4,400
125 MX	200	500	1,400	2,900	3,900	4,900
175 Enduro	200	500	1,400	2,400	3,400	4,400
175 Hare Scrambler.	200	500	1,400	2,400	3,400	4,400
250 Enduro	200	500	1,400	2,900	3,900	4,900
250 Hare Scrambler.	200	500	1,400	2,900	3,900	4,900
250 MX	200	500	1,400	2,900	4,400	5,700
320 Trials	200	500	1,400	1,900	2,900	3,900
370 Enduro	200	500	1,400	2,400	3,900	5,400
370 Hare Scrambler.	200	500	1,400	2,400	3,900	5,400
370 MX	200	500	1,400	2,900	4,400	5,700

1981
RS125 TLNW Trail	200	500	1,400	1,900	2,900	3,900
RS175 GSTF1	200	500	1,400	2,400	3,400	4,400
RS250 GSTF1	200	500	1,400	2,400	3,400	4,400
RS250 MCTF4	200	500	1,400	2,900	4,900	6,900
RS320 TLNW Trail	200	500	1,400	2,400	3,400	4,400
RS440 GSTF1	200	500	1,400	2,900	4,900	6,900
RS440 MCTF1	200	500	1,400	3,400	5,400	7,400

1982
RS80 TLNW Trail	200	500	900	1,400	2,000	2,600
RS125 GSTF3	200	500	1,400	1,800	2,200	2,600
RS125 TLNW Trail	200	500	1,100	1,500	2,000	2,500
RS175 GSTF3	200	500	1,400	1,700	2,200	2,700
RS240 TLNW Trail	200	500	1,400	1,900	2,900	3,900
RS250 GSTF3	200	500	1,400	2,400	3,400	4,400
RS250 MCTF6	200	500	1,400	2,900	4,900	6,900
RS320 TLNW Trail	200	500	1,400	2,400	3,400	4,400
RS440 GSTF3	200	500	1,400	2,900	4,900	6,900
RS440 MCTF6	200	500	1,400	3,400	5,400	7,400

1983
RS125 GS.	200	500	1,400	1,900	2,900	3,900
RS125 MC	200	500	1,400	2,900	3,900	4,900

	6	5	4	3	2	1
RS175 GSTF3	200	500	1,400	1,800	2,200	2,600
RS240 TLNW	200	500	1,400	1,900	2,900	3,900
RS250 GS.	200	500	1,400	2,400	4,400	6,400
RS250 MCTF6	200	500	1,400	2,900	4,900	6,900
RS320 TLNW	200	500	1,400	2,400	3,400	4,400
RS350 TLNW Jumbo	200	500	1,400	2,400	3,400	4,400
RS440 GSTF3	200	500	1,400	2,900	4,900	6,900
RS440 MCTF6	200	500	1,400	3,400	5,400	7,400
1984						
MC125 S2.	200	500	1,400	2,900	3,400	3,900
RS240 TLNW	200	500	1,400	1,900	2,900	3,900
GS250 S1.	200	500	1,400	2,400	2,900	3,400
MC250 S2.	200	500	1,400	2,900	3,900	4,900
RS320 TLNW	200	500	1,400	1,900	2,900	3,900
RS350 TLNW	200	500	1,400	2,400	3,400	4,400
TRIUMPH						
1907						
Single (475cc).	2,000	4,000	8,000	12,000	16,000	20,000
1914						
Model H (550cc).	1,500	2,500	4,000	5,500	7,000	8,500
1915						
Junior (225cc single)	1,500	2,300	3,400	4,500	6,000	7,500
1916						
Belt Drive	4,000	8,000	12,000	16,000	20,000	25,000
1920						
Model H 500 (500cc single)	−4,000	−8,000	−12,000	−16,000	−20,000	−25,000
1925						
Model P (494cc).	1,000	2,000	3,500	5,000	6,500	8,000
Model W (494cc)	−1,500	−3,000	−5,000	8,000	−11,000	−14,000
1926						
Model T (498cc).	2,000	4,000	8,000	12,000	16,000	20,000
1927						
Model N (494cc).	1,000	2,000	3,500	5,000	6,500	8,000
Model P (494cc).	1,000	2,000	3,500	5,000	6,500	8,000
1929						
Model CSD (500cc).	1,000	2,000	3,500	5,000	6,500	8,000
Model CN (500cc).	1,000	2,000	3,500	5,000	6,500	8,000
1930						
Model CSD (500cc)	1,000	2,000	3,500	5,000	6,500	8,000
1932						
Model CD (500cc).	2,000	4,000	8,000	12,000	16,000	20,000
1934						
Model XO (147cc).	1,000	2,000	3,500	5,000	6,500	8,000
Side Valve 5/3 (350cc single)	2,000	3,000	4,000	5,000	7,500	9,500
Model 3/1 (348cc single)	1,800	2,700	4,100	5,400	7,200	9,000
1935						
Model 2/1 (249cc single)	1,000	2,000	3,500	5,000	6,500	8,000
1936						
Model 2/1 (249cc single)	1,000	**2,500**	**4,000**	5,500	**7,000**	**8,500**
Model 3/1 (348cc single)	1,800	2,700	4,100	5,400	7,200	9,000
T70 Tiger (250cc single).	**2,000**	3,000	4,000	5,000	7,500	9,500
T80 Tiger (350cc single).	1,800	**3,000**	4,500	6,000	8,500	11,000
T90 Tiger (500cc single).	2,600	3,900	5,900	7,800	10,400	13,000
6/1 (650cc twin)	3,600	5,400	8,100	10,800	14,400	18,000
1937						
T70 Tiger (250cc single).	−1,000	**2,500**	**4,000**	5,500	**7,000**	**8,500**
2H (250cc single)	−1,000	**2,500**	**4,000**	5,500	**7,000**	**8,500**
T80 Tiger (350cc single).	1,800	2,700	4,100	**6,000**	**9,000**	**12,000**
3H (350cc single)	**2,000**	3,000	4,000	5,000	7,500	9,500
3S (350cc single)	**2,000**	3,000	4,000	5,000	7,500	9,500

	6	5	4	3	2	1
T90 Tiger (500cc single)	2,600	3,900	5,900	7,800	10,000	13,000
5H (500cc single)	2,400	3,600	5,400	7,200	9,600	12,000
5T Speed (500cc twin)	4,000	6,000	10,000	**15,000**	**20,000**	**25,000**
1938						
T70 Tiger (250cc single)	−1,000	**2,500**	**4,000**	5,500	7,000	8,500
2H (250cc single)	−1,000	**2,500**	**4,000**	5,500	7,000	8,500
2HC (250cc single)	−1,000	**2,500**	**4,000**	5,500	7,000	8,500
T80 Tiger (350cc single)	**2,000**	**3,000**	−4,000	−5,000	7,500	9,500
3H (350cc single)	**2,000**	**3,000**	**4,000**	5,000	7,500	9,500
3S (350cc single)	**2,000**	**3,000**	**4,000**	5,000	7,500	9,500
3SC (350cc single)	1,700	2,600	3,900	5,200	6,900	8,600
T90 Tiger (500cc single)	2,600	3,900	6,000	9,000	12,000	15,000
T100 Tiger (500cc twin)	4,000	7,000	12,000	18,000	24,000	30,000
5H (500cc single)	2,400	3,600	5,400	7,200	9,600	12,000
5T Speed (500cc twin)	4,000	6,000	11,000	16,000	22,000	28,000
6S (600cc twin)	3,600	5,400	8,100	**12,000**	**16,000**	**20,000**
1939						
T70 Tiger (250cc single)	−1,000	**2,500**	**4,000**	5,500	7,000	8,500
2H (250cc single)	−1,000	**2,500**	**4,000**	5,500	7,000	8,500
2HC (250cc single)	−1,000	**2,500**	**4,000**	5,500	7,000	8,500
T80 Tiger (350cc single)	1,800	2,700	4,100	5,400	7,200	9,000
3H (350cc single)	**1,800**	**2,700**	**4,100**	**5,400**	**7,200**	**9,000**
3S (350cc single)	**1,800**	**2,700**	**4,100**	**5,400**	**7,200**	**9,000**
3SC (350cc single)	**1,800**	**2,700**	**4,100**	**5,400**	**7,200**	**9,000**
3SW (343cc single)	1,400	2,200	3,200	4,300	5,800	7,200
T90 Tiger (500cc single)	2,600	3,900	5,900	8,000	11,000	15,000
T100 Tiger (500cc twin)	4,000	7,000	12,000	18,000	24,000	30,000
5H (500cc single)	2,400	3,600	5,400	**8,000**	**11,000**	**14,000**
5S (500cc single)	2,400	3,600	5,400	**8,000**	**11,000**	**14,000**
5T Speed (500cc twin)	4,000	6,000	11,000	16,000	22,000	28,000
6S (600cc twin)	3,600	5,400	8,100	**12,000**	**16,000**	**20,000**
1940						
T70 Tiger (250cc single)	−1,000	**2,500**	**4,000**	5,500	7,000	8,500
T80 Tiger (350cc single)	1,800	2,700	4,100	5,400	7,200	9,000
3H (350cc single)	**1,800**	**2,700**	**4,100**	**5,400**	**7,200**	**9,000**
3S (350cc single)	**1,800**	**2,700**	**4,100**	**5,400**	**7,200**	**9,000**
3SE (350cc single)	**1,800**	**2,700**	**4,100**	**5,400**	**7,200**	**9,000**
T100 Tiger (500cc twin)	4,000	7,000	12,000	18,000	24,000	30,000
5S (500cc single)	2,400	3,600	5,400	7,200	9,600	12,000
5SE (500cc single)	2,400	3,600	5,400	7,200	9,600	12,000
5T Speed (500cc twin)	4,000	6,000	11,000	16,000	22,000	28,000
1941						
WD/3HW (350cc single)	1,800	2,700	4,100	5,400	7,200	9,000
WD/3SW (350cc single)	**2,000**	**3,000**	−4,000	−5,000	7,500	9,500
WD/5SW (350cc single)	2,400	3,600	5,400	7,200	9,600	12,000
1942						
WD/3HW (350cc single)	1,800	2,700	4,100	5,400	7,200	9,000
WD/3SW (350cc single)	**2,000**	**3,000**	−4,000	−5,000	7,500	9,500
WD/5SW (350cc single)	2,400	3,600	5,400	7,200	9,600	12,000
1943						
WD/3HW (350cc single)	1,800	2,700	4,100	5,400	7,200	9,000
WD/3SW (350cc single)	**2,000**	**3,000**	−4,000	−5,000	7,500	9,500
WD/5SW (350cc single)	2,400	3,600	5,400	7,200	9,600	12,000
1944						
WD/3HW (350cc single)	1,800	2,700	4,100	5,400	7,200	9,000
WD/3SW (350cc single)	**2,000**	**3,000**	−4,000	−5,000	7,500	9,500
WD/5SW (350cc single)	2,400	3,600	5,400	7,200	9,600	12,000
1945						
WD/3HW (350cc single)	**1,800**	**2,700**	**4,100**	**5,400**	**7,200**	**9,000**

	6	5	4	3	2	1
WD/3SW (350cc single)	**2,000**	**3,000**	−4,000	−5,000	**7,500**	**9,500**
WD/5SW (350cc single)	2,400	3,600	5,400	7,200	9,600	12,000
1946						
3T (350cc single)	1,700	2,600	4,000	6,000	9,000	12,000
T100 Tiger (500cc twin)	3,200	5,000	8,000	12,000	16,000	20,000
5T Speed (500cc twin)	3,600	5,000	8,000	12,000	16,000	20,000
1947						
3T (350cc single)	1,700	2,600	4,000	6,000	9,000	12,000
T100 Tiger (500cc twin)	3,200	5,000	8,000	12,000	16,000	20,000
5T Speed (500cc twin)	3,600	5,000	8,000	12,000	16,000	20,000
1948						
3T (350cc single)	1,700	2,600	4,000	6,000	8,000	10,000
Grand Prix (500cc twin)	6,200	10,000	14,000	21,000	28,000	35,000
T100 Tiger (500cc twin)	3,000	5,000	8,000	12,000	16,000	20,000
TR5 Trophy (500cc twin)	2,400	5,000	10,000	15,000	20,000	25,000
5T Speed (500cc twin)	4,000	6,000	8,000	12,000	16,000	20,000
1949						
3T (350cc single)	1,700	2,600	4,000	6,000	8,000	10,000
Grand Prix (500cc twin)	6,200	10,000	14,000	21,000	28,000	35,000
TR5 Trophy (500cc twin)	2,400	5,000	10,000	15,000	20,000	25,000
T100 Tiger (500cc twin)	3,000	5,000	**8,000**	**12,000**	**16,000**	**20,000**
TRW (500cc twin)	1,200	2,000	**4,000**	**6,000**	**8,000**	**10,000**
5T Speed (500cc twin)	1,500	4,000	7,000	10,000	14,000	18,000
6T Thunderbird (650cc twin)	3,000	**7,000**	**14,000**	**21,000**	**28,000**	**35,000**
1950						
3T (350cc single)	1,700	2,600	4,000	6,000	8,000	10,000
Grand Prix (500cc twin)	6,200	10,000	14,000	21,000	28,000	35,000
T100 Tiger (500cc twin)	3,000	5,000	**8,000**	**12,000**	**16,000**	**20,000**
TR5 Trophy (500cc twin)	2,400	5,000	10,000	15,000	20,000	25,000
TRW (500cc twin)	1,200	2,000	**4,000**	**6,000**	**8,000**	**10,000**
5T Speed (500cc twin)	1,500	4,000	7,000	11,000	15,000	19,000
6T Thunderbird (650cc twin)	3,000	**7,000**	**14,000**	**21,000**	**28,000**	**35,000**
1951						
3T (350cc single)	1,700	2,600	4,000	6,000	8,000	10,000
T100 Tiger (500cc twin)	3,000	5,000	**8,000**	**12,000**	**16,000**	**20,000**
TR5 Trophy (500cc twin)	2,400	5,000	10,000	15,000	20,000	25,000
TRW (500cc twin)	1,200	2,000	**4,000**	**6,000**	**8,000**	**10,000**
5T Speed (500cc twin)	3,400	5,100	7,700	11,000	14,000	18,000
6T Thunderbird (650cc twin)	4,000	6,000	8,000	12,000	16,000	20,000
1952						
T100 Tiger (500cc twin)	3,000	5,000	**8,000**	**12,000**	**16,000**	**20,000**
TR5 Trophy (500cc twin)	2,400	5,000	10,000	15,000	20,000	25,000
TRW (500cc twin)	1,200	2,000	**4,000**	**6,000**	**8,000**	**10,000**
5T Speed (500cc twin)	3,400	5,100	7,700	1,000	14,000	18,000
6T Thunderbird (650cc twin)	4,000	6,000	8,000	12,000	16,000	20,000
1953						
T15 Terrier (150cc single)	1,000	1,500	2,300	3,500	5,000	6,500
T100 Tiger (500cc twin)	3,000	5,000	**8,000**	**12,000**	**16,000**	**20,000**
TR5 Trophy (500cc twin)	2,400	5,000	10,000	15,000	20,000	25,000
TRW (500cc twin)	1,200	2,000	**4,000**	**6,000**	**8,000**	**10,000**
5T Speed (500cc twin)	3,400	5,100	7,700	1,000	14,000	18,000
6T Thunderbird (650cc twin)	4,000	6,000	8,000	12,000	16,000	20,000
1954						
T15 Terrier (150cc single)	1,000	1,500	2,300	3,500	5,000	6,500
T100 Tiger (500cc twin)	3,000	5,000	**8,000**	**12,000**	**16,000**	**20,000**
TR5 Trophy (500cc twin)	2,400	5,000	10,000	15,000	20,000	25,000
TRW (500cc twin)	1,200	2,000	**4,000**	**6,000**	**8,000**	**10,000**
5T Speed (500cc twin)	3,200	4,800	7,200	9,600	13,000	16,000
T110 Tiger (650cc twin)	3,200	**5,000**	8,000	11,000	14,000	**17,000**
6T Thunderbird (650cc twin)	4,000	6,000	8,000	12,000	16,000	20,000

	6	5	4	3	2	1
1955						
T15 Terrier (150cc single)	1,000	1,500	2,300	3,500	5,000	6,500
T100 Tiger (500cc twin)	2,800	4,200	6,300	9,000	12,000	15,000
TR5 Trophy (500cc twin)	**3,200**	**4,800**	**7,200**	**9,600**	**13,000**	**16,000**
TRW (500cc twin)	1,200	2,000	**4,000**	**6,000**	**8,000**	**10,000**
5T Speed (500cc twin)	−2,000	−3,000	−6,000	−9,000	−12,000	−15,000
T110 Tiger (650cc twin)	−2,000	−3,000	−6,000	−9,000	−12,000	−15,000
6T Thunderbird (650cc twin)	2,000	3,000	6,000	9,000	12,000	15,000
1956						
T15 Terrier (150cc single)	1,000	1,500	2,300	3,500	5,000	6,500
T100 Tiger (500cc twin)	2,800	4,200	6,300	9,000	12,000	15,000
TR5 Trophy (500cc twin)	**3,200**	**4,800**	**7,200**	**9,600**	**13,000**	**16,000**
TRW (500cc twin)	1,200	2,000	**4,000**	**6,000**	**8,000**	**10,000**
5T Speed (500cc twin)	3,200	4,800	7,200	9,600	13,000	16,000
T110 Tiger (650cc twin)	−2,000	−3,000	−6,000	−9,000	−12,000	−15,000
TR6 Trophy (650cc twin)	2,200	5,000	8,000	11,000	14,000	18,000
6T Thunderbird (650cc twin)	2,000	3,000	6,000	9,000	12,000	15,000
1957						
T20 Tiger Cub (200cc single)	1,000	1,500	3,000	4,500	6,000	7,500
T20C Tiger Cub (200cc single)	1,000	1,500	3,000	4,500	6,000	7,500
T100 Tiger (500cc twin)	2,800	4,200	6,300	9,000	12,000	15,000
TR5 Trophy (500cc twin)	**3,200**	**4,800**	**7,200**	**9,600**	**13,000**	**16,000**
TRW (500cc twin)	1,200	2,000	**4,000**	**6,000**	**8,000**	**10,000**
5T Speed (500cc twin)	3,200	4,800	7,200	9,600	13,000	16,000
T110 Tiger (650cc twin)	−2,000	−3,000	−6,000	−9,000	−12,000	−15,000
TR6 Trophy (650cc twin)	2,200	5,000	8,000	11,000	14,000	18,000
6T Thunderbird (650cc twin)	2,000	3,000	6,000	9,000	12,000	15,000
1958						
T20 Tiger Cub (200cc single)	1,000	1,500	3,000	**6,000**	**9,000**	**12,000**
T20C Tiger Cub (200cc single)	1,000	1,500	3,000	4,500	6,000	7,500
3TA Twenty One (350cc twin)	1,200	2,000	3,500	5,000	7,500	9,000
T100 Tiger (500cc twin)	2,800	4,200	6,300	9,000	12,000	15,000
TR5 Trophy (500cc twin)	**3,200**	**4,800**	**7,200**	**9,600**	**13,000**	**16,000**
TRW (500cc twin)	1,200	2,000	**4,000**	**6,000**	**8,000**	**10,000**
5T Speed (500cc twin)	3,000	4,500	6,800	9,000	12,000	15,000
T110 Tiger (650cc twin)	−2,000	−3,000	−6,000	−9,000	−12,000	−15,000
TR6 Trophy (650cc twin)	2,200	5,000	8,000	11,000	14,000	18,000
6T Thunderbird (650cc twin)	2,000	3,000	6,000	9,000	12,000	15,000
1959						
T20 Tiger Cub (200cc single)	1,000	1,500	3,000	4,500	6,000	7,500
T20C Tiger Cub (200cc single)	1,000	1,500	3,000	4,500	6,000	7,500
3TA Twenty One (350cc twin)	−1,000	−1,500	3,000	**6,000**	**9,000**	**12,000**
T100 Tiger (500cc twin)	2,600	3,900	5,900	7,800	10,000	13,000
TRW (500cc twin)	1,200	2,000	**4,000**	**6,000**	**8,000**	**10,000**
5TA Speed (500cc twin)	−2,800	−4,200	−6,300	−8,400	−11,000	−14,000
T110 Tiger (650cc twin)	2,800	4,200	6,300	8,400	11,000	14,000
T120 Bonneville (650cc twin)	4,300	6,300	10,000	15,000	**21,000**	**28,000**
TR6 Trophy (650cc twin)	2,200	**5,000**	**8,000**	**11,000**	**14,000**	**18,000**
6T Thunderbird (650cc twin)	3,000	4,500	6,000	9,000	12,000	16,000
1960						
T20 Tiger Cub (200cc single)	1,000	1,500	3,000	4,500	6,000	7,500
T20S Tiger Cub (200cc single)	1,000	1,500	3,000	4,500	6,000	7,500
3TA Twenty One (350cc twin)	−1,000	−1,500	3,000	**6,000**	**9,000**	**12,000**
T100A Tiger (500cc twin)	2,600	3,900	5,900	7,800	10,000	13,000
TRW (500cc twin)	1,200	2,000	**4,000**	**6,000**	**8,000**	**10,000**
5TA Speed (500cc twin)	−2,800	−4,200	−6,300	−8,400	−11,000	−14,000
T110 Tiger (650cc twin)	−1,000	−1,500	−3,000	−6,000	−9,000	−12,000
T120 Bonneville (650cc twin)	−3,000	**6,000**	**10,000**	**14,000**	**18,000**	**22,000**
TR6 Trophy (650cc twin)	2,200	3,300	5,000	6,600	10,000	14,000
6T Thunderbird (650cc twin)	2,000	3,000	4,500	6,000	10,000	14,000

	6	5	4	3	2	1
1961						
T20 Tiger Cub (200cc single)	1,000	1,500	3,000	4,500	6,000	7,500
T20S/L Tiger Cub (200cc single)	1,000	1,500	3,000	4,500	6,000	7,500
T20T Tiger Cub (200cc single)	1,000	1,500	3,000	4,500	6,000	7,500
3TA Twenty One (350cc twin)	1,200	**2,000**	**4,000**	**6,000**	**8,000**	**10,000**
T100A Tiger (500cc twin)	2,400	3,600	5,400	7,200	9,600	12,000
TRW (500cc twin)	1,200	2,000	**4,000**	**6,000**	**8,000**	**10,000**
5TA Speed (500cc twin)	−1,000	−1,500	−3,000	−6,000	−9,000	−12,000
T110 Tiger (650cc twin)	2,800	4,200	6,300	8,400	11,000	14,000
T120 Bonneville (650cc twin)	−3,000	**6,000**	**10,000**	**14,000**	**18,000**	**22,000**
T120R Bonneville (650cc twin)	−3,000	**6,000**	**10,000**	**14,000**	**18,000**	**22,000**
TR6 Trophy (650cc twin)	2,000	3,000	4,500	6,000	10,000	14,000
6T Thunderbird (650cc twin)	2,000	3,000	4,500	6,000	10,000	14,000
1962						
T20 Tiger Cub (200cc single)	1,000	1,500	3,000	4,500	6,000	7,500
T20S/H Tiger Cub (200cc single)	1,000	1,500	3,000	4,500	6,000	7,500
T20S/S Tiger Cub (200cc single)	1,000	1,500	3,000	4,500	6,000	7,500
TR20 Tiger Cub (200cc single)	1,000	1,500	3,000	4,500	6,000	7,500
3TA Twenty One (350cc twin)	1,200	**2,000**	**4,000**	**6,000**	**8,000**	**10,000**
T100SS Tiger (500cc twin)	2,400	3,600	5,400	7,200	9,600	12,000
TRW (500cc twin)	1,200	2,000	**4,000**	**6,000**	**8,000**	**10,000**
5TA Speed (500cc twin)	2,800	4,200	6,300	8,400	11,000	14,000
T120 Bonneville (650cc twin)	−3,000	**6,000**	**10,000**	**14,000**	**18,000**	**22,000**
T120R Bonneville (650cc twin)	−3,000	**6,000**	**10,000**	**14,000**	**18,000**	**22,000**
TR6 Trophy (650cc twin)	2,000	3,000	4,500	6,000	**10,000**	**14,000**
6T Thunderbird (650cc twin)	2,000	3,000	4,500	6,000	**10,000**	**14,000**
1963						
T20 Tiger Cub (200cc single)	1,000	1,500	3,000	4,500	6,000	7,500
T20S/H Tiger Cub (200cc single)	1,000	1,500	3,000	4,500	6,000	7,500
T20S/S Tiger Cub (200cc single)	1,000	1,500	3,000	4,500	6,000	7,500
T90 Tiger (350cc twin)	−1,000	−1,500	**3,000**	**4,500**	**6,000**	**7,500**
3TA Twenty One (350cc twin)	1,200	1,800	3,000	4,000	6,000	8,000
T100SC Tiger (500cc twin)	2,200	3,300	5,000	6,600	**9,000**	**12,000**
T100SR Tiger (500cc twin)	2,200	3,300	5,000	6,600	8,800	11,000
T100SS Tiger (500cc twin)	2,200	3,300	5,000	6,600	8,800	11,000
TRW (500cc twin)	1,200	2,000	**4,000**	**6,000**	**8,000**	**10,000**
5TA Speed (500cc twin)	−2,200	−3,300	−5,000	−6,600	−9,000	−12,000
T120 Bonneville (650cc twin)	3,600	5,400	8,100	11,000	14,000	18,000
T120C Bonneville (650cc twin)	−3,000	−5,000	**8,000**	**12,000**	**16,000**	**20,000**
T120R Bonneville (650cc twin)	3,600	5,400	8,100	11,000	14,000	18,000
TR6 Trophy (650cc twin)	2,000	3,000	4,500	6,000	**10,000**	**14,000**
6T Thunderbird (650cc twin)	−1,500	3,000	**6,000**	**9,000**	**12,000**	**15,000**
1964						
T20 Tiger Cub (200cc single)	1,000	1,500	3,000	4,500	6,000	7,500
T20S/H Tiger Cub (200cc single)	1,000	1,500	3,000	4,500	6,000	7,500
T20S/S Tiger Cub (200cc single)	1,000	1,500	3,000	4,500	6,000	7,500
T90 Tiger (350cc twin)	−1,000	−1,500	**3,000**	**4,500**	**6,000**	**7,500**
3TA Twenty One (350cc twin)	1,200	1,800	3,000	4,000	6,000	8,000
T100SC Tiger (500cc twin)	2,000	3,000	4,500	6,000	**9,000**	**12,000**
T100SR Tiger (500cc twin)	2,000	3,000	4,500	6,000	8,000	10,000
T100SS Tiger (500cc twin)	2,000	3,000	4,500	6,000	8,000	10,000
5TA Speed (500cc twin)	−2,000	−3,000	−4,500	−6,000	−9,000	−12,000
T120 Bonneville (650cc twin)	3,200	4,800	**7,000**	**10,000**	**13,000**	**16,000**
T120 Bonneville Thruxton (650cc twin) . . .	4,100	6,200	9,200	12,000	16,000	21,000
T120C Bonneville (650cc twin)	−3,000	**5,000**	**8,000**	**12,000**	**16,000**	**20,000**
T120R Bonneville (650cc twin)	−2,000	−4,000	**7,000**	**10,000**	**13,000**	**16,000**
T120TT Bonneville TT Special (650cc twin) .	**3,600**	**5,400**	**8,100**	**11,000**	**14,000**	**18,000**
TR6 Trophy (650cc twin)	2,000	3,000	4,500	6,000	**9,000**	**12,000**
TR6S/C Trophy (650cc twin)	2,000	3,000	4,500	6,000	**9,000**	**12,000**

	6	5	4	3	2	1
TR6S/R Trophy (650cc twin)	2,000	3,000	4,500	6,000	9,000	12,000
TRW (500cc twin)	2,000	3,000	4,500	6,000	9,000	12,000
6T Thunderbird (650cc twin)	−1,500	3,000	6,000	9,000	12,000	15,000
1965						
T20 Tiger Cub (200cc single)	1,000	1,500	3,000	4,500	6,000	7,500
T20S/H Tiger Cub (200cc single)	1,000	1,500	3,000	4,500	6,000	7,500
T20S/M Tiger Cub (200cc single)	1,000	2,000	4,000	5,500	7,000	8,500
T20S/S Tiger Cub (200cc single)	1,000	1,500	3,000	4,500	6,000	7,500
T90 Tiger (350cc twin)	−1,000	−1,500	3,000	4,500	6,000	7,500
3TA Twenty One (350cc twin).	1,200	1,800	3,000	4,000	6,000	8,000
T100SC Tiger (500cc twin)	2,000	3,000	4,500	6,000	9,000	12,000
T100SR Tiger (500cc twin)	2,000	3,000	4,500	6,000	8,000	10,000
T100SS Tiger (500cc twin)	2,000	3,000	4,500	6,000	8,000	10,000
5TA Speed (500cc twin).	−2,000	−3,000	−4,500	−6,000	−9,000	−12,000
T120 Bonneville (650cc twin)	3,600	5,400	8,100	11,000	14,000	18,000
T120 Bonneville Thruxton (650cc twin) . . .	4,100	6,200	9,200	12,000	16,000	21,000
T120C Bonneville (650cc twin)	−3,000	5,000	8,000	12,000	16,000	20,000
T120R Bonneville (650cc twin)	3,600	5,400	8,100	11,000	14,000	18,000
T120TT Bonneville TT Special (650cc twin).	−3,000	5,000	8,000	12,000	16,000	20,000
TR6 Trophy (650cc twin)	2,000	3,000	4,500	6,000	9,000	12,000
TR6S/C Trophy (650cc twin)	2,000	3,000	4,500	6,000	9,000	12,000
TR6S/R Trophy (650cc twin)	2,000	3,000	4,500	6,000	9,000	12,000
TRW (500cc twin)	2,000	3,000	4,500	6,000	9,000	12,000
6T Thunderbird (650cc twin)	−1,500	3,000	6,000	9,000	12,000	15,000
1966						
T20 Tiger Cub Bantam (200cc single). . . .	1,000	2,000	3,000	4,000	5,500	7,000
T20S/H Tiger Cub (200cc single)	1,000	1,500	3,000	4,500	6,000	7,500
T20S/M Tiger Cub (200cc single)	1,000	2,000	4,000	5,500	7,000	8,500
T20S/S Tiger Cub (200cc single)	1,000	1,500	3,000	4,500	6,000	7,500
T90 Tiger (350cc twin)	−1,000	−1,500	3,000	4,500	6,000	7,500
3TA Twenty One (350cc twin).	1,200	1,800	3,000	4,000	6,000	8,000
T100C Tiger (500cc twin)	1,800	2,700	4,100	5,400	7,200	9,000
T100R Tiger Daytona (500cc twin)	1,900	3,000	6,000	9,000	12,000	15,000
5TA Speed (500cc twin).	2,500	3,800	5,600	7,500	10,000	13,000
T120 Bonneville (650cc twin)	−1,900	−3,000	−6,000	9,000	12,000	15,000
T120R Bonneville (650cc twin)	3,600	5,400	8,100	11,000	14,000	18,000
T120TT Bonneville TT Special (650cc twin).	−3,000	5,000	8,000	12,000	16,000	20,000
TR6 Trophy (650cc twin)	2,000	3,000	5,000	8,000	11,000	14,000
TR6C Trophy (650cc twin)	−1,900	3,000	6,000	9,000	12,000	15,000
TR6R Trophy (650cc twin)	2,000	3,000	5,000	8,000	11,000	14,000
TR6S/C Trophy (650cc twin)	−1,900	3,000	6,000	9,000	12,000	15,000
TR6S/R Trophy (650cc twin)	2,000	3,000	5,000	8,000	11,000	14,000
6T Thunderbird (650cc twin)	2,000	3,000	5,000	8,000	11,000	14,000
1967						
T20S/C Tiger Cub (200cc single)	1,000	2,000	4,000	5,500	7,000	8,500
T90 Tiger (350cc twin)	−1,000	−1,500	3,000	4,500	6,000	7,500
T100 Tiger (500cc twin)	1,800	2,700	4,050	5,400	7,200	9,000
T100R Tiger Daytona (500cc twin)	1,900	3,000	6,000	9,000	12,000	15,000
T120 Bonneville (650cc twin)	−1,900	−3,000	−6,000	9,000	12,000	15,000
T120R Bonneville (650cc twin)	3,200	4,800	6,500	9,000	12,000	15,000
T120TT Bonneville TT Special (650cc twin).	−3,000	5,000	8,000	12,000	16,000	20,000
TR6 Trophy (650cc twin)	2,000	3,000	5,000	8,000	11,000	14,000
TR6C Trophy (650cc twin)	−1,900	3,000	6,000	9,000	12,000	15,000
TR6R Trophy (650cc twin)	−1,900	3,000	6,000	9,000	12,000	15,000
1968						
T20S/C Tiger Cub (200cc single)	1,000	2,000	4,000	5,500	7,000	8,500
TR25W Trophy (250cc single).	800	1,300	2,000	3,000	4,000	5,500
T90 Tiger (350cc twin)	−1,000	−1,500	3,000	4,500	6,000	7,500
T100C Tiger (500cc twin)	2,000	3,000	4,500	6,000	9,000	12,000

	6	5	4	3	2	1
T100R Tiger Daytona (500cc twin)	1,900	**3,000**	**6,000**	9,000	12,000	15,000
T100S Tiger (500cc twin)	1,800	2,700	4,050	5,400	7,200	9,000
T120 Bonneville (650cc twin)	1,000	2,500	6,500	8,000	10,000	12,000
T120R Bonneville (650cc twin)	1,000	2,500	6,500	**9,000**	**12,000**	**15,000**
TR6 Trophy (650cc twin)	2,000	4,000	7,000	10,000	13,000	16,000
TR6C Trophy (650cc twin)	2,000	4,000	7,000	10,000	13,000	16,000
TR6R Trophy (650cc twin)	−1,000	−2,500	6,500	9,000	12,000	15,000
1969						
TR25W Trophy (250cc single).	800	1,300	**2,000**	3,000	4,000	5,500
T90 Tiger (350cc twin)	−1,000	−1,500	3,000	4,500	6,000	7,500
T100C Tiger (500cc twin)	**2,000**	**3,000**	4,500	6,000	9,000	12,000
T100R Tiger Daytona (500cc twin)	1,900	**3,000**	**6,000**	9,000	12,000	15,000
T100S Tiger (500cc twin)	1,800	2,700	4,050	5,400	7,200	9,000
T120 Bonneville (650cc twin)	1,000	2,500	6,500	8,000	10,000	12,000
T120R Bonneville (650cc twin)	**2,000**	**4,000**	7,000	10,000	13,000	16,000
TR6 Trophy (650cc twin)	−1,000	−2,500	6,500	8,000	10,000	12,000
TR6C Trophy (650cc twin)	2,000	4,000	7,000	10,000	13,000	16,000
TR6R Trophy (650cc twin)	−1,000	−2,500	6,500	9,000	12,000	15,000
T150 Trident (750cc triple)	1,000	2,500	6,500	8,000	10,000	12,000
1970						
T25SS Street Scrambler (250cc single). . .	−800	1,300	2,000	3,000	4,000	5,500
T25T Blazer (250cc single)	−800	1,300	2,000	3,000	4,000	5,500
TR25W Trophy (250cc single).	800	1,300	**2,000**	3,000	4,000	5,500
T100C (500cc twin)	−1,000	−2,500	6,500	8,000	10,000	12,000
T100R Tiger Daytona (500cc twin)	−1,000	−2,500	6,500	9,000	12,000	15,000
T100S Tiger (500cc twin)	1,800	2,700	4,050	5,400	7,200	9,000
T120 Bonneville (650cc twin)	**2,000**	**4,000**	7,000	10,000	13,000	16,000
T120R Bonneville (650cc twin)	3,600	5,400	8,100	11,000	14,000	18,000
T120RT Bonneville (US) (650cc twin)	1,000	2,500	6,500	**9,000**	**12,000**	**15,000**
TR6 Trophy (650cc twin)	1,800	2,700	4,100	6,000	8,000	10,000
TR6C Trophy (650cc twin)	**2,000**	**4,000**	7,000	10,000	13,000	16,000
TR6R Trophy (650cc twin)	−1,000	−2,500	6,500	9,000	12,000	15,000
T150 Trident (750cc triple) (350 made) . . .	1,000	2,500	6,500	9,000	12,000	15,000
1971						
T25SS Street Scrambler (250cc single). . .	−800	1,300	2,000	3,000	4,000	5,500
T25T Blazer (250cc single)	−800	1,300	2,000	3,000	4,000	5,500
T100C (500cc twin)	−1,000	−2,500	6,500	8,000	10,000	12,000
T100R Tiger Daytona (500cc twin)	−1,000	−2,500	6,500	8,000	10,000	12,000
T120 Bonneville (650cc twin)	1,000	2,500	6,500	8,000	10,000	12,000
T120R Bonneville (650cc twin)	1,000	2,500	4,000	6,000	8,000	10,000
TR6C Trophy (650cc twin)	1,800	2,700	4,100	5,400	7,200	9,000
T150 Trident (750cc triple)	1,000	2,000	4,000	6,000	8,000	10,000
1972						
T100R Tiger Daytona (500cc twin)	−1,000	−2,500	6,500	8,000	10,000	12,000
T120R Bonneville (650cc twin)	1,000	2,500	4,000	6,000	8,000	10,000
T120RV Bonneville (650cc twin)	1,000	2,500	4,000	6,000	8,000	10,000
T120V Bonneville (650cc twin)	1,000	2,500	4,000	6,000	8,000	10,000
TR6C Trophy (650cc twin)	1,800	2,700	4,100	5,400	7,200	9,000
TR6CV Trophy (650cc twin)	1,800	2,700	4,100	5,400	7,200	9,000
TR6R Trophy Sports (650cc twin).	1,900	2,800	4,200	5,600	7,400	9,300
T150 Trident (750cc triple)	1,000	2,500	4,000	6,000	8,000	10,000
T150V Trident (750cc triple).	1,000	2,500	4,000	6,000	8,000	10,000
1973						
T100R Tiger Daytona (500cc twin)	−1,000	−2,500	6,500	8,000	10,000	12,000
TR5T Adventurer (500cc twin)	−1,000	−2,500	−4,000	6,000	8,000	10,000
T120R Bonneville (650cc twin)	1,000	2,500	4,000	6,000	8,000	10,000
T120RV Bonneville (650cc twin)	1,000	2,500	4,000	6,000	8,000	10,000
T120V Bonneville (650cc twin)	1,000	2,500	4,000	6,000	8,000	10,000
TR6C Trophy (650cc twin)	1,800	2,700	4,100	5,400	7,200	9,000

	6	5	4	3	2	1
TR6CV Trophy (650cc twin)	1,800	2,700	4,100	5,400	7,200	9,000
TR6R Trophy Sports (650cc twin)	1,900	2,800	4,200	5,600	7,400	9,300
T140RV Bonneville (750cc twin)	1,000	2,000	3,000	**6,000**	**8,000**	**10,000**
T140V Bonneville (750cc twin)	1,000	2,000	3,000	**6,000**	**8,000**	**10,000**
T150V Trident (750cc triple)	1,000	2,500	4,000	6,000	8,000	10,000
TR7RV Tiger (750cc twin)	–1,000	2,500	4,000	**6,000**	**8,000**	**10,000**
X75 Hurricane (750cc triple)	3,000	6,000	12,000	17,000	23,000	29,000
1974						
T100R Tiger Daytona (500cc twin)	–1,000	–2,500	**6,500**	**8,000**	**10,000**	**12,000**
TR5MX Avenger (500cc twin)	–1,000	–2,500	–4,000	**6,000**	**8,000**	**10,000**
TR5T Adventurer (500cc twin)	–1,000	–2,500	–4,000	**6,000**	**8,000**	**10,000**
T120R Bonneville (650cc twin)	2,000	3,000	4,000	6,000	8,000	10,000
T120RV Bonneville (650cc twin)	2,000	3,000	4,000	6,000	8,000	10,000
T120V Bonneville (650cc twin)	2,000	3,000	4,000	6,000	8,000	10,000
T140RV Bonneville (750cc twin)	1,000	2,000	3,000	**6,000**	**8,000**	**10,000**
T140V Bonneville (750cc twin)	1,000	2,000	3,000	**6,000**	**8,000**	**10,000**
T150V Trident (750cc triple)	1,000	2,500	4,000	6,000	8,000	10,000
TR7RV Tiger (750cc twin)	–1,000	2,500	4,000	**6,000**	**8,000**	**10,000**
1975						
T120RV Bonneville (650cc twin)	2,000	3,000	4,000	6,000	8,000	10,000
T120V Bonneville (650cc twin)	2,000	3,000	4,000	6,000	8,000	10,000
T140RV Bonneville (750cc twin)	1,000	2,000	3,000	**6,000**	**8,000**	**10,000**
T140V Bonneville (750cc twin)	1,000	2,000	3,000	**6,000**	**8,000**	**10,000**
T150V Trident (750cc triple)	1,000	2,500	4,000	6,000	8,000	10,000
T160 Trident (750cc triple)	1,000	2,500	**6,500**	**8,000**	**10,000**	**12,000**
TR7RV Tiger (750cc twin)	–1,000	2,500	4,000	**6,000**	**8,000**	**10,000**
1976						
T140V Bonneville (750cc twin)	1,000	2,000	3,000	**6,000**	**8,000**	**10,000**
T160 Trident (750cc triple)	1,000	**2,500**	**6,500**	**8,000**	**10,000**	**12,000**
TR7RV Tiger (750cc twin)	–1,000	2,500	4,000	**6,000**	**8,000**	**10,000**
1977						
T140J Bonneville Silver Jubilee (750cc twin)	1,000	2,500	**6,500**	**9,000**	**12,000**	**15,000**
T140V Bonneville (750cc twin)	1,000	2,000	3,000	**6,000**	**8,000**	**10,000**
TR7RV Tiger (750cc twin)	1,000	2,000	–3,000	**6,000**	**8,000**	**10,000**
1978						
T140E Bonneville (750cc twin)	1,000	2,000	3,000	**6,000**	**8,000**	**10,000**
T140V Bonneville (750cc twin)	1,000	2,000	3,000	**6,000**	**8,000**	**10,000**
TR7RV Tiger (750cc twin)	1,000	2,000	–3,000	**6,000**	**8,000**	**10,000**
1979						
T140D Bonneville (750cc twin)	1,000	2,000	3,000	**6,000**	**8,000**	**11,000**
T140E Bonneville (750cc twin)	1,000	2,000	3,000	**6,000**	**8,000**	**10,000**
TR7RV Tiger (750cc twin)	–1,000	2,000	–3,000	**6,000**	**8,000**	**10,000**
1980						
T140 Executive Bonneville (750cc twin)	1,000	2,000	3,000	**6,000**	**8,000**	**10,000**
T140D Bonneville (750cc twin)	1,000	2,000	3,000	**6,000**	**8,000**	**11,000**
T140E Bonneville (750cc twin)	1,000	2,000	3,000	**6,000**	**8,000**	**10,000**
T140ES Bonneville Electro (750cc twin)	1,000	2,000	3,000	**6,000**	**8,000**	**10,000**
TR7RV Tiger (750cc twin)	–1,000	2,000	–3,000	**6,000**	**8,000**	**10,000**
1982						
T140ES Bonneville (750cc twin)	1,000	2,000	4,000	6,000	8,000	10,000
T140ES Royal (750cc twin)	**2,000**	**3,000**	**5,000**	**7,100**	**9,000**	**12,000**
T140ES Executive (750cc twin)	**2,000**	**3,000**	**5,000**	**7,100**	**9,000**	**12,000**
1983						
T140ES Bonneville (750cc twin)	1,000	2,000	3,000	**6,000**	**8,000**	**10,000**
T140TSX (750cc twin)	2,500	3,500	4,300	6,300	8,300	11,000
T140TSS Eight Valve (750cc twin)	–2,000	–3,000	–5,000	**8,000**	**11,000**	**14,000**
T140ES Executive (750cc twin)	**2,000**	**3,000**	**5,000**	**7,100**	**9,000**	**12,000**
1995						
Tiger SE (885cc triple)	1,000	2,000	3,500	5,000	6,500	8,000

	6	5	4	3	2	1
Trident 900SA (885cc triple)	1,000	2,000	3,000	4,000	5,500	7,000
Sprint SD (885cc triple)	1,000	2,000	3,500	5,000	6,500	8,000
Thunderbird SJ (885cc triple)	1,000	2,000	3,500	5,000	6,500	8,000
Speed Triple SG (885cc triple)	1,000	2,000	4,500	6,000	7,500	9,000
Daytona 900SC (885cc triple)	1,000	2,000	3,500	5,000	6,500	8,000
Super III SH (885cc triple)	1,000	2,000	3,500	5,000	8,000	11,000
Daytona 1200VS (1,180cc four)	1,000	2,000	4,500	6,000	7,500	9,000
Trophy 900SB (885cc four)	1,000	2,000	3,500	5,000	6,500	8,000
Trophy 1200VA (1,200cc four)	1,000	2,000	3,500	5,000	6,500	8,000
1996						
Tiger (885cc triple)	1,000	2,000	3,500	5,000	6,500	8,000
Trident 900 (885cc triple)	1,000	2,000	3,000	4,000	5,500	7,000
Sprint (885cc triple)	1,000	2,000	3,500	5,000	6,500	8,000
Thunderbird (885cc triple)	1,000	2,000	3,500	5,000	6,500	8,000
Adventurer (885cc triple)	1,000	2,000	3,500	5,000	6,500	8,000
Speed Triple (885cc triple)	1,000	2,000	4,500	6,000	7,500	9,000
Daytona 900 (885cc triple)	1,000	2,000	3,500	5,000	6,500	8,000
Daytona Spr III (885cc triple)	1,000	2,000	3,500	5,000	8,000	11,000
Trophy 900 (885cc four)	1,000	2,000	3,500	5,000	6,500	8,000
Daytona 1200 (1,180cc four)	1,000	2,000	3,500	5,000	6,500	8,000
Trophy 1200 (1,200cc four)	1,000	2,000	3,500	5,000	6,500	8,000
VELOCETTE						
1922						
EL3 (220cc single)	1,000	2,000	4,000	6,000	9,000	12,000
1927						
KSS (350cc)	3,000	6,000	9,000	12,000	15,000	18,000
1929						
KN (348cc)	2,000	4,000	8,000	12,000	16,000	20,000
KTT (348cc single)	7,000	11,000	16,000	21,000	28,000	35,000
1930						
KTT (348cc single)	7,000	11,000	16,000	21,000	28,000	35,000
1934						
KSS (350cc)	3,000	6,000	9,000	12,000	15,000	18,000
1935						
MSS	3,000	5,000	7,000	9,500	11,500	13,500
KTT (348cc single)	7,000	11,000	16,000	21,000	28,000	35,000
1937						
GTP	1,000	2,000	4,000	6,000	8,000	10,000
KSS	3,000	6,000	9,000	12,000	15,000	18,000
1938						
MAC (349cc single)	2,500	4,000	5,300	6,500	8,000	10,000
MSS (500cc single)	1,500	3,000	6,000	10,000	14,000	18,000
KTT (348cc single)	7,000	11,000	16,000	21,000	28,000	35,000
1946						
GTP (249cc single)	2,000	3,000	4,500	6,000	8,000	10,000
KSS (350cc single)	2,000	3,000	4,500	6,000	8,000	10,000
1947						
KTT (348cc single)	7,000	11,000	16,000	21,000	28,000	35,000
KSS MK II (349cc single)	2,000	3,000	4,500	6,000	**9,000**	**12,000**
MAC (349cc single)	1,400	2,100	4,000	**5,500**	**7,000**	**8,500**
1948						
LE (150cc twin, shaft drive)	1,000	1,800	2,600	3,500	5,000	6,500
KTT (348cc single)	7,000	11,000	16,000	21,000	28,000	35,000
KSS MK II (349cc single)	2,000	3,000	4,500	6,000	**9,000**	**12,000**
MAC (349cc single)	1,400	2,100	4,000	**5,500**	**7,000**	**8,500**
1949						
LE (150cc twin, shaft drive)	**1,000**	**1,800**	**2,600**	**3,500**	**5,000**	**6,500**
KTT (348cc single)	7,000	11,000	16,000	21,000	28,000	35,000
MAC (349cc single)	1,400	2,100	4,000	**5,500**	**7,000**	**8,500**

	6	5	4	3	2	1
1950						
LE (150cc twin, shaft drive)	1,000	1,800	2,600	3,500	5,000	6,500
KTT (348cc single)	7,000	11,000	16,000	21,000	28,000	35,000
MAC (349cc single)	1,400	2,100	4,000	5,500	7,000	8,500
1951						
LE (200cc twin, shaft drive)	800	1,500	3,000	4,500	6,000	7,500
KTT (348cc single)	7,000	11,000	16,000	21,000	28,000	35,000
MAC (349cc single)	1,400	2,100	4,000	5,500	7,000	8,500
1952						
LE (200cc twin, shaft drive)	800	1,500	3,000	4,500	6,000	7,500
KTT (348cc single)	7,000	11,000	16,000	21,000	28,000	35,000
MAC (349cc single)	1,400	2,100	4,000	5,500	7,000	8,500
1953						
LE (200cc twin, shaft drive)	800	1,500	3,000	4,500	6,000	7,500
KTT (348cc single)	7,000	11,000	16,000	21,000	28,000	35,000
MAC (349cc single)	1,400	2,100	4,000	5,500	7,000	8,500
1954						
LE (200cc twin, shaft drive)	800	1,500	3,000	4,500	6,000	7,500
MAC (349cc single)	1,400	2,100	4,000	5,500	7,000	8,500
MSS (499cc single)	−1,000	−2,000	4,000	6,000	8,000	10,000
1955						
LE (200cc twin, shaft drive)	800	1,500	3,000	4,500	6,000	7,500
MAC (349cc single)	1,400	2,100	4,000	5,500	7,000	8,500
MSS (499cc single)	−1,000	−2,000	4,000	6,000	8,000	10,000
1956						
LE (200cc twin, shaft drive)	800	1,500	3,000	4,500	6,000	7,500
MAC (349cc single)	1,400	2,100	4,000	5,500	7,000	8,500
Viper (349cc single)	−1,000	−2,000	4,000	6,000	8,000	10,000
MSS (499cc single)	−1,000	−2,000	4,000	6,000	8,000	10,000
Venom (499cc single)	2,000	4,000	6,000	8,000	10,000	12,000
1957						
LE (200cc twin, shaft drive)	800	1,500	3,000	4,500	6,000	7,500
Valiant (200cc twin, shaft drive)	1,400	2,100	4,000	5,500	7,000	8,500
MAC (349cc single)	1,400	2,100	4,000	5,500	7,000	8,500
Viper (349cc single)	−1,000	−2,000	4,000	6,000	8,000	10,000
MSS (499cc single)	−1,000	−2,000	4,000	6,000	8,000	10,000
Venom (499cc single)	2,000	4,000	6,000	8,000	10,000	12,000
1958						
LE (200cc twin, shaft drive)	800	1,500	3,000	4,500	6,000	7,500
Valiant (200cc twin, shaft drive)	1,400	2,100	4,000	5,500	7,000	8,500
MAC (349cc single)	1,400	2,100	4,000	5,500	7,000	8,500
Viper (349cc single)	−1,000	−2,000	4,000	6,000	8,000	10,000
MSS (499cc single)	−1,000	−2,000	4,000	6,000	8,000	10,000
Venom (499cc single)	2,000	4,000	6,000	8,000	10,000	12,000
1959						
LE (200cc twin, shaft drive)	800	1,500	3,000	4,500	6,000	7,500
Valiant (200cc twin, shaft drive)	1,400	2,100	4,000	5,500	7,000	8,500
MAC (349cc single)	1,400	2,100	4,000	5,500	7,000	8,500
Viper (349cc single)	−1,000	−2,000	4,000	6,000	8,000	10,000
MSS (499cc single)	−1,000	−2,000	4,000	6,000	8,000	10,000
1960						
LE (200cc twin, shaft drive)	800	1,500	3,000	4,500	6,000	7,500
Valiant (200cc twin, shaft drive)	1,400	2,100	4,000	5,500	7,000	8,500
MAC (349cc single)	1,400	2,100	4,000	5,500	7,000	8,500
Viper (349cc single)	−1,000	−2,000	4,000	6,000	8,000	10,000
MSS (499cc single)	−1,000	−2,000	4,000	6,000	8,000	10,000
1961						
LE (200cc twin, shaft drive)	800	1,500	3,000	4,500	6,000	7,500
Valiant (200cc twin, shaft drive)	1,400	2,100	4,000	5,500	7,000	8,500
Viper (349cc single)	1,600	2,400	4,000	6,000	8,000	10,000

	6	5	4	3	2	1
MSS (499cc single)	1,600	2,400	3,600	5,000	7,500	9,000
MSS Scrambler (499cc single)	−1,600	−2,400	−3,600	−5,000	7,500	9,000
1962						
LE (200cc twin, shaft drive)	800	1,500	3,000	4,500	6,000	7,500
Valiant (200cc twin, shaft drive)	1,400	2,100	4,000	5,500	7,000	8,500
Viper (349cc single)	1,600	2,400	4,000	6,000	8,000	10,000
MSS (499cc single)	1,600	2,400	−3,600	5,000	7,500	9,000
MSS Scrambler (499cc single)	−1,600	−2,400	−3,600	5,000	7,500	9,000
1963						
LE (200cc twin, shaft drive)	800	1,500	3,000	4,500	6,000	7,500
Valiant (200cc twin, shaft drive)	1,400	2,100	4,000	5,500	7,000	8,500
Vogue (200cc twin, shaft drive)	1,400	2,100	4,000	5,500	7,000	8,500
Viper (349cc single)	1,600	2,400	3,600	5,000	7,500	9,000
MSS (499cc single)	1,600	2,400	3,600	5,000	7,500	9,000
MSS Scrambler (499cc single)	−1,600	−2,400	−3,600	−5,000	7,500	9,000
1964						
LE (200cc twin, shaft drive)	800	1,500	3,000	4,500	6,000	7,500
Valiant (200cc twin, shaft drive)	1,400	2,100	4,000	5,500	7,000	8,500
Vogue (200cc twin, shaft drive)	1,400	2,100	4,000	5,500	7,000	8,500
Viper (349cc single)	1,600	2,400	4,000	6,000	8,000	10,000
MSS (499cc single)	1,600	2,400	3,600	5,000	7,500	9,000
MSS Scrambler (499cc single)	−1,600	−2,400	−3,600	−5,000	7,500	9,000
Thruxton (499cc single)	5,000	10,000	15,000	20,000	25,000	30,000
Venom (499cc single)	2,000	4,000	8,000	12,000	16,000	20,000
1965						
Viceroy Scooter (200cc single)	900	1,400	2,000	3,000	4,300	5,500
LE (200cc twin, shaft drive)	800	1,500	3,000	4,500	6,000	7,500
Vogue (200cc twin, shaft drive)	1,400	2,100	4,000	5,500	7,000	8,500
MSS Scrambler (349cc single)	1,600	2,400	3,600	5,000	7,500	9,000
Viper (349cc single)	1,600	2,400	−3,600	−5,000	−7,500	−9,000
MSS (499cc single)	1,600	2,400	3,600	5,000	7,500	9,000
MSS Scrambler (499cc single)	−1,600	−2,400	−3,600	−5,000	7,500	9,000
Thruxton (499cc single)	5,000	10,000	15,000	20,000	25,000	30,000
1966						
Viceroy Scooter (200cc single)	900	1,400	2,000	3,000	4,300	5,500
LE (200cc twin, shaft drive)	800	1,500	3,000	4,500	6,000	7,500
Vogue (200cc twin, shaft drive)	1,400	2,100	4,000	5,500	7,000	8,500
MSS Scrambler (349cc single)	1,600	2,400	3,600	5,000	7,500	9,000
Viper Clubman (349cc single)	1,600	2,400	3,600	5,000	7,500	9,000
MK II Venom (499cc single)	−1,600	−2,400	4,000	6,000	8,000	10,000
MSS (499cc single)	1,600	2,400	3,600	5,000	7,500	9,000
MSS Scrambler (499cc single)	−1,600	−2,400	−3,600	−5,000	7,500	9,000
Thruxton (499cc single)	5,000	10,000	15,000	20,000	25,000	30,000
1967						
LE (200cc twin, shaft drive)	800	1,500	3,000	4,500	6,000	7,500
Vogue (200cc twin, shaft drive)	1,400	2,100	4,000	5,500	7,000	8,500
MSS Scrambler (349cc single)	1,600	2,400	3,600	5,000	7,500	9,000
Viper Clubman (349cc single)	1,600	2,400	3,600	5,000	7,500	9,000
MK II Venom (499cc single)	−1,600	−2,400	4,000	6,000	8,000	10,000
MSS (499cc single)	1,600	2,400	−3,600	−5,000	7,500	9,000
MSS Scrambler (499cc single)	−1,600	−2,400	−3,600	−5,000	7,500	9,000
Thruxton (499cc single)	5,000	10,000	15,000	20,000	25,000	30,000
1968						
LE (200cc twin, shaft drive)	800	1,500	3,000	4,500	6,000	7,500
Vogue (200cc twin, shaft drive)	1,400	2,100	4,000	5,500	7,000	8,500
MSS Scrambler (349cc single)	1,600	2,400	3,600	5,000	7,500	9,000
Viper Clubman (349cc single)	1,600	2,400	3,600	5,000	7,500	9,000
MK II Venom (499cc single)	1,700	2,600	3,800	6,000	9,000	12,000
MSS (499cc single)	1,600	2,400	4,000	6,000	8,000	10,000

	6	5	4	3	2	1
MSS Scrambler (499cc single)	−1,600	−2,400	−3,600	−5,000	7,500	9,000
Thruxton (499cc single)	5,000	10,000	15,000	20,000	25,000	30,000
1969						
LE (200cc twin, shaft drive)	800	**1,500**	**3,000**	4,500	6,000	7,500
MSS Scrambler (349cc single)	−1,600	−2,400	−3,600	−5,000	7,500	9,000
Viper Clubman (349cc single)	1,600	2,400	3,600	**5,000**	7,500	9,000
MK II Venom (499cc single)	1,700	2,600	3,800	**6,000**	9,000	12,000
Thruxton (499cc single)	5,000	10,000	15,000	20,000	25,000	30,000
1970						
LE (200cc twin, shaft drive)	800	**1,500**	**3,000**	4,500	6,000	7,500
MK II Venom (499cc single)	−1,500	**3,000**	**5,000**	8,000	11,000	14,000
Thruxton (499cc single)	5,000	10,000	15,000	20,000	25,000	30,000
VESPA						
1953						
Twin.	300	600	1,200	1,800	2,400	3,000
1954						
125 (125cc)	1,000	2,000	3,000	4,000	5,000	6,000
1955						
150 (150cc)	1,000	2,000	3,000	4,000	5,000	6,000
1962						
VBB (150cc).	400	800	1,600	2,400	3,200	4,000
1963						
150cc	1,000	2,000	3,000	4,000	5,000	6,000
GS160.	750	1,500	2,500	4,000	5,500	7,000
1964						
150cc	1,000	1,500	1,900	2,300	2,700	3,200
1965						
Gran Turismo (125cc).	1,000	2,000	3,000	4,000	5,000	6,000
VBB2T	300	6,000	1,000	1,500	2,000	2,500
150cc	500	1,000	2,000	3,000	4,000	5,000
1968						
150cc	300	6,000	1,000	1,500	2,000	2,500
1970						
V46	1,000	2,000	3,000	4,000	5,000	6,000
1971						
Rally.	1,000	2,000	3,000	4,000	5,000	6,000
1974						
Rally 200	1,000	2,000	3,000	4,000	5,000	6,000
1976						
Rally.	1,000	2,000	3,000	4,000	5,000	6,000
1978						
Special 4 Speed (49cc single).	200	400	600	800	1,100	1,400
Special (90cc single)	200	400	600	800	1,200	1,600
Primavera (125cc single)	200	500	800	1,200	1,600	2,000
P125X (125cc single)	200	500	800	1,200	1,600	2,000
Super 6V Electric (150cc single)	200	500	800	1,200	1,600	2,000
Sprint 6V Electric (150cc single)	200	500	800	1,200	1,600	2,000
P200E (200cc single)	200	500	800	1,200	1,700	2,200
Rally (200cc single)	200	500	800	1,200	1,700	2,200
1979						
Ciao (49cc single)	100	200	400	600	900	1,200
Bravo (49cc single)	100	200	400	600	900	1,200
Grande (49cc single)	100	200	400	600	900	1,200
P125X (125cc single)	200	500	800	1,200	1,600	2,000
Primavera (125cc single)	200	500	800	1,200	1,600	2,000
P200E (200cc single)	200	500	800	1,200	1,700	2,200
1980						
Ciao (49cc single)	100	200	400	600	900	1,200
Bravo Super Deluxe (49cc single).	100	200	400	600	900	1,200
Si Special (49cc single)	100	200	400	600	900	1,200

	6	5	4	3	2	1
Grande Super Deluxe (49cc single)	100	200	400	600	900	1,200
Special 3 Speed (49cc single)	200	400	600	800	1,200	1,600
Sport (100cc single)	100	300	500	900	1,300	1,700
P125X (125cc single)	200	500	800	1,200	1,600	2,000
P200E (200cc single)	200	500	800	1,200	1,700	2,200
1981						
Ciao Special (49cc single)	100	200	400	600	900	1,200
Si Deluxe (49cc single)	100	200	400	600	900	1,200
Si Special (49cc single)	100	200	400	600	900	1,200
Grande (49cc single)	100	200	400	600	900	1,200
MX Super Deluxe (49cc single)	100	200	400	600	900	1,200
Special 3 Speed (49cc single)	200	400	600	800	1,200	1,600
Sport (100cc single)	100	300	500	900	1,300	1,700
P125X (125cc single)	200	500	800	1,200	1,600	2,000
P200E (200cc single)	400	700	1,100	1,700	2,500	3,300
1982						
Bravo (49cc single)	100	200	400	600	900	1,200
Ciao (49cc single)	100	200	400	600	900	1,200
Si (49cc single)	100	200	400	600	900	1,200
Grande (49cc single)	100	200	400	600	900	1,200
Grande Super Deluxe MX (49cc single) . . .	100	200	300	500	700	1,100
Special 3 Speed (49cc single)	200	400	600	800	1,200	1,600
Sport (100cc single)	100	300	500	900	1,300	1,700
P125X (125cc single)	200	500	800	1,200	1,600	2,000
Rally (200cc single)	200	400	600	800	1,200	1,700
P200E (200cc single)	200	500	800	1,200	1,700	2,200
1983						
P200E (200cc single)	200	500	800	1,200	1,700	2,200

VINCENT

	6	5	4	3	2	1
1934						
Series A Comet (499cc single)	5,000	10,000	20,000	35,000	50,000	65,000
Series A Meteor (499cc single)	5,000	10,000	20,000	35,000	50,000	65,000
1935						
Series A Comet (499cc single)	5,000	10,000	20,000	35,000	50,000	65,000
Series A Comet Special (499cc single) . . .	−5,000	10,000	20,000	35,000	50,000	65,000
Series A Meteor (499cc single)	5,000	10,000	20,000	35,000	50,000	65,000
Series A TT Replica (499cc single)	10,000	15,000	25,000	35,000	50,000	65,000
1936						
Series A Comet (499cc single)	5,000	10,000	20,000	35,000	50,000	65,000
Series A Comet Special (499cc single) . . .	−5,000	10,000	20,000	35,000	50,000	65,000
Series A Meteor (499cc single)	5,000	10,000	20,000	35,000	50,000	65,000
Series A TT Replica (499cc single)	10,000	15,000	25,000	35,000	50,000	65,000
Series A Rapide (998cc twin)	30,000	45,000	68,000	90,000	120K	150K
1937						
Series A Comet (499cc single)	5,000	10,000	20,000	35,000	50,000	65,000
Series A Comet Special (499cc single) . . .	−5,000	10,000	20,000	35,000	50,000	65,000
Series A Meteor (499cc single)	5,000	10,000	20,000	35,000	50,000	65,000
Series A TT Replica (499cc single)	10,000	15,000	25,000	35,000	50,000	65,000
Series A Rapide (998cc twin)	30,000	45,000	68,000	90,000	120K	150K
1938						
Series A Comet (499cc single)	5,000	10,000	20,000	35,000	50,000	65,000
Series A Meteor (499cc single)	5,000	10,000	20,000	35,000	50,000	65,000
Series A TT Replica (499cc single)	10,000	15,000	25,000	35,000	50,000	65,000
Series A Rapide (998cc twin)	30,000	45,000	68,000	90,000	120K	150K
1939						
Series A Comet (499cc single)	5,000	10,000	20,000	35,000	50,000	65,000
Series A Meteor (499cc single)	5,000	10,000	20,000	35,000	50,000	65,000
Series A Rapide (998cc twin)	30,000	45,000	68,000	90,000	120K	150K
1946						
Series B Rapide (998cc twin)	5,000	10,000	20,000	30,000	40,000	50,000

	6	5	4	3	2	1
Series B Rapide Touring (998cc twin). . . .	5,000	10,000	20,000	30,000	40,000	50,000
1947						
Series B Rapide (998cc twin)	5,000	10,000	20,000	30,000	40,000	50,000
Series B Rapide Touring (998cc twin). . . .	5,000	10,000	20,000	30,000	40,000	50,000
1948						
Series B Black Shadow (998cc twin)	15,000	25,000	40,000	55,000	70,000	85,000
Series B Black Shadow Touring (998cc twin)	15,000	25,000	40,000	55,000	70,000	85,000
Series B Rapide (998cc twin)	5,000	10,000	20,000	30,000	40,000	50,000
Series B Rapide Touring (998cc twin). . . .	5,000	10,000	20,000	30,000	40,000	50,000
Series C Black Lightning (998cc twin). . . .	50,000	75,000	100K	150K	175K	200K
Series C Black Shadow (998cc twin)	15,000	30,000	45,000	60,000	75,000	90,000
Series C Black Shadow Touring (998cc twin)	15,000	30,000	45,000	60,000	75,000	90,000
Series C Rapide (998cc twin)	5,600	8,400	15,000	30,000	45,000	60,000
Series C Rapide Touring (998cc twin). . . .	5,600	8,400	15,000	30,000	45,000	60,000
1949						
Series B Meteor (499cc single)	4,200	6,300	10,000	20,000	30,000	40,000
Series C Comet (499cc single)	3,000	7,000	14,000	21,000	28,000	35,000
Series C Comet Touring (499cc single) . . .	3,000	7,000	14,000	21,000	28,000	35,000
Series C Grey Flash (499cc single)	10,000	17,000	24,000	31,000	38,000	45,000
Series B Black Shadow (998cc twin)	15,000	25,000	40,000	55,000	70,000	85,000
Series B Black Shadow Touring (998cc twin)	15,000	25,000	40,000	55,000	70,000	85,000
Series B Rapide (998cc twin)	5,600	8,400	15,000	30,000	45,000	60,000
Series B Rapide Touring (998cc twin). . . .	5,600	8,400	15,000	30,000	45,000	60,000
Series C Black Lightning (998cc twin). . . .	50,000	75,000	100K	150K	175K	200K
Series C Black Shadow (998cc twin)	15,000	30,000	45,000	60,000	75,000	90,000
Series C Black Shadow Touring (998cc twin)	15,000	30,000	45,000	60,000	75,000	90,000
Series C Rapide (998cc twin)	5,600	8,400	15,000	30,000	45,000	60,000
Series C Rapide Touring (998cc twin). . . .	5,600	8,400	15,000	30,000	45,000	60,000
1950						
Series B Meteor (499cc single)	4,200	6,300	10,000	20,000	30,000	40,000
Series C Comet (499cc single)	3,000	7,000	14,000	21,000	28,000	35,000
Series C Comet Touring (499cc single) . . .	3,000	7,000	14,000	21,000	28,000	35,000
Series C Grey Flash (499cc single)	10,000	17,000	24,000	31,000	38,000	45,000
Series B Black Shadow (998cc twin)	15,000	25,000	40,000	55,000	70,000	85,000
Series B Black Shadow Touring (998cc twin)	15,000	25,000	40,000	55,000	70,000	85,000
Series B Rapide (998cc twin)	5,600	8,400	15,000	30,000	45,000	60,000
Series B Rapide Touring (998cc twin). . . .	5,600	8,400	15,000	30,000	45,000	60,000
Series C Black Lightning (998cc twin). . . .	50,000	75,000	100K	150K	175K	200K
Series C Black Shadow (998cc twin)	15,000	30,000	45,000	60,000	75,000	90,000
Series C Black Shadow Touring (998cc twin)	15,000	30,000	45,000	60,000	75,000	90,000
Series C Rapide (998cc twin)	5,600	8,400	15,000	30,000	45,000	60,000
Series C Rapide Touring (998cc twin). . . .	5,600	8,400	15,000	30,000	45,000	60,000
1951						
Series C Comet (499cc single)	3,000	7,000	14,000	21,000	28,000	35,000
Series C Comet Touring (499cc single) . . .	3,000	7,000	14,000	21,000	28,000	35,000
Series C Grey Flash (499cc single)	10,000	17,000	24,000	31,000	38,000	45,000
Series C Black Lightning (998cc twin). . . .	50,000	75,000	100K	150K	175K	200K
Series C Black Shadow (998cc twin)	15,000	30,000	45,000	60,000	75,000	90,000
Series C Black Shadow Touring (998cc twin)	15,000	30,000	45,000	60,000	75,000	90,000
Series C Rapide (998cc twin)	5,600	8,400	15,000	30,000	45,000	60,000
Series C Rapide Touring (998cc twin). . . .	5,600	8,400	15,000	30,000	45,000	60,000
1952						
Series C Comet (499cc single)	3,000	7,000	14,000	21,000	28,000	35,000
Series C Comet Touring (499cc single) . . .	3,000	7,000	14,000	21,000	28,000	35,000
Series C Black Lightning (998cc twin). . . .	50,000	75,000	100K	150K	175K	200K
Series C Black Shadow (998cc twin)	15,000	30,000	45,000	60,000	75,000	90,000
Series C Black Shadow Touring (998cc twin)	15,000	30,000	45,000	60,000	75,000	90,000
Series C Rapide (998cc twin)	5,600	8,400	15,000	30,000	45,000	60,000
Series C Rapide Touring (998cc twin). . . .	5,600	8,400	15,000	30,000	45,000	60,000

	6	5	4	3	2	1
1953						
Series C Comet (499cc single)	3,000	7,000	14,000	21,000	28,000	35,000
Series C Comet Touring (499cc single) . . .	3,000	7,000	14,000	21,000	28,000	35,000
Series C Black Lightning (998cc twin). . . .	50,000	75,000	100K	150K	175K	200K
Series C Black Shadow (998cc twin)	15,000	30,000	45,000	60,000	75,000	90,000
Series C Black Shadow Touring (998cc twin)	15,000	30,000	45,000	60,000	75,000	90,000
Series C Rapide (998cc twin)	5,600	8,400	15,000	30,000	45,000	60,000
Series C Rapide Touring (998cc twin). . . .	5,600	8,400	15,000	30,000	45,000	60,000
1954						
Firefly	3,000	7,000	14,000	21,000	28,000	35,000
Series C Comet (499cc single)	3,000	7,000	14,000	21,000	28,000	35,000
Series C Comet Touring (499cc single) . . .	3,000	7,000	14,000	21,000	28,000	35,000
Series D Black Knight (998cc twin)	15,000	23,000	40,000	60,000	80,000	100K
Series C Black Lightning (998cc twin). . . .	50,000	75,000	100K	150K	175K	200K
Series D Black Prince (998cc twin)	15,000	25,000	50,000	75,000	100K	125K
Series C Black Shadow (998cc twin)	15,000	30,000	45,000	60,000	75,000	90,000
Series C Black Shadow Touring (998cc twin)	15,000	30,000	45,000	60,000	75,000	90,000
Series C Rapide (998cc twin)	5,600	8,400	15,000	30,000	45,000	60,000
Series C Rapide Touring (998cc twin). . . .	5,600	8,400	15,000	30,000	45,000	60,000
1955						
Series C Black Lightning (998cc twin). . . .	50,000	75,000	100K	150K	175K	200K
Series D Black Knight (998cc twin)	15,000	23,000	40,000	60,000	80,000	100K
Series D Black Prince (998cc twin)	15,000	25,000	50,000	75,000	100K	125K
Series D Black Shadow (998cc twin)	15,000	23,000	40,000	60,000	80,000	100K
Series D Rapide (998cc twin)	5,600	8,400	15,000	30,000	45,000	60,000

WHIZZER						
1939						
Motorbike	2,000	3,500	5,000	6,500	8,000	10,000
1940						
Schwinn DX.	1,500	2,500	3,500	4,500	5,500	7,000
1945						
Assembled	500	1,000	2,000	3,000	4,000	5,000
1946						
Schwinn.	500	1,000	2,000	3,000	4,000	5,000
Monark	500	1,000	2,000	3,000	4,000	5,000
Hiawatha	700	1,000	1,300	1,800	2,500	3,500
1947						
Schwinn.	1,000	2,000	3,000	4,000	5,000	6,000
Model H.	700	1,000	1,300	1,800	2,500	3,500
1948						
Pacemaker	2,000	4,000	5,000	7,500	10,000	12,500
Model J.	1,500	2,500	3,500	4,500	5,500	7,000
Model WZ.	1,000	2,000	3,000	4,000	5,000	6,000
1949						
Schwinn.	2,000	3,500	5,000	6,500	8,000	10,000
Model J.	1,500	2,500	3,500	4,500	5,500	7,000
Model WZ.	1,000	2,000	3,000	4,000	5,000	6,000
Wasp	800	1,500	2,200	2,900	3,600	5,000
1950						
Schwinn.	800	1,500	2,200	2,900	3,600	5,000
Roadmaster.	700	1,000	1,300	1,800	2,500	3,500
Sportsman.	1,000	2,000	3,000	4,000	5,000	6,000
1951						
Pacemaker	1,000	2,000	3,000	4,000	5,000	6,000
Ambassador.	2,000	3,500	5,000	6,500	8,000	10,000
Special	2,000	3,500	5,000	6,500	8,000	10,000
Sportsman.	1,000	2,000	3,000	4,000	5,000	6,000
1952						
Schwinn.	1,500	3,000	4,500	6,000	7,500	9,000
Pacemaker	1,000	2,000	3,000	4,000	5,000	6,000

	6	5	4	3	2	1
Sportsman.	1,000	2,000	3,000	4,000	5,000	6,000
1953						
British Tandem	1,500	3,000	4,500	6,000	7,500	9,000
1954						
Special (138cc)	500	1,000	2,000	3,000	4,000	5,000
1955						
Road Runner	1,500	3,000	4,500	6,000	7,500	9,000
Pacemaker	1,000	2,000	3,000	4,000	5,000	6,000
1956						
Sportsman.	1,000	2,000	3,500	5,000	6,500	8,000
Red Ryder.	1,000	2,000	3,000	4,000	5,000	6,000
1957						
Delivery Cycle.	400	800	1,600	2,400	3,200	4,000
Schwinn B6	1,000	1,800	2,600	3,400	4,200	5,000
1960						
Wasp (6 made)	1,000	2,000	3,000	4,000	5,000	6,000
YAMAHA						
1956						
YA2 (123cc single)	1,000	2,000	3,500	5,000	6,500	8,000
1959						
YA3 (123cc single)	900	1,400	2,000	2,700	3,600	4,500
1961						
MF1 (50cc single)	500	800	1,100	1,500	2,000	2,500
MF2 (50cc single)	500	800	1,100	1,500	2,000	2,500
YA2 (125cc single)	500	800	1,100	1,500	2,000	2,500
YA3 (125cc single)	500	800	1,100	1,500	2,000	2,500
YC1 (175cc single)	500	800	1,200	1,600	2,200	2,700
YD2 (250cc twin)	900	1,400	2,000	2,700	3,600	4,500
YDS1 (250cc twin)	900	1,400	2,000	2,700	3,600	4,500
1962						
MJ2 (55cc single)	400	600	1,000	1,300	1,700	2,100
YA5 (125cc single)	500	800	1,200	1,600	2,100	2,600
YD3 (250cc single)	900	1,400	2,100	2,800	3,700	4,600
YDS2 (250cc twin)	900	1,400	2,100	2,800	3,700	4,600
1963						
YG1 (73cc single)	500	800	1,200	1,600	2,100	2,600
YG1T (73cc single)	500	800	1,200	1,600	2,100	2,600
YDT1 (250cc twin).	900	1,400	2,100	2,800	3,700	4,600
1964						
MJ2S (55cc single)	400	600	1,000	1,300	1,700	2,100
MJ2T Trail (55cc single).	400	600	1,000	1,300	1,700	2,100
YJ1 (60cc single)	400	600	1,000	1,300	1,700	2,100
MG1T (73cc single)	500	800	1,200	1,600	2,100	2,600
YG1 (73cc single)	500	800	1,100	1,500	2,000	2,500
YA5 (125cc single)	500	800	1,200	1,600	2,100	2,600
YA6 (125cc single)	500	800	1,200	1,600	2,100	2,600
YD3 (250cc single)	900	1,400	2,100	2,800	3,700	4,600
YDS2 (250cc twin)	1,200	1,800	2,700	3,600	4,800	6,000
TDS3 (250cc twin)	1,400	2,100	3,200	4,200	5,600	7,000
YDT1 (250cc twin).	1,000	1,500	2,300	3,000	4,000	5,000
1965						
U5 (50cc single)	400	600	900	1,200	1,600	2,000
MJ2T (55cc single)	400	600	900	1,200	1,600	2,000
YJ2S (60cc single)	400	600	1,000	1,300	1,700	2,100
YGS1 (73cc single)	500	800	1,100	1,500	2,000	2,500
MG1B (80cc single)	500	800	1,200	1,600	2,100	2,600
YL1 (98cc twin)	600	900	1,350	1,800	2,400	3,000
TD1B (250cc twin).	2,600	3,900	5,900	7,800	10,000	13,000
TD1C (250cc twin)	2,600	3,900	5,900	7,800	10,000	13,000
YD3C Big Bear Scrambler (250cc twin)	1,200	1,800	2,800	3,700	4,900	6,100

	6	5	4	3	2	1
YDS3 (250cc twin)	1,400	2,100	3,200	4,200	5,600	7,000
YM1 (305cc twin)	800	1,200	1,800	2,400	3,200	4,000
1966						
US Step Thru (50cc single)	400	600	900	1,200	1,600	2,000
MJ2T Omaha Trail (55cc single)	400	600	900	1,200	1,600	2,000
YJ2 Riverside (60cc single)	400	600	900	1,200	1,600	2,000
YGK Rotary Jet (73cc single)	500	700	1,100	1,400	1,900	2,400
YGTK Trailmaster (73cc single)	500	700	1,100	1,400	1,900	2,400
MJ1T Omaha Trail (80cc single)	500	800	1,100	1,500	2,000	2,500
YL1 (98cc twin)	500	800	1,100	1,500	2,000	2,500
YA6 Santa Barbara (125cc single)	400	600	900	1,200	1,600	2,000
TD1 Daytona Road Racer (247cc single) . .	2,600	3,900	5,900	7,800	10,000	13,000
YDS3C Big Bear (250cc twin).	1,000	1,500	2,300	3,000	4,000	5,000
YDSM Ascot Scrambler (250cc twin) . .	1,000	1,500	2,300	3,000	4,000	5,000
YM1 Big Bear Scrambler (305cc twin). . . .	800	1,200	1,800	2,400	3,200	4,000
1967						
U5 Newport (50cc single)	400	600	900	1,200	1,600	2,000
YJ2 Campus (60cc single)	400	600	900	1,200	1,600	2,000
YG1K Rotary Jet (73cc single)	500	700	1,100	1,400	1,900	2,400
MG1T Omaha Trail (80cc single)	500	700	1,100	1,400	1,900	2,400
YL1 (98cc twin)	500	700	1,100	1,400	1,900	2,400
YL2C (98cc single)	500	800	1,100	1,500	2,000	2,500
YA6 Santa Barbara (125cc single)	500	800	1,100	1,500	2,000	2,500
YCS1 Bonanza (180cc twin)	500	700	1,100	1,400	1,900	2,400
TD1 Daytona (247cc single).	2,600	3,900	5,900	7,800	10,000	13,000
DT1 Enduro (250cc single)	1,000	1,800	2,600	3,400	4,200	5,000
YDS3 Catalina (250cc twin).	1,000	2,000	3,000	4,000	5,000	6,000
YDS3C Big Bear (250cc twin).	700	1,000	1,500	2,000	3,000	4,000
YDS5 Catalina Electric (250cc twin). . . .	400	700	1,000	1,300	1,800	2,200
YM1 Cross Country (305cc twin)	500	800	1,200	1,600	2,200	2,700
YM2C (305cc twin)	500	800	1,100	1,500	2,000	2,500
YR1 Grand Prix (350cc single)	600	900	1,350	1,800	2,400	3,000
1968						
U5 Newport (50cc single)	400	600	900	1,200	1,600	2,000
YJ2 Campus (60cc single)	400	600	900	1,200	1,600	2,000
YG5T (73cc single)	500	700	1,100	1,400	1,900	2,400
YL1 (98cc twin)	400	700	1,000	1,300	1,800	2,200
YL2CM (98cc single)	400	700	1,000	1,300	1,800	2,200
YAS1C (125cc twin).	500	700	1,000	1,400	1,800	2,300
YCS1C (180cc twin	500	700	1,100	1,400	1,900	2,400
TD1 Daytona (247cc twin).	2,600	3,900	5,900	7,800	10,000	13,000
DT1 Enduro (250cc single)	1,000	1,800	2,600	3,400	4,200	5,000
YDS5 Catalina Electric (250cc twin). . . .	400	700	1,000	1,300	1,800	2,200
YM1 Cross Country (305cc twin)	500	800	1,200	1,600	2,200	2,700
YR2 Grand Prix (350cc single)	600	900	1,350	1,800	2,400	3,000
YR2C Street Scrambler (350cc single) . . .	500	800	1,200	1,600	2,200	2,700
1969						
U5 Step Thru (50cc single)	400	600	900	1,200	1,600	2,000
YJ2 (60cc single)	400	600	900	1,200	1,600	2,000
G5S (73cc single)	500	700	1,100	1,400	1,900	2,400
U7E (75cc single)	500	700	1,000	1,400	1,800	2,300
L5T Trail (98cc single).	400	700	1,000	1,300	1,800	2,200
YL1 (98cc twin)	400	700	1,000	1,300	1,800	2,200
AT1 Trail (125cc single).	500	700	1,100	1,400	1,900	2,400
AT1M (125cc single)	500	700	1,100	1,400	1,900	2,400
YAS1-C Street Scrambler (125cc twin) . . .	500	800	1,200	1,500	2,000	2,600
CT1 Trail (175cc single).	500	800	1,100	1,500	2,000	2,500
YCS1-C Street Scrambler (180cc twin) . . .	400	700	1,000	1,300	1,800	2,200
DT1B Trail (250cc single)	1,000	1,800	2,600	3,400	4,200	5,000
DT1S (250cc single).	500	700	1,000	1,400	1,800	2,300

	6	5	4	3	2	1
YDS6C Street Scrambler (350cc single) ..	500	800	1,200	1,600	2,200	2,700
YM1 (305cc twin)	600	900	1,350	1,800	2,400	3,000
R3 (347cc twin)	600	900	1,350	1,800	2,400	3,000
YR2-C Street Scrambler (350cc single) . . .	500	800	1,200	1,600	2,200	2,700
1970						
G6SB (73cc single)	500	700	1,000	1,400	1,800	2,300
HS1 (90cc single)	500	700	1,100	1,400	1,900	2,400
HT1 Enduro (90cc single)	500	700	1,100	1,400	1,900	2,400
L5TA (98cc single)	500	700	1,100	1,400	1,900	2,400
YL1E (98cc single)	500	700	1,100	1,400	1,900	2,400
YL2 (98cc single)	500	700	1,100	1,400	1,900	2,400
AS2C (125cc twin)	500	800	1,100	1,500	2,000	2,500
AT1B Enduro (125cc single)	500	800	1,100	1,500	2,000	2,500
AT1BMX (125cc single)	500	800	1,100	1,500	2,000	2,500
CT1B Enduro (175cc single)	500	800	1,100	1,500	2,000	2,500
CS3C (198cc twin)	400	700	1,000	1,300	1,800	2,200
DS6B (247cc twin)	400	700	1,000	1,300	1,800	2,200
DT1C Enduro (247cc single)	**1,000**	**1,800**	**2,600**	**3,400**	**4,200**	**5,000**
DT1CM (247cc single)	400	1,000	1,500	2,000	2,500	3,000
TD2 (247cc single)	2,700	4,100	6,100	8,100	11,000	14,000
RT1 Enduro (250cc single)	600	900	1,400	1,900	2,500	3,100
R2C (347cc twin)	400	700	1,000	1,300	1,800	2,200
R5 (347cc twin)	500	800	1,200	1,500	2,000	2,600
RT1M (360cc single)	400	700	1,000	1,300	1,800	2,200
XS1 (654cc twin)	1,500	2,000	3,000	5,000	7,000	9,000
1971						
G6SB (73cc single)	500	700	1,000	1,400	1,800	2,300
HS1B (90cc single)	500	700	1,100	1,400	1,900	2,400
HT1B Enduro (90cc single)	500	700	1,100	1,400	1,900	2,400
HT1MX (90cc single)	500	700	1,100	1,400	1,900	2,400
AT1C Enduro (125cc single)	500	800	1,100	1,500	2,000	2,500
AT1MX (125 single)	500	800	1,100	1,500	2,000	2,500
CT1C Enduro (173cc single)	500	800	1,100	1,500	2,000	2,500
CS3B (198cc twin)	500	700	1,100	1,400	1,900	2,400
TD2B (247cc single)	2,700	4,100	6,100	8,100	11,000	14,000
DT1E Enduro (250cc single)	**1,000**	**1,800**	**2,600**	**3,400**	**4,200**	**5,000**
DT1MX (250cc single)	400	700	1,000	1,300	1,800	2,200
R5B (347cc twin)	500	800	1,200	1,600	2,200	2,700
RT1B Enduro (360cc single)	500	800	1,200	1,600	2,200	2,700
RT1MX (360cc single)	500	800	1,100	1,500	2,000	2,500
XS1B (654cc twin)	1,300	1,800	**3,000**	**4,500**	**6,000**	**7,500**
1972						
JT2 (60cc single)	600	1,200	1,700	2,200	2,700	3,200
G7S (73cc single)	400	700	1,000	1,300	1,700	2,200
U7E (75cc single)	400	700	1,000	1,300	1,700	2,200
LS2 (98cc single)	400	700	1,000	1,300	1,800	2,200
LT2 Enduro (98cc single)	400	700	1,000	1,300	1,800	2,200
LT2M (98cc single)	400	700	1,000	1,300	1,800	2,200
AT2 Enduro (125cc single)	500	700	1,100	1,400	1,900	2,400
AT2M (125cc single)	500	700	1,100	1,400	1,900	2,400
CT2 Enduro (173cc single)	500	700	1,100	1,400	1,900	2,400
CS5 (198cc twin)	500	800	1,200	1,500	2,000	2,600
DS7 (247cc twin)	400	600	900	1,200	1,600	2,000
DT2 Enduro (247cc single)	400	700	1,000	1,300	1,800	2,200
DT2MX (247cc single)	400	700	1,000	1,300	1,800	2,200
TD3 (247cc single)	2,700	4,100	6,100	8,100	11,000	14,000
R5C (347cc twin)	500	800	1,200	1,600	2,200	2,700
RT2 Enduro (360cc single)	500	800	1,200	1,600	2,200	2,700
RT2MX (360cc single)	500	700	1,100	1,400	1,900	2,400
XS2 (654cc twin)	1,000	1,500	2,500	3,500	5,000	6,500

	6	5	4	3	2	1
1973						
GT1 (73cc single)	300	500	700	1,000	1,300	1,600
GTMX (73cc single)	300	500	700	1,000	1,300	1,600
LT3 (98cc single)	300	400	600	800	1,100	1,400
LTMX (98cc single)	300	500	600	800	1,100	1,400
AT3 (125cc single)	300	500	600	800	1,100	1,400
ATMX (125cc single)	300	400	700	900	1,200	1,500
CT3 (173cc single)	300	500	800	1,000	1,400	1,700
DT3 (247cc single)	400	600	900	1,200	1,600	2,000
MX250 (247cc single)	400	800	1,500	2,500	3,500	4,500
RD250A (247cc twin)	400	600	900	1,200	1,600	2,000
TA250 (247cc twin)	2,100	3,200	4,700	6,300	8,400	11,000
RD350 (347cc twin)	**1,000**	**2,000**	**3,000**	**4,000**	**5,000**	**6,000**
TZ360 (347cc twin)	2,600	3,900	5,900	7,800	10,000	13,000
MX360 (360cc single)	300	500	800	1,000	1,400	1,700
RT3 (360cc single)	600	900	1,350	1,800	2,400	3,000
MX500 (500cc single)	400	600	1,000	1,300	1,700	2,100
SC500 (500cc single)	400	600	1,000	1,300	1,700	2,100
TX500 (500cc twin)	600	900	1,350	1,800	2,400	3,000
TX650 (654cc twin)	1,200	1,700	2,500	3,500	4,500	6,000
TX750 (743cc twin)	1,000	1,400	2,000	2,600	4,000	5,000
1974						
GT80A (73cc single)	300	500	700	1,000	1,300	1,600
GTMXA (73cc single)	300	500	700	1,000	1,300	1,600
TY80A (73cc single)	300	500	700	1,000	1,300	1,600
YZ80A (73cc single)	300	500	700	1,000	1,300	1,600
DT100A (98cc single)	300	400	600	800	1,100	1,400
MX100A (98cc single)	300	400	600	800	1,100	1,400
DT125A (123cc single)	300	400	700	900	1,200	1,500
MX125A (123cc single)	300	400	700	900	1,200	1,500
TA125A (125cc twin)	1,700	2,600	3,800	5,100	6,800	8,500
YZ125A (125cc single)	300	500	600	800	1,100	1,400
DT175A (171cc single)	300	500	700	1,000	1,300	1,600
MX175A (171cc single)	300	500	700	1,000	1,300	1,600
RD200A (195cc twin)	400	600	1,000	1,300	1,700	2,100
DT250A (246cc single)	500	700	1,100	1,400	1,900	2,400
MX250A (246cc single)	500	800	1,500	2,500	3,500	4,500
RD250A (247cc twin)	500	800	1,200	1,500	2,000	2,600
TY250A (247 cc twin)	300	700	1,000	1,500	2,000	2,500
TZ250A (247cc twin)	2,400	3,600	5,400	7,200	9,600	12,000
YZ250A (247cc single)	300	500	600	800	1,100	1,400
RD350A (347cc twin)	**1,000**	**1,800**	**2,600**	**3,400**	**4,200**	**5,000**
RD350B (347cc twin)	600	800	1,200	1,700	2,200	2,800
TZ350A (347cc twin)	2,600	3,900	5,900	7,800	10,400	13,000
DT360A (352cc single)	400	600	900	1,200	1,600	2,000
MX360A (352cc single)	300	500	700	1,000	1,300	1,600
YZ360A (360cc single)	400	600	900	1,100	1,500	1,900
SC500A (500cc single)	400	600	900	1,100	1,500	1,900
TX650A (654cc twin)	1,100	1,600	2,400	3,200	4,500	5,500
TZ700A (698cc four)	1,500	3,000	6,000	9,000	12,000	15,000
TX750 (743cc twin)	1,000	1,400	2,000	2,600	4,000	5,000
1975						
GT80B (73cc single)	300	500	700	1,000	1,300	1,600
GTMXB (73cc single)	300	500	700	1,000	1,300	1,600
TY80B (73cc single)	300	500	700	1,000	1,300	1,600
YZ80B (73cc single)	300	500	700	1,000	1,300	1,600
DT100B (98cc single)	300	400	600	800	1,100	1,400
DT100B5 (98cc single)	300	400	600	800	1,100	1,400
MX100B (98cc single)	300	400	600	800	1,000	1,300
DT125B (123cc single)	300	400	700	900	1,200	1,500

	6	5	4	3	2	1
MX125B (123cc single)	300	400	700	900	1,200	1,500
RD125B (125cc twin)	300	400	600	800	1,100	1,400
TA1 (125cc twin)	1,800	2,700	4,100	5,400	7,200	9,000
YZ125B (125cc single)	300	400	600	800	1,100	1,400
DT175B (171cc single)	300	500	700	1,000	1,300	1,600
MX175B (171cc single)	300	500	700	1,000	1,300	1,600
TY175B (171cc single)	300	500	700	1,000	1,300	1,600
RD200B (195cc twin)	400	600	1,000	1,300	1,700	2,100
DT250B (246cc single)	500	700	1,100	1,400	1,900	2,400
MX250B (246cc single)	500	800	1,500	2,500	3,500	4,500
RD250B (247cc twin)	500	700	1,100	1,400	1,900	2,400
TZ250B (247cc twin)	2,400	3,600	5,400	7,200	9,600	12,000
YZ250B (247cc single)	300	400	600	800	1,100	1,400
RD350B (347cc twin)	1,000	1,800	2,600	3,400	4,200	5,000
TZ350B (347cc twin)	2,600	3,900	5,900	7,800	10,400	13,000
YZ360B (360cc twin)	400	600	900	1,100	1,500	1,900
DT400B (397cc single)	400	1,000	1,500	2,000	2,500	3,000
MX400B (397cc single)	400	600	1,000	1,500	2,000	2,500
XS500B (499cc twin)	700	1,000	1,500	2,000	2,600	3,300
XS650B (654cc twin)	1,100	1,600	2,400	3,200	4,500	5,500
TZ750B (750cc four)	4,000	6,000	9,000	12,000	16,000	20,000
1976						
GT80C (73cc single)	300	500	700	1,000	1,300	1,600
GTMXC (73cc single)	300	500	700	1,000	1,300	1,600
YZ80C (73cc single).	300	500	700	1,000	1,300	1,600
RS100C (97cc single).	300	500	700	1,000	1,300	1,600
DT100C (98cc single)	300	500	700	1,000	1,300	1,700
YZ100C (98cc single)	300	500	700	1,000	1,300	1,700
DT125C (123cc single)	300	500	800	1,000	1,400	1,700
MX125C (123cc single)	300	500	800	1,000	1,400	1,700
RD125C (125cc single)	400	600	900	1,100	1,500	1,900
YZ125C (125cc single)	400	600	900	1,200	1,600	2,000
YZ125X (125cc single)	400	600	900	1,200	1,600	2,000
DT175C (171cc single)	400	600	900	1,200	1,600	2,000
TY175C (171cc single)	400	600	900	1,200	1,600	2,000
YZ175C (174cc single)	400	600	900	1,200	1,600	2,000
RD200C (195cc twin)	400	600	1,000	1,300	1,700	2,100
DT250C (246cc single)	500	700	1,100	1,400	1,900	2,400
TY250C (247cc twin)	500	700	1,100	1,400	1,900	2,400
TZ250C (247cc twin)	2,400	3,600	5,400	7,200	9,600	12,000
YZ250C (247cc single)	400	600	900	1,200	1,600	2,000
XS360C (358cc twin)	400	600	900	1,200	1,600	2,000
RD400C (399cc twin)	500	1,000	1,500	2,500	3,000	4,000
YZ400C (399cc single)	400	600	900	1,100	1,500	1,900
TT500C (499cc single)	400	1,000	1,500	2,000	2,500	3,000
XS500C (499cc twin)	450	650	900	1,300	1,800	2,500
XT500C (499cc single)	900	1,800	2,600	3,400	4,200	5,000
XS650C (654cc twin)	900	1,300	1,900	2,500	3,400	4,500
XS750C (747cc triple)	700	1,200	1,900	2,500	3,500	4,500
TZ750C (750cc four)	4,000	6,000	9,000	12,000	16,000	20,000
1977						
GTMXD (73cc single)	300	500	700	900	1,200	1,500
YZ80D (73cc single).	300	500	700	900	1,200	1,500
DT100D (98cc single)	300	500	700	900	1,200	1,500
YZ100D (98cc single)	300	500	700	900	1,200	1,500
YZ125D (125cc single)	300	500	700	1,000	1,300	1,600
IT175D (171cc single).	300	500	700	1,000	1,300	1,600
TY250D (243cc twin)	400	500	800	1,100	1,400	1,800
DT250D (243cc twin)	400	500	800	1,100	1,400	1,800
IT250D (246cc single).	400	500	800	1,100	1,400	1,800

	6	5	4	3	2	1
TZ250D (247cc twin)	2,200	3,300	5,000	6,600	8,800	11,000
YZ250D (247cc single)	400	600	900	1,100	1,500	1,900
XS360D (358cc twin)	400	600	900	1,200	1,600	2,000
XS400D (392cc twin)	400	600	900	1,200	1,600	2,000
DT400D (397cc single)	400	600	1,000	1,300	1,700	2,100
IT400D (399cc single)	400	600	1,000	1,300	1,700	2,100
RD400D (399cc twin)	500	1,000	1,500	2,500	3,000	4,000
YZ400D (399cc single)	2,400	3,600	5,400	7,200	9,600	12,000
TT500D (499cc single)	400	1,000	1,500	2,000	2,500	3,000
XS500D (499cc twin)	500	700	1,100	1,400	1,900	2,400
XT500D (499cc single)	**900**	**1,800**	**2,600**	**3,400**	**4,200**	**5,000**
XS650D (654cc twin)	900	1,300	1,900	2,500	3,400	4,500
XS750D (747cc triple)	800	1,200	1,700	2,250	3,000	3,700
TZ750D (750cc four)	3,600	5,300	7,800	11,000	14,500	18,000
1978						
GT80E (73cc single)	300	500	700	900	1,200	1,500
YZ80E (73cc single)	300	500	700	900	1,200	1,500
DT100E (98cc single)	300	500	700	900	1,200	1,500
YZ100E (98cc single)	300	500	700	900	1,200	1,500
DT125E (123cc single)	300	500	700	900	1,200	1,500
YZ125E (125cc single)	300	500	700	900	1,200	1,500
DT175E (171cc single)	400	500	800	1,100	1,400	1,800
IT175E (171cc single)	400	500	800	1,100	1,400	1,800
DT250E (246cc single)	400	600	900	1,100	1,500	1,900
IT250E (246cc single)	400	600	900	1,100	1,500	1,900
TZ250E (247cc twin)	2,400	3,600	5,400	7,200	9,600	12,000
YZ250E (247cc single)	400	600	900	1,100	1,500	1,900
XS400-2E (392cc twin)	400	600	1,000	1,300	1,700	2,100
XS400E (392cc twin)	400	600	1,000	1,300	1,700	2,100
DT400E (392cc twin)	400	600	900	1,200	1,600	2,000
IT400E (397cc single)	400	600	900	1,200	1,600	2,000
RD400E (399cc twin)	500	1,000	1,500	2,500	3,000	4,000
YZ400E (399cc single)	400	600	900	1,200	1,600	2,000
SR500E (499cc single)	500	800	1,500	2,000	2,500	3,000
TT500E (499cc single)	500	1,000	1,500	2,000	2,500	3,000
XS500E (499cc twin)	500	700	1,000	1,300	1,700	2,100
XT500E (499cc single)	**900**	**1,800**	**2,600**	**3,400**	**4,200**	**5,000**
XS650E (654cc twin)	900	1,300	1,900	2,500	3,400	4,500
XS650SE (654cc twin)	900	1,300	1,900	2,500	3,400	4,500
XS750E (747cc triple)	800	1,200	1,700	2,300	3,000	3,700
XS750SE (747cc triple)	800	1,200	1,700	2,300	3,000	3,700
TZ750E (750cc four)	3,600	5,300	7,800	11,000	14,500	18,000
XS1100E (1,101cc four)	1,100	1,600	2,400	3,200	4,500	5,400
1979						
GT80F (73cc single)	300	500	700	900	1,200	1,500
GTMXF (73cc single)	300	500	700	900	1,200	1,500
YZ80F (73cc single)	300	500	700	900	1,200	1,500
DT100F (98cc single)	300	500	700	900	1,200	1,500
MX100F (98cc single)	300	500	700	900	1,200	1,500
YZ100F (98cc single)	300	500	700	900	1,200	1,500
DT125F (123cc single)	300	500	700	900	1,200	1,600
RS125 (125cc single)	300	500	700	900	1,200	1,600
YZ125F (125cc single)	300	500	700	900	1,200	1,600
DT175F (171cc single)	300	500	800	1,000	1,400	1,700
IT175F (171cc single)	300	500	800	1,000	1,400	1,700
MX175F (171cc single)	300	500	800	1,000	1,400	1,700
DT250F (246cc single)	400	500	800	1,100	1,400	1,800
IT250F (246cc single)	400	500	800	1,100	1,400	1,800
YZ250F (247cc single)	400	600	900	1,100	1,500	1,900
XS400-2F (392cc twin)	400	600	1,000	1,300	1,700	2,100

	6	5	4	3	2	1
IT400F (399cc single)	400	600	900	1,200	1,600	2,000
RD400F (399cc twin)	500	1,000	1,500	2,500	3,000	4,000
RD400F Daytona Special (399cc twin) . . .	900	1,300	1,800	2,400	3,200	4,000
YZ400F (399cc single)	400	600	900	1,200	1,600	2,000
SR500F (499cc twin)	400	600	1,500	2,000	2,500	3,000
TT500 (499cc single)	400	600	900	1,100	1,500	1,900
XT500F (499cc twin)	900	**1,800**	**2,600**	**3,400**	**4,200**	**5,000**
XS650-2F (654cc twin)	900	1,300	1,900	2,500	3,300	4,200
XS750-2F (747cc triple)	800	1,200	1,700	2,300	3,000	3,700
XS1100F (1,101cc four)	1,100	1,600	2,400	3,200	4,500	5,400
XS1100SF (1,101cc four)	1,100	1,600	2,400	3,200	4,500	5,400
1980						
YZ50G (49cc single)	300	400	600	800	1,000	1,300
GT80G (73cc single)	300	500	700	900	1,200	1,500
MX80G (73cc single)	300	500	700	900	1,200	1,500
YZ80G (73cc single)	300	500	700	900	1,200	1,500
DT100G (98cc single)	300	500	700	900	1,200	1,500
MX100G (98cc single)	300	500	700	900	1,200	1,500
YZ100G (88cc single)	300	500	700	900	1,200	1,500
DT125G (123cc single)	300	500	800	1,100	1,400	1,800
IT125G (125cc single)	300	500	700	900	1,200	1,600
YZ125G (125cc single)	300	500	700	900	1,200	1,600
DT175G (171cc single)	300	500	700	900	1,200	1,600
IT175G (171cc single)	300	500	700	1,000	1,300	1,600
MX175G (171cc single)	300	500	700	1,000	1,300	1,600
IT250G (246cc single)	400	500	800	1,100	1,400	1,800
YZ250G (247cc single)	400	**600**	**1,200**	**1,800**	**2,400**	**3,000**
XT250G (249cc single)	400	500	800	1,100	1,400	1,800
SR250G (250cc single)	400	600	900	1,200	1,600	2,000
TT250G (250cc single)	400	600	900	1,200	1,600	2,000
XS400G (392cc twin)	400	700	1,000	1,300	1,800	2,200
XS400SG (392cc twin)	400	700	1,000	1,300	1,800	2,200
IT425G (425cc single)	400	600	1,000	1,300	1,700	2,100
YZ465G (465cc single)	500	700	1,100	1,400	1,900	2,400
SR500G (499cc single)	400	900	1,500	2,000	2,500	3,000
TT500G (499cc single)	400	600	1,000	1,300	1,700	2,100
XT500G (499cc single)	500	**800**	**1,600**	**2,400**	**3,200**	**4,000**
XJ650G (653cc four)	500	700	1,000	1,400	1,800	2,300
XS650G (654cc twin)	900	1,300	1,900	2,500	3,300	4,200
XS650SG (654cc twin)	900	1,300	1,900	2,500	3,300	4,200
XS850G (826cc triple)	900	1,300	1,900	2,500	3,300	4,200
XS1100G (1,101cc four)	900	1,300	1,900	2,500	3,300	4,200
XS1100SG (1,101cc four)	900	1,300	1,900	2,500	3,300	4,200
1981						
SR185 Exciter (185cc single)	200	500	800	1,100	1,400	1,800
SR250T Exciter (250cc single)	300	500	800	1,100	1,400	1,800
SR250 Exciter (250cc single)	300	500	800	1,100	1,400	1,800
XS400 Special II (400cc twin)	300	500	800	1,100	1,400	1,800
XS400S (400cc twin)	300	500	800	1,100	1,400	1,800
SR500 (500cc twin)	400	900	1,500	2,000	2,500	3,000
XJ550 Maxim (550cc four)	400	700	1,000	1,300	1,600	2,000
XJ550R Seca (550cc four)	400	700	1,000	1,300	1,600	2,000
XS650 Special II (650cc twin)	400	700	1,000	1,500	2,000	2,500
XS650S (650cc twin)	400	700	1,000	1,500	2,000	2,500
XJ650 Maxim (650cc four)	400	600	1,000	1,200	1,500	1,900
XJ650L Midnight Maxim (650cc four)	400	600	1,000	1,200	1,500	1,900
XV750 Virago (750cc twin)	500	800	1,200	1,500	1,800	2,200
XJ750R Seca (750cc four)	500	800	1,200	1,500	1,800	2,200
XS850S (850cc triple)	500	800	1,200	1,500	1,800	2,100
XS850L Midnight Special (850cc triple) . . .	800	1,200	1,800	2,400	3,200	4,000

	6	5	4	3	2	1
XS850 Venturer (850cc triple)	800	1,200	1,800	2,400	3,200	4,000
XV920R (920cc twin)	800	1,200	1,800	2,400	3,200	4,000
XS1100S Eleven Special (1,100cc four). . .	900	1,300	1,900	2,500	3,300	4,200
XS1100L Midnight Special (1,100cc four). .	900	1,300	1,900	2,500	3,300	4,200
XS1100 Venturer (1,100cc four).	900	1,300	1,900	2,500	3,300	4,200
1982						
SR185 Exciter (185cc single)	300	500	700	800	900	1,100
SR250 Exciter (250cc single)	300	500	900	1,000	1,100	1,200
XS400S Heritage Special (400cc twin) . . .	400	700	1,000	1,200	1,300	1,500
XS400 Maxim (400cc twin)	400	600	900	1,100	1,300	1,600
XS400R Seca (400cc four)	400	700	1,000	1,200	1,400	1,700
XZ550R Vision (550cc twin).	500	800	1,200	1,400	1,700	2,000
XJ550 Maxim (550cc four)	400	700	1,000	1,400	1,700	2,000
XJ550R Seca (550cc four)	400	700	1,100	1,400	1,700	2,100
XS650S Heritage Special (650cc twin) . . .	600	800	1,200	1,500	1,800	2,300
XJ650 Maxim (650cc four)	400	700	1,000	1,400	1,800	2,200
XJ650R Seca (650cc four)	400	700	1,000	1,500	1,900	2,500
XJ650L Seca Turbo (650cc four)	700	1,000	1,500	2,000	2,500	3,000
XV750 Virago (750cc twin)	500	900	1,200	1,600	2,100	2,700
XJ750 Maxim (750cc four)	500	800	1,100	1,500	2,100	2,700
XJ750R Seca (750cc four)	500	800	1,200	1,600	2,200	2,900
XV920 Virago (920cc twin)	600	900	1,300	1,900	2,500	3,000
XV920R (920cc twin)	600	900	1,300	1,900	2,600	3,100
XJ1100 Maxim (1,100cc four)	700	1,000	1,400	2,200	3,000	3,800
1983						
XS400 Maxim (400cc twin)	400	600	900	1,300	1,600	1,950
XS400R Seca (400cc twin)	400	700	1,100	1,300	1,700	2,100
XV500 Virago	500	800	1,100	1,400	1,800	2,200
XJ550 Maxim (550cc four)	400	700	1,100	1,600	2,100	2,600
XJ550R Seca (550cc four)	500	800	1,200	1,700	2,200	2,700
XZ550R Vision (550cc twin)	500	800	1,200	1,800	2,600	3,300
XS650S Heritage Special (650cc twin) . . .	500	800	1,200	1,500	2,000	2,500
XJ650 Maxim (650cc four)	400	700	1,100	1,700	2,300	3,000
XJ650L Seca Turbo (650cc four)	700	1,100	1,500	2,300	3,100	4,000
XV750 Virago (750cc twin)	600	900	1,300	1,800	2,300	2,850
XJ750 Maxim (750cc four)	500	800	1,200	1,700	2,400	3,000
XV750M Midnight Virago (750cc twin) . . .	600	900	1,300	1,800	2,600	3,100
XJ750M Midnight Maxim (750cc four). . . .	600	900	1,300	1,800	2,600	3,300
XJ750R Seca (750cc four)	500	900	1,200	2,000	2,800	3,700
XJ900R Seca (900cc four)	700	1,000	1,400	2,100	2,800	3,700
XV920 Virago (920cc twin)	600	1,000	1,400	1,900	2,600	3,300
XV920M Midnight Virago (920cc twin) . . .	600	1,000	1,400	2,000	2,700	3,600
XVZ12T Venture (1,200cc four)	1,200	1,700	2,300	3,300	4,400	6,000
XVZ12TD Venture Royale (1,200cc four) . .	1,500	2,000	2,700	3,500	4,600	6,100
1984						
RZ350 (350cc twin)	1,500	2,000	3,000	4,000	5,000	6,000
FJ600 (600cc four)	500	700	1,100	1,600	2,200	2,900
XV700 Virago (700cc twin)	1,000	1,300	1,800	2,200	2,600	3,100
XV1000 Virago (1,000cc twin).	1,000	1,300	1,800	2,700	3,600	4,500
FJ1100 (1,100cc four).	1,000	1,400	1,900	3,000	4,000	5,000
XVZ12LR/R Venture (1,200cc four)	1,300	1,700	2,300	3,800	4,900	6,600
XVZ12D Royale (1,200cc four)	1,600	2,000	2,700	4,100	5,300	6,700
1985						
PW50 Y-Zinger Mini (50cc single).	100	150	200	300	400	500
PW80 Y-Zinger Mini (80cc single).	200	300	400	500	600	700
YZ80 (80cc single)	200	500	700	900	1,000	1,100
YZ125 (125cc single)	300	500	800	1,200	1,500	1,900
IT200 (200cc single).	300	500	800	1,200	1,500	1,800
YZ250 (250cc single)	400	600	900	1,500	2,000	2,500
XT350 (350cc single)	300	600	900	1,300	1,600	2,000

	6	5	4	3	2	1
TY350 (350cc single)	400	600	1,000	1,500	2,000	2,500
RZ350 (350cc twin)	1,500	2,000	3,000	4,000	5,000	6,000
YZ490 (490cc single)	400	600	900	1,500	2,000	2,600
TT600 (600cc single)	400	600	900	1,500	2,000	2,500
XT600 (600cc single)	400	600	900	1,400	1,900	2,400
FJ600 (600cc four)	500	700	1,000	1,700	2,300	2,900
XJ600 Maxim (600cc four)	700	1,000	1,400	2,000	2,500	3,000
XV700 Virago (700cc twin)	1,000	1,300	1,800	2,200	2,600	3,150
XJ700X Maxim X (700cc four).	700	1,000	1,500	2,200	3,000	4,000
FZ750 (750cc four)	800	1,200	1,700	2,700	3,700	4,600
XV1000 Virago (1,000cc twin)	1,000	1,400	1,900	2,800	3,700	4,500
FJ1100 (1,100cc four).	1,000	1,400	1,900	3,000	4,000	5,000
VMX12 V-Max (1,200cc four)	2,050	2,800	4,000	6,000	8,000	10,000
XVZ12D Venture Royale (1,200cc four). . .	1,600	2,000	2,700	4,000	5,300	6,900
1986						
PW50 Y-Zinger Mini (50cc single).	100	200	300	400	500	600
YZ80 (80cc single)	200	300	700	800	900	1,100
YZ125 (125cc single)	400	600	900	1,300	1,700	2,100
IT200 (200cc single).	300	500	900	1,300	1,700	2,000
TT225 (225cc single)	400	600	900	1,200	1,500	1,800
YZ250 (250cc single)	500	700	1,100	1,600	2,200	2,800
TT350 (350cc single)	400	600	900	1,400	1,900	2,400
TY350 (350cc single)	400	600	1,000	1,500	2,100	2,700
XT350 (350cc single)	400	600	900	1,400	1,800	2,300
YZ490 (490cc single)	500	700	1,000	1,600	2,200	2,900
TT600 (600cc single)	400	600	1,000	1,600	2,200	2,800
XT600 (600cc single)	400	600	1,000	1,500	2,000	2,600
YX600 Radian (600cc four)	600	900	1,400	1,900	2,500	3,000
SRX600 SRX (600cc single)	800	1,100	1,600	1,900	2,200	2,600
FZ600 (600cc four)	500	800	1,200	1,700	2,400	3,200
XJ700 Maxim (700cc four)	700	1,000	1,400	1,900	2,500	3,200
XV700S Virago (700cc twin)	1,000	1,300	1,800	2,300	2,700	3,300
XV700C Virago (700cc twin)	1,000	1,400	1,900	2,400	2,800	3,400
FZ700 Fazer (700cc four)	1,000	1,300	1,800	2,200	2,800	3,500
FZX700 (700cc four)	1,000	1,400	1,900	2,300	2,900	3,500
XJ700X Maxim X (700cc four).	1,000	1,200	1,500	2,200	2,900	3,700
FZ750 (750cc four)	900	1,300	1,800	2,700	3,500	4,600
XV1100 Virago (1,100cc twin).	1,100	1,600	2,200	2,900	3,700	4,500
FJ1200 (1,200cc four).	1,100	1,600	2,200	3,000	4,000	5,200
VMX12 V-Max (1,200cc four)	2,000	2,800	4,000	6,000	8,000	10,000
XVZ13D Venture Royale (1,300cc four). . .	1,700	2,300	3,000	4,200	5,500	7,200
1987						
PW50 Y-Zinger Mini (50cc single).	100	200	300	400	500	600
YSR50 (50cc single)	700	900	1,200	1,500	1,800	2,100
YZ80 (80cc single)	300	500	800	900	1,000	1,200
YZ125 (125cc single)	400	600	1,000	1,400	1,800	2,300
TW200 Trailway (200cc single)	300	500	800	1,200	1,400	1,700
TT225 (225cc single)	400	600	1,000	1,300	1,600	2,000
SRX250 SRX (250cc single)	600	800	1,200	1,500	1,800	2,200
YZ250 (250cc single)	500	700	1,100	1,700	2,300	2,900
TT350 (350cc single)	400	600	1,000	1,500	2,000	2,500
XT350 (350cc single)	400	600	1,000	1,500	2,000	2,500
YZ490 (490cc single)	500	800	1,100	1,700	2,300	3,000
XV535 (535cc twin)	800	1,100	1,600	1,900	2,300	2,700
XT600 (600cc single)	500	700	1,000	1,600	2,200	2,800
YX600 Radian (600cc four)	700	1,000	1,400	1,900	2,400	2,800
FZ600 (600cc four)	600	900	1,300	2,000	2,800	3,600
XV700C Virago (700cc twin)	1,000	1,400	2,000	2,500	3,000	3,700
FZX700 Fazer (700cc four)	1,100	1,500	2,100	2,700	3,400	4,200
FZ700 (700cc four)	1,100	1,400	1,900	2,800	3,700	4,600

	6	5	4	3	2	1
FZR1000 (1,000cc four)	1,400	1,800	2,400	3,400	4,500	5,800
XV1100 Virago (1,100cc twin)	1,200	1,700	2,200	3,000	3,800	4,800
FJ1200 (1,200cc four)	1,200	1,700	2,250	3,300	4,400	5,700
XVZ13 Venture (1,300cc four)	1,600	2,100	2,800	4,400	5,700	7,300
XVZ13D Venture Royale (1,300cc four)	1,800	2,500	3,400	4,700	6,100	7,500
1988						
DT50 DT L/C (50cc single)	200	400	700	800	1,000	1,100
YSR50 (50cc single)	600	700	800	900	1,000	1,200
YZ80 Mini (80cc single)	300	500	800	900	1,100	1,300
YZ125 (125cc single)	400	700	1,000	1,500	2,000	2,500
TW200 Trailway (200cc single)	400	600	900	1,200	1,500	1,800
XV250 Route 66 (250cc twin)	600	900	1,300	1,500	1,800	2,100
YZ250 (250cc single)	500	800	1,200	1,800	2,400	3,100
XT350 (350cc single)	500	700	1,000	1,500	2,000	2,600
FZR400 (400cc four)	1,000	1,400	1,900	2,600	3,300	4,000
FZR400S (400cc twin)	1,100	1,600	2,100	2,700	3,400	4,100
YZ490 (490cc single)	500	900	1,300	1,800	2,400	3,000
XV535 Virago (535cc twin)	800	1,200	1,600	2,000	2,500	2,900
XT600 (600cc single)	500	800	1,150	1,700	2,300	3,000
YX600 Radian (600cc four)	700	1,000	1,450	1,900	2,400	2,900
FZ600 (600cc four)	1,000	1,400	1,900	2,500	3,100	3,700
XV750 Virago (750cc twin)	1,300	1,700	2,300	2,800	3,300	3,900
FZR750 (750cc four)	1,100	1,500	2,100	3,000	3,900	4,900
FZR1000 (1,000cc four)	1,400	1,900	2,550	3,500	4,600	5,900
XV1100 Virago (1,100cc twin)	1,300	1,700	2,300	3,100	4,000	5,000
VMX12 V-Max (1,200cc four)	2,000	2,500	3,000	4,000	6,000	8,000
XVZ13 Venture (1,300cc four)	1,600	2,100	2,900	4,500	5,800	7,400
XVZ13D Venture Royale (1,300cc four)	2,000	2,600	3,450	4,800	6,200	7,600
1989						
DT50 DT L/C (50cc single)	300	500	700	900	1,100	1,300
YSR50 (50cc single)	600	800	1,000	1,200	1,500	1,800
YZ80 Mini (80cc single)	300	500	800	1,000	1,200	1,500
YZ125 (125cc single)	500	800	1,100	1,700	2,400	3,100
TW200 Trailway (200cc single)	400	600	900	1,300	1,600	2,000
XV250 Route 66 (250cc twin)	700	1,000	1,400	1,700	2,100	2,500
YZ250 (250cc single)	600	900	1,300	2,100	2,900	3,700
YZ250WR (250cc single)	600	900	1,300	2,100	2,900	3,900
XT350 (350cc single)	500	800	1,100	1,600	2,200	2,800
FZR400 (400cc four)	1,100	1,500	2,100	2,900	3,700	4,600
FZR400S (400cc twin)	1,200	1,700	2,300	3,000	3,900	4,800
YZ490 (490cc single)	600	900	1,300	2,000	2,700	3,500
XT600 (600cc single)	500	900	1,200	1,900	2,600	3,300
YX600 Radian (600cc four)	700	1,100	1,500	2,100	2,800	3,500
FZ600 (600cc four)	1,000	1,500	2,000	2,900	3,900	4,900
XV750 Virago (750cc twin)	1,200	1,800	2,400	3,000	3,600	4,300
FZR1000 (1,000cc four)	1,600	2,000	2,700	4,000	5,500	7,600
XV1100 Virago (1,100cc twin)	1,200	1,800	2,400	3,300	4,300	5,500
FJ1200 (1,200cc four)	1,400	1,900	2,600	3,700	5,000	6,400
VMX12 V-Max (1,200cc four)	2,000	2,500	3,000	4,000	6,000	8,000
XVZ13D Venture Royale (1,300cc four)	2,000	2,600	3,500	4,900	6,300	7,800
1990						
DT50 DT L/C (50cc single)	300	500	800	1,000	1,200	1,400
PW50Y-Zinger Mini (50cc single)	200	300	400	500	600	700
YSR50 (50cc single)	700	1,000	1,100	1,300	1,500	1,800
BW80 Big Wheel (80cc single)	300	500	800	900	1,000	1,100
YZ80 Mini (80cc single)	400	600	900	1,100	1,300	1,600
RT100 (100cc single)	300	500	800	1,000	1,100	1,300
YZ125 (125cc single)	500	800	1,200	1,800	2,500	3,300
RT180 (180cc single)	300	500	800	1,000	1,250	1,600
TW200 (200cc single)	400	700	1,000	1,400	1,700	2,100

	6	5	4	3	2	1
XV250 Route 66 (250cc twin)	700	1,000	1,500	1,900	2,300	2,700
YZ250 (250cc single)	700	1,000	1,400	2,200	3,000	3,900
YZ250WR (250cc single)	700	1,000	1,400	2,300	3,200	4,100
XT350 (350cc single)	500	800	1,200	1,700	2,300	2,900
FZR400 (400cc four)	1,100	1,600	2,200	2,900	3,900	4,900
YZ490 (490cc single)	700	1,000	1,400	2,100	2,800	3,600
XV535 (535cc twin)	900	1,200	1,700	2,300	2,900	3,700
XT600 (600cc single)	600	1,000	1,300	2,000	2,900	3,800
YX600 Radian (600cc four)	800	1,100	1,500	2,200	2,900	3,700
FZ600R (600cc four)	1,100	1,600	2,100	3,100	4,100	5,200
XV750 Virago (750cc twin)	1,400	1,800	2,400	3,000	3,700	4,500
FZR1000 (1,000cc four)	1,500	2,200	2,900	4,500	6,000	7,900
XV1100 Virago (1,100cc twin)	1,400	1,800	2,400	3,500	4,600	5,800
FJ1200 (1,200cc four)	1,500	2,000	2,700	4,000	5,300	6,700
VMX12 V-Max (1,200cc four)	2,000	2,500	3,000	4,000	6,000	8,000
XVZ13D Venture Royale (1,300cc four) . . .	2,100	2,700	3,600	5,100	6,400	8,000
1991						
PW50Y-Zinger Mini (50cc single)	200	300	400	500	700	800
YSR50 (50cc single)	800	1,100	1,200	1,400	1,600	1,900
PW80Y-Zinger Mini (80cc single)	200	400	700	800	900	1,000
YZ80 Mini (80cc single)	400	600	900	1,200	1,400	1,700
YZ125 (125cc single)	600	900	1,300	2,000	2,700	3,500
RT180 (180cc single)	300	500	800	1,100	1,400	1,600
TW200 (200cc single)	400	700	1,100	1,500	1,900	2,300
YZ250 (250cc single)	800	1,100	1,500	2,300	3,100	4,000
WR250Z (250cc single)	800	1,100	1,500	2,400	3,200	4,200
XT350 (350cc single)	600	900	1,300	1,900	2,500	3,200
XT600 (600cc single)	700	1,000	1,500	2,100	3,000	4,000
FZR600 (600cc four)	1,200	1,700	2,300	3,100	3,900	4,900
XV750 Virago (750cc twin)	1,300	1,900	2,500	3,200	3,900	4,700
FZR1000 (1,000cc four)	1,700	2,300	3,000	4,500	6,000	8,100
XV1100 Virago (1,100cc twin)	1,400	1,900	2,500	3,600	4,700	6,100
FJ1200 (1,200cc four)	1,600	2,200	2,900	4,100	5,500	7,050
VMX12 V-Max (1,200cc four)	2,400	3,000	4,000	5,000	6,500	8,500
XVZ13D Venture Royale (1,300cc four) . . .	2,100	2,800	3,700	5,200	6,700	8,200
1992						
PW50Y-Zinger Mini (50cc single)	200	400	600	700	800	900
YSR50 (50cc single)	800	1,100	1,300	1,500	1,700	2,000
PW80Y-Zinger Mini (80cc single)	200	400	700	800	1,000	1,100
YZ80 Mini (80cc single)	400	600	1,000	1,300	1,600	1,900
RT100 (100cc single)	300	500	800	1,000	1,300	1,500
YZ125 (125cc single)	700	1,000	1,400	2,200	3,000	3,700
RT180 (180cc single)	400	600	900	1,200	1,500	1,800
TW200 (200cc single)	500	800	1,200	1,600	2,000	2,500
WR200 (200cc single)	800	1,100	1,500	2,200	2,900	3,600
XT225 Serow (225cc single)	600	900	1,300	1,800	2,400	3,000
YZ250 (250cc single)	900	1,200	1,600	2,500	3,400	4,300
WR250 (250cc single)	900	1,200	1,600	2,500	3,400	4,300
XT350 (350cc single)	700	1,000	1,400	2,000	2,700	3,400
WR500 (500cc single)	800	1,100	1,500	2,500	3,500	4,500
XT600 (600cc single)	800	1,100	1,600	2,400	3,300	4,200
XJ600 Seca II (600cc four)	1,000	1,500	1,900	2,600	3,300	4,000
FZR600 (600cc four)	1,200	1,700	2,400	3,300	4,300	5,300
FZR600VH (600cc four)	1,400	1,900	2,600	3,700	4,800	6,000
XV750 Virago (750cc twin)	1,400	1,900	2,500	3,200	4,000	5,000
TDM850 (850cc twin)	1,500	2,000	2,700	4,000	5,300	6,800
FZR1000 (1,000cc four)	1,900	2,400	3,200	4,600	6,400	8,300
XV1100 Virago (1,100cc twin)	1,400	1,900	2,600	3,700	4,800	6,400
FJ1200 (1,200cc four)	1,700	2,300	3,000	4,200	5,600	7,500
VMX12 V-Max (1,200cc four)	2,400	3,000	4,000	5,000	6,500	8,500

	6	5	4	3	2	1
FJ1200A (1,200cc four)	1,900	2,500	3,300	5,000	6,800	8,700
XVZ13D Venture Royale (1,300cc four). . .	2,200	2,900	3,900	5,300	6,900	8,500
1993						
PW50Y-Zinger Mini (50cc single)	200	400	600	700	800	900
PW80Y-Zinger Mini (80cc single)	200	400	700	800	1,000	1,100
YZ80 (80cc single)	400	600	1,000	1,300	1,600	1,900
RT100 (100cc single)	300	500	800	1,000	1,300	1,500
YZ125 (125cc single)	700	1,000	1,400	2,200	3,000	3,700
RT180 (180cc single)	400	600	900	1,200	1,500	1,800
TW200 (200cc single)	500	800	1,200	1,600	2,000	2,500
XT225 Serow (225cc single)	600	900	1,300	1,800	2,400	3,000
YZ250 (250cc single)	900	1,200	1,600	2,500	3,400	4,300
WR250 (250cc single).	900	1,200	1,600	2,500	3,400	4,300
XT350 (350cc single)	700	1,000	1,400	2,000	2,700	3,400
WR500 (500cc single).	800	1,100	1,500	2,500	3,500	4,500
XV535 (535cc twin)	800	1,200	1,700	2,300	3,300	4,300
XT600 (600cc single)	800	1,100	1,600	2,400	3,300	4,200
XJ600S Seca II (600cc four)	1,000	1,500	1,900	2,600	3,300	4,000
FZR600R (600cc four)	1,200	1,700	2,400	3,300	4,300	5,300
XV750 Virago (750cc twin)	1,400	1,900	2,500	3,200	4,000	5,000
TDM850 (850cc twin)	1,500	2,000	2,700	4,000	5,300	6,800
FZR1000 (1,000cc four)	1,900	2,400	3,200	4,600	6,400	8,300
GTS1000A (1,000cc four)	2,000	3,000	4,200	5,300	6,400	7,500
XV1100 Virago (1,100cc twin).	1,400	1,900	2,600	3,700	4,800	6,400
FJ1200A (1,200cc four)	1,900	2,500	3,300	5,000	6,800	8,700
VMX12 V-Max (1,200cc four)	2,400	3,000	4,000	5,000	6,500	8,500
XVZ13D Venture Royale (1,300cc four). . .	2,200	2,900	3,900	5,300	6,900	8,500
1994						
PW50Y-Zinger Mini (50cc single)	200	400	600	700	800	900
PW80Y-Zinger Mini (80cc single)	200	400	700	800	1,000	1,100
YZ80 (80cc single)	400	600	1,000	1,300	1,600	1,900
RT100 (100cc single)	300	500	800	1,000	1,300	1,500
YZ125 (125cc single)	700	1,000	1,400	2,200	3,000	3,700
TW200 (200cc single)	500	800	1,200	1,600	2,000	2,500
XT225 (225cc single)	600	900	1,300	1,800	2,400	3,000
YZ250 (250cc single)	900	1,200	1,600	2,500	3,400	4,300
WR250Z (250cc single)	900	1,200	1,600	2,500	3,400	4,300
XT350 (350cc single)	700	1,000	1,400	2,000	2,700	3,400
XV535 (535cc twin)	800	1,200	1,700	2,300	3,300	4,300
XV535S (535cc twin)	800	1,200	1,700	2,300	3,300	4,300
XT600 (600cc single)	800	1,100	1,600	2,400	3,300	4,200
XJ600S Seca II (600cc four)	1,000	1,500	1,900	2,600	3,300	4,000
FZR600R (600cc four)	1,200	1,700	2,400	3,300	4,300	5,300
XV750 Virago (750cc twin)	1,400	1,900	2,500	3,200	4,000	5,000
YZF750R (750cc four	1,000	1,800	2,600	3,400	4,200	5,000
FZR1000 (1,000cc four)	1,900	2,400	3,200	4,600	6,400	8,300
GTS1000A (1,000cc four)	2,000	3,000	4,200	5,300	6,400	7,500
XV1100 Virago (1,100cc twin).	1,400	1,900	2,600	3,700	4,800	6,400
VMX12 V-Max (1,200cc four)	2,400	3,000	4,000	5,000	6,500	8,500
1995						
PW50Y-Zinger Mini (50cc single)	200	400	600	700	800	900
PW80Y-Zinger Mini (80cc single)	200	400	700	800	1,000	1,100
YZ80 (80cc single)	400	600	1,000	1,300	1,600	1,900
RT100 (100cc single)	300	500	800	1,000	1,300	1,500
YZ125 (125cc single)	700	1,000	1,400	2,200	3,000	3,700
RT180 (180cc single)	300	500	800	1,100	1,400	1,800
TW200 (200cc single)	500	800	1,200	1,600	2,000	2,500
XT225 (225cc single)	600	900	1,300	1,800	2,400	3,000
YZ250 (250cc single)	900	1,200	1,600	2,500	3,400	4,300
XV250 (250cc twin)	500	900	1,400	1,900	2,400	3,000

	6	5	4	3	2	1
WR250Z (250cc single)	900	1,200	1,600	2,500	3,400	4,300
XT350 (350cc single)	700	1,000	1,400	2,000	2,700	3,400
XV535 (535cc twin)	800	1,200	1,700	2,300	3,300	4,300
XV535S (535cc twin)	800	1,200	1,700	2,300	3,300	4,300
XT600E (600cc single)	800	1,100	1,600	2,400	3,300	4,200
XJ600S Seca II (600cc four)	1,000	1,500	1,900	2,600	3,300	4,000
FZR600R (600cc four)	1,200	1,700	2,400	3,300	4,300	5,300
YZF600R (600cc four).	800	1,500	2,300	3,100	3,900	4,700
XV750 Virago (750cc twin)	1,400	1,900	2,500	3,200	4,000	5,000
FZR1000 (1,000cc four).	1,900	2,400	3,200	4,600	6,400	8,300
XV1100 Virago (1,100cc twin).	1,400	1,900	2,600	3,700	4,800	6,400
VMX12 V-Max (1,200cc four)	2,400	3,000	4,000	5,000	6,500	8,500
1996						
PW50Y-Zinger Mini (50cc single)	200	400	600	700	800	900
PW80Y-Zinger Mini (80cc single)	200	400	700	800	1,000	1,100
YZ80 (80cc single)	400	600	1,000	1,300	1,600	1,900
RT100 (100cc single)	300	500	800	1,000	1,300	1,500
YZ125 (125cc single)	700	1,000	1,400	2,200	3,000	3,700
RT180 (180cc single)	300	500	800	1,100	1,400	1,800
TW200 (200cc single).	500	800	1,200	1,600	2,000	2,500
XT225 (225cc single)	600	900	1,300	1,800	2,400	3,000
YZ250 (250cc single)	900	1,200	1,600	2,500	3,400	4,300
WR250Z (250cc single)	900	1,200	1,600	2,500	3,400	4,300
XV250 (250cc twin)	500	900	1,400	1,900	2,400	3,000
XT350 (350cc single)	700	1,000	1,400	2,000	2,700	3,400
XV535 (535cc twin)	800	1,200	1,700	2,300	3,300	4,300
XV535S (535cc twin)	800	1,200	1,700	2,300	3,300	4,300
XJ600S Seca II (600cc four)	1,000	1,500	1,900	2,600	3,300	4,000
FZR600R (600cc four)	1,200	1,700	2,400	3,300	4,300	5,300
YZF600R (600cc four).	800	1,500	2,300	3,100	3,900	4,700
XV750 Virago (750cc twin)	1,400	1,900	2,500	3,200	4,000	5,000
YXF750R (750cc twin)	1,000	2,000	3,500	5,000	6,500	8,000
XV1100 Virago (1,100cc twin).	1,400	1,900	2,600	3,700	4,800	6,400
XV1100 Virago Special (1,100cc twin) . . .	1,400	2,000	2,700	3,800	4,900	6,600
XVZ13A Royal Star (1,300cc four)	1,000	2,000	4,000	6,000	8,000	10,000
XVZ13AT Royal Star Classic (1,300cc four).	1,200	2,500	4,500	6,500	8,500	10,500
YANKEE						
1970						
Boss Scrambler Twin 500	900	1,500	2,100	3,800	5,500	7,300
Boss ISDT Twin 500	900	1,900	2,700	3,600	5,100	7,100
1971						
Boss Scrambler Twin 500	900	1,500	2,100	3,800	5,500	7,300
Boss ISDT Twin 500	800	1,800	2,500	3,200	5,300	7,500
1972						
Boss ISDT Twin 500	800	1,800	2,500	3,200	5,300	7,500
1973						
Z Twin 500	600	1,500	3,100	5,900	7,000	8,200
1974						
Scrambler Single	900	1,500	3,200	5,700	7,500	9,300
Z Twin 500	600	1,500	3,100	5,900	7,000	8,200
ZUNDAPP						
1933						
K800	5,000	10,000	15,000	20,000	25,000	30,000
1935						
K800	5,000	10,000	15,000	20,000	25,000	30,000
KK200.	1,500	3,000	6,000	9,000	12,000	15,000
1936						
K800	5,000	10,000	15,000	20,000	25,000	30,000
1937						
DBK200	1,500	3,000	6,000	9,000	12,000	15,000

	6	5	4	3	2	1
1938						
K800	1,500	3,000	6,000	9,000	12,000	15,000
KS600.	1,000	2,000	4,000	6,000	8,000	10,000
1939						
KS600.	1,000	2,000	4,000	6,000	8,000	10,000
1940						
KS600.	1,000	2,000	4,000	6,000	8,000	10,000
1941						
KS600.	1,000	2,000	4,000	6,000	8,000	10,000
KS750.	5,000	10,000	15,000	20,000	25,000	30,000
1942						
KS750.	5,000	10,000	20,000	30,000	40,000	50,000
1943						
KS750.	5,000	10,000	20,000	30,000	40,000	50,000
1944						
KS750.	5,000	10,000	20,000	30,000	40,000	50,000
1950						
KS601.	1,500	3,000	6,000	9,000	12,000	15,000
1951						
KS601.	1,500	3,000	6,000	9,000	12,000	15,000
1952						
KS601.	1,500	3,000	6,000	9,000	12,000	15,000
1953						
KS601.	1,500	3,000	6,000	9,000	12,000	15,000
1954						
KS601.	1,500	3,000	6,000	9,000	12,000	15,000
R150S.	1,000	2,000	3,000	4,000	5,000	6,000
1955						
KS601.	1,500	3,000	6,000	9,000	12,000	15,000
1956						
DB200.	1,000	2,000	3,000	4,000	5,000	6,000
1957						
891	1,000	1,500	2,000	2,500	3,000	3,500
Bella R203	1,000	2,000	3,000	4,000	5,000	6,000
1958						
R154K.	1,000	2,000	3,000	4,000	5,000	6,000
1959						
Falconette (70cc)	500	1,000	1,500	2,000	2,500	3,000
Super Sabre (250cc)	500	1,000	2,500	4,000	5,500	7,000
1960						
Bella R204	1,000	2,000	3,000	4,000	5,000	6,000
Super Sabre (250cc)	500	1,000	2,500	4,000	5,500	7,000
1961						
Bella R204	1,500	3,000	6,000	9,000	12,000	15,000
Super Sabre (250cc)	500	1,000	2,500	4,000	5,500	7,000
1972						
KS50	1,000	2,000	3,000	4,000	5,000	6,000
MC125	500	1,000	2,500	4,000	5,500	7,000

230

Notes

Notes

Notes

Notes

Notes

Notes

Notes

Notes

Notes

Notes

Notes